CARRY IT ON

CARRY IT ON

The War on Poverty
and the Civil Rights Movement
in Alabama, 1964–1972

Susan Youngblood Ashmore

The University of Georgia Press   Athens and London

© 2008 by the University of Georgia Press
Athens, Georgia 30602
All rights reserved
Set in Minion Pro and Interstate by
   Graphic Composition, Inc., Bogart, Georgia
Printed and bound by Thomson-Shore
The paper in this book meets the guidelines for
permanence and durability of the Committee on
Production Guidelines for Book Longevity of the
Council on Library Resources.

Printed in the United States of America
12 11 10 09 08 C 5 4 3 2 1
12 11 10 09 08 P 5 4 3 2 1

Library of Congress Cataloging-in-Publication Data

Ashmore, Susan Youngblood, 1961–
Carry it on : The war on poverty and the civil rights
movement in Alabama, 1964–1972 / Susan Youngblood
Ashmore.
         p. cm.
   Includes bibliographical references and index.
   ISBN-13: 978-0-8203-3007-5 (hardcover : alk. paper)
   ISBN-10: 0-8203-3007-8 (hardcover : alk. paper)
   ISBN-13: 978-0-8203-3051-8 (pbk. : alk. paper)
   ISBN-10: 0-8203-3051-5 (pbk. : alk. paper)
   1. Civil rights movements—Alabama —History—20th century.
   2. African Americans—Civil rights—Alabama—History—20th century.
   3. African Americans—Alabama—Social conditions—20th century.
   4. Poverty—Alabama—History—20th century.
   5. Alabama—Race relations—History—20th century.
   6. Alabama—Social conditions—20th century.
   7. Alabama—Social policy. I. Title
      E185.93.A3A74 2008
      323.1196'0730761—dc22   2007044587

British Library Cataloging-in-Publication Data available

"Carry It On," words and music by Gil Turner, TRO
© copyright 1964 (renewed) Melody Trails, Inc. New York, N.Y.
Used by permission.

For Rob

Carry It On

There's a man by my side walkin',
There's a voice within me talkin',
There's a word that needs a sayin'.
Carry it on, carry it on, carry it on, carry it on.

They will tell their lyin' stories
Send their dogs to bite our bodies
They will lock us into prison,
Carry it on, carry it on, carry it on, carry it on.

All their lies be soon forgotten
All their dogs are gonna lie there rottin'
All their prison walls will crumble,
Carry it on, carry it on, carry it on, carry it on.

If you can't go any longer
Take the hand held out by your brother
Every victory gonna bring another,
Carry it on, carry it on, carry it on, carry it on.

"Carry It On," by Gil Turner, 1964

[The southerner's] social situation demands more of him than that elsewhere
in the country. It requires considerable grace for two races to live together,
particularly when the population is divided fifty-fifty between them and when
they have a particular history. It can't be done without a code of manners based
on mutual charity. [The] old manners are obsolete, but the new manners will
have to be based on what was best in the old ones—in this real basis of charity
and necessity. . . . For the rest of the country, the race problem is solved when the
Negro has his rights, but for the Southerner, whether he's white or colored, that's
only the beginning. The South has to evolve a way of life in which the two races
can live together with mutual forbearance. You don't form a committee to do this
or pass a resolution; both races have to work it out the hard way. In parts of the
South these new manners seldom make the papers.

Flannery O'Connor

Contents

Illustrations

Abbreviations

ACHR	Alabama Council on Human Relations
ADC	Alabama Democratic Conference
AIDP	Alabama Independent Democratic Party
ASCS	Agriculture Stabilization and Conservation Service (USDA)
BACDEO	Birmingham Area Committee for the Development of Economic Opportunity
CAA	Community Action Agency
CAP	Community Action Program
CDGM	Child Development Group of Mississippi
COAPO	Confederation of Alabama's Political Organizations
CORE	Congress of Racial Equality
DCIFVO	Dallas County Independent Free Voters Organization
DCVL	Dallas County Voters League
FHA	Farmers Home Administration (USDA)
FSA	Farm Security Administration
LCCMHR	Lowndes County Christian Movement for Human Rights
LCDC	Lawyers Constitutional Defense Committee
LCFO	Lowndes County Freedom Organization
MFDP	Mississippi Freedom Democratic Party
NAACP	National Association for the Advancement of Colored People
NDPA	National Democratic Party of Alabama
OEO	Office of Economic Opportunity
RAP	Rural Advancement Project (ACHR)
SCLC	Southern Christian Leadership Conference
SCOPE	Summer Community Organization and Political Education Project (SCLC)
SEASHA	Southeast Alabama Self-Help Association
SHAPE	Self-Help against Poverty for Everyone

SIP	Selma Inter-Religious Project
SNCC	Student Nonviolent Coordinating Committee
SWAFCA	Southwest Alabama Farmers Cooperative Association
USDA	U.S. Department of Agriculture
VISTA	Volunteers in Service to America

Acknowledgments

When I began the research for this manuscript, I was not aware of how many people and institutions I would rely on before I completed it. It is wonderful to finally have the chance to recognize those who have been so generous with moral support, time, and money. The history department at Auburn University provided me with an important foundation and supportive circle of professors and colleagues from which to learn American and southern history. My major professor, Larry G. Gerber, saw this work through in its initial phase as a dissertation. His example as a scholar, teacher, and mentor have set the standard for what a professor should be. Donna Bohanan and Wayne Flynt have given me so much. While I was studying at the University of Virginia, Patricia Sullivan and Waldo Martin introduced me to the richness of civil rights history. Pat became a mentor and friend; I appreciate her invitation to join this ongoing conversation. Robert Abzug and Louis Gould inspired me as an undergraduate at the University of Texas at Austin.

I thank the LBJ Foundation, the Friends of the Alabama Archives, and the Milo Howard Fund of the Auburn University History Department for providing research grants to support this project. My former dean, Dana Greene, and my current academic dean, Kent Linville, at Oxford College of Emory University have provided encouragement, monetary aid, and a sabbatical leave that assisted in the final stages of writing. I am also indebted to Norwood Kerr and Debbie Pendleton at the Alabama Department of Archives and History, Linda Hansen Seelke at the Lyndon Baines Johnson Library, Jim Baggett and Don Veasey at the Birmingham Public Library, and the other archivists and staff members whose work is so important at the many different libraries and archives I used. I am particularly thankful to all of the people who spent time telling me their stories in oral history interviews. Their willingness to share has helped me make sense out of a complicated story. Rev. Francis X. Walter was especially generous in allowing me to read his diary and use documents and photographs from his collection. Jack Willis provided me with a copy of his excellent documentary, *Lay My Burden Down: A Look at the Life Today of the Southern Rural Negro*. David Carter, Joseph Crespino, and Kent Germany were kind enough to share their manuscripts with me before they were published. Mark Griffith of the Oxford College IT division helped me prepare the illustrations for publication. The University of Alabama Press has graciously allowed me to use a revised version of an essay that appeared in *History and Hope in the Heart of Dixie: Scholarship, Activism, and Wayne Flynt in the Modern South* (chapter 1 in this book).

Those who have read this book in various phases have helped to make it better. Mary G. Rolinson and Patricia Sullivan read all or parts of the manuscript in its many developmental stages. Joe Crespino offered early advice on the introduction. I thank Kay Mills and an anonymous reader who provided comments for the University of Georgia Press. Ellen Goldlust-Gingrich gave invaluable suggestions as my copyeditor and saved me from many potential embarrassments. All of their recommendations were priceless in helping me sharpen my argument and clarify my prose. In the end, however, any interpretation or documentation errors are my own. Working with Nicole Mitchell, Derek Krissoff, Jon Davies, and John McCloud at the University of Georgia Press has been a wonderful experience.

Other friends and family have given me gracious support and steadfast encouragement. Special thanks go to my graduate school colleagues—at Auburn, Dixie Dysart, Glenn and Jeannie Feldman, and James "Buddy" Sledge, and at UVa, Catherine OBrion, Angie Parrot Howard, and Joe Sinsheimer. I learned more from them than they probably realize. Dixie Dysart in Auburn, Marynell and John Walker in Austin, and Ron and Ann Lewis in Washington, D.C., opened their homes to me for many weeks—probably more than I should have asked. Friendships through the years have made this work more meaningful. I owe a great deal to Jane Read Gherardi, Leslie Harris, Martha Harris, Janet Hudson, Adriane Ivey, Averill Jones, Susan McGrath, Ester Mouton, Milton Pullen, Mary G. Rolinson, Amy Stephenson, Carrie Stockard, A. J. and Carol Tanet, Melinda Taylor, Faye and Francis Walter, Ken Wheeler, Marny, and all the good folks at Oxford College. I hope my brother and sisters and their spouses—Linda, Tom, Carey, Jim, and Cindy—will see their influence in these pages. I was lucky to know all four of my grandparents well. In long conversations around the Sunday dinner table, they taught me about Texas and the South and the aspirations of people caught up in circumstances outside of their control. I am indebted to my parents, Jim and Katie Youngblood, who provided so many opportunities for their suburban children to see the world and get to know people beyond our community in the shadow of NASA. They have been my guiding star. Who knew the combined effects of singing Pete Seeger songs on car trips and visiting Chester, Texas, and points beyond? Finally, I dedicate this book to my husband, Rob Ashmore, who has supported me generously and cheered me on all these many years.

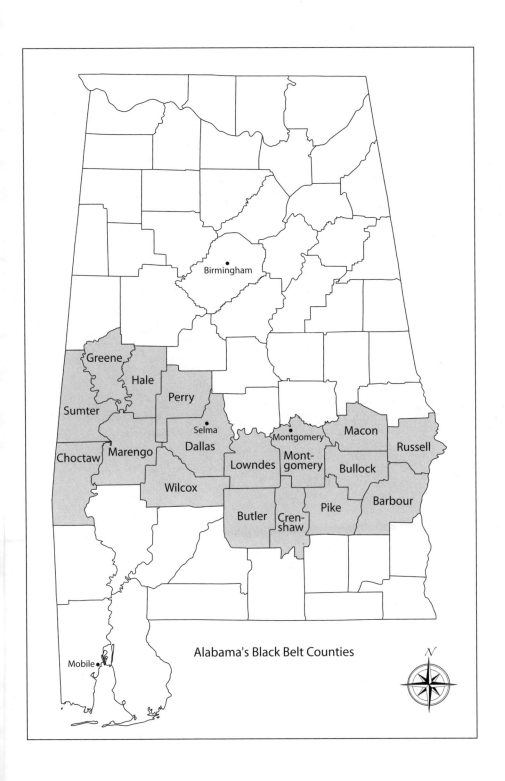

Alabama's Black Belt Counties

CARRY IT ON

From April to June 2006, the High Museum of Art in Atlanta exhibited quilts from Gee's Bend, Alabama, that had been touring the country. The curators chose the new wing of the museum as the site for a display of sixty quilts made by four generations of women. The space set off the quilts nicely with expansive ceilings, large rooms, and plenty of natural light coming through special skylights. Modern art hung in other galleries nearby, providing a reminder that despite being handmade using traditional skills, these quilts could be considered modern. Part of the introductory text made it plain that "improvisational designs, asymmetry, multiple patterns, and an almost minimalist aesthetic characterize these quilts." Visitors to the exhibit were greeted by a wall full of large black-and-white photographs of the artists—some had gray hair, others were middle aged or younger; all had faces that conveyed dignity, openness, and sincerity. Michael Shapiro, the museum's director, narrated the audio tour. He described meeting some of the quilt makers when he visited Gee's Bend for the first time. "When we arrived at the community center, they sang 'Swing Low Sweet Chariot,' we ate a southern feast and were greeted warmly by the women." The curators wanted visitors to know that the quilters were authentic black southerners.[1]

The quilts were grouped within the gallery's rooms based on aspects of the way the quilts were designed—work clothes, patterns, housetop, Sears corduroy. But as museumgoers progressed through the rooms, they were not provided with a way to understand the circumstances that explained the harsh realities of the quilt makers' poverty or how these "isolated" women became known throughout the country for their quilts. Issues of power, dominance, and politics were hidden, tucked away like sheets under a spread. Instead, visitors were called to marvel at the artists' perseverance and creativity while living under adverse conditions. The introductory text revealed that Gee's Bend "occupied land some five miles across and seven miles deep, cut off on three sides from the outside world inside a horseshoe-shaped bend in the Alabama River." Post–Civil War isolation preserved "the community's customs and folkways . . . virtually unchanged well into the twentieth century."[2]

The display text beside one of Loretta Pettway's quilts vividly spoke to viewers: "I didn't like to sew. Didn't want to do it. Had to go to the field. Had to walk about fifty miles in the field every day. Get home too tired to do no sewing. My grandmamma, Prissy Pettway, told me 'you better make quilts, you going to need them.' I said 'I ain't going to need no quilts.' But when I got me a house, a raggedy old house, then I needed them to keep warm." After reading this text, one patron offered a quiet comment that revealed that the exhibit needed more explanation: "Fifty miles in the field. Wow. Well, Grandma knew best." The quilt's description said that Loretta Pettway was born in 1942 and implied that she still lived in Gee's Bend. Beyond imparting the information that she was poor, the text failed to explain why she had to work so hard in the cotton fields, why her house was "raggedy," and why she needed to make quilts to keep warm.[3]

Lutisha Pettway constructed a quilt from work clothes that "were mended many times before they were used" as quilting material. The exhibit also revealed that "she was a descendant of slaves, worked in cotton fields as a child, and had little schooling. She was independent and supported her children on her own. One of her joys was singing in the Friendship Baptist Church." But visitors were left wondering why did she not receive an education. How did she support herself and her children under these circumstances? Beside another quilt made from used flour sacks, the text reported, "This quilt testifies to a way of life that has almost disappeared." While the dignity of these women was never in question, the exhibit curators assumed that the audience naturally carried enough knowledge about rural life, including tenant farming and sharecropping, that a more complete explanation was not necessary. There was no need to account for the injustices of the southern agricultural system other than to note that it was hard on those African Americans who lived under it and that it has disappeared.[4]

One piece provided an opportunity to furnish some needed historical context; however, museum officials gave only limited information. This quilt revealed that the civil rights movement had touched Wilcox County directly. The materials used in the quilt made this obvious. Irene Williams chose for her design red, white, and blue cotton with the word *vote* repeated throughout the housetop pattern. Williams created the quilt ten years after hearing Dr. Martin Luther King Jr. speak in February 1965 at the Pleasant Grove Baptist Church in Wilcox County. While the gospel song "How We Got Over" played in the background, the audio tour related that "Gee's Benders took part in the Selma march and tried to register to vote in Camden." Apparently because of this activism, white people stopped operating the ferry that connected Gee's Bend to the rest of Wilcox County, so area residents "had to drive one hour to get to Camden." Finally, the tour explained, "Mules from Gee's Bend were used in Dr. King's funeral." No further history was offered so that visitors could understand the context of the quilt. The exhibit focused on the quilters' determination rather than on how Williams and her neighbors in Wilcox County took part in giving meaning to the civil rights movement in their lives and in their communities.[5]

The exhibit's patrons would have benefited from the knowledge that Rev. Francis X. Walter, a white Episcopal priest who grew up in Alabama, learned about the quilts through his civil rights work in the county. This information would have given viewers a clearer understanding that many of these women sought to transform their surroundings beyond making beautiful quilts to keep warm. When he began documenting the evictions that occurred after people participated in the movement, he noticed the quilts—draped on clotheslines or spread across corn-husk beds—in the many houses he visited. Many of these women contributed their time and energy to the local movement; some had been arrested for their activism. He recognized that they had a marketable skill, and his relationship with local Southern Christian Leadership Conference activists and Office of Economic Opportunity officials had contributed to his knowledge of the effectiveness of cooperatives. In 1966, he helped organize the Freedom Quilting Bee handicraft co-op as a way for many of these women to earn a living after they or their husbands had been fired because of their commitment to the black freedom movement.[6]

How museums—even those that focus on art—tell their stories is important because they often reveal the way a region chooses to remember its past. This exhibit did a wonderful job of highlighting the significance of isolation and family ties in the creative process and of making the link between outsider art and modern art. But its silences reinforced a hackneyed view of Jim Crow and the struggle for civil rights—life was hard, black families overcame with the help of their religious faith and Martin Luther King Jr., and that world now has all but disappeared. The exhibit's neglect of the complexities of the history through which these quilt makers lived conveyed that we do not need to know the messy details of how we got to where we are today as long as we honor those who struggled. It no longer matters who employed these families, why they chose to stay in the region, what they thought about the federal civil rights laws, and how they acted to change their part of the South. The exhibit's broad message was that poverty and isolation led to the creation of amazing vernacular art. While these women have made a significant contribution to southern

Figure 1. Two quilts made by members of the Freedom Quilting Bee. Francis X. Walter Personal Papers, Sewanee, Tenn.

culture that is worthy of acknowledgment across the country, I was left wanting another part of their story to be told.[7]

Reflecting on my museum visits, I saw something else—artistic expressions of Black Power, Alabama style. Williams's quilt beckoned people to vote, literally calling out in ways the other quilts did figuratively. Elizabeth Walter, Rev. Walter's wife at the time, first saw some of these quilts in 1966 and remembered the experience vividly: "What grabbed [me] initially was the boldness, the aggressiveness, the assertive patterns so different from white Appalachian quilts that are tight, sometimes tedious and seem introverted. These were extroverted quilts. The contrast was evident immediately." The fact that all of the quilts exhibited at the High Museum share this vividness says something about the region as a whole. Just as these women found their own ways to design quilts to keep warm using new variations on an old form, people in the rural Black Belt constructed their own way after 1964 using new patterns with old systems of democracy. They gave meaning to the Civil Rights Act and the Voting Rights Act, creating lives that expressed Black Power. Not in paramilitary style like Robert Williams in Monroe, North Carolina, or the Deacons of Defense in Bogalusa, Louisiana, but boldly and assertively through small and large decisions—to register to vote, to develop antipoverty programs through the Office of Economic Opportunity, to create a third political party, to file a lawsuit, to join a cooperative, to run for elected office. These were expressions of freedom; civil rights encompassed all of these actions. When Williams made her quilt in 1975, she had many reasons for encouraging people across the Black Belt to vote in an effort to preserve what they had gained.[8]

How Will Freedom Come?

When Americans talk about poverty, some things remain unsaid. Mainstream discourse about poverty, whether liberal or conservative, largely stays silent about politics, power, and equality. But poverty, after all, is about distribution; it results because some people receive a great deal less than others. Descriptions of the demography, behavior, or beliefs of subpopulations cannot explain the patterned inequalities evident in every era of American history. These result from styles of dominance, the way power is exercised, and the politics of distribution. Poverty is no longer natural; it is a social product.
    Michael B. Katz

Two months after the Selma march culminated at the Alabama State Capitol, *New York Times* reporter Gay Talese returned to the Black Belt town. His essay for the paper's Sunday magazine, "Where's the Spirit of Selma Now?" provided a snapshot of where the movement for civil rights stood in May 1965. From his perspective, the Selma march had created "a strange new hope that after the bridge had been crossed, after Montgomery finally had been reached, everything would somehow be all right, a kind of miracle would occur—it would be like Lourdes and the faithful might toss away their crutches." Instead of a new day, he found the community filled with a mundane sameness. The schools, the YMCA, the pool, the jail, and most of the churches, restaurants, and hotels remained segregated. The voter registration drive had not immediately produced the hoped-for swell of potential black voters. "Those Negroes who twice each month line up outside the Dallas County Courthouse," he reported, "are kept waiting, they say, five and six hours in the sun; and then, if they are a minute late in reporting to the registrar's desk after their number has been called, or if they did not hear it . . . they are told to come back in two weeks because they were too late." The city denied requests to hire black police officers, claiming a

Figure 2. This Coca-Cola sign portrays the way Selma's elites wanted the city to be known. The civil rights campaigns beginning in 1965 provided evidence to the contrary. Photo by John F. Phillips.

tight budget and no plans for new hires. Job opportunities were equally bad. Talese found that "Negro chances for fair employment in skilled positions in Selma businesses have not, so far, been improved by the civil rights demonstrations last March." The mayor of Selma summed up the reporter's findings: "Things are pretty much back to normal." "He says it," Talese noted, "as many white leaders in Selma today say it: with a knowing nod, a half-smile, a Southerner's sense of Northern hypocrisy."[1]

From his short visit to Selma, Talese concluded that the black people of Selma had been abandoned. The leaders and freedom fighters "have either returned to New York, Los Angeles, Chicago, or Atlanta; or perhaps they have found a new cause in another town." Despite this fact, his interviews with local people who had been involved in the movement revealed a more perceptive evaluation of the campaign's significance. While standing on the sidewalk near the Brown's Chapel African Methodist Episcopal Church, Gerald Turley explained that the march was not the sum total of the movement. "The white people came down here and demonstrated, then went back North feeling very good that they had come. . . . The whites felt they did their share, and they did a lot. Some of them have sent money back to Selma, and clothes, and they helped focus attention on the problem of Selma, and we appreciate that. But they shouldn't feel that they solved anything, because they didn't. The problem is still here." Mary Lamar took the long view when thinking about the campaign, telling the *New York Times* reporter that "Selma, with all its faults and hypocrisy and unfulfilled promises, has made a lasting impression in the South and beyond it." Her neighbor, Mabel Evans, explained, "Selma did something. It did something that's hard to explain, but it's inside where you can't see it. . . . I mean, you remember when Jim Clark said there wasn't gonna be no march to Montgomery except over his dead body? Well, we marched, didn't we? And a lot of other things happened here that we thought we never gonna see happen . . . and maybe it will help change the thinking of the Negroes not now . . . but years from now."[2]

Talese's piece clearly showed that a difficult road lay ahead. How could the hope and momentum inspired by those heady days in March be sustained? In what ways would white southerners maintain their traditions of white supremacy, political dominance, and economic oppression? If the more famous civil rights leaders left, who would support the movement to change the South? In other words, how would freedom come?

Talese's cursory visit to Alabama could not have provided him with foreknowledge of the complicated events that would unfold in the wake of the spring 1965 protests. This history has been eclipsed by wider events, often referred to as the "great unraveling," that captured the nation's attention—destructive urban riots, the escalating Vietnam War and the rise of the movement opposing it, assassinations of beloved leaders. This book reveals what has been overshadowed, examining what happened in the region after the passage of landmark federal legislation. Focusing on Alabama after 1964 and using the War on Poverty as a lens offers insight into the challenges southerners faced during a time of real transition. President Lyndon Baines Johnson's Economic Opportunity Act, combined with the civil rights laws, provided new levers that local people could pull as political actors in an effort to gain control over their lives and define their citizenship on their own terms. This moment seemed to offer real possibility for change. Rev. Francis X. Walter, director of the Selma Inter-Religious Project, described the sense of expectation: "None of us knew what we were going to do, but we all knew that there was a tremendous energy there, and it was the hope that many things could be done." This study details the interaction of people who worked on the federal, state, and local levels; the variety of responses by the black and white communities to the shifting ground; the transformative nature of black people's struggle for freedom; and the assortment of perspectives held by federal bureaucrats, state officials, white landowners and their local leaders, and rural African Americans and their black neighbors in towns and cities across the state. The Civil Rights Act of 1964 and the Voting Rights Act of 1965 generated a political and economic struggle in Alabama to test the applicability of these new laws and ownership of the local government in the wake of the fall of legal segregation.[3]

One way to better understand this post-1964 period is to trace the influence of civil rights laws on other federal initiatives that played out at the grassroots level as part of President Johnson's Great Society. Local people in Alabama saw these federal programs as an opportunity to create communities that reflected their sense of democracy and social justice. Walter had come to Selma as part of a project sponsored by the Episcopal Society for Cultural and Racial Unity. He had planned to replace seminarian Jonathan Daniels when he returned to school in the fall of 1965, but when Tom Coleman murdered Daniels on August 20, 1965, Walter agreed to serve in what he called a "ministry of presence" in a consortium of religious groups under the name Selma Inter-Religious Project (SIP). "The idea was, we can't let this ministry stop," he later explained. Growing up in Mobile, he had become aware of the damaging effects of white supremacy when he was in high school and college in the late 1940s and early 1950s. Walter became an Episcopal priest after earning his undergraduate degree at Spring Hill College and graduate degrees at the University of the South in Sewanee, Tennessee, and the General Theological Seminary in New York City. After he became the SIP's director, he offered support to the civil rights movement, using Selma as his base. He explained that the SIP would "remain as a consultative-type organization that assists the self-help groups that exist all over the Black Belt but more or less in southwest Alabama."[4]

Some of his early work involved seeking funds from the Office of Economic Opportunity (OEO) for Wilcox County residents who had been evicted from their tenant farms because they registered to vote in the winter of 1965–66. In December 1965, Walter concluded, "The Negro is no longer needed or wanted in Wilcox County. Perhaps a few years ago he was not needed but he was not unwanted. The grand plan is to get him out of Wilcox County." Because the county lacked federal housing, when planters evicted their tenants, they had few options except to leave the area. He found that county extension agents and local banks colluded to foreclose on black borrowers who registered to vote or identified with the civil rights movement. "Eviction is a potent tool," he wrote in his diary. "The purpose of all this is no longer to terrify but simply to aggravate. Life becomes intolerable in Wilcox so a move is made to Chicago or Detroit. This is the white plan." His "ministry of presence" eventually enabled him to link the work of local Southern Christian Leadership Conference (SCLC) leaders such as Rev. Daniel Harrell Jr. and his wife, Juanita, in Camden, Alabama, with sympathetic OEO officials on the national and regional levels that would eventually lead to federal support for programs in Wilcox County.[5]

The January 1967 issue of *Harper's Magazine* included an article written by renowned southern historian C. Vann Woodward, "What Happened to the Civil Rights Movement?" Woodward sought to explain why the civil rights movement had lost its way after 1966. Although the magazine published no letters to the editor in response to Woodward's article, he received correspondence from Virginia Durr, a friend of his since the early 1940s. Her experience in Alabama enabled her to correct his sense of the direction of the struggle for civil rights. She told him that the antipoverty programs in Montgomery provided another avenue from which to try to change the South and that this approach looked familiar to her from her activism during the 1930s. "I am engaged in a fight now over Head Start," she explained to her friend, "as I am one of the few white people on the board, and we are trying to keep community participation, rather than have it turned over to white and some Negro social workers to be run on a mass scale from the top." She feared that funds for the antipoverty program would be cut as the result of a conservative backlash. Such a cut would constitute a real blow because these programs "have so far done a lot of good," she noted. "They have given people hope and aroused their responsibility and made them feel their government has some concern for them, as did [the Works Progress Administration] back in the old days, but I think the Republican–Pole Cat combination will ruin them if it can, and it probably can."[6]

Durr recognized this work as part of the struggle for racial equality. As she wrote to Woodward, "I agree with you that Civil Rights has now become déjà vu but I do not agree with you that it is over or even weaker." "I think the great mass demonstrations are over," she explained, "BUT all of this has left in its wake a new spirit and a new determination on the part of the Negroes to get their due as Americans. It has come down to the nitty gritty, and on the local level there are fights going on all the time."[7]

Durr also noted the changes wrought by the new federal civil rights laws. She could see that participation in civil rights activities had been a transformative experience for many people: "I hate to say there is a 'New Negro' because that is absurd, but the old Negro no longer feels so hopeless or beat down or pathetic or apathetic, and when people change their feelings about themselves, then I think a big change has come." Yet her letter also reveals her sense that the revolution was not complete. White southerners might have acknowledged the change, but they did not necessarily accept this new day without attempting to maintain the familiar continuity of white supremacy. "And you find it everywhere which is evident in listening to any private conversation of any white Southerner, one way or another, who may be integrationist or most of course, segregationists," she stated plainly, "but they realize the Negro is not what he used to be." In closing her letter, she used her knowledge of events around her to expand on Woodward's views: "I agree the wave has receded but it left a lot of residue and I do not believe that will be swept away. Still hopeful."[8]

The same year that Durr wrote to Woodward, the Southwest Alabama Farmers Cooperative Association (SWAFCA) was formed through the organizing work of Albert Turner, Lewis Black, and Shirley Mesher and the financial and technical support of the Demonstration Division of OEO. The cooperative conducted its business in ten contiguous counties across the Black Belt (Choctaw, Dallas, Greene, Hale, Lowndes, Marengo, Monroe, Perry, Sumter, and Wilcox) and had two thousand members at its peak. The organizers hoped that SWAFCA would create a regional economic base that would free those who had depended on white people for employment. SWAFCA's supporters dreamed that this economic freedom would lead to political change that would ultimately alter the region's future for the better.

Turner, the director of the SCLC in Alabama, explained that the organizers saw the co-op "as the economic arm of the civil rights movement." He had grown up in the Black Belt in Perry County, the fifth of his parents' twelve children, and civil rights had tangible meaning for him. Turner had known all his life that racial justice included receiving an education and gaining economic independence. Black, director of the Alabama Council on Human Relations' Rural Advancement Project, summed up his SWAFCA activity in October 1967: "I feel that we have had a wide gap in society—that Negroes, in spite of the legislative movements that have been made, the Negroes are far behind and they are going to continuously be far behind unless the civil rights movement can work fast to get an economic base for the minority groups." A resident of Hale County, like Perry County part of Alabama's Black Belt, Black knew that work still remained despite the fact that African Americans had won "the right to be seated," "school rights," and "voting rights." He emphasized that "the civil rights movement should move more, trying to give people a continued economical base." Through the development of cooperatives and the use of federal agencies, Black explained, "we can build a society where the minority can live and vote as they please, vote rightfully, where they can live in a society where they can better perpetuate."[9]

Mesher came to the Black Belt in 1965 to participate in the Selma campaign as part of a delegation from San Francisco "to be a body for demonstrations." Prior to her work in Alabama, she had been on the staff of the Congress of Racial Equality (CORE) for its western region, working in the areas of housing and job discrimination. After her arrival in Dallas County, the SCLC tapped Mesher's public relations skills to handle the reporters who had come to cover the dramatic events. Although she realized the march's importance in supporting the right to protest, the right to assemble, and the right to petition the government, she also saw this activism as incomplete. She stayed in the area after the march, eventually becoming a member of the SCLC staff based in Selma. Through this work she found that "people unfortunately felt terribly self-satisfied and they felt, well, like we've solved the problem of Selma." "I think this is rather unfortunate," she lamented. "I think most people went home and that was their responsibility and the salvaging of their consciences for a lifetime." Similar to Talese's observations in May 1965, Mesher's assessment was that "things essentially became worse for these people, people who were still working in the laundry for thirty-six cents an hour—they were still working on the farm since they were farm laborers for a dollar a day." When the cameras left, she said, "It wasn't glamorous anymore; there was no romance to it. It was just grinding head-on work. . . . You were dealing now with the real guts issues. You couldn't keep looking at a man who earned his dollar a day in the field or couldn't get a job at all." From her perspective, the Selma campaign was important "for tearing open an area." "But I think what needs to be realized and perhaps is realized now," she clarified, is "that once you tear open an area, you leave it to a worse fate if you don't have an intention to build an indigenous community organization that's going to be able to fight the battle on from there." The farm co-op served as part of that community-building initiative, reinforcing a web of activities linking economic development with political power across the Alabama Black Belt in the eight years after the passage of the Civil Rights Act.[10]

Local white elites understood the economic and political implications of SWAFCA's collective effort. After OEO agreed to fund the co-op venture, Selma's mayor, Joe Smitherman, joined in a campaign to reverse the decision, which he feared would lead to the takeover of all Black Belt agricultural operations by African American farmers. Louis B. Whitfield, owner of Alabama's only pickle-processing plant, the Whitfield Pickle Company, also knew that he was engaged in a fight to define the meaning of the new civil rights laws. He had a lot to lose if the co-op organized vegetable growers in his region, and he wrote to U.S. senator Lister Hill to express his worries about the co-op's funding. No less than the entire free enterprise system was at stake, according to Whitfield, if black people voted together as a bloc.[11]

By examining the dynamics of the "nitty gritty," as Durr put it, we are able to observe how the federal government addressed the structural issues associated with poverty—lack of industrial growth, loss of jobs, underfunded schools, deficient health facilities, a regressive state tax structure, corrupt political parties entrenched in old ways of doing business. Alabamians understood these matters as key components of white supremacy, which meant that the War on Poverty opened another territory that black and white Alabamians could fight over and wrestle with in their effort to define for themselves the precise meaning of the civil rights revolution. An examination of federal poverty programs enables an understanding of the national government's various roles in the black freedom struggle. The federal government's engagement was crucial to the success of those who worked to implement the new laws. In many ways, this upheaval brought true changes, but familiar patterns also persisted, which helps to explain why portions of the state remain some of the nation's poorest places.

This book provides historical context for the rise of Black Power in the Alabama Black Belt and its connection to the earlier phases of the civil rights movement. Many studies have chronicled SCLC and SNCC's activities in Alabama but have not exposed the variations within these organizations in the small towns and rural communities across the state after 1965, when the national organizations moved on to new campaigns. Among Alabama's many local civil rights activists, the means for reaching their collective goals were varied, often divisive, and rarely unified by race alone—sometimes splitting along class lines, other times breaking along the borders that separated rural areas from towns and cities. By 1972, significant numbers of African Americans had begun to hold public office, histories of this period usually note, but this volume explains who some of these people were, how they got elected, and why their elections could not solve the problems of poverty in the region.

In addition to issues associated with racial inequality, in 1965 the Alabama Black Belt stood at the end of an agricultural transformation that fueled the anxiety of many of the region's citizens—from powerful white landowners to black tenant farmers and landless sharecroppers. By 1966, many planters had stopped growing cotton and begun planting soybeans for new markets, pasture grasses for beef cattle, or timber for the expanding paper mill industry. This change displaced many black people whose families had worked on the land for generations. Throughout this economic upheaval, conflicts arose between the U.S. Department of Agriculture, which saw its role as assisting the development of agribusiness, and OEO, which viewed its purpose as lending a hand to small farmers. The former had its origins in the nineteenth century, while the latter started after the passage of the Civil Rights Act. Members of these federal bureaucracies had differing views of the legitimacy of the civil rights movement and the federal government's role in supporting the struggle for racial justice. What happened on the land and the economic consequences that followed became entwined with the black freedom movement throughout the region and form a significant part of this history.

This book also offers a more complete picture of those people who stood in opposition to the civil rights movement. Familiar characters appear here, including Smitherman and Alabama governor George Wallace, but the story also involves business leaders, state government bureaucrats, and small-town elected officials who used their jobs and influence against the enforcement of federal civil rights laws. In addition, the work of a handful of white supporters of racial justice has often remained unseen and unrecognized. This picture of white Alabamians provides another corrective to the standard historical narrative, revealing a variety of perspectives on the progress of the freedom movement.

Finally, this history refocuses attention on Alabama by noting how the civil rights movement and the War on Poverty destabilized traditional race and class relationships that ultimately affected the state's politics, culture, and economics. During the crucial eight years after 1964, the struggle for civil rights became fully engaged, as federal bureaucrats, state officials, and local residents tried to use federal laws to remap the southern landscape. This period saw real hope as well as real despair. In many ways, the civil rights movement carried on, but so did the forces of white supremacy.

This history has multiple layers. At its base it is a story of how public policy worked, but telling that story requires including the history of the modern South and the civil rights movement. This story is also linear, but it is linear like the Alabama River. At times it will double back to pick up another line of explanation before rejoining the current. It begins in Washington, D.C., in the halls of power, with the high politics of Lyndon Baines Johnson's administration. It then winds through the bureaucracy of OEO and the Alabama state government, based in Montgomery, as well as local governments. The officials charged with implementing the mandates of the Economic Opportunity Act and the new federal civil rights laws faced continual challenges from those bureaucrats in Alabama who had no interest in complying. Finally, the story flows to the grassroots of the Alabama Black Belt, the poorest part of the state financially but the richest in civil rights activism. This history looks at how the meanings of economic justice, morality, and democracy were interpreted, distorted, and reinterpreted as the antipoverty programs reached the grassroots. Chapter by chapter, the complex story unfolds from the apex of the U.S. political power structure to the very poorest Americans. The years after 1964 left their mark on the way people lived in the Alabama Black Belt. Many individuals seized what was their first opportunity to assume leadership roles in their communities.

As Durr noted in her letter to Woodward, his position in New Haven, Connecticut, did not afford him the chance to see what was happening in places such as the Alabama Black Belt. He was not alone; national newspapers and television failed to notice most of this activism and its complexity. Scholars today criticize the War on Poverty because it fell short of its goals. Common complaints point out that OEO ignored the structural nature of poverty and focused instead on job training; when OEO attempted to redistribute political power through the Community Action Program (CAP), Congress weakened this effort with the 1967 Green Amendment. One journalist, Nicholas Lemann, has concluded that the War on Poverty failed politically because the rhetoric that surrounded it could never be turned into reality: the War on Poverty "set itself up to seem as if it had ended in defeat when it didn't vanquish all poverty." President Ronald Reagan reinforced this image of the Great Society program when he quipped in a State of the Union address, "We waged a War on Poverty, and poverty won."[12]

Even though OEO programs did not end rural poverty in Alabama's Black Belt, antipoverty critics have used too broad a brush, painting over important details that enhance our comprehension of the region's history. Both the black freedom struggle and the fight against poverty were community based and in practice involved interactions among Washington, Alabama, and local people. A study that looks at the civil rights movement and the War on Poverty on the community level can contribute to our knowledge of both. This history provides a more complete understanding of how southerners worked it out the hard way to define for themselves how freedom would come during the years shaped by the civil rights movement.

CHAPTER ONE

Southern Accents

The Politics of Race and the
Economic Opportunity Act of 1964

If you're saying, "Did civil rights have an influence?" I'd say the answer is, "Sure." That was part of the context of the times.
William B. Cannon, Bureau of the Budget and Member of the President's Task Force in the War Against Poverty

There's nothing done in the world that isn't political.
Donald M. Baker, Counsel to the Labor Subcommittee, Senate Committee on Labor and Public Welfare

On January 8, 1964, in his first State of the Union address, President Lyndon Baines Johnson laid out his administration's plans in the aftermath of the assassination of John F. Kennedy. LBJ connected civil rights for African Americans with support for the broader federal programs that would become the cornerstone of his policies. This speech is remembered most for articulating his commitment to pass the stalled civil rights bill to honor the slain president. However, LBJ also used this national occasion to reshape Kennedy's New Frontier into something that could be identified more closely with Johnson's style of governing. He began his speech by asking the Eighty-eighth Congress to envision itself as an active body that would go down in history as having done more for civil rights than previous Congresses, as having enacted a far-reaching tax cut, and as having "declared all-out war on human poverty and unemployment in these United States." Johnson used the attack on poverty to illustrate the direction his administration would take, initially by linking poverty with racism. "Unfortunately, many Americans live on the outskirts of hope—some because of their poverty, and some because of their color, and all too many because of both." He then proclaimed, "This administration today, here and now, declares unconditional war on poverty in America. . . . It will not be a short or easy struggle, no single weapon or strategy will suffice, but we shall not rest until that war is won. The richest Nation on earth can afford to win it. We cannot afford to lose it."[1]

Johnson's bold support for civil rights thus merged with his call to end poverty. Even though a different chief executive had initiated both of these ideas, the speed with which LBJ's administration brought legislation forward showed the nation that the president had greater ambitions and would take bigger strides than Kennedy had. Two key components of Johnson's Great Society— the Civil Rights Act and the Economic Opportunity Act—signaled the president's intention to use the strength of the federal government in new ways. Johnson had cut his political teeth during the New Deal, and his attempt to exceed Roosevelt's legacy altered the balance of power in the federal system in ways FDR could not have imagined. In the South, the potential to undermine the old Jim Crow order was lodged within this antipoverty effort. The Civil Rights Act provided mandates that would alter all federal legislation. For example, when combined with the provisions of the Economic Opportunity Act, these new directives changed the traditional relationship between the federal government and the states. In many cases, the antipoverty legislation enabled administrators within the Office of Economic Opportunity (OEO) to deal directly with citizens, independent of state and local elected officials. While the social and political dynamics between these officeholders and newly enfranchised black people remained unsettled, federal bureaucrats—including those in OEO—were called on to mediate between the rival forces, with, in many cases, hundreds of thousands of dollars hanging in the balance. As the Johnson administration moved forward, observers realized that other Great Society initiatives could implement some of the civil rights movement's goals.

A focus on the legislative history and initial implementation of the Economic Opportunity Act of 1964 highlights the civil rights movement's influence on the political landscape of the South. The drafters of the bill believed that state-level politicians would not incorporate their African American constituents into the antipoverty fight because of the massive resistance of white southerners that followed the Supreme Court's 1954 *Brown v. Board of Education* decision. As a result, the antipoverty legislation enabled the federal government to circumvent these local officials to bring all the voices of the poor into the federal initiative.

While Congress debated the legislation during the summer of 1964, the presidential campaign entered its final stages. The Republican nominee, Arizona senator Barry Goldwater, signaled a new conservatism with a harder edge and passionate base. During the early 1960s, the GOP began to split over its traditional supportive stance on civil rights. Historian Joseph Crespino has explained that this process resulted from the belief "that as the white South evolved beyond Jim Crow, southern segregationists would realize that what they believed was much closer to the new conservatism than to the platform of the Democratic Party." Goldwater and his supporters sought to create a new Republican Party committed to a strict order of conservative ideology. At the June 22, 1963, Republican National Committee meeting in Denver, the rift between the progressive northeastern branch of the party and the more conservative western and heartland branches became more apparent with the recent addition of white southern Republicans. Journalist Robert Novak reported that many of those in attendance in Denver were bothered by "unmistakable signs that party leaders from outside the industrialized states of the eastern seaboard were seriously contemplating transforming the Republican Party into the White Man's Party." Southern and western GOP members made it known during this meeting that they intended to overtake the party, nominate Goldwater, and adopt the most conservative party platform since the 1920s. As a part of the GOP strategy, this new group of leaders intended to take a neutral stand with regard to the civil rights of African Americans. Indeed, Goldwater's candidacy attracted voters in the Deep South based on his commitment to states' rights and his opposition to federal civil rights laws.[2]

During the hearings on the antipoverty bill, members of the GOP raised questions about the legislation to draw attention to the federal government's new power to assist poor, black southerners. Republican members of Congress took this calculated stance to use race to attract conservative Democrats into their party. The Arizona senator's growing popularity among white southerners made it increasingly difficult for many Dixie Democrats to maintain their political fidelity, especially after the passage of the Civil Rights Act. Bill Moyers, a presidential adviser, remembered that on the night Johnson signed the landmark legislation, he said, "I think we just delivered the South to the Republican Party for a long time to come." President Johnson and his aides realized that they were operating in uncharted territory, and the fight to pass the Economic Opportunity Act reveals the way they maneuvered under these new conditions while trying to retain as many southern Democrats as possible. In the end, compromises had to be made, and the changes in the legislation played a significant role in the way the War on Poverty would be fought in the South, especially in Alabama. The wrangling for votes to pass the antipoverty legislation exposed a pattern replicated on the state and local levels as the people in Alabama—black and white—struggled to redefine their positions within the polity under these new circumstances.[3]

The details of the antipoverty legislation and the Johnson administration's strategy to gain the measure's passage reveal the new reality brought about by the civil rights movement in areas that may initially appear to have nothing to do with race. In the summer of 1964, many southern politicians had difficulty finding their way as the political ground moved beneath their feet. Race has always been a fault line within American society, especially in the South, and the cracks in the political surface that formed during the 1940s and 1950s widened and began to move in unpredictable ways after 1964, causing politicians to reexamine their positions on the new terrain. The debate over how to wage the War on Poverty underscores the manner in which the president as well as southern federal elected officials tried to maintain control over this process. The Democratic Party was reforming, but the details of that reformation remained unclear.

The Senate's August 11, 1964, approval of the Economic Opportunity Act signaled that a Second Reconstruction was under way. However, as in the 1870s, the southern accents of Dixie's politicians had not been ignored. Amendments to the legislation accommodated the demands of states' rights supporters. After a summer of negotiating the bill, the Johnson administration was willing to have people believe that the racial issues initially associated with the bill had been removed. The *Atlanta Constitution* described the legislation as "primarily an education bill aimed at training people now on relief rolls and potential welfare recipients—particularly the young—for employment." While accurate only in the most limited way, this narrow assessment highlights the nature of the Second Reconstruction as the manifestation of the civil rights movement in federal public policy. In formulating legislation, executive and congressional leaders made changes and cut deals to ensure passage. For decades, southern white politicians altered proposals to suit their social mores and economic power, and this bill shared that tradition. Yet even after late-night meetings and closed-door sessions, the ground had indeed shifted because of the Civil Rights Act. On the surface, the final version of the Economic Opportunity Act may have seemed to give southern politicians their way once again. But the heavy-handed actions of a few southern governors—those from Alabama, Florida, South Carolina, and Texas—led to future amendments to the legislation that ultimately strengthened federal power at the expense of local and state authority. As a result, by 1973, when OEO's doors closed, this federal initiative clearly had played a supporting role in the Second Reconstruction, especially in George Wallace's home state.[4]

Why Focus on the Poor in 1964?

Johnson used Kennedy's legislative agenda for the election year but made these plans his own after occupying the Oval Office for just over six weeks. The day after JFK'S assassination, the new president met with Walter Heller, chair of the Council of Economic Advisers, to discuss the Kennedy administration's unfinished business, including the proposed program to fight poverty, which was being called "Widening Participation in Prosperity." LBJ asked Heller to continue working on this initiative: "That's my kind of program. . . . Move full speed ahead." Few people outside of the Kennedy administration knew about the plans to fight poverty, and Johnson could use this issue to emerge from the shadow cast by the national grief over JFK's death. "We've got to use the Kennedy program as a springboard to take on the Congress, summon the states to new heights, create a Johnson program, different in tone, fighting and aggressive," he told one of his aides. "Hell, we've barely begun to solve our problems. And we can do it all. We've got the wherewithal. . . . There's nothing we can't do, if the masses are behind us." Winning the fight against poverty would prove that Johnson deserved to occupy the White House. This legislation would also enable him to use the powers of the federal government to better people's lives, a goal that defined LBJ's liberalism. The possibility of success also motivated the president. He told Richard Goodwin, "I'm sick of all the people who talk about the things we can't do. Hell, we're the richest country in the world, the most powerful. We can do it all, if we're not too greedy; that's our job: to persuade people to give a little so everyone will be better off." Johnson summed up all these motivations in his memoirs: "I believed a program that eliminated poverty—or even reduced it—would strengthen the moral and economic fiber of the entire country. It was on that basis that I prepared to move forward and commit the resources and prestige of the new administration."[5]

In addition, Johnson apparently planned to use the antipoverty program to address the needs of black southerners without having to proclaim that goal outright. LBJ's entire career in government had been geared toward pulling the South into the mainstream of American society through programs that supported modernization and economic growth. He knew that white southern racism played a leading role in the region's slow advance. Prior to becoming president, LBJ had a mixed record with regard to publicly supporting the aspirations of African Americans. Johnson took clandestine actions on behalf of his black constituents in the National Youth Administration in Texas during the New Deal and in his early years in the House of Representatives, where he made sure that black farmers from his district received the same Farm Security Administration (FSA) loans as did white farmers. Milo Perkins, an FSA official, said that Johnson "was the first man in Congress from the South ever to go to bat for the Negro farmer." In the Senate, however, Johnson developed a close relationship with Richard Russell of Georgia, an unabashed advocate of racial segregation who used the filibuster and other Senate rules to his advantage. As Senate majority leader, Johnson managed the passage of the Civil Rights Act of 1957, but the amendments to the measure he allowed severely weakened its ability to increase black voting or protect other African American civil rights. Each of these actions in one way or another confirmed his purpose of modernizing the South. He shrewdly took what he could get from a piece of legislation and looked for more the next time. By 1964, he believed, the Economic Opportunity Act might be that "next time." The civil rights bill before Congress sought to end racial segregation in the South, a monumental achievement but one that would not, however, address the economic woes of those who had lived under Jim Crow's boot. In May, Johnson expressed his concern about the Civil Rights Act's reception across the country: "The thing we are more afraid of than anything else," he told Hubert Humphrey, "is that we will have real revolution in the country when this bill goes into effect. . . . It took us ten years to put this Supreme Court decision into effect on education. . . . Unless we have the Republicans joinin' us and helpin' put down this mutiny, we'll have mutiny in this goddamn country. So we've got to make this an American bill and not just a Democratic bill." Fighting poverty, a problem that affected more white Americans than black, could serve as another way to Americanize the aims of the Civil Rights Act. The War on Poverty would address some real needs in the country—the out-of-work Appalachian coal miner, the neglected inner-city teenager, and the displaced southern sharecropper.[6]

In this regard, Johnson took his cues from Kennedy, who had initially based his attack on poverty on stimulating the economy. Following the lackluster performance of the Area Redevelopment Act, the Manpower Development Training Act, and the economy in general, the idea for a tax cut took center stage in December 1962. Knowing that the cut in taxes would primarily benefit people in the upper- and middle-income brackets, Heller advised the president that adding something developed specifically for poor Americans might be politically prudent. As historian Carl Brauer has explained, "Heller was concerned about protecting the Kennedy administration's left flank."[7]

Another faction of that "left flank" led the president to more directly connect unemployment and racism. By the summer of 1963, the president found it increasingly difficult to hold the direct-action campaigns for civil rights at arm's length. Many leaders within the civil rights movement feared that Kennedy would wait until after the 1964 election to introduce a federal civil rights bill; on June 9, therefore, they began to plan for the March on Washington for Jobs and Freedom, intended to generate national support for their cause. Events in Birmingham, Alabama, ultimately seized the attention of the nation and the president. "For two years [Attorney General] Robert Kennedy had attempted to deal with each racial crisis on an ad hoc basis," Adam Fairclough has explained. The brutal attacks on demonstrators in Alabama led by Police Commissioner Eugene "Bull" Connor "finally convinced him that crises would recur with such frequency and magnitude that the federal government, unless it adopted a more radical policy, would be overwhelmed. . . . There was a direct connection, therefore, between SCLC's demonstrations and the introduction of the civil rights bill."[8]

On June 19, 1963, JFK committed himself to take action, ending two and a half years of indecision. He laid out his plans for federal civil rights legislation in a special message to Congress on civil rights and job opportunities. He wanted to provide a full equal right to vote, legal remedies for the denial of certain individual rights, and legislation to improve the training, skills, and economic opportunities of the "economically distressed and discontented, white and Negro." By connecting equal rights with job opportunities, Kennedy revealed his understanding of the civil rights crisis. The president clearly staked out his position: "There is little value in a Negro's obtaining the right to be admitted to hotels and restaurants if he has no cash in his pocket and no job." By placing the demands of the civil rights movement within an economic framework, the president disclosed how he hoped to deal with these pressing issues. He could confront the intransigent problems of racism that the civil rights movement dramatized through a program that also addressed unemployment. This approach would enable him to meet African Americans' needs by focusing on the economic distress of poor people in general, increasing the likelihood that the legislation would pass Congress. The dramatic August 1963 March on Washington, in which 250,000 people called for jobs and freedom through peaceful protest in front of the Lincoln Memorial, was beamed via television across the nation, validating the goals of the civil rights movement for many Americans for the first time. By forging civil rights with employment, Kennedy planned to open the door of opportunity wider to include the needs of other "forgotten" Americans. In September, White House officials concluded that the 1964 legislative package should include a poverty bill. A Kennedy adviser rationalized that "having mounted a dramatic program for one disadvantaged group [through civil rights legislation] it was both equitable and politically attractive to launch one specifically designed to aid other disadvantaged groups."[9]

The intellectual justification for the fight against poverty appeared in the January 1964 *Economic Report of the President,* which proposed the passage of legislation that would take the country beyond the New Deal programs by reaching out to poor Americans. Robert Lampman, a member of the Council of Economic Advisers, wrote the report's second chapter, "The Problem of Poverty in America," in which he made the case that poverty had become a national problem. He also stressed that the South stood poised as one of the prime targets for improvement. In 1960, 16,305,000 of the 31,775,000 poor people in the United States (51.31 percent) lived in the South. Dixie's politicians had been aware of their poor constituents for many decades, and the statistics in the report probably did not surprise many of them. In the 1930s, FDR declared the region "the nation's number one economic problem," and the South benefited greatly from the New Deal. Many southern congressmen acquired liberal reputations because they supported progressive legislation such as the creation of public housing, farm subsidies, hospital construction, and rural electrification that improved the living standards for many of their constituents. Historian Wayne Flynt has noted that "in the 1940s and 1950s no state congressional delegation did more [than Alabama's] to expand federal powers to assist the nation's weakest and most vulnerable people." In fact, in 1950 and in 1955, U.S. senator from Alabama John Sparkman, the son of a tenant farmer who paid for his University of Alabama education by shoveling coal, conducted the Joint Economic Committee's first Senate hearings on the persistence of rural poverty. Yet although the Alabama congressional delegation had no problem creating federal assistance for poor whites, such aid often ignored their poverty-stricken black neighbors.[10]

When Johnson became president, the South's congressional representatives might have been expected to be among the first to support his antipoverty plan. Unanimous southern support, however, did not materialize. Past events had made southerners in Congress skeptical. At the end of the New Deal, liberalism became closely associated with racial equality, a process further solidified when President Harry S. Truman accepted a strong civil rights platform in his 1948 presidential campaign. The Democratic Party split that year, with states' rights supporters forming the Dixiecrat Party in protest. The Supreme Court's 1954 *Brown v. Board of Education* decision, which declared the doctrine of separate but equal unconstitutional in public education, and the Civil Rights Act of 1957, which was the first federal legislation for racial justice in the twentieth century, added further fuel to the flames of southern Democratic discontent. "The one issue that threatened everything was race," LBJ aide Harry McPherson explained. "It was pervasive, insistent, and aroused unequaled passion." By the early 1960s, assistance from the federal government held racial overtones—as evidenced in Lampman's report linking poverty and racial discrimination—that many southern politicians found distasteful. Kari Frederickson, a historian of the Dixiecrat revolt, has concluded that those southerners who stayed within the Democratic fold did so by "convincing the white voters that party loyalty in congressional elections was the best means by which to safeguard their economic and their racial interests." Only as loyal members of the Democratic Party could they ensure the ability to alter legislation to avoid threatening the racial status quo. Many southerners held powerful positions in the House of Representatives and the Senate that would enable them to contain the tide that the civil rights revolution created. Despite the South's heavy concentration of poor people, many of the region's representatives in Congress cast a dubious eye at Johnson's plans for a War on Poverty. While the new president's administration prepared for the antipoverty effort, the hearings and the floor debate on the 1964 civil rights bill stormed through the Capitol. For some politicians from Dixie, these fierce fights punctuated the fact that assistance to the poor could promote both racial and economic equality. Since 1963, first Kennedy and then Johnson had said as much in speeches to gain support for civil rights legislation. As appealing as many Americans may have found this connection, it dismayed dyed-in-the-wool racists who resisted change as well as southern moderates who took a more gradual approach. Both would now oppose federal aid under these circumstances. By 1964, the risks in publicly backing efforts against poverty had become too great unless the legislation could be altered to protect states' rights and diminish the expanding powers of the federal government.[11]

LBJ rarely sent legislation up to the Hill without first knowing where he stood with the Congress. Johnson recognized that southern congressmen held the key to his success. He had been willing to take on the South to get a civil rights bill; the Economic Opportunity Act could serve as his way to offer southerners a reason to stay in his party. LBJ realized that northern Democrats would support the legislation because their urban constituency would clearly benefit from it. Early on, many Republicans voiced their opposition. Senator Goldwater attacked the president's motives, calling him the "Santa Claus of free lunch." With the Congress divided between liberal forces made up of northern Democrats and Republicans and conservative heartland and western Republicans, the president saw that the bill's fate rested with the southern members of his party. He hoped to court them with enough federal assistance that they might look beyond their racial anxieties and take another step into modernity.[12]

The Development of the Economic Opportunity Act

A force from the old South confronted LBJ in mid-January, before the antipoverty effort got under way. Prior to Kennedy's death, Senator Harry F. Byrd (D-VA), chair of the Finance Committee, had demanded that the 1965 fiscal budget total less than $100 billion before he would let the tax-cut legislation out of the Rules Committee. In December, Johnson met with Byrd, and the Virginian presented the new president with a scenario similar to the one that he had offered JFK. Byrd would let the bill proceed if LBJ met with Byrd's committee and the House Ways and Means Committee before submitting the budget. In addition, the total budget would still have to fall below $100 billion, and it had to be offered to Congress before the tax bill became law. The president and his aides whittled the budget to $97.9 billion, thereby enabling the passage of the bill to cut federal taxes by $10 billion over two years. The horse-trading had already begun. The War on Poverty would now be fought with almost $1 billion instead of the $11 billion originally called for in the *Economic Report of the President*. As a result, instead of reforming programs that already existed within the federal bureaucracy, the antipoverty program would operate as a separate organization within the executive branch because no existing organization could take the necessary time to plan the program and then get it through Congress. Some observers argued that having the new organization so closely identified with the president might quell the anticipated criticism—the antipoverty fight could never be mistaken as anything other than Johnson's program. Under these financial constraints, LBJ abandoned a jobs program to assist in civil rights implementation and gambled that the tax cut and the antipoverty program would adequately address the needs of the poor.[13]

Johnson next needed a specific bill that would plan and manage this domestic war. To lead this new program, the president tapped R. Sargent Shriver, who had proven his ability to create new programs and to get legislation through Congress. Shriver's work for the Peace Corps had impressed LBJ. "In planning that organization," the president remembered, "he had personally visited and briefed many Senators and Congressmen, obtaining a measure of congressional respect not always given to a bureaucrat." President Kennedy credited the passage of the Peace Corps Act to his brother-in-law's lobbying skills. In addition, speed was essential. LBJ had declared the War on Poverty in early January, but a month later, no program was in sight. The president told Shriver, "We don't have a year. This thing has to work. And it has to . . . get through Congress, and then . . . it has to work right away." Johnson believed that Shriver, with his experience in creating new programs, a successful record with Congress, and the know-how to work the political system, could work both quickly and effectively.[14]

Not everyone in Washington found Shriver so appealing. During Kennedy's presidential campaign, Shriver and Harris Wofford worked as the candidate's civil rights advisers. As director of the Peace Corps, Shriver had instituted a nondiscrimination policy and an affirmative action plan that prevented southern universities that declined to admit black students from offering training sessions for Peace Corps volunteers. In January 1963, African Americans occupied 7.4 percent of the agency's higher-echelon positions, far better than the dismal 0.8 percent figure for other federal government bureaus. Black people filled 24 percent of the Peace Corps's lower-level positions, compared to only 5.5 percent in other federal agencies. Shriver's minority-employment policies made good sense for an agency that worked with impoverished people of color all over the world, especially as a counterweight in the Cold War struggle for the hearts and

Figure 3. OEO director R. Sargent Shriver and President Lyndon Baines Johnson in the Oval Office, April 5, 1965. Photo by Yoichi R. Okamoto, A213-2A, Lyndon Baines Johnson Library, Austin, Tex.

minds of people in developing countries. Shriver also sought to challenge the federal government's traditional hiring practices. The Peace Corps's employment policies may not have alarmed southern politicians because they affected only a small segment of the federal bureaucracy in the secretary of state's office. But given the proposed scope and high profile of the new federal antipoverty program, Shriver's new role might enable him to accelerate changes in the racial status quo.[15]

Johnson formally appointed his new poverty chief on February 1, 1964. The president told Shriver to encourage joint planning, joint programs, and joint administration wherever feasible. Johnson also said that he wanted to "propel a program through Congress immediately" and that he wanted the plan "to produce visible results, so that there would be no question about Congress' continuing the effort with adequate funding" in the future. Johnson warned Shriver of the effort this would take: "You'll have a billion dollars to pass out. . . . So you just call up the Pope and tell him you might not be on time every morning for church . . . but you're going to be working for the good of humanity."[16]

To accomplish Johnson's charge, Shriver formed the President's Task Force in the War Against Poverty, a fluid organization made up of a variety of people who came and went as the weeks and months passed. High-level bureaucrats, economists, and sociologists constituted the majority of task force members, and a core group of people worked steadily with Shriver throughout the planning period. A handful of the members of this inner circle had backgrounds that would draw the attention of some conservative southern members of Congress, giving credence to their fears that the War on Poverty could help implement the new civil rights legislation. Adam Yarmolinsky, Shriver's deputy, found himself targeted for particular contempt. He had come to the task force from the Department of Defense, where he served as a special assistant to Secretary Robert McNamara. While working at the Pentagon, he had helped carry out the Gesell Report, which focused on widening the desegregation process on military bases across the South by declaring segregated facilities in nearby towns off-limits to service personnel. Assistant secretary John Baker represented the U.S. Department of Agriculture on the task force. Baker had begun working for the department in the 1930s, when he was involved in New Deal programs that sought to combat rural poverty. As part of the controversial Resettlement Administration, Baker attempted to aid sharecroppers and tenant farmers, and he was involved in efforts by the FSA to provide loans and grants to poor farmers. Baker remained with the Agriculture Department until 1951, when he began a ten-year stint as the director of legislative services for the National Farmers Union, a progressive organization that offered an alternative to the conservative Farm Bureau. With Kennedy's election, Baker had returned to government service. Jack Conway joined the task force in its final stages, when the legislation had been sent up to Congress and the hearings had begun. He came from Chicago and had been a labor activist since the 1940s, first with the United Auto Workers and later with the Industrial Union Department of the AFL-CIO. He joined the Kennedy administration as a deputy administrator of the Housing and Home Finance Agency, where he streamlined the approval procedure for applicants to the Area Redevelopment Administration. In 1963, he left government service to represent Walter Reuther on the committee planning the March on Washington. Conway also lobbied Congress in support of the civil rights bill through the Leadership Conference on Civil Rights.[17]

From early February until mid-March, the President's Task Force in the War Against Poverty developed what would become the Economic Opportunity Act of 1964, an omnibus bill to fight poverty. All the sections of the bill shared a common grassroots goal—expanding opportunity for the poor so that they could change their own lives. Some observers have criticized the legislation because it did not redistribute wealth or offer a large jobs program. Alice O'Connor has pointed out that without a targeted employment program, the focus on individuals "effectively skirted the systemic nature of social inequality and economic change." The task force sought to combat poverty through federally

sponsored programs that would benefit people on the local level, not by restructuring society to assist those left behind by capitalism's cruelty. Yet even in its
less ambitious and less coherent format, the proposed economic opportunity
bill harbored enough transforming possibilities to threaten entrenched local
power structures, especially in the South, where the welfare system had habitu-
ally excluded many of the people who needed the most assistance.[18]

The bill had seven titles. Title I concentrated on youth programs, primarily
the Job Corps, the Neighborhood Youth Corps, work training, and work-study.
Title II encompassed the urban and rural Community Action Program (CAP),
which offered funds directly to communities through local governments or
private nonprofit agencies to devise projects that would alleviate poverty and
which required the "maximum feasible participation of the residents served" in
planning and implementing programs. Title III focused on several programs to
combat poverty in rural areas, and Title IV centered on employment and investment incentives operated by the Small Business Administration. Programs in
Title V sought to expand the opportunities for work, training, and basic education. Title VI resurrected Kennedy's National Service Corps as the Volunteers
in Service to America (VISTA), creating a volunteer force that could bring the
War on Poverty to poor people all over the country. Finally, Title VII contained
provisions relating to administration and appropriations, creating OEO in the
Executive Office of the President with a $962.5 million budget for fiscal 1965.[19]

The two titles that would eventually cause southern members of Congress
the most consternation were the CAP (Title II) and the Rural Poverty Program
(Title III). An explanation of these initiatives provides some insight into the
potential problems in persuading southern Democrats to accept the legislation as written by the task force. Those who worked on the body of Title II
knew that the Community Action Program could spur big changes in impoverished communities, especially in the South. For example, participants in task
force discussions realized that not all local governments operated the same way
and that the legislation therefore needed to address that issue. A debate began
over local government involvement in community action agencies (CAAs) and
whether the bill should require government participation. When the conversation focused on the South, some members of the task force wondered how poor
black southerners could be guaranteed involvement in antipoverty programs in
a segregated society. "We had a problem," William Cannon explained; "we knew
we couldn't get community action agencies in the established governmental
structure in the South." As a result, task force members were comfortable with
the idea that some CAAs should be able to bypass the local power structure to
protect the rights of poor minorities. A compromise developed that permitted
the CAP to offer funds to both local governments and nonprofit agencies. The

federal government thus could evade segregationist state and local governments to support CAAs that would benefit poor African Americans.[20]

Title II's "maximum feasible participation" phrase provided another avenue through which to bring in the talents of poor black and white people into the operation of CAAs. Daniel Patrick Moynihan, a task force participant from the Labor Department, said that he agreed to the inclusion of this phrase because he "saw it as a way of ensuring that the Southern black poor would not be denied any of the benefits of the poverty legislation." If the requirement to include local residents in the program became part of the law, then Washington could intervene if the preconditions of the legislation were not being met. Shriver agreed because he knew of other areas in the country where the poor could be excluded: "It isn't only in the South, the same thing was true in Appalachia, or . . . in Chicago, or in San Francisco." As Baker explained, maximum feasible participation could also be used with different types of service providers: "The Extension Service . . . really felt that if you wanted to have a community action program, you must turn it over to them and they'd do it. They needed to be disabused of that. . . . They would do it for the poor and to the poor, but not with the poor." The maximum feasible participation clause enabled the poor to be their own agents in mitigating poverty.[21]

In a May 4, 1964, discussion draft on "The Role of Indigenous Organizations in Community Action Programs," Fred O'R. Hayes, a task force member from the Urban Renewal Administration, tried to define the genesis of the maximum feasible participation clause and exactly what the task force meant by it. In his examination of the benefits of this new approach, he indicated that the possibility of political confrontation also existed. According to Hayes, the requirement for the participation of the poor was based on a number of widely accepted and interrelated hypotheses that were applicable to varying degrees depending on the situation of the community involved.[22]

The first premise supposed that the members of the American middle class did not understand the poor and were therefore incapable of devising an effective antipoverty program without their involvement. Some who developed the community action concept also thought that the poor resented dominant community institutions, a belief that resulted in low participation rates in programs created for impoverished people. To remedy this situation, the poor needed to be involved in the process of program development and administration. This new approach to welfare would reduce dependency, and those living in poverty would develop the "capacity and opportunity to make [their] own way." A new sense of dignity would grow out of participation and could not be obtained in a program that worked on rather than with the poor. In addition, as they redirected their energies toward the community and away from themselves, the poor would enhance the community. And finally, an effective antipoverty program would assist in revolutionizing the existing welfare agencies, which were dominated by bureaucracies resistant to change. Organization would provide the poor with increased political power, which, in turn, would enable them to press their needs with their elected officials and community bureaucracies.[23]

Based on Hayes's memo, the task force members discussed some anticipated consequences of involving the poor in local CAAs. All agreed that a CAA could interfere with a city's power structure. Hayes warned of the potential for trouble when he wrote in his draft discussion memo, "We hope to unite and at the same time to divide. We insist upon a community consensus but would also like to have politically potent and potentially effective criticism of programs as directed." This approach might create problems for the antipoverty agency because "we wish to have an administratively simple program but are willing, at least tentatively, to disrupt the administrative integrity of local programs to develop and give strength to the critics representing the views of the poor." Hayes also realized that politicians could benefit from as well as be hurt by the contributions of poor citizens working on their own behalf: "Finally, we offer the political leadership of our cities a program which can redound to their political credit and at the same time would encourage the creation of organizations which almost inevitably would be politically competitive and destructive of the support of the existing political power structure." Surprisingly, some members of the group overlooked the possibility that such opposition might be anything other than constructive. "Our discussion of the implications of participation of the poor did not assume the kind of confrontations that later developed," Yarmolinsky remarked. "We didn't really talk about" that possibility. James Sundquist later observed, "Nobody, as of February or March, anticipated the direction it eventually went, or if they did anticipate it, there's absolutely nothing on the record or in anybody's recollection."[24]

The deputy director must not have been present the day Hayes presented his memo, and Sundquist must not have been on Hayes's distribution list. The potential for conflict existed, and some task force members had been debating and discussing it. Hayes wrote his memo in early May, which may have been too late for anything to be done about the problem since the bill had gone to the Hill in mid-March. When the task force drafted the legislation, most members commented that they viewed black poverty in the geographical context of the South, not in the ghettos of the nation's largest cities, and they felt comfortable with the possibility of enhancing Dixie's chances to change its ways. The southern civil rights struggle dominated the scenario of racial conflict at this time. Since the South seemed to be the problematic region with regard to race, Hayes's prophetic warning did not resonate enough to induce changes in the legislation. "The Negro protest throughout this country is illustrative," Hayes cautioned, "and Negro protest will be embodied in neighborhood and group organizations with which the anti-poverty program must deal. The low income white neighborhood which finds its common ground in protection against the Negro encroachment will be no less difficult."[25]

In addition to concern over the CAP, plans for the rural poor also had the potential to raise some red flags. Title III concentrated on the poorest farmers who lived beyond the reach of the city. Through loans, grants, landownership, and development of cooperatives, task force members from the Agriculture Department hoped to curtail the stream of rural poor who migrated into the nation's larger cities, where some on the task force believed "they . . . accomplished nothing but a relocation of their poverty." In each of these programs lay the chance for a reformation of the rural southern landscape.[26]

Farm families represented 16 percent of the U.S. poor in 1964. Many lived at a subsistence level. One family in rural Montgomery County, Alabama, had eight people living in a house that had a dirt floor and no glass windows; wooden shutters provided some protection but did not close tightly. A federal employee, Mary Drake, found that many of the houses in this part of the county leaned in such a way that doors could not shut properly, occupants pasted paper on the walls to keep out the wind, and indoor plumbing was not available. She described housing conditions as "the worst I have ever seen." At a hearing sponsored by the U.S. Commission on Civil Rights, Rebecca Ward of Akron, Alabama, testified that four of her children could not go to school because they lacked proper shoes and clothes. She earned twelve dollars a week and could not afford to spend money on such things. The night before her testimony, she fed her family biscuits and syrup for dinner. Pattie Mae Haynes of Shorter, Alabama, explained that her family drew water from a local spring and did not even have an outhouse: "We just go way down in the woods somewhere." Many of the rural poor existed on the outskirts of society, unable to take advantage of safety-net programs offered by the Farmers Home Administration because they had too few assets to qualify for credit.[27]

The drafters of Title III believed that they needed to make money available so that the poorest farm families could improve their standards of living through capital improvements such as the purchase of milk cows or small tractors. Title III offered fifteen-hundred-dollar grants and twenty-five-hundred-dollar loans to enable farm families to expand their operations and enhance their living standards. But Bureau of the Budget officials objected to the grant/loan idea, which they feared southern members of Congress would see "as a way of giving grants to poor Negro sharecroppers in the South," in Charles Schultze's words. "Under the community action program this could have been done without spelling it out with specific language in the bill." As Schultze's anxiety indicates, the South's votes were key to the legislation's passage.[28]

Figure 4. A typical Alabama Black Belt house inhabited by a sharecropper or tenant farmer, with an uneven porch floor and damaged roof, late 1960s. The washtub indicates that the house lacks running water. Photo by Nancy Redpath. Francis X. Walter Personal Papers, Sewanee, Tenn.

The family farm corporations section of Title III, described by its critics as the land reform section, promised to establish nonprofit corporations that would buy land and then sell it to poor farmers in individual allotments. Not planned as a central part of Title III, this program would have provided some people with land on which they could live more comfortably. In the South, this idea had serious ramifications. The crop-lien system had kept sharecroppers and tenants economically and politically powerless since the days of Reconstruction. Enabling people who had never owned property to buy land free and clear would have offered a level of independence unthinkable even in the early 1960s. Those who opposed the civil rights bill, including Alabama governor George Wallace, feared that the transfer of land would be one repercussion of the legislation. He told a crowd at a Jackson, Mississippi, rally that the proposed civil rights measure demonstrated that the federal government was "well on its way to 'land-reform' legislation under which people will be called upon to redistribute the real estate which they have labored so hard to accumulate." Southern Democrats who agreed with Wallace were unlikely to support this part of Title III.[29]

The last section of Title III to assist the rural poor emphasized the support cooperatives could give to this target population. Acknowledging that impoverished farmers had the greatest need for strong marketing, purchasing, and consuming organizations, Title III sought to provide financing for these group endeavors. This program also might unite southern black farmers who had not been able to organize on their own. Having to buy seed and fertilizer from companies that had a monopoly on the local market kept poor farmers from gaining much ground. Many marginal farmers would benefit from a cooperative, thus potentially threatening traditional business practices in some parts of Dixie.[30]

The president did not personally contribute to the drafting of the economic opportunity bill other than approving the ideas presented to him. After the bill was written, LBJ reviewed it and formulated his own opinions about what it would accomplish. He understood the concept of the Job Corps, with its job training facilities and conservation camps. This resembled the National Youth Administration, which had provided vocational training for unemployed and unskilled young people in workshops and resident training centers during the Great Depression. Kermit Gordon and Walter Heller explained the CAP to the president, and Johnson remembered that they "warned me of the risks—particularly the political risks—that might make the outcome uncertain. I was willing to take the chance." Johnson later claimed that he knew that this program might rattle many existing institutions, "but I decided that some shaking up might be needed to get a bold new program moving. I thought the local governments had to be challenged to be awakened."[31]

The president anticipated opposition to the legislation. Elizabeth Wickenden Goldschmidt, a friend of Johnson's from his days as a New Deal congressman and a veteran of federal social welfare policy, warned him that the CAP was "intrinsically divisive" and cautioned his advisers about keeping it in the legislation. Johnson thought he could handle the criticism, especially if it came from those areas of the government—federal, state, or local—that had traditionally been managed, as he told Shriver, by "people who were either apathetic, entrenched or ignorant, or scared, or all those things put together." The president rationalized that in these cases, it was "both necessary and legitimate to shake the place up," but he warned that he did not want the CAP to "burn the barn down." When the legislation moved from the task force to Congress, LBJ shifted gears, thinking less about the substance of the economic opportunity bill and more about the political problems of getting it approved.[32]

The Politics of Race and the Passage of the Economic Opportunity Act of 1964

Finding sponsors for the bill became the first item of business on the president's agenda. Johnson knew that the Republican opposition to the bill would be fierce, especially in the climate of election-year politics. More importantly, he realized that his GOP opponents had been quite successful in aligning with southern Democrats to form a powerful conservative coalition in Congress. The coalition would no doubt use tactics with the economic opportunity bill that resembled those used against earlier civil rights legislation, "stirring the Southerners' fears that certain provisions would enforce integration," as he recalled. After discussing the realities of this issue with his chief congressional liaison, Larry O'Brien, LBJ asked Georgia congressman Phil Landrum to manage the bill in the House and Alabama senator Lister Hill to sponsor it in the Senate. Landrum accepted; Hill declined.[33]

Landrum was a good choice for the president's plan to attract southern Democrats to the bill. He served a district located in the foothills of the Appalachian Mountains in North Georgia, and some bills he supported focused on conservative issues. He consistently voted in favor of federal public works and worked to curb some of the power of organized labor, most notably with the 1959 Landrum-Griffin Act, which aimed to control union corruption by safeguarding democratic procedures within labor unions and penalizing the misuse of union funds and the coercion of members. Landrum could openly support the economic opportunity bill. Georgia's Ninth Congressional District had a substantial white majority, and the rural poverty there meant that many of Landrum's constituents could benefit from the bill's proposed programs. He also had an outspoken advocate in his district's newspaper, the *Gainesville Daily Times*. On March 17, 1964, editor Sylvan Meyer wrote proudly about what Landrum's recruitment as bill sponsor would mean for the region: "All this tends to put Mr. Landrum in a most favorable position and at the same time cannot help but accrue to the advantage of people in this district. . . . We feel good about our congressman's having such a key role in a bill that reflects the country's conscience and common sense going to work to attack a major problem." With this type of backing in the local press, Landrum did not risk his House seat by managing the bill.[34]

Landrum exemplified the type of southern politician Johnson favored, one who could see that the benefits of the antipoverty effort outweighed the political liabilities associated with race. The president's Senate choice, however, could not follow a similar path. Hill's constituency kept him trapped in a Jim Crow ravine. Since the late 1940s, Alabama's political climate had hampered federal legislators' support for any program that could infringe on the state's racist customs. Governor George Wallace's meteoric rise in national politics boosted his standing at home and made it harder for Senator Hill to pull himself out of the segregationist ditch in which he had placed himself out of political expediency. According to Gerry Boulard, "Terrified that he should ever be associated with some political movements calling for better race relations, Hill went out of his way to demonstrate his fealty to the Old Confederacy." Not surprisingly, therefore, the senior senator from Alabama turned down LBJ's request to manage the

Figure 5. In the 1964 congressional elections, challenger Zell Miller tried to tie incumbent congressman Phil Landrum with Johnson's Great Society, but as this cartoon shows, praise of Landrum as the "South's Greatest Liberal" and a "Two-Fisted Poverty Fighter" left Miller in the dust. Editorial cartoon by Clifford H. "Baldy" Baldowski (*Atlanta Constitution,* n.d.), Phil M. Landrum Papers, Offices of Susan Landrum and Phil Landrum Jr., Jasper, Ga.

bill in the upper chamber. As chair of the Labor and Public Welfare Committee and fifth in seniority in the Senate, Hill distanced himself even further from the legislation when he refused to sit on the subcommittee that conducted the hearings, the only member of the Labor and Public Welfare Committee to do so. This was the position of a southern moderate.[35]

Hill's retreat from publicly supporting national Democratic Party causes illustrates the southern opposition that the Johnson administration faced and the political climate of a Deep South state such as Alabama. In 1947, two years after Truman's ascendancy to the presidency, Hill resigned as party whip. In the Senate, he did not vote for any measure that could be construed as supporting the civil rights cause, including legislation abolishing the poll tax and antilynching legislation. Historian Tony Badger has found that Hill signed the Southern Manifesto against the *Brown* decision without even reading it, a decision explained by Alabama congressman Carl Elliott: "When that Manifesto came along, neither those [Deep South] colleagues nor my constituents back in Alabama cared about moderation. You were either with them or against them. And if you were against them, you were gone. Voted out. Politically excommunicated. . . . I knew there was no way I could survive and I hadn't yet achieved what I came to Congress to do. It was that knowledge . . . that grabbed me as I decided to add my signature to the others. . . . I'd probably make the same decision again." Both Alabama senators and its Democratic loyalist representatives were conspicuously absent from the 1960 Democratic National Convention. Two years later, racial politics put Senator Hill's career on the line. Hill's Republican opponent accused him of being "soft" on civil rights, and he responded by assuring white Alabama voters that he could protect their way of life. He bragged to crowds that he had killed ten "integration" bills in his committee, and he warned that Republicans had elected a "Negro" legislator in Georgia. The trump worked—just barely. Hill won his last election by a 1 percent margin. After 1962, staff members, friends, and even a White House aide noticed that Hill seemed shaken and uncharacteristically bitter that his constituents had nearly rejected him. During the filibuster against the civil rights bill, Hill served as a team captain, working twelve-hour shifts to block cloture. Johnson could not easily change Hill's position by offering more federal assistance to Alabama's poor, not as long as the Civil Rights Act promised to alter the way that help would be administered. As Hill's biographer has noted, "The price of power for Lister Hill—his stand against civil rights—cast a lasting shadow over his long record of public service."[36]

The committee hearings began in the lower chamber, which the administration thought harbored more hostility toward the bill. Meeting over a six-week period from mid-March until the end of April, the Democrats dominated, controlling who testified, monopolizing the questions asked, and restraining the opposition whenever possible. Committee chairman Adam Clayton Powell (D-NY) gave his Republican colleagues only three days to call witnesses. Eighty-five people testified during the hearings, including twenty-nine members of the administration or original members of the task force and every member of the president's cabinet. Yarmolinsky, Shriver's deputy, was noticeably absent.[37]

Resistance to the antipoverty bill came exclusively from the Republican members of the committee and subcommittee and nine witnesses—from the U.S. Chamber of Commerce, a state manufacturing association delegate, the Farm Bureau Federation, and two educators. The GOP concentrated on six key issues: the omnibus nature of the bill, which they thought should have required other committees to review the legislation; the duplication of programs already in existence in other departments; the commandeering of authority of the other cabinet officers by the proposed "poverty czar"; OEO's ability to bypass state governments, especially in Title II; the unnecessary creation of a new layer of government; and the bill's focus on race, with charges that it could enforce integration and primarily benefited black Americans.[38]

The intraparty debate that had begun at the 1963 Republican National Committee meeting in Denver continued in the halls of Congress. As a result, GOP members of the House Subcommittee on the War on Poverty dealt with the issue of race in a variety of ways. The progressive wing supported the civil rights aspects of the antipoverty bill, while the conservative wing used the hearings to highlight the bill's capacity to infringe on state authority. Regardless of the rift within the Republican ranks, each time legislators and hearing participants brought up the subject of civil rights, it underscored the connection between fighting poverty and supporting racial equality. For example, on March 20, Congressman Charles Goodell (R-NY) sought reassurance from Agriculture Secretary Orville Freeman that Job Corps facilities conducting conservation projects would be fully integrated. "To the extent that you use local facilities or personnel, it is not going to be trying to set up any separate but equal routine?" he asked. Freeman reassured Goodell that such would not be the case. Serving as the voice for the conservatives, Peter Frelinghuysen (R-NJ) tried to get Walter Reuther to admit that the president's program targeted mainly black Americans: "You also say that the Negro's position is deteriorating even though there has been a general improvement in the situation nationwide. Is it your feeling that this Landrum bill should be aimed primarily at alleviating the problems of the Negroes or that this would be a primary effect in passage of the legislation of this kind?" Reuther, head of the United Auto Workers, was a longtime supporter of civil rights and had difficulty avoiding Frelinghuysen's trap. "Obviously, the fight against poverty should be colorblind," the labor leader said, "but the Negroes, because they have been denied, disadvantaged, and discriminated against more than any other group, would get a larger benefit out of this program, because they are the victims of poverty more than any other group."[39]

That same day, Landrum took the GOP to task for using the predicament of poor black Americans in its effort to win southern opposition to the bill: "I want it clearly understood with reference to this bill under my name, and I am proud to have my name upon it, that any assistance it may provide toward eliminating the plight of poverty affecting Americans of all races is a source of pride for me. I am not ashamed of it." Landrum called the Republican strategy inflammatory and opportunistic and continued, "I come from a section of the country that has been bombarded with a great deal of demagoguery. . . . I want it clearly understood that my efforts . . . are directed toward relieving poverty that affects both white and Negro Americans. I want the record made crystal clear on this point." The next day, Marjorie Hunter reported in the *New York Times* that the Georgia congressman "would not be scared off from the anti-poverty program by GOP efforts to picture it as largely of benefit to Negroes."[40]

After the hearings, the full committee met on April 30 to redraft portions of the bill. The CAP dominated the deliberations. The committee revised Title II, introducing an allotment formula for allocation of funds to the states. About

60 percent of the money would be distributed equally among the states but still channeled through OEO, while the remainder would be left for use at the agency's discretion. The committee also limited funding to one year. Beyond the changes to Title II, there were no casualties; even the Title III Family Farm Development Corporation survived this initial stage. The committee completed the redrafting process on May 26, but the legislation stalled when conservative congressman Howard Smith (D-VA), chairman of the Rules Committee, held the bill hostage for the entire month of June. If the president wanted his bill passed before the Democratic National Convention in August, the Senate would have to debate the legislation first.[41]

Hearings began in the Senate on June 17. Senator Patrick V. McNamara (D-MI) had agreed to sponsor the bill after Hill refused. The administration decided that the best strategy for passage of a Senate bill would be to operate with the version drafted in the House. On the first day of testimony, McNamara explained that the Select Committee on Poverty would meet to question witnesses for only four days because the House had conducted lengthy hearings and printed copies of that testimony were available.[42]

The Senate hearings resembled those in the House. Most of the witnesses came from the administration and the same outside interest groups. Frelinghuysen appeared as a witness, making the Senate hearings noteworthy to interested southern senators. Frelinghuysen complained about Shriver's future role as poverty czar and about the new federal powers associated with the bill. He described the Title II CAP as opening "the way for direct Federal involvement in the activities of every private organization in every community in this country without the necessity for participation or approval of either State or local government." As he finished his testimony, he wondered what would happen if a southern state refused to cooperate in a community effort to desegregate its school system. McNamara replied that the War on Poverty had nothing to do with desegregation: "There is nothing to say that it [does] not," the New Jerseyan replied. "I think it might well be part of the poverty war." He then concluded by linking Landrum's hometown with a fictitious CAP brought about by a civil rights organization: "I think it would be very unwise to give the Federal Government the power to give to the NAACP, or a local citizens group which might not even be representative of the community, Gainesville, Georgia, wherever it is, that the Federal money to do something that the community or the State does not want." McNamara responded by dismissing Frelinghuysen's fears, stating, "I don't believe . . . that we have civil rights or integration or segregation problems involved in this bill."[43]

When the hearings ended and the bill moved into the Rules Committee, the southern bloc had plenty of evidence to support its fears. The Senate Select

Committee on Poverty made some changes to the bill after the hearings. It revised Title II, requiring that the CAP also use the maximum feasible participation of public agencies and private nonprofit organizations primarily concerned with the community's poverty problems. This change addressed Frelinghuysen's concern that any community group could receive poverty funds for an area. In a July 7 Labor and Public Welfare Committee meeting, Senator Jacob Javits (R-NY) tried to amend the bill so that state welfare agencies would be involved in the antipoverty effort. His amendment failed, but Senator Harrison "Pete" Williams (D-NJ) predicted that there would be an amendment on the floor requiring governors' approval of projects. Senator McNamara feared that this requirement would prevent action rather than offer greater coordination.[44]

The floor debates began in both houses of Congress at the height of an active summer session. The Civil Rights Act had passed on July 2, and Shriver remembered that the task force members felt that "psychologically it would then be easier to ride [the economic opportunity bill] through in the wake and on the euphoria ... that [the civil rights legislation] produced." The press predicted that the vote would be close, especially after the GOP nominated Goldwater for president. In late July, the *Wall Street Journal* reported that conservative southern Democrats feared "being swept out of office in November by a Goldwater vote tide throughout most of their region in these race-troubled days, and they're acting in self-defense." Opposition to the bill from southern congressmen became even more predictable as the summer dragged on. Johnson hoped that if the Senate passed the bill first, "some waverers" in the House might be influenced to lend their support.[45]

All levels of the administration became involved in the effort to pass the antipoverty bill. The president worked closely with his congressional liaison staff, telephoning members of Congress to get endorsements and contacting leaders in the private sector to lobby their representatives to support the bill. On the eve of the Senate vote, Shriver counted on fifty Democrats and seventeen Republicans to back the economic opportunity bill. He might have been right in his predictions of support, but Shriver missed the key point that some southern senators would alter the legislation before accepting it.[46]

The Senate debated the bill over two days, July 22 and 23, and considered amendments intended to curb the more provocative aspects of the legislation. Senators Winston Prouty (R-VT) and George Smathers (D-FL) offered governors' veto amendments to remedy the bypassing of the states in Title I and Title II programs. Smathers called for a governor's approval before OEO could set up Job Corps conservation camps or training centers. McNamara did not want to accept Smathers's amendment but agreed when Democratic leaders recommended that the amendment go forward. "Of course, that had the civil rights aspects to it, too," Larry O'Brien, White House congressional liaison, later admitted. For him this was a political accommodation. "It was a way of getting around the corner. . . . [Y]ou have to accept it for what it was; it was a [political] maneuver." Prouty submitted an amendment allowing governors to approve Title II programs before they could begin operating in states. Upon reconsideration, the Senate rejected Prouty's version of a governors' veto.[47]

The states' rights issue did not die, however. Later on July 23, Strom Thurmond (D-SC) resurrected it while serving in his role as the conservative spokesman of the South. He warned that the CAP would allow the federal government to establish direct control over programs functioning on the local level. Thurmond picked up Frelinghuysen's line of reasoning using more colorful language: "Under the innocent sounding title of 'Community Action Program,' the poverty czar would not only have the power to finance the activities of such organizations as the National Council of Churches, the NAACP, SNCC, and CORE, but also a SNOOP and a SNORE which are sure to be organized to get their part of the green gravy." Thurmond bemoaned the fact that the economic opportunity bill addressed issues that touched on racial discrimination. "I naively thought the Congress had finished with legislation on racial matters last month." He tried to highlight the bill's intent, describing it as "pregnant with racial overtones. . . . [T]he community action programs will be aimed at what [Shriver] considers to be America's poverty of spirit as well as economic poverty. Never has there been such arbitrary and discretionary grants of power, free of congressionally imposed guidelines, vested in a nonelective Federal official." These battles must have had an effect on the South Carolina senator. Before the year came to a close, Thurmond would switch to the Republican Party.[48]

Also on July 23, Senator John Stennis (D-MS) entered into the record a letter from a constituent who refused to take a training position under the Manpower Development Training Act because it would have been conducted at the Tuskegee Institute, "an all-Negro institution": "My safety would be endangered if I attended such a place of training," the young man wrote. The Mississippi conservative used this anecdote to point out to his like-minded colleagues that the economic opportunity bill could "force" integration along the lines of the Manpower Development Training Act.[49]

On the heels of these complaints, Smathers crafted another version of Prouty's governors' veto amendment, this time with more precise language. Richard Russell (D-GA) wanted this amendment in the bill, and he let Shriver know about it. "Richard Russell was one of the behemoths, one of the giants of the Senate," Shriver recounted, "and normally wouldn't even have concerned himself with a peripheral thing like the War on Poverty." The future OEO director reasoned that Russell became involved because he wanted to maintain the traditional states' rights doctrine of the South. The new amendment called for the OEO director to establish procedures to "facilitate effective participation of the State in Community Action Programs." It authorized the director to make grants to or contract with appropriate state agencies to provide technical assistance. And this change did not allow grants to private institutions or nonprofit organizations within a state "except when said institution operate[d] in conjunction with or under authority of a public agency, unless a plan setting forth the proposed program has been submitted to the Governor of the State, and he has not disapproved [within] thirty days of submission." Unlike Prouty's earlier offering, Smathers's amendment passed resoundingly by a vote of eighty to seven. Senator Albert Gore (D-TN) was the only southerner to vote against the amendment.[50]

To keep the omnibus legislation intact, the White House apparently worked out a compromise with the southern supporters of a governors' veto. Yarmolinsky remembered that administration officials were "getting beat on" to include this accommodation. According to Cannon, the White House agreed to this compromise as a consequence of fears that the South would derail the entire antipoverty effort: "I was worried to death that we wouldn't get any program, because the South would hold us up for ransom, so I was willing to pay even more than [the governors' veto]." Senator Herman Talmadge (D-GA) told Shriver that the inclusion of the veto would allow southern senators to tell their constituents that they had upheld the states' rights doctrine. Shriver remembered that Talmadge also predicted that the veto would not be used: "They're not going to disapprove of many of them," Talmadge concluded, "because the governors all want to have the money come to their states."[51]

The Family Farm Development Corporation provision of Title III became the next casualty of the Senate debates. Not surprisingly, Senator Thurmond attacked this clause with as much spite as he had the Title II programs, this time using anticommunist language. He described the "land reform" program as a replica of the 1930s farm resettlement program that had been investigated by a select committee of the House Agriculture Committee in 1944. Using effective phrases from this report, he shrouded his racism with Cold War rhetoric. He linked the Title III land-buying program with the New Deal's FSA, which had been accused of financing "communistic resettlement projects" and operating as "an experiment station of unAmerican ideas and economic and social theories of little or questionable value." Thurmond then indicted the Farm Development Corporation by associating it with the National Farm Commission of the Communist Party of the USA, which in 1955 proposed that "sharecroppers and tenants, Negro and white, should be aided to become owners. The government [is] to buy up tracts of land and make productive farms available to sharecroppers, tenants, and farm workers on a low-cost basis." The former Dixiecrat proclaimed, "It is adding insult to injury for future generations for us to engage in deficit spending to implement these reactionary, alien, duplicative, Socialistic and collectivist programs." To remove any last doubts about where he stood, Thurmond closed by calling this provision a "Trojan horse filled with socialism and collectivism on the American people." The South Carolina senator could not be ignored. Frank Lausche (D-OH) killed the program with an amendment that narrowly passed, forty-nine to forty-three. Reflecting on the Lausche amendment, John Baker recalled, "We just considered that was kind of an expected casualty, and the overall was worth getting" even without the Family Farm Development Corporation. The Senate's last amendment replaced all Title III grants for farmers with loans.[52]

On July 23, the Senate closed its debate and voted on the economic opportunity bill, which passed by a vote of sixty-one to thirty-four. The southern bloc had been appeased. Nine southern Democrats, including all four senators from North Carolina and Tennessee, supported the bill. The *Wall Street Journal* pointed out that only two of these nine faced GOP challenges in the upcoming fall elections—Tennessee's Gore and Texas's Ralph Webster Yarborough—and described both as having "trodden too far down liberal paths to retreat now." Twelve southerners, including all six senators from Alabama, Mississippi, and Virginia, voted against the bill. The Arkansas, Florida, Georgia, Louisiana, and South Carolina delegations split their votes. Dixie's most vocal senators during the floor debate and backroom negotiations were the same men who had led the fight against the earlier civil rights bill—Russell, Stennis, and Thurmond. Those southern senators who voted for the bill must have thought they had tamed the more provocative aspects of the legislation and seen that it could do some good for their region. That almost half of the senators from the old Confederacy voted against the bill, even in its amended form, indicates that many recognized and feared the bill's potential to support change in the South despite the fact that it could benefit many of their impoverished constituents.[53]

Debates began in the House of Representatives on August 5. The administration remained anxious about the chances of passing the bill. On July 31, O'Brien reported to the president that the House stood deadlocked, with thirty southerners still undecided.[54]

The economic opportunity bill's potential to enforce the new civil rights legislation became a primary subject of the House debates. Congressman Smith took up the cause supported earlier by Senator Thurmond. On the first day of debate, Smith let his fellow southerners know where he stood: "I want to say to the members from the South who are going to vote for this bill—and I know there are a lot who are going to vote for it—that they are voting to implement the civil rights bill that they opposed and voted against." He warned that the antipoverty programs would not be "popular south of the Potomac River." Like Thurmond, Smith sought to undermine support for the bill by associating an established civil rights organization with extreme groups that OEO might finance as a result of the bill. "Can they set up a project to help the Ku Klux Klan, can they turn money over to the NAACP, can anybody find anything in this bill that would stop them from sponsoring the establishment of a nudist colony in your State or county?" he asked.[55]

To counter these charges, Landrum gave his reasons for backing the bill, voicing his support with a disturbing message that confirmed the opinions of many southern conservatives. He saw "not anything but conservatism" in the program. He championed the legislation for the savings it would generate for the country instead of for the support it would offer to those below the poverty line. He estimated that the price tag for public assistance on the federal level amounted to just over $4 billion, while indirect costs stood at $25 billion. In the wake of a mid-July riot in Harlem in response to the killing of an African American youth by a white New York City policeman, Landrum admonished his fellow representatives to concentrate on what would happen if they did nothing about this national problem: "Does it give you any pause, that these human beings are reproducing in their own images? Are you concerned that the frustration may develop into violence and anarchy?" To move the debate along, he minimized the bill's more progressive policies. In his judgment, the legislation constituted nothing more than an education and training bill that offered some hope in the federal effort to stem welfare expenses. The Johnson administration's acceptance of the compromises reveals the new circumstances the Civil Rights Act had created in Congress. Elected officials were willing to use whatever means were necessary to get legislation passed on their terms, threatening the intent and spirit of the original legislation. The Johnson administration chose to maneuver as best it could under the circumstances.[56]

In an effort to streamline the process, Landrum offered an initial amendment to substitute the Senate version of the bill that passed on July 23 for the measure that the House was considering. This brought the problem of the governors' veto out onto the House floor and harvested the bitter fruit that had been planted in earlier hearings. Goodell argued that instead of a states' rights amendment, it was a segregationist amendment: "It means in effect that in any State where a program is designed to help a particular type of people the Governor can simply say, 'No, if you are going to do it that way, I veto it; I do not want that kind of program here.'" Frelinghuysen also objected to the Senate version of the governors' veto, complaining that "this so-called veto by Governors would allow a Governor to forbid a federally financed project to come into his

State, without giving any reasons for his veto. It does absolutely nothing . . . to give the local community any control at all." He went on, "It would only be a negative power, probably acted upon . . . because a Governor would not like to see a federally financed program which does not practice discrimination in his State." Admitting that states' rights had many forms, Frelinghuysen continued his lecture: "This would not be the kind of participation in any sense that we talk[ed] about. . . . A veto does not in any way pull in either the State or local government." No matter how exact these Republican assessments of the amendment may have been, the Democratic leadership could not let them remain in that light. GOP criticisms made it clear that the president's approval of the bill included acceptance of the veto amendment, which put LBJ in a bind.[57]

Landrum came to the administration's defense by trying to blunt the Civil Rights Act's role in the antipoverty fight. Countering the Republicans' assessment, he stated that the civil rights bill "is an accomplished fact" and as public officials, members of Congress must acknowledge "facts as facts." There was no need for further discussion. "To do so is only to fill the RECORD with inflammatory material designed to build prejudice where tolerance would be more desirable and more constructive." The administration apparently had spent a lot of its political capital during the debates regarding the civil rights bill, and the White House accepted the governors' veto as a necessary compromise to ensure passage of the legislation. The administration must have hoped that the new civil rights law could keep governors from discriminating against their minority constituents. The *Elberton Star,* a newspaper in Landrum's district, reported that Democrats, including southerners, gave Landrum an ovation when he finished speaking.[58]

Trying one last time to rid the bill of the governors' veto, William Ryan (D-NY) pointed out that many southern governors had used their veto pens when other federal welfare legislation had encroached into their states. He reminded his colleagues that Louisiana had refused to sign an agreement with the federal government for Manpower Development Training programs and that Mississippi had halted the distribution of federal surplus food in LeFlore County after a voter registration drive in Greenwood in 1963. "What reason is there to believe that there is a willingness to raise the general standard of living of the Negro population in 1964?" he asked. Such arguments could not sway the majority of House members, who agreed to accept the Senate version of the bill with the governors' veto intact. Nevertheless, these disputes foreshadowed the approach four southern governors—Haydon Burns of Florida, John Connally of Texas, Donald Russell of South Carolina, and George Wallace of Alabama— would take in implementing the antipoverty program in their states. As a result of their heavy-handed actions, Congress would reconsider the governors' veto in 1965, giving the OEO director override powers and thus the final say in Title II funding issues.[59]

After two days of debate, the governors' veto would not go away. In the midst of another day of arguing about its consequences, the administration revealed the lengths to which it would go to placate the South in an effort to get the omnibus bill passed. While he had the floor, Representative William Ayres (R-OH) pointed out that Yarmolinsky had discussed an alternative view of the power of the governors' veto in a June 13 memorandum. Landrum interrupted his colleague and pointed out that as far as he was concerned, "this gentleman, Mr. Yarmolinsky, will have absolutely nothing to do with the program. And second, I wish to state that I have been told on the highest authority that not only will he not be appointed, but that he will not be considered if he is recommended for a place in this agency." Yarmolinsky had been sacked; Landrum used Ayres's testimony as the occasion to announce the final concession made to gain southern votes for the bill.[60]

The night before, Mendel Rivers (D-SC), a powerful member of the House Armed Services Committee, and Harold Cooley (D-NC), chairman of the Agriculture Committee and seventh-ranking member in the House, met in Speaker John McCormack's office with the House Democratic whips, Landrum, other congressmen from the Carolinas, and Shriver. Rivers and Cooley told the group that eight representatives from their state delegations would not vote for the bill unless they received assurance that Yarmolinsky would not be involved in OEO. According to Shriver, the whips said that "if they did not have the votes of these congressmen . . . they couldn't get the legislation through the Congress." To avoid betraying his colleague and friend, Shriver told those gathered that he did not know if he would be OEO's director, so he had no control over Yarmolinsky's position. Shriver's dodge failed—someone told him to call the president. Shriver later recalled, "I stepped into a little room adjoining the Speaker's office, and I called the White House." Shriver explained the situation and told LBJ, "I don't want to kowtow to these guys." Johnson said, "That's okay. Don't worry about them. You just tell them that the President will act on these matters in his own judgment." This evasion did not work either. Shriver had to call the president back, and he later described this episode as "the most unpleasant experience I ever had in the government of the United States. . . . I felt then as if I ought to go out and vomit, it was such a despicable proceeding." In the end, the president agreed to sever Yarmolinsky's ties with OEO in exchange for eight votes. Although Shriver felt horrible for capitulating to these members of Congress, he rationalized his actions: "It was a question of whether we have this bill and the benefits which it will bring to hundreds of thousands or maybe millions of poor people," or Yarmolinsky.[61]

In the early days of the Task Force in the War Against Poverty, Yarmolinsky had agreed to leave the Defense Department with the understanding that he would be appointed deputy director when the bill became law. "I felt that it would be a mistake to leave my post," Yarmolinsky explained, "without having a definite post as deputy special assistant to the President." Johnson had agreed but had initially told Yarmolinsky that the official appointment would come after the bill was signed because the president did not want the White House payroll to be too large. This gentleman's agreement vanished when the task force deputy became the target of southern bigotry and anti-Semitism. His past work to integrate southern military bases, combined with his hard-hitting manner, his Russian last name, his Jewish faith, and the undeserved taint of "radicalism" that followed him, raised the suspicions of these southern members of Congress. When Landrum announced on the House floor that Yarmolinsky would not be considered for an OEO position, Donald Baker of the OEO general counsel's office thought that "the agency was in no position—nor was the White House, in fact—to make a liar out of him. . . . The fact of the matter is once that statement had been made on the floor of the House, the matter was accomplished." The White House believed that the vote would be close, and LBJ did not want to lose the first piece of major legislation that he could call his own. This episode revealed the dark side of Washington politics—no one in the Carolina delegations knew Yarmolinsky personally, but they smeared his reputation to justify their votes to their constituents and exact a price for his earlier efforts to confront segregation. In 1956, Rivers declared his membership in the White Citizens' Council, and his actions with regard to Yarmolinsky represented a familiar Citizens' Council tactic. Yarmolinsky's absence eventually left a crucial void in the management of OEO.[62]

Over the course of his long political career, President Johnson had perfected the art of hardball Washington deal making. During a press conference held a week later, LBJ denied that Yarmolinsky had been offered a place on the OEO team. One of Johnson's biographers has explained that through thirty years in government service, Johnson viewed politics as a dirty business in which only the most manipulative succeeded. Thus he believed that he got the better end of the deal. As Secretary of Defense Robert McNamara explained, "The important lesson here . . . is this. When the President, or one of his major programs, is involved, none of us is important. Everyone's expendable." This was the brutal reality of Washington. A government bureaucrat was dispensable; legislation was not.[63]

After these backroom deals were concluded, the House ended its debate on August 8 and voted 226 to 185 in favor of the bill. As in the Senate, the House members from Dixie split almost equally in their support for the legislation, with 51 voting for it and 49 (12 Republicans and 37 Democrats) voting against it. Only the Mississippi delegation, representing one of the poorest states in the nation and a state with a strong tradition of opposing civil rights for its black citizens, voted unanimously against the bill. The Alabama delegation's voting record highlights the great flux in the Deep South in the aftermath of the passage of civil rights legislation and in the midst of Goldwater's presidential campaign. Three of Alabama's eight House members—Carl Elliott, Robert E. Jones, and Albert Rains—voted for the economic opportunity bill. Later in the fall, Elliott lost his congressional seat as part of the Goldwater tide, and Rains did not run for reelection. Jones came from the Fifth District in the northern part of the state, a white-majority area similar to Phil Landrum's North Georgia district. Jones kept his congressional seat. Four Alabama representatives voted against the bill: Armistead Selden, whose district stood in the state's Black Belt, won reelection as a Democrat in 1964, as did George William Andrews, whose district bordered the Georgia state line. Opposition to this bill and other progressive issues did not save George Huddleston Jr. and Kenneth Roberts, both of whom were defeated by Republicans in November. Democrat George M. Grant did not cast a vote on the economic opportunity bill, but he too lost to a Republican in the fall. This election constituted a sea change for Alabama's federal officials. Prior to the 1964 election, they had been a unanimous Democratic delegation; after November, five of Alabama's eight congressional representatives were Republicans. When the Civil Rights Act became law and the GOP became a viable alternative for conservative voters in places such as Alabama, congressional Democrats had increasing difficulty mounting the argument that party loyalty enabled them to alter legislation to protect white supremacy. Many Deep South politicians continued to use their power to weaken the force of civil rights legislation, but they now did so in more clandestine ways and in the Republican Party.[64]

The Senate concurred with the House, voting to accept the Economic Opportunity Act on August 11. The margin of victory was wider than the Johnson administration had expected. Donald Baker thought that congressional support came from members who had been stymied for the preceding fifteen years in their fight to pass social welfare legislation: "These were people who had for many years seen a great need for programs of this kind and they just fell in behind and supported it." Other members of the administration felt that Johnson got his bill because he had a tremendous amount of goodwill at the time and because senators would have had trouble justifying their opposition to the president during an election year. The wide margin of victory, however, led some in his administration to criticize the president's actions with regard to Yarmolinsky. Yet as Norbert Schlei later explained, "It's fair to say that many times once you're over the top you get a lot more votes that you wouldn't have got if you weren't over the top. So I am not in a position to say that it was an unnecessary decision."[65]

The bill still had to go through the appropriations process, the administration's final hurdle. Congress would not hold these hearings until late September, so the president again confronted the dilemma of the changing South and the variety of the region's voices that demanded his attention at the Democratic National Convention. LBJ's response to the seating of the Mississippi delegation disclosed his view of how injustices should be remedied and the manner in which the Democratic Party should reform. This process clearly demonstrates that Johnson did not fully appreciate the essence of the black freedom struggle and instead continued the balancing act he had maintained since putting his full support behind the civil rights legislation. Johnson's lack of appreciation for the civil rights movement's meaning to those who had been working for freedom reverberated throughout his presidency.[66]

The convention featured a controversy between the white elected delegates from Mississippi's regular Democratic Party and sixty-four delegates from the Mississippi Freedom Democratic Party (MFDP), which had held separate elections because the state Democratic Party barred black voters. The president worried that a floor fight over the seating of the delegation would lead to a walkout by representatives not only from the Deep South states but from important border states as well: "I've got to carry Georgia," Johnson told Reuther over the telephone, "and [Georgia governor] Carl Sanders can't go if he throws 'em out. He has to go with 'em. I've got to carry Texas. [Texas governor] John Connally will go. . . . We don't want to cut off our nose to spite our face." Connally told the president, "If you seat those black buggers, the whole South will walk out." Johnson viewed the world through the lens of politics and believed that a compromise could be found for every situation. In this process, he minimized the deeper meaning of the MFDP challenge, which revealed the injustice and hypocrisy of Mississippi democracy and the Freedom Democrats' loyalty to the national party. "If they give us four years," Johnson reasoned with Reuther, "I'll guarantee the Freedom delegation somebody representing views like that will be seated four years from now. But we can't do it all before breakfast."[67]

By August 25, a compromise had been proposed. The MFDP would receive two at-large seats, the remaining delegates would be "honored guests" of the convention, and only the regular Democrats who signed a loyalty oath to the national party would be seated. The national party pledged to end racial discrimination in all state delegations for future conventions. The offer pleased neither group from Mississippi, but a floor fight had been averted. In a conference call with Reuther and Hubert Humphrey, who had forged the compromise,

LBJ offered his view of the Democratic Party's place in American political life. "I think it's a good solution," he told them in a relieved voice. "Our party's always been a group that you can come to with any bellyache and injustice, whether it was a pecan-shelling plant that paid four cents an hour or sweatshop wages or usurious interest rates or discrimination to vote or Ku Klux Klan whipping somebody. . . . That's what the Democratic party's for. That's why it was born. And that's why it survives." He made himself available to the demands of the people through the political process and used his power to provide them with solutions he deemed appropriate. "Long as the poor and the downtrodden and the bended know that they can come to us and be heard. And that's what we're doing. We're hearing 'em. . . . We passed a law back there in '57 and said it was the first time in eighty-five years that everyone was going to have a chance to vote. . . . And we're going to say it again in the convention in '64. . . . Get ahold of these people and say to 'em, 'For God's sakes, we've tasted from the cup of injustice ourselves.'" He wanted Reuther and Humphrey to reassure the MFDP delegates and their supporters that they would have someone on whom to rely in Washington: "You're going to have a President and . . . a Vice President . . . that you trust. You're going to have Congress. . . . Let's all get out there in the precincts. . . . [W]e'll start out next January and do enough about . . . economic and social and other interests that we can go in there and send a fellow like Humphrey down to make a speech now and then and cry with 'em a little." This was a case of pure principle meeting pure politics. The ethos of local people seeking a voice in the way decisions were made was not a part of LBJ's political Bible.[68]

The president had not completely ignored the MFDP delegates. He knew they had been wronged. "Mississippi's seated!" he told Connally. "She gets every damned vote she's entitled to. She oughtn't to be seated. She wouldn't let those nigras vote. And that's not right. . . . Now she says, 'I'm gonna be a goddamn dog in the manger.'" LBJ's candor with his Texas friend clearly shows that the MFDP delegates' idealism and faith in the democratic process were lost on the president.[69]

At the convention, as in the fight for passage of the Economic Opportunity Act, Johnson displayed his approach to politics and power. For him, the ends justified the means. If Americans elected Goldwater, all of Johnson's plans for the country would be scuttled, especially those that would help African Americans, poor people, and other future beneficiaries of his Great Society. The MFDP delegates' desire for full participation in the electoral process came at too high a price for the president. He feared that their efforts would split the Democratic Party. Winning national elections counted to LBJ, not who participated in a nominating convention or who chose the delegates. "What we want to do is elect some Congressmen to keep 'em from repealing this [civil rights] act," he told Reuther. "And who's seated at this convention don't amount to a damn." For the MFDP delegates, in contrast, the process mattered as much as the outcome. They cared about being equal participants in a democracy. Their version of the political game did not follow the same compass as LBJ did. Not surprisingly, therefore, in the wake of the passage of the Civil Rights Act, the Democratic Party did not transform into a party that honored the democratic aspirations of its grassroots members such as those from the Magnolia State.[70]

Some of the Mississippi challengers saw a connection between Johnson's actions at the convention and the funds available through the Economic Opportunity Act. Upon reflection, Bob Moses, an activist with the Student Nonviolent Coordinating Committee and one of the architects of the MFDP challenge, thought that Johnson was trying to reform the Democratic Party in the wrong way. "They were trapped in issues of money," he explained. Convention delegates "were wrapped up trying to get money for the War on Poverty." Moses reasoned that if the Freedom Democrats had been seated, the party could have reorganized by creating "a way for the grassroots foundation of the party" to flourish instead "of the middle class." When Humphrey offered the compromise for seating the Mississippi delegation, Moses felt that there was no place in the Democratic Party for the energy from local activists like those from the MFDP. "If you were going to be a part of the machinery of the War on Poverty," he explained, "you had to be part of the team, so you could not reach out to the MFDP" and help its delegates receive official recognition. The struggle over seating the Mississippi convention delegates revealed another feature of the Second Reconstruction that resembled its predecessor nearly a hundred years earlier. As in the post–Civil War era, the federal government acknowledged the legal rights of black southerners but left the finer points of citizenship participation to be worked out over time on the local level, outside of the purview of high-level federal officeholders.[71]

Moses was not the only disgruntled activist from Mississippi. Charles Pickering, a white conservative, believed that "the people of [Mississippi] were heaped with humiliation and embarrassment at the Democratic Convention." Soon after the convention, he switched from the Democratic Party to the GOP and put his energy into building up his new party in his state. He was not alone. Walking out of the Atlantic City convention, one Mississippi delegate remarked, "We didn't leave the national party. It left us." These issues associated with political restructuring would continue throughout Johnson's presidency, especially in the Deep South. LBJ ultimately would not be able to control the direction in which the party moved because it—functioning simultaneously on the national, state, and local levels—was bigger than anything he could manage single-handedly.[72]

After receiving the Democratic nomination, Johnson prepared his budget for fiscal 1965, which included funding for the War on Poverty. At the convention, he had placated the white Mississippi Democrats and at the same time signaled to all the southern delegations his willingness to continue to strike deals. Congress held hearings in late September and marked up the president's budget, removing $15 million from the original $962.5 million request for the Economic Opportunity Act. Johnson signed the appropriations bill on October 8, but he would not allow members of the newly created OEO to spend any of the allocated money until after the November election to avoid any appearance that government spending bought votes. Almost twelve months elapsed as the omnibus legislation was drafted and passed Congress. LBJ achieved a major piece of his Great Society legislation but paid a high price. The concessions made to obtain southern support weakened the bill, especially with the governors' veto, the stipulation for annual funding, and the firing of Yarmolinsky. Johnson had declared the War on Poverty in early January, the legislation passed nine months later, and programs did not get under way until early November. This lengthy implementation process contributed to the War on Poverty's initial inability to live up to both rich and poor Americans' high expectations for it.[73]

Throughout the legislative process, the South held center stage as the key player in the bill's passage. The civil rights movement had altered southern politics, putting many forces in play. As an element of the Second Reconstruction, the Economic Opportunity Act revealed how much had changed and how much had stayed the same. Southern politics forced Johnson to strike a bargain to enable the antipoverty program to move forward without overtly challenging Dixie's racism. The addition of the governors' veto, the firing of Yarmolinsky, the removal of the Family Farm Corporation, and the replacement of grants with loans to poor farmers left some southern congressmen with the impression that they had addressed the more provocative elements of the bill. For the South's poorer citizens, these alterations diminished the hopes raised by Titles II and III but did not curtail overall expectations for the Economic Opportunity Act. Shriver's appointment as head of OEO as well as his earlier selection of progressive task force members and OEO staffers increased the likelihood that the South's poor—black and white—would benefit from the legislation, regardless of the amendments attached to it. The new Civil Rights Act would provide OEO with weapons that enabled it to enforce equal treatment, and Shriver created the Civil Rights Division and the Inspection Division within the agency to ensure that the needs of poor minorities would receive close attention.

As the War on Poverty began, however, the Economic Opportunity Act did not really address the structural issues that had nothing to do with individual character or a culture of poverty. As was the case with the New Deal programs of the 1930s, politicians assumed that capitalism could still accommodate all Americans; neither the legislative nor the executive branch, therefore, addressed these structural issues—such as strip mining that displaced coal miners or technological advances that eliminated the livelihoods of tenant farmers and sharecroppers—in this specific legislation. This bill sought to provide economic opportunity, not to restructure the American economy. So despite the fact that people living in pockets of poverty across America needed more than individual opportunity to meet their economic needs, the architects of the War on Poverty chose a different battle plan. Congress further tied OEO officials' hands by creating an annual funding process. The struggle against poverty thus remained in the political arena, a situation that prevented OEO from fighting this domestic war above the fray of Washington politics.

More than one southern accent could be heard across the region as the Johnson administration launched its War on Poverty. After August 11, 1964, grassroots organizations could access a federally funded program as part of their efforts to change the South. The mixed signals of accommodation to the white South that had emanated from 1600 Pennsylvania Avenue became clarified as southern governors implemented antipoverty programs. People at the grass roots would need to mount an organized effort to continue the struggle for equal access to this federal program. In many cases, they would have important allies within OEO who worked to make sure that the voices of the black poor could be heard.

CHAPTER TWO

At the Crossroads

The Programs of the Office of Economic Opportunity and Civil Rights in the South

Poverty claims victims among all racial groups. Indeed, the majority of the poor in America are white. But, one-half of the non-white population is poor, and the solutions to the problems of poverty are closely interrelated with the solutions to the barriers to civil rights. . . . Poverty cannot be substantially eliminated until the problems of racial discrimination are more nearly solved; until opportunity is more nearly equal for all of our citizens.
Sargent Shriver

The Office of Economic Opportunity (OEO) officially opened on October 8, 1964. As a federal agency created after the 1964 Civil Rights Act, OEO faced the issue of civil rights compliance from its inception. Title VI of the Civil Rights Act stipulated, "No person in the United States shall, on the ground of race, color, or national origin, be excluded from participation in, be denied the benefits of, or be subjected to discrimination under any program or activity receiving Federal financial assistance." The Civil Rights Act required departments that distributed federal funds to formulate rules, regulations, or orders to meet the conditions of the legislation. As a result, not only did fighting poverty compel OEO to be concerned with the needs of the nation's impoverished minority population, but federal legislation required that OEO make sure no one received discriminatory treatment. Several departments within OEO, particularly the General Counsel's Office, the Inspection Division, and the Civil Rights Division, made it a priority to keep the agency within the letter of the law.[1]

Other events also kept OEO officials aware of the civil rights component of fighting poverty: the Selma march that contributed to the passage of the Voting Rights Act in 1965; the urban riots that followed that landmark legislation and erupted periodically from 1965 through 1969; the 1967 disclosure of severe malnutrition among Mississippi's poor population; and the Poor People's Campaign mounted by the Southern Christian Leadership Conference (SCLC), which culminated with the building of Resurrection City in Washington, D.C., in 1968. These occasions highlighted the plight of African Americans and often tied racial discrimination to poverty.

By 1966, OEO openly associated the achievement of civil rights as one measure of the antipoverty program's success. As an agency reference guide stated, "While some progress in the elimination of poverty is possible at the current level of progress in civil rights, poverty cannot be substantially eliminated until the problems of racial discrimination are more nearly solved; until opportunity is more nearly equal for all of our citizens." Of course, confronting problems stemming from racial discrimination was not OEO's only tactic for fighting poverty. Civil rights organizations, however, continually compelled OEO to address this issue because several groups sought to use antipoverty programs to benefit their constituents.[2]

The National Association for the Advancement of Colored People (NAACP) began considering how to use antipoverty programs even before the legislation creating OEO was enacted. In October 1964, NAACP executive director Roy Wilkins explained to the presidents of the association's branches and state conferences that it expected "to involve its administrative and branch structure, its personnel, its leaders and its members in a vigorous and continuing effort to implement the Anti-Poverty Act in every community where the possibility exists." He thought that taking this new direction was absolutely necessary if the NAACP wanted to maintain a leadership position within the civil rights movement. Wilkins wanted the branches to spearhead local antipoverty efforts by serving as a coordinating agency in the African American community. He envisioned association branches initiating, developing, and operating OEO-funded programs. Wilkins also hoped that his organization could "serve as a watchdog in the community during the development and implementation of each phase of the various programs" to ensure that the NAACP received adequate representation on community action agency (CAA) boards. Wilkins considered it essential that "the Association be thought of as the responsible spokesman of the Negro community."[3]

After Congress passed the Economic Opportunity Act, the NAACP moved into action. In the Southeast, regional director Ruby Hurley reported in the spring of 1965 that throughout the region, African Americans who were not representative of the black community had been appointed to CAAs. The Jacksonville, Florida, branch and the Georgia State Conference protested these practices, and the South Carolina State Conference planned to demonstrate at the State Capitol. To alleviate future problems, Hurley developed a relationship with OEO's southeast regional office in Atlanta, and some improvements resulted by the fall. Hurley's office stopped funds from going to the Clarendon County, South Carolina, CAA by notifying OEO in Washington that politicians and segregationists had taken over the program.[4]

In late 1964, the National Urban League sponsored a symposium in Washington, D.C., to bring OEO activities to the attention of group leaders from across the country. Sargent Shriver attended this conference and answered participants' questions regarding OEO's plans. The Urban League also held meetings across the South to publicize antipoverty programs and to teach people how to apply for grants. In the winter of 1965, the league joined forces with Birmingham progressives. Organizing under the name "Alabama State Economic Opportunity Conference Planning Committee," this group held a statewide meeting to explain how to take advantage of the Economic Opportunity Act. The following spring, the Urban League hosted a similar meeting in Jackson, Mississippi.[5]

Not to be overshadowed by the older civil rights organizations, the Southern Christian Leadership Conference (SCLC) and the Student Nonviolent Coordinating Committee (SNCC) also capitalized on antipoverty activities to further their efforts in the South. As a part of its Summer Community Organization and Political Education (SCOPE) project, the SCLC worked to organize communities around the issues of political disfranchisement, educational deprivation, and poverty. Administered by Hosea Williams, chair of the SCLC's Voter Registration and Political Education Department, SCOPE expected to bring the War on Poverty to one hundred southern counties where the annual median individual income for African Americans stood at less than eight hundred dollars. Williams planned to introduce community action programs (CAPs) and Neighborhood Youth Corps projects to these impoverished counties with the help of summer volunteers recruited from college campuses from around the country. In November 1965, Martin Luther King Jr. wrote to tell OEO officials of his organization's continued intention to sponsor antipoverty programs.[6]

Just as the NAACP brought a more representative body of the black community onto the CAA board of Clarendon County, South Carolina, the SCLC's efforts also bore some fruit in this area in the fall of 1965. In Gadsden, Alabama, the SCLC helped achieve legitimate grassroots representation on the local CAA board. Four of the twenty-one board members were black, most importantly Dr. J. W. Stewart, also a member of the Gadsden Civic Center. A product of the SCLC's community development work, the Civic Center confronted local politicians when they refused to sponsor a summer Head Start program. After obtaining a court order against the mayor, the members of the Gadsden Civic Center operated the Head Start program themselves. With the support of the Goodyear Rubber Company (whose officials had a quiet but influential role in improving race relations in the community) and the Catholic Church through Sister Peter Claver, the Gadsden CAA achieved a consensus rarely seen in Alabama. By the spring of 1966, the SCLC worked on community development projects through OEO Title II programs in six of the state's Black Belt counties—Dallas, Greene, Hale, Marengo, Perry, and Wilcox.[7]

SNCC members continued to maintain ties to communities in which they had been operating since 1963. These young people also saw the benefits available through the War on Poverty. Having worked in Alabama, Arkansas, Georgia, Maryland, Mississippi, North Carolina, and Virginia, SNCC workers established freedom schools, community centers, citizenship training and education programs, adult literacy projects, and programs assisting rural people in forming cooperatives and small businesses. All of these activities seemed to coincide with the Economic Opportunity Act's goal of enlisting people to form programs to help themselves. Instead of directly sponsoring OEO activities, SNCC encouraged local people to create or join CAAs.[8]

As these organizations carried out their plans, it became obvious that War on Poverty programs served as a new medium in which the civil rights movement could operate. In Alabama, the CAP, Head Start, and projects administered through the U.S. Department of Agriculture (USDA) provided new opportunities for confronting civil rights concerns. Predictably, these programs provoked cultural and political changes.

On the other side of the equation, OEO's support for the civil rights cause became more than the simple matter of distributing funds. Civil rights compliance would not have been expected to be difficult to manage, since OEO was a new agency. Nevertheless, factors such as agency personnel, the director's management style, and legislative authorization and amendments affected OEO's overall ability to enforce civil rights in a comprehensive manner.

Events beyond the purview of the agency also added to the difficulty of OEO's civil rights tasks. From 1964 to 1969, existing fissures within the civil rights movement widened, especially after Congress passed key legislation. As a result, implementing the stipulations of the Civil Rights Act while carrying out OEO activities often meant choosing among the movement's various factions. OEO officials increasingly found that even though they followed the provisions of the civil rights law, they still received criticism for funding one group rather than another. When these instances arose, both the political Left and the Right often attacked the antipoverty agency, thus putting it on the defensive. Understanding how the War on Poverty became a new medium for the civil rights movement and how OEO responded clarifies the antipoverty effort's role as the black freedom movement entered a new phase. Because poverty programs functioned on a local level but received funding from the federal government, it

mattered who worked in the various departments of OEO and how they interpreted their mandate to fight poverty. Knowledge of these inner workings of the
"permanent government" help explain the decision-making process within the
Office of Economic Opportunity and how those decisions affected people on
the local level in places such as Alabama.

More than a Bureaucrat: Community Action and Civil Rights Enforcement

The War on Poverty became a vehicle for the civil rights movement in the South
through its programs, which started in late 1964 and early 1965. As spelled out
in the legislation, OEO managed the Job Corps, CAP, and the Volunteers in
Service to America (VISTA). OEO's southeast region had no Job Corps centers
as a result of the governors' veto provision in the Economic Opportunity Act.
With the requirement of integrated housing and working conditions, southern
governors did not want Job Corps facilities in their states.[9]

VISTA—Title VI of the Economic Opportunity Act—harbored the potential to support civil rights components in the antipoverty campaign. Volunteers
received small government stipends and lived and worked in the communities
they served. Glenn Ferguson, VISTA's first director, described a volunteer as
a "conduit," someone who brought time, skills, concern, and insight to assist
people in making judgments about how to accomplish community goals to alleviate poverty. Most recruits to this program were young, middle class, and well
educated. Just as local groups under the CAP had to discover the best ways to
solve the problems associated with poverty, VISTA volunteers had to create
their own assignments based on their understanding of the community and its
needs. Many worked in conjunction with other OEO-affiliated projects, such as
Head Start, Legal Services, Community Action, and the Job Corps. VISTA assistant director Edgar May highlighted the program's potential for creating controversy when he described a volunteer's actions on an Indian reservation that
did not receive services from the water authority in the nearest town: "Once you
figured out there's something the matter with the public system, and if you're
there to do something about poverty, you begin showing up at the water authority meetings, and you say things that they really don't want to hear. That's when
the genie's out of the bottle." In this capacity, a VISTA worker could be an agent
of change. During the summer of 1964, parts of the South—especially Georgia, Louisiana, and Mississippi—witnessed what came to be known as Freedom
Summer. Black and white volunteers worked in conjunction with CORE, the
NAACP, the SCLC, and SNCC to organize black communities to confront Jim
Crow and gain the right to vote. Some southerners subsequently concluded that
VISTA workers looked suspiciously like outside agitators.[10]

VISTA, however, never got very big, especially in the South, and consequently did not have a large effect across the region. In addition, VISTA was weakened in some southern states by the fact that the legislation gave governors the right to approve VISTA activity in their states. Mississippi hosted no volunteers during OEO's existence, while North Carolina had eighty-six volunteers in 1967 alone. Even though the program remained small, it could be unruly. OEO and Congress brought VISTA to heel by mandating policy changes within the agency. After a group of VISTA workers in New York organized a protest against the Vietnam War, OEO officials ruled that volunteers could not use the VISTA name while "exercising their political rights as citizens." Congress stepped in after complaints about the activities of Appalachian VISTA volunteers reached a fever pitch. Federal legislators amended the Economic Opportunity Act in 1966 to forbid voter registration campaigns as part of the CAP's fight against poverty. May described this as a "crippling blow" for OEO because it kept the poor from becoming a distinct part of the political system.[11]

In the absence of the Job Corps or a strong VISTA presence, the poverty programs that provided the greatest opportunity for civil rights activity in the South were the Title II CAPs (which later included Head Start) and the Title III programs that dealt with rural poverty. As the heart of the Economic Opportunity Act, CAP offered something new in the fight against poverty. People would assess the problems in their community that fostered poverty, develop ideas for solving those problems, and apply for funds from Washington to accomplish their tasks. The CAAs worked to mobilize the poor to develop and implement plans to combat poverty and coordinate local antipoverty resources at all levels. OEO staff hoped that the CAAs would speak on behalf of the poor to focus different approaches and resources simultaneously on the multifaceted problems of poverty while reorienting existing programs more effectively to meet the needs of low-income people.[12]

In addition to the unique feature of federal government programs operating independently on the local level, the Community Action Program's other distinguishing attribute—the stipulation that CAPs utilize the maximum feasible participation of the residents of the areas and members of the groups served—also attracted people with connections to the civil rights movement. In this provision resided the concept of participatory democracy that had served as the dynamo providing much of the current to the grassroots civil rights movement. This requirement involved poor people in the development, operation, and administration of programs. The poor could serve on CAA boards, participate on agency policy committees, work as subprofessionals on antipoverty projects, and operate neighborhood councils that advised the CAAs. Many within OEO believed that poor people's participation in planning and carrying out programs on their behalf would result in more effective programs because low-income people knew their own needs, what worked best, and what new techniques could succeed.[13]

Richard Boone, the member of the President's Task Force in the War Against Poverty who introduced the phrase *maximum feasible participation* into the legislation, explained that he developed this concept in light of the growing civil rights struggle. "The 'movement' has been an historic rejection of second-class citizenship. It was and is a rejection of both exclusion and paternalism," Boone stated. "The maximum feasible participation section of the Economic Opportunity Act of 1964 could not have been written before the flowering of the Civil Rights Movement. In a substantial degree it was written because of that movement." The participatory clause brought into the process of fighting poverty many people who had previously been excluded from taking part in any government-sponsored community service. David Grossman, a member of the CAP staff in Washington, thought that the legislative combination of the Civil Rights Act and the Economic Opportunity Act "had much to do with the way the maximum feasible participation phrase was interpreted by Negroes . . . and other minority groups."[14]

OEO officials often described maximum feasible participation using appealing American jargon as a way of defusing the phrase's potential for controversy. "This is simply a statement of the principles that we assume in a democracy—that people should have some say in what happens to them," an OEO reference guide asserted. "If it sometimes results in stress, it is stress that is necessary to democracy." The antipoverty agency also considered the maximum feasible participation clause to be part of the country's political ideals—another way to create consensus. Power would be shared by poor residents of an area and others in the community who held an interest in alleviating poverty, including local elected officials, people who worked with social welfare, business executives, religious organizations, and philanthropists. At no time did OEO staff view the participatory concept as the poor controlling the local community action projects. Regardless of who dominated local CAAs, many agency officials knew that arriving at consensus might involve confrontation. Initially, no fixed percentages were established for determining how many poor representatives should sit on CAA boards. However, by 1966 OEO generally viewed a strong community action board as one that had about 30 percent of its members representing the targeted population. Finally, OEO did not require those people who spoke on behalf of their poor neighbors to be impoverished themselves. What mattered most to CAP administrators was that these persons truly represented their poor constituents.[15]

Under these conditions, Community Action Programs clearly had the potential to stir up changes in the South. If successful, a CAP could achieve a variety of objectives. In addition to providing programs to help people out of poverty, a CAP could give poor black southerners a voice in structuring those projects and the power to decide where federal money would be spent. "The CAP in a southern community," George Esser, an OEO official, explained, "is perhaps the only institution for change that would provide a focal point for opening up all aspects of the community in terms of opportunities for the Negro, in terms of giving the community a place where real dialogue can take place."[16]

Some CAPs created quite a stir when they began operating. Many CAAs caused mayors and other local elected officials anxiety because they did not have complete control over these organizations: in Shriver's words, "Nobody in politics liked that." However, several hundred CAPs functioned without controversy or conflict. Whether contention arose or consensus reigned, including poor people in this new assault on poverty had many benefits. May credited the maximum feasible participation clause with the discovery of "a whole host of very bright poor people." The poor also acquired new skills that could be applied to future jobs. Throughout the antipoverty agency's history, OEO received criticism that it did not do enough to bring more poor people into the process. Yet assistant director of management William Kelly defended OEO's efforts. At a December 1965 meeting of the National Advisory Council, he said, "You know a year ago there were exactly zero poor people involved in anything in this nation. Now we've got about eight hundred to nine hundred Community Action Agencies, and poor people represent twenty-seven percent of all the boards that we've got. I think we've come a hell of a distance."[17]

The initial personnel who worked on the Community Action Program in Washington greatly influenced OEO policy. These individuals focused on incorporating formerly marginalized people into the agency's programs. Jack Conway, the CAP's first director, came to the agency with a commitment to grassroots organizing that dated from his work for the organized labor movement. He supported the terms of Title II and planned for his office to take seriously the maximum feasible participation clause. "I took the objectives as they were very clearly set out, and we designed a program and put it on the boards and hit with as strong a mule kick as we could," Conway remembered. "Now if that's radicalizing it, that's what we did." He truly believed that meeting the program's objectives would require some "shaking up," especially in the South. He supported the idea of enlisting local governments in CAA programs; however, if elected officials refused to cooperate, Conway was willing to work within the private sector. Meeting with the president in November 1964, Conway explained his plans for carrying out his part of the antipoverty program. Johnson's reaction to this overview forecast the CAP's future. LBJ warned, "There are a lot of these places where civilization is pretty thin, and you have to be sure you don't ride

Figure 6. OEO published brochures to explain the Community Action Program. This one said, "Let's discuss our problems. Let's invite everyone to a meeting maybe at a nearby church, school, or home. Let's work together to solve our problems. Let's elect officers. And let's decide on a plan of action!" Records of the Field Office, CAP, Ala. and S.C. District Offices, OEO Multi-Purpose Training Center of Atlanta University, Box 1, Office of Economic Opportunity Papers, RG 381, National Archives and Records Administration, Southeast Division, Morrow, Ga.

roughshod over people and create your own problems." Conway interpreted this statement to mean that if the CAP "hit too hard, too fast and [in] too many places that we'd create our own counterrevolution . . . and give him too many problems to deal with, as well as ourselves."[18]

Several people Conway hired held similar ideas about CAP's role in addressing the social problems brought about by poverty. Richard Boone and Fred O'R. Hayes continued working for CAP after serving on the task force that drafted Title II. Boone came to the President's Task Force in the War Against Poverty after serving on John F. Kennedy's President's Committee on Juvenile Delinquency. He had long seen the connection between juvenile delinquency and poverty, having studied the subject while doing undergraduate and graduate work in sociology and criminology at the University of Chicago. In the mid-1950s, he became a captain in the Cook County sheriff's Juvenile Bureau, and later in the decade he did intensive work with youth gangs through the YMCA of Metropolitan Chicago. Boone joined the staff of the juvenile delinquency program in 1962 as a consultant and developed the ideas for the National Service Corps. Experiences from his early career flowed into his work there and influenced his definition of poverty. Like others on the staff of the President's

Committee on Juvenile Delinquency, Boone blamed structural problems within society for trapping people in poverty. He had seen social programs that had been developed to assist the poor become dominated by professional employees and elected officials. Both groups found ways to use these programs to their own advantage or to benefit powerful supporters rather than to alleviate poverty. Boone believed that the traditional welfare institutions could be changed from within if they started utilizing the poor they served in planning and delivering services. He thought that this approach would keep the welfare agency focused on the constituents served as well as benefit the recipients by increasing their ability to earn a living.[19]

Boone headed the CAP's Program Policy and Planning Division. He handled inquiries, applications, and related material for demonstration projects and processed background material on programs. Some people referred to his area as the CAP's "idea side." Not surprisingly, Boone employed people who agreed with his belief in maximum feasible participation. In the demonstration division, staffer Eric Tolmach recalled, "we tried out new methods of bringing poor people into the operation of programs." These approaches involved low-income people in the various aspects of the CAAs by reserving jobs for them in entry-level positions as well as staff-level duties. In this way, officials hoped to provide on-the-job training and educational enrichment for the targeted population that would upgrade their skills and lead to jobs with greater responsibility. Neither local CAAs nor any other person or agency had to approve a demonstration project before OEO would fund it. If such approval had been required in places such as the Alabama Black Belt, Tolmach explained, "we never would have been able to make the kinds of experiments that we did make." If a demonstration project succeeded, the CAP division planned to replicate it in other communities. Ideas focusing on education, housing, and health were just a few of the demonstration programs on which Boone and his staff worked. In the Alabama Black Belt, a demonstration program that received funding in 1967 had important ramifications for the region both economically and politically.[20]

Hayes controlled the operations side of CAP—receiving inquiries, applications, and related materials for program and technical assistance. He held graduate degrees from Harvard in public administration and in political economy and government. He initially entered federal government service as a fiscal economist for the Bureau of the Budget but left in 1961 to become an assistant commissioner in the Urban Renewal Administration. Three years later, he joined the antipoverty task force, helping to draft Title II of the legislation. At that time, he acknowledged, he "really didn't know very much about" the President's Committee on Juvenile Delinquency and Youth Crime, and he admitted that he grew skeptical about relying on the abilities of the inner-city poor as the main effort to wage a war on poverty. "We knew from experience with urban renewal and other programs that we could expect, at most, only a handful of communities to create antipoverty agencies with these capabilities." As the staff person responsible for CAP in the field, Hayes felt strongly about quickly funding as many programs as possible. Samuel Yette, the head of OEO's Civil Rights Division, characterized Hayes as an efficiency person concerned with processing applications in a timely manner. According to Yette, Hayes often said, "Let's get this [grant] out of here, sign the thing, don't worry about all that stuff." Hayes did not want perceived foot-dragging over civil rights compliance to dampen enthusiasm for CAP across the country.[21]

In these early days of community action, conflicts soon arose between Hayes and Boone regarding how to achieve maximum feasible participation. No guidelines had yet been developed, and some OEO officials therefore used the original CAP grant applications as learning tools on which to base decisions. According to Edgar Cahn, an attorney who played a leading role in creating OEO's Legal Services program, Hayes wanted the agency to have a presence in as many communities as possible. In March 1965, for example, Hayes's contacts in Alabama reassured him that "if the federal government insists on what it wants in Community Action organizations, the vast majority of the communities will comply and will, themselves, be able to take care of any problem this creates in the State House." He told Theodore M. Berry, an African American who had just succeeded Conway as the CAP's director, that Governor George Wallace had shown no interest in the poverty program except in Birmingham. Therefore, Hayes concluded, OEO "should begin funding eligible programs in Alabama without further delay." In his haste, however, Hayes miscalculated. Wallace had every intention of keeping a tight rein on the War on Poverty in his state and managing these programs for his political benefit. Alabamians who had been trying to start OEO programs in their communities made this clear at a hearing sponsored by the U.S. Civil Rights Commission: "In our judgment, Mr. Yette, the manner in which the funds are funded in Alabama are organized in such a manner so as to deprive the people for whom the legislation was actually passed."[22]

Boone agreed that funds needed to be widely distributed. He thought the ideal bargaining leverage for bringing the poor into these programs, however, occurred at the front end of the grant process, before the application had been approved. "That's when we ought to hold the line as tough as we can," Cahn remembered Boone saying. Quality, not quantity, served as the ruling force in his decision-making process.[23]

The Inspection Division became a third force in this conflict. Created as the "eyes of the king" for Shriver, this division, which fell under the purview of the director's office, served as an early warning system, alerting him to potential problems in any OEO project before the press reported on it. In the Peace Corps, Shriver had set up an independent source of intelligence to keep him informed regarding what was happening out in the field. He installed a similar operation within OEO.[24]

William Haddad served as the first inspector general. He had been an award-winning investigative reporter for the *New York Post* and the *New York Herald Tribune* before working with Shriver at the Peace Corps. In his new role at OEO, Haddad felt strongly that the Inspection Division needed to enforce the maximum feasible participation clause of CAP with regard to poor people as well as minorities. In early 1965, one staff member reviewed programs in the South and reported to Haddad that the "OEO's programs seem to me an extremely promising stimulus to racial progress in the south, at this time." Haddad agreed. He viewed the poor as the "newest minority . . . to be melted into the pot of democracy." He saw their desire to be fully American in the context of past immigrants who had fought for their place in the wider society. In his judgment, this phenomenon was part of "the tradition of urban politics and nothing more." In an effort to gain as much information on minority representation as possible, Haddad reached out to civil rights organizations. He wrote to the NAACP's assistant director for details on how OEO programs were functioning in Alabama, Georgia, Louisiana, and Mississippi. To establish a direct line of communication, Haddad asked the NAACP official to contact him at any time. "If you get anything you want to talk about, please call me collect," he closed.[25]

Members of Haddad's staff investigated CAP projects and reported their findings to the director. In some cases, they alerted Shriver to the consequences of unchecked CAP programs. One investigator warned of escalating problems if issues in Georgia were neglected: "If the present trend toward nonrepresentation is allowed to harden," he advised, "we might just as well kiss off the rest of the Deep South as far as getting meaningful Negro participation in decision making roles." These reports occupied a significant place within the antipoverty agency. Shriver claimed to have read every one and determined the worthiness of grant applications and program continuation based on these accounts.[26]

In an effort to avoid blindly funding programs, Shriver established a sign-off procedure. He convened meetings of his senior staff and asked for information about each grant, basing his final decision on what he heard. Thus, reports from Haddad's office carried great weight within the agency. Haddad also sent reports to the General Counsel's Office and the Civil Rights Division, where officials often reviewed the reports before anyone in the CAP division saw them. Each of these branches of OEO took part in these sign-off sessions and valued the Inspection Division's findings and recommendations. Yette thought that the inspection reports and participation in the grant approval process were essential to his staff's ability to enforce civil rights within OEO's programs. Modifications in grant applications sometimes would occur during these sessions to ensure that poor people and minorities could participate fully in the program before funds were approved. At other times, however, Shriver supported CAP staff members who objected to the findings of the General Counsel's Office, the Inspection Division, or the Civil Rights Division.[27]

In March 1965, the Inspection Division conducted a survey of the Community Action Program in the South; the results contradicted Hayes's approach to funding CAPs. Jack Gonzales, a member of Haddad's staff, reported on the difficulties faced by the region's CAP officials, who could not scrutinize each CAA for compliance. Instead, regional staff members tried "to get one or two 'good' programs started" and hoped that future CAPs in a state would emulate those models. Gonzales concluded, however, that this strategy did not work: "It has produced tokenism: one or two safe Negroes on a board, or parallel Negro subcommittees that meet to approve the minutes of the main board." He warned that the agency was "being kidded badly by many Southern CAP's, I suspect, and we are kidding ourselves about the way our programs are heading in the South because we want so badly for them to work." One CAP staff member explained the frustration that arose from reports such as Gonzales's. The CAP "representatives would agree to one set of conditions only to have Inspection overturn them. Then there would be a battle back and forth" while the local people had to wait for the issue to be resolved within OEO. Some southern CAAs complained about this problem directly to OEO. David Hughes of the Northeast Georgia Area Planning and Development Agency argued that OEO's civil rights policies were inconsistent—various people within the agency interpreted OEO guidelines differently. He insisted that "OEO seems to think integration has got to be all or nothing, with no allowance for local situations." Hughes also accused OEO bureaucrats of "pre-judging Southern projects. . . . [J]ust by virtue of locale," OEO would not "take people in certain areas on good faith." He saw this process as merely another form of prejudice. The Inspection Division's David Swit believed that some of these charges were valid, but the Georgia official "sounded as sincere as an undertaker trying to look sad at a $8,000 funeral." For his part, Conway considered these reports an infringement on the CAP's function and on his authority.[28]

Tension mounted between OEO's two divisions, with Conway believing that Haddad had overstepped his bounds. As the head of CAP, Conway supervised the spending of funds for his operation, yet Haddad's investigators caused increasing difficulty in approving grants on a timely basis, and the process of grant approval stretched from sixty days to about six months. Senior OEO staff lacked a great deal of respect for bureaucratic hierarchy, which contributed to the battleground atmosphere of the grant sign-off sessions. One OEO official remembered that "every issue had to be fought out time and time again." To remedy this situation, Shriver abandoned the formal grant sign-off sessions in August 1965 and instead circulated grant packages to interested offices for comment.[29]

This conflict continued to simmer throughout OEO's history. Some agency officials pushed to accelerate programs, while others called for cautious implementation. The clash later widened to include the Civil Rights Division and the General Counsel's Office. Yette viewed Hayes as an adversary: "Whenever I saw a package I had to be sure that Fred once more was not trying to rush something through." Yette took the position that the Civil Rights Division would concentrate on maximum participation and let "the other guys worry about the feasibility." As a result, Yette felt that many other agency staffers regarded him as an antagonist. He later concluded that Hayes advised the director to leave Yette out of the decision-making process, often trying to go around the Civil Rights Division's recommendations.[30]

The General Counsel's Office became the brakes on the CAP funding machine. OEO general counsel Donald Baker saw his staff as "the last protection . . . for the director," a viewpoint that caused more discord with the program people. CAP employees accused OEO's lawyers of meddling beyond the parameters of their duty, while Baker justified his position by saying that "we are not authorized by Congress to be using bad judgment with the taxpayers' money." Kelly, who agreed more closely with Hayes, remembered that there "was always the terrible problem that administrators in this agency had, that you were selling out because all of a sudden you approved a board in which there were 30 percent poor, and somebody thought it ought to be 35 percent." This dispute highlights the difficulty OEO personnel faced in reaching agreement on interpretations of the spirit of the Economic Opportunity Act as well as in following the letter of the law. Officials encountered difficulty forging a consensus on how effectively to implement these federal laws. The issue resolved itself to some degree as a result of staff resignations and promotions as well as amendments to the Economic Opportunity Act, which in 1967 established percentages for representation on CAA boards.[31]

Despite his disagreement with Haddad in OEO's internal turf wars, Conway remained committed to bringing more targeted people into CAP projects. Conway recruited Boone and Hayes as well as other staff to join the CAP office. Brendan Sexton came on board to manage the training side of CAP, also known as Program Support. He was joined by Fred Hoehler, Judah Drob, and Tom Cosgrove, all of whom had been labor educators and knew Conway before he joined OEO. This labor union experience served an important purpose. "Just as we had trained illiterate working people to become effective union people," Conway said, "we trained illiterate, inexperienced blacks and Chicanos and Indians to become effective leaders in their own right and to take on responsibilities." Sexton resolved that in the South his group would work only with interracial programs. To that end, he tried to organize a consortium of universities and colleges that "previously have been either all white or all Negro" to provide CAP training centers. For example, he wanted to have the Tuskegee Institute and the University of Alabama work together and to organize a New Orleans consortium including Dillard, Xavier, Loyola, and Tulane. Sexton also recruited an African American to work in the South "so our section will be represented in negotiations and developments by persons who are acutely aware of this problem." In his critique of CAP, Daniel Patrick Moynihan blamed Conway and his staff for expanding the involvement of the poor in community action programs to be "as much as possible, at all stages, and for every purpose." But Conway did not view Moynihan's contention as criticism; instead, he saw the "enfranchisement, the empowerment, of literally hundreds and thousands of people who had been out of it before" as CAP's permanent contribution to the War on Poverty.[32]

In February 1965, Conway accepted a position as Shriver's deputy. This promotion altered the dynamics within the Community Action Division. By March, the Kentucky-born Berry, who had strong ties to the NAACP and the Urban League, replaced Conway. Berry held a law degree and had many years of experience in the city government of Cincinnati, where he developed a community action plan that brought him to the attention of Shriver and others at OEO. Berry proved to be a committed poverty warrior, but his approach differed from Conway's.[33]

After arriving at OEO headquarters, Berry first had to figure out how to fund CAP programs that met OEO's standards, a process made more difficult by the fact that many of the applications did not conform to the language of the statute. With only three months remaining in the fiscal year, CAP still had 50 percent of its allocation to spend. This predicament increased the friction between the factions of "idea people" and "program people." Enormous pressure mounted to use all the money Congress had designated for the War on Poverty by approving more grant proposals. Many believed that placing CAAs far and wide created a critical mass of people with vested interests in OEO. With more supporters, the agency would have a better chance of gaining congressional reauthorization. In its haste to spend the budgeted money, however, OEO funded some programs that later created trouble.[34]

Under Berry's leadership, CAP guidelines were put into writing and program policies became more routine. These guidelines defined the types of projects that fit under the CAP concept, interpreted what OEO meant by "maximum feasible participation," and explained how to form a CAA. Berry described the CAP's position at this time as intended to foster harmony, not division, in clarifying to groups what the antipoverty agency regarded as "community action." While trying to encourage slow-moving communities to share in the decision-making process, Berry also explained that confrontation in and of itself was not the goal of community action. As a part of this consensus building, OEO officials for the first time decided not to reject a government-sponsored applicant for CAA funding in favor of a competing private group. The General Counsel's Office supported this policy. Donald Baker and his staff did not think that CAP would benefit if it started with the most militant southern civil rights requests. Baker believed that having two or three black people serving on a CAA board in the South not only represented an achievement but "probably indeed was the maximum feasible at that particular time." He reasoned that more progress could be made by "pleading and cajoling and threatening over time" to get greater minority representation. Baker had anticipated that CAP would bring trouble to OEO, and he tried to distance the agency from as much conflict as possible. Norbert Schlei, who helped draft the Economic Opportunity Act, saw the benefits of working within the local governmental structure. "Maybe you could defy them," he argued, "and go and do your thing, but they would keep undoing it or uprooting it unless they were brought in."[35]

This policy had repercussions in the South, especially in Alabama, where many CAAs foundered as a consequence of the lack of support from the local government or failed to include black people who represented the poor community. OEO at times ended up supporting people who had been directly involved in thwarting the progress of the civil rights movement. In Mississippi, Sunflower County's chief of police became chair of the CAA board. In Alabama, Selma's mayor, Joe Smitherman, appointed the local CAA director. Eventually the antipoverty agency agreed to fund nongovernmental CAAs in the South only after local governmental officials refused to cooperate, a solution that often led to direct confrontation between the governor and OEO.[36]

B. B. Mayberry, dean of the School of Agriculture at the Tuskegee Institute, wrote to Shriver in early 1966 to highlight the consequences of this policy. Mayberry pointed out that twelve Alabama counties had populations that were both 50 percent African American and 50 percent living on family incomes of less than twenty-five hundred dollars per year. "Not one of these counties has received one dime of CAP funds," he explained, "except Macon where Tuskegee Institute is located." Mayberry concluded that no OEO programs had been organized in these counties because "of the failure of the community to organize or otherwise establish a community action committee through the democratic process." He blamed this failure on the apathy of the local power structure and its resentment of "federal participation in progressive programs at the local level." Mayberry asked OEO to intervene to change some of the CAP's guidelines to enable the creation of poverty programs in his region of Alabama. Without these modifications, he feared, program development would remain frozen in the state's most economically deprived counties. Although OEO guidelines were essential for a uniform grant application process, the new policies had unintended consequences in the South.[37]

After Haddad left OEO in the fall of 1965, Shriver promoted Edgar May, who had previously served as an assistant director of VISTA and subsequently as Shriver's special assistant, to lead the Inspection Division. May brought impressive credentials to his new position. He had published a book on poverty, *The Wasted Americans,* based on a series of Pulitzer Prize–winning investigative reports he had written for the *Buffalo Evening News.* May's promotion eventually influenced the dynamics between the Inspection Division and CAP.[38]

Under May's supervision, the Inspection Division gradually changed its focus. The antipoverty agency, no longer operating like a newborn department, tried to develop means to check on developing programs. Instead of serving as a restraint on OEO's programming function, May's Inspection Division shifted to evaluating the effectiveness of OEO projects that were already up and running. Division staff wrote comprehensive reports on the Job Corps, VISTA, and CAP instead of merely verifying compliance. During 1966 and 1967, inspectors also responded to the many complaints that arose from a variety of sources regarding CAP. Under May's supervision, his staff "followed the dollar to where it was being used," going directly to OEO programs and interviewing all parties involved to get to the bottom of the accusations. Unlike other federal agencies, which relied on state branches to conduct investigations, May's inspectors personally checked up on federal agencies operating on the local level. He remembered that when his staff investigated a welfare office in the South, the state's welfare commissioner called him to complain, "You can't have your man in there." May responded, "Well, then, we can't have our money in there. You make the choice." Unlike Haddad, who sent his findings directly to Shriver, May reported his staff's conclusions to OEO operating officials and regional directors before notifying Shriver. This change eased the long-standing tension between the Inspection Division staff and the CAP personnel.[39]

One further change, however, exacerbated friction between the Inspection Division and the Civil Rights Division. In an effort to remove his division from the programming business, May pulled his staff out of the grant sign-off loop. But this change removed an essential check from the pre-grant review process, greatly annoying Yette. At times he could tell from reading a grant application that the CAP needed to be checked before the grant could be approved; under the new sign-off policies, however, Yette had few options. "I have neither the staff nor the function to investigate that program's board before signing off. Neither has the program been investigated by anyone at OEO, according to CAP," Yette complained. "It seems foolish indeed for us either to (a) refuse to fund such programs out of ignorance or (b) to fund them in ignorance, then sit and wait for the earth to crumble under us." Shriver responded to this quandary by asking Yette, May, and southeast regional director Frank Sloan to make an inspection from a civil rights point of view before approving a grant. Bertrand Harding, who became Shriver's deputy in 1966, supported May's struggle to get the Inspection Division to operate in a more streamlined fashion. In the end, the Civil Rights Division initiated examinations through the Inspection Division when civil rights officials believed such an inspection was needed. As OEO matured into a more regulated bureaucracy, the combined rapid response to civil rights claims from CAP, the Inspection Division, and the Civil Rights Division faded. The conflicts involving May, Harding, and Yette were characteristic of the interdepartmental frictions within OEO. These frictions came to a head when LBJ requested a management survey of OEO, a process that led to Harding's assignment as Shriver's deputy. May was a member of Shriver's inner circle, and Shriver tended to rely greatly on the opinions of his core staff. As a result, May's influence trumped Yette's call for more staff. Yette and his office were left to hold the fort on their own and to hope that backup support would be there when they called.[40]

By the spring of 1967, Shriver seemed pleased with the state of CAP's management. Conway, Boone, and Hayes had left the agency; May had replaced Haddad; and Harding had been serving as Shriver's deputy for a year. "In CAP for two and a half years there's been a consistent policy—to fight any policy made by the Director which CAP disapproves," complained the OEO director. "Fortunately . . . we now have a top trio who have enough sense to execute policies, and enough loyalty to follow the Director's decisions." The Community Action Division continued to have problems, but it seemed much more under control than it had been during the chaotic days of late 1964 and early 1965.[41]

Jump-Starting Community Action: National-Emphasis Programs as a Way In

To accelerate the formation of community action projects, OEO at first tried to enlist state governments. The agency sponsored conferences in Washington that focused on such topics as rural poverty and migrant and seasonal farm workers. Shriver invited governors to attend (or send representatives) to learn how to utilize the antipoverty programs in their states. OEO also provided money so that states could form technical assistance agencies to help local communities develop and administer CAPs. This desire to enlist the states in helping OEO obtain higher-quality grant applications had a low success rate. Because OEO had not developed the CAP guidelines until late 1965, the states had too little expertise to aid citizens in applying for assistance. Governors who did not support the antipoverty agency because it could bolster their political rivals often did not provide staff and assistance to parallel federal programs. An investigation found that many southern governors had appointed "amiable hacks" to run the state OEO offices and that these appointees could not provide the information eager communities needed. As a consequence, people sought assistance from private sources, further threatening the governors' position. This political wrangling stifled much of local people's initial enthusiasm for the Community Action Program. Finally, some personnel within OEO viewed state agencies as another bureaucracy blocking direct communication between Washington and the local community. As a result, OEO staff members often avoided using such state-level organizations.[42]

The antipoverty agency tried another tactic to acquire more comprehensive CAP grant applications without becoming too mired in planning. This approach also became a way to address the conflict between the "idea" people and the "program" people within CAP. The program's strength—developing locally controlled responses to poverty—also became its chief vulnerability. Communities were not always up to the challenge of creating solutions to relieve poverty. As a result, OEO offered communities program-development grants. With this seed money, a director and small staff could be hired to research the community's needs and formulate concrete ideas for fighting poverty. Offering this first step also enabled the CAP staff and other OEO personnel to monitor the progress of the anticipated plans. Dealing with problems arising from the maximum feasible participation clause would be more easily resolved at this early stage than after a full-blown community action project had been funded. In Mobile, Alabama, Haddad's office took this approach. "After speaking with Mayor [Charles S.] Trimmier of Mobile," Haddad told Berry, "and reviewing his city council resolution, we have decided to do a full (but quick) check on the situation there. Also, the awarding of a planning grant gives us time to watch the situation develop." Communities that met OEO's standards at this first stage could then apply for CAP grants to fund planned programs. The federal government would pay up to 90 percent of the project's cost for the first two years, while the community could make up the remainder with cash or in-kind services. Even these changes did not seem to do enough. By the spring of 1965, some OEO officials still felt that the Community Action Program had not gotten off to a strong start. As a result, OEO turned to what became known as national-emphasis programs to serve as building blocks for community action.[43]

National-emphasis programs originated in Washington instead of on the local level. Shriver and some of his advisers thought that these programs would assist communities in starting the War on Poverty in areas that had not previously generated any activity. Many officials hoped that the creation of a national-emphasis program would serve as a catalyst for more antipoverty ventures. This "prepackaged" approach bothered some of the agency's CAP enthusiasts because it did not coincide with the original concept of community action—people developing solutions to their own problems. Conway thought that real institutional change could not occur outside of the procedure of citizens meeting and developing ideas and programs to deal with poverty. For him, the process was just as important as the end product. When Washington offered preplanned projects, part of CAP's original intent had been undermined. Politics also played a role in this decision. Boone concluded "that these strategies evolved from the need to get something highly visible and action-oriented before the American public and Congress." So that Congress would renew the legislation, OEO developed several of these programs over the years—Head Start, Legal Services, Upward Bound, Foster Grandparents, and Comprehensive Health Services.[44]

Although these projects may have fostered a service rather than organization and mobilization approach for CAP, they still had the potential to induce important change in a community. Supporters reasoned that national-emphasis programs offered a balance "between individual decision making and some assurance of a quality standard that would result in a good program." In some parts of the country, better services for the poor could have revolutionary results. Head Start programs addressed the problems associated with early childhood development; Legal Services gave the poor access to the unfamiliar legal system; and Comprehensive Health Services provided medical care to people who lacked the benefits of routine visits to a doctor. All of these projects had the capacity to equip people from poor communities with the tools needed to confront institutional obstacles and thereby improve the quality of life. The national-emphasis programs had to follow CAP's legislative regulations, including the maximum feasible participation clause. This simple fact kept them from becoming the equivalent of the traditional federal bureaucratic response to poverty.[45]

An examination of Head Start offers a case in point. Beginning an early childhood development program required contact with several different parts of a community—education, social services, health care—and thus brought in people who might not otherwise have been involved in a broad-based CAA.

Head Start programs enabled "the nation's attention [to] be focused upon the effects of poverty on young children," Berry pointed out. "If we can get the educational institutions and private institutions interested in this, and if they will take the idea of involving parents, it would, in effect . . . be Community Action in microcosm." Berry reasoned that by beginning with a single-purpose CAA organized around Head Start, the concept of community action would make more sense to the community and would ultimately spread to other programs. Shriver credited these projects with protecting CAP from its critics, "because a lot of people liked Head Start . . . Foster Grandparents [and] Upward Bound [even though] they don't like Community Action."[46]

Plans for Head Start began in the winter of 1965 with an eight-week summer project intended to prepare impoverished children for school. Unlike a day-care program, Head Start was to follow a comprehensive curriculum that included education, medical care, social services, and nutritional help, thereby attempting to meet all of poor children's emotional, medical, nutritional, and societal needs. The architects of Head Start wanted the program to "intervene at a point in the life of the child in ways which would keep deficits from developing in that child[, making] it possible for him to achieve his maximum potential in later life." Planners hoped to accommodate 100,000 children during the program's first summer, but 560,000 enrolled. A sampling of 55,500 of those participants found that 70 percent received their first medical or dental examinations from the program: more than 44 percent had cavities, 60 percent had no immunization against measles, and 32 percent had no smallpox vaccination. Just like other CAP projects, Head Start programs were organized and administered by local communities. The program's success depended on parents' involvement—by working as teachers' aides, taking special courses to improve the home environment, or advising in program development and administration. OEO covered 80 percent of the cost for Head Start programs, which eventually grew to include summer sessions for children aged five and six; a full-year program for three-, four-, and five-year-olds; parent and child centers for children up to two years old; and a school follow-through program for children from six to eight. OEO publicized its new program across the country to get people interested in sponsoring a project. Yette wrote to Wilkins about the program, reassuring him that it would be operated "strictly on a non-discriminatory basis as regards race." Haddad also wrote to Wilkins to recruit the NAACP to monitor potential problems in Head Start: "We are beginning to get a number of applications from the southern states and border areas. My estimate is that one hundred will be from 'problem' communities. We would like to confidentially send to you details on these communities and enlist your help in developing information on them." The inspector general explained that even though Head Start programs had to sign civil rights compliance forms, OEO planned to "go behind the signature to see if the communities understand what they signed and understand that we mean to enforce the requirements." The NAACP agreed to help, sending Haddad a list of field directors for the southern states as well as regional directors.[47]

In the South, Project Head Start met head on with the fallout from the 1965 Elementary and Secondary Education Act, another component of LBJ's Great Society. This education relief bill provided federal monies for public education nationwide based on the number of poor people living in a school district. To get the aid, school districts had to comply with the Civil Rights Act as a means of increasing the pace of school integration. Even though Head Start was not a Department of Health, Education, and Welfare program, some southern leaders recognized that it could foster acceptance of desegregation. Shriver initially thought the child development program would be the key to OEO's entrance into Dixie: "Basically, I thought that Head Start would be a terrific way to get into the South in a non-confrontational mode and begin to do something very beneficial for the poor whites and the poor blacks who are a huge proportion of the poverty population in the South." He believed that southerners "had friendly feelings toward little black children," thereby enabling OEO to "cut across a lot of the opposition which would otherwise exist in the South to anything we did to help poor people." The OEO director could not have been more off base.[48]

Friendly feelings aside, some southern communities embraced Head Start but tried to manipulate the program to fit in with the region's racial mores. In the most celebrated case, Senator John Stennis charged that the Child Development Group of Mississippi (CDGM), which began in May 1965 with eighty-five centers in forty-five counties enrolling six thousand children, was a front for the Mississippi Freedom Democratic Party and that it geared its programs exclusively toward poor African American children. The CDGM's leaders were proud of their civil rights activism, and they viewed this OEO program as an opportunity to provide education to poor children while advancing the civil rights movement. During the ensuing two-year battle, OEO issued funds, retracted support, and then helped create a second organization to operate the Head Start program in Mississippi. It was not one of OEO's finest hours, and the agency has received much justifiable criticism for its handling of this project. This episode caused an enormous amount of friction within OEO and led to many resignations, including Yette's.[49]

Despite the problems in Mississippi, the antipoverty agency had some success in supporting civil rights enforcement through Head Start. Historians generally cite the CDGM incident as a key example of the relations between Head Start and civil rights. The larger story of Head Start in other parts of the South has yet to be told. Throughout the region, what some southern officials perceived as an integrated program looked like segregation from the perspective of Washington, D.C. This caused the Office of the General Counsel, the Civil Rights Division, and the Inspection Division to work closely with the people approving Head Start grant proposals to verify that none operated in a segregated manner.

OEO issued guidelines that clearly indicated that the agency would fund only those projects that did not discriminate. These regulations encompassed all aspects of the program—the location of the Head Start Center, the eligibility of participants, the recruitment and placement of staff, transportation, and publicity. The guidelines stated unequivocally, "The burden shall be on the applicant and sponsor to take such measures as may be necessary to insure the program is operated in a completely nondiscriminatory manner." At a hearing sponsored by the Alabama State Advisory Committee to the U.S. Commission on Civil Rights, Yette explained OEO's procedures to ensure that Head Start programs fostered integration: "We require every applicant file with us an assurance of non-discrimination." Yette also asked that anyone who wanted to file a complaint contact his office.[50]

Haddad also set up a special Head Start task force to investigate complaints of discrimination and telephone applicants where there was reason to believe that segregated practices might prevail. After a review of programs in Louisiana and Florida, inspector Don Petit reported to Haddad that "the Southern superintendent is inclined to try to con us, in many instances, and to see how far he can go and how far he can push us in doing as little as possible in this area." Petit warned that OEO needed to be consistent in its policies and not back down with regard to civil rights enforcement: "I believe if we show any relaxing in regard to compliance, the Superintendent will quickly detect it and use it as precedent in future contacts; other OEO programs which contain the compliance feature could be influenced by what we do initially in a community on this point." After the first summer ended, the Inspection Division created standards for future programs, establishing the necessity to recruit all children—black and white—in the targeted areas and requiring greater parent participation. Finally, in the spring of 1966, the Inspection Division recruited twenty-five law students to work as summer Head Start inspectors. Their findings resulted in the denial of fifty-nine applications that failed to comply with civil rights requirements.[51]

The General Counsel's Office also became involved in setting policy to ensure that Head Start programs complied with the Civil Rights Act. OEO lawyers knew that following the procedures of Title VI as it applied to schoolchildren would not be effective for Head Start. If the violating project asked for the full hearing process required by law, the summer would end before a decision had been made. OEO's attorneys took a different tack. They focused on the hiring policies of Head Start faculty, citing the discrimination violation occurring against the student as a beneficiary instead of against the teacher as an employee. OEO's lawyers also broadly interpreted civil rights compliance. They held prospective grantees to a higher standard beyond ending segregation. Head Start projects—and later all CAP programs—would have an "affirmative duty" to recruit minorities for service on governing boards and to provide enrollment on an integrated basis. OEO legal staff sought to end de facto segregation in OEO-sponsored programs even where no deliberate local policy of segregation existed.[52]

The General Counsel's Office interpreted the separation of church and state to the benefit of OEO programs as well. The Economic Opportunity Act did not distribute general aid to education, a practice that was prohibited by the legislation. Instead, Congress allowed the antipoverty agency to offer "special, remedial and non-curricular educational assistance." Under these terms, OEO could support programs operated by parochial schools, an interpretation that had special significance in the South. When a school district refused to sponsor a Head Start program or when a school had been denied funds because it refused to comply with OEO's nondiscrimination requirements, parochial schools could step in to fill the void.[53]

As the summer Head Start programs got under way, OEO began to hear complaints from black southerners who thought they had received discriminatory treatment. Officials in the Civil Rights Division and the General Counsel's Office worked with Head Start personnel to respond to the objections. In some places, hot meals were not provided; in others, too little parental involvement occurred; in still others, a doctor could not be found to give physical examinations. Baker initially took a gradual approach to remedying these problems: "All right, so the first year you can't do it, but a little bit of progress every year is the way we've been trying to approach all of these things. And where there has been no progress or where there's a retrogression, we have cut off grants, and refused to renew them." Baker drafted a form letter under Shriver's name that explained OEO's civil rights expectations. The letter opened, "Among the most gratifying aspects of the summer Head Start program just completed was the high level of compliance with the legal requirement that there be no racial discrimination in Head Start programs. Only a very small minority of the 2300 programs proved disappointing in this respect. Regrettably, your agency's program was among this small minority." Then Shriver got to the point: "I must inform you that your failure to comply with the nondiscrimination requirement this past summer, despite your written word of honor accepting clear instructions to do so, will be considered strong evidence of your intention not to comply with this requirement in the future." The letter stipulated that subsequent applications from the recipient would be subject to special grant review procedures. The offending grantee would have to provide a detailed statement spelling out the positive steps taken to ensure nondiscrimination in all aspects of the program. Shriver closed his warning by stating, "We are sorry that our trust in your word last summer was misplaced. But we remain hopeful that you will develop specific plans of action to insure nondiscrimination in future programs." Receipt of this letter definitely alerted southern officials that OEO intended to enforce civil rights laws.[54]

In December 1965, Douglas Brown, the mayor of Ozark, Alabama, wrote emotionally to Shriver to express disappointment at being denied Head Start funds: "If it required the City of Ozark or the Ozark City Board of Education [to] get on their knees to you . . . to try to give our children every educational opportunity that may be available to them, then we must decline to deal with you. We are not so hungry for money that we are willing to take your insults and unjust accusations without expressing the resentment that we feel and have felt since receiving your letter."[55]

Two years later, correspondence from other Head Start programs in the South revealed the continued difficulty in meeting OEO's requirements. The southeast regional office had 180 applications for summer Head Start programs waiting for review. Two problems dominated in these applications—site selection and recruitment of low-income children of both races. OEO officials predicted that grant denials would occur in Alabama, Florida, Georgia, Mississippi, South Carolina, and Tennessee. One CAA coordinator in Alabama explained that he had contacted the local armories, the housing authorities, and the school boards in his three-county region but could not get permission to use a racially neutral facility. After all of this effort, he could establish Head Start centers only in African American sections of his area: "I submit this in defense of your statement, and the use of the word 'Designed.' These were the best facilities available and I feel sure that we would have had a fine Head Start Program as we had in 1966." He went on to explain that "freedom-of-choice" integration plans hindered his ability to completely desegregate Head Start classrooms. Finally, he asked for OEO's understanding on the importance of only minimal faculty integration, since "this is the first time in this area where a Negro teacher taught in a white center." The coordinator closed his letter with a plea for understanding. He thought that "wonderful cooperation" had occurred and that the situation would further improve "as time goes on. I am sure that the Benefits from this program will far overshadow the inefficiencies in this program. 750 children will never have this opportunity again." The Inspection Division had been monitoring this CAP program for two years and did not trust that its director was sincerely trying to comply with the law. In this case, a little compliance simply was not enough. OEO officials knew that "freedom of choice" really meant integration avoidance.[56]

Some Head Start recipients asked their senators to intervene on their behalf. Georgia's U.S. senator Herman Talmadge wrote to Shriver, explaining that the Head Start civil rights compliance letter caused distress for officials in Schley, Sumter, and Worth Counties and in the city of Americus, where if a program administrator "failed to meet the nondiscrimination requirements, it was not intended." OEO's congressional-relations staff handled these problems, sometimes supplying the member of Congress with a more complete explanation than the one offered by the constituent. William Phillips told Talmadge that the Worth County Head Start program had been completely segregated—"all Negro," with no white students, faculty, or staff. The superintendent "did not make any substantial effort to obtain white staff members and indicated that it was impossible to change anything." Phillips closed by pointing out that OEO's requirements had been explicitly set forth as conditions of the grant, which Worth County officials had accepted.[57]

Head Start in the South provided civil rights activists with many opportunities to confront problems associated with segregation in the classroom as well as in the community. Although this prepackaged program was created in Washington, it had the capacity to organize local people to oppose the entrenched caste and class system.

Working across the Federal Bureaucracy: Rural Antipoverty Programs

OEO's delegated programs also challenged institutions that had contributed to the complex problems associated with poverty. Title III of the Economic Opportunity Act authorized the USDA to offer low-interest loans with long-term repayment schedules to poor rural families so that they could raise or at least maintain their incomes and standards of living. This program sought primarily to bring income-producing resources and management counseling to poor rural people. The Farmers Home Administration (FHA) distributed the funds—known as economic opportunity loans—to enable the purchase or improvement of land, to strengthen the operation of family farms, to enable low-income rural dwellers to participate in cooperative associations, and to finance nonagricultural enterprises that would supplement a family's income. Individual loans were limited to twenty-five hundred dollars and could be paid back over fifteen years at 4.125 percent interest. Cooperatives could also qualify for economic opportunity loans if two-thirds of the members qualified as having low incomes, with such loans granted at the same 4.125 percent interest rate and to be repaid over thirty years.[58]

This financial opportunity met some important needs for rural black southerners. In 1960, 1.5 million African Americans lived on farms, and 3.2 million black people lived in the rural nonfarm South. These people made up a major element of an arc of poverty that curved down the southeastern portion of the country from Maryland to Texas—the country's largest geographic and social concentration of the poor. Sixty-two percent of rural black families lived on less than two thousand dollars a year, more than double the 26 percent rate for rural white families. Most rural blacks lived in homes that lacked modern toilet, bathing, and kitchen facilities, and 30 percent of African American rural residents lived in dilapidated or deteriorating housing. Pattie Mae Haynes's house in Shorter, Alabama, had a leak in the roof, allowing rain to soak one of her two beds. She and her six children lived in one room, and she shared a bed with three of them. She grew collards, turnips, tomatoes, and okra to feed her family. To wash their clothes, she carried water up a steep hill about one hundred yards from her house. She used the same washtub to clean clothes and bathe her children. Even when the Food Stamp Program began, recipients originally purchased food stamps based on their income, and many rural African Americans lacked the money to participate. Helen Randale, from Greene County, in Alabama's Black Belt, had six children and no reliable income source. She depended on her neighbors' charity and her sons' ability to cut wood to earn enough cash to get by. Elizabeth Hutton, from Eutaw, Alabama, testified at a U.S. Commission on Civil Rights hearing in Montgomery that for between two and three weeks each month, she had no money. By the end of the school year, her children's clothes were worn out: "We wasn't able to buy no more," she explained. She did not even have enough chairs for all of her children to sit around their table: "They have to eat on the floor, take their plates and sit down on the floor and eat." She participated in civil rights activities and explained, "What am I marching for? To get jobs, and hope we have better jobs." The need obviously was great.[59]

OEO could not address the long-term problems associated with this structural poverty, and the economic opportunity loans served as a way for OEO to assist residents in these areas of changing economic circumstances. Many people used these loans to develop new opportunities for themselves. One Mississippi farmer used his loan to operate a farm machinery repair shop, which increased his annual income by nearly one thousand dollars. By 1966, 43 percent of the individual loans made in the South went to African American families, and nearly 60 percent of all farm borrowers in the South were African American. Of all the southern states, Mississippi received the most FHA loans that year, followed by Arkansas and North Carolina. In 1967, the plight of black Mississippians became the focus of a congressional study on poverty. Many in this target population were malnourished because they could not afford to buy into the new federal food stamp program after the state revoked the commodities food surplus program, which had provided food at no charge. As a result of the investigation, OEO made economic opportunity loans available to enable poverty-stricken families in seven southern states to buy food stamps.[60]

Despite this rosy picture of economic assistance, many people were denied access to the Title III loan program. Just as Head Start in the South led to confrontations over the desegregation of public schools, the economic opportunity loan program brought to light the discriminatory practices of the USDA, known around Washington as the "last bastion of the Confederacy" because it was beholden for appropriations to congressional committees dominated by southerners who did not mind programs that benefited only white farmers. Many OEO officials distrusted the department: as James Sundquist, who headed the rural poverty task force within OEO and had experience in the USDA, remembered, "They thought we were a department of racists and that the best thing we could do for the program was get out of it." Not everyone at USDA held white supremacist beliefs, but many working within the Agriculture Department clearly had some answering to do.[61]

During the 1930s, federal legislation had sought to improve tenant farmers' position by extending credit, developing soil conservation practices, and encouraging crop diversification and landownership. Three USDA agencies—the FHA, the Soil Conservation Service, and the Agricultural Stabilization and Conservation Service (ASCS)—began operating to assist people in becoming successful farm owners. The FHA offered low-cost credit and technical assistance to help farmers buy land and equipment. The Soil Conservation Service worked to solve the problems of soil exhaustion and erosion, and the ASCS organized the crop allotment program to reinforce production restraints. These new programs worked in conjunction with the Cooperative Extension Service, formalized in 1914 through the Smith-Lever Act, which educated farm and rural families about farming practices and health and nutrition. All of these agencies received federal funds, but people on the community level controlled the decision-making processes, sometimes through locally elected committees or federally appointed boards, other times through state-supported land-grant colleges and universities. The USDA built this local control into its programs to ensure flexibility and responsiveness to grassroots needs. In the South, however, local control led to segregated programs that were not funded equally, did not represent black and white rural farmers democratically, and enabled white farmers to prosper at the expense of their black neighbors.[62]

The FHA managed the Economic Opportunity Loan Program for OEO because the FHA had experience in helping farmers obtain land, equipment, and operating funds. The FHA also offered technical assistance along with its loans to teach farmers techniques for making their operations more viable. This USDA agency functioned through state and county offices, but its personnel were federal employees who could be compelled to follow federal laws.[63]

The FHA's practices contained embedded oddities, however, that served as obstacles for black farmers seeking assistance. To get an FHA loan, prospective borrowers had to appear before a committee of three local residents appointed by the state FHA director and establish that they had good character, were capable of repaying the loan, and could not acquire credit on reasonable terms on the commercial market. FHA staffers rather than borrowers decided which loan route to take. The FHA county supervisor counseled local borrowers, hearing their needs and recommending whether they should buy land, seek enlarged allotments, find off-farm employment, or use extension specialists. In most areas of the country, this sort of supervision led to an improvement in the farmer's standard of living. In many parts of the South, however, the local committee (with the ability to decide who was of good character) and the FHA county supervisor (with the power to decide which loan would be best) became gatekeepers for the racial status quo. The U.S. Commission for Civil Rights found that the two races received different types of service, "with Negro farmers receiving for the most part subsistence loans with limited supervision, while white farmers received supervised loans for capital expenditures." When OEO added economic opportunity loans to the varieties of assistance the FHA offered, a new day had not necessarily dawned for the USDA.[64]

During the 1960s, organizations concerned with black farmers' needs began to confront the USDA. In 1961, the NAACP conducted a study of the USDA's "mass racial bias." Two years later, officials with the National Sharecroppers Fund wrote a memorandum to Secretary of Agriculture Orville Freeman spelling out the fund's findings of discriminatory practices in his agency's programs, especially the FHA and the ASCS. To remedy these policies, the Sharecroppers Fund asked Freeman to do several things: (1) instruct state administrators to appoint qualified African Americans to serve on committees in counties that had large numbers of black-operated farms; (2) make an effort to address the needs of small farmers whose present operations might not be considered viable and who might be ineligible for FHA credit (perhaps the prototype for Title III's economic opportunity loans); (3) recruit qualified black people for employment at USDA agencies on the local level; and (4) revise informational materials so that people of all educational levels could understand the available programs.[65]

Prior to the passage of the 1964 Civil Rights Act, Freeman found some of these requests difficult to accomplish. The structure of some USDA programs led to acquiescence to the segregated practices of southern society. County extension agents received half of their pay from local communities and half from the state and federal governments. As a result, the secretary of agriculture lacked direct authority over the entire Extension Service program, which hindered his ability to make changes within the agency. Further, the Cooperative Extension Service's experiment stations operated out of segregated universities, which planned and conducted racially separate training meetings. Finally, people who had profited from the Jim Crow system ran many of these programs. Armed with Title VI of the Civil Rights Act, Freeman developed rules and regulations to take corrective action, but he did not use the full force of his office to implement these new initiatives. For example, historian Pete Daniel has found that when the federal Extension Service held an Alabama meeting to establish criteria for compliance with Title VI, black people were excluded.[66]

With such a far-flung bureaucracy wielding enormous power through the disbursement of millions of federal dollars, Freeman found enforcement to be a difficult task. According to Daniel, "The tracks of racism and discrimination led from local committees and agriculture offices to state offices, to land-grant schools, to experiment stations, and on to Washington to disappear into the trackless bureaucratic wilderness where untamed racism flourished, where men and women alienated from the land punished the clientele they were hired to help." Freeman took some steps to change his agency. He held heads of departments and staff offices personally responsible "for positive and affirmative direction in carrying out this program," and he asked his General Counsel's Office to provide agencies with legal interpretations regarding compliance procedures. Further, he met with leaders of civil rights organizations—CORE, SNCC, the Urban League, the National Association of Colored Women's Clubs, SCLC, the Women's Committee on Civil Rights, and the NAACP—and made a personal commitment to eliminate inequities within USDA programs, but he rarely followed up on these initial contacts. He created a new position and hired William Seabron as assistant secretary for civil rights but gave Seabron little power to implement his duties. Many bureaucrats openly ignored his requests. The situation was so bad that Seabron had to hand carry memos to the secretary's office to make sure that they were delivered. "Clearly," Daniel wrote, "too much power resided in the agencies and not enough in Seabron's office."[67]

OEO's Title III programs provided opportunities for the USDA to come to terms with its approval of the segregated customs of some of its agencies. Black farmers who had been denied economic opportunity loans voiced their complaints at hearings conducted by the U.S. Commission on Civil Rights. OEO officials attended these hearings and responded by seeking remedies within the USDA. Antipoverty agency staffers also tried to join forces with the USDA to compel civil rights compliance. Edgar May tried to borrow USDA inspectors to help OEO enforce civil rights compliance in Mississippi but, as he recalled, "I got fourteen different excuses why they couldn't do that." However, he continued, "The real reason was that, hey, they weren't going to get crosswise with a bunch of southern congressmen who were their bread and butter, and they weren't going to send any damn inspectors in to enforce civil rights. But we were, and did." In this case, an OEO program provoked change in an old-line federal bureaucracy.[68]

Other issues beyond the Economic Opportunity Loan Program refocused the nation's attention on poor people living outside metropolitan areas. In 1967, after two consecutive summers of destructive urban riots, government officials began to look for answers to the complicated problems of the nation's inner cities and thought one solution lay beyond the cities. Many of these officials wanted to formulate programs that would keep rural Americans from moving to overpopulated urban centers. In 1967, President Johnson developed the National Advisory Committee on Rural Poverty to assist rural America and stem the tide of migration. OEO responded by creating the Office of Rural Affairs to focus even more attention on the rural poor. Amendments to the Economic Opportunity Act for 1967 reinforced this approach by designating CAP to provide programs "to enable the poor living in rural areas to remain in such areas and become self-sufficient therein." John Baker recommended this amendment to the legislation because USDA economists "believed that the way to increase farm income per capita was by reducing the denominator, not increasing the numerator." The amendment explained that congressional studies had concluded that "to encourage the rural poor to migrate to urban areas . . . is frequently not in the best interests of the poor and tends to further congest the already overcrowded slums and ghettos of our Nation's cities." The Council of Economic Advisers also called on the USDA to differentiate its efforts to target commercial farmers, low-income farmers, farm laborers, and rural nonfarm residents.[69]

Instead of directly confronting the structural issues associated with urban poverty—discriminatory lending practices, dislocation associated with urban renewal, lack of public transportation, shrinking job opportunities—OEO programs were brought in as a measure for short-term relief. OEO planned to strengthen rural CAAs after 1967. The antipoverty agency assigned a rural specialist to each OEO regional office to provide technical assistance to CAAs in organization, management, programming, and planning. The USDA joined in to assist CAP development, creating the Rural Poverty Task Force within the agency, with Sundquist as its head. Sundquist had a distinguished record in government service: he had suggested to Shriver the need for a rural title in the economic opportunity bill to counteract the dominant urban focus. Sundquist's

Rural Poverty Task Force used a team of people from the Office of Rural Areas Development to target specific states to form more CAPs. John Baker credited this group with bringing community action out to the countryside. "Sundquist was very effective . . . in getting things down over at the Budget Bureau or OEO." The USDA also directed its state and county staff to work with CAAs to ensure that agriculture programs reached low-income people.[70]

Indeed, OEO's Title II and Title III programs provided new opportunities for civil rights activities in the South. Armed with new federal civil rights legislation and monetary support through federal antipoverty programs, workers from all over the region put their energies into expanding the movement's goals to include the pursuit of economic justice. CAP, with its emphasis on people coming together to fix local problems and the maximum feasible participation clause, seemed an ideal place to start. Other people who had been organizing communities in the South also viewed the Title III programs as a chance to seek important institutional changes within the USDA agencies. Activists laboring in the South were keenly aware of the inequities lodged within the FHA, the ASCS, the Soil Conservation Service, and the Extension Service and looked to OEO to overcome these obstacles. The programs were in place; organized individuals would bear responsibility for making the War on Poverty work for them.

The antipoverty agency's ability to respond to the demands of poor black southerners would be a crucial factor in determining how much the civil rights movement would endorse the work of OEO officials. Agency infighting over CAP funds indicated poverty officials' difficulty in unabashedly advocating civil rights. Events outside of the agency in the Deep South would further circumscribe OEO's ability to lend strong backing to grassroots civil rights organizations in their struggle for racial and economic justice. Standing at the crossroads, OEO would not be able to go arm in arm down the same road with civil rights supporters. In the end, the agency could only furnish activists with some of the means needed to get where they wanted to go.

Alabama witnessed important events in the modern civil rights movement—the Montgomery Bus Boycott, the Birmingham campaign, the Selma to Montgomery march, the creation of the Lowndes County Freedom Party. The War on Poverty's arrival in the state provided movement supporters with a new resource with which to implement the Civil Rights Act and the Voting Rights Act. Looking at the manner in which the civil rights movement and the War on Poverty intertwined to confront Alabama's old order provides clear examples of how the movement carried on after 1965.

CHAPTER THREE

Wallace's Infrastructure

Alabama State and Local Government Defiance of Federal Civil Rights Laws

You heard correctly that I will not aid in the enforcement of the Civil Rights Bill, however, that was only a portion of my statement. I said that it was not the duty or the responsibility of the Governor of the State to enforce the federal laws—this is a matter for the Justice Department—the Federal Courts and the Federal Government. I said that I had all that I could do enforcing the laws of the State. . . . I only said that it would not be the duty and responsibility of the Governor to enforce the federal law. I have in no instance ever called for willful disobedience of any law whether I liked the law or not. This law, however, is going to be either universally violated or we will have to have a police state to enforce the same. . . . I agree with you that we must, of course, have law and order and this must be maintained. However, I again reiterate that it is not the responsibility of the Governor of any state to enforce the federal law—this is the job of the federal folks.
Governor George C. Wallace to Lieutenant Gordon M. Williams, July 7, 1964

The War on Poverty did not reach most of the Alabama Black Belt until 1966, two years after President Lyndon Baines Johnson signed the Economic Opportunity Act. As one of the country's poorest regions, the area should have been one of the first strategic battles in the president's domestic war. In the Alabama Black Belt, however, the federal antipoverty program became entangled with the burgeoning political revolution that followed the passage of the Voting Rights Act and the agricultural transformation that had been altering the rural landscape since the New Deal. "The number of farms in Alabama decreased from 212,000 in 1950 to 93,000 in 1965," the state's agriculture commissioner, Richard Beard, bragged. "The size of farms is growing larger each year. Our farmers are becoming more efficient, are using more machinery and equipment, and producing more per worker." Figures for capital improvements explain the increase in efficiency. In 1950, Alabama farmers invested $1.3 billion in capital development; fifteen years later, that figure had more than doubled to $2.8 billion. The consolidation of the countryside came at the expense of small farmers—owners, renters, and sharecroppers. This turmoil stymied the launching of federal poverty programs in the region.[1]

The post–World War II boom that boosted the economy of the industrial areas of Alabama passed over the rural communities of the Black Belt. As a result, living conditions for the majority of the region's citizens remained dismal. Most of these counties had significant African American populations, ranging from 45 percent in Pickens County to 81 percent in Lowndes County. In 1960, 85 percent of the region's black families earned significantly less than three thousand dollars a year (the federal definition of poverty), and 67 percent of the adults older than twenty-five had less than a sixth-grade education. In Dallas County, the 1960 census found that between 85 and 90 percent of the black community was poor, compared with 25 percent of the white community. More than half of the African Americans classified as poor earned less than one thousand dollars a year. These statistics reflected the consequences of the state's 1901 constitution and its amendments, such as the 1946 Boswell Amendment, which effectively disfranchised most black residents through poll taxes, literacy tests, property tests, lengthy residency requirements, and understanding clauses. Without a voice politically and subjugated to second-class citizenship socially, many African Americans in the Black Belt renewed their hope for themselves and their communities by participating in the civil rights movement.[2]

By 1965, the region stood in the throes of enormous social and political change. Although the 1964 Civil Rights Act and the 1965 Voting Rights Act gave the federal government power to change long-practiced injustices, time and enormous effort would be required to alter the entrenched misuse of local government that had traditionally tilted the scales in favor of the white community. When civil rights activists enlisted the federal government's assistance in an effort to create a more equitable society, most white Alabamians feared the consequences. Many white people did what they could—legally and illegally—to hold back the tide of change. This scenario unfolded most dramatically in the Black Belt, where, more than in any other part of the state, many white people had prospered at the expense of their black neighbors. Through violence and intimidation, the tenets of white supremacy gripped the region, convincing many white people that they deserved their special status and therefore that they had the right to maintain the racial status quo at all costs. African Americans knew otherwise and tried to garner federal support—through the Department of Justice, the Department of Agriculture, and the Office of Economic Opportunity (OEO)—to break down those state-protected barriers. Those people who joined the civil rights movement hoped that this federal backing would assist them in obtaining what other Americans had—decent housing, good-paying jobs, vibrant public schools, and effective police protection.[3]

When the War on Poverty came to Alabama in 1964, it entered this tense environment, which also spawned the next phase of the civil rights movement. The timing of the antipoverty legislation was crucial to the struggle for civil rights. Federal grants issued through OEO provided much-needed support to people who continued the local fight for equal justice as leaders of the national movement left the region after 1966. Scholars have found this to be the case in Louisiana and Mississippi, and, not surprisingly, similar events happened in Alabama.[4]

Although many Alabamians hoped that new federal laws would transform the white-supremacist culture that had dominated the state since its founding, those who had benefited from the Jim Crow way of life were less optimistic about the future. The state's metamorphosis would not take place without a struggle. A collective siege mentality set in among those who resisted the aims of the civil rights movement, thus affecting the manner in which OEO could wage the War on Poverty in Alabama. Dave Marlin, a Department of Justice official working in the civil rights division, warned OEO director Sargent Shriver about the difficulties of fighting poverty in the South: "Southern Negro poverty involves problems having nothing to do with race—the whole question of the rural farm, education, job skills, motivation, etc.—but race is at the bottom." Marlin continued, "To constructively remedy this would tax the skill of persons dedicated to the proposition that whites and Negroes should be treated as one. There are hardly any white southerners who feel that way and they are rarely in a position to work their will. It will take constant supervision from Washington for any worthwhile results." As the white power structure continued to erect barricades of defiance, OEO officials would have to alter their plans to effectively implement federal poverty programs. In the interim, Alabama's black citizens—especially those residing in the Black Belt—became more committed to the movement and more sympathetic to the call for Black Power.[5]

Throughout this period, OEO officials negotiated among Alabama's various factions to reconcile the racial breach, a daunting task because Governor George C. Wallace and the state and local bureaucracy stood firm as formidable opponents. The intersection of the antipoverty programs with civil rights made OEO's job in Alabama arduous. The provisions of the Economic Opportunity Act and the Civil Rights Act had changed the traditional relationship between the federal government and the states. In many cases, OEO dealt directly with citizens, independent of state or local elected officials. The social and political dynamics between these officeholders and newly enfranchised black citizens remained unsettled following the passage of the federal civil rights legislation. OEO staff often had to mediate among rival forces while hundreds of thousands of dollars hung in the balance. "In a number of places," Edgar May, OEO's inspector general from the fall of 1965 until 1968, explained, "you got into fiefdoms, and you got into power struggles, and you got into who had the action, who didn't, and then, when the dollars started to come in, who got the dollars and who didn't." Understanding the extent to which the state and local bureaucracy resisted implementing civil rights legislation helps to clarify the widening racial divide and why black and white southerners continued to have difficulty working together after the passage of federal civil rights laws. OEO's ability to operate directly with local people also explains why the antipoverty program seemed to be an effective tool for civil rights activists to use in their search for ways to pry open southern society and why those in power tried to prevent such an opening. Looking at the way the state managed its voting, public schools, and farming programs shows examples of this defiance, helping to provide an understanding of the political climate that OEO entered.[6]

Voting

Since the early twentieth century, the Black Belt had wielded disproportionate power within the state. The legislature did not reapportion districts, so the less populated Black Belt had as many representatives as the more inhabited northern section of the state. Moreover, Black Belt counties did not pay their fair share of taxes. In 1955, the fourteen most industrialized counties paid nearly 80 percent of the state's total ad valorem taxes. When the 1960 census revealed that Alabama's population had declined, however, congressional districts had to be redrawn. In the fight to create new boundaries, the old coalition between the agricultural Black Belt elites and the large industrial interests in Birmingham—known as the Big Mules—broke apart. The courthouse gangs and agriculturally privileged soon realized that their place in the hierarchy of power had been cut down. By 1968, the Alabama commissioner of agriculture and industries lamented the rural bloc's loss of status: "Once upon a time much of our legislation could not be passed in Montgomery without the approval of farm senators and representatives—but here, as in Washington, the town folks are now in control."[7]

As the region lost political ground in the redrawn legislative districts, parts of the state and county governmental apparatus continued to foster officially sanctioned racism. The governor, the state tax assessor, and the state commissioner of agriculture and industries each appointed one person to each of Alabama's sixty-seven county boards of voter registrars. In many instances, these officials appointed people who had supported their campaigns and could be trusted to maintain the wall of black disfranchisement.

In 1962, J. Webb Cocke, an attorney from the Black Belt town of Greensboro, wrote to A. W. Todd, the new commissioner of agriculture, seeking reappointment to his position on the registration board for Hale County. Cocke explained, "I have done all in my power to keep these Negroes off our poll lists, and with my board I have been able to do it in such a manner that [Attorney General] Bobby [Kennedy] and his crowd when they were down here could do nothing about it. I would like very much to have the board left as it is, as our work is harmonious and without disagreeableness." When Ruth Hicks asked Todd for an appointment to the Chilton County Board of Registrars, she expressed her happiness that "Little Judge Wallace" won the governorship. "I worked hard for him too," she told the commissioner. "If at any time I can be of assistance to you . . . please feel free to call on me. I am available." Both B. V. Hain, a member of the Alabama House of Representatives, and Dallas County sheriff Jim Clark recommended the appointment of bank executive Aubrey Allen as a registrar in 1963. When Wallace wanted to organize all of the voter registrars across the state to lessen the chances of federal prosecution, Allen disagreed. "Personally," he advised, "I feel that it would be far safer for all the Boards of Registrars in Alabama to get in sixty-seven different boats and paddle in sixty-seven directions."[8]

Nevertheless, Wallace implemented his idea in 1964 and appointed Huntsville journalist and Madison County registrar Martha Witt Smith as his voting consultant. Paid by the State Sovereignty Commission—a state-funded organization Wallace started in 1963 to oppose the impending federal support for civil rights—Smith's position was really a subterfuge to avoid compliance with the 1964 Civil Rights Act. Wallace did not believe that his attorney general, Richmond Flowers, was preparing the registrars for a strong defense against Department of Justice lawsuits and consequently instructed Smith to make sure the boards of registrars knew the relevant federal laws and to "get the state out of federal court and keep it out." He ultimately wanted Alabama to evade the mandates of the new civil rights legislation—in June 1964, the Justice Department cited thirty-seven counties for discriminating in voter registration. Smith blamed the lack of state supervision of boards of registrars as the "real cause of the state losing the qualifications of literacy, character, and witnesses for registration." She hoped to assist Alabama in gaining back some of its power to control voter qualifications and to protect state registrars in the process. "Whatever the state can do to help in any problems will be done," she reassured the registrars of Montgomery County, warning, "NONE of us can consider ourselves safe from federal suit no matter how fair we may actually be conducting registrations!"[9]

While Congress considered the voting rights bill, the Wallace administration intensified its effort to obstruct the federal government. The Sovereignty Commission argued that the legal term "the right to vote" should be applied only to people who met the state's requirements for registration. "Voting is not a 'right' in the sense that a person is born entitled to it," the commission argued, "else we would register the babies to vote!" Administration officials traveled to Washington to testify before the Senate Judiciary Committee against the proposed legislation. Frank Mizell, a private attorney who represented Alabama in voting cases filed by the Justice Department, raised the specter of the chaos that would follow when illiterates received voting privileges: "Who can seriously contend that it will benefit either white or Negro to subject nine counties in the State of Alabama to the political domination by a majority which is illiterate?" Mizell further predicted that a virtual voting war would be touched off. "Action begets action," he contended. "The registration of vast numbers of Negroes who are not qualified from the standpoint of literacy will inevitably tend toward the development of a bloc vote to counteract the expected bloc vote of federally registered illiterates." In the end, these arguments had little credibility because observers generally accepted that Alabama's literacy test did not accurately evaluate reading ability. State registrars had previously rejected black citizens with high school diplomas, college educations, and graduate degrees on the grounds of illiteracy.[10]

After President Johnson signed the Voting Rights Act in August 1965, federal examiners immediately came to Alabama to register voters, beginning in four counties that qualified for this assistance under the new law—Dallas, Hale, Lowndes, and Marengo. One elderly man from Dallas County expressed his relief at the presence of the federal officials. Before their arrival, he explained, "I went down [to the Dallas County Courthouse] so much it began to seem like my home. But I never got inside to register." His chance finally came in mid-August. Literacy tests were outlawed; instead, federal examiners asked each applicant his or her name, age, address, length of residence in Alabama, length of residence at the present address, and precinct of residence. Applicants were also to answer whether they had ever been convicted of a felony. "The old way I just didn't know the questions," one black woman lamented, "They're so hard." But with the presence of federal registrars, "Everybody pass now," she said. "They so glad." After the questions were answered, federal registrars immediately told applicants whether they qualified. The federal registrars produced sudden results in Lowndes County, qualifying 1,328 black voters by the middle of September 1965. Local registrars had previously signed up no African Americans. By February 1966, federal officials in Alabama had registered 49,492 black people, and the county registrars had accepted another 46,700 black voters.[11]

Alabama lost its argument when the voting rights bill passed in August, but that did not stop the attempts to slow implementation of the intent of the new law. In September 1965, Choctaw, Dallas, Hale, Perry, and Wilcox Counties asked a federal court for permission to purge the names of all registered voters from registration lists and to reregister citizens using literacy tests and the old "voucher" system, which required that two county residents attest to, or vouch for, the applicant's length of residence in the county. Both of these requests violated the Voting Rights Act. Arguing on behalf of the State Sovereignty Commission, Mizell also wanted those who failed these two tests to be prohibited from reapplying "until others have been given ample opportunity" to register.[12]

Wallace's "voting consultant" also continued to meet her objectives for the Sovereignty Commission. Working with Cecil Jackson Jr., Wallace's executive secretary, and Hugh Maddox, the governor's legal adviser, Smith developed manuals and guidelines for Alabama's boards of registrars. In one handbook, she advised poll watchers to carry egg timers that "will alarm when three minutes have passed." Watchers could then make sure officials knew that state law limited voters to only five minutes to cast their ballots. Legislators passed the law on September 30, 1965, a month after President Johnson signed the Voting Rights Act, ostensibly because not everyone would have enough time to vote if illiterates had unlimited time to mark their ballots. The law also had the intended effect of intimidating newly registered illiterate voters. "If a person refuses to leave the machine," Smith explained to the registrars, "he shall be removed by the election officials under state law (Section 105). If a person refuses to leave the machine, it is the duty of the officials to enter, turn the switch opening the curtains and thus end voting by that voter." In addition to the *Watchers Handbook,* Smith wrote two other publications: a *State Voting Handbook,* and *Assistance for Illiterates in Alabama Elections on Voting Machines and Paper Ballots.*[13]

Wallace continued to use the power of the governor's office to curtail what he saw as the impending bloc vote of the growing black electorate. In August 1965, he assured one of his supporters that he would test the new federal voting law. The removal of literacy qualifications bothered him: "If a person is not literate enough to go into the armed services of this country," he wrote, "then he should not be considered literate enough to vote on the policies which this country will follow." Avoiding blatantly racist language, he conjured up Cold War fears that "liberals and pro-Communist federal agents" were behind the new legislation, which had the effect of "making it a Federal crime for voting officials to follow State law designed to prevent fraudulent voting." From his perspective, "these facts illustrate the extent of our march down the road to totalitarian government." By portraying himself as the new law's victim, Wallace rationalized the need to use his power as governor to disobey the measure in any way possible.[14]

He directed Eli Howell, the secretary of the Sovereignty Commission, to ask the two hundred thousand people who had previously written to him to make sure they and their family members had registered to vote. In early January 1966, U.S. attorney general Nicholas Katzenbach wrote to all the voter registrars in Alabama, explaining in detail that they must make accommodations to register all Alabama citizens in time for "the next significant state-wide election." Later in the month, lawyers from six southern states argued before the U.S. Supreme Court against the Voting Rights Act. On behalf of Alabama, Mizell trotted out more of his ineffective arguments. This time he was joined by Richmond Flowers, who testified that the law was unconstitutional "because it required only certain states to abandon their own laws against illiterates' voting." Wallace then asked Earl C. Morgan, the circuit solicitor of the Tenth Judicial Circuit Court, to issue an injunction to keep the names of illiterate voters off the rolls. Jackson and Howell discussed whether the governor should issue a proclamation based on "an emergency situation created by irresponsible and illegal massive registration of illiterates and others not qualified to vote under Alabama law." They reasoned that this action could stimulate registration of white people throughout the state and highlight Wallace's "leadership in opposing high handed federal government procedures." Finally, the governor permitted the Sovereignty Commission to use $3,750 in state funds to print pamphlets urging white people to register to vote. The commission distributed these pamphlets exclusively to children who attended white public schools, with the idea that these children would bring the information home to their parents.[15]

The U.S. Constitution ultimately stood in the way of Wallace and the state bureaucracy. In March 1966, federal district judges Frank M. Johnson and Richard T. Rives pulled down some planks from the state's barricade of defiance. They ruled that the Alabama poll tax violated the Fifteenth Amendment of the Constitution. The Justice Department also sent federal registrars to Greene, Perry, and Wilcox Counties, which had not originally been included in the law's implementation. The governor and his administration, however, created an atmosphere of anxiety that heightened white Alabamians' fears and pushed them into the voter registrars' offices. In 1965, 23 percent of Alabama's eligible African Americans were registered, along with 78 percent of white Alabamians; by 1970, just over 65 percent of black voters had registered, as had 96 percent of whites.[16]

Public Schools

The governor, state legislature, and county school superintendents also joined forces to thwart the process of school desegregation after the Civil Rights Act passed. Ten years after the Supreme Court ruled segregated schools unconstitutional, Alabama continued operating dual systems that were obviously separate and unequal. According to the State Board of Education's 1964 Annual Report, in Wilcox County, in the far western part of the Black Belt, for example, 50 white teachers taught 15 percent of the school-age population (955 white students, an average of 19 per teacher) while 160 African American teachers taught the remaining 85 percent (4,987 black students, an average of 31). Only three of the fifteen schools for black children had indoor toilet facilities; the rest had outhouses. Science equipment was almost nonexistent at the high school for black students—a pickled frog served as the only piece of laboratory material for the seventh through twelfth grades. For transportation, the district spent $18.50 per black child and $41.11 per white child. This discrepancy led to dangerous traveling conditions for some African American children. One bus carried 105 students, 40 children more than capacity.[17]

Officials with the federal Department of Health, Education, and Welfare hoped to remedy some of the problems associated with segregated public schools. Agency employees met with state and local officials starting in the summer of 1964 to explain the requirements of the Civil Rights Act. If public schools hoped to receive federal funds under the 1965 Elementary and Secondary Education Act, school officials had to formulate specific arrangements for desegregation. Most Alabama school districts responded with "freedom-of-choice" plans that put the burden of integration on black parents, who had to complete applications to transfer their children to white schools. That first year of desegregated public education in Alabama found between one thousand and twelve hundred black children attending formerly white schools, "only a token of tokenism," in the words of a special report by the Alabama Council on Human Relations (ACHR). This pitiful attempt at desegregation involved only .3 percent of the total African American school population of 300,000 attending integrated schools. The slow pace of Alabama's school desegregation could be laid at the doors of the governor's mansion and State Capitol.[18]

In August 1964, the Alabama legislature passed a law providing $185 per pupil in state tuition grants for parents who wanted to send their children to private, nonparochial schools. The legislature budgeted $1.7 million for 1965–66 and $2 million for 1966–67 to implement the law. On September 2, 1964, the governor, acting as chair of the State Board of Education, issued a resolution recommending that Alabama school boards stop complying with Title VI regulations until the federal lawsuit filed by the Bessemer City School Board had been resolved. At a meeting of the state's city and county school superintendents held in Montgomery five days later, Wallace urged school administrators to go no further than the "law and court decisions" require. During this gathering, Lieutenant Governor James B. Allen forthrightly stated, "We're in favor of maintaining the dual school system in Alabama by whatever means that is peaceable, legal and honorable." The federal Office of Education ultimately approved eighty-four desegregation plans, rejected sixteen, and accepted nine court-ordered plans and one assurance of compliance.[19]

On closer inspection, the freedom-of-choice plans revealed that the ploy was being used to avoid authentic integration. In Lowndes County, only five of the thirty-five black students who applied for admittance to Hayneville High School for the fall of 1965 were accepted. When African American students tried to enter Greene County High School in September 1965, state troopers turned them away, telling them, "Get the hell out of here." The principal eventually enrolled twelve of the eighty-seven who sought entrance and told the rest that "there wasn't any more room." In the city of Marion, in Perry County, black children were told to go back to their old schools, apply for admittance to white schools, and wait ten days for a response. Children from Monroe County could enroll in the school of their choice as long as it was not "overcrowded." If the school board deemed a school too full, students were chosen on the basis of proximity to the school, "without regard to racial consideration," according to the county's desegregation plan. Twenty-seven pupils applied to attend Greensboro High School in Hale County. Only six got in, all of them girls from the same three families.[20]

Some parents of children who submitted freedom-of-choice applications received veiled threats from their employers and people with whom they did business. In July 1965, for example, William Joe White applied to have his three children attend Hayneville High School for the upcoming term. His boss, Julian Bryant, told White to take his children off the list. "You can let that woman [White's wife] and them children go," Bryant suggested, "if they don't go over and take their names off." White stood his ground. Oliver "Buddy" Woodruff and Brady Ryan visited Gully Jordan to see why he had signed up his daughter, Wilma Jean Pate, to attend Hayneville High School. Woodruff asked Jordan, "What kind of shit" he was "trying to run over him?" Ryan warned Jordan to pay attention to who drove by his house. "We didn't bother about y'all registering," he told Jordan. "We didn't bother you about going to mass meetings. But I'll be goddamn if this shit is going over this time. We going to stop it." Both Ryan and Woodruff then told Jordan that they would no longer help him with his business enterprises. Before leaving, Woodruff asked one last time, "Can't you have her name erased off the book?" Jordan answered simply, "No." LaRue Haigle evicted Cato Lee and his family from his tenant farm after Lee attempted to send his children to a formerly all-white school in Lowndes County. Robert Harris received a visit from a man who identified himself only as a "teacher from Hayneville High School." The man told Harris that if he did not withdraw his daughter's request, he would not be advanced another year by his landlord. "He asked would I go up there and take her name off the roll," Harris explained. "I told him no."[21]

In Greene County, four black people—Elizabeth Hutton, Cora Richardson, John Anthony, and John H. Chambers—sued the sheriff, school superintendent, school board, and director of public safety on behalf of their children, seeking a permanent injunction against denying them entrance to the white public schools. The lawsuit stated that 3,000 African American students and 530 white students attended the public schools and that no steps had been taken until 1965 to remedy the discrepancy between the two systems. On the first day of school, an empty bus came to pick up Mattye Lee Hutton, an African American, to take her to the white high school. Two cars followed the bus, which frightened Hutton's mother, who chose instead to drive her daughter to school that day. When they arrived at the campus, Alabama state troopers would not let the Huttons enter. The principal asked why Hutton did not ride the bus and explained that she should expect various kinds of discriminatory treatment at the school. He then told the girl's mother to come back on August 30 to register her daughter. The Greene County sheriff followed up and told Hutton to call him on Monday because "the white men around the school were Klansmen." In this atmosphere, the plaintiffs sued to obtain complete integration without intimidation, harassment, or discrimination. They also asked for adequate police protection against anyone trying to keep them from attending the schools of their choice.[22]

Beginning in January 1966, the federal government began to lose patience with southern school districts that refused to comply with the new law. Alabama proved to be one of the most recalcitrant. At this point, of the eleven southern governors, Wallace was the only one who urged public school districts not to comply with Title VI of the Civil Rights Act. As a result, the Department of Health, Education, and Welfare revised its policies for school desegregation plans. If a school district wanted to keep its freedom-of-choice plan, it had to show substantial achievements. Teachers and staff also had to be integrated. Small, inadequate schools created for black students had to be closed. If school districts did not take these steps, the federal government would cut off its support. School officials now bore responsibility for making the plans work and ensuring that they were in compliance with the law. Harold Howe II, U.S. commissioner of education, thought that these revised guidelines represented "a step toward providing public schools which are neither Negro nor white—but simply public schools attended by Americans without regard to race." But Alabama political leaders instead chose to go down swinging in support of massive resistance.[23]

At that same time, Black Belt school districts began receiving letters from the Justice Department informing officials that they were not in compliance with the Civil Rights Act. After attending a school desegregation conference at Florida State University, Wilcox County superintendent Guy S. Kelly wrote to Wallace suggesting that the state not comply: "If I ever heard Hitler speak, and I did," he told the governor, "I heard him matched on Saturday, March 5, in Tallahassee, Florida." Kelly wanted all the Alabama school superintendents to "do nothing further to comply" with the directives and "let us all go to court together." In May, the Justice Department asked the Fifth Circuit Court of Appeals to use the new guidelines as a model for court-ordered desegregation plans for three Birmingham-area systems. The governor quickly formulated a plan of defiance. The next month, he held a meeting of Alabama school board members and superintendents, with a special session of the legislature called in July to draft legislation interposing the state between the federal government and local school boards. Before the legislators assembled, Wallace went on television to describe his proposed law, which would declare "that it is the Legislature's determination that the integration guidelines . . . are illegal in that they go beyond the law." Wallace intended to pronounce the guidelines "null and void in this state." The governor also used the occasion to seek contributions to support "people in our state who are being forced to conduct private schools because of the destruction of their public schools." Finally, he exploited the circumstances to back his wife's campaign for governor, indirectly telling viewers that she would be willing to stand up for them in the same manner. Some of Alabama's congressional representatives jumped on the antiguidelines bandwagon. Representative James Martin, also a gubernatorial candidate, sent Wallace a telegram affirming that he had "urged School Boards in my district not to sign compliance with federal guidelines." He wanted the governor to know that "my position has been made widely known and I shall continue to urge this course of action." Even Representative Bob Jones, viewed as a moderate, reassured Wallace, "I will continue to make every effort to countermand the implementation of the announced guidelines by the Office of Education." This rebellious plan put the state at risk of losing up to $38 million in federal funds per year if all districts refused to obey the guidelines.[24]

Wallace's defiance had gone too far: even Alabama's major newspapers did not support these measures of state encroachment on local government. The *Birmingham News* found the governor's tactics a "tragedy of extremism" and warned readers to look beyond Wallace's words to understand what was really happening: "The governor is taking Alabama on a political snipe hunt." According to the *News,* the real issue was Lurleen Wallace's candidacy for governor "and what it could mean to his power at home and his opportunities to trot around the nation making a phony run for president." The *Montgomery Adver-tiser* hoped that the federal courts would "spare Alabama some of the conse-quences of the reckless legislation and not lower the federal yoke on all our school systems." The paper's editors saw the bill as a "much more serious pre-emption of local control by the state."[25]

Just in time for the new school year, both houses of the state legislature fol-lowed the governor's lead, passing his bill by wide margins on September 2, 1966. The legislation forbade local school systems from signing compliance agreements with the federal government and established a governor's commis-sion to serve as the new authority to make decisions regarding desegregation. If a school district lost federal funding, the state would replace the money through the Alabama Special Educational Trust Fund, but eligibility was limited only to those programs in existence prior to the adoption of the Elementary and Secondary Education Act of 1965. Senator Neil Metcalf of Geneva did not sup-port the bill, but as a seasoned politician he acquiesced to the trap Wallace set. "Sooner or later someone is going to rule it illegal anyway so why should we filibuster?" Metcalf reasoned. "If we won, Wallace would talk about what he could have done with the law and blame it all on us. Then we'd have all that mess on our shoulders," he said. As Metcalf predicted, lawsuits soon followed, filed by the National Association for the Advancement of Colored People (NAACP) and by the Justice Department. Wallace and the state school board countersued, claiming that the 1966 guidelines were illegal. The governor's effort only delayed the inevitable, but it did, however, have a lasting impact on the state's public schools, image, and citizens. In late December 1966, Alabama led the nation in school segregation: only 2.4 percent of the African American student popula-tion attended formerly white schools.[26]

Farming

The state and county bureaucracy that administered U.S. Department of Agri-culture (USDA) programs and Alabama's Commission of Agriculture and Industries also resisted enforcement of civil rights legislation. This opposition had long-standing consequences for African American farmers in the Black Belt.

Black farmers often did not receive the same assistance as white farmers from the Extension Service, which in Alabama separated from the research station at Auburn University in 1920. Luther N. Duncan directed the pro-gram, making it a semi-independent and "highly political" agency. Duncan also organized the Alabama Farm Bureau, which became active in all of the state's sixty-seven counties by 1930. When Edward O'Neal III took the reins of the Farm Bureau from Duncan, the two used their agencies to form a political machine. According to Wayne Flynt, "O'Neal and Duncan worked closely together, making it hard to decide where the extension service ended and the farm bureau began." As a result, extension agents—paid with federal and state funds—became involved in political campaigns that created the "single most powerful lobby in Alabama for the next half century." The state Extension Service developed cooperative financing and administration with county governments, thereby enabling county officials to locate Extension Service offices in segregated facilities. The operating budget of the Lowndes County Extension Service revealed the discrepancy in these separate and unequal county offices. The white Lowndes County Extension Service had a budget of $4,488 for October 1, 1964, through March 31, 1965, while the black Lowndes County Extension Service had to make do with just $600.[27]

The Farmers Home Administration (FHA), like the Extension Service, offered its assistance in a biased manner. The FHA helped farmers obtain land, equipment, and operating funds. It gave technical advice along with financial assistance in an effort to implement modern techniques that would make farm operations more viable. The Alabama commissioner of agriculture and industries credited the FHA with helping to modernize the state's agriculture: "Without FHA loans and other sources of financial aid," Beard told FHA employees, "most of our farmers would not have been able to mechanize and continue to increase production without increasing the cost of farm products to the consumer and processor." Beard, like most agricultural executives, saw USDA programs as benefiting agribusiness, not those small farmers who had been left behind by the agricultural revolution. In his view, the new ways of farming freed labor to "work in industry, to fight wars, to produce products that have made this the most comfortable and healthiest civilization ever known." The FHA, like other USDA agencies, operated through state and county offices, but its personnel were federal employees who could be compelled to follow federal laws. Such enforcement would be difficult in Alabama, where Robert C. "Red" Bamberg served as head of the FHA offices beginning in 1964. Bamberg had previously occupied the post of state commissioner of agriculture and industries and had no qualms about maintaining the accepted racial mores of the day. Evidence of Bamberg's abuse of the system could be seen on his own forty-two-hundred-acre plantation. He acted as a furnishing agent to the twenty-five families who worked on his farm. The staff director of the U.S. Commission on Civil Rights reported to Agriculture Secretary Orville Freeman that Bamberg "advances seed, fertilizer, insecticides and cash during the planting and growing season for which he charges six percent interest until September 1st." As the state director of the FHA, Bamberg knew that farmers had access to similar loans at 5 percent interest.[28]

Certain FHA practices served as obstacles for black farmers seeking assistance while living in a segregated society. African American farmers often had difficulty qualifying for FHA loans. According to Lillian McGill of Lowndes County, the FHA denied people credit because they could get loans elsewhere—but at 10 or 12 percent interest. "It's not for us to say that ten percent is not a reasonable rate," Orville O'Shields, the FHA's state economic opportunities officer, told her. The FHA county supervisor for Greene and Hale Counties, J. D. Pattillo, manned his post at the white supremacy gate quite effectively. He would not provide an economic opportunity loan to a tenant or sharecropper unless the borrower could prove he had insurance and had no judgments against him and his landlord provided papers stipulating the terms of their rent or share agreement. Thus, landowners could prevent tenants from receiving financial assistance by refusing to provide the FHA with the necessary paperwork. Rev. Percy McShan described the treatment he and fellow tenants received at the FHA office in Greene County: "Many of these farmers that went to this particular place to borrow money," McShan explained, "were told they couldn't get a loan if the landlord didn't want them to have a loan, and there was one landlord in particular had already gone to the office and told Mr. Pattillo that he didn't want his people to have the loan." The FHA supervisor then explained that anyone who received financial support would get a check in Pattillo's name, and he would manage the money for the borrower. Pattillo also refused to assist black farmers, many of whom could not read or write very well, in filling out loan applications: according to McShan, Pattillo and his staff "would give people the loan application form, which have some complex questions, and tell the farmers to fill it out himself, and then return it."[29]

Like the FHA, the Agriculture Stabilization and Conservation Service (ASCS) played an important role in Black Belt farm communities. This USDA agency administered—through farmer committees on the state, county, and community levels—the farm programs dealing with conservation, crop allotments, and price supports. Most Alabama farmers who had crop allotments received price-support payments for corn, cotton (upland and extra-long staple), and peanuts. Farmers also received technical advice about protecting their land from erosion by planting new grasses and other ground cover and about developing water sources for livestock and irrigation. ASCS funds had an enormous effect on communities. In 1967, ten Alabama Black Belt counties received $249,669 in Cotton Form A loans, $1,073,456 from the Agriculture Conservation Program, $121,549 for participating in the Conservation Reserve Program, $7,292,318 from the Upland Cotton Program, $4,548,808 in price-support payments for upland cotton, and $2,743,510 in diversion payments for upland cotton. In one year, the ASCS allocated $16,029,310 to farmers in these ten Alabama counties and $96,000,000 statewide.[30]

With so much money on the line, the USDA devised a democratic way to distribute it throughout the country. Each year, eligible farmers (owners, tenants, and sharecroppers) were supposed to vote through the mail to elect three farmers from each ASCS-designated community to serve as committeemen. These community committeemen in turn gathered to elect the ASCS county committee, which set policy at that level. The actions of this committee could determine whether a farmer succeeded or failed in his endeavors, since the group's responsibilities included appointing the county office manager, determining the size of a farmer's crop allotment, adjusting program benefits between landlords and tenants, and hearing appeals from farmers who objected to cuts in their allotments.[31]

The USDA's plans may have looked good on paper, but in the cold, hard reality of Alabama racial practices, the ASCS became a program for white farmers who owned large farms. Just as state-appointed voter registrars skewed their duties in favor of white citizens and freedom-of-choice plans kept the number of black children in integrated public schools very low, the ASCS state, county, and community committees also distorted their official mandate.

In 1965, the U.S. Commission on Civil Rights found that the secretary of agriculture had never appointed any of the South's 266,000 black farmers to a state committee. Many black farmers never received information regarding the importance of the ASCS elections or their eligibility to run for a committee position, and some landlords had coerced tenants into voting for particular candidates. Some Black Belt landowners also insisted that their tenants and sharecroppers sign over their ASCS cotton allotment checks to them. Lillian McGill of Lowndes County said that the ASCS officials there had not told black farmers about the program and its services: "We didn't know anything about the programs. We didn't even know they had programs. Nobody knew how Negroes or any farmer became eligible for participation in the programs." Black farmers reported that the ASCS county officials mismeasured property when determining crop allotments, forcing farmers to plow up good crops when too much was planted. During a hearing on the ASCS program in Alabama, Robert Valder, director of the Alabama Council on Human Relations, summed up the extent of racial bias within this agency: "ASCS is guilty of fostering and maintaining a pervasive pattern of discrimination," he testified. "This is true about employment, it is true about the entire election process, and it is true about programs, benefits, and services." According to Valder, "Negroes are excluded and discriminated against on a massive scale by Federal, State, and County ASCS offices and personnel." He deduced that ASCS officials on the local level had deliberately decided that this program was "for white folks" and had then oriented "their work on that decision."[32]

Beyond the federal agricultural programs that operated on the state, county, and local levels, the state of Alabama had its own agriculture department that offered about as much assistance to black farmers as the USDA programs did. The Alabama Commission on Agriculture and Industries functioned as a regulatory agency to "protect the farmer, agriculture generally, and the consuming public," according to Beard, who headed the agency from 1967 to 1971. The commission also ran on a dual track, working through the state with state funds but sometimes implementing federal-state agreements relating to agricultural marketing and statistics, farm produce grading and inspection, animal and plant diseases, and pest control. This part of the state bureaucracy was quite large, with twenty-three separate divisions, yet the legislature kept its appropriations inadequately low because many commissioners used the office as a springboard for a gubernatorial run.[33]

Some officials who were assigned to work with federal programs on the state level harbored contempt for the changes brought about by the new civil rights legislation. James L. Lawson, head of the Agriculture Industries Division, was one such individual. He came to the Commission of Agriculture and Industries in 1961 after organizing the State Rural Development Committee in 1955 as one of his duties while serving as associate director of the Auburn University Extension Service. President Dwight D. Eisenhower had asked that states form committees to help stem the migration of rural people into the nation's cities. Lawson's committee severed its ties with the federal government and changed its name to the Alabama Resource Development Committee after President Johnson took office. Lawson's experience at the Extension Service served him well in his new position with the state commission, where his department oversaw the development of agribusiness in Alabama. As a member of the Rural Areas Development Committee, he worked with other state officials to distribute loans and grants from federal programs such as the Area Redevelopment Administration, the Small Business Administration, and later OEO. After reviewing the Economic Opportunity Act in September 1964, Lawson anticipated that "parts of this program will probably be highly controversial," although he thought that Alabama could benefit from OEO programs when Governor Wallace initially announced that they would be operated through the state bureaucracy.[34]

As the agriculture official in charge of rural development, Lawson was in a position to let his personal opinions of the civil rights movement and the federal antipoverty effort affect the amount of support African Americans from the Black Belt could expect. As a Wallace supporter and an unreconstructed southern racist, he vehemently opposed these measures and did not shy away from expressing his feelings on the subject. Lawson blamed both political parties for the new civil rights legislation. "However," he wrote, "the Democratic Party has been able to out bid the Republicans for the beatniks, ne'er-do-wells, Negroes, foreigners and others who expect the government to support them." He warned Alabama's junior U.S. senator, John Sparkman, that President Johnson lacked popular support not because of his policies in Vietnam but because of "his 'We Shall Overcome' speech, [which] will always be remembered." Lawson told Alabama's senior U.S. senator, Lister Hill, that Sparkman had won re-election because many feared that Senator Paul Douglas of Illinois would gain seniority if Sparkman lost. "Conservative people," Lawson explained, "had seen [Douglas's] wife participate in the Selma to Montgomery march and were disgusted by her embracing a filthy Negro man on television in front of the Capitol." Lawson thought Alabama's junior senator was "too much of a Johnson-Kennedy Democrat" but voted for him out of "force of habit."[35]

By 1966, Lawson viewed the War on Poverty as the "most stupid and wasteful government program ever devised." Ironically, given that he did not object when he received federal largesse, he complained that minority groups were interested only in promoting their own welfare. He thought that the federal antipoverty programs caused "our lowest class of people to multiply while those who work and pay taxes are, through necessity, limiting the size of their families." He deduced that federal social welfare programs were a waste because "there is no way to avoid the effects of heredity despite those who say a change in environment, integration, housing, race-mixing, etc., will cure all evils." He was also unsympathetic to USDA programs designed to fight hunger and malnutrition. After reviewing publications on these programs, he wrote to Beard, "This needs no comment and is best suited to the files." Not content to sit on the sidelines and throw rocks, Lawson worked in his community to hold back change. He served on the Auburn Housing Authority "to give the conservative membership a majority and a veto power over some of the left-wing extremists" he thought lived in the city.[36]

As the 1960s ended, Lawson's opinions reflected the "silent majority" Richard Nixon tapped for his successful presidential bid. Lawson continued to support Hill but grew disenchanted with the national Democratic Party. Lawson wrote to Chicago mayor Richard Daley to praise his actions during the 1968 Democratic Convention. "However, I can never again vote the National Democratic ticket," he told Daley, "so long as it does not stand for law and order. We have long seen, here in the South, and have suffered from, Communists such as Martin Luther King, [SCLC leader Ralph] Abernathy, and all their tribe." By

1968, Lawson's disgust with the civil rights struggle had even led him to form a new church in Auburn. Unhappy with his pastor, Rev. Powers McLeod, a leader in the ACHR, and "the socialistic doctrine of the Methodist leadership," Lawson and others split off from the United Methodist Church and formed an independent Methodist church. They bought an abandoned church building and hired a minister who had also left the denomination because he did not want to "preach the new doctrine."[37]

The culture of white supremacy seeped into almost every crevice of the state and local governmental apparatus in Alabama. Wallace stood out as the leader in this cause, but bureaucrats in local offices also played an important part in sustaining the wall of defiance. The structure of Alabama's state and local governments and the people who worked in them would make the transition from Jim Crow to equal justice a difficult task. So many layers of society—voter registrars, school administrators, farm program bureaucrats, and local elected officials, among others—needed to reform. Civil rights activists realized the problem and tried to attack it where they believed they had a chance of succeeding.

The War on Poverty Begins in Alabama

The Office of Economic Opportunity entered Alabama's atmosphere of defiance in 1964. Many Alabamians had difficulty accepting this federal presence in their state, especially as civil rights activists pushed for equal treatment. Wallace could not completely dominate the War on Poverty in Alabama as he had the voting, education, and farm programs, although he certainly tried.

OEO attempted to enlist state governments in its early efforts. The agency provided states with money to form state technical assistance agencies, which would help local communities develop and administer community action programs (CAPs). The federal government paid 90 percent of the cost of operating these agencies. By offering to support state offices, OEO officials hoped to assuage the suspicions some governors harbored regarding the federal antipoverty effort.[38]

Governor Wallace appointed Claude Kirk to study the possible benefits of OEO programs for Alabama. After becoming convinced that the antipoverty program could help his state, Wallace selected Kirk (who had no experience in working with the poor or with federal programs) to coordinate the effort across Alabama. OEO approved a $134,000 grant to the Alabama Office for Economic Opportunity. The agency, however, initially distributed only $30,000 of the grant to Kirk's office because no specific funding guidelines had been developed, and OEO administrators did not want to commit large amounts of money before they knew they could adequately enforce the agency's policies.

Alabama would have to reapply for the remainder of the funds to operate its statewide office after February 28, 1965.[39]

Wallace envisioned the War on Poverty as a form of patronage for his state-wide political machine, not as a program to empower the poor. His advisory committee consisted of state bureaucrats, and his first public announcement regarding the program specified that he wanted "no part of anti-poverty funds that require race mixing." As a first step in initiating the War on Poverty in Alabama, the governor's executive secretary, Cecil C. Jackson Jr., compiled a list of fourteen jobs with salaries ranging from $3,720 to $14,500 that the governor could offer to people who would work in the state antipoverty office.[40]

In the beginning, the governor instructed Kirk to operate his office passively, responding to requests for information on the federal antipoverty program but not promoting any activity. As interest grew, however, Wallace asked his poverty coordinator to contact only individuals friendly to his administration to keep the federal program in check. Kirk mailed out letters informing Wallace supporters how to set up community action agencies (CAAs). By March, Kirk had made contacts in forty-five of the state's sixty-seven counties and reassured Jackson, "This office is on guard at all times to see that no political factions are entering into the efforts to get community action programs started in each community of the State of Alabama." In his correspondence to interested parties, Kirk made it clear that Wallace planned for the federal antipoverty effort to remain under the control of the governor and local elected officials, a viewpoint that stood in direct conflict with the spirit of the Economic Opportunity Act. "Except in extraordinary circumstances," Kirk relayed, "the Governor will either veto or accept the particular plan based on the advice given by said governing bodies."[41]

Wallace often wrote to tell Kirk whom to contact and hire. In mid-December, the governor asked Kirk to employ Matt Colley of Troy as deputy director. Throughout February and March, Wallace's office asked his poverty coordinator to retain individuals in various counties to serve as administrators. Writing on behalf of Leroy Porter of Geraldine, for example, the governor's press secretary, Bill Jones, told Kirk, "This is one man we really want to try to find something for in this program. The Governor is extremely interested that this be done as soon as possible." He also asked that W. S. Hoit be hired as a community economic opportunity consultant because he "is well qualified for this work and he has been a strong supporter of our Administration." In Coosa County, the governor had Kirk contact Jesse and James Hamil, who agreed to form a contact group to discuss forming a CAP in their area. As they sent out word of an upcoming organizational meeting, the Hamil brothers discovered that Judge Mac Thomas had already established the Coosa County Advisory Committee for Economic Opportunity, which the county commission had approved. The Hamils suspected that "Sargent Schriver [*sic*] could be the force behind a move of this sort" and asked Wallace to intercede on their behalf. Jackson arranged a meeting between Kirk and the Coosa County delegation, telling the poverty coordinator "that we were interested in seeing that Mr. Hammel and his delegation received the fullest cooperation from him."[42]

When OEO approved community action grants, Kirk contacted the governor, seeking his approval of people hired as administrators for the local CAA. After announcing the funding of the Talladega, Clay, and Randolph Counties CAP, Kirk listed the four top administrators and asked for the governor's advice on whom to hire for "the project assistant director, at a salary of $6,500 a year . . . and four counselors at $3,900 each." Jackson suggested that Kirk get in touch with Wallace coordinators in Clay and Randolph Counties "and see that we get Wallace people for all five of these jobs." Jackson also wanted Kirk to provide evidence that "Wallace people" were ultimately hired. The heavy hand of the governor's office did not go unnoticed. OEO officials began to suspect his actions in late March, and a federal employee in Alabama alerted members of President Johnson's staff to Wallace's plans: "It appears that the poverty program in Alabama is being organized along strictly political lines with 100% Wallace forces as co-ordinators in every case, and with most executive committee members being Wallaceites," he warned. "We have been told by certain key Wallace supporters that only a co-ordinator acceptable to Wallace will be placed on the payroll."[43]

Evidence of the governor's attempt to manipulate the antipoverty effort could be seen clearly in the state's second-largest city. Even before LBJ had signed the Economic Opportunity Act, some Mobile leaders were eager to establish these programs. Mayor Joseph N. Langan received a copy of Johnson's proposed program in March 1964. He hoped the city's participation in the War on Poverty would be a way to develop a program that combined job training with school dropout prevention. He envisioned a city works project with an educational component. Langan reasoned that if members of the black community increased their ability to participate in the city's economic life, racial tensions would be eased. He later described economic disparity as the "underlying problem of race relations," with "one off setting the other." Langan called a public meeting for September 1, 1964, to begin coordinating the activities of various agencies within Mobile County to prepare an OEO grant application. Three days later, he contacted Sargent Shriver to schedule a meeting to discuss establishing a program in Mobile.[44]

Langan's interest in federal funds to fight poverty came as no surprise. A New Deal Democrat, he was confident in the government's ability to assist those in need, telling one newspaper reporter in 1965 that the "government is the only agency that has the scope to do it." A devout Catholic and graduate of Spring Hill College, a four-year Jesuit institution in Mobile, he had earned a reputation as a racial moderate during his service as Mobile's state senator in the mid-1940s and as a city commissioner beginning in 1953. While Langan was on the commission, the city hired its first black policemen, in 1954. Two years later, Langan formed a human relations committee after observing Montgomery's troubles during its bus boycott. Langan wanted this group to study housing, recreation, education, and political rights with the idea of maintaining the "separate but equal" concept. Taking even these small steps made him an easy mark for racist reactionaries, however. He became the target of a White Citizens' Council "Joe Must Go" campaign, but the attack failed to keep Langan from winning reelection as a commissioner in 1961.[45]

Unfortunately for the city's poor, Langan was not the only commissioner interested in the new federal antipoverty program. Between September 1964 and March 1965, a total of six other groups, including one led by commissioner Charles S. Trimmier, arose to compete to become the city's CAA.[46]

The structure of Mobile's city government explains this confusion. The city commission comprised three commissioners elected at large to four-year terms. The specific responsibilities of each position were not assigned by law. As a result, the commissioners had the power to decide who would oversee the various functions of city government. The commissioners rotated as the city's mayor, with each commissioner serving for a year. Although the system was seen as progressive when it was established in 1911, flaws surfaced when the commissioners disagreed. Such was the case after the 1961 election, in which Trimmier barely defeated incumbent Charles Hackmeyer by tapping into white fears of racial change. Trimmier had accused Hackmeyer of holding onto his seat by virtue of the "bloc-vote," a euphemism for the voting strength of Mobile's African American political wards. George McNally also won a position on the commission, the first Republican elected in Mobile since Reconstruction. McNally and Trimmier often lined up together, leaving Langan the odd man out.[47]

At the beginning of 1965, Trimmier moved into the mayor's seat; he also faced an August reelection campaign. He stood on shaky ground as he faced a possible federal income tax indictment and realized he had alienated the black vote in his last bid for office. In an effort to repair the breach and to appear to be an effective commissioner, he established himself as coordinator of the Mobile Area Economic Commission. Trimmier formed a biracial executive committee that included power brokers from the black community, among them Clarence Montgomery, president of the Mobile branch of the NAACP; Bishop William Smith of the African Methodist Episcopal Zion Church; and John LeFlore, a civil rights activist since World War II and a caseworker for the Nonpartisan Voters League, the organization created in Mobile after Alabama banned the NAACP in 1956. His commission also included labor and business representatives. In March, Trimmier headed to Washington to meet with OEO officials, hoping to gain favor for his plan. The mayor made a good impression on Bill Haddad, OEO's inspector general. "He says that the political situation is such that Wallace won't veto," Haddad told CAP director Theodore Berry. "Board looks good (negro, poor) and the money requested ($50,000) is modest enough. His attitude, too, seems okay." Just to be sure, the inspector general sent two investigators to Mobile to verify Trimmier's claims.[48]

After inviting county commissioner Leroy Stevens to participate in this antipoverty initiative, Mayor Trimmier learned that the county had the governor's blessing to organize a separate agency. Wallace had asked Stevens to set up a board to serve as the only CAA in Mobile County. Following OEO directives, the county commissioner established a biracial group, but the twenty-seven-person board included only four African Americans. Such numbers meant that independent black initiatives could easily be quashed. The *Mobile Register,* whose editor was a known Wallace supporter, had reported that Trimmier's autonomous efforts had minimized the governor's role. This was a shot across the bow. By early April, the governor made it clear that he backed the Stevens committee. In an attempt to influence OEO's decisions, Wallace wrote to Shriver to offer support for the county group: "I will be willing to waive the thirty-day waiting period set up under section 209c when the application has been accepted by you and has been sent to me for my action."[49]

While all of this jockeying for position was taking place, other Mobile residents had been organizing on their own, outside of Wallace's reach. On October 22, 1964, the Catholic archbishop of Alabama and North Florida, Thomas J. Toolen, hosted a meeting to discuss the new antipoverty program. Father Thomas Nunan, director of the diocese's Catholic Charities, planned and organized the gathering. He viewed the federal program as "a practical means of spreading God's kingdom on earth." Nunan had been an active member of the National Catholic Charities board, a position that had afforded him the chance to learn about the Economic Opportunity Act. He later explained that the "word was very clear coming from the national office," where charities officials realized that the antipoverty effort was going to be something new. Nunan remembered being told that "any group . . . is a legitimate contender . . . for funds from this." He also knew that the Catholic Charities office gave him an established mechanism from which to begin developing antipoverty programs.[50]

More than one hundred pastors, heads of charitable institutions, and hospital and school personnel gathered in Montgomery to hear Maurice Hartmann of the National Catholic Community Service in Washington explain how Catholic clergy and laypeople could become involved. Hartmann suggested that Alabama Catholics form a group to coordinate diocesan projects and that parish priests could aid the effort by opening their facilities to the community, identifying people in need of assistance, and encouraging parishioners to join in. After lunch, the meeting attendees broke up into six groups to make specific plans. Langan led a group discussion on the Economic Opportunity Act's various titles and the ways in which local communities could utilize them. At the close of the day, Archbishop Toolen appointed a diocesan executive committee on poverty, chaired by Father Nunan, to coordinate the statewide plans and assigned people to serve on five local committees that would operate in the diocese's various districts.[51]

The week after the meeting, participants from Mobile, led by Nunan, began forming a diocesan antipoverty committee for their city. By November, this group called itself Archbishop Toolen's Anti-Poverty Committee. Nunan worried that the archbishop would not wholeheartedly endorse the program and consequently named the organization after Toolen, hoping to seal the archbishop's support. In preparation for a meeting to seek approval of his plans for Mobile, Nunan gave the archbishop a draft of his ideas with the name of the organization printed on the top of the document. "Everyone's got an ego," Nunan later explained. "It was deliberate, and whether it helped or not, I will never know." After their discussion, Toolen authorized Nunan to move ahead and told him that his efforts would be supported. One program Nunan hoped to bring to Mobile was the newly formed Project Head Start.[52]

Since Kirk did not have a broad mandate from the governor to take the antipoverty message across the state, Rev. Nunan's group and others filled the void. OEO officials had also contacted people in Birmingham before the Economic Opportunity Act had passed so that Alabama's largest city would be prepared to launch antipoverty programs immediately after Congress enacted the legislation. William C. Hamilton, Mayor Albert Boutwell's executive secretary, and C. H. Erskine Smith, a thirty-year-old attorney who had been active in reforming Birmingham's municipal government in 1963, collaborated to plan for a CAP. Smith traveled to Washington at his own expense to obtain detailed information from OEO administrators and used his skills as a lawyer to draw up the necessary documents at no charge to the city.[53]

Smith had been committed to helping Birmingham become a more modern city since the late 1950s. He lived in Los Angeles during World War II, attending school with Mexican American and African American children. The family moved to Birmingham in 1947, when Smith was thirteen, and Erskine's younger brother, Paul, recalled being "shocked" by the "totally different way of life" they encountered in Alabama. From their arrival at night, when they "were confronted with the blast furnace out there and the steel mill lighting up the sky," the Smiths felt as though they were entering a new world. Erskine Smith began forming his opinions regarding racial matters while he was a teenager. When Erskine and Paul rode city buses to pick up newspapers for their paper route, they hated seeing black women standing behind the Jim Crow signs that divided the bus even when the section reserved for white people remained empty. "Erskine and I both, we used to move those signs," Paul recalled. "I'm surprised, but the drivers never said anything to us about it." Erskine Smith was acutely aware of the injustices of Jim Crow segregation and the harm it did to the city's citizens and its progress.[54]

Smith worked his way through undergraduate school at George Washington University as an administrative assistant in Alabama congressman Laurie Battle's office. Smith then attended the University of Alabama law school and returned to Birmingham to start practicing real estate law. He served as the Kennedy-Johnson campaign chair for the Ninth Congressional District, which encompassed all of Jefferson County. In 1963, Smith joined other young attorneys in an effort to change the city's political structure that kept Eugene "Bull" Connor in office as police commissioner. "They wanted to 'create opportunity at home,'" historian Glenn Eskew has explained, "so they focused on political reform, and their campaign became a 'crusade for good government, led by a new generation.'" The group of young Turks instigated a November 1962 referendum that turned out the city commission form of government and ushered in the mayor–city council model. Smith also worked with David Vann to negotiate a settlement to the boycott led by the Southern Christian Leadership Conference (SCLC) and to the demonstrations that rocked the city in 1962 and 1963. When President Johnson announced his plans for the War on Poverty, it seemed natural that Erskine Smith would try to find a way for Birmingham to participate. He was keenly aware that the city needed this type of federal support to make the transition from an industrial city to one more oriented toward a service economy.[55]

On January 5, 1965, Mayor Boutwell appointed Smith to chair the newly incorporated Birmingham Area Committee for the Development of Economic Opportunity (BACDEO). Following the civil rights laws, the BACDEO formed a biracial twenty-member board, and Boutwell made it clear that board members served at his pleasure. In his new role, Smith went to meetings around the city explaining how the Community Action Program worked, and he advised Mobile and Huntsville leaders seeking to submit grant applications to OEO. By late January 1965, the BACDEO submitted an application for a one-hundred-thousand-dollar program development grant to start the War on Poverty in

Birmingham. The committee wanted to develop twenty-two recreational, educational, and social service centers in poor neighborhoods.[56]

Despite OEO's intention to support new approaches to alleviating poverty, the Birmingham plans would not progress smoothly because the governor stood between the city and the federal agency. Smith's history of participating in progressive activities that opposed the traditional way of doing business in Alabama countered Wallace's modus operandi. Predictably, the governor's office tried to outflank the BACDEO's plans for Jefferson County. At a February BACDEO meeting, board members agreed to widen the antipoverty program by including other parts of Jefferson County that would have an interest in the Birmingham program. Smith asked Bessemer mayor Jess Lanier to consider serving on the antipoverty board, to which Lanier replied, "We are not in the position at this time to commit ourselves, and if we decide to participate with you and your committee we will advise you." Two days later, on February 19, Lanier, a close political ally of the governor, wrote to Bill Jones, Wallace's press secretary, to ask the governor's office to contact every mayor in Jefferson County to form a countywide CAP that would dilute Birmingham's power to operate on its own. Wrote Lanier, "I am positive this will give us the impetus we need to put this program over."[57]

Unaware of this latest move, Claude Kirk and Earl Redwine, OEO's southeast regional director, asked the BACDEO to sponsor a statewide workshop to explain to interested communities how to utilize the War on Poverty programs. Birmingham seemed the ideal place to hold such a meeting, since Smith knew so much about the Economic Opportunity Act and had developed strong contacts in Washington. The young attorney agreed and scheduled the conference for February 26 and 27 at the Dinkler-Tutwiler Hotel. In mid-February, Smith and Frieda Coggin, the conference's program director, invited Governor Wallace to welcome the participants. Smith also placed Kirk on the agenda to address the gathering on the opening day of the conference. Unbeknownst to Coggin, Smith had also invited the National Urban League to cosponsor the statewide event with the BACDEO, calling it the Alabama State Economic Opportunity Conference.[58]

On February 25, the *Birmingham Post Herald* reported on the upcoming meeting, listing the speakers and the agenda and revealing the Urban League's involvement. This information must have found its way to the governor's office, where it provoked an immediate and fiery response from Kirk. He wired top officials at OEO in Washington, Coggin, WBRC-TV, WAPI-TV, and Smith that Smith lacked the authority to "call a meeting indicating that it is in any way sanctioned by the Alabama Advisory Committee for Economic Opportunity of which I have been duly appointed as the state coordinator." This statement directly contradicted the reality of the situation: Kirk and Redwine had asked Smith to convene the conference. But Kirk was undeterred: "I have no intention of standing by and letting you and other liberal left wingers in Alabama take over this program," he admonished Smith. Kirk then tried to inhibit the gathering's success by advising other community action committees in Alabama "that this meeting has not been called by me and such meeting will only serve to confuse and retard the entire anti-poverty program in the state of Alabama." Kirk's response had some immediate results. Coggin resigned from the board of the BACDEO, and the director of the CAA in Calhoun County decided not to attend the meeting, as did a delegation from Tuskegee.[59]

Despite Kirk's rebuke and Coggin's departure, about four hundred people representing forty communities attended the conference, as did top OEO officials from Washington. Jack Conway, OEO's deputy director, and Theodore Berry, the director of CAP, explained how the War on Poverty could be waged in Alabama. The locals who spoke included Milton Cummings, chairman of the Huntsville–Madison County Community Action Committee; Dr. Joseph F. Volker, vice president of the University of Alabama; Dr. Lucius Pitts, president of Miles College; John C. Barnette, international representative of the United Auto Workers; and Robert W. Block, president of the Birmingham Community Service Council. Acknowledging that the governor could veto some OEO programs, the *Birmingham News* reported that "program ideas are limited only by the imagination of the local citizens. The idea is to eliminate poverty and the government feels that local citizens know best what their needs will be." Participants were also told that all federal antipoverty projects fell under the regulations of the Civil Rights Act.[60]

Harold J. Wershow, a social worker from the Birmingham suburb of Mountain Brook, described to Shriver the meeting's importance: "It was the most inspiring event in which I had ever participated in my professional career, it was a true mobilization of common people from all walks of life, gathered together to discuss what they could do about their problems, rather than wait for Social Welfare Councils and public agencies to get around to them—to the back of the line, their customary place." The information distributed at the conference ran counter to the governor's plans for the War on Poverty. People who had not been informed about the program now had the material they needed to access OEO and start programs in their communities, independent of Wallace's office, as Wershow understood. He relayed to the OEO director the potential problems the situation could cause those in the power structure: "Here is . . . the nub of the problem. . . . Neither government nor private agencies, with their lily-white boards . . . want the poor, Negro or white, to organize, to by-pass the organized social agencies (which plan to use the program to 'strengthen' their own programs), to develop group relation skills." He hoped that Shriver could find a way to keep control of the war on poverty in the hands of the local committees and away from state officials and agencies.[61]

Some Alabamians came to refer to the two-day conference as the Urban League's takeover of the Economic Opportunity Conference. Three days after the workshop closed, Lanier hosted a meeting of the Jefferson County municipal mayors and the county commission so that Kirk could explain to them how to form a CAA. Threatened by the BACDEO/Urban League conference, the Bessemer mayor intended to get ahead of any other Jefferson County group and wrest control of the antipoverty program from local people and put it in the hands of more "responsible" elected officials. "The purpose of the meeting," Lanier revealed, was "to organize and consolidate the interests and efforts of all the Municipalities in Jefferson County in order to afford an organization which would be better able to serve the interests of all the Mayors." Lanier dominated the meeting. After the mayors elected him chairman, they authorized him to appoint the five members of the executive committee. Only after Lanier had gained control of the Jefferson County effort did Kirk explain to the group how to apply for a community action grant.[62]

Other, more significant waves developed in the wake of the statewide conference. Boutwell asked Smith to resign as chairman of the BACDEO. The mayor believed that the young attorney had acted unilaterally in bringing the Urban League in as cosponsor of the statewide workshop and told the press that he was "unalterably convinced that Mr. Smith grievously impaired the future operation of the committee, unintentional though it may have been, by planning, programming and conducting the workshop conference without advising with his full committee and by failing to ask for and get their approval for his specific plans and program." Smith then tendered his resignation, effective March 12, giving as his reasons Boutwell's lack of confidence as well as a desire to avoid jeopardizing the success of the Birmingham antipoverty program. "With my resigning there's at least the possibility of the Governor's approving the programs," Smith reasoned. "The important thing is to keep the committee functioning." Boutwell accepted Smith's resignation on March 10, but the resignation did not mean that Smith would really step aside.[63]

Smith had privately harbored doubts about Boutwell from the beginning. According to Paul Smith, Erskine "had some concerns about the mayor. . . . I guess that's an understatement. . . . He was one of the old guard. . . . He wasn't a bad man, he just . . . didn't want change." Boutwell had been involved in state and local politics since 1946. In the 1950s he chaired the Interim Legislative Committee on Segregation in the Public Schools. Alabamians also elected him lieutenant governor in 1958. In spite of his segregationist past, Boutwell was more progressive than George Wallace, but the mayor knew how political wheels turned in the state and what needed to be done to keep his administration on track. He received support from the local newspaper when it editorialized that "Smith was wrong in his handling of the chairmanship, he tried to go too far, too fast, and he upset the boat." Smith suspected that the mayor's request had been prompted by the governor's office and that political plums had been offered in exchange for his removal. He told the *New York Times* that Wallace "wished to control the Federal program throughout the state for his own political advantage" and that Smith had stood in Wallace's way with a different political philosophy and by bringing in black people to participate. Smith also thought that Wallace had threatened to withhold state and federal grants from Birmingham for a needed road-building program.[64]

National newspapers' coverage of Smith's resignation enabled him to voice his fears regarding Wallace's manipulations, thereby putting OEO's integrity on the line. "I am very strongly concerned that the Johnson Administration will seek its normal accommodations—the President being the great accommodator—and may just accommodate Governor Wallace to give the illusion that the program is working in Alabama," he told one reporter. Washington was on high alert regarding anything that happened in Alabama after the violent March 7 "Bloody Sunday" confrontation on the Edmund Pettus Bridge, which sparked national interest in the Selma voting rights campaign. Under such circumstances, OEO administrators could not easily ignore the events in Birmingham.[65]

Boutwell received letters from constituents seeking to change his mind about Smith's removal. One man pointed out the absurdity of the mayor's approach, declaring himself "shocked and amazed" at Boutwell's "hasty action and attitude toward Attorney Erskine Smith," especially in light of the fact that the two-day conference "had an official welcome from your office and it was profitable and informative." BACDEO board members also contacted the mayor to voice their opinions. Robert H. Aland told Boutwell that he recognized the mayor's deeds as a capitulation to Governor Wallace. "Your act of political cowardice in submission to the pressure from Montgomery was reprehensible beyond words," he chastised. "At a time when you should have risen to the defense of one of your finest appointees, you chose to surrender." Other Birmingham residents encouraged Shriver to hold up the grant until the issue had been fully resolved. "Having attended that meeting I can only say that the road to success will be a long hard one," Winthrop R. Wright wrote to the OEO director, "and it will take patient coercion by men like you to lead Birmingham out of the wilderness."[66]

OEO officials responded in several ways. First, they assumed that "the request for Smith's resignation was, directly or indirectly, dictated by Wallace."

Operating under that supposition, Holmes Brown of the antipoverty agency's public relations office said that the Birmingham program development grant hinged on its chairman remaining in office. He worried that if Smith resigned, black board members might also depart and the committee would thus not be representative of the community served. Orzell Billingsley, an African American attorney and chairman of the Alabama Democratic Conference, reassured OEO that he and the other black board members would not abandon ship. Billingsley did, however, want Smith to remain on the board even if he stepped down as its leader and asked that OEO expand the committee to include people from poor neighborhoods to provide some balance. CAP administrators then placed two stipulations on the city's grant to protect the integrity of the board from "arbitrary or pressured change of its membership or officers." OEO would have to approve any change in the directors of the CAP board for the duration of the grant, except in the case of the majority of the board voting for the change, and within thirty days after the grant had been approved, representatives from Birmingham's impoverished areas had to be selected to serve on the board.[67]

In light of these developments, the BACDEO asked the mayor to rescind his request for Smith's resignation. The mayor wanted OEO to fund the grant before final decisions were made about the BACDEO chairman. Smith agreed to this approach because he thought that the controversy drained enthusiasm from the program's supporters. The mayor and the BACDEO board never met to decide Smith's fate. On April 14, OEO approved Birmingham's program development grant for $66,349, along with those for Huntsville–Madison County, Anniston–Calhoun County, and Tuskegee. The antipoverty agency deliberately waited until after the Selma to Montgomery march to announce these grant approvals. OEO officials would not know for about a month whether the compromise over Smith's position had been smoothed over, since the Economic Opportunity Act permitted Wallace to take thirty days to announce whether he would veto the program. When a reporter asked Kirk if he would recommend that Wallace approve the Birmingham grant, he responded, "I don't endorse. My job is to provide technical assistance to communities that want to set up programs. And that's what I've been doing." His statement highlighted what OEO administrators already knew: Kirk was subservient to the governor. This issue had to be addressed.[68]

The state technical assistance grant for the Alabama Office for Economic Opportunity came up for renewal on February 28. OEO administrators from Washington and the southeast regional office used this deadline as an opportunity to reassess the office's functioning, especially after Wallace's actions in Selma and with regard to the antipoverty program in Birmingham. One official stated that the agency had received "some disturbing reports" about the way in which CAPs and committees were being set up "in several areas of Alabama." Some of those in OEO found that Kirk, despite his lack of qualifications for the job, was an enthusiastic supporter of the War on Poverty and tried to work with him to get around the governor's obstinacy. Wallace would not allow Kirk to hire an integrated staff for the state office, and OEO would not release funds for the state technical assistance program unless it functioned on a nondiscriminatory basis. This situation put OEO on shaky ground. Funding the Alabama state antipoverty office in accordance with Wallace's strictures would violate Title VI of the Civil Rights Act as well as the intent of the Economic Opportunity Act. The refusal to offer a grant would hand the governor an issue with which to bash OEO, and the chances of any antipoverty programs moving forward in Alabama would decrease dramatically.[69]

Frederick O'R. Hayes and Brendon Saxton, CAP administrators in Washington, worked out two compromises with Kirk. First, they allowed him to hire African American office staff under the subterfuge that they were "consultants." This special status enabled these employees to avoid taking the state merit exam, which purported to be offered on a nonracial basis but was not. OEO personnel also agreed that these black administrators could work in a separate office away from the Public Safety Building out of which Kirk worked. Hayes and Sexton rationalized this agreement to their skeptical OEO colleagues by arguing that it would be a temporary situation that would enable the agency to push for a completely desegregated staff at a later time. Second, the two Washington officials agreed to form a consortium among five Alabama colleges and universities—Alabama A & M, Auburn University, Troy State College, Tuskegee Institute, and the University of Alabama, Tuscaloosa—that could offer training programs on a biracial basis in an office at the University of Alabama, Montgomery. Antipoverty funds issued to colleges and universities were not subject to a governor's veto. By funding a program of this nature, OEO officials reasoned, they could offer the needed technical assistance to interested Alabamians yet bypass Wallace's objection to an integrated office staff environment and avoid the governor's political appointments.[70]

As was the case with many other federal programs that tried to operate in Alabama, these concessions did not work out as planned. By June 1966, OEO officials had tired of the state's refusal to desegregate the statewide office. Even though Kirk had left his post and been replaced by a retired air force general, Ralph P. Swofford, the racial segregation in the state office did not change. At this stage in the War on Poverty, Alabama was the only state that still temporized about employing black people. Surprisingly, Swofford blamed OEO for this practice, claiming that he found it difficult to attract qualified personnel when OEO withheld funds as a consequence of his office's noncompliance issues. In addition, the first director of the consortium, Dr. D. L. Howell of the University of Alabama, did not get his program up and running. The southeast regional office's Redwine described Howell as "a segregationist and a weak man." He was slow to hire staff members to offer technical assistance to those interested in the program, and he did not hire any African Americans, precisely the reason OEO had created the consortium. Finally, Howell did not take an active role in bringing information to people across the state. Instead, much like Kirk in the state office, Howell only responded to requests for assistance. Swofford hired a new director in the summer of 1966, and he immediately asked three black people to join the staff. Under these circumstances, OEO continued to fund the Alabama Office for Economic Opportunity on an interim basis, never giving the state the full grant amount in one lump sum. By mid-1967, however, the stalling tactics continued. When OEO tried to get the consortium merged into the state office, thus creating one place for technical assistance, Maddox informed the federal agency that OEO had no power to require the consolidation. Ted Berry, as the head of the Community Action Program in Washington, understood the difficulties inherent in trying to set up successful CAPs in Alabama and told OEO's assistant director that it was "extremely doubtful that any institution which depends on the state for funds will become militantly aggressive in espousing the cause of citizen involvement in community action" there. These problems remained unresolved as late as 1970.[71]

While waiting for Governor Wallace to make his decision about the Birmingham program, OEO officials sought ways to continue the antipoverty effort in Alabama. CAP officials in Washington decided that "OEO must avoid publicly or in actuality involving itself in any degree with Wallace or his state coordinator." When doing so was unavoidable, administrators wanted to make sure they never gave "public evidence within one situation of yielding to the governor." Therefore, antipoverty officials developed less defiant means of supporting programs that the governor did not endorse. One option was funding a single-purpose agency when no CAA was available. OEO followed this track in Mobile by approving two single-purpose programs—a Head Start program and a Neighborhood Youth Corps—through Archbishop Toolen's Antipoverty Committee as various groups across the city vied to become Mobile's CAA. The archbishop had desegregated the parochial schools in the diocese in 1964, and the Catholic Church's ability to operate integrated Head Start programs made it an ideal place to get the antipoverty program under way in a large city that had not received funds as a result of the governor's interference. Officials within OEO's Civil Rights Division also wanted to take more "positive action to reach out into the community." Markham Ball suggested that agency administrators work with FHA officials to require county agents to meet with the poor and publicize antipoverty programs. Members of the Inspection Division also recommended that OEO fund CAP grants through the Migrant Workers/Seasonal Farmers programs under Title III (b) and direct grants to universities, out of the reach of the governor's veto.[72]

Finally, the administrators within the federal agency thought that the regional headquarters could begin to work directly with local people in Alabama, thereby enabling OEO to sidestep the state office. One official rationalized that this approach would pit Wallace against local antipoverty groups rather than against Washington, a stratagem that would be less politically fulfilling. This option did not reap the harvest OEO had planned.[73]

OEO's southeast regional office, located in Atlanta, at times seemed more preoccupied with supporting programs that would pass Wallace's scrutiny than with backing effective antipoverty projects. Regional officials sometimes would not enforce civil rights legislation. After the national Inspection Division sought compliance from the Huntsville Head Start program, Picot Floyd of the Atlanta office stepped in. "Huntsville then told us to go to hell," Jack Gonzales told his boss at the OEO Inspection Division in Washington, "and has not budged to this date, ending with a worse program from the Civil Rights point of view than ninety percent of Alabama, including backwoods areas."[74]

This sort of interference infuriated Bill Haddad, head of the Inspection Division. "Sarge," Haddad implored, "you're putting a massive, unresponsive bureaucracy between your ideas and judgments and the people you're trying to help." The regional office continued selectively to comply with the wishes of the national agency. Alabama native Mary Grice of the southeast regional office joined forces with Matt Colley in the Alabama Office for Economic Opportunity to create community action agencies that could be acceptable to both organizations. They divided the state into "areas," pairing Black Belt counties with adjacent counties, effectively diluting the strength of the African American majority. For example, Area 23 combined two Black Belt counties, Bullock and Pike, with Coffee and Geneva Counties. When Bullock and Coffee Counties tried to apply separately for CAP funds, the Atlanta office declined to fund the effort unless Pike and Geneva were included. Area 11 combined two Black Belt counties, Hale and Perry, both of which had black majorities, with Bibb, Chilton, and Shelby Counties, creating an overall area in which blacks comprised 37 percent of the total population. To the dismay of the Black Belt's African Americans and OEO's Washington officials, this arrangement prevented black people from forming a majority to operate antipoverty programs. Such compromises kept Wallace at bay and satisfied the Atlanta office, which had to comply with Title VI Civil Rights Act enforcement. Floyd defended this "district plan" to

Rev. Francis X. Walter of the Selma Inter-Religious Project, noting that the idea had "emanat[ed] from the Alabama office." Floyd thought that putting together "liberal whites and eager Negro groups" provided a promising beginning for antipoverty efforts in the state and explained that this arrangement put "counties with professional skills (equals white county eg. Shelby) into group with no skills (eg: Hale)." Walter noted in his diary, "I was not convinced."[75]

Despite this type of support on the regional level, Bessemer's Lanier voiced his disapproval of the federal antipoverty program in late April, calling it a "come-on deal" and a "political football" and stating that he would prefer to drop Jefferson County's plans to form a CAA. Lanier may have been sending a message that the governor should veto Birmingham's plans as well, and Wallace complied in a May 7 letter to Shriver. Wallace based his decision on two issues: the BACDEO did not include the entire county, and the board of directors did not constitute a representative group from across the entire county area. The governor took the opportunity to share his judgment of the federal effort. After complaining that OEO stood outside "the traditional principles of government as we have known it," he claimed that the program seemed to help "those who would direct and prepare the studies rather than the poor themselves." Of course, Wallace himself was guilty of using federal antipoverty efforts in that manner.[76]

The governor's veto of the BACDEO grant revealed his true desires for the program. He had approved applications in Anniston, Huntsville, Mobile, and Tuskegee, all of which had biracial committees, so race was not necessarily the overriding factor in Wallace's disapproval of Birmingham's approach. Political control, pure and simple, provided the rationale for standing against Boutwell and Smith. Wallace would play the race card to make his point, but it was not the sole reason for his opposition to the antipoverty program.

Three of the CAPs the governor approved bear out this contention. In Anniston, Dan Gray, county commissioner and head of the board of voter registrars, spearheaded the antipoverty program. Three African Americans chosen by the black community served on the board. As board members, they were not afraid to voice their opinions, but they also formed a distinct minority on a seventeen-person board. In addition, the governor did not need to confront Gray, who managed the voter registration office. Huntsville's CAA was dominated by Milton K. Cummings, the president and CEO of Brown Engineering and Senator Sparkman's brother-in-law. The CAP board had black members, but they were easily outnumbered. Dr. John Cashin, an African American leader in the area, told OEO that "Cummings had no intention of ever letting the Huntsville program become an outlet for genuine Negro aspirations." As a wealthy man with powerful connections, Cummings dealt with but did not fear

Wallace. The governor clearly did not want to cross Cummings and felt that this program did not threaten his basic agenda.[77]

Why the governor did not veto the grant for the Head Start program sponsored by Archbishop Toolen's Anti-Poverty Committee is less obvious. However, the project appeared nonthreatening—it started out small, in only two centers—and according to program director Sara Kaffer, the archbishop "was not anybody's notion of a liberal at all." Rev. Thomas Weise speculated that the governor probably had an exaggerated view of Catholic power in Mobile. "If you ever knew Archbishop Toolen," he explained, "you wouldn't want to confront him." Langan agreed, theorizing, "I just think he thought it wasn't any real threat to his overall programs and that it might, by letting it go, win him some brownie points in the long run" with the Catholic vote. Finally, Nunan remembered that at this time "there was an awful lot of regard for Archbishop Toolen," and longtime diocesan lawyer Vince Kilborn was also a close friend of Wallace's. Nunan imagined that Kilborn told the governor, "You'll have more problems if you decide to do something about it," so let it go—"it's quiet enough."[78]

Although no written evidence explains the governor's actions, the annual celebration of Christ the King Sunday illustrates an outsider's image of the Catholic presence in Mobile. On October 30, 1966, for example, an estimated ten thousand black and white Catholics met in the City Auditorium after walking through the streets of downtown in a solemn procession with clergy in full vestments, children in brightly colored parochial school uniforms, and service clubs—the Knights of Columbus and the Knights of Peter Claver—represented. After a public recitation of the Rosary, group members sang hymns, listened to Father Nunan speak, and heard Archbishop Toolen preach. A makeshift altar had been erected inside the civic building, transforming it into a sacred space, so that Mass could be held and those present could take Holy Communion. This annual event permitted Catholic Mobilians overtly to claim the city as their own, with Archbishop Toolen standing out as their leader. In this climate, Wallace's political instincts may have led him not to oppose the Catholic-sponsored Project Head Start.[79]

Birmingham offered a sharp contrast to Anniston, Huntsville, and Mobile. Smith, the chair of the board, could not be put on Wallace's leash, as he had proven in 1963. Mayor Boutwell, however, could be brought to heel by the governor's threats, and Wallace could profit in the process of vetoing the grant.

Smith spoke out to the local press about Wallace's actions. Because people from outside of the city served on the board, according to Smith, one of the governor's reasons for vetoing the grant became moot. The BACDEO chairman said he had no intention of resigning and instead planned to expand the board membership to meet Wallace's standards. Lanier's earlier maneuvers made doing

Figure 7. Archbishop Thomas J. Toolen in his vestments, n.d. To avoid confrontation with
the archbishop, Governor George Wallace did not veto the Head Start program sponsored by
Archbishop Toolen's Anti-Poverty Committee even though it operated the only integrated public
education program in the state's second-largest city. Birmingham Public Library Department of
Archives and Manuscripts, Birmingham, Ala. (portraits collection).

so difficult, since a countywide group was already in the works and was not
interested in cooperating with Smith. A way to break the logjam between the
powers in Montgomery and those in Birmingham had to be found. Boutwell's
executive secretary urged OEO officials not to offer any extreme comments on
Wallace's veto and stated plainly that "the Mayor has no stomach for a direct
confrontation with the Governor." Boutwell agreed to reorganize the BACDEO
to include the entire county, create a new charter, and have the new board of
directors elect its own officers. This would take care of the main sticking point
of Smith's leadership and bring Wallace allies into the effort. Operating as the
Jefferson County Committee for Economic Opportunity, the new board elected
Sheldon Schaffer as chairman.[80]

Smith told OEO administrators that he did not want to step down as chairman because the mayor offered only his partial cooperation to the antipoverty
effort and the county officials gave the program mere lip service. He thought

that if he resigned, the program would not be carried on in the spirit of the Economic Opportunity Act. In some ways, Smith was right. Now operating as a board member and not chairman, in late May he told the mayor that to receive the planning grant, two people from the area's poor community had to serve on the board. Four days later, Alan Drennen, one of Boutwell's advisers, responded, "How poor is poor?" Drennen suggested that the mayor appoint James Cotton, who worked in the printing department of the Protective Life Insurance Company. Drennen found Cotton attractive because "he is not directly connected with the Jefferson County Democrat organization, and as such might be in a sense a little more independent than some of the Negro appointees." By the middle of June, the Jefferson County antipoverty program submitted a new grant application to OEO, which the federal agency approved in October. Having been placated by Smith's removal and the addition of Jefferson County officials, Wallace waived the thirty-day waiting period, and the Jefferson County Committee for Economic Opportunity received its first grant nearly a year after originally planned. In one final dig at Smith, the governor wanted to make sure that the Jefferson County Committee for Economic Opportunity did not employ the former BACDEO chairman in a staff position on the CAP. Schaffer assured Kirk that Smith would not be hired.[81]

Although Wallace managed to dominate Birmingham's antipoverty program, Smith may have had the last word. The national attention Alabama garnered in the aftermath of Selma and the governor's vociferous veto of the BACDEO grant had far-reaching consequences. Wallace's actions took place while Congress debated the reauthorization of funding for the Economic Opportunity Act. The day after Alabama's governor vetoed the Birmingham grant, Representative John Brademas (D-IN) tacked an amendment onto the bill that would enable OEO's director to override a governor's veto of CAPs and the establishment of Neighborhood Youth Corps projects. In its final form, the amendment restored the governors' ability to object to these two programs plus adult basic education classes, but Shriver could overrule those vetoes based on racial discrimination, political manipulation, or "some other kind of undue influence." Congress attributed the amendment against the governor's veto to Wallace's handling of the Birmingham grant, even though Texas governor John Connally and South Carolina governor Donald Russell had also used their veto power against OEO programs.[82]

Armed with the ability to override a governor's veto, OEO administrators knew that Wallace would continue to seek confrontations with the federal agency for political gain. By February 1966, only twelve areas in the state had received OEO funding. Not surprisingly, the poorest counties had been passed over because they were part of the Black Belt, where African Americans could outnumber white board members and control the CAA's policymaking. Local government officials in the poorest part of the state consequently dragged their feet in seeking assistance from the federal antipoverty program. Wallace had strong support from white voters in this region and reassured local governments that he would not fund programs to which they objected. As a member of the technical assistance consortium, the dean of the school of agriculture at Tuskegee Institute, B. B. Mayberry, asked Shriver to rework OEO's guidelines to enable Black Belt residents to receive direct support from the agency when local governments did not want to start antipoverty programs. Mayberry wanted the OEO director to raise from $750 to $2,000 the maximum average income at which residents could qualify for 100 percent federal funding. If this became the rule, impoverished communities would not have to rely on local governments to put up 10 percent of the funding to receive OEO support. He also wanted Shriver to allow CAPs to receive federal assistance without local government involvement.[83]

Many civil rights activists pinned their hopes first on changing the political structure in a region where African American voters could affect the outcomes of elections. Economic improvements, it was hoped, would follow. "Money means economic power," SNCC chairman John Lewis explained. "In order to get and to maintain economic power we have to bargain. Bargaining means political power. . . . So it took us three years to understand that political power insures the stability of economic power." Dr. Martin Luther King Jr. also put his faith in an emerging black vote that could alter southern society. He believed that these new voters would curb the violence of many segregationist leaders elected to office, shift the balance of power to a coalition of white liberals and African Americans, and undermine the South's oligarchical rule in national politics. SNCC had been operating in Alabama's Black Belt region since 1962, and SCLC had been active in and around Selma since 1964. Both organizations believed that advancements could be made if the political participation of the newly enfranchised majority of black residents could be channeled to create effective change. In the Black Belt region, politics and economics intertwined as the civil rights movement carried on after the passage of key federal legislation. Civil rights activists and Black Belt residents would bear responsibility for pushing against the dominant force of white supremacy to weaken its grip on the state. The route taken in the search for social and political equality would touch on issues involving voter registrars, agricultural officials, and the Alabama Office of Economic Opportunity. Civil rights activists would look to programs offered through the Economic Opportunity Act to take them from a Jim Crow culture to a society that honored equal rights, defining the meaning of freedom for themselves.[84]

CHAPTER FOUR

In Selma's Wake

Organizing for Change in the Alabama Black Belt after the Selma to Montgomery March

In the cities and small towns of Alabama many Negroes will now begin to exercise rights promised them for almost a century. But change will not come easily. "For the Right: White Supremacy" is the official slogan of the Alabama Democratic Party. The political structure of Alabama is built on racism, and it will not easily crumble. The state has woven a cotton curtain around its borders to keep out new ideas. That curtain has become the shroud of isolation and ignorance. . . . But change will come, and from a single source—the government of the United States. With the registration of Negro voters, at last the people of Alabama have an opportunity to free themselves from the bondage of prejudice and poverty. . . . The Voting Rights Act of 1965 carries with it tragedy for some and hope for many. With the new law, registration will not be easy, nor will voting. The hard lines of history must still be broken. But an era in the history of the state which practiced slavery, and in so doing enslaved itself, is closed.
    Charles Morgan, 1965

Workers in the civil rights movement of the Black Belt renewed the effort to change Alabama's political system in the early 1960s. Local people had been working in the area since the 1940s and welcomed the assistance provided by new national organizations. Activists with the Student Nonviolent Coordinating Committee (SNCC) came to Selma in 1962, and members of the Southern Christian Leadership Conference (SCLC) arrived in late 1964 to work on voter registration. Each organization used a different means to reach the goal of black enfranchisement. SNCC tried to organize the communities in Selma and Dallas County to develop local leaders in an effort to resolve community problems, while SCLC used direct-action techniques and marches to draw attention to black citizens' exclusion from the political process. The combined efforts of African Americans from Selma and its surrounding communities reached the national stage on March 7, 1965, with a violent confrontation on the Edmund

Pettus Bridge between civil rights protesters and city, county, and state law enforcement officials. Americans across the country watched the brutal showdown as television networks interrupted local programming to show the events as they unfolded live in Selma. Later that month, Dr. Martin Luther King Jr. utilized the nation's shock at "Bloody Sunday" to gain support for the continuation of the march to Montgomery to give the governor the movement's demands for fair voting rights. Approximately thirty-two hundred people from all over the nation joined in the first leg of the fifty-mile trek down Highway 80, thus helping to persuade Congress to pass the Voting Rights Act and President Lyndon Baines Johnson to sign it on August 6, 1965. At the end of the five-day demonstration, twenty-five thousand people entered Montgomery to hear King speak on the steps of the State Capitol, where he called the nation's response to Selma "a shining moment in the conscience of man."[1]

Not everyone in the civil rights movement agreed with the SCLC leader—what he saw as the end of the Alabama journey, others perceived as more like the halfway point. Many people throughout the country and in the civil rights movement viewed the Selma march and subsequent passage of the Voting Rights Act as the crown of victory. Yet slight fissures among the various civil rights organizations—and even among individuals within each group—that had been present all along now began to look more like definite cracks.

A break between SCLC and SNCC began to appear most clearly to those involved in the final stages of the Selma campaign. In March 1965, SNCC's Selma project director, Silas Norman, and John Love explained their disagreements with King's organization. They wanted voter registration with no literacy requirement, which was not part of SCLC's agenda. SNCC also favored starting a third political party in Alabama, as it had done in Mississippi, while SCLC endorsed directing newly registered black voters into the established Democratic or Republican Party. The dispute between the two groups boiled down to one of organizational style. SCLC opted to link up with traditional local black leaders, while SNCC hoped to develop leadership among individuals who had not normally had a say in their communities. Many SNCC workers did not even agree with the principles of the demonstration that had begun on the Edmund Pettus Bridge. Alabama SNCC staff thought that the march's objectives did not justify the danger and the resources involved in carrying it out. John Lewis, SNCC's chairman, wrote to King on March 7 that from then on, SNCC planned to maintain and develop its own Alabama programs and set up offices separate from those of SCLC.[2]

The quarrel between the two organizations grew after the Selma to Montgomery march later in the month. James Bevel explained that King wanted to declare victory and stop SCLC's involvement in the Selma campaign after the five-day march ended. He canceled a planned national economic boycott of Alabama and its products and instead supported a summer project to register voters in the Alabama Black Belt. Conversely, Stokely Carmichael, an Alabama SNCC field worker, thought it unfortunate that local people had not controlled the march and that many viewed it as a success. Not surprisingly, SNCC would make other plans for its work in the state while capitalizing on the new excitement brought by the Selma campaign.[3]

In spite of these differences, the recent events in the Black Belt motivated black citizens of the area who joined in the civil rights struggle. Both SCLC and SNCC sought to tap into the new energy generated by the Selma voting rights campaign to create more just communities.

Working within the System

During the summer of 1965, SCLC created the Summer Community Organization and Political Education Project (SCOPE), which used college-student volunteers from northern states to register voters and provide political education throughout the South. SCLC leaders planned to work in 113 counties across Alabama, Georgia, South Carolina, North Carolina, and Virginia. Hosea Williams directed this multistate program; James Orange, Daniel Harrell Jr., Albert Turner, and Richard Boone served as codirectors for Alabama, where the project covered fifteen counties and utilized eighty volunteers and twelve full-time staff members. At an orientation session for SCOPE volunteers, SCLC conducted workshops on farm labor in the South, the War on Poverty in the South, and community organization. Despite this nod to broader plans for the summer workers, SCOPE primarily emphasized voter registration. SCLC leaders reasoned that most of the problems faced by Alabama's black people—poor education, high unemployment, police brutality, bad housing—stemmed from disfranchisement and lack of political representation. Thus, voter registration and subsequent political participation seemed to be the keys to unlocking the doors that kept black people out. Many people had a strong faith in the federal government's ability to assist in this change. Reflecting back on this period in 1968, SCLC Selma staff member Shirley Mesher remembered, "When I came here three and a half years ago, going on four, people really had faith in the federal government, they really believed that that was their saving [grace]. The commentary was, 'If only they knew, they would correct things. If only they knew what their own agencies were doing; if only they knew the collusion between their agencies and the power structures here; if only they knew that the federal funds are being misspent and were being used for maintenance of segregation and bigotry and of course inferior services and everything else to

the black people. Then the federal government would surely correct it.'" The
SCOPE effort would be impeded, however, because Congress did not pass the
voting rights bill until August, leaving intact traditional obstacles to registering
voters until the SCOPE campaign had nearly ended.[4]

SCLC staff members became the backbone of the summer campaign that
lasted from June 15 through August 29. Williams told them to "be *the* bosses" in
their communities and interpret the campaign's actions and activities, especially
the work being done by northern white volunteers, for the local people. SCOPE
required SCLC staff to circulate from county to county—what one scholar has
called "hit-and-run tactics"—a strategy that met with greater success in registering people to vote than in organizing communities. For example, when
Turner tried to find out why the Greenville voter registrar's office was closed,
courthouse officials forced him out of the building at gunpoint. Later that morning, the office opened, but police officers, the county sheriff and deputies, and
state troopers surrounded the courthouse. Turner tried and failed to get the law
enforcement officials to leave the area, fearing that their presence would scare
off potential voter applicants, but SCOPE volunteers continued with their plans,
driving carloads of people into town to register. In Choctaw County, SCOPE
volunteers helped almost half of all the eligible black voters get on the rolls.
However, the voter registration activity died down after the volunteers left at
the end of the summer.[5]

In Hale County, SCOPE workers joined an SCLC project already in progress.
Hale was the nation's thirteenth-poorest county, and roughly 70 percent of its
residents were black. As a part of SCLC's Direct Action Alabama campaign,
people tried to register to vote in large numbers starting in February 1965. One
month later, the 4,824 white voters continued to far outnumber the 236 African
Americans who had registered. Rev. A. T. Days, pastor of St. Matthew's African
Methodist Episcopal Church in Greensboro, headed the Hale County movement through the Hale County Improvement Association. Working with SCLC,
this association conducted voter registration schools, encouraged people to register, and sponsored demonstrations in Greensboro objecting to the slow progress of the county voter registrars.[6]

The Hale County protests intensified along with the temperature. In July,
the voter registrars promised to open for business for five extra days to process
voter applications but did not honor their commitment. On July 6, Rev. Days;
Lewis Black, a leader of the Hale County movement; and Rev. Orange spoke to a
crowd of five hundred and led them in a march to the county courthouse. Days
continued to direct protest marches through downtown Greensboro, sparking
violent responses from some local white people and from Ku Klux Klan members, who wore placards that read, "Fight Communism, Fight Race Mixing, and

Protect the American Way." On July 15, a gang of white men carrying sticks, hammers, and rubber hoses attacked the protesters, sending seventeen to the Good Samaritan Hospital in Selma. Two days later, arsonists burned Days's church and the Elwood African Methodist Episcopal Zion Church in Akron, whose pastor, Rev. Farredin, had also been active in the demonstrations.[7]

As a result of the escalating violence, the Hale County Board of Registrars conceded to the protesters' demands and canceled the literacy test as a qualification for voter registration, but the Hale County Improvement Association continued the demonstrations, now focusing on the burning of the churches, the registrars' failure to extend their operating hours, and the continued slow pace at which applications were processed. In an effort to defuse the impending disorder, the local police tried to alter the route of the marches, keeping them out of the downtown area. A standoff ensued at a police barricade that blocked off Main Street to four hundred marchers. Turner advised the crowd members to "love that barrier down." After the demonstrators refused to leave, the law enforcement officials used tear gas to break up the protest.[8]

By the end of July, 435 people had been jailed. Just before President Johnson signed the voting rights bill, Black felt pessimistic about the new legislation. "The voting bill won't make any difference," he told a reporter for the *New York Times*. "The whites already are spreading the word among Negroes that the civil rights movement is run by Communists, they will suffer financial reprisals if they join it, and that they will lose their job if they try to vote." In some ways, he was right; the legislation did not calm the charged atmosphere in his hometown. Members of the Hale County Improvement Association filed a motion for a temporary restraining order against local officials. Federal District Judge Dan Thomas ruled on August 13 that the demonstrators must be allowed to continue picketing downtown businesses but limited the marches to groups of four. He also called for the police to offer the best available protection to the marchers. Nevertheless, the violence continued. Someone fired a gun into Days's house in late August, landlords evicted tenants, and white families fired black maids who were involved in the demonstrations.[9]

At an SCLC executive staff meeting, Williams summed up SCOPE, concluding optimistically that the work in Alabama had been very successful and that "it is now possible to elect Negro public officials in many communities." After the summer ended, SCLC continued its work in Alabama. By the fall, Turner had been promoted to Alabama field secretary. He had been active in voter registration efforts in the years since he returned to Perry County after earning his bachelor's of science degree from Alabama A & M. When registrars refused his voter application, he began working with others in West Perry, where many black people owned property, to become qualified voters. This group became the Perry County Civil League. When SCLC expanded its work beyond Dallas County during the Selma campaign, it coordinated with existing organizations, including Turner's. SCLC asked him to join the staff, and he worked with Orange in Marion throughout the SCLC voter campaign. In the fall of 1965, he joined a team of fifteen that carried on where the SCOPE project had left off, registering voters in anticipation of the May 1966 primaries.[10]

The Alabama SCLC workers signed up record numbers of new voters and sent daily tallies to the Atlanta headquarters. Turner's October 1965 report showed 285 registered in three days in Barbour County, 116 in four days in Greene County, 157 in four days in Choctaw County, 10,000 in Dallas County, and 1,277 in Montgomery. SCLC staffers also drew up county maps of Alabama and marked the legislative districts that contained African American majorities. Turner had high hopes for the work he and his staff performed, writing in his 1965 annual report, "With proper organizing we should be able to say who will be the next Governor of Alabama." Although this goal may have been overly ambitious, by 1966 the dominant position so long held by white Alabamians was facing challenges on many fronts.[11]

In addition to his SCLC work, Turner maintained his connections in Perry County. Working through the Perry County Civil League, Lawrence C. Johnson and James Carter Lenys wrote to the Office of Economic Opportunity (OEO) in August, requesting a technical assistance grant to form a community action program (CAP). Johnson had been the Extension Service's black county agent for twenty-five years, a position that gave him a great deal of knowledge about the benefits of federal programs as well as ties to both the black and white communities. His commitment to getting along with Perry County's white elites changed, however, as the civil rights movement entered his hometown and turned violent. White officials called on Colonel Al Lingo, head of the Alabama State Troopers, when the Selma campaign moved out of Dallas County and into surrounding areas. On February 18, 1965, during a night march to the Perry County Courthouse to demand the right to register to vote, state troopers shot Jimmie Lee Jackson, who died eight days later. Turner, Johnson, and Lenys knew the benefits of OEO programs and formed the Perry County Community Committee. Although the committee invited white community leaders to all its meetings, none came. Turner, Johnson, and Lenys asked Sargent Shriver to join Perry County to Greene and Hale Counties if OEO would not fund the request for the technical assistance grant.[12]

In August, the Perry County committee combined forces with Hale County's Lewis Black to apply for a CAP grant. Black had a history of working for the economic advancement of African Americans. He had taught in the county's public schools for sixteen years, was a farmer, and served as the secretary-treasurer of the Greenala Citizens Federal Credit Union, which Black and seven others had created in 1961 because Greensboro's blacks found it difficult to get credit at reasonable interest rates. By May 1966, the credit union had grown to one thousand members and had acquired eighty thousand dollars in liquid assets. An OEO inspector described the credit union as "the center of all Negro activity in the county," and the effort earned Black the enmity of Hale County's white population. The credit union had to put its money in a bank in Moundsville because the banks in Greensboro would not accept it. His participation in the summer protests further confirmed him as one of Hale County's civil rights leaders.[13]

Black formed the Hale County Progressive Association to sponsor the antipoverty effort and set up districts with community action coordinators who worked to organize black neighborhoods and communities, an effort OEO officials considered "rather sophisticated community action work" for Alabama. But the state's antipoverty organization had other plans for Hale County. Black learned that the Alabama Office for Economic Opportunity had joined Hale and Perry Counties to the non–Black Belt counties of Bibb, Chilton, and Shelby as part of Area 11 in an attempt to limit African Americans' ability to control the programs. Civil rights leaders in Hale and Perry Counties initially fought back by attempting to alter the composition of the Area 11 Committee's county groups. Black invited people from the white community to come together to form a biracial community action agency (CAA). The four who came—the probate judge, the county attorney, a principal from the white high school, and Greensboro's mayor/police chief—refused to accept a board with equal representation for both races. No white people attended the meeting called by the Perry County Poverty Program Committee, so group members decided to move ahead on their own to try to get OEO funding for a Hale–Perry County community action grant that would be separate from the Area 11 Committee. Members of the OEO Inspection Division viewed Black as the leader of this effort: "Every Negro in Hale County knows who he is and that he fights for them," Frank Prial told his bosses in Washington. "Black is no rose," Prial concluded, "but if the Klan doesn't kill him, it's hard to see how any county [community action committee] could exclude him."[14]

Following OEO guidelines, the Area 11 Committee selected representatives from each county to act as area directors. In Perry County, the committee asked Obie Scott, whose daughter, Coretta, had married Martin Luther King Jr., to serve. He declined to avoid being so closely associated with the white power structure that had cracked down so harshly on the black community during the February demonstrations. Next, white leaders turned to Robert (Boysie) Tubbs, an undertaker and onetime baseball star with the Birmingham Black Barons. Tubbs agreed to serve and found ten other African Americans to sit on the board. Members of the Perry County Community Committee became outraged, because the leaders of the Area 11 county committee, including chair James Wheller, a strong Wallace supporter, and R. Leigh Peagues, the mayor of Marion, refused to allow the black community to select its own board members. "If we let them pick their own representatives," Peagues told an OEO official, "they will pick the same ones who led those riots. I'd quit before I'd sit down with any of those rabble rousers." Peagues's objections also stemmed from his fears of losing his political position: he thought that Turner was planning to run for mayor and had no intention of furthering those efforts by letting him serve on the community action committee. "Listen," he told Prial, "the whites in this county don't want the poverty program in the first place. We sold it to them by assuring them we'd be in charge. Where would we be if we sold out to that SCLC . . . crowd?" The mayor's obstinacy led to an impasse for OEO funding of any program in Perry County. Johnson, the chair of the Perry County Community Committee, told OEO, "We know that having our own program would only make tensions around here worse." He was even willing to accept a minority position on the community action committee, but only if African Americans could choose their own representatives.[15]

In Hale County, Victor Poole, president of the Bank of Moundville and a member of the White Citizens' Council, agreed to serve as area director for the Area 11 program despite the fact that the county's white leaders did not want to be a part of the antipoverty program. Prial discovered that white elites in the southern part of Hale County did not want to offer any assistance to their poor African American neighbors. "We like our Nigras," Greensboro newspaper editor Hamner Cobbs told Prial, "but we can't afford to keep 'em around. The county's economy can't take it." Cobbs feared that the poverty program would encourage Hale County's black people to stay in the area rather than "go up the road . . . where they are accepted." Poole agreed to form a biracial committee to represent Hale County on the Area 11 Committee. Poole was from the northern part of the county, which had more interracial interaction, and consequently could find white people willing to join him. In spite of his segregationist attitudes, Poole thought the antipoverty program could benefit Hale County, declaring, "I don't agree with all of it myself, but I've taken a stand for it." Using his banker's mind, he reasoned that if the War on Poverty could double the income and improve the finances of Hale's black citizens, "we're going to get a share of it, too." Four black men—Norman Cephus, principal of the Moundville Negro high school; Sam Tooson, a farmer and school bus driver; Clinton Brassfield; and Willis Jones—agreed to serve on his twenty-four-person committee, but none came from Black's Hale County Progressive Association. Poole paid a price for his antipoverty activities, even though he avoided working with militant African Americans. Account holders removed their money from his bank, and members of the Ku Klux Klan visited him one night.[16]

The two groups from Hale and Perry Counties lodged protests against the Area 11 Committee with OEO's southeast regional office in Atlanta: "We refuse to be humiliated by being subjected to a CAP which, in information, policy-making, planning composition and control has eliminated Negroes who represent the community, and have given their time continually to the cause of social change and economic improvement in Hale and Perry Counties." The two groups united to submit an application to OEO as the Hale-Perry Area Coordinating Committee for Economic Opportunity, with the sponsorship of the Alabama Federation of Civic Leagues.[17]

Harvey Burg served as an intermediary among the Hale–Perry County group, OEO, and his boss, Orzell Billingsley, a Birmingham-based attorney who represented the Federation of Civic Leagues and served as the chairman of the Alabama Democratic Conference (ADC). A law student at Columbia University, Burg volunteered his legal services for the summer to people throughout the Black Belt, using Billingsley's contacts. African Americans formed the ADC in 1963 to work in conjunction with the Democratic National Committee and through the Southern Democratic Conference. President John F. Kennedy wanted to bring newly registered black voters to the Democratic Party, and the ADC would be the mechanism for doing so. Many of Alabama's traditional leaders in black politics joined the ADC, including Billingsley, Charles G. Gomillion, John L. Cashin, Amelia Boynton, and Arthur Shores. The ADC tried to find ways to work within the national Democratic Party in an effort to enter the mainstream of politics. As head of the ADC, Billingsley knew many of the state's traditional black leaders. The ADC also had strong connections with SCLC, which shared similar political strategies, especially the willingness to work within the existing political party structure. In addition to meeting the needs of the poor, Billingsley had other motivations for seeking Burg's assistance in creating federal poverty programs throughout the Black Belt. After the Mississippi Freedom Democratic Party challenge at the 1964 Democratic National Convention, the Democratic National Committee mandated the inclusion of black people in all state Democratic parties. Billingsley looked through this crack in the door and envisioned the black vote transforming Alabama's Democratic Party. As head of the ADC, he imagined himself as a power broker armed with a large bloc vote that could decide what those changes would be. In anticipation of the 1966 primaries, he wanted to round up as many black voters into his camp as possible. Through Burg's work, OEO programs developed in the Black Belt could corral those voters.[18]

In addition to helping Hale and Perry Counties, Burg worked with local civil rights organizations in Dallas, Greene, Lowndes, Marengo, and Sumter Counties to stymie local officials' attempted takeover of poverty programs. In

Figure 8. Attorney Orzell Billingsley, n.d. Billingsley sought to use his position as the chairman of the ADC to create a unified bloc of black voters that would transform the state's political system and saw the antipoverty programs as one way to do so. Birmingham Public Library Department of Archives and Manuscripts, Birmingham, Ala. (1565).

a memorandum to Randolph T. Blackwell, the SCLC's program director, Burg explained CAP's importance in the wake of the Voting Rights Act, which had finally given black people political power: "If a politician can control a community action coordinating committee which can obtain funds from the Office of Economic Opportunity, he then controls the influx of thousands of dollars into his community, a reservoir of needed community services, and a source of jobs." By commanding these federal funds, Burg noted, "a poverty program can provide the vehicle for change." Moreover, the person running the Title II program would have "his hands on the pulse of community life." By 1966, SNCC workers in Sumter County grew suspicious of Billingsley's intentions with regard to the development of antipoverty programs, reporting that "Billingsley was using the poverty program as the vehicle for his power in the state, particularly the rural black belt and organizing the movement leadership in the various counties into the ADC."[19]

By protesting the actions of the Alabama Office for Economic Opportunity, Burg hoped to create a confrontation between OEO, the Hale-Perry Area Coordinating Committee for Economic Opportunity, and the Area 11 Committee. An OEO inspector explained to Burg that the southeast regional office was reluctant to fund an all-black program out of fears that doing so would "only divide the two communities further, and bring down the wrath of the whites on a lot of undeserving Negro heads." "Good," said Burg. "When they push us around now, there is nothing we can do. When they start interfering with a Federally financed program, we can go right to the Justice Department. It will give us a defensive tool we've never had before." Burg's strategy revealed the faith many people had in the federal government's ability and willingness to support civil rights activists' efforts. Yet this approach would have few results for the poor people of the Black Belt as long as federal funds were not forthcoming. In the end, Burg could not force the antipoverty agency to follow his plan.[20]

OEO officials still had not made a decision about the Area 11 Committee in October 1965. However, Black and Turner used the experience working with Burg to their benefit. Both hoped to run for office in the 1966 primaries, and their community work provided opportunities to reach out to potential voters.[21]

Working Outside the System

Although SNCC activists often complained that SCLC put too much emphasis on leading and not enough on organizing, Turner's efforts in Perry County show that this paradigm was too simplistic. Some people associated with the Alabama SCLC project did community development work, but these people—ministers, schoolteachers, and businesspersons—usually were already perceived as leaders. In contrast, SNCC workers wanted to seek out local people who had not been a part of the traditional black leadership class and give them the tools they needed to have a voice in their community's future. The group of young activists had planned to expand SNCC's efforts in the Alabama Black Belt beyond Dallas County, but at an executive committee meeting in Holly Springs, Mississippi, just after the Selma to Montgomery march, SNCC leaders reassessed the situation. The last month of the Selma campaign had caused some confusion within the organization. Between fifty and sixty people came from SNCC's Mississippi program to participate in the March 7 demonstration, even though Alabama SNCC staff members did not support this strategy. Then, when the final march to Montgomery became a reality, Bernard Lafayette acted as spokesman for SNCC in Alabama, ignoring Silas Norman's position as Alabama project director. Ivanhoe Donaldson became a marshal of the march despite the fact that he opposed the rationale for the demonstration. Executive secretary Jim Forman also took a public role throughout the long walk to Montgomery, as did the group's chairman, John Lewis. At the Holly Springs meeting, the executive committee wanted to make sure that if a similar situation arose in the future, SNCC leaders would not come in and take over a local project. Although these young activists took pride in their bottom-up organizing style, it became increasingly difficult to use within SNCC itself, as evidenced by the Holly Springs discussions. Some decisions were being made from the top down, and SNCC had to finesse these realities into its own management style.[22]

After the Selma march, SNCC staff and volunteers moved into eight counties across the Alabama Black Belt. In addition to Norman in the state headquarters office in Selma, two people per county worked in Calhoun, Greene, Hale, Lowndes, Perry, Pickens, Sumter, and Wilcox Counties. Carmichael, who had begun working in Lowndes County, tried to motivate those at the Holly Springs conference to commit to what he called "radical" programs. "We are supposed to work outside the structure," he reminded the staff. "People came to SNCC because of radical programs." Carmichael worried that the Voting Rights Act would "squash a lot of SNCC work." Along the same lines, others wanted to make sure that voting per se did not become the movement's purpose but rather the means to achieve the true goal. Lee Bankhead suggested associating the right to vote with economic issues. Carmichael also knew that SCOPE would be going on simultaneously in counties where SNCC planned to operate. "The problem is one of two groups, differently oriented, working in virgin territory," he concluded, suggesting that SNCC attempt to subvert Williams's project: "You can't ignore them and set up a different program to compete with them." Instead, he proposed, "We go and work the counties and we control their program." The Holly Springs conference produced no decision regarding SNCC's future in Alabama. Rather, state staffers formulated their plans at a later workshop.[23]

Carmichael chose to work in Lowndes County, situated southeast of Dallas County, to focus on developing "radical programs." He wanted people in the movement to pass on their acquired skills and information to local people, who would then make decisions about their future. "It's not radical if SNCC people get political offices, or if M. L. King becomes President, if decisions are still made from the top down," Carmichael reasoned. "If decisions get made from the Bottom up, that's radical." He wanted to assist in creating a third political party, akin to the Mississippi Freedom Democratic Party, that would give local black people a say in how their communities functioned. The party itself would not necessarily be radical, but the concept of African Americans taking control of their lives was revolutionary for Alabama in the mid-1960s.[24]

Residents of Lowndes County became swept up in the SCLC/SNCC voter registration campaign that surrounded Selma in the spring of 1965. The Selma to Montgomery march passed through Lowndesboro on Highway 80, in the northern section of the county, where on the last day of the demonstration, four Klansmen shot and killed Viola Liuzzo, a Michigan woman who was driving marchers back to their homes. The county had classic Black Belt characteristics—tenants operated about 50 percent of the farms, African Americans comprised almost 81 percent of the total population, the typical family earned $1,387, and the average citizen had about a sixth-grade education. The agricultural revolution hit the county hard, and the number of farms had declined since 1940 as a consequence of low income, farm mechanization, and high beef prices. Beef cattle became the county's largest source of agricultural income as farmers replaced their cotton crop with pasture and grazing cattle displaced tenant farmers. Cotton production continued to slide into the hands of large, highly mechanized farm operations. A few small farmers in the southern part of the county restored some of their income by growing cucumbers and okra.[25]

Carmichael came to Lowndes County on March 27, 1965, the day after Liuzzo was killed, intent on nurturing local leaders to organize the community. In mid-March, Andrew Young and James Bevel, part of SCLC's Direct Action Alabama campaign, had begun working with a group of local people to form the Lowndes County Christian Movement for Human Rights (LCCMHR). This group planned to promote voter registration and to support the alleviation of the black community's grievances. SCLC leaders offered the LCCMHR little assistance, and Carmichael soon stepped in to fill the void.[26]

Lowndes County residents noticed Carmichael after he confronted policemen who answered a call from R. I. Peers, the principal of one of the black public schools. Carmichael wanted to publicize a mass meeting and decided to pass out leaflets to students at school so that they could deliver the announcement to their parents. When the police told him that he should not be on the school grounds and that he could be arrested, Carmichael responded, "If you're going to arrest me, do it, if not don't waste my time. I got work to do. I can't be bothered listening to your lectures." The policemen ultimately did not arrest Carmichael, and word spread through the black community that he had stood his ground against the authorities. "After that day," he remembered, "whenever we went canvassing, people would always say, 'Are you those civil rights fighters that cussed the cops out? . . . Well I'm sure glad to meet you all.'" He used the police confrontation as an organizing tool, an informal introduction that enabled him to then talk about the importance of attending upcoming mass meetings. "So when we got it together," he recalled, "we had three hundred people there. They liked to shock the shit out of us. . . . We were expecting a grand total of about seventy-five people." By mid-April, SNCC workers Bob Mants, Scott B. Smith, Willie Vaughn, and Judy Richardson had joined Carmichael in Lowndes. According to Smith, the young activists worked with the LCCMHR members in SCLC's absence: "We got the people to realize they could organize themselves and run their own movement." In one month of work, the activists set up a library for schoolchildren, helped three hundred people try to register to vote, and held two Sunday night mass meetings attended by about two hundred people. Matthew Jackson of the LCCMHR let the SNCC staff live in his house until they set up two freedom houses, one in Trickom and one in Hayneville, the county seat. The LCCMHR soon organized the county by communities, with each community electing two community chairmen. These officials, in turn, served on the LCCMHR's board of directors.[27]

The LCCMHR's leaders had developed talents and significant experience with black protest prior to the 1965 Selma campaign. The SNCC staff soon realized they were not working with novices. John Hulett, the thirty-eight-year-old chairman of the new organization, had left the county soon after graduating from high school in 1946. Working in a Birmingham foundry, he joined a labor union and later served two terms as its president. After the war, civil rights activities bubbled to the surface in Birmingham, and Hulett joined in, becoming a member of the National Association for the Advancement of Colored People (NAACP). After the state attorney general banned the civil rights group, Hulett joined the Alabama Christian Movement for Human Rights. These organizations brought the Lowndes County native into contact with important leaders in the city's civil rights movement, including W. C. Patton of the NAACP, Fred Shuttlesworth of the Alabama Christian Movement for Human Rights, and Martin Luther King Jr. Hulett did not join in the direct-action campaigns in Birmingham, but he registered to vote and encouraged others to do the same. With these affiliations, it is not surprising that the LCCMHR took a name similar to that of Shuttlesworth's grassroots Birmingham organization.[28]

Hulett was not the only member of the LCCMHR with experience in civil rights activity. Robert L. Strickland joined the Montgomery Bus Boycott in 1955 while working for a construction company. He and his wife, Willie Mae, participated in the Montgomery Improvement Association and ferried people in their cars to support the boycott of the city's bus system. In 1957, the Stricklands and their five children moved back to Lowndes County, Willie Mae Strickland's home, and bought a one-acre lot in the county seat. Strickland kept his job in Montgomery and thus retained an element of financial independence from Lowndes County's white people. Described as a big, powerful man, the forty-two-year-old had confronted the injustice of white supremacy at a young age. When he was sixteen, four white boys chased and threw rocks at him. A few days later they came after him again at the grocery store where he worked. Strickland ran into a neighbor's house, grabbed a shotgun, and fired as two of the white boys approached the front door and two others tried to come in the back door. He hit one of the attackers. An investigator's notes reported that as the victim lay on the operating table, he told his mother that Strickland had shot him after he "ran that Nigger down the hill and hit him with a beer bottle." Two weeks after the boy died, an all-white jury convicted Strickland of premeditated murder and handed down a harsh sentence of life in prison. In 1945, after serving five years, he received parole, and in 1957, Governor James Folsom, a racial moderate, granted a full pardon that restored Strickland's citizenship rights. Black people's lack of political power bothered him, and he intended to do what he could to change Lowndes County's old ways. He unsuccessfully tried to register to vote in 1958 and agreed to serve in a leadership position with the LCCMHR in 1965.[29]

Like Hulett, Charles Smith was born in Lowndes County and left to take advantage of the job opportunities provided by World War II. He helped build the shipyard in Pascagoula, Mississippi, and then moved to Mobile, where he became a hull erector for the Alabama Dry Docks and joined a CIO labor union and the NAACP. In 1948, he returned to his hometown, Calhoun, to live on forty acres of land he had bought with his wartime savings. Smith also bought a truck and began a logging business. After the Montgomery Bus Boycott began, he occasionally drove to the capitol to keep abreast of the situation. When white landowners learned that Smith supported the Montgomery protest, they stopped buying his timber, thus forcing him out of the logging business and back into farming. He also worked as an insurance agent, earning about two thousand dollars a year from both jobs combined. The fifty-one-year-old farmer was eager to see changes in Lowndes County when the LCCMHR formed.[30]

Women also held leadership positions in the new organization. Sarah Logan came from the Gordonsville section of the county, where her husband farmed his own land. After having six children, she attended Alabama State University in Montgomery and earned a degree in 1958, becoming a teacher. She joined the NAACP and later became a leader in the push to integrate Lowndes County's public schools. Lillian McGill grew up in the White Hall area of the county. Her father had been employed by the Western Alabama Railroad, a job that enabled him to send Lillian to high school at Selma University's boarding school. After graduation, she too attended Alabama State. She married in the mid-1950s, and she and her husband took an active role in the Montgomery Bus Boycott. When her mother died, the McGills moved back to Lowndes County to care for her father. When the LCCMHR formed, Lillian McGill served as its first secretary.[31]

Other members of the LCCMHR included William J. Cosby, Jesse W. Favor, Frank Haralson, Matthew Jackson, and Sidney Logan Jr. Few of these activists had ever voted, but many had registered in the spring of 1965. They gained important experience in Alabama's organized labor and early civil rights movements. Their parents had some economic independence and gave their children strong foundations from which to grow. Some took leadership positions in their churches. By the 1960s, many of the LCCMHR members owned their own homes, freeing them from some of the economic reprisals the county's white people often used to keep civil rights protest at bay. The combined experiences of LCCMHR's leaders put them in an excellent position to take advantage of the whirlwind that blew their way after the Selma campaign and the passage of the Voting Rights Act.[32]

The Lowndes County activists formed an antipoverty program action committee to apply for a CAP grant in August 1965. OEO standards ranked Lowndes County as 100 percent rural, and LCCMHR members felt they could develop programs to assist the poor. Hulett, Frank Miles Jr., and McGill headed up a committee to launch the project. "We wish to declare our intention to take the initiative in Lowndes County to bring a community action program to our county," they wrote to Shriver. They explained that the LCCMHR could represent many areas of the community: "It is open . . . to others who wish to contribute to bring change and improvement to our county which ranks among the poorest in the country." They told Shriver that although their plans originated in the black community, the committee members intended to invite their white neighbors to join in the antipoverty program. But "if the white community rejects our offer to cooperate in immediately moving forward," the group warned, "we plan to move ahead and apply for a grant." Burg offered his legal advice to the LCCMHR in its quest for OEO funds. Aware of the multitude of problems that the governor had created for people in the Black Belt, the sponsors of the proposal asked Shriver to fund a program in Lowndes County only or join Lowndes and Wilcox Counties together, echoing the approach taken by Hale and Perry Counties. "We cannot afford to await the initiative of others," they told the OEO director. "We want to and must help ourselves by acting now."[33]

Their suspicions of the white community were not unfounded. After writing to Shriver in early August, the committee sent letters to local government leaders, merchants, farmers, teachers, bankers, policemen, and lumbermen in an effort to form a biracial CAA, as required by the CAP guidelines. Like Black and Turner in Hale and Perry Counties, the members of the LCCMHR were surprised to learn that plans had already begun for an antipoverty program in the county. Lowndes County would be joined with Covington, Butler, and Crenshaw Counties to form Area 22. Mayor Stagger of Benton responded to Hulett's letter with the information that Lowndes County would be represented by Ralph Norman Jr., Hulda Coleman, Fred Holladay, and Sam Bradley.[34]

On August 22, the LCCMHR antipoverty committee sent a telegram to Shriver and CAP director Theodore Berry, protesting Area 22's application. Upon receiving the wire, Berry wrote to one of his aides, "Hold Everything—Investigate and advise!" Two days earlier, Tom Coleman had shot and killed Jonathan Daniels, an Episcopal seminary student and volunteer in the civil rights movement, at point-blank range outside a small store in Hayneville. Coleman's sister, Hulda, served on the Area 22 committee and was the Lowndes County school superintendent. This incident must have heightened OEO officials' concerns about the progress of the antipoverty program in the county. Historian Charles Eagles has concluded that Daniels's death also made the black people involved in the local civil rights movement even more dedicated to changing Lowndes County.[35]

Hulett also sent a formal protest letter to Berry, charging that the Area 22 board members had no interest in "the changes and conditions of the poor people" of Lowndes County. Hulett went on to explain that the LCCMHR had formed a countywide movement with representatives from every community in the county, whereas the Area 22 committee had not even tried to contact members of the LCCMHR's antipoverty committee. "The one negro whom we have been informed is on this so called bi-racial committee," Hulett complained, has "never come out to see what the poor and needy people wants and think or need." "We no longer wish to be spoken for without being asked what is best for poor people and how we will be governed in relation to Federal funds," Hulett advised. He challenged Berry to consider the consequences of OEO's acceptance of the Area 22 plan. If OEO funded this program, Hulett thought, it would not change the county's impoverished conditions, a situation that "could prove detrimental to the President's Anti-poverty program and embarrass both the president and the United States of America." Nevertheless, the LCCMHR's first attempt to operate an OEO program failed, as the agency turned down the initial application for a CAP grant, probably because of a reluctance to fund programs opposed by local officials. Undaunted, the LCCMHR members continued to search for a way to get OEO support for a program that could not be blocked by local officials or vetoed by the governor.[36]

Using the Franchise

As the summer progressed, SNCC searched for new ways to engage potential voters. Taking a page from the organizing book of the 1964 Mississippi Summer Project (also known as Freedom Summer), SNCC's Alabama staff planned to have local people participate in the fall Agriculture Stabilization and Conservation Service (ASCS) community committee elections as a first step in utilizing the right to vote. "As more and more Negroes are registered to vote, the lesson of the ASCS election is an important one," reported Edward Rudd in the *Southern Courier*. "It is not enough to be given the right to vote. It is not enough to put Negro names on the ballot. Negroes must work and plan together if they want their vote to do them any good." SNCC leaders reasoned that after black farmers understood what was at stake in the ASCS program, local people would become involved in the voting process, as had occurred in Mississippi in 1964. As part of Freedom Summer, the Council of Federated Organizations, which consisted of SNCC, SCLC, the NAACP, and CORE, ran candidates in ASCS elections in twelve Mississippi counties. The results of the foray into U.S. Department of Agriculture (USDA) local elections were not too promising—no black candidates won a majority of the community elections in any Mississippi county. Nevertheless, according to one SNCC volunteer, "what we did was present the idea . . . , get some men nominated, and . . . relied upon people who attended the meeting to get the word out to their friends." The task in Alabama would be just as difficult. At a summer statewide ASCS meeting held in Mobile, several men claimed that black farmers did not hold important posts because "most Negro farmers prefer to have whites running the ASCS."[37]

SNCC took the lead in using the ASCS elections as an organizing tool in Alabama beginning in July 1965. SNCC workers knew how the crop allotment and conservation program operated because they had attended a fall 1963 conference sponsored by the South Carolina Council on Human Relations and the National Sharecroppers Fund. SNCC's annual conference that year took as its theme food and jobs. Field staff received briefings on the programs offered by the federal government that could relieve some of the economic distress of rural communities. In the summer of 1965, the Alabama organizers understood that millions of dollars were at stake. If black farmers and tenants could serve on local ASCS committees, some of the economic resources available to white farmers might be made accessible on a more equitable basis. The ASCS county committee set policy goals, implemented the program, supervised elections, and hired personnel. If a black farmer were to be elected to a seat on this committee, he would hold a position of power at the grass roots.[38]

Elmo Holder worked out of the Selma headquarters getting the necessary information from the state ASCS office on election procedures and dates. He found the state ASCS handbook ambiguous and tried to pin down the state director, B. L. Collins, on key matters such as who was eligible to vote, the residency requirements for holding office, the ASCS's definition of *sharecropper* and *tenant farmer*, and whether women could participate. Holder asked Collins how the ASCS planned to secure the ballots after they had been mailed but before they were counted. Collins offered little assistance, telling Holder that "he was at a loss to know how to prevent tampering with the ballots." Holder also warned Collins that based on experience with ASCS elections in Mississippi, SNCC wanted to make sure that the community committee nominating meetings did not overload the ballots with black farmers not nominated by those present at the meeting. "In areas where Negroes put up their own candidates," Holder explained, "there is absolutely no legitimate reason why the committees should put up additional Negro candidates." Holder brought to Collins's attention tactics the ASCS had previously used to weaken the black vote, which SNCC hoped to avoid. Collins refused to give Holder the exact date of the election, which caused the SNCC worker to ask for a guarantee that it would not take place before October 1. Finally, Holder asked if SNCC representatives could start attending regular ASCS meetings to avoid missing important information regarding the upcoming elections. In short, Holder tried to prepare for all contingencies. In case Collins remained evasive, Holder enlisted the aid of Bruce Rogow of the Lawyers Constitutional Defense Committee (LCDC) in Jackson, Mississippi, to obtain definite answers to his questions from Ray Fitzgerald, the deputy director of state and county affairs at the USDA's Washington offices.[39]

At the July Alabama SNCC staff meeting, participants decided to hold a workshop on the ASCS elections to help local people obtain answers regarding the USDA program and participation in the upcoming elections. SNCC hoped to use this workshop as an opportunity to assist black farmers in getting the technical assistance they needed as well as information that they could share with their neighbors. The members of the state field staff agreed to attempt to generate interest by talking about the ASCS workshop in the counties where they worked.[40]

Collins finally replied to Holder's questions on August 10, with a short letter that reported that the USDA required ballots to be postmarked or returned in person by November 12, with the ballots to be counted on November 15 and the county convention to be held on November 19. The USDA announced that for the 1965 ASCS elections, every county ballot had to include the same percentage of black farmers as lived in the county and that all ballots must be cast through the mail. On the surface, these new regulations looked like advancements for a nondiscriminatory election, but in reality these changes could still serve to overwhelm and intimidate black voters. Voting by mail presented many potential problems. This requirement did not ensure that all of the ballots would be counted, that all of the ballots would arrive at the ASCS office, or that ballots could not be replaced by other ballots. The percentage rule also opened the door for local ASCS county committees to flood the ballots with black nominees and limit the number of white candidates, facilitating the election of white farmers by splitting the black vote.[41]

SNCC held the ASCS elections workshop in mid-September 1965 at St. Paul's Methodist Church in Selma. The attendees saw an ASCS filmstrip and heard a brief history of southern agriculture. Jack Wasserman and James Mays of the National Sharecroppers Fund discussed the ASCS program. Charles Smith of the LCCMHR explained how to set up farmer meetings and workshops and gave an overview of events in each county represented at the workshop. Holder reported on the information he gathered from state and federal ASCS officials. African American farmers from several counties talked about their problems. One man complained that he could not make much profit from his cucumber crop. James Mays of the Sharecroppers Fund told the farmer about a Mississippi cooperative that received five cents a pound for its cucumbers. All of the nineteen farmers who came to the meeting had previously participated in ASCS elections but had not seen much value in them. After this workshop, many participants expressed interest in running for their county committees. "Whether win, lose, or draw," a SNCC staff member explained, "the important thing is that folks are really interested in the elections and see ways of attempting to get their own people elected." The young activists distributed flyers explaining the importance of the ASCS program and planned to continue holding weekly community meetings with the farmers until the ASCS elections. Historian Pete Daniel has described SNCC activists here as "unofficial extension workers" because "they condensed complicated USDA programs and translated them into layman's language, often with graphic aides to help farmers understand committee structures and county organizations."[42]

That fall, articles appeared in the *Southern Courier* (a weekly newspaper started by northern students who had participated in the Mississippi Summer Project and written specifically for Alabamians interested in civil rights activities) emphasizing the importance of the ASCS program and of the upcoming vote. To generate interest, SNCC worker Chris Wiley described to reporter Edward Rudd how the ASCS committee parceled out the cotton allotment. In Hale County, according to Wiley, large landowners received an average cotton allotment of thirty-nine acres, "while the smaller and poorer Negro farmers [got], on the average, less than nine acres." Wiley said that if poor farmers were elected to the committees, they "would divide the pie much differently." Holder, whom Rudd also interviewed for his article, warned black farmers about the pitfalls of the new percentage regulations and suggested that "Negroes should agree on a slate of candidates" to avoid splitting their votes.[43]

Twenty-five SNCC staff people worked feverishly in Barbour, Dallas, Greene, Lowndes, and Wilcox Counties, canvassing for eligible voters, recruiting farmers to run for the ASCS committee positions, and obtaining signatures for petitions to place interested farmers on the ballot. Running for ASCS committee positions required great courage on the part of black farmers, who faced the potential wrath of people threatened by a fair vote. In her door-to-door effort, Janet Jermott, a SNCC activist in Lowndes County, said she met people who had never even heard of the ASCS committee: "All they see is Mr. Charlie who comes around and takes their cotton away." As Election Day approached, SNCC held workshops to answer questions about casting votes and watching the tabulation of ballots. At one meeting, Jack McNair, who owned a 130-acre farm in Wilcox County, remarked, "I've always wondered why was it that they didn't put some colored on the committee as well as white." He decided to run for a committee position to change that practice.[44]

As expected, the local ASCS officials did not comply with the rules set out in the ASCS handbook. Only six signatures on a petition were required to place someone on the community committee ballot. In Greene County, however, the ASCS county offices disqualified eleven candidates because "an insufficient number of eligible voters" had signed the nominating petitions. But most of these petitions had carried twelve signatures in case some of the signatories were ineligible, calling into question the disqualifications. The rejected nominees had until October 28 to appeal but were not told of their ineligibility until the day before. The same day, when Wendy Turner, a SNCC worker based in Greene County, went to inquire about the petitions, workers in the ASCS county office would not let her enter. And on October 28, the Greene County ASCS office closed at noon without notice. By the time the ballots were counted, nine families had been evicted from their land as a consequence of their participation in the Greene County ASCS elections. In Hale County, the ASCS office rejected all seven African American nominees. Several families whose members signed nominating petitions were thrown off the plantations where they worked and lived. Some Hale County candidates were too frightened to sign affidavits identifying their intimidators.[45]

In Lowndes County, the African American nominees fared better. Twenty-four of the thirty seats on the community committee had black candidates. But the county ASCS committee nominated black farmers in addition to those supported by the movement. In one community, sixty-nine African Americans appeared on the ballot alongside three white farmers. Likewise, in those communities where black farmers had not nominated anyone, the county ASCS committee did not add nominees from the black community, although "if they were following the rule straight," commented SNCC staffer John Liutkus, "they would have put Negroes on the ballot in proportion to whites." Also, the new home of a candidate named Harris burned to the ground in a suspicious October 30 fire. Wilcox County farmers could choose African American candidates for thirty-six out of forty available seats. The Wilcox County ASCS office, however, developed a novel approach to voting: voters had to mark the five candidates they wanted to elect and then cross out all the other names. Anyone who did not read very well would find this process confusing and difficult, thereby increasing the likelihood that a ballot would be thrown out because of an error.[46]

Liutkus tried to head off further problems before the ballots were cast by meeting with the members of the state ASCS committee, the state advisory committee to the U.S. Civil Rights Commission, the ASCS southwestern regional director, the administrative assistant to the ASCS administrator, and the associate director of the ACHR (the state affiliate of the Southern Regional Council).

The group drew up a list of five proposals to solve anticipated problems associated with the upcoming elections. The state ASCS committee approved the recommendations and sent them to Fitzgerald, who rejected the suggestions and instead said that a state official would monitor the counting of ballots in each county office.[47]

This first attempt to elect African American farmers to Alabama's ASCS committees had mixed results. While some blacks gained seats on their community committees, most won only as alternates, not as full-fledged committee members. In Wilcox County, ten black farmers gained seats on the community committee, including four as community committeemen, which enabled them to be delegates to the county convention, and six as alternates. In Lowndes County, one community elected an all-black slate of five men. Three other communities elected two African American alternate members each. One black farmer was elected as an alternate committeeman in Greene County, but no African Americans won seats in Hale or Barbour Counties.[48]

Despite these accomplishments, SNCC filed fraud charges because of the many abnormalities in the voting process. The deception and deceit had the suspicious patina of official sanction, which only exacerbated the polarization between the races that already existed in the region. "We did it fair and square," Carmichael noted. "We believed in them, and they cheated us." After the election, SNCC found that the chicanery of the ASCS officials ran deep. A number of black farmers in Lowndes County received ballots for communities other than the ones where they were eligible to vote. Some received correct ballots from the county ASCS office, while others reported being chased out of the office when they tried to exchange their incorrect ones. In some communities, the election results were close; thus, these wrong ballots could have made a difference in the final outcome. In three communities in Wilcox County, 120 voters selected the same 3 white men from among 5 white and 2 black candidates, while no voters selected the other 2 white or 2 African American men whose names appeared on the ballot. SNCC workers interviewed people who had cast ballots in these communities and found that some had indeed voted for the black candidates. And one SNCC worker heard the state ASCS official overseeing the counting of ballots in Wilcox County say that he had come to offer moral support to the county officials, making it clear he would not act on any complaints of irregularities. In Greene County, ASCS officials initially allowed only one person to witness the counting of the ballots. After Liutkus complained to Collins, four black farmers were allowed to watch, but they were made to sit against the wall, where they lacked a good view of the tabulations.[49]

The USDA requested that the Office of the Inspector General conduct a thorough and detailed investigation into SNCC's charges. Such an inquiry would do little immediate good, however, since the county conventions were scheduled to meet on November 19. The trickery continued at these conventions. In Lowndes County, ASCS officials skirted guidelines by allowing farmers to run for positions on the county committee even if they had not won seats in the community committee elections. As a result, white farmers maintained their majority status on the community committees by keeping black alternates from advancing into open seats that would have been vacated by those elected to the county committee. Five white farmers won seats on the Lowndes County committee, which served as the focal point of control in local ASCS programs. This ruse further weakened whatever power the newly elected African Americans might have had in administering the program.[50]

In the aftermath of the disappointing fall ASCS elections, much remained to be done. "We had big plans for those farm subsidies," Carmichael said. He thought that if black farmers had been elected to positions of power within the ASCS, many African Americans could have supported themselves with farm subsidies and thus would not have needed to move out of the Black Belt. Now something else would have to be done. SNCC set up a tent city in Lowndes County for twenty families who had been evicted for participating in the ASCS elections, trying to register to vote in general elections, or attempting to enroll their children in the white public schools. Threddie Lee Stewart won an alternate spot on his ASCS community committee and was forced from his farm but nevertheless planned to stay in the county: "My grandfather was born on this land. I've worked on this land, and I'm going to stay on the land." Buster Haigler, chairman of the Lowndes County ASCS committee, foreclosed on Cato Lee's mortgage after Lee refused to stop his civil rights activity. Doug and Tina Harris, SNCC workers based in Selma, thought that the only hope for small African American farmers would be to form cooperatives for raising cattle or growing vegetables.[51]

Rev. Daniel Harrell Jr., an SCLC staff member, agreed. He had been trying to launch a self-help housing program in Wilcox County since August to assist thirty-two families evicted from their homes for participating in the spring civil rights demonstrations and ASCS elections. "I feel like I've been on this place so long, I feel like I'm lost, regardless of my former position," recounted a seventy-year-old woman expelled from her tenant home in Wilcox County. Harrell anticipated even more problems after the fall harvest because one hundred families had received word that their services would no longer be needed after that time. Harrell raised three thousand dollars through donations from local African Americans and SCLC and purchased some land to begin the housing program. He also contacted the Farmers Home Administration (FHA) for assistance in setting up a cooperative for farmers to grow corn, peas, okra, and squash. A processing plant in Uniontown promised to buy the crops.[52]

Harrell moved to Wilcox County during SCLC's Direct Action Alabama campaign to assist in voter registration and community organizing. He had been involved in the civil rights movement since 1963, working in Louisiana with Major Johns and SCLC. Wilcox County ranked as Alabama's third poorest and the country's twentieth poorest. Before federal registrars came to the county, no black people's names appeared on the voter rolls. By the fall of 1965, Harrell's efforts to start a CAP faced obstacles similar to those in Hale, Lowndes, and Perry Counties. After he tried to form a biracial organizing committee, white leaders in Wilcox and neighboring Marengo took control of the antipoverty effort. A group led by the two state senators from each county handpicked a coordinating committee that did not represent either the poor or the black community. The Wilcox County SCLC members—John Cook, Albert Gordon, Daniel Harrell, Carl Jones, and Thomas L. Threadgill—protested these actions to OEO in Washington, to no avail. The antipoverty program stood dead in its tracks as evictions mounted and winter closed in.[53]

Harrell received support for his work in Wilcox County from Rev. Francis X. Walter, director of the Selma Inter-Religious Project. He admitted that "it's an ambiguous role for a white person to play, the role that I play." Walter maneuvered on this challenging ground by living in Tuscaloosa and maintaining an office in Selma while working across the Black Belt. "I've been more effective as someone who simply comes into the community and has a service to offer if anybody needs it. I perform my service; I may spend three or two nights . . . with some regularity [as] I do in Wilcox County. I spend about two nights a week in Wilcox County in one place. But I'm not saying to the community that 'I've come down here to live with you all.'"[54]

In early October 1965, Walter went to Atlanta to see OEO officials in the southeast regional office. He met with Vernon Jordan, who was working as a consultant in the Community Action Division. The black attorney gave Walter advice about how southern African Americans could get support through the War on Poverty. Walter noted in his diary that Jordan "suggested Black Belt or Negroes generally in Alabama ask for *special* projects. Does not mean have to give up their claim to be the whole or only local group in area. But after filing for that distinction should ask for special project which would later be incorporated into the overall program." By November, Walter met with Mew Song Li of SCLC's economic development department to discuss a poverty program for Wilcox County. Li had contacted Picot Floyd in OEO's southeast regional office, and he had promised that "he would personally push through a single purpose grant for Wilcox" on the basis of emergency needs arising from the more than ninety eviction cases that occurred in the county. They put together a three-component project that involved a marketing cooperative for one hundred farmers who had lost their tenant farms. They planned to grow cucumbers,

Figure 9. Francis X. Walter in his study in Tuscaloosa, Alabama, 1970. Photo by Nancy Redpath. Francis X. Walter Personal Papers, Sewanee, Tenn.

peas, and okra on six hundred acres. OEO would supply the funds for seeds, fertilizer, equipment, and insecticides. The income from this venture would provide the capital for FHA loans to finance a cooperative housing project. The second and third parts of the project included the development of a credit union and a large Head Start program. Li viewed SCLC's voter registration and anti-poverty efforts as "crucial to a new day in Wilcox."[55]

But OEO officials allowed these plans to fall through, too. Floyd left the regional office for a position at the University of Georgia, and his replacement, James May, did not feel compelled to honor Floyd's commitment. The winter of 1965–66 looked foreboding. Throughout December, Walter traveled across Wilcox County with Juanita Harrell and Ella Saulsbury, documenting eviction cases and sending affidavits to Charles Morgan, an attorney with the American Civil Liberties Union office in Atlanta, and to the Justice Department. In one case, Addie Lee Farish notified her four tenants that they had to vacate their homes by January 13 because they had been active in demonstrating or registering to vote. Walter recorded his sense of frustration at the way these farmers had to live: "Today I was plunged into the world of rent, lease, parity, debt, rent receipts, pasture rent and loans, loans, loans. It is impossible for these people to state their income. Even if they understand the concept, the tangle of tenant-landlord finance is so artfully constructed that its impossible to know how a man can owe over $3,000—twice his theoretical income is hard to grasp. Mr. Parker is expected to move off land he has occupied all his life by Jan 13 and pay off this debt by Feb. Nice Xmas!" In spite of these sad injustices, Walter found some simple pleasures that helped him keep going as he made his way in the region. That night he noted that many women in the area displayed a talent for making beautiful quilts that could possibly be sold outside of Wilcox County as a means of earning a living. After discussing this idea with Ella Saulsbury, he wrote that he "enjoyed a supper with the Henrys—squirrel perloo, blackeyed peas, cornbread and preserved peaches. To bed very satisfied."[56]

Walter attended a precinct meeting at Annemanie that took place in a Masonic building, "clap board, unpainted, in [the] middle of nowhere." He described this as "a strange and romantic night." Seeing local people gaining their political voices moved him. "They talked and learned politics," he con-fided in his journal. They planned their strategy. "What is the white man trying to do next, how can we out wit him?" Walter witnessed something important that night. "The depths of these peoples democracy is so sweet and primitive," he wrote, "it reminds one of what we imagine Greek city democracy might have been. We stated our reasons for being there. Collected another case and led to plead ignorance to several questions on [Veterans Administration], Small Busi-ness Loans, Old Age Pension, and so forth." By early January, morale stood at an all-time low in the Wilcox County SCLC offices. The two local people hired to work in the office, Saulsbury and Gordon, had not been paid in six weeks. They had sent nearly seventy-five complaints to Morgan, and federal investiga-tors had met with Gordon and Li, but only twice. Wilcox County SCLC lead-ers decided to follow the Justice Department's advice and to encourage people to refuse to move even when told to do so by their landlords. This plan worried some tenants. On the Farish plantation, Walter found that "the folk there were not too happy about tempting the Sheriff to put them off. A note of distrust of the Camden SCLC came out—a feeling [that] a promise to supply a house might not materialize. I couldn't blame them." By the middle of February, the Wilcox County SCLC chapter was back at the drawing board, and spring plant-ing needed to begin shortly. Li worried that she had led these local people astray, leaving them "prey to evictions, foreclosures and false hopes in a new economy we can't really promise them."[57]

Daniel Harrell organized the farm cooperative between December and Feb-ruary without the OEO grant. Montgomery's W & W Pickle Company built two grading sheds in the county—in Gee's Bend and in Camden—for the coopera-tive's produce. At the same time, however, SCLC pulled back on its financial support to Wilcox County. Since August 1965, the Atlanta headquarters had sent Harrell only $140 to cover $500 in expenses. Turner told Harrell that no further funds were earmarked for Wilcox County. Harrell used his own money to buy seeds for the new cooperative. When he complained to Andrew Young, his grievances fell on deaf ears. Young blamed Harrell for harboring jealous feelings toward Turner. In spite of this neglect from SCLC headquarters, the Wilcox County field worker carried on, telling the board of directors, "This is one time SCLC is going to get credit for staying with a county until the job is completely done, and after the job is done I do not mind going to Egypt."[58]

Harrell and other Wilcox County SCLC workers decided to apply for an OEO grant for a self-help housing and family education project under Title III (b) of the Economic Opportunity Act, following Jordan's earlier advice to seek assistance as a special project. Title III (b) enabled local communities to apply for funds to develop programs for seasonally employed and migrant farm workers, which OEO administered through CAP. Broadly interpreting Title III's intent, local people could utilize these programs to assist sharecroppers, tenants, and small farmers in need of assistance.[59]

The Wilcox County SCLC's antipoverty committee reasoned that sharecroppers and tenants could qualify as seasonal workers and thus could receive benefits from this portion of the OEO program. After some debate, antipoverty officials in Washington agreed with this explication of Title III (b). The Wilcox County SCLC planned to ask OEO for fifteen-hundred-dollar grants to qualified families, which would enable them to access FHA credit. This group would then hire a building contractor, who could teach them how to build homes. Harrell even enlisted the SIP to find churches, synagogues, clubs, and labor unions that would be willing to cosign FHA loans for the chosen families. Harrell anticipated receiving more than half a million dollars from OEO by the middle of May 1966. But unbeknownst to the SCLC activist, Washington officials in OEO had grown weary of the southeast regional office's plan to pair Black Belt counties with white majority counties that bordered the region in an effort to dilute the black majority. Funding this grant was a way to counteract this misguided plan.[60]

The educational component involved programs for adults and children. The adults would learn reading and math to prepare them for future employment, and the children would participate in an eight-month early childhood education program. Ten teacher aides, chosen from among the seasonal farm workers, would assist this program. The project seemed feasible, and OEO in Washington appeared supportive. Several months would pass, however, before OEO processed the Wilcox County SCLC's application.[61]

In Eutaw, a group formed the Greene County Community Fund to assist people who had nowhere to go after their landlords failed to renew long-standing tenant agreements for 1966. "To make a living and to keep our vote in the county," Raymond Morrow explained in a fund-raising letter, "we established the Greene County Community Club Fund." Realizing that cattle would soon replace cotton in the local fields and sensing that their white neighbors wanted to decrease the percentage of black people in the county, the Greene County Community Fund planned to raise money to buy land, build housing, and start a cooperative business for the landless tenants. As more and more people became displaced because of their participation in civil rights activities, the group shifted its plans, using the money raised to erect a tent city in Forkland to serve as temporary housing. Borrowing the idea from the Wilcox County SCLC, the Greene County activists hoped to receive Title III (b) funds from OEO to establish a self-help housing program. The Greene County NAACP, headed by Rev. William Branch, also tried to assist the newly homeless black tenants and sharecroppers. He set up Operation Rehabilitation, which used money raised by the NAACP and private donations to help farmers buy land and build houses.[62]

At this juncture in the struggle for civil rights in the Alabama Black Belt, activists chose several avenues to address the issues of local people who faced repercussions as a consequence of their participation in the movement. Some, like Harrell in Wilcox County and Branch in Greene County, confronted the immediate needs of those displaced from their homes. Others focused on the long-term solutions that the spring primaries and fall elections seemed to offer. In early January, a group of Black Belt residents attended a statewide conference on governmental antipoverty and other programs to aid low-income rural people, forming the Alabama Rural Areas Development Council. The participants elected Lewis Black of Greensboro to head this organization. In February, this grassroots effort at rural development received more than moral support from the ACHR and the National Sharecroppers Fund. With a twelve-thousand-dollar grant from the Southern Regional Council, the ACHR sponsored the Rural Advancement Project and hired Black as its director. The Sharecroppers Fund agreed to offer technical support whenever he asked for such help. The ACHR had chosen Black for several reasons. He had connections to civil rights organizations, valuable experience in forming the Greenala Federal Credit Union, and knowledge of federal programs through his efforts to start the Hale–Perry County CAP. In his new position as the director of the ACHR's Rural Advancement Project, he planned to help local groups start credit unions and cooperatives, assist with school desegregation, organize antipoverty programs funded by OEO, and prepare for the 1966 ASCS elections.[63]

In assessing the first nine months of work in the Alabama Black Belt after the Selma to Montgomery march, many civil rights activists and local people realized that roadblocks would continue to be placed in their path as long as the political system remained the same. The governor and the state bureaucracy controlled too many aspects of the local government—voter registrars, the ability to obtain OEO funds, and the USDA farm programs, to name just three. Seeking remedies through the court system, although important, took a long time. Black people's greatest asset was strength in numbers. In several Black Belt counties, they made up a large percentage of the population. As fall turned to winter, local people involved in Alabama's civil rights movement focused on the spring primaries for the statewide elections, hoping that African Americans would win political offices. In the Black Belt, federal poverty programs would become part of the artillery used by both sides in the battle over political representation that began with the 1966 statewide elections.

CHAPTER FIVE

In the Rurals

The Civil Rights Movement, the War on Poverty, and the 1966 Statewide Elections in the Alabama Black Belt

When I talk about Black Power, I talk about black people in the counties where they outnumber [white people, working] to get together, to organize themselves politically and to take over those counties from white racists who now run it. . . . And then you can talk about integration. We are propertyless people in this country. . . . So we grasp that political power now and then we see . . . how we can work with that political power to then achieve economic power.
    Stokely Carmichael, 1966

If anything, the next period will be more serious and difficult than the preceding ones. . . . It takes very little imagination to understand that the Negro should have the right to vote, but it demands much creativity, patience, and political stamina to plan, develop, and implement programs and priorities. . . . It is here that we who advocate coalitions and integration and who object to the "black-power" concept have a massive job to do. . . . It is up to the liberal movement to prove that coalition and integration are better alternatives.
    Bayard Rustin, 1966

Social and political change through black enfranchisement had been the principal aim of the civil rights movement in the Alabama Black Belt. As the spring 1966 primaries and fall election approached, more direct efforts to prepare for the first post–Voting Rights Act election got under way. It was now time to harvest the hard work of the past three years, but the reaping would be done in conflict, not in unity, because the relationship between the Alabama staffs of the Southern Christian Leadership Conference (SCLC) and the Student Nonviolent Coordinating Committee (SNCC) had broken down.

Members of SNCC did not trust the established political parties—too much water had passed under the bridge. Both national parties seemed more concerned with other domestic issues and the war in Vietnam than in creating public policy that would assist those living in rural Alabama. "Negroes want a steam heated house, food on the table, and a decent education," Stokely

Carmichael explained, "but the nation isn't interested in that." Barry Goldwater's hawkish stance and lack of support for civil rights legislation tainted the Republican Party, and SNCC's list of grievances with the Democratic Party grew longer with each passing month. First, LBJ had refused to seat the Mississippi Freedom Democratic Party delegates at the 1964 National Convention until the party forged a compromise that pleased only a limited few. Second, many SNCC members felt that the Johnson administration moved too slowly in implementing the Civil Rights Act and the Voting Rights Act. SNCC especially criticized the U.S. Department of Education's overdue enforcement of the Civil Rights Act's Title VI to desegregate the schools and the U.S. Department of Justice's slow pace of placing federal voter registrars across the South—by 1966, only thirty-seven of more than five hundred eligible counties had received registrars. Finally, the obstructionist actions of the U.S. Department of Agriculture (USDA) further confirmed SNCC workers' suspicions regarding the Democratic Party. Instead of supporting the national parties, SNCC pinned its hopes on forming "freedom parties" that aimed to seize the reins of power on the county level.[1]

The staff of SCLC felt differently. "When SNCC goes around talking about a third party," Hosea Williams said, "we don't want no part of it." Many people in SCLC saw the national Democratic Party as offering hope because it had sponsored the Civil Rights Act and the Voting Rights Act. With strong ties to the Alabama Democratic Conference (ADC), SCLC wanted to transform the Alabama party by infiltrating the state organizations through the 1966 elections. For Williams, now director of SCLC's Voter Education Program, it all came down to numbers: "We are only thirty-five percent of the people in Alabama, and ten percent in the nation," he argued. "We can't go pitting race against race. We've got to take over the Democratic Party; we've got to take over the Republican Party." Both strategies had merit—SNCC's made more sense in the Black Belt counties, and SCLC's had more appeal on the state and national levels. Regardless of the value of each plan, both organizations had enormous mountains to climb because the opposition in Alabama continued to loom large. After failing to convince the state legislature to amend the state constitution to enable a governor to serve consecutive terms in office, Governor George Wallace decided that his wife, Lurleen, should run in his place. Predictably, the governor would use newly registered black voters as a key ingredient in his political demagoguery to see that Lurleen Wallace occupied the governor's office come November.[2]

Freedom Parties, Political Coalitions: Black Power, Alabama Style

SNCC took the first steps to implement its political strategy in the Alabama Black Belt, where it had been working with a fairly sophisticated organization. The Lowndes County Christian Movement for Human Rights (LCCMHR) had incorporated in November 1965 and began to make concrete plans to change the quality of life in the county, meeting every Sunday night in various places around the county. The needs of the people living in the tent city set up just outside of Lowndesboro had to be addressed, and living conditions there were quite bad. Each tent had only two beds and a rudimentary heating unit; the fabric walls did not keep out the cold and offered even less protection from white supremacists: "They're defenseless," SNCC worker George Greene stated. "Living in canvas tents, there is no possible way [a] bullet might be deflected." There was no running water, and the twenty families shared a single outhouse and cooking facilities. Despite the conditions, many residents remained in the temporary housing because they did not want to diminish the strength of the black vote in the upcoming elections.[3]

One way to remedy these housing needs was to seek help from the federal government. Members of the LCCMHR decided to reapply for an OEO grant, hoping this time to receive aid beyond the reach of the governor's veto. Immediately after incorporating, the LCCMHR set up a housing committee including locals William Cosby, John Hulett, Matthew Jackson, Arthur Johnson, Charles Smith, and Robert L. Strickland. Like the Wilcox County SCLC antipoverty committee, the LCCMHR's housing committee applied for funds for a self-help housing and training program for low-income seasonally employed farm workers under Title III (b) of the Economic Opportunity Act.[4]

The Lowndes County activists planned to offer fifty farm workers training in basic construction skills so that they could build homes for themselves by sharing in the labor. The beneficiaries would also receive basic education in home management, tool use and safety, community development, and citizenship. The members of the LCCMHR housing committee planned to serve as instructors for the program. Hulett and Strickland could teach carpentry and masonry, and Johnson wanted to act as the project's contractor and staff director. Ken Brown of OEO told Greene that "the applications from Lowndes County have been given triple A priority." Yet Greene still worried about the tent dwellers' ability to survive the winter before OEO funding became available.[5]

Members of the LCCMHR made their boldest move in late December 1965. Realizing that most of their community needs had to be fulfilled on the county level—public education, just law enforcement, paved roads, decent housing—they decided to form a new political party, the Lowndes County Freedom Organization (LCFO). A third political party would enable the activists to develop the means to address community issues at the county courthouse and witness the tangible results based on services delivered on a daily basis. The LCFO's members hoped that effectively using the local political structure would transform the county into the society they wanted. The Republican Party was basically nonexistent in Lowndes County, and white supremacists who had

Figure 10. A woman and child living in the tent city near Lowndesboro, Alabama, 1966. They were among twenty families who chose to stay in the county despite being evicted from their homes for participating in the civil rights movement. Photo by John F. Phillips.

no interest in accepting newly enfranchised voters dominated the Democratic Party. "We had to find some ways or means to get our own people on the ballot," Hulett explained. LCCMHR members also thought that if they won seats in the various county offices, they could more equitably distribute state and federal resources owed to the county. Taking this step made perfect sense to one Lowndes County farmer, who said, "We must use the vote to get out of the cotton fields, and we can't do that by voting for the boss man." The LCFO planned to nominate candidates for sheriff, tax assessor, tax collector, and the school board in the May primaries.[6]

Every political party in Alabama had to have a corresponding logo that voters could recognize. The LCFO took a provocative stand when it chose the black panther as its party symbol. Carmichael saw the panther as "a bold, beautiful animal, representing strength and dignity of black demands today." Hulett viewed the panther in defensive terms, describing it as "a vicious animal" that "never bothers anything" unless it is cornered. "We aren't asking any longer for protection," Hulett explained. "We won't need it—or for anyone to come from the outside to speak for us, because we are going to speak for ourselves . . . from now on."[7]

The choice of the black panther logo was tied up in the thorny issues of integration. Carmichael's experience in Mississippi and Alabama influenced his opinions about desegregation, which he believed would accomplish little for the poor, low-skilled, uneducated masses of the Black Belt. "The main result of [civil rights] protest has been an opening up of the society to Negroes who had one of the criteria for upward mobility," he wrote in the *New Republic*. In another article for the *New York Review of Books,* he reasoned that the plight of the masses in places such as the Alabama Black Belt and inner-city ghettoes would not change "until black people have power. . . . Then Negroes become equal in a way that means something, and integration ceases to be a one-way street." If a member of the LCCMHR was elected as the sheriff of Lowndes County, Carmichael envisioned that "even a Governor Wallace will have to deal with him." In Carmichael's reasoning, integration did not address the problems of poverty; it dealt only with the issue of skin color, usually in a despicable way, leaving black people with the concept that they had to forsake their communities to be desegregated. Thus, the symbolic strength of the black panther became more than a logo for voters to recognize; it reinforced the positive aspects of being an African American in the Alabama Black Belt. Regardless of how much sense it made to form the LCFO and use the panther as its emblem, these choices left the party open to attack from the Alabama Democratic Party and the coalition-oriented mainstream black voters who were not ready to venture so far out.[8]

Soon after forming the LCFO, members of the LCCMHR began preparing for the spring primaries. On January 3, 1966, several members filed a complaint in U.S. District Court against their county elected officials. The plaintiffs wanted the court to invalidate the 1964 general elections because no blacks, who comprised a majority in the county, were registered to vote at that time. The plaintiffs asked the judges to accelerate to 1966 the scheduled 1968 and 1970 elections for the members of the county board of revenue, the county superintendent of schools, the circuit judge, and the probate judge. A week later, Morton Stavis of the American Civil Liberties Union filed a lawsuit on behalf of twenty tenants and sharecroppers against thirteen Lowndes County landowners who had evicted their farm workers. He charged that the owners had "entered into a conspiracy with numerous persons . . . to intimidate, threaten, and coerce the Negro citizens of Lowndes County by evicting them or threatening to evict them from their homes and lands, denying them credit . . . and otherwise denying them their livelihoods" because they tried to register to vote. The plaintiffs eventually lost both of these cases, but bringing such issues to federal court proved that Lowndes County's blacks were not afraid to seek justice for themselves and confront two sources of white elite power.[9]

A month later, the LCCMHR won some important victories in the same courtroom. Federal district judges H. Hobart Grooms, Frank Johnson, and Richard Rives issued a permanent restraining order against the justice of the peace of Lowndes County, preventing him from trying Hulett on reckless driving charges. The court ruled that the justice of the peace had a direct, personal, and substantial interest in convicting Hulett, thereby denying him due process of law. Two days after handing down this ruling, the same court ordered in favor of the plaintiffs in *White v. Crook*. This case (a tangential product of Tom Coleman's trial for the murder of civil rights activist Jonathan Daniels) addressed the issue of black people denied the right to serve on juries in Lowndes County. The judges ruled that the Lowndes County jury commission and its clerk could no longer discriminate by reason of race or color in the selection of jurors. Judges Clarence Allgood, Johnson, and Rives also required the jury commission to place no fewer than one thousand names in the jury box at each refilling and directed that Alabama's qualifications for jury service—especially those relating to good character and sound judgment and the ability to read English—be imposed fairly and objectively in a nondiscriminatory manner.[10]

Lowndes County's white people of course reacted to the formation of the LCFO and the judicial decisions that favored the LCCMHR. The Democratic Party chair raised the entry fees on Democratic candidates for sheriff, tax assessor, and tax collector from fifty dollars to five hundred dollars and the entry fees for the board of education from ten dollars to one hundred dollars. He claimed the fee hike was necessary because "we've got a lot of opposition and the party needs more money to combat it with." His actions simply bolstered the LCFO's argument for the necessity of a third party. Members of the Ku Klux Klan also burned down the uncompleted new home of a member of the LCCMHR, and someone shot at Matthew Jackson's home near the tent city.[11]

In April the LCFO formally organized by electing officers, declaring candidates, and discussing plans for the May 3 primary. Hulett explained the reasoning behind the third party and its logo. He understood the criticism of the black panther symbol "because it implies there's no place for whites." "But things have been white for too long now," he told the audience. "Why can't they be all black for a while?" Strickland then discussed the complicated procedure that had to be observed to qualify as a third party for the November general election. Following Alabama law, on the day of the primary, fifty or more members of the LCFO had to convene in Hayneville, the county seat, to nominate one candidate for each open seat. To make sure that their efforts would not later be disputed, LCFO leaders decided that people should not vote in the May 3 Democratic primary if they wanted to participate in the LCFO nominating meeting. After candidates had been selected, the new third party would give the names of the nominees to the county registrar to be placed on the ballot for the November election. If LCFO candidates lost in the fall election but received 20 percent of the vote, the LCFO would become a bona fide political party under Alabama law. SNCC planned to encourage other Black Belt counties to follow the LCFO's lead and form freedom parties to run candidates in the May primaries.[12]

The LCFO, its black panther logo, and its members' assertive use of the federal court system sent shock waves through black and white communities across the state. More mainstream black leaders knew that their dream of a bloc vote of newly registered African Americans now stood in jeopardy. Albert Turner worried that the LCFO could hurt the candidacies of moderate white and black candidates in other parts of the state. Orzell Billingsley of the ADC and Hosea Williams, SCLC's voter registration and political education director, responded negatively to the Lowndes County community's independence, seeking to shore up their own power bases. To the average white Alabamian, words such as *black panther* and later *Black Power* easily conjured up fearful images of "black rule" from the mists of the collective memory of Reconstruction. Wallace too used the LCFO to agitate his anxious followers and strengthen his wife's run for the governorship.[13]

Billingsley's commitment to the national Democratic Party remained strong. When John Cashin and Charles Morgan Jr. wanted the ADC to form a statewide third party in late 1965, Billingsley resisted their idea in favor of giving the Alabama Democrats a chance to integrate their party. He focused on changing

VOTING

What is the vote?

VOTING IS THE WAY A CITIZEN CHOOSES PEOPLE TO REPRESENT HIM IN HIS
COUNTY, STATE AND FEDERAL GOVERNMENT. WHEN A CITIZEN VOTES, HE SPEAKS
FOR HIMSELF ABOUT THINGS THAT CONCERN HIS OWN WELFARE.

Why vote?

IF YOU DON'T VOTE, YOU GIVE UP YOUR RIGHT TO DECIDE FOR YOURSELF
HOW YOU WANT THINGS TO BE DONE IN YOUR GOVERNMENT. YOUR VOICE NEVER
GETS HEARD IN POLITICS IF YOU DON'T VOTE.

How does voting work?

FIRST, YOU HAVE TO BE REGISTERED. THIS MEANS YOU HAVE TO GO TO
HAVE YOUR NAME PUT ON A LIST ALONG WITH OTHERS WHO WANT TO VOTE IN
ELECTIONS IN YOUR COUNTY OR STATE. THEN YOU MUST PAY THE POLL TAX.

Can YOU vote?

YES. ANY PERSON CAN BE A QUALIFIED VOTER IF HE OR SHE IS AT LEAST
21 YEARS OLD, HAS LIVED IN THE STATE AT LEAST ONE YEAR, IN THE COUNTY
SIX MONTHS AND IN THE PRECINCT THREE MONTHS.

Figure 11. To gain support for the Lowndes County Freedom Organization, SNCC published a guidebook that resembled a civics lesson in the elements of participatory democracy. It explained the essentials of voting and politics and the benefits of taking part in the electoral process. 1044.1.45, Selma Inter-Religious Project Papers, Birmingham Public Library Department of Archives and Manuscripts, Birmingham, Ala.

the Alabama Democratic Party's logo, a white rooster with a banner that read, "White Supremacy for the Right." The Birmingham lawyer began his campaign in his own community. Meeting in secret with Jefferson County Democrats loyal to the national party, ADC members voiced their complaints about the party's logo in late December. In early January 1966, ADC members and party loyalists from across the state gathered in the Parliament House Motor Hotel in Birmingham to hammer out a deal. The dozen ADC members convinced the group, presided over by Judge Roy Mayhall, chair of the state Democratic Executive Committee, that between 170,000 and 200,000 black voters would not support the Democratic Party unless the motto changed. By mid-January, the stage was set for the final showdown. Governor Wallace tried to persuade the loyalists to retain the logo, but when he realized he would not prevail, he backed off. His states' rights friends made one last attempt to sway the group. "You are destroying the Democratic Party of Alabama today," argued Henry Sweet of Bessemer, calling it "a sad time" to change the party label "under pressure from radicals, and anarchists, and street walkers." The change narrowly passed by a vote of thirty-nine to thirty-two. One loyalist commented that the "third party down in the Black Belt" had pressured the white Democrats to make a move. "We cannot afford to take a stick and run off 150,000 to 170,000 people who might vote for us," commented Charles McKay of Sylacauga. The Alabama Democrats—loyalists and ADC members—agreed to keep the rooster and change the motto to "Democrats for the Right." After the meeting adjourned, one committee member asked another, "Are you running for anything?" "Yeah," the other answered, "the state line."[14]

In the wake of his success, however, Billingsley could not harness the winds of change that blew through his own organization. He did not survive a power struggle that developed at the April ADC convention. Members split over whether to endorse Richmond Flowers, the state's attorney general, or Democratic Congressman Carl Elliott for the governorship. Before the primary vote, Joe Reed, a protégé of Rufus Lewis, who had worked in the Montgomery Improvement Association during the Montgomery Bus Boycott, called for a new election of ADC officers, and Billingsley was voted out as the group's leader. The convention chose Lewis as chairman and Birmingham's Peter Hall as vice chairman. Even though both men were Elliott supporters, the delegates endorsed Flowers. Reed's call for a leadership change signaled the end of an era for the ADC as Billingsley's tenure came to an end.[15]

In the spring of 1966, the ADC took another hit, losing its status as the voice of Alabama's black vote. Williams called a meeting in Selma to form a state-wide confederation of black voter organizations that could ensure a bloc vote in the 1966 primaries. "We must let the Negro vote hang there like ripe fruit,"

Figure 12. The logo used by the Alabama
Democratic Party prior to 1966.
1044.1.45, Selma Inter-Religious Project
Papers, Birmingham Public Library
Department of Archives and
Manuscripts, Birmingham, Ala.

he told the group, "and whoever is willing to give the Negro the most freedom can pluck it." He envisioned the SCLC-sponsored confederation serving as a patronage clearinghouse. Candidates could exchange jobs and political favors for endorsements. Leaders from eleven Black Belt counties attended this first meeting and agreed to form the new coalition. Williams viewed the confederation as a way to push the ADC into the background. "They don't have the ear of the masses," he said, "even in the city." Williams imperiously reported that black voters felt more loyalty to SCLC than to any other organization in Alabama. "The person who registered them controls them," he said. "As far as I'm concerned we've got the Black Belt sewed up tonight." His hubris would ultimately blind him to the difficulties of electing black candidates.[16]

Williams named the new association the Confederation of Alabama's Political Organizations (COAPO). Although he helped to organize the group, Williams vociferously claimed "this is not an SCLC organization." The COAPO's raison d'être, however, displayed characteristics of Williams's overbearing personality. "We've got to say, 'White folks, what you going to give us?' We've been selling our vote all along," Williams reasoned. "Now we've got to sell it for freedom." His secretary kept all the records for the group, and a month after the election of officers, Williams continued to set rules for the confederation and to promote certain candidates for office. The COAPO would be run by three elected committees, one to interview candidates to see what they could do for black voters in Alabama, one to decide which candidates to support, and the third to dispense the anticipated political favors and jobs after the election. The new group began recruiting local leaders across the state, some of whom had been working with Billingsley's ADC. Fifteen counties across the southern half of the state sent representatives to the COAPO's second organizational meeting. The third meeting drew people from twenty-six counties. The participants elected Rev. T. Y. Rogers of Tuscaloosa as president. Adopting a militant tone, Rogers said that the COAPO would be looking for candidates "who will really represent us at the local and state levels in this land which is rightfully ours." He said that the COAPO offered something new in black leadership. "We formed this organization because we were tired of being led by men who told us one thing and told the white power structure something else." Rogers called on all blacks to vote like they were "upset," continuing, "and we're gonna vote together this time." Although leaders of this organization spoke with a new voice of black unity, the substance of their words sounded much like the traditional practice of southern politics. This was a long way from the transformation of the political system that SNCC leaders had envisioned.[17]

Rogers's call for a unified vote would be difficult to achieve. The COAPO did not include representatives from Lowndes County or Macon County (home of Tuskegee University), and SNCC, the ADC, and the older State Coordinating Committee for Registering and Voting did not agree with SCLC's approach. Some members of SCLC's Alabama staff also did not go along with the COAPO plan. Shirley Mesher, SCLC's project director for Selma, questioned the value of joining with the COAPO and established political parties. Her attempts to bring an antipoverty program to Dallas County brought to light continued divisions not only between the black and white communities but also among the different classes of African Americans. In the aftermath of this struggle over federal funds, a third political party would organize in Selma, too. At the center of Alabama's civil rights struggle, the various Black Belt strategies for the 1966 elections appeared in bold relief.[18]

The Economics of Black Power: The War on Poverty Comes to Selma

After the spring 1965 Selma to Montgomery march, civil rights activities died down in the Dallas County seat. As in other parts of the Alabama Black Belt, schools, restaurants, and hotels remained segregated. Even the voter registration drive slowed before the SCOPE project started in the summer. The torpor brought an uneasiness to the community that had put so much on the line just a few months earlier. Selma mayor Joe Smitherman held a series of Wednesday meetings between white and black leaders two months after the march in an effort to find common ground to end the divide the spring demonstrations had wrought. The African American attendees presented the mayor with seven demands. By the end of May, the group had stopped meeting. "The segregation-ists thought that Negro demands were too militant," David M. Gordon reported. "The Negroes felt that the whites were not sincere." Selma's blacks had reasons to doubt the mayor's candor.[19]

In March, Smitherman had applied for an OEO community action grant with an all-white governing board and only tentative plans for a biracial policy committee. These actions shut out precisely the people who needed the most assistance from the War on Poverty. When Randolph Blackwell visited the city in early May, he reported back to SCLC headquarters that local black people were "confused, divided, and often hostile towards the SCLC." Many missed the strong presence of Martin Luther King Jr. "Oh, if Dr. King could only stay here we'd have no problems," lamented Mary Lamar. "Dr. King is a second Moses. And he could come here and say, 'We're going to all march in the Alabama River,' and we'd all do it." By July, more confusion arose within Selma's black community after a grand jury indicted Rev. Frederick D. Reese, the chairman of the Dallas County Voters League (DCVL), on charges that he had embezzled $1,650 from his organization.[20]

King sent Rev. Harold Middlebrook to Dallas County to try to reassemble the Selma movement. Shirley Mesher, a white woman in her midthirties who had grown up in Seattle, joined him as an SCLC field staff member. SCLC's Selma staff occupied an office one floor below SNCC's Alabama headquarters at 31½ Franklin Street, where Doug and Tina Harris, Susan and Elmo Holder, Janet Jermott, Silas Norman, Martha Prescott, and Willie Emma Scott worked. The SNCC activists concluded that the DCVL had not done a good job of represent-ing the needs of the local people and made plans to work outside of Selma in the rural parts of the county. Sharing office space near these young people influenced SCLC's approach in Dallas County. Much work remained to be done. In 1960, 65–70 percent of all county residents lived in poverty, and 85–90 percent of the black population eked out a living on less than three thousand dollars a year. The Census Bureau classified only 46 percent of the houses in the county as sound and 25 percent as dilapidated. Sixty-six percent of the county's rural areas had African American residents, while the city of Selma had a population that was 49 percent black. Many observers believed that effective political participation might enable Dallas County's black citizens to change some of these harsh living conditions. Both SNCC and SCLC staffers began to reach out to assist mem-bers of the black community in changing the area's traditional way of life. These activists believed that the issues that needed to be addressed were the structural consequences associated with poverty—racial discrimination, educational defi-ciencies, unemployment, declining opportunities in agriculture, substandard housing, neglected infrastructure, lack of health facilities—not the individual characteristics of the rural folk tagged as mired in a culture of poverty.[21]

SNCC began organizing in East Selma to help people there address the problems in their neighborhoods. "Basically," the Harrises and Jermott explained, "we believe that voter registration alone can't begin to deal with many of these problems." Tina Harris had met a woman named Mrs. Strong in jail during the spring demonstrations, and the East Selma resident offered her backyard to the SNCC staff for meetings. They organized the East Selma People's Convention so that people could plan ways to improve their community. Doug Harris emphasized the need to stop waiting for "leaders" to make decisions; rather, residents had to solve their own problems. The East Selma organization invited the area's city councilman to talk about the lack of city services in the neighborhood and subsequently sent representatives to the city council meeting to make sure he correctly reported the results of their assembly to the city government.[22]

For the next year, SCLC's Selma office buzzed with activity, much like the city's SNCC headquarters. In September, SCLC staff—in particular, Mesher—began to organize an antipoverty committee to counter the mayor's all-white program. They worked through Dallas County's rural churches, distributing handbills, visiting farms, and attempting to contact every poor person in the county. Earning twenty-five dollars a week from SCLC, Mesher initially lived with families in the community and tried to organize around issues that local people wanted addressed. This process brought her into contact with A. D. Bush, Joe Johnson, Pearl and Will Moorer, and Clara Walker, among many others. She later explained that she "appreciated how smart those people were out in the rurals, how much it took to get by when they had nothing."[23]

During the fall months, civil rights organizations in Selma applied to the USDA to serve as the local representative to distribute surplus commodities. Faced with this expression of African American autonomy, Dallas County elected officials agreed to support the food program, and the result was the first federal food distribution center in the Alabama Black Belt. Mesher often sent letters on behalf of needy people to the county commodity supervisor, trying to convince him that they qualified for the free food.[24]

SCLC promoted Mesher to Selma project director in early 1966. She continued her efforts to represent local people in their pursuit of equal justice, often clashing head-on with white business leaders. In the spring of 1965, moderates within the Chamber of Commerce viewed industrialization as the path the county should follow in the wake of federally enforced civil rights legislation. The Dan River Mills textile company located in Selma in September 1964, and the Hammermill Paper Company arrived the following February. Historian J. Mills Thornton has noted the logic behind this plan: "moderates" sought to balance the black and white populations so that African Americans could not dominate the area politically. Selma's city attorney, McLean Pitts, argued that "attracting industry to Selma, and the new white voters who would follow it, was the most effective way of dealing with the threat of black [voter] registration." In mid-February 1966, Mesher filed a complaint about discriminatory hiring practices at the Dan River Mills, asking the Labor Department to investigate whether the textile mill violated the 1964 Civil Rights Act when it refused to hire trained African American spinners and weavers but instead employed untrained white workers. Her actions brought unwanted publicity to Selma, and she became a fly in the ointment of white city leaders' business plans.[25]

Mesher also began to learn about USDA programs that could assist Dallas County's sharecroppers and tenant farmers. Many of these black farmers knew that federal programs existed to help with the development of agriculture, but they did not know the names of these programs or the specific ways they operated. "I would go day after day, learning from the farmers about programs," she remembered. "I didn't know what they were called. They didn't know what they were called, but they knew what the program was." Through this work, people in the rural part of the county began to hear that they could get assistance in the SCLC office. "I'll never forget," Mesher recalled, "the two big guys who came up the stairway and into the office." They asked her to come out to the plantation owned by J. A. Minter in Tyler "to meet with the people . . . in their church." SCLC workers learned that these farmers "had cotton, they had corn growing up to their doorsteps, and they never got the payment for it." As part of his agreement with his tenants, Minter required that farmers sign over their cotton allotment checks from the ASCS cotton program. According to Arthur Brown and Elijah Green, they "couldn't stay on the land if [they] didn't sign over [their] subsidy check[s] to him." Rev. Francis X. Walter helped take affidavits from Minter tenants for use in a lawsuit. He remembered feeling physically threatened when he went out to their rural church: "I know there were some edgy nights cause Minter was very, very angry. . . . They had guards out . . . and nobody knowing whether or not somebody was going to shoot" into the church. Mesher eventually found legal representation for the tenants through the Lawyers Constitutional Defense Committee (LCDC) of the American Civil Liberties Union and tried to find them a place to live and work when Minter evicted them.[26]

A year after she started working in Selma, Mesher reported to SCLC that eleven thousand black people had registered to vote in Dallas County; that every rural community in the county had been organized, with meetings held once a week to discuss problems; that she had counseled people on matters of welfare, federal housing, and federal farm programs; that the LCDC had decided to set up an office in Selma; and that a free-lunch program had been established for children attending county schools. Many of these local people had not participated in the earlier civil rights campaigns in the region prior to 1965; this change reveals how the civil rights movement had the capacity to inspire and change people—in this case, both Shirley Mesher and the local people. Initially, Mesher recalled, "these people had not registered, they hadn't voted. They hid in the bushes when the march went by. They didn't participate in anything. And that was true largely of the rurals. The rurals were largely untouched." But when the people living out in the county came forward, the SCLC activist found them to be "much stronger than the people in the city. . . . They knew adversity." One woman said that she had learned a great deal from Mesher during her first year working in the rural areas, to which Mesher replied, "'No, Mrs. Harris, I learned it from you.' And she said, 'Oh, but we didn't know we could tell it.'" Mesher's relationships with local people sustained her: "I have no idea what kept the people going, but they kept me going," she explained, "because there were many times I can assure you that I was very down, very low." Much of Mesher's organizational work grew out of the communitywide effort to start a CAP in Dallas County.[27]

From the beginning, the bid for antipoverty funds in Selma faced problems as a consequence of community divisions along not only racial lines but along social lines—between the various classes of African Americans residing in Selma and out in the rural parts of the county. Harold Middlebrook first sought information on CAP from the USDA in late July 1965. As other SCLC volunteers talked up the idea of an antipoverty program among county residents, Rev. F. D. Reese of the DCVL spoke out against these actions. Chuck Fager, an SCLC volunteer, reported to Randolph Blackwell in SCLC's Atlanta headquarters that the DCVL had "announced that no projects are to be initiated or even meetings scheduled, without prior consultation with them." Fager wanted to make his position clear to Blackwell in case altercations arose later with the DCVL. Reese had taken similar stands as part of his effort to serve as the Dallas County black community's political power broker in Selma. After SNCC conducted the East Selma People's Convention, he told the citizens of Ward 5 that they had "no right to go off on their own without consulting him." Ignoring Reese's domineering style, however, Middlebrook formulated a plan for winning OEO funds for Dallas County by the fall. He created the Dallas County Economic Employment Opportunity Committee, which, Middlebrook said, would "take over the white folks' program—which we think is very good—add our own proposals to it, and submit the whole thing to OEO." The next challenge involved bringing in white people from Selma to join the SCLC effort.[28]

At the second organizational meeting held in October, William Zierden, a field representative from OEO's southeast regional office, came down to oversee the process and answer any questions. Because of the mayor's obstinate behavior,

Zierden's office decided to give technical support to the SCLC plan, with the idea of funding single-purpose programs that would not need the backing of the city or county governments. Zierden urged the participants to "not let the race problem stand in the way of the anti-poverty program." The SCLC anti-poverty committee asked thirty white people to come to the gathering. Seven accepted, including Arthur Capell, managing editor of the local newspaper, the *Selma Times Journal,* two city council members, and the superintendent of the Selma schools. At the end of the evening, Rev. Ernest Bradford, who chaired the committee, put several of the white attendees on the spot, asking them to tell the group how they would help in the antipoverty effort. Most of the whites present agreed to join one of the antipoverty committees and gave a statement of support for the program. By November, the mayor challenged this biracial committee that had begun to encroach on his territory.[29]

On November 4, Smitherman sponsored a public meeting at the Selma Armory to discuss the War on Poverty program and to reveal his ideas for creating a biracial committee. Black and white people attended, but few of those present were poor. The mayor announced his complicated plan. He wanted eleven men from the black community to select fifty African Americans to serve on the county's one-hundred-person antipoverty committee. Smitherman announced that he and the probate judge, Bernard Reynolds, would have final approval of the fifty black representatives. Smitherman and Reynolds would then choose a thirty-five-member board of directors from among the one hundred members of the antipoverty committee. The board of directors would control the money for the programs. Many African American attendees thought that the mayor's concessions sounded like the familiar tune of the white power structure maintaining its hold over the black majority. When black leaders balked at his plan, Smitherman told them, "You've got to start somewhere with good faith. This is the key to it. Until proven otherwise, I think this is the route we should take." The black community had good reason to be suspicious of the mayor. In August, the *Southern Courier* had reported that he told the delegates of the Alabama League of Municipalities that the way to avoid civil rights conflict was by "building up leadership among local Negroes to keep the civil rights people from taking over." Before the spring 1965 unrest in Selma, Smitherman had tried his hand at this strategy. He called in three Selma black men and told them "we would build them up as leaders." All three left his office, never to return. By mid-November, however, things had changed so much in the city that Smitherman now found a willing participant in the DCVL's chair, Reese.[30]

The SCLC-led antipoverty committee regrouped for a third organizational assembly at the Greene Street Baptist Church on November 9. This time, more poor black people attended. Rev. Reese told those gathered that he favored the mayor's plan. Not surprisingly, Rev. Bradford disagreed with the DCVL leader, and the meeting broke up before any decisions were made. Rev. Walter, who also came to the meeting, recorded his thoughts in his journal: "Many more prosperous Negroes (I guessed) wanted to accept. From the acknowledged accurate report of the meeting between Mayor and committee of this group I don't see how anybody could accept his proposal." Walter also thought "Alabama Public Safety men and/or [Alabama Bureau of Investigation] men" took pictures of the demonstration, and "I was an attraction as a new and unknown face." The SCLC-led group, now going by the name Self-Help against Poverty for Everyone (SHAPE), tried to convince Smitherman to change his plan. A week later, about one hundred SHAPE supporters held a protest march that began at the First Baptist Church and proceeded to the probate judge's office and the mayor's office. Neither public official met with the marchers, but those gathered read a statement of their grievances outside the courthouse and carried placards stating their positions. A mass meeting followed that night. On December 4, two dozen SHAPE members met with the mayor and suggested that people elected at mass meetings manage the program. The SHAPE representatives wanted "NO formal education requirements" for board members: it was "*not* necessary that a person be able to read or write" to serve. The only requirement was that "people in the area feel that the persons they select will faithfully and fairly represent their interests and do a good job." Smitherman dismissed the group members, telling them that he would study their plan.[31]

Four days later, SHAPE met to hammer out a complete strategy for selecting a board of directors. In addition to representatives of the traditional governmental, public welfare, and nonprofit organizations, SHAPE wanted to include representatives of the poor, an equal number of city and rural residents, and white and black people in numbers that reflected their percentages of the population. After the areas and numbers of people to serve from each community had been set, SHAPE held neighborhood meetings in which local people elected their representatives to the board of directors. SHAPE's plan took to heart the OEO mandate of "maximum feasible participation of the residents served." An OEO official later commented that SHAPE's method "led to the most effective elections by the poor that have been held in the South, and perhaps in the nation." SHAPE members thought they had executed a good plan. The board would include members from the middle class and the poor as well as from government and social welfare groups. Under the SHAPE proposal, the community action agency (CAA) would have been composed of 155 people, 90 blacks and 65 whites, numbers that reflected the county's population (58 percent black, 42 percent white). Poor people would have a larger voice than had ever before been the case.[32]

In a December 15 letter, Bradford asked the mayor to reconsider the structure of the antipoverty committee and to attend a meeting with other members of the white community on December 20 at the Selma Holiday Inn. Bradford called Smitherman to see if he planned to accept SHAPE's invitation. "He told me a meeting would not be granted to me," Bradford said, "but only to people of good faith." Smitherman wrote to SHAPE and explained that he regarded SHAPE's membership as "representative of a segment of the community" but not as "being 'broad base' in the overall concept of the Office of Economic Opportunity." Furthermore, the mayor thought, a broadly based organization had to be assembled before anyone could discuss the CAA's structure. "I think that the only guidelines necessary at this point [are] an understanding by both the Negro and white communities that each will have equal representation from top to bottom in whatever structure evolves," he told Bradford. The mayor closed his correspondence by letting Bradford know that SHAPE's efforts would be disregarded. He planned to form an antipoverty committee after January 1 "without further reliance upon your organization, as such to provide recommendations for the Negro representation on it." SHAPE had failed to create a biracial program supported by both the African American poor and city and county elected officials.[33]

The SHAPE members moved on with their plans. "We won't try to make contact with him any more," Rev. Bradford said. "There might be meetings with other representatives of city and county government, but I'm not saying yes." The mayor and OEO's southeast regional office moved on, too. An official with OEO's Inspection Division later reported that "when it became apparent that no meeting could be held, Atlanta began working more closely with the Mayor, who had agreed to go to any reasonable length to get a program." Atlanta OEO officials planned to hold an open meeting to elect sixty representatives of the community who could sit down with sixty representatives of the mayor's office and thus work out a solution with the regional office. SHAPE complained to the antipoverty agency about this meeting, and an OEO representative reported that he told the SCLC activists that they could elect people to this committee, just as anyone else could. But this person had also been told that "SCLC, SNCC, and the other way out groups just don't have the support of the majority of the Negro population." Echoing the attitude found in other Black Belt counties, one of the southeast regional office administrators snidely remarked that the OEO representative in Selma doubted "that SCLC could get even one bus-load of Selma Negroes to ride to Washington in their behalf."[34]

The divisions within Dallas County's black community became more clear at a January 18 SHAPE meeting. Father J. P. Crowley of the Catholic Society of Saint Edmund Mission, located in Selma, announced that Smitherman's plan must mean that the mayor was now ready to form a biracial group with "no strings attached." "Once they get together," the Catholic priest naively argued, "the mayor will have no control over it." He thought this new approach would give white liberals "a chance to raise their heads." Rev. Bradford had a different interpretation: "The mayor hasn't done anything so far without being pushed." One middle-class African American said, "We don't think people who make under $4,000 a year can go downtown and talk to the mayor. We don't want them to represent us." Not surprisingly, the impoverished black people at the meeting distrusted their better-off neighbors.[35]

Rev. P. H. Lewis of Brown's Chapel African Methodist Episcopal Church chaired the nominating committee that chose the delegates for the compromise sixty-person group. Twelve people on his list had no previous connection to SHAPE. Others complained that Lewis's committee chose delegates on their behalf when local meetings could not be organized. Flabbergasted by these events and remarks, Mesher pointed out their ramifications: "It is ironic that the poor black people are now hearing from the black middle class the same thing they heard from the white power structure." Because of these decisions, SHAPE split. Those who agreed to attend the meeting with the mayor diverged from those who wanted to apply to OEO without the support of city and county officials. This division could be summed up by the statements of Mesher and Rev. J. D. Hunter. "The purpose of the whole program is really that people do things for themselves," Mesher told the group. "Nobody is trying to shove the poor people out," Rev. Hunter replied. "But when I go to court I want a lawyer, and when I go to church I want a preacher." Hunter implied that he thought someone from the middle class should speak for the black community in meetings with the mayor.[36]

According to Walter, the conflict within the black community over the antipoverty program involved issues of leadership style. His assessment reveals how much had really changed as a result of the black freedom movement. Community leaders before the struggle for civil rights came to the region had intended to maintain their positions after the Selma campaign ended. "I don't want to take away anything from a man like Reese who's suffered personally, who could be killed any time or hit over the head or put in jail," Rev. Walter explained. "When the tide went out, they felt they had to consolidate. And what were they going to do now? Well economic things, register to vote, try to get political structure set up." Walter reasoned that these activists thought they could accomplish these goals only by strengthening their leadership and providing assurances that they "are going to be the leaders in this community." Men such as Reese and Lewis had in mind leadership qualities established before 1964. "And that . . . was an error," Walter noted, "because the movement had brought to the common Negro the idea . . . of a mass meeting, where the group makes the policy. And the idea of the open meeting in the Negro church . . . was just unheard of."[37]

Another important part of the old form of leadership included the idea of allegiance to the leader. "You show loyalty to the organization by showing loyalty to the leader. And that one of the ways you show loyalty to the leader is by unquestioning loyalty, unquestioning obedience," Walter explained. "If he's the one who keeps the books, and he says the money's all accounted for in a meeting, you just don't stand up and say, 'Well, I'd like to examine the books' or 'I'd like to question that.'" Under this structure, a slippery slope of blame easily developed. "Then the leader can stand up and say, 'You do not back the XYZ improvement association because you question me and therefore you don't back the civil rights movement and therefore you don't back Martin Luther King and God, . . . so sit down.'" Walter remembered hearing that many months after the march to Montgomery ended, a man "from the country" stood up in a meeting and disagreed with a prominent black minister in Selma. The minister's response included an insult about the man's use of English. "He stood up and said, 'You don't even know how to talk good English.' In other words, 'How can you have an opinion about that?'" Those present at the meeting told Walter that the audience booed the minister. "Well, that's what the movement did," he clarified. "This is a mass movement, of course how this happens nobody ever knows, but the decisions are made by the whole group, no closed meetings, and then the idea [that] the fellow of the rural could stand up, and he could say for the first time in his life, he could stand up just like any preacher and voice his opinions and his opinion carried just as much weight because he had discovered that he was a man. Well, if you're an old-time leader, how do you make the adjustments to this new kind of stuff? And I think that's what happened . . . and why people got put off in Selma." Walter defined the group-centered leadership style "personally by the personality of Shirley Mesher," which created conflict with the traditional black leaders in the city. "You've just got automatic conflict, fireworks and everything else," Walter surmised.[38]

SNCC and SCLC's renewed activities in Dallas County had created a flash point within Selma that threatened to reignite the smoldering coals from the previous spring that had not been completely extinguished. The *Selma Times Journal* made sure that if Smitherman made any compromises in accordance with SHAPE's demands, his actions would be viewed as capitulation and a step in the wrong direction. The editors of the local newspaper threatened to withdraw their tentative support for the program if it did not stay in the hands of elected officials. Their willingness to back the antipoverty program hinged on the cooperation of city and county officials working with OEO to organize a program to benefit the entire area. "From the start, unfortunately, there have been brazen efforts by individual SCLC and SNCC professionals to torpedo any structure that failed to place their man—a Negro preacher named Bradford—in a position at the elbow of those who dispense the goodies," the newspaper complained. "This, of course, under the ever watchful eyes and outstretched palms of SCLC and SNCC." The newspaper warned of dire consequences if members of civil rights organizations sat on the CAA. "The question is whether Sargent Shriver has any business helping to shake up anybody else's city hall," the editors announced to their readers. "The question is also whether, in the name of local flexibility, Mr. Shriver should help impose federally financed revolutionary movements that could become, given enough money, local quasi-governments." In this charged atmosphere, the mayor put together a biracial CAA with the help of OEO's southeast regional office. Smitherman's actions effectively divided the black community between those people willing to work with him and those who continued to distrust his motives. Lewis and Reese withdrew their support for SHAPE and started holding separate meetings with the mayor.[39]

By the end of March, a CAA had been formed with a forty-eight-member board. It had an equal number of black and white members, with one-third coming from public and private agencies, one-third from private leadership, and one-third from the poor. Lewis and Reese chose the sixteen poor members from among the ninety-eight representatives previously elected by SHAPE, telling an OEO inspector that they picked "those with whom they felt they could deal most effectively." Although four of the sixteen had supported Bradford, they were now completely outnumbered on the new CAA. Smitherman did not sit on this board, but probate judge Reynolds did. The mayor kept his finger on the pulse of the new organization by placing his friend, thirty-four-year-old Joseph S. Knight, in the executive director's chair of the new Dallas County–City of Selma CAA. Knight admitted to OEO officials that he would remain loyal to the mayor.[40]

To no one's surprise, SHAPE protested the creation of the new CAA. The grassroots organization complained that its initial work had been taken over by the "white power structure with their chosen minute faction of the Negro community" with the official sanction of OEO's regional office in Atlanta. "We protest all of this and more on the grounds of DISCRIMINATION against the Negro and against the poor," SHAPE angrily stated in its long letter of complaint. The protest seemed to fall on deaf ears in the OEO Washington headquarters because achieving a biracial group with local government support took priority over establishing a truly autonomous, integrated, multiclass organization. After an investigation, OEO officials concluded that Smitherman's committee looked good on paper: "It includes political leadership, charitable and service organizations, civil rights leaders, and representatives of the poor elected from all areas of the county." From OEO's perspective, a breakthrough had been achieved—an integrated antipoverty program in the city that stood out as one of the nation's icons of racial hatred and polarization. "This CAP is probably the only one in the South in which the militant civil rights leaders will sit on the Board of Directors with the power structure," OEO inspector Robert L. Martin reported to his boss in Washington. It is not clear how much Martin knew about the internal leadership struggle taking place within the black community. Lewis and Reese could indeed be called militant leaders in the context of the Selma to Montgomery march. Brown's Chapel had served as the movement's head-quarters during the spring campaign, and Reese led the local civil rights organization in Selma and lost his job as a science teacher as a consequence of his activism. Yet much had transpired since March 1965. When OEO confronted issues brought up by Bradford and Mesher, officials in the antipoverty agency blamed the two activists for being unable to negotiate. "Miss Mesher is aware that OEO funded the Child Development Group of Mississippi—a non–power structure, civil rights oriented group, and cannot be persuaded that conditions which dictated formation of CDGM do not exist in Selma," Martin relayed back to Washington. "Her reasoning is that SHAPE unquestionably represents the Negro poor, and that OEO will not fund a program which is positively opposed by the poor." By papering over the sharp differences within the black community, OEO's actions helped spark a third-party movement among those black people who had been left out of the new community action agency similar to the Lowndes County Freedom Organization.[41]

The actions taken by members of the DCVL against SHAPE reinforced SNCC's desire to create a Dallas County freedom organization that would become a third political party, as in Lowndes County. Not surprisingly, Mesher and SCLC's Selma office supported the idea, too. In mid-March, about one hundred people gathered to form the Dallas County Independent Free Voters Organization (DCIFVO) and elected temporary officers. Most of the third party's supporters came from the rural areas where black people more significantly outnumbered white people than was the case in the city of Selma. Their experience organizing SHAPE paid off in the creation of this independent political party. Participants chose Clarence Williams for party chairman. He was a shop steward at the Curtis, King and McKensey Products Company, the first unionized plant in Selma with a black voting majority, and set up a base of "soul folk" that SNCC contacted in its effort to organize the county. A. D. Bush, Mary Jane Sims, and Nathan Payne rounded out the new party's board; all but Sims had been elected to the original SHAPE board before the mayor's plan commandeered it. Those attending the meeting also chose the party's slogan and symbol, a black-and-white diamond in a circle of chain with the words "Strength through Unity." Although not as provocative as the LCFO's black panther, this image conveyed the message of black political independence. Because of her political activism, Sims's landlord evicted her and her brother from their home.[42]

At the organizational gathering for the new party, many attendees voiced their disappointment that the twenty-year-old DCVL was not running African American candidates for all of the county offices in the upcoming May Democratic Party primaries. Shortly after Reese agreed to work with Smitherman on the antipoverty program, Circuit Judge L. S. Moore dropped the charges pending against the minister for misusing funds contributed to the DCVL. Many in the black community wondered if Reese's legal problems contributed to the DCVL's decision to back Selma's police chief, Wilson Baker, for Dallas County sheriff in his bid against the notorious incumbent, Jim Clark. The DCIFVO members also thought that registered black voters would not be in a majority in time for the May 3 vote but might be for the November general election, thereby enhancing the chances of electing black people to office through a third party. Finally, the motivations for a new political party stemmed from the DCVL's middle-class nature. "We find that people out in the rurals have never heard of the Dallas County Voters League," Williams told a reporter, but many people had been contacted through SHAPE's earlier work and could be recruited again to support the third party.[43]

To mark the first anniversary of the Selma to Montgomery march, the DCIFVO sponsored an April 11 Freedom Rally at the National Guard Armory. Comedian Dick Gregory addressed the crowd and spoke in support of the third-party movement. He warned listeners not to fall for the argument that voting for Baker would be giving their support for "the lesser of two evils." Gregory illustrated his point in graphic detail: "If a man has a choice between marrying a girl that's a prostitute seven days a week and one that's only a prostitute on the week-ends, he might decide to take the lesser of two evils," the comedian quipped. "But even if he takes the week-end prostitute, he's still married to a whore." Gregory also criticized Reese for attacking the Dallas County third-party movement in the local newspaper. "Watch out for the preachers. Captain'll double-cross you with the Bible when it's his rent gotta be paid," Gregory warned. SNCC's Julian Bond also participated in the rally, and Stokely Carmichael and John Hulett came over from Lowndes County to lend their moral support. In defense of their bold move, Williams commented, "People say this is black democracy and that that's bad. But how could black democracy be any worse for us than the white democracy we've been living under for the last 100 years?"[44]

Speakers from various Dallas County grassroots organizations also addressed the crowd, reinforcing the third-party effort by proving that people from rural communities could make changes for themselves outside of the political mainstream. Bradford told those present about his experiences dealing with white elected officials. He said that his organization had been formed by "the Negro people themselves," but he blamed the mayor's biracial committee for handpicking as Dallas County's representatives in the War on Poverty only those African Americans who would be "responsive to the whites." Pearl Moorer then told those gathered about the Dallas County Farmer Movement, which was trying to address the needs of evicted tenants who refused to sign their allotment checks over to their landlords, such as those from the J. A. Minter plantation, including Moorer's husband, Will. Documentary filmmaker Jack Willis captured Pearl Moorer giving such a speech in his film, *Lay My Burden Down*. Addressing a crowd of about seventy-five people, she said, "Y'all just might as well get ready to get right side me. I'm fightin for y'all; I ain't fightin for myself." "Y'all just might as well get ready to get some nerve," she admonished, "if you have to, get you a drink of whiskey. . . . [T]hat will get your nerve up, . . . and say, 'I'm goin on with Mrs. Moorer.'" She took the men in the mass meeting to task. "We're gonna stand up, and we want these men to stand up and be men." She mocked those who talked bravely while in their own communities but "when the white man come around," she said, crossing her arms and lowering her head, "be like 'Yeah, sir, boss.'" She wanted the people to get organized. "The thing for us to do, us got to get movin now cause the time is drawing near."[45]

Five days after the rally, SNCC sponsored political workshops in a variety of Dallas County communities, including Brantley, Everdale, Potters Station, Sardi, Selma, and Selmont. Participants discussed the legalities of forming a third party following Alabama law and decided that weekly meetings would be held in each area until the May 3 primary. DCIFVO supporters also printed flyers to explain the details of forming the third party and the reasoning behind the political movement. "The white people will not help us win control of our government. They will not give us candidates to vote for who will work for our welfare," one handbill proclaimed. "The Democrats will not represent us. They will give us Jim Clark and Wallace over and over again if we let them, or they will give us Toms who will work for them, not us. We have to choose our own people, if we want to win." The announcements also encouraged people to "talk to everybody we meet," so that they would understand the plans for Dallas County. Williams was not completely satisfied with the help he received from SNCC. Complaining to Cleveland Sellers in Atlanta, Williams wrote, "We don't need people we have to train like James Patterson and wife, Bill Hobbs, or people like Gloria Larry and Stu House, whom you can't get to go out in the county and work, or when you need transportation—you can't find them, this we cannot afford." He also felt neglected by the SNCC Atlanta office. Since February 1966, SNCC had only four cars in Alabama, which explained the origins of Williams's frustration. "People find themselves in new counties without any possible way of moving back and forth across the county," George Greene told Stokely Carmichael and James Forman. "One of the major problems is that people at this point have not gotten contacts in the community where they can get community people to carry them around or will let them borrow the cars. The workers then find themselves stranded in one community because they are unable to move freely." Nevertheless, the DCIFVO took what help it could and did its best to prepare for the May 3 primaries.[46]

Days of Reckoning: The 1966 Elections

People had risked life and limb to participate in the election process, and now the day of reckoning approached. Much was riding on the spring primary, the first statewide election since the passage of the Voting Rights Act. Independent party supporters, interracial coalitionists, and traditional white supremacists hoped the primary would strengthen their respective positions within the state's political system. In most Black Belt counties, African Americans appeared on the primary ballot alongside fellow white Democrats, but in three counties— Dallas, Greene, and Lowndes—independent third parties held organizational meetings on the day of the primary to place candidates on the November ballot. In the Democratic primary for governor, Richmond Flowers campaigned as a racial moderate against First Lady Lurleen Wallace, whose political position was clear since she ran as her husband's stand-in. The attorney general hoped the newly registered black voters across the state would give him the edge he needed to defeat his opponent.[47]

The divide between the political strategies of SCLC and SNCC, now firmly established, came out publicly during the run-up to the May primaries. Despite Mesher's position in Selma, most SCLC members campaigned openly against the third-party movement. Some people made this criticism part of their own campaigns for office. Albert Turner, who ran for state representative, told a mass meeting in Perry County that "SNCC doesn't register voters, doesn't care about registering voters" and blamed the young civil rights activists for splitting the black vote. As the SCLC's Alabama director, Turner also lobbied against the freedom organizations in other counties. SNCC labeled his tactics "black-baiting" because he tagged freedom party supporters with outrageous accusations. In an attempt to scare voters away from the third party, Turner claimed that SNCC workers had chased SCLC staff members out of Greene County at

gunpoint. In late April, Martin Luther King Jr. announced his plans to conduct a seventeen-stop tour through Alabama to rally people to vote in the primary, meaning that he did not back the third-party drive. Andrew Young went
to Dallas County in an attempt to bridge the gap between the coalitionists in
the DCVL and the third-party supporters of the DCIFVO. He spoke of the
rift in the Selma black community as a family argument and tried to convince
third-party supporters to vote for Baker and Flowers because SCLC saw a difference between these candidates and their opponents. Reese did not agree wholeheartedly with SCLC's peacekeeping effort because it trespassed on his political
turf. When Hosea Williams distributed sample COAPO ballots throughout
Selma, Reese dispatched people to intercept the leaflets and destroyed them.
For different reasons, Carmichael stated clearly that he did not back the SCLC
coalition plan, describing "asking a Negro to join the Democratic Party" as akin
to "asking a Jew to join the Nazi Party." Carmichael also criticized SCLC for
running Democratic candidates because he thought most black voters were not
"politically educated enough" to pick out black candidates from a long Democratic ticket.[48]

SCLC backed Democratic candidates in Autauga, Barbour, Bullock, Choctaw, Dallas, Greene, Hale, Macon, Marengo, Perry, Sumter, and Wilcox Counties for the offices of tax collector, tax assessor, sheriff, county commissioner,
board of education, and Democratic Executive Committee. Turner ran for Place
1 in the Alabama House of Representatives race for the Twenty-seventh District (Marengo, Perry, and Sumter Counties), and Sumter County NAACP chair
Rev. F. N. Nixon campaigned for Place 2 in the Twenty-seventh District. Lonnie
Brown of Alberta was the only African American to run for the State Senate,
aiming for Senator Roland Cooper's seat in the Nineteenth District (Clarke,
Conecuh, Monroe, and Wilcox Counties). The night before the primary, LeRoy
Randolph from the Pine Hill precinct in Wilcox County gave members of his
church many reasons to elect one of their black neighbors to office. "We've been
on the outside of the mainstream for America's life. We've been on the outside
of society. We've been on the outside of education. We've been on the outside of
jobs," he told them at a mass meeting. "But we can change that tomorrow. All
we got to do is get some black faces over there." His encouraging words were
full of hope for what the newly registered voters could bring. "I don't want you
to march tomorrow. But I want you to make some Xs tomorrow, and make it
beside those Negro names. Because we are tired of the white man's power. We
are tired of being called 'nigger.' We're tired of being the last hired and first fired.
We're tired of all the injustices that the white man been putting on us. So let's do
something about it tomorrow. Just put some Xs beside those boys' names."[49]

Greene County seemed to offer a good chance for success: the thirty-four hundred registered black voters far outnumbered the two thousand white voters on the rolls. Rev. Thomas Gilmore, SCLC's project director, ran as a Democratic candidate for sheriff against incumbent William E. Lee. "The reason I want to be sheriff," Gilmore explained, "is to give my children and the rest of the children in the Negro community somebody they can look up to without being afraid." The candidate sounded a conciliatory tone: "I'm not looking for any trouble. When someone has to be arrested, I'll call him up and ask him to come in. I'm not planning to go gunning for anyone," he said. The two men had faced off during demonstrations in Eutaw during the summer and fall of 1965. Alberta Branch ran for tax collector, Rev. Percy McShan campaigned for tax assessor, Rev. Woodson Lewis Jr. sought to join the Democratic Executive Committee, and Rev. Peter J. Kirksey pursued a seat on the board of education. Kirksey said that he wanted a position on the school board because "after working with the civil rights group here, my boy was thrown in jail for four days. I couldn't get any consideration from the school officials or the board. After I got him out, I decided if there was someone on the board, some of our people, maybe we'd get more consideration." Yet as primary day neared, SCLC workers in the county decided to cover all their bases by having the black Democratic candidates also be the nominees from the area's SNCC-backed third party. This move guaranteed that black people would appear on the November ballot. The Greene County Freedom Organization agreed and nominated the same African American candidates when supporters met on May 3 to form their party.[50]

In Dallas County, the divisions created by the formation of the Dallas County–City of Selma CAA continued to play a role in the spring political campaign. The DCVL supported black Democrats for the various county offices except sheriff, where the league backed Selma's police chief, Baker, against Clark. Rev. Lewis campaigned against B. V. Hain for Hain's Twenty-eighth District seat in the state House of Representatives. Following the Alabama Code for forming a third party, thirty members of the DCIFVO met on primary day to put together a slate of candidates to appear on the November 3 ballot. Samson Crum, a postal worker who lived in Selmont but worked in Birmingham, agreed to run for sheriff. Nine other people, including two members of the original SHAPE board of directors, came forward to seek county positions. The Dallas County third party also nominated two candidates, Jimmy L. Stanley and Pearl Moorer, to run for the Alabama House of Representatives from the Twenty-eighth District.[51]

In Lowndes County, the LCFO had a monopoly on black candidates. The new party planned to run nominees for most of the county offices but faced a

Figure 13. Rev. Thomas E. Gilmore (right) campaigning for Greene County sheriff on the Democratic Party ticket, 1966. © Flip Schulke/Corbis.

difficult task. The Black Panther Party had to convince interested members to stay away from the Democratic primary and instead vote exclusively at its nominating convention. As the members of the new party gathered, a young SNCC activist spoke to the determined crowd of mostly middle-aged people dressed in their Sunday best—hats, jewelry, ties, dresses, pressed shirts and slacks, and clean overalls. "I don't care nothin when the first thing they say is 'I was raised with a Negress. I grew up with colored folks.' That's right, you grew up with them." "That's right," he reminded them. "You out there working in some cracker's field when some of you ladies in there takin care of that white nasty baby." The SNCC worker rallied his listeners to transform their community: "You've got to change that. Right now you've got the power. You've got the power." He then led the crowd in a movement song. To the tune of "The Battle Hymn of the Republic," the assembled people sang, "The Movement's Moving On." The last verse captured the spirit of the momentous day:

> Many noble dreams are dreamed by small and voiceless men
> Many noble deeds are done for righteous to depend
> We're here today, John Brown to say
> We'll triumph in the end
> And our movement's moving on.

All of those in the crowd joined their voices together to sing the chorus, creating a sense of unity:

> Move on over or we'll move on over you
> Move on over or we'll move on over you
> Move on over or we'll move on over you
> And the movement's moving on.

Although this was a political rally, the mood was not jovial or lighthearted. Instead, this was a day for serious action.[52]

SNCC reported that more than 850 of the county's 2,000 registered black voters cast ballots for freedom candidates. Some of the office seekers ran provocative campaigns. Running for tax assessor, Alice Moore told a crowd at Mount Moriah Church, "Tax the rich to feed the poor—that's my slogan." Moreover, she reasoned, "If everyone had been taxed their share we'd have better schools and good roads today." Sidney Logan Jr. said that he had wanted to be sheriff "ever since the deputy stood in the [courthouse] doorway and said, 'Go home,'" during the voter registration drives of 1965. The LCFO also placed five other candidates on the November ballot: Frank Miles Jr. for tax collector; John Hinson, Robert Logan, and Willie Mae Strickland for board of education; and Emory Ross for coroner. Anticipating the worst and with the murders of Jonathan Daniels and Viola Liuzzo still fresh in many people's minds, some LCFO affiliates prepared to protect themselves during the nominating meeting. "I remember when that minister got shot here," recalled a sixty-seven-year-old World War I veteran. He told a reporter, "We gonna protect our friends this time," pulling three shotgun shells from the pocket of his overalls.[53]

The results of the May 3 primaries disappointed many African Americans. In some precincts voting irregularities surfaced. In Selma, voting officials placed black stickers on votes cast by African Americans. Clark locked up six boxes containing more than sixteen hundred ballots from black neighborhoods, charging that he had found them unattended and that they thus should be discarded as tainted goods. In Greene County, white people who had moved out of the county years earlier and who were no longer on the voting rolls appeared at the polls and cast ballots. SCLC reported that some employers "suggested" that their black workers vote for Wallace and Lee. Voting officials in Greene County prohibited illiterate black voters from using sample ballots and instead instructed them on how to cast their votes, sometimes against their wishes. Voting officials in Wilcox County moved one polling place from a main road to Harvey's Fish Camp, a white-owned cafe and bait shop far off the paved roads, making it difficult to both find and reach. When Robert Crawford reported for duty as a poll watcher in Pine Apple in Wilcox County, state election inspectors

Figure 14. Voters cast their ballots for Lowndes County Freedom
Organization candidates, May 3, 1966. Both men are wearing hats
and starched white dress shirts under their overalls, indicating the
seriousness of the occasion. The Black Panther logo appears on
their ballots. © Flip Schulke/Corbis.

forced him to leave. Crawford, however, located federal observers, who over-ruled the Alabama officials' decision and had his position restored in time for the election.[54]

The results of the primary served as a hard lesson in politics. Even a black majority in a county did not guarantee an African American candidate's election. "It's going to take some time for the vote to change anything in Wilcox County because really our peoples are still divided here," LeRoy Randolph explained. "They still go by largely what the white man says. They've grown accustomed to being afraid of the white man and just going on and being afraid of him." Some black Democrats lost close elections: Gilmore lost to Lee in the race for Greene County sheriff by just 297 votes. In several contests, black Democrats received enough votes to advance to the May 31 runoff, but when those ballots were counted, twenty-two more black candidates had lost, leaving only four African Americans remaining on the Democratic ticket for the November election. In Macon, Lucius D. Amerson became the first African American to gain the Democratic nomination for sheriff of an Alabama county, while L. A. Lock-lair overwhelmed his opponent for tax collector and Harold W. Webb barely took the District 1 Board of Revenue seat. Kirksey stood for the school board in Greene County, where the schools were not yet desegregated. Also in Greene, Gilmore and McShan, who had lost in the primary, got their names to appear on the Greene County Freedom Organization ticket for the November elections. In Dallas County, the U.S. Justice Department filed a complaint against Sheriff Clark's actions with regard to the six boxes of ballots. Judge Daniel Thomas ruled that those ballots must be counted, clearing the way for Baker's victory over Clark. Finally, six African Americans won seats on Choctaw County's Democratic Executive Committee. Only in Lowndes and Dallas Counties, where the third-party movement was strongest, did significant numbers of black candidates remain on the November 3 ballot. Despite losing Greene, Hale, and Macon Counties, Wallace dashed Flowers's hopes of being elected governor, taking 52 percent of the overall vote and thus avoiding a runoff.[55]

Governor George Wallace attempted to derail the Black Panther Party train in time for the fall election, hoping to boost his wife's chances against her Republican opponent, Congressman James Martin. The local people involved in the civil rights movement would have to face the governor's actions without the strong presence of SNCC and SCLC. After the May primaries, King shifted his focus northward to Chicago, and by June only a skeleton SCLC staff continued to work in Alabama. The largest number of SCLC activists would remain in Selma under the direction of Stoney Cook, but if Mesher's experience was any indication, Cook would receive little assistance from the organization. In her year-end report to the SCLC board of directors, Mesher complained that she

Figure 15. George and Lurleen Wallace on the campaign trail in Mount Meigs, Alabama, 1966. Although Lurleen Wallace is running for office, her husband is speaking to the crowd, an indication of the accepted belief that Lurleen Wallace would be governor in name only. The all-white audience expected entertainment at these events, as the pedal steel guitar on the stage indicates. Birmingham Public Library Department of Archives and Manuscripts, Birmingham, Ala. (portraits collection).

did her work in the Dallas County seat with no staff and no financial assistance from the Atlanta headquarters. "This lack of support quite often gets down to not having paper to write on," she complained. "This kind of frustration seems unfair and unnecessary[,] [w]hen there is yet so much work to be done." Mesher resigned from SCLC but remained in Selma, working independently in shared office space with LCDC attorneys, who came to Selma in June at her urging.[56]

SNCC also began reorienting its overall goals as a result of discussions during a May 8 conference at Kingston Springs near Nashville. Inspired by Carmichael's successes in Lowndes County, the SNCC executive staff elected him chairman. SNCC's gain would be Lowndes County's loss, because Carmichael relocated to Atlanta and turned his attention away from the local movement. As he took on a national persona, his manner would become more provocative and at times even jeopardize his hard-won accomplishments in Alabama. For example, he announced that for the November election, SNCC planned to bring to the Alabama Black Belt observers from Watts in Los Angeles and from Chicago's South Side. SNCC maintained a thirteen-person Alabama staff through the summer and early fall, but by the November election, doubts had arisen about whether anyone from the organization would remain in the state.[57]

As SNCC's chairman, Carmichael joined other civil rights leaders in Mississippi to continue the "march against fear" that James Meredith had begun in early June but had abandoned after he was shot and injured by Aubrey James Norvell. Meredith had initiated the march "to challenge the all pervasive and overriding fear" that still characterized Mississippi. Meredith wanted to convey that black people could safely register and vote, and after he was attacked, other civil rights leaders took up his march to prevent violence from stopping his message. On June 16, after being released from the LeFlore County jail, where he had been held after being arrested for camping without a permit, Carmichael addressed a large crowd, telling them, "This is the twenty-sixth time I have been arrested. I ain't going to jail no more." He told them that their demands for freedom for the past six years had gotten them nothing. "What we gonna start saying now is 'black power.'" He repeated the slogan, and each time the crowd shouted it back. Three days later, Carmichael appeared as a guest on the CBS program *Face the Nation,* where he clarified what he meant by Black Power and pushed the federal government to enforce its civil rights laws, especially in the upcoming fall elections.[58]

He explained that in Lowndes County, black citizens outnumbered their white neighbors four to one and "are going to try to achieve taking over the power structure according to the democratic processes in this country." When asked if he advocated violence, Carmichael responded a bit ambiguously: "I don't organize around violence or nonviolence." He later reiterated, "I have never rejected it." The upcoming elections represented a crucial juncture in the civil rights struggle, and Carmichael believed that the federal government had a responsibility to ensure that the people of Lowndes County could participate in free and fair elections. "Now if this country neglects to do that then it seems to me that the responsibility of assuring free elections lies in the hands of the black people in Lowndes County and anybody else in the country who is willing to have free elections there." Although he used a confrontational style, Carmichael's message was really an endorsement of the fair practice of democracy by people who had been denied it for too long.[59]

James Doyle of the *Boston Globe* asked the twenty-six-year-old activist to explain what he meant when he said during the Meredith march that "every court house in Mississippi should be burned down tomorrow so we can get rid of the dirt." Carmichael began his answer by explaining that Mississippi's black people had never received justice from their state's courthouses, from the murder of Emmett Till in the 1950s to Meredith's recent shooting. He then explained that his statement was meant as an analogy, that black people should get "rid of the people inside those court houses." He wanted Black Power to convey that "in the counties where black people outnumber white people in the majority . . . they have the right to organize themselves politically and . . . via the vote seize the power." Every time the interviewer asked Carmichael if he believed that black people should resort to violence if they could not get what they wanted otherwise, he answered unequivocally, "On the contrary. I have never said that." Carmichael wanted to make clear that the Voting Rights Act could bring real change for the black southerner, who "now has at his disposal via the voting rights bill political power. He grasps that political power and then he starts through that, seeing what terms he can use. He controls the CAP Board . . . if he has the political power so that the chief of police of Indianola, who is the chief of police last year that beat up black people, who is now the CAP director in Sunflower County, Mississippi, will not have that power." Now that black citizens were armed with the right to vote, the civil rights struggle would no longer operate solely by moral persuasion but would be backed up by political power.[60]

Carmichael's friends in Lowndes County asked him to be more prudent. Alice Moore admonished him to "do more work and les[s] talk, for you have done a good job here and we really want to see you move on." She asked that he plan his speeches with the entire SNCC staff lest "you hurt yourself, SNCC and also Lowndes County." "You must try to listen to us now for you know that we do care about you and want you to know it," Moore wrote. Carmichael reassured Moore, telling her that he had decreased his attention to the LCFO because "now I speak for SNCC and the tone has to be different." Overlooking her suggestions that he stop being so provocative, he told Moore not to worry about what she read in the newspaper "because most of the time I haven't said that."[61]

No matter how much he explained himself, Carmichael could not control how others interpreted or used the Black Power slogan. What some listeners heard as a motivating message to become involved, others heard as a violent message to "get whitey." Metaphors of burning courthouses could be deciphered as literal commands, and the longer laws went unenforced, the higher frustration levels mounted, affecting the way people understood the slogan. This roving definition came to light when OEO revealed that it would grant the Title III funds to Lowndes and Wilcox Counties. Governor George Wallace used Carmichael's connections to the Alabama Black Belt and the Black Power slogan against the two antipoverty programs.

In this charged atmosphere, OEO took some risks in funding programs in the Black Belt; however, the agency's integrity stood on the line because poverty undeniably engulfed the region. On June 28, Sargent Shriver announced that his office intended to give scaled-down Title III (b) grants to Lowndes and Wilcox Counties. The Anti-Poverty Coordinating Committee of the Wilcox County SCLC received $302,081 for the educational portion of its proposal. Dr. Robert Green, SCLC's director of citizenship education and a professor at Michigan State University who had published articles on adult literacy, became the staff director for the Wilcox antipoverty effort. The Wilcox County SCLC planned to hire teachers fired for their participation in the civil rights movement as instructors for the family education program. OEO also awarded $240,640 to the LCCMHR to teach reading, writing, and math skills. William Strickland, the group's vice chairman, felt that OEO's approval also represented an endorsement of his organization: "The government realizes that we are not radical or extremists as some newspaper columnists and others have said." Although OEO funded a narrower program than the original self-help housing plan, Strickland felt hopeful about what the federal support meant for the county. "Getting the grant shows that the federal government is concerned with the welfare of the people in Lowndes," he said.[62]

SCLC had been lobbying OEO to approve the grants since March. The holdup seemed to revolve around the interpretation of Title III (b) and whether it could be used for tenants and sharecroppers. Samuel Yette, the director of OEO's Civil Rights Division, warned Shriver that "if we do not fund them our reasons should be sound enough to withstand considerable criticism and agitation." The Black Belt grants represented the first time the agency had used the broad interpretation of the farm workers program. Aware of George Wallace's history of blocking antipoverty programs that he could not control, Shriver's press release described the two grants innocuously, explaining that both programs sought to prepare unskilled workers for anticipated new industries coming into the region, such as the Millers Ferry Dam and the Dan River Mills. "In this two-county area," Shriver emphasized, high poverty levels and low education rates made "programs for adult education and pre–vocational training" necessary so "that the seasonal farm workers can participate in the expanding economy." When questioned about civil rights organizations' connections to the two grants, an OEO spokesman replied that officials had concluded that "the organizations have a much wider base and purpose than just civil rights." Right after OEO announced its approval of the Lowndes and Wilcox plans, a member of the Inspection Division reported that local newspapers in both counties had reported favorably on the antipoverty grants.[63]

On July 18, Wallace spoke out against the OEO grants. He claimed that the antipoverty agency had circumvented the law by funding programs in the Black Belt through Title III rather than Title II, which he could veto. With the November election just over three months away, the governor complained that

the grant to the Wilcox County SCLC had gone to "a group which has created turmoil, strife and disharmony since its organization." He claimed that "its
sole interest, as shown by the application, seems to be to establish Black rule in
Wilcox County." Wallace told Shriver that the OEO money essentially "would
be subsidizing a partisan political activity bent on establishing 'black power' in
Wilcox County." He used similar logic in opposing the Lowndes County grant.
"The Lowndes County Christian Movement for Human Rights, Inc. is closely
associated with the 'Black Panther Party,'" Wallace warned. This "party advocates 'Black Power' not only in Lowndes County, Alabama, but in the entire
nation." Using a report compiled by the Alabama Legislative Commission to
Preserve the Peace, Wallace laid bare what he saw as suspicious connections
linking the LCCMHR to the LCFO and its leaders to Stokely Carmichael. In the
governor's logic, every word uttered by the SNCC chairman provided further
proof of the sinister motives behind the Lowndes County civil rights organization and thus the antipoverty program it planned to operate. "I repeat," Wallace
emphasized to Shriver, "through unorthodox procedures your office is making
a grant to a group which advocates 'Black Power,' violence, turmoil and disorder, bordering on treason, in this nation." He wanted to send the OEO director evidence and documentation to back up his claims. For example, the Peace
Commission report professed to have certifiable proof that Carmichael planned
on "November 8, 1966, to create in Alabama, through the use of 'the toughest
Negroes in Chicago, New York, Watts, Philadelphia, and Washington' a situation calculated to create riot, lawlessness, and possibly bloodshed."[64]

Wallace continued to lash out at the Black Belt antipoverty programs in a
televised press conference aired across the state on July 19. He focused his criticism exclusively on the Lowndes County grant, repeating the arguments he
had used in his complaint to Shriver but adding the extreme claim that "the
founders and leaders of the 'Black Panther Party' constitute the leadership of
the 'Black Power' movement in this country." He used the old Cold War tech-
nique of creating fear through guilt by association, claiming that the LCCMHR's
poverty program had ties to SNCC leaders such as Carmichael, James Forman,
John Lewis, and Cleveland Sellers, "all of whom are people who are well known
for having fed the seeds of discord and strife throughout this country." Wallace then said that Carmichael had called for Black Power on national television during the "so-called Mississippi march" and had "indicated that he is not
opposed to the use of violence to accomplish his 'Black Power' purposes."[65]

Having linked the LCCMHR antipoverty grant to national SNCC leaders,
the governor then proceeded to smear the people of Lowndes County, alleging that Hulett served as the president of the Black Panther Party and signed
the incorporation documents of the LCCMHR. Wallace then dragged out

Strickland's murder conviction from the 1940s without giving any context: "Robert L. Strickland is a convicted murderer and has served time in the penitentiary," he warned his viewers before describing both Hulett and Strickland as close associates of Carmichael. These scathing accusations bolstered his claim that OEO was indeed financing "those who advocate actions which border on treason." In classic Wallace style, he claimed to be outraged at this evidence of a "breakdown of law enforcement authority and the basic principles upon which our society was founded" before closing by stating that his office had informed OEO of these associations prior to the announcement of the poverty grants. As a result, this folly could be attributed to the antipoverty agency's incompetence.[66]

The governor's demagoguery had its anticipated effect. He could stand upright as the defender of Alabama against the federal government and its support of "black rule" while subliminally reminding voters that this defense could continue under his watchful eye if Lurleen Wallace became governor. One of his aides reassured his colleagues in the Wallace administration that the governor's calculated response hit the anticipated target, telling Cecil Jackson Jr. and Hugh Maddox that the administration was gaining politically "as a result of Lowndes Wilcox publicity." He continued accurately, "As a result of the Lowndes-Wilcox press conference you received miles of national press and T.V. exposure." Wallace's supporters drank up the elixir he poured out to them. A physician from Mobile praised him for protecting Alabama: "You are a remarkable man, and we admire you for your courage! The stand you have taken with the Poverty Program is heart warming!" A couple from Collinsville were proud of the governor and of the state. Another supporter asked God to "guide and strengthen [Wallace's] every effort for a clean government." Beyond serving his own political ambitions, the televised statement also stymied the antipoverty program in the Black Belt. The governor had no veto power over the two Title III programs, but the widespread publicity had virtually the same effect.[67]

A cry of protest arose across the state against OEO's actions. The *Alabama Journal* could not believe the federal antipoverty office would have made such a blunder by mistake unless it was "so heavily infiltrated with black Kluxers that it knew exactly what it was doing." The *Birmingham Post-Herald* asked whether program participants would "be instructed in reading and writing or . . . in how to demonstrate and protest?" The Birmingham newspaper called on Wallace to fund a state-operated program for the illiterate people of the Black Belt. For three days, Montgomery's WSFA-TV editorialized about the antipoverty applications, warning of the serious nature of the governor's charges and asking for an investigation of the matter. The NBC affiliate later deduced that "at best, the federal allocations in question appear to be a muddled mess of improper planning and inadequate administration." On the third day of opinion giving, Channel 12 said that things would get better "when civil rights organizations start leading Negroes instead of lashing out at whites." Wallace clearly had struck a chord and had set the tone of the debate. Newspapers as far away as Dallas, Texas, and Muncie, Indiana, reported on the governor's actions. The *Dallas Morning News* opined that Alabama could have used the money but that Wallace's actions also might "have averted the financing of mob rule. The sacrifice appears amply justified," the conservative Texas editors reasoned.[68]

U.S. senator Lister Hill received telegrams from white constituents who expressed deep concern over the grants. One woman from Lowndes County told Hill that "Robert Strickland . . . and his wife have a most truculent, discourteous, and arrogant attitude toward white people" and passed on rumors that "Strickland has been heard to say that he will shoot to kill." Moreover, she wanted her senator to know, "Strickland and his wife openly associate with Stokely Carmichael. Their house periodically teems with strangers, both Negro and white, people unknown to this community and county. . . . I understand he has quite an armory in his home." She suggested that if OEO funded the Lowndes County program, the same amount of money should be sent to the Republican and Democratic Parties. She pleaded for Hill to do something soon: "We are in a state of shock."[69]

The mayor of Lowndesboro sent a petition signed by seventy-seven people urging Hill to "prevent this quarter of a million dollars being funded to the LCCMHR which is a Civil Rights organization dedicated to creating black-power, anti-white chaos in this area." The senior senator suggested that Shriver reconsider the grants because of the "political involvement of the organization, the background of its Director, and the fact that the project was not coordinated through local and State officials." He asked Shriver for a detailed report. State senator Roland Cooper of Camden charged that the Wilcox County SCLC was "not representative of the people of Wilcox County" and that all but one of its board members were also SCLC members. "One of the purposes of SCLC in Wilcox County," he claimed, "is political activity. They voted as a bloc here in the primary elections." Republican U.S. representative Glenn Andrews wanted to know why OEO had funded the grants when the boards lacked white representation. Martin, the Republican gubernatorial candidate, also took a swipe at the program, stating that the Wilcox and Lowndes County grants were "typical of the abuse" in which Democrats were engaging throughout the country "to build political machines." He suggested that the only way to stop "this abuse and misuse of the people's money" was to defeat Lyndon Johnson and Hubert Humphrey. "You have got to remember," he told the *Birmingham News*, "that this is the whole outline and platform of the Democrat Party to take money from hardworking taxpayers and squander it on socialistic programs."[70]

"Man, This Ain't A Hangin'—It's A Resurrection."

Figure 16. Governor George Wallace demonized the Black Power
aspirations of Black Belt residents with his complaints about OEO's
funding of the Lowndes and Wilcox County antipoverty programs.
The exposure the governor received in the national press and on
television pleased Wallace's advisers. This political cartoon drawn by
Bill Mauldin of the *Chicago Sun Times* was reprinted in the *Alabama
Journal* on August 9, 1967. Copyright 1967 by Bill Mauldin. Courtesy of
the Mauldin Estate.

In addition to these shrill outcries from Alabama, Shriver received dire warnings from OEO's southeast regional office. Confidential sources informed him that if the two Black Belt antipoverty programs received federal aid, Alabama would fight OEO in Congress and on national television. Alabama officials (probably the Peace Commission) claimed to have more photographs, affidavits, letters, and other materials documenting Black Power and "Communist link-up allegations" and threatened to release those materials to the public. Bureaucrats in OEO's Atlanta office did not back the program. James May, OEO's regional official responsible for the state, told an Alabama newspaper that he had known about the potential problems in Lowndes County for weeks but that no one in Washington seemed interested. Frank Sloan, OEO's southeast regional director, asked Shriver to consider the other sixty-five counties in Alabama before he agreed to fund the Lowndes and Wilcox County grants: "At the present time we have been informed that all new programs in Alabama are being scrutinized by the Governor's office with the hope of embarrassing the Office of Economic Opportunity and then vetoing the projects." He suggested that white people be brought into each of the antipoverty programs before any money was transferred. Shriver had to take seriously these threats, especially since they could be used against the antipoverty program in the upcoming election cycle. He felt that OEO had been caught flat-footed. He wanted facts on the situation in Lowndes County and expressed his disappointment that the agency had not received them prior to announcing the grants.[71]

The day after Wallace's televised press conference, the OEO director answered the accusations. Shriver thanked the governor for his communications and announced that he had ordered an investigation of all of Wallace's allegations and objections. He also said that since no funds had yet been disbursed, they would be held pending the completion of an investigation. Shriver rebutted the governor's accusations point by point, trying to take the sting out of Wallace's charges. He pointed out that no other governor had criticized the Title III programs operating in their states and noted that both the Wilcox County SCLC and the LCCMHR had been formed a year before "the so-called 'Black Panther Party' came into existence" and were chartered under Alabama law to "provide assistance for poor and needy families." The need remained great in both of these counties, Shriver explained. Lowndes County was Alabama's poorest (twelfth in the country), while Wilcox County ranked as the state's third poorest (twentieth in the country). In closing, Shriver confronted Wallace's actions head-on. "I feel that it is unfortunate that Governor Wallace has equated this self-help and training program with social and political movements he dislikes." Shriver clarified that "OEO has regulations restricting political activities by any recipients of OEO money," and he reassured the governor that those regulations would be enforced. Wallace refused to comment on the suspension of funds from the two antipoverty programs but must have been pleased with the outcome of his calculated grandstanding. He had limited the strength of the Black Belt movement that had been trying to parlay economic power into political action.[72]

OEO's Inspection Division conducted its investigation of the Lowndes and Wilcox County grants over the next few weeks. The LCCMHR's chair, Hulett, wrote a memo to the members of the organization clarifying the situation. He told them that Wallace sought to keep federal money out of the hands of people he could not dominate. "Who will control the lives of black people in Alabama?" Hulett asked. "Will it be the whites who have been controlling our lives since we were born? Or will it be us?" In Lowndes County, he stated plainly, "WE . . . DO NOT INTEND TO LOOK IN GOVERNOR WALLACE'S FACE OR ANYBODY ELSE'S TO SEE WHETHER HE OR SHE IS VEXED OR PLEASED." Hulett called on the LCCMHR members to remain unified: "If we are not for ourselves who can be for us?" Shriver received telegrams of support for the two programs from Martin Luther King Jr., the Alabama Council for Human Relations, Lewis Black, and the Selma Inter-Religious Project. By the middle of August, OEO officials had made their decision.[73]

Shriver received advice from his top officials in the Community Action Program, the Inspection Division, and the Office of Civil Rights. CAP director Theodore Berry recommended that the grants be held until a director for each had been found. He also reiterated that membership in a political organization had not disqualified other people from serving on CAP governing boards in other parts of the country and consequently should not be used as a basis for rejecting a proposal in Alabama. He saw the LCFO as a "by-product of the racial exclusion procedures of the Alabama Democratic Party" and reasoned that the Lowndes group did not endorse violence but instead supported the right of the majority to control their own future. He also thought bringing Strickland's criminal record into the mix was irrelevant. Berry concluded that if OEO denied funds on this basis, "It would show the very people we are trying to help across this country that their past mistakes will never be forgiven." He even offered the Title III program in Lowndes his office's technical assistance so that it could become a "model for the teaching of adult literacy" in the Deep South. Members of the Inspection Division suggested that the two boards of the LCFO and the LCCMHR antipoverty committee remain separate, forcing Hulett, Sidney Logan Jr., Frank Miles Jr., and Strickland to choose on which board to serve. Edgar May, the director of the Inspection Division, also wanted to bring in an independent auditing firm to review both grantees' operations, and he thought OEO should have some input into the choice of staff directors for both programs.[74]

In Wilcox County, the main issue of contention involved getting the white people who had initially agreed to sit on the Wilcox County SCLC antipoverty program board to continue to serve in the wake of Wallace's attacks. As early as July 27, Shriver felt confident enough about this program to state, "I'm ready to announce Wilcox County immediately!" Although he ultimately waited, Shriver felt certain enough about both programs to release the grant funds. In a nod to political considerations, however, he did not distribute the money until after the November elections.[75]

As OEO conducted its investigations, both communities continued to prepare for the November elections without the boost of the poverty programs, just like most other Black Belt counties. The African Americans who remained on the November 8 ballot had to fight voter apathy as a result of the fact that the ballot offered few black candidates and encourage people to vote even though there were few chances to elect African Americans to office. Lowndes and Dallas Counties still had a viable chance to elect sizable numbers of independent third-party candidates to office.

Two months before election day, the LCFO held a campaign kickoff rally at which Black Panther candidates spoke about their platforms. The LCFO printed flyers that described the seven candidates and their campaign promises. Running for Lowndes County sheriff, Sidney Logan Jr. explained that "the time has come for us, who have not been protected by the law, but brutalized by it, to begin to take action to see that justice is done without fear or favor." Willie Mae Strickland advocated equitable funding for education in her race for Place 5 on the county board of education. The Sunday before election day, LCFO candidates spoke on radio station WRMA, seeking to entice voters to come to the polls. Logan spoke optimistically about his new party's chances: "We have enough registered people in Lowndes County to win." When asked about SNCC's role in the LCFO, school board nominee John Hinson replied, "Stokely Carmichael and the rest of the SNCC fellows haven't ever made any decisions in Lowndes County." He clarified that "the help they have given us is in courage . . . letting you know you are an American."[76]

Dallas County's third party faced a serious setback in early October when Samson Crum withdrew from the race for sheriff. DCIFVO chairman Clarence Williams explained that Crum's job in the postal service kept him from campaigning. With Crum's departure, the DCIFVO decided not to endorse anyone for that office. Like the third-party supporters in Lowndes, those in the Selma area distributed leaflets encouraging people to vote for the party that favored "strength through unity." In an attempt to catch the eye of as many potential voters as possible, the flyers stated that SNCC, SCLC, COAPO, and the DCIFVO backed the third-party candidates in Dallas County. The third party offered a true contrast to the DCVL, which supported the Democratic ticket from top to bottom, including Lurleen Wallace. Reese wanted to make sure that Baker won the sheriff's office over Clark's write-in campaign, but this stance turned many people away from supporting viable black candidates from the DCIFVO. Reading the writing on the wall, Albert Turner now seemed to understand why SNCC had supported the third-party movement. He wanted newly registered voters to go to the polls on November 8 to knock down the "wall of segregation, discrimination, and injustice." He said that "we can't knock it down by bowing to 'bag men,' Democratic parties, Republican parties, or any other kind of parties. We must use our strength anywhere it will help us."[77]

As Election Day approached, tension mounted in Selma. Carmichael came down from Atlanta to offer his moral support to the third-party movement. On November 6, he rented a sound truck to rally people to head to the polls on Tuesday. Mayor Smitherman had Carmichael and two others arrested when they refused to move the truck, claiming that Carmichael had "lunged" at a police officer. The Dallas County sheriff formally charged the three men with inciting a riot. This official crackdown foreshadowed Election Day events. Several people reported questionable behavior at polling places. In one precinct, white men opened the curtains of the voting machine to look in on black people while they cast their ballots. One man, Andrew Jones, was beaten inside his precinct in Fort Deposit while a local police officer stood by. Poll watchers from the DCIFVO reported being chased away from their stations. Only two federal poll observers served in Dallas County.[78]

The expectations of the third-party candidates had faded by the time the polls closed. None won in either Lowndes or Dallas Counties. Sheriff Frank Ryals defeated Sidney Logan Jr. by 517 votes, and Charlie Sullivan beat Alice Moore by 677 votes. The DCIFVO candidates lost by wider margins, receiving too few votes to be considered a bona fide political party. "We're not concerned with being listed as a party," Clarence Williams said. "We're to establish a democratic system in the county. The next four years will determine what the Negro does with himself, where he'll be placed." To the DCIFVO's chairman, the process was what mattered: "We intend to stand up politically, any way we can. We're going to keep fighting." The LCFO captured enough votes to become the Lowndes County Freedom Party. Sounding like Williams, Lowndesboro resident James Jones said that the county's black people had not been discouraged by the losses at the polls. "We're on the move," he exclaimed. "We are the second party in Lowndes County now. We polled more votes than the Republican Party."[79]

The bright spots of the November election for the Black Belt came in Macon and Greene Counties, through the Democratic Party. Amerson won his bid for

Figure 17. Voters line up outside the Sugar Shack in Peachtree, in Wilcox County, 1966. People dressed in their best clothes for the occasion, which for many people was the first time they had voted. © Bettmann/Corbis.

sheriff despite a last-minute write-in campaign by Harvey Sadler, and Locklair and Webb were victorious in the elections for tax collector and county board of revenue, respectively. Rev. Kirksey held onto his school board seat by a one-hundred-vote margin. The other big Democratic winners came as no surprise. Lurleen Wallace beat her Republican challenger by a two-to-one margin; Albert Brewer, running unopposed, became lieutenant governor; and MacDonald Gallion trounced his GOP opponent to become the attorney general. Democrats also won all but 1 of the 141 seats in the state legislature.[80]

In the wake of the elections, Shriver felt confident enough to release the OEO funds to Lowndes and Wilcox Counties. Both antipoverty programs consented to OEO approval of their staff directors. An Atlanta accounting firm agreed to supervise the projects' account books and to conduct periodic audits, and no member of the governing boards of the antipoverty effort would be an official or a candidate of any partisan political organization. John Hulett, Robert Logan, and Frank Miles stepped down from the LCCMHR poverty committee, while Robert Strickland removed himself as the LCFO's vice chairman. Shriver noted that every member of the governing bodies of both groups was a long-term resident of Alabama: "OEO considers this a striking example of indigenous leadership and participation in an anti-poverty program." Finally, the OEO director put Strickland's murder conviction into context and explained that he met all the qualifications for board membership. The two Black Belt antipoverty programs received a total of $544,000 in federal funds on November 17.[81]

Shriver's delay seemed the politically prudent response, as did the alteration of the antipoverty programs to focus on vocational education. The Washington OEO's support of the two programs indicated its willingness to override the regional OEO's concerns. Yet the antipoverty agency's caution did not offer the best program for the poor people of Lowndes and Wilcox Counties; the self-help housing plan would have better served these two communities. The Dallas County–City of Selma CAA also offered politically safe programs without extending much hope for real change in the county. In August, the antipoverty program received $256,247 for Operation Draino, which planned to install and improve a citywide drainage system. This program did nothing for the county's rural poor, especially those displaced by the changes in agriculture, who were truly in distress. Thus, many of the structural problems of poverty in the rural Alabama Black Belt remained unaddressed. "Along with the ballot, we need economic security," said Rev. William Branch, president of the Greene County NAACP. "Voting doesn't help a man who gets thrown off his land."[82]

The year 1966 marked the end of a strong presence by national civil rights organizations in the Alabama Black Belt. Local people would be left to carry on by themselves in their effort to bring about political and economic change. Those who stayed involved continued to view the federal antipoverty program as an avenue that could take them in the direction they wanted to go.

CHAPTER SIX

Agriculture Is More Than Farming

The Southwest Alabama Farmers Cooperative Association and the National Democratic Party of Alabama

We need a farm agency that will get down to us like this white agency with these white agents is getting down to white people—We need people who can speak in a language we can understand. I used to wonder how all my white neighbors got such fine cows and fine pastures and fine tractors. I kept snooping around and I found out my white neighbors were getting loans from the government. My agent hadn't told me that!
     Rev. Solomon Seay, 1966

The essential elements of the "coalition" which Southern Negroes must eventually seek are two. First, an independent organizational base which will enable them to bargain with their potential allies from a position of strength. Second, a new vision of what their coalition should work toward, a vision which goes beyond the welfare state and equality of opportunity, looking towards a political and social reconstruction in which everyone can "make it" simply because he is human. Para-governmental institutions can be the political base for the first of these activities and the experimental context for seeking the second. Without them, the best we can hope is that another generation of struggle will bring the Deep South to the dubious utopia of Maryland or Kentucky.
     Christopher Jencks and Milton Kotler, *Ramparts Magazine*

After the disappointing results of the 1966 statewide elections in the Black Belt, some local activists continued to look for new ways to transform the region. The evictions that began in 1965 continued after the fall vote. In November, fourteen families from Rev. John Rice's congregation in western Greene County were told to vacate their rented land by January 1. "The notice come unexpected on us," tenant Jack Bizzell told a reporter. "I wasn't through with my crop." These fourteen families joined twenty others displaced in Greene County that winter alone. They all faced a grim future. Most of these small farmers knew little about modern farming; many were middle-aged or older and had few skills for jobs outside of agriculture.[1]

Several of the dislocated farmers blamed their plight on anxious landlords who did not like their tenants exercising their new right to vote. "I think the real cause for the eviction was that the Negroes got registered to vote, and this is a backlash," Rev. Thomas Gilmore of Greene County explained. "People don't really care what happens to that land." Although such statements were true in some cases, other reasons for eviction abounded. More than likely, these tenants had gotten entangled in the second wave of an agricultural transformation that had been working its way through the region since the 1930s. Increased mechanization was one culprit. With new machinery and better herbicides, large landowners could plant, grow, and pick more crops without the aid of their tenants. Other landlords decided to transition out of cotton and into less labor-intensive land uses, such as growing timber or soybeans and raising cattle. In many cases, civil rights activity was the final straw, causing landlords to decide that it was time to send tenants packing.[2]

Gilmore, who had lost his bid to serve as Greene County sheriff, tried to assist some of these homeless tenants by starting a cinder block factory, reasoning that affordable homes could be built with this new material for just thirty-five hundred dollars each. Using funds received from the Southern Rural Action Project of the Citizens Crusade against Poverty, Gilmore and civil rights worker Paul Bokulich bought machinery and supplies to produce fifteen hundred cinder blocks a day. Nevertheless, more would clearly have to be done to help those displaced by the agricultural revolution. What happened across the Black Belt revealed the structural nature of rural poverty and showed that it was tied to a changing economy and not, as some might have wanted to believe, the result of the character flaws of the impoverished. For these rural Alabamians, civil rights included seeking both economic progress and political power. Rev. Rice continued to pin his hopes on the ballot box. "If there's any power in the vote, that's what it's about," he explained. "This county has a majority, eighty-five percent Negroes. Naturally, if there's anything they (white people) can do to you, they do it." Although the statewide elections had not yet brought this strategy to fruition, people involved in the civil rights movement continued to focus on this plan. Many others joined Rice in believing that electing black people to office would one day ease the burdens of the vast majority of those living in the Black Belt.[3]

Another important election had taken place in the fall of 1966, bringing people together from across the western part of the state to design new ideas for the region's future. Local people again tried to elect black farmers to the important Agriculture Stabilization and Conservation Service (ASCS) county committees. In response to the unsatisfactory outcome of the 1966 ASCS vote, local civil rights activists formed a vegetable-producing and -marketing cooperative that operated in Choctaw, Dallas, Greene, Hale, Lowndes, Marengo, Monroe, Perry, Sumter, and Wilcox Counties. With the support of the Office of Economic Opportunity (OEO), some of the organizers of the Southwest Alabama Farmers Cooperative Association (SWAFCA) envisioned that their new venture would recast the livelihoods of low-income farmers and displaced tenants. The co-op would teach better farming practices and give farmers the ability to shift out of cotton and corn and into more lucrative truck crops that required less land. This development, in turn, would assist the low-skilled farm workers who had been evicted, enabling them to stay in their hometowns and avoid moving to overcrowded northern cities.[4]

The co-op's organizers ultimately hoped to create an economic base that would release those who had been dependent on white people and thereby enable them to vote for candidates who would represent the interests of their new constituency. William Harrison explained the cooperative's purpose in testimony before the U.S. Commission on Civil Rights in the spring of 1968: "The whole idea behind SWAFCA is to create some kind of economic basis by which people will be able to think for themselves. . . . [I]f a man is able to feed himself he votes the way he wants to. Not only is this true, but he does anything else he wants to, and my feeling is that basically the power structure, especially in the South here, wants to continue to create that master-servant relationship. As long as it exists, you can control the very destiny of people." "We saw it as the economic arm of the civil rights movement," explained Albert Turner, the Alabama director of the Southern Christian Leadership Conference (SCLC). This economic foundation would keep people from having to move away and would thereby ensure the preservation of black voter strength. According to SWAFCA board member Ezra Cunningham, some of the cooperative's leaders concluded that Alabama's political power centered in the northern and southern parts of the state. But "if we could organize these blacks in the center," he said, "then the white power structure got to jump over us . . . and this is some of the reasons that the co-op movement was put together." Rev. Percy McShan, also a SWAFCA board member, agreed: "What is happening is that the white man is trying to get into the majority, but if the Negro can maintain and stay in the county and live on what land they have, I think we might be able to do so. The whole problem is getting the Negro out to vote."[5]

The farmers' cooperative had the potential to assist more than a thousand small landowners, renters, and displaced tenants who struggled to remain on the land. Because the co-op would be supported by a federal agency and operated by African Americans who had been active in the civil rights movement, its row would not be an easy one to hoe. Local, state, and federal elected officials from Alabama joined forces to block the rural readjustment project in a bitter fight that lasted several years. White officeholders' animus pushed many supporters of the cooperative into another third-party movement—the National Democratic Party of Alabama—this time on a statewide level. By 1970, SWAFCA put the region on a path to change the Black Belt from its segregationist past to a more open society represented by black elected officials. Like so many other episodes in the story of the civil rights movement, however, those who led this passage to a fuller democracy would not reap all the benefits they had envisioned for their communities.

Trying Again: Lewis Black and the 1966 ASCS Election

In early February 1966 the Alabama Council on Human Relations (ACHR) hired Hale County activist Lewis Black as the first director of its Rural Advancement Project (RAP). The Southern Regional Council and the National Sharecroppers Fund supported this three-year initiative in an effort to improve rural living conditions through federal and state programs. The ACHR wanted Black and the RAP to develop rural leadership and community organization, report local needs to appropriate federal and state agencies, bring information about available government-sponsored programs to people in need, and fight public agencies' discriminatory practices with regard to low-income farmers and other rural people. Being well versed in the culture of the Alabama Black Belt, Black knew this job would be difficult. A change in the ASCS rules in March, however, kept him from contemplating the problem for too long: He had to get to work quickly in an effort to aid poor tenant farmers in Sumter County.[6]

New regulations for the domestic cotton allotment program refueled interest in trying to gain seats on the ASCS county committees across the Black Belt. The updated rules required that landlords share with their tenants the proceeds received from the federal government for diverting specific crops—cotton, corn, peanuts, and tobacco. A landowner could no longer keep diversion payments owed his workers without their written permission. Although this new regulation sought to give tenants a larger monetary share in the U.S. Department of Agriculture (USDA) program, it left a loophole. If a tenant signed over his check to his boss, the USDA did not require the landowner to give the worker an itemized statement of expenses charged against the assigned check. As a result, a landlord could compel his renters and tenants to give their checks to him in exchange for rent and expenses without proving that the entire diversion payment had been advanced to the hired farmer. Landowners could also adjust their tenants' crop allotments at their discretion without the approval of the county ASCS office. In both of these instances, renters and tenants remained vulnerable to the whims of landlords who participated in the ASCS program.[7]

Barnes Rogers; his son, John; and Barnes's two sisters owned twenty-four hundred acres in northern Sumter County and had rented parts of their property to tenants for thirty years. In January 1966, they decided to shift to timber production when the Hammermill Paper Company offered as much as three times the amount their renters had been paying. The new arrangement did not allow the tenants to work the land, although they could continue to pay rent for their housing. Left without any cotton acreage, several farmers had no way to support themselves. R. W. Williams had lived on his place for fifty-one years under a handshake agreement that rolled over year after year until January 1966. He rented six acres from the paper company, paying $105 a month for land and a sharecropper house, so he could at least grow his own food.[8]

Not all of the Rogers's renters fell under this new arrangement. Some worked on property not reserved for the paper company. Robert Thomas lost the ability to farm his usual thirteen acres when he inquired about his cotton allotment check. When Barnes Rogers tried to get Thomas to sign over his ASCS check, Thomas refused because his landlord would not give him enough time to read the document. According to Thomas, Rogers "just wanted us to go on and sign it. He just have a mark there for you to sign." Thomas did not budge. "Yeah, I wanted to know how much it was and he didn't want to tell me," Thomas later testified to the Alabama State Advisory Committee to the U.S. Commission on Civil Rights, "and I told him I was going to see about the check. Well, it wasn't too long before I got a letter that he wasn't going to rent me any more land. . . . [A]ll I could see was he got mad about that." The cotton farmer had also participated in mass meetings conducted by the Sumter County Movement for Human Rights, and he believed that Rogers had canceled their agreement in part because of those civil rights activities.[9]

Some of these displaced families moved to Tuskegee, while others headed north to Chicago and about twenty families moved in with relatives in Sumter County. The National Association for the Advancement of Colored People (NAACP) sent the tenants one thousand dollars in emergency funds. The Sumter County Movement for Human Rights then filed a lawsuit against the Rogers family on behalf of the evicted tenants, seeking their share of the cotton diversion payments. Although the tenants eventually won the case, they did not receive any monetary gains because Rogers claimed the renters owed him the money for past debts. Lewis Black helped form the Panola Land Buyers Cooperative for those evicted farmers who remained in Sumter County. They ultimately purchased enough land on which to live independently from white landlords.[10]

Similar events took place in Dallas County in early April 1966. Twenty tenants of J. A. Minter, an owner of fourteen thousand acres in Tyler, claimed that when they refused to assign their ASCS checks to him, their rent agreements changed and they were required to provide an up-front cash payment. Minter asked any of his tenants who could not afford this new expense to vacate his property in sixty days. Minter allowed some of the tenants to continue living in their houses—their families had farmed on this land for generations—but he would not let them continue growing crops on any of his land. Clemon Barlow tried to reason with his landlord: "Let me sign the check and have it come direct to me," Barlow suggested, and he would "pay the rent from that check as it came up." But Minter said, "No, I can't go on that." When Barlow continued to withhold his signature, he received a registered letter telling him that the ASCS office had been notified that Minter had taken over Barlow's share of his land. "He say, 'y'all gonna have to sign the check to me,'" Will Williams explained. "I told him, 'Mr. James, why are you changin' that a way? You've been takin' a mortgage on my mule when I plow with a mule. My wagon, what not, you've been takin a mortgage on that, and I've made my crop.' I say, 'when I got rid of plowing with mules and bought a tractor, you took a mortgage on my tractor.' And he told me, 'No, I'm not taking a mortgage on that junky stuff. I'm takin good security now.'" Williams continued to hold out hope that he could work out a new arrangement with Minter. "I told him, 'well Mr. James,' I said, 'if you can't rent me the land . . . I can't help that. I can't sign that check to you.' That's what I told him. That's how we left it. Me and him haven't had no more talk since then. No more."[11]

These tenants had good reason to distrust their landlord. Minter managed his farm workers in the style of a late nineteenth-century Bourbon planter. He tried to dominate them, as evidenced by his reaction to the new ASCS rule. He required his tenants to process their cotton at his gin, where they were paid in checks made out to him. When the tenants brought the gin checks to the Minter store, he paid them in scrip that they could spend only there. "You can't trade nowhere else and you never know what nothing cost," Pearl Moorer complained. Minter even had charge over the federal food stamps that some tenants received because his store also served as the local post office. Finally, he made his tenants buy their fertilizer from him at the rate of fifty-six dollars a ton, nineteen dollars more than if they had bought it somewhere else in the county. At a hearing conducted by the Alabama Advisory Committee to the U.S. Commission on Civil Rights, one questioner asked Moorer, "Do you mean to say that you think Mr. Minter would actually steal from you?" She curtly answered, "That is how he got the chance to wear a white shirt and necktie."[12]

The tenants from Minter's plantation tried to get the diversion checks owed to them. Alvin J. Bronstein of the Lawyers Constitutional Defense Committee (LCDC) in Jackson, Mississippi, wrote to Secretary of Agriculture Orville

Freeman, seeking relief for the farmers. Later in the month, Moorer attended the second annual meeting of the Citizens' Crusade against Poverty in Washington, D.C., where she met Vice President Hubert Humphrey and told him about her neighbors' predicament. While in the nation's capitol, Moorer also went to the USDA, seeking a remedy for her landlord's injustices. Some department administrators told her that more inspectors would be sent from Washington to investigate.[13]

Minter denied the charges made by his farm workers and claimed his innocence by virtue of the fact that they were renters, not tenants. "Let's get one thing straight," he exclaimed, "I don't even have any sharecroppers." Instead, he classified the renters as individual farmers. He admitted that he had his farmers assign their ASCS money to him but claimed that this had been the standard practice. "I've never threatened to throw anyone off the land," he protested. "I have a theory of what this is but I think it'd be better to keep it to myself."[14]

Minter's "theory" might have involved the civil rights activism of the tenants he evicted. All of the twenty families he released had been described as involved in the movement. Will Moorer, Pearl's husband, had been the first black person to register to vote in Dallas County after the Selma campaign ended. Pearl Moorer had worked to integrate the white schools in rural Dallas County, and she had had a white man arrested for slapping one of her children. When she checked at the courthouse and discovered no record of the assault, she contacted the FBI. When no appropriate response was forthcoming, she went to the Dallas County jail and told the men there that "if they come out hanging around my house [then] I will kill them." The Moorers later joined the Dallas County Farmer Movement, organized by Shirley Mesher after she left the SCLC in May 1966. In June, Mesher encouraged the LCDC to open an office in Selma. Donald A. Jelinek, a young New York attorney who had been on the LCDC staff in Mississippi, came to work in Dallas County. He offered free legal services to anyone who had a grievance arising out of civil rights activism. Jelinek set up his office in the old SCLC headquarters in Selma and filed a lawsuit against Minter on behalf of the evicted tenants, seeking their diversion payments. As a consequence of this suit, the LCDC formed the Southern Rural Research Project to investigate the discriminatory nature of USDA programs across the Alabama Black Belt.[15]

Under these conditions, some activists increased their interest in the upcoming ASCS elections. Similar eviction stories had been reported in Greene and Lowndes Counties. "Well, any number of things might have caused this in my opinion," Charles Smith of Lowndes County explained, "and ASCS . . . is one of them. . . . [T]hose that had guts to ask for payments did and we did not only lose the checks that were coming to us but we lost the farm also." Alabama staff members of the SCLC and the Student Nonviolent Coordinating Committee (SNCC) continued to put their faith in trying to get African Americans onto the local ASCS committees. In the 1966 ASCS elections, this effort received needed support from the ACHR. Having black farmers on county committees seemed to offer a solid chance to change the course of the federal farm support program in the region. Black, as director of the ACHR's Rural Advancement Project, spearheaded the organizational process across the Black Belt. The veterans of the 1965 farm program elections knew to be wary of the USDA local officials; 1966 proved only slightly different. The Alabama ASCS committee first moved the election date from its usual time in November to August. Although perfectly legal—the ASCS regulations required that the elections occur sometime between July and December—it was not the traditional practice. This change put a cloud of suspicion over the entire procedure. Under the new date, ballots would be due on August 16. Civil rights activists had to scramble to get farmers ready in time.[16]

In an attempt to buy some time, SCLC, SNCC, and a number of black farmers filed suit against the USDA, seeking to move the ASCS election date to December. Jelinek represented the group in a Washington federal court. Twenty local farmers traveled to the Capitol, where some testified. Peter Agee of Marengo County told the judge that he had been bribed to keep from seeking an ASCS committee position: "I'll give you ten acres of the best farming land and show you how to get free loans if you get out and put some of those scared Negroes in," a white farmer had told Agee. John Rice of Greene County recounted that his local all-white ASCS committee used fraud and intimidation to keep black farmers off the ballot. Jelinek argued that the ASCS had "totally failed" to properly educate farmers about how to participate in the elections; therefore, his clients needed more time to prepare. The federal judge seemed persuaded by this argument and ruled that the ASCS elections would take place on September 15. Arthur Brown, an ASCS committee nominee from Dallas County, felt good about this trip. "I like Washington," he said. "I'm going to try to take some of the freedom here back home."[17]

After returning to Magnolia, Alabama, Agee received a threat against his life, and some white men fired two shots into his store as they drove by. Someone also shattered the picture window of Black's Greensboro office. Such attempts to intimidate civil rights supporters did not slow the organizational effort, but they do reveal that this activism threatened the position of many white people in the region. With the election date settled, other ASCS regulations had to be followed closely to make sure no votes would be lost on technicalities. For the 1966 election, the farm subsidy program required each ballot to list between six and ten nominees, with the proportion of black nominees equal to the percentage of

African Americans in the county. This new ruling sought to remedy the ballot packing that had taken place in the 1965 vote and had diluted the black vote.[18]

Black obtained a $1,650 grant from the Southern Regional Council's Voter Education Project to fund the effort to get competent black farmers on the ASCS ballots. He set up a county coordinator system for twelve counties that echoed his system for obtaining representatives as part of his failed attempt to create a Hale–Perry County community action agency. Black worked out of the Selma LCDC office as well as his office in Greensboro. He paid the county coordinators $15 a week to organize meetings in each ASCS community to explain the election process and how to correctly mark and mail the ballots. Each coordinator also encouraged those gathered to choose a slate of five and to spread the word to their neighbors who had not come to the meeting. Each county coordinator also passed out leaflets publicizing the ASCS election and attended church services to explain the importance of the upcoming vote. Throughout the weeks leading up to the election, Black met with his coordinators so that they could exchange information about their experiences and offer each other suggestions and support. As Election Day approached, Black asked the coordinators to go door to door to reach as many voters as possible to verify that they had voted and to assist them in casting their ballot if asked to do so. At the final coordinators' meeting, John Vance, the ASCS's Washington-based southeastern area director, came to Selma to answer any last-minute questions.[19]

After all ballots had been submitted, Black assigned the county coordinators to observe the counting process and keep a written record of any violations and of the election results. He also set up a complaint headquarters in the Selma office so he could forward protests to Vance, who had come to the ASCS office in Montgomery for this purpose. Black arranged for Vance to contact the appropriate county office as soon as he received a grievance. This system proved useful, especially when Macon County observers reported that the ballots had not been sealed in a locked box. Vance invalidated the Macon election at once and ruled that another vote had to be conducted.[20]

The cancellation of the Macon County vote turned out to be the bright spot in the 1966 farm support program elections. "In general everyone was very disappointed and somewhat surprised at the poor showing in this year's ASCS elections," ACHR director Bob Valder and Black reported, "especially in the Black Belt." Eighteen African Americans won election to their community committees, and voters selected seventy-six black farmers as alternates. Seven African Americans would serve on Wilcox County community committees, but no black people were elected to any positions in Hale, Perry, and Sumter Counties.[21]

As in the 1965 ASCS election, fraud and intimidation forced their way into the process, despite the presence of the ASCS Washington administrator. In

Sumter County, some black people were barred from witnessing the vote counting. The Hale County ASCS office changed the definition of an eligible voter to a farmer who raised cotton or rented from the government. This erroneous interpretation of the regulations—any legitimate farmer could legally cast a ballot—kept Black from voting in his community. The Greene County ASCS office listed one man in seven different communities. In Dallas County, Mesher reported that the ASCS officials counted the ballots selectively. "If a man was listed in one community [and] his ballot came in from another community, the committee would sit there and decide, 'Should we count it in this community, or shall we wait and see what was going on in the balloting in the other community?'" The concerted effort by Black and his county coordinators did not pay off as they had hoped. When all the ballots had been tallied, the ASCS county committees across the Black Belt remained lily-white.[22]

When asked if he felt disappointed by the results, Black answered that he had not expected "as many [to be elected] as last year." He felt that the civil rights movement had begun to leave Alabama. "Negroes are losing hope and going back to the old ways," Black lamented. "There weren't as many [civil rights] folks in here to work anyway. Not as many young people joined in. There wasn't as much curiosity," he added.[23]

At hearings held by the Alabama Advisory Committee to the U.S. Commission on Civil Rights, the testimony of ASCS county officials revealed that the old ways of doing business remained entrenched. The compliance supervisor for the Dallas County ASCS office thought that any representative of the federal government who tried to enforce civil rights was an "outside agitator." Jack Bridges, the chair of the state ASCS committee, testified that the white county committees were responsive to the needs of low-income black and white farmers. M. H. Mashburn, a state ASCS field worker, thought that the assistance large landowners received eventually trickled down to their tenants. "Every one of them has from one to three milk cows and several beef cattle and they are running that man's pasture just as if it were their own," he told the panel. "They say the big man gets it all, that is not true. The tenant benefits." The Sumter County ASCS office manager, Woodson Ennis, claimed that no black people served on his county's ASCS committee because "colored people would prefer that the white man carry out their business activities than they would their colored friends."[24]

For Black and other activists, the answer clearly lay somewhere beyond the ASCS community elections. "You gotta have a lot of Negroes pulling together to get just one man in power," Black said. "They got tricks they been using for a hundred years. You can't beat 'em in one year. We gotta keep working on education." Since July, some people in the area had been trying to form a multicounty vegetable producers' cooperative. The outcome of the 1966 statewide elections and the ASCS vote seemed to fuel the fire for this new approach. Black's contacts across the state and in Washington would provide valuable assets in getting this effort off the ground.[25]

Working under New Banners

Throughout the summer of 1966, Mesher had been holding meetings with farmers—tenants who rented and those who farmed on shares—in Dallas County to talk about their problems and look for solutions. Most of those who participated in the discussions did not live near each other and did not have telephones, which kept them isolated. Mesher tried to learn as much as possible about the various USDA farm programs in an effort to improve the economic opportunities of these low-income farmers. Through this Farmer's Aid Committee, Mesher realized that many people had not been aware of most of the USDA farmers' programs, especially those offered through the ASCS and the Farmers Home Administration (FHA).

Mesher repeatedly heard stories of the misinformation and obfuscation the USDA officials handed out to low-income black farmers. She learned that most had not heard of the ASCS storage program, did not know how the ASCS county committee assigned allotments, and had not received information on the ASCS conservation program. The FHA office in Dallas County made no effort to help farmers fill out complicated loan applications. Mesher deduced that "they don't feel the person needs the loan to begin with." When those who inquired about such opportunities went to their county's various USDA offices, they were instructed to discuss their needs with their landlords.[26]

In other cases, USDA officials seemed to be working in collusion with large white landowners. Some black farmers surrendered their assigned allotments back to the ASCS when farming such small acreage no longer seemed worthwhile. They were never told that they could have rented the land or sold it to someone else within the county. Some African American farmers also did not know what happened to cotton they placed in ASCS-operated warehouses. In some cases, the cotton had been removed without the tenant's permission. Mesher testified that "on some of these cotton producers['] notes . . . the landowner signed a waiver notice saying that there was no liens against that cotton that the tenant was putting in. Yet in every case the checks were made out to the landlord and not to the tenant when his cotton entered the compress." When some tenants asked for copies of the cotton diversion assignments they signed over to their landlords, S. H. O'Hara, the Dallas County ASCS office manager, replied that "Washington did not provide enough copies" for the tenants to have one. When investigators came down from Washington to look into Mesher's complaints, she saw no follow-up: "No one has ever had their share withheld, nothing has ever happened to people that have ever been found to be in violation," she said. As the number of evictions mounted, tenants perceived landlords as having even more power, and workers consequently had increasing difficulty convincing farm workers to confront these wrongful practices. These farmers clearly were not going to receive what they needed as long as they continued to operate in isolation.[27]

While Mesher began to formulate ideas in Dallas County to assist low-income farmers, Black started making plans in Hale and Perry Counties. In early 1966, he had already made contact with the Cooperative League of the United States of America. That spring, Al Ulmer of the Southern Regional Council and representatives from the Cooperative League met with Black in Marion to discuss the formation of a cooperative in several Black Belt counties. Black thought a co-op "was the thing that we needed to bound together the farmers['] resources in order that one can be helped through the other." Starting in Greene, Hale, Perry, and Sumter Counties, the RAP director envisioned forming a vegetable-producing and -marketing co-op for farmers who had small plots of land. Black then ventured beyond these four counties to see if others across the region would be interested in the idea. Ezra Cunningham was his contact in Monroe County. "[We] would have these meetings to decide what in the heck we were going to do with these people that had been kicked off the land," Cunningham explained. "I started working with my county to see what I could do with it, and the other guy working in his county, then they called us all together and we all got together to see what we can come up with." Some Wilcox County farmers had been growing cucumbers cooperatively since 1965. Farmers who remained on Barnes Rogers's plantation in Sumter County wanted to join after their landlord refused to rent them land. The SCLC's Alabama state director, Albert Turner, became interested in the idea, too, because he felt accountable to those people who had been dislocated because of their civil rights activity. "We felt that it was our responsibility to a large extent to try to provide for these people after they had made these sacrifices," he explained. Low-income farmers already knew how to work the land; they merely needed technical assistance to modernize their agricultural know-how and resources to purchase materials. Through the work of Mesher, Black, and Turner, a vegetable-producing and -marketing cooperative started to take shape across the Black Belt by the end of July 1966.[28]

The members of the cooperative chose to call the new venture the Southwest Alabama Farmers Cooperative Association. The Orrville Cooperative in Dallas County served as the co-op's interim board of directors until a full board could be elected. Plans were made to coordinate the planting of cucumbers, okra, and field peas beginning in August. Organizers fanned out across the region, distributing survey sheets to gather information about land quality and future needs for fertilizer, seeds, and insecticides. The group of farmers also started a limited county-by-county education program to teach people about the cooperative method and how it could benefit members. Through this combined effort, about eight hundred farmers expressed interest in joining SWAFCA.[29]

A focus on growing vegetables made sense. The Alabama Commission of Agriculture and Industries had been promoting this idea for some time. The Montgomery-based Whitfield Pickle Company had bought cucumbers from Black Belt farmers in the past and wanted to increase its acreage beginning in 1965. The Auburn Extension Service even produced a publication promoting the growth of the state's vegetable industry. This venture could prove risky, however. Close attention had to be paid to finding markets for the vegetables and ensuring proper crating and shipping. Even though many of the cooperative's potential members knew how to work hard, few had the skills to effectively market crops. SWAFCA's initial attempt at growing vegetables cooperatively did not fully take into account all of these factors, although it did have enough small landowners to grow the new crops. In late July, the cooperative submitted a $218,900 grant application to OEO, seeking assistance to become a more viable organization. SWAFCA leaders knew that the co-op needed to hire an experienced cooperative educator, a horticulturist, a vegetable-marketing expert, a full-time manager, and technical advisers for each county. In the grant application, SWAFCA organizers described the co-op as "a tool . . . to solve [the region's] immediate and long range problems." OEO turned down this initial proposition and instead sent advisers to assist the cooperative in formulating a more complete proposal.[30]

The perseverance of local people throughout the Black Belt appeared finally to be paying off. After earlier attempts to secure OEO funding had ended in rejection, the SWAFCA project might be a breakthrough for the Black Belt poor. SWAFCA's organization could not have come about at a better time. OEO had begun to place more emphasis on rural poverty as a result of congressional amendments to the Economic Opportunity Act in 1966 for the 1967 fiscal year. The legislation called for the antipoverty agency to develop programs that would assist the rural poor and thus prevent them from migrating to the nation's overcrowded cities. Alabama's Black Belt elected officials had also managed to keep the War on Poverty at bay through November 1966. Something had to be done for the region, and the initial grassroots organization of SWAFCA made it a perfect candidate for OEO's support. After the cooperative was better organized, several OEO administrators backed the plan. "All divisions of CAP realize its merit, strongly support it, and urge its funding," Community Action Program (CAP) director Theodore Berry told Sargent Shriver. "Accordingly, those OEO officials who have worked directly with SWAFCA committed themselves openly to do everything possible with their authority to get this project funded."[31]

For two days during the week of Christmas 1966, Peter Mickelsen, an OEO rural specialist, met with various farmers and the co-op organizers to discuss SWAFCA and its expansion. They laid out a schedule for the next fourteen days to finalize the co-op's future plans. Dividing into county groups, they decided to conduct a survey of interested farmers. Organizers needed to know how much land would be available for planting and what crops would be grown. A multi-county coordinating and planning board had to be formed by selecting two people from each participating county. On January 5, representatives from five counties gathered in the LCDC offices in Selma to meet with Bruce Kashdon from OEO's Migrant Division. John Zippert from the Grand Marie Cooperative in Louisiana spoke about the details of producing and marketing vegetables. Those present agreed to have Black, Mesher, and Turner serve as the cooperative's advisers, with Black acting as the field coordinator and Mesher working as the office coordinator. They wanted to get one hundred people interested in joining the co-op from each of the ten counties, enabling SWAFCA to claim one thousand farmer-members. The group then elected a former member of Self-Help against Poverty for Everyone (SHAPE), Joe R. Johnson of Dallas County, as the temporary chairman of the board. The Cooperative League of the United States of America gave the fledgling group five hundred dollars to conduct this initial organizing drive.[32]

On January 14, 1967, SWAFCA held another meeting, this time with private and governmental agencies to see what type of assistance the cooperative could receive. Representatives came from various federal departments, including the USDA Farmers Cooperative Service, the Department of Labor, and the Economic Development Administration, indicating that the project was being taken seriously. State and county FHA, ASCS, and Extension Service officials also received invitations. SWAFCA organizers invited educators and personnel from private foundations, including Tuskegee Institute's dean of agriculture and staff from Auburn University's Extension Service and Research Station, Alabama A & M, Southern University, the Cooperative League of the United States of America, the National Sharecroppers Fund, the Southern Regional Council, the Southern Rural Action Project, and the LCDC. Support also came from local civil rights activists Jimmy Lytle, George Green, Paul Bokulich, Rev. Francis X. Walter, and Rev. Ernest M. Bradford.[33]

Miles Hollister, OEO's deputy director of community service cooperative planning, opened the meeting with a discussion of the Black Belt's need for a rural readjustment program. He admitted that the antipoverty program and the USDA had not done a good job of helping people left behind by the changes taking place in agriculture. He offered OEO's commitment to assist local people in getting needed federal and private resources to benefit the South. Mesher then explained the basis for SWAFCA's formation. The group broke up into governmental and private organizations to discuss what could be offered to strengthen the cooperative. The governmental officials, excluding those from OEO, stated that they were not ready to help SWAFCA until it became better organized, perhaps in a year. Orville L. O'Shields, chief of operating loans for the Alabama FHA office, stated that he did not have enough personnel to lend the co-op any assistance. This meeting foreshadowed SWAFCA's difficulty in garnering support from state and local USDA programs. After more discussion, Clyde Markeson of the USDA Farmers Cooperative Service offered to send a representative from his office to Selma to aid in the co-op's development.[34]

Participants from private organizations offered more resources to the co-op. The ACHR gave Black's services, and the SCLC financed Turner's activity. Ulmer said that the Southern Regional Council could donate between five hundred and eight hundred dollars, and the Cooperative League agreed to send one of its staff members to Selma to work with the co-op development. Even though OEO endorsed the SWAFCA plan, one of its representatives, Dr. Joseph Bradford of the Rural Programs Division of the CAP, would not support the co-op because he thought it should broaden its leadership base and target group. "A strongly reinforced structure can certainly lessen the economic and political pressures that exist, and will be applied," he warned. He was skeptical about the co-op's future, pointing out that its organizers "have practically no history in cooperative production and marketing failure can be easily built into the effort." Bradford judged the SWAFCA idea harshly. He said that "Alabama's Blackbelt, with its hostile environment is no place to take chances. To ignore these facts is simply begging trouble." This tough location, however, was precisely where OEO needed to be working. Antipoverty officials ignored Bradford's advice and moved forward to strengthen the project.[35]

For three months, SWAFCA organizers worked feverishly to shore up the cooperative and make it a viable enterprise. They distributed flyers advertising the co-op plan and inviting people to attend meetings. Cooperative representatives held weekly gatherings in each of the co-op's ten counties and elected a board of directors. More than half of the members of the twenty-person board had direct ties to the civil rights movement. William Harrison of Choctaw County had run for office in 1966 and served on his county's community action committee. McShan had made a bid for tax assessor on the Freedom Party ticket in Greene County, and John Chambers had joined a lawsuit to integrate the Greene County public school. The daughter of Richard Daniel Jr. of

Hale County had tried to desegregate Greensboro High School in 1965. The two Lowndes County representatives, Matthew Jackson and Charles Smith, participated actively in the Lowndes County Christian Movement for Human Rights (LCCMHR) and the Lowndes County Freedom Party. The Perry County board members, James Avery and James Carter, had tried to organize a CAP for their area. George Mason served as an officer in the Sumter County Movement for Human Rights. Joe Johnson and Freeman Berry of Dallas County had been active in the attempt to get a CAP through SHAPE. For three months, the SWAFCA board met at various locations throughout the ten-county region so that farmers could get to know their co-op leaders and the board could learn more about the co-op's participating communities. The *Southern Courier* announced SWAFCA's formal organization in mid-February and encouraged white and black farmers to join in the effort. "We are working to save our farms, our homes, our lives," SWAFCA chairman Joe Johnson told the newspaper. "Without a massive crash program to help solve our problems, many of us will be driven to the Northern ghettos. . . . We are fighting to stay on the land."[36]

Most of SWAFCA's members either rented their land or owned their property. Only 0.2 percent of the co-op's members were classified as sharecroppers. The average renter worked 38 acres, and the typical landowner farmed 63 acres. Even those who owned their land could not be considered prosperous, however. Johnson, for example, lived on a small farm deep in Dallas County that lacked a telephone, running water, and electricity. When he attended co-op meetings, he walked three miles to the highway to hitch a ride. Many women participated in the cooperative while their husbands worked outside of the Black Belt in places such as Mobile and Montgomery. The husband of Clara Walker, of Marion Junction in Dallas County, worked in Mobile while she ran their 173-acre farm. When asked why she and her husband had decided to stay in rural Alabama instead of moving north, she replied, "Well, we could see there wasn't anything any better. And if we left the farm and went to the cities, we would be in just as bad a shape or probably worse. So we just decided to stay on where we are and use what we have best." Mesher found that when the co-op members were tenants or sharecroppers, the men were the active co-op members in their families. When landowners participated, many women ran the farms for the co-op venture. Throughout February, Black, Mesher, and Turner encouraged SWAFCA members to conduct soil tests on their land. Dr. Asa Sims of Southern University in Baton Rouge, Louisiana, agreed to process the tests so that farmers could know what type of fertilizer to use. SWAFCA also located a source of seeds and fertilizer so that spring planting could begin on time.[37]

Some cooperative members also tried to obtain economic opportunity loans from their FHA county offices to buy supplies to start planting. In Sumter County, the FHA supervisor advised those seeking credit to stay away from the

Figure 18. The interior of Willie Abrams's house, Wilcox County, Alabama, ca. 1968. Abrams's living room decorations were typical of those of many Black Belt residents, showing the value she placed on her family members, Jesus Christ, Martin Luther King Jr., and Coretta Scott King. Photo by Nancy Redpath. Francis X. Walter Papers, Sewanee, Tenn.

Figure 19. A white landowner's house near Safford, Alabama, 1970. Photo by Nancy Redpath. Francis X. Walter Personal Papers, Sewanee, Tenn.

co-op. To remedy this problem, the cooperative's three advisers and board chairman met with state FHA officials, seeking financial assistance for SWAFCA's members. However, the FHA administrators refused to make definite commitments to the group until it provided a proposed operating budget, a permit to operate, a list of the board of directors, the co-op's bylaws and articles of incorporation, and all of the member survey forms.[38]

The state USDA affiliates obviously did not view SWAFCA as a worthy investment. These federal administrators would lend assistance only if the co-op functioned like more established commercial cooperatives. According to assistant secretary of agriculture John Baker, not only racial attitudes but also class issues contributed to USDA administrators' dislike of the self-help venture. The USDA "system was top down," he explained, but Shriver and OEO were "turning society upside down." Baker also explained that since 1945 his department had been supporting more efficient ways to farm by decreasing the amount of labor: "It's almost as if they didn't care what happened to these people after they left." Historian Pete Daniel has described the symbiotic relationship between "agribusiness" and "agrigovernment" that "cooperated—conspired, some might argue—to replace labor-intensive with capital-intensive farming operations." These connections between "federal agricultural policy and laborsaving science and technology became tools that ruthlessly eliminated sharecroppers, tenants, and small farmers." For Daniel, this tragedy of "human dislocation" was made worse by the fact that USDA officials hid it with "an upbeat and sterile bureaucratic vocabulary of progress." The SWAFCA concept contradicted this reasoning because the cooperative sought to employ as many small landowners and displaced tenants as possible. Nevertheless, white supremacy and the threat to local processors stood out as predominant reasons that these officials failed to lend assistance to the cooperative. On February 1, 1967, Robert C. "Red" Bamberg, the state director of the FHA who had served as the Dallas County farm agent in the early 1940s, wrote to the Alabama commissioner of agriculture and industries to explain the availability of economic opportunity loans to cooperatives, describing a project similar to SWAFCA as worthy of support: "I can envision communities in the state that are producing certain vegetables such as cucumbers where a local station might be established for the members of the cooperative to bring their products for grading and preparing for this product to be picked up by a buyer." Bamberg indicated that these loans could provide assistance where none had been offered in the past. He committed his agency's resources to this endeavor: the FHA "stands ready to assist in any way possible in helping the rural population of this state increase their income." Bamberg assured the commissioner that "we stand ready with our entire force." Such a reversal of policy could only be explained by the fact that SWAFCA consisted of black farmers whose talents contradicted the convictions of white supremacy and whose organization would come at the expense of local buyers.[39]

In February, Mickelsen met with the CAP administrators in the southeast regional OEO office. They agreed that the SWAFCA demonstration program seemed encouraging and worthy of support. Black attended a weeklong conference sponsored by the National Sharecroppers Fund during which he visited the Panola Cooperative in Batesville, Mississippi. He met the co-op's board members and learned details of its operation. A month later, SWAFCA applied for a $503,460 CAP demonstration grant to begin a rural readjustment project starting April 1. Black felt extremely hopeful about what SWAFCA could do for the region. "It could be the point to change the history of farming and change the history of the economical struggle for Negroes," he reported. "It could be the thing to [liberate] Negroes through its economic stability and their political inspiration in the United States." John Hulett, the chairman of the Lowndes County Freedom Party, thought SWAFCA's formation contributed to the political evolution of his county. Speaking in New York City, Hulett said that the co-op proved that his party could improve conditions in the county even without holding office. Birmingham attorney C. H. Erskine Smith helped draft SWAFCA's charter and filed its incorporation papers at the Dallas County Courthouse on March 21. Later that month, the local elected officials from the ten SWAFCA counties received word that OEO planned to fund the cooperative.[40]

Fear of Losing Control: Organized Opposition to SWAFCA

When it became known that SWAFCA might receive a half-million-dollar OEO grant, Selma mayor Joe T. Smitherman quickly organized an opposition. He had fought back the rural community's challenge to his authority earlier in 1965 by co-opting SHAPE's grassroots organizing work and incorporating part of it into the Dallas County–City of Selma community action agency. Smitherman probably thought he had made it into the clear when OEO funded the city's CAP. When SWAFCA emerged with Mesher as one of its advisers, he moved into action, using all of his political clout in a campaign to keep the cooperative from obtaining any federal funds. In this concerted effort to oppose OEO's first rural readjustment project, members of the opposition revealed their fears about the changes that an increasingly organized rural voting bloc could bring to the region.[41]

Smitherman and Dallas County probate judge B. A. Reynolds first met with their newly elected congressman, Bill Nichols. The Democratic representative had his own history with agribusiness, having served as vice president of the Parker Fertilizer Company and as president of the Parker Gin Company in Sylacauga since 1947. Nichols agreed to set up a meeting with antipoverty administrators in Washington so the Black Belt opposition group could voice its objections to SWAFCA. The Dallas County officials then hosted a meeting of thirty-five men—fellow probate judges, members of boards of revenue, city council members, mayors from eight of the ten SWAFCA counties, and representatives from two vegetable-processing companies—to decide what to tell OEO. After unanimously adopting a resolution opposing the SWAFCA grant, the participants agreed to ask for an FBI investigation of the co-op's leadership and to seek the assistance of all available state investigative resources "in preparing a full, public report on these professional troublemakers we are dealing with." The *Selma Times Journal* contributed to the heightened anxiety over SWAFCA by calling it a "collective" in a headline, thereby reminding readers of communism instead of the more benign agriculture cooperative common throughout the region. Smitherman and Reynolds claimed to be conducting this effort to protect those "well-intended, good citizens" who had joined the co-op without knowing the "dangerous aspects of it." Before leaving for Washington, Selma's mayor disclosed one of his key fears about the federally supported co-op. "This would be only the beginning," he predicted. "The initial grant for one year would permit them to get their feet in the door and eventually take over agricultural operations in the Black Belt. Each succeeding year's funding could be larger than the year before." Millions of dollars were at stake—in a single year, Alabama farmers received $195 million in USDA price supports and diversion payments.[42]

On April 5, eleven men from Alabama joined the state's U.S. senators and four members of its congressional delegation in a meeting with Gerson Greene, director of research and demonstration, and Bertrand Harding, OEO's deputy director, at the agency's headquarters. The group held court for three hours. Alabama's U.S. senator, Lister Hill, made a lengthy speech protesting the proposed grant. The governor's office supplied the investigative powers of the state's Legislative Commission to Preserve the Peace, which provided OEO with a memorandum that probed into the past of SWAFCA affiliates in an effort to stop the grant. The Alabamians cited six main reasons why the federal government should turn down the co-op's application. They saw a violation of OEO regulations, since SWAFCA would be independent from the Selma–Dallas County CAP, and they thought the co-op duplicated existing services, since the local USDA offices offered assistance to any farmer. They found the character of SWAFCA's leadership "highly suspicious," citing instances in Mesher's work history that proved she was "too-radical." The commission was bothered by the white activist's connections to SCLC and SNCC, especially her association with James Bevel, who "now openly espouses 'Black Power,'" and her office, which had Black Panther emblems painted on the door and windows. They also argued that the project would create community disharmony and was economically unfeasible. Moreover, opponents claimed it might serve as a "screen for a subversive movement." But what worried the group the most was its belief that "SWAFCA is a 'black panther' group."[43]

For these members of the Black Belt elite, the SWAFCA project touched many nerves that had been exposed since 1960. All measures had to be brought to bear against the large cooperative; otherwise, they thought, their way of life stood in jeopardy. Their region had already lost some of its prestige in state politics when the legislature redrew the boundaries for congressional seats after the 1960 census. Agricultural businesses also feared what the co-op would do. The Whitfield Pickle Company had been buying cucumbers cheaply from small farmers across the region. If SWAFCA organized these people, the company would have to pay more for the produce it needed. A drought in the area since 1965 made increased competition from a cooperative seem even more problematic. State agriculture commissioner Richard Beard reported that 1967 "was the worst cotton year in [the] history of Alabama." On top of these agricultural and political worries, the group could not escape the fact that they lost ground almost daily in their fight to uphold segregation. On March 22, the federal district court in Montgomery issued a strong reminder of the federal government's powerful presence in the form of an injunction against Governor Lurleen Wallace and the state superintendent of education in an effort to advance school integration.[44]

The political threat that SWAFCA posed lay at the root of the opposition. If the cooperative could organize thousands of rural black voters through its programs, then civic power could change hands. Since the early 1960s, Selma leaders had planned to attract new industry to the region in an effort to balance the black and white populations. This large cooperative did not coincide with these plans to diversify the region. A handful of SWAFCA's directors had run for office in 1966, and many supported local civil rights organizations that worked to elect black people. This strong activism threatened the white power structure across the Black Belt. If African Americans sat in these offices formerly held by white men, other lucrative positions, such as seats on the ASCS county committees, could also be transferred to black citizens.

The Peace Commission had been monitoring Mesher's activities since the fall of 1966. Its investigators erroneously reported that her work on the ASCS elections might indicate "a first move toward organizing an affiliate of the National Farm Workers Association," which the commission described as "supported by Walter Reuther's money." The staff director of the commission, Ed Strickland, told George Wallace that the farm workers union had organized marches and wage-hour demands in Wisconsin and Texas, "and its leaders announced that it would organize in the South." He thought that Mesher's involvement with area farmers proved that such a plan was under way. Strickland claimed that SNCC's Alabama staff helped the Farm Workers Association's organizational efforts in California by sending two-way car radios. By March, the Peace Commission deduced that the organization of SWAFCA indicated that the Farm Workers Association "has recently become active in Alabama, though they have not used the label to date." Strickland marked Mesher as the force behind this activity.[45]

As a result of this faulty investigative work, Mesher became the focus of the SWAFCA opposition. She had participated in the Selma to Montgomery march, which made her suspect in the eyes of the Peace Commission, and the Alabama Sovereignty Commission produced a movie that alleged that communists played a major role in the event. State representative John Hawkins, who headed the Peace Commission, had previously warned that "the civil rights movement was the vanguard of the revolutionary thrust of international Communism." Fearing that a potential communist lived inside every tenant and small farmer's house, the Peace Commission conducted self-fulfilling research that produced the desired results. Although many other local people involved in the formation of SWAFCA had been equally dedicated to the civil rights movement across the ten-county area, the Peace Commission homed in on Mesher's activities. Perhaps investigators had difficulty believing that Alabama's black people could conduct sophisticated organizing on their own. She may also have been targeted because as a white woman from the West Coast, she stood out starkly. Historian Adam Fairclough has explained that "visible examples of interracialism contradicted and subverted the ideology of white supremacy; they also emboldened others to resist." Mesher's earlier work in SHAPE, the Dallas County Independent Free Voters Organization (DCIFVO), the Farmers Aid Committee, and the ASCS elections put her in the center of the opposition's bull's-eye. Rev. Francis Walter explained that many white Alabamians disliked Mesher because "she destroys the myth of the white woman." He continued, "Shirley hasn't got time to be a Southern lady. She just believes in helping people. She is the most honest person I've ever met. Her cause is to assist people to run their own affairs and to have power, and when you do that you automatically cut yourself out of the reward." A Peace Commission report described her as "very intelligent and fiercely dedicated," not to be "underrated." The members of the Alabama delegation opposing SWAFCA may also have focused on Mesher because they knew that OEO would disregard comments made about African American participation in civil rights activity in light of the Lowndes and Wilcox County OEO grants approved in November 1966.[46]

The opposition feared the future political consequences that SWAFCA might engender. In Smitherman's words, the organization was a "black power group vying for political power." He predicted that "if they get federal funds, they will demonstrate to other Negroes that they are the group to join." Black Belt elites demonized Black Power because they knew that in their region, it meant enabling black residents to participate freely in elections and live independently in society. Louis B. Whitfield clearly described his fears to Senator Hill: "I further understand that there are some 12,000 white votes in this ten county area and some 11,000 Negro votes. If these people get this money given to them, it will be used to the detriment of the white people over there and they will control this Negro vote as a bloc and they will vote to the disadvantage of private enterprise and excessive taxation of established business."[47]

OEO backed the SWAFCA idea because it seemed to offer some hope for the rural poor and relief for overcrowded cities by offering small landowners and landless tenants an opportunity to make a living in the Black Belt. "The project is so designed that it will open doors to both Federal and private fund sources, heretofore unavailable to individuals in this area," a memorandum on SWAFCA explained. The cooperative's stated goal also enhanced the chances of maintaining a black majority in some of these counties. Turner thought this was the real reason that SWAFCA generated opposition: "If they had succeeded, it would have meant that these people would have been run out of the Black Belt," he argued. "That, I think, when you get down to it, was the reason. Because their real reason for eviction in the first place was to get rid of the black majority of the Black Belt." The week before the Alabama group came to Washington, Stokely Carmichael had addressed a group of students at Stillman College, a four-year liberal arts school in Tuscaloosa. Newspapers reported that the SNCC chair told the group, "If you want to be free you've got to say 'to hell with the laws of the United States.' This country has law and order, but it doesn't know a damn thing about justice." Such statements embittered SWAFCA's opposition. Linking the co-op's farmers to Black Power and Black Power to Carmichael seemed to make perfect sense to the Alabama delegation. Trying to stop the OEO grant to SWAFCA represented an obvious attempt to protect white economic and political self-interest. Other members of the black community found it convenient to make these associations as well.[48]

Another source of resistance to SWAFCA came from a quieter corner, but it also exposed the cooperative's potential to alter the traditional way of doing business in the Black Belt and the revolutionary nature of the civil rights movement. Some members of the Dallas County Voters League (DCVL) voiced opposition to the co-op, including Rev. Fred Reese, Amelia Boynton, and her son, Bruce. League members had been active in the Selma campaign for voting rights; the mayor considered them militants. Led by Reese, the DCVL had decided to work through the City of Selma–Dallas County Economic Opportunity Board to effect change from within the system. DCVL members' rejection of the SWAFCA approach was rooted in thirty years of experience as the power brokers for Selma's black community. "Many of the rural black elite," sociologist Hardy T. Frye has explained, "saw the rise of any type of new political or civil rights organization as a threat to the carefully worked-out race relations that existed in their particular county or region." Many SWAFCA members had previously been involved in SHAPE and the third-party movement in Dallas County that opposed the leadership of the DCVL in the 1966 statewide elections. The cooperative represented a substantial threat to the future power of Reese's organization.[49]

Orzell Billingsley also wrote to OEO to express his negative opinions of the co-op. He made his case in an April 3 letter, claiming that SWAFCA "draws too heavily on those who do not seem to have any leadership potential to develop and ignores and drives away those leaders of stability. . . . The cooperative idea is not a concept which lends itself to quickie and roving leadership." Billingsley had tried to form a co-op through his own organization, the Alabama Farmers and Rural Development Council. He wanted OEO to utilize "the Negro-oriented colleges, the successful businessmen, the responsible and trustworthy leadership," in its USDA-directed programs. Bradford, the OEO official who had voiced negative opinions about SWAFCA in January, had been working with Billingsley and agreed with his approach. The Birmingham attorney must have resented the fact that traditional black leaders had not been included in SWAFCA's formation. He might have feared the co-op's potential negative impact on the strength of the Alabama Democratic Conference (ADC). ADC chair Rufus Lewis joined Billingsley in opposing the co-op. At eight hundred members and growing, SWAFCA could populate the Black Belt with people who did not feel beholden to established leaders and organizations such as Billingsley, Lewis, and the ADC. A supporter of Senator Hill's relayed a rumor that the Birmingham attorney planned to threaten Shriver with a lawsuit if OEO funded SWAFCA.[50]

As with the criticisms lodged by the white power structure, Billingsley's judgments against the co-op carried a certain veneer of self-interest. The cooperative, with its base and leadership firmly secured in the grass roots of the rural community, threatened him. The co-op's members were not the people who had been groomed to lead the black community. "The golden words of conservative black politics," Frye has explained, "have been moderation, consensus, respectability, persuasion, and access." SWAFCA challenged all of these notions by operating without the consensus of local leadership and the respectability and access that middle-class black leaders offered. The co-op contested the established way of doing business in the Black Belt and thus generated opposition among seemingly disparate groups opposed to it.[51]

The opposition to SWAFCA received coverage in newspapers across the state. The *Selma Times Journal* published the details of the co-op's grant application and indicated that there were reasons to be skeptical about the co-op's intentions based on the amount of money budgeted for travel expenses. The *Birmingham Post Herald* thought that the fact that the cooperative had applied for assistance from OEO rather than "from recognized agriculture organizations" demonstrated "political motivation . . . from the outset." The Birmingham newspaper editors suggested that the grant should be "put on the shelf until some other less costly, and perhaps less political, ways are tried." Throughout the two years of SWAFCA's formation and development, Alabama newspapers published articles that put the cooperative in a bad light. Only one weekly publication, the *Southern Courier,* printed pieces that reflected the co-op's goals and objectives from the perspective of the black farmer. "Under the SWAFCA program small farmers in ten Black Belt counties would get higher prices for their crops, and would learn modern farming methods. Certainly, there is nothing subversive about that," the Montgomery-based newspaper reported. Editors sympathized with the need that the co-op filled in the region, writing, "It is true that SWAFCA is a revolutionary approach to the problems of destitute tenant farmers. But it is time for a revolution in the Black Belt. SWAFCA's peaceful revolution has been carefully planned by responsible people. It should be given a chance."[52]

After returning to Alabama, Smitherman and Reynolds crowed about their productive meeting with OEO officials. "We feel that we were not only successful in this present effort," the mayor of Selma said, "but also achieved a closer working relationship between OEO and local officials." They must have been convinced by their own testimony. Harding agreed to conduct an investigation of SWAFCA to "look into" whether "subversive elements are involved" but clarified that his investigation would be looking only for communists: membership by board members in a Black Panther political party would not disqualify SWAFCA from receiving the grant. Rudy Frank, Gerson Greene's assistant, indicated that the two Dallas County officials might have missed their mark. He said after the meeting that OEO appreciated hearing the Alabama group's objections; however, Frank hoped that Wallace would not veto the project because OEO officials were "tremendously concerned" about the displacement of farmers who were too old for job retraining, too young for Social Security, and "too proud" for welfare. These statements indicated that OEO would continue its commitment to the co-op.[53]

In the face of such strong protest, however, the antipoverty agency agreed to reevaluate the co-op project. Agency staffers who had worked closely with SWAFCA to develop the grant proposal urged Shriver to go forward. L. Sylvester Odum explained the director's dilemma to Ted Berry: "To withdraw is to turn our backs on hundreds of poor farmers who have created a form of community action in the midst of a community action vacuum." He thought that SWAFCA's members had a proven need for the program, and he recognized that if OEO moved forward, it would do so in the face of "the political and economic power structure in Alabama." Nevertheless, he believed in the program's viability. "As in the past, we will suffer great recrimination, *but the program should be funded*." The earlier contacts made by SWAFCA and the Selma Inter-Religious Project (SIP) with national organizations and civil rights groups also paid off, as many of these institutions sent telegrams in support of the project and lobbied OEO to fund the program.[54]

Local people from Selma also tried to give the antipoverty agency another view of the region that ran counter to that of the SWAFCA opposition. Three priests from the Society of Saint Edmund Mission, based in Selma, took out a full-page advertisement in the *Selma Times Journal* to explain their support of the SWAFCA grant. Using pointed headlines and a photograph of a black farmer sitting beside his house, the priests tried to convey the co-op's legitimacy. Father John Crowley wrote directly to Shriver to explain that the vocal opposition to SWAFCA could "confuse what is essentially a simple effort by the poor to better their condition." Crowley diffused the Smitherman-led opposition with humor. He explained that the accusations that Mesher was a communist were as valid as the "'rumor' that Lurleen Wallace is a Go-Go Girl." What mattered more to the Catholic priest was SWAFCA's potential impact on the Black Belt. "For the small poor farmers to have any financial independence at all is an historic development in this area," he explained. Crowley endorsed the cooperative and hoped that Shriver would do so, too.[55]

The members of SWAFCA did not sit back and wait for OEO to act. At the co-op's board meeting in late March, the group agreed to continue its operations. Board members choose as the co-op's manager Calvin Orsborn, a black businessman who owned a cotton gin in Selma and seemed to have the experience the cooperative needed. The board also decided to seek money from other sources so that co-op members could begin planting their crops. SWAFCA received a five-thousand-dollar loan from Operation Freedom and a twenty-five-thousand-dollar loan from the International Foundation for Independence. The cooperative, in turn, loaned this money to its members so they could buy supplies and begin farming during the first two weeks in April. Turner and Black distributed fertilizer. These loans kept the cooperative afloat while it waited for OEO to make its decision. This concerted effort also indicated the local people's determination to get their endeavor under way, with or without the OEO grant.[56]

The co-op's leaders sent their own delegation to Washington to lobby for support on April 12. Using money donated by the SIP, eleven SWAFCA farmers and Rev. Walter drove from Alabama in two cars to meet with various OEO administrators in an effort to rebut opposition claims. In a newsletter for SIP members, Walter noted that "Joe Johnson deserves tremendous praise for a most skillful, diplomatic, and reasoned piece of defense." Sims told the antipoverty officials that SWAFCA's plans were sound and feasible. Tuskegee attorney Fred Gray came along to verify that the co-op was not a Black Panther organization. The members of the SWAFCA delegation explained that their efforts had been well advertised. Anyone could have participated in the planning; no one was purposefully excluded. After lobbying OEO, the group went to make its case with both Alabama senators as well as Senators Joseph Clark (D-PA), Jacob Javits (R-NY), and Robert Kennedy (D-NY).[57]

On May 11, OEO announced that it would fund the program but with some concessions. Instead of issuing almost half a million dollars to the cooperative, OEO granted $399,967. After the April 5 meeting with the Alabama delegation, the agency agreed to request an FBI investigation of the cooperative's board members and advisers to quell the charges that the project harbored subversives and violent Black Power advocates. The probe revealed the false charges made by the Alabama Peace Commission. Harding explained to the Alabama officials, "No federal agency could make a grant to a State, municipality, college or university, or any other grantee, if all personnel of that grantee had to forswear their constitutional privilege of political participation." To keep the program from receiving further criticism as a consequence of her activities, Mesher agreed to withdraw from the program after it received the funds. She would not serve either on the co-op staff or on the board. The antipoverty agency maintained veto power over hiring for all staff positions for SWAFCA, and the co-op agreed to try various methods to recruit eligible white farmers as members. The grant also included $60,000 in loan insurance capital, which OEO intended SWAFCA to use to secure loans for agricultural supplies. Agency administrators knew that Alabama officials feared the political strength that SWAFCA could generate through the economic independence of its members but viewed this phenomenon as part of the solution to curing poverty. Harding tried to explain to SWAFCA's opposition why his agency had backed the co-op: considering the "desperate problems of the poor farmers in the area," the grant was needed.[58]

In spite of the decision to issue SWAFCA a demonstration grant, OEO officials still had two points of concern. Berry warned that people hostile to the co-op might try to prevent its crops from being marketed. He thought the cooperative's members had enough experience with living in a belligerent environment to cope with this problem. Moreover, said Berry, "If the potential for interference prevents Negro farmers in the South from earning a livelihood, it is important that this fact be made known to this agency, and to the country." The CAP director's comments indicated the level of support that OEO was willing to give SWAFCA. Nevertheless, antipoverty agency bureaucrats had no idea of the extent to which antagonistic forces would work to thwart the co-op's success. OEO's second sticking point related to the first. Officials knew that SWAFCA's success hinged on the presence of skilled advisers who would assist the co-op in crop diversification, financial affairs, crop marketing, and the administration of social service programs. As a result, the antipoverty agency kept a watchful eye on SWAFCA through monthly reviews provided by the Continental-Allied Company. In spite of this backing, one of the main challenges to the cooperative would be its ability to function isolated from the technical services that local USDA officials routinely offered Black Belt white farmers and cooperatives. The vegetable-producing and -marketing cooperative faced enough challenges in its operations; functioning as a parallel structure would be an added burden for the organization to bear. Both of these issues would have repercussions for the cooperative's long-term viability.[59]

Shriver received support for SWAFCA from other federal agencies, providing him some political cover for issuing the grant. Assistant secretary of agriculture John Baker urged OEO not to retreat from the proposal. He offered the services of various USDA programs to keep the development of the co-op on track. The Extension Service agreed to provide field assistance to SWAFCA members through the Alabama state director of extension. The Farmers Cooperative Service would continue helping the co-op, and the FHA agreed to make a "special effort to provide Economic Opportunity loans and farm operating loans" to cooperative farmers. Baker also submitted a variety of resource materials—films, bulletins, pamphlets—for SWAFCA to distribute to members.[60]

The assistant secretary of agriculture had been committed to helping small family farmers since his early days with the department during the Great Depression. In 1961, he established a rural areas development advisory committee and asked Fay Bennett of the National Sharecroppers Fund and Elizabeth Herring of the National Council of Agricultural Life and Labor to serve with him. "We were just absolutely . . . convinced," Baker disclosed, "that in [a] really tough social structure intertwined with economic structure, . . . the only solution for poor folk was to get co-ops with competent management to be on their side." He knew the distance SWAFCA had to travel to succeed in this venture, but he was willing to lend his support. "Alabama hadn't decided that black folks were as good as white folks yet," Baker remembered. "They were still supported by their governor . . . I couldn't see anything wrong with" SWAFCA. He then made sure that Agriculture Secretary Orville Freeman agreed. Freeman told Baker, "Have at!" but "Don't quote me." In addition to this veiled endorsement from the head of the USDA, OEO received supportive statements from the Economic Development Agency and two economic consulting firms that confirmed the cooperative's feasibility.[61]

Beyond the merits of the demonstration grant, OEO had other reasons for backing the Black Belt co-op. First, the Alabama delegation lacked credibility. Smitherman and the rest of his coalition obviously were not interested in fostering the economic independence of their black neighbors. These white officials wanted only community action agencies that they could control. The Selma mayor made this clear when he closed the city's CAP office with a padlock on April 17 when the assistant director moved his African American secretary into the front portion of the office. OEO also learned through a board member of the Selma–Dallas County CAP, Rev. Louis Lloyd Anderson, that Smitherman had spoken without consulting the CAP's board. Anderson admitted that the local CAP had not done enough to help the poor and said that he therefore wholeheartedly supported SWAFCA. "The only thing our CAP Board has done," he relayed, "is to provide minimal, temporary relief-type programs whose small benefit . . . ends when the project terminates." He confessed, "We have not been a success." Anderson reassured the OEO director that SWAFCA would not be competing with the local CAP since it did not offer programs to people in the rural sections of the county. "SEVERAL groups working would NOT even begin to dent the vast wall of problems," he told Shriver. "WE NEED THEM ALL!"[62]

Donald Baker, OEO's general counsel, understood that the opposition also feared the economic consequences of the co-op. "It was not an accident," the attorney explained, "that the local pickle manufacturer who had been paying a very minimum for the cucumbers he bought, was the only businessman, non-politico, to make the trip up here." Also, unlike Mississippi senators John Stennis and James O. Eastland, who used their power to cut off OEO funding for the Child Development Group of Mississippi (CDGM) Head Start program in September 1966, neither Alabama senator was willing to fight the project beyond offering the delegation a chance to air its grievances. Hill protested and released statements to Alabama newspapers but went no further. Hill and Sparkman may have chosen not to become more involved because they were formulating new political tactics for operating in a new political world after the passage of the Civil Rights Act. Historian Joseph Crespino has found that in Mississippi, "practical segregationists" tried to work in a new way to protect white supremacy. By not taking a hard line and instead supporting realistic approaches, they hoped to reduce federal interference and then "have some stake in controlling where, when and how desegregation would actually occur." Without any hard evidence to account for the actions of Senators Hill and Sparkman, this idea of "practical segregation" could offer an explanation. Maybe they realized that it was not worth spending their political capital to fight SWAFCA. Finally, the Wallace administration had opposed the antipoverty agency almost continually since 1965. This obstruction meant that OEO could justify overriding Governor Lurleen Wallace if she vetoed the project.[63]

The co-op also fit into OEO's larger plan for the country's fight against poverty. The urban riots of 1965 and 1966 led to a renewed focus on rural areas in an attempt to curtail the stream of migrants to the nation's larger cities. President Johnson worried that these uprisings would slow his Great Society plans and sought a way to relieve the cities without seeming to reward the rioters. One way to do so would be to fund rural economic programs that assisted people enough to prevent them from searching for a better life in the city. Support of cooperatives had been a part of the antipoverty legislation from the beginning, but in 1966 Congress amended the Economic Opportunity Act to devote more attention to rural poverty. SWAFCA seemed to offer answers to some of the difficult questions associated with rural poverty. OEO expected the demonstration project to assist the federal government in learning new ways of alleviating poverty through self-help programs that could then be applied to other southern states.[64]

Finally, OEO had suffered severe criticism for its handling of the Mississippi Head Start program. The debacle left the agency bruised by the condemnation it received when it funded a more moderate group in an effort to phase out the CDGM. The National Sharecroppers Fund and the National Farmers Union told OEO's Civil Rights Division that it had "better not make another CDGM" out of the SWAFCA grant. The antipoverty agency issued its last check to CDGM in 1967. The grant to the Alabama Black Belt co-op may have represented an attempt by OEO to restore its reputation as a governmental program that supported the needs of the rural black poor.[65]

When the antipoverty agency announced the SWAFCA grant, local officials continued to attack the co-op. Shriver sent Donald Baker to Selma in an effort to explain why SWAFCA had received the federal grant despite the Alabama delegation's objections. Baker emphasized the demonstration features of the co-op, which would not be allowed to spend money for any other purpose, including civil rights activity, politics, or even food to feed hungry people. Local elected officials kept Baker under fire for ninety minutes and walked out in "disgust" at the federal attorney's answers to their questions. "We might be whipped already

and just don't know it," Smitherman warned Baker, "but we aren't through fighting this program yet."[66]

As Smitherman had predicted, after Baker left Selma, the attack against
the cooperative continued. The mayor first sought the authority to place an
injunction on OEO funds after they were sent to the Selma-based co-op. When
it became clear that he could not get such power, he claimed to have found
proof that the cooperative had ties to SNCC. At a news conference later in May,
he displayed a briefcase that supposedly belonged to a member of SNCC and
contained documents linking the cooperative to the civil rights organization.
He then called for an FBI investigation of the entire OEO. "It looks like some
of them have communist connections," he charged. Johnson, the chair of the
co-op's board, tried to respond to the mayor's theatrics. "No political group or
race is shut out of the coop," he told a reporter. "We are a farmers' organization.
If you are a poor white farmer, hurry on and pay your dollar membership dues,
and start raising peas and greens." Instead of Black Power, Johnson explained,
"We are interested in green power." Smitherman was not the only person who
continued protesting the grant: the Dallas County FHA Office reduced the
amounts of loans it had issued to two SWAFCA-affiliated farmers. When they
brought their first bill from SWAFCA for supplies to the FHA supervisor they
were told their loan had been reduced to $360.[67]

The opposition to the co-op extended beyond the confines of the Black Belt.
The Alabama Senate passed a resolution protesting the grant. The three sponsoring legislators, Walter Givhan, Roland Cooper, and John Hawkins, asked
their colleagues to seek a congressional investigation of OEO's approval of the
grant, claiming that it amounted to "another waste of federal funds." The resolution also said that OEO was financing the "lawless Black Panther movement
designed to overthrow the government of this country and particularly the governments of Southern states." Using an interesting choice of words, the resolution described Shriver as a "weak tool of his brother-in-law, Bobby Kennedy,"
and labeled the grant "nothing more than a cheap political move designed to
blacken Alabama."[68]

In June, the *Birmingham News* ran a series on SWAFCA headlined "Black
Belt Tempest: Politics and Poverty." The five articles reiterated the Peace Commission's complaints about the co-op and implied that it duplicated services
available elsewhere in the region. One article questioned Mesher's motivations
in gathering USDA information for local farmers. The reporter reinforced the
idea that reasons existed to doubt SWAFCA's ability to succeed and laid the
entire organizing effort on Mesher's shoulders. The series gave Smitherman
another forum in which to speak out against the cooperative. One reporter
claimed that the Selma mayor found SWAFCA "a nightmare nest of duplicity

and subversion, waste and do-gooderism; a conglomerate of agricultural ama-
teurs who'll draw excessive salaries while promoting a program which is more
interested in financing Black Pantherism and Negro racist causes with federal
money." In the fourth article in the series, reporters claimed that the Extension
Service had integrated its programs and therefore could reach all farmers who
wished to help themselves. At no time did the reporters research the difficulties local black farmers faced in accessing USDA programs. The paper never
challenged the basic criticisms of SWAFCA put forth by the Peace Commission
and Smitherman but merely repackaged them for a wider audience. The newspaper layout also had an effect. Articles surrounding this investigative series
reinforced the dramatic changes that were taking place that also explain the
siege mentality that was setting in among Alabama's white population: accom-
panying pieces noted President Johnson's nomination of Thurgood Marshall as
the first African American to serve on the U.S. Supreme Court, the Supreme
Court's decision to overturn state-imposed bans on interracial marriages, and
accusations by authorities in Prattville, just outside of Montgomery, that Stokely
Carmichael had touched off a gunfight there.[69]

Governor Lurleen Wallace predictably vetoed the SWAFCA grant on June 8,
further threatening the co-op's chances to make its first crop. Taking a page from
her husband's political Bible, Wallace used the most inflammatory language to
explain her reasons for rejecting the program. She claimed to have evidence that
linked the co-op with "the violent Black Power organization . . . whose leaders
called for the assassination of me, my husband, and my child." In addition to citing technicalities of OEO regulations, the governor used information provided
by Alabama's FHA director, Bamberg, to object to the cooperative. Bamberg
reported that the FHA already loaned money to small farmers to produce okra,
peas, corn, and cucumbers in the SWAFCA area, although the loans were available only to farmers who had contracts with the King Pharr Canning Company
and the Whitfield Pickle Company. From the governor's perspective, only those
farmers deserved funding: "It is obvious that those farmers with a reasonably
sound farming operation could get needed credit here or from other sources
in the area." While Alabamians waited for Shriver to respond to Wallace's veto,
SWAFCA members continued to work in their fields.[70]

Making a Go of It: The Co-op in Action

As the spring progressed to summer, SWAFCA members tended their crops.
Some families arranged safety nets by having one member find paid employment while another worked the land. Some people lived in town and went back
and forth to farm on a piece of land provided by other members. Turner recalled

that in some areas, women were more involved than men. "They were the ones who grew the crops more or less. . . . The men would migrate out and try to find a job in the sawmill or something, and [the women] would stay home and grow the cucumbers." Cunningham offered 102 acres of his land to nineteen families who wanted to grow vegetables: "I had land available, I had the tractor, I had a little credit that I could get the fertilizer and seeds and stuff like that." After picking the crop, each family marked its name on the sacks of produce, and Cunningham and Prince Black (Lewis's brother and a SWAFCA board member from Monroe County) loaded the produce onto their trucks and delivered it to Selma, where it was graded and shipped. "We would be there all night, sometimes through to the next day, trying to get it graded," Cunningham said. "It was a religion kind of thing. . . . The point was helping these people that had the children, giving them something to do and some money in the summer . . . when farmers don't get money." Joe Johnson thought that SWAFCA "meant life to the poor people in the beginning of it. . . . It done a real tremendous job in getting people back on their feet." Prior to joining the co-op, one family had earned only $22.84 by growing four acres of cotton that season; another man had to kill rabbits with a stick to provide his eleven children with some meat— he did not have enough money to buy shotgun shells. From its beginnings, SWAFCA clearly served as a way for some of its members to survive. The co-op would have to expand beyond this level if it was going to transform the rural landscape.[71]

As co-op members marketed their crops in anticipation of making a better living, the opposition to their effort did not abate. With its first harvest on the way, SWAFCA leaders had to find markets for the produce. Beginning in May, Lewis Black worked with marketing specialist Ben Fink to contact produce companies across the country, trying to secure contracts for the co-op's produce; ten companies signed up. For the first three weeks of June, the cooperative sold its members' cucumbers for 40 percent more per ton than they had received before joining the organization. "They are making $95 a ton where they used to make $60 a ton," Turner told a reporter. But by the middle of June, the companies backed out of the agreement, a decision Black blamed on Alabama officials. "For one week all of us were running around like a chicken with his head cut off trying to find a market for the Co-op. During this struggle we lost 20 tons of cucumbers," he recounted. Fink found markets in Michigan and Wisconsin that agreed to accept the produce, enabling operations to continue.[72]

OEO funds were vital for the co-op's future. Without this support, SWAFCA had trouble operating its large produce venture. Members lacked transportation to bring their crops to Selma, where it could be graded and shipped. At times, crops spoiled on their way to Selma and could not be sold because they had traveled up to ninety miles in the sun. The co-op also did not have enough people to properly grade the produce; in one instance, the wrong size cucumbers were sent to market and were rejected by the processor. Each county needed a grading shed, but the co-op could not afford to build them. SWAFCA members also required technical assistance. Many knew how to grow cotton but did not know the details of raising vegetables. The cooperative was late in delivering seeds for the next crop to many of its members. In some cases farmers had plowed their ground in anticipation of planting but had to wait until the seeds arrived to continue. In spite of these difficulties, SWAFCA managed to sell twenty-five thousand dollars' worth of cucumbers in June, but leaders knew that the co-op faced a precarious future without the OEO grant.[73]

Secretary of Agriculture Orville Freeman visited the Black Belt in late June. SWAFCA leaders invited him to "drop by for an extended visit and conference at the co-op headquarters." Freeman did not want to exacerbate the debate that surrounded the cooperative, so he compromised, driving by SWAFCA headquarters in Selma, where Orsborn and Johnson got onto his bus to discuss the co-op's needs. OEO's director of rural services, Ira Kaye, accompanied Freeman and sat on the bus with the three men as they discussed SWAFCA. After hearing about the cooperative's problems, the agriculture secretary agreed to send someone from the Farmers Cooperative Service to help out. This news led SWAFCA members to hope that Shriver planned to override the governor's veto.[74]

The official harassment of SWAFCA continued after Freeman's visit. Shriver wrote to Smitherman, indicating that OEO would probably fund the cooperative. "I wish to make clear also in order to avoid misunderstanding," the OEO director emphasized, "that I do not consider an appropriate ground for rejecting the program that public officials may allow their hostility to the program to express itself in the form of an improper harassment of the project and its beneficiaries." Alabama officials did not heed Shriver's warning. The two processors who had traditionally bought produce from individual Black Belt farmers cut off purchases from SWAFCA members. Not content to stop there, the processors also tried to prevent these farmers from finding other outlets for their crops. In early July, Alabama state troopers stopped two eighteen-wheelers full of SWAFCA produce for traffic violations. The state police kept the trucks waiting until they ran out of fuel, which turned off the cooling mechanisms inside the carriers. This action ruined the cucumbers and kept them from being sold. The local telephone company tried to charge SWAFCA seven hundred dollars for the installation of telephones in its headquarters. Fertilizer bought from a local white cooperative became unavailable to black farmers, and lime trucks ceased deliveries to SWAFCA members. In addition to threatening the cooperative's ability to continue, this type of intimidation sent a message to co-op members that serious repercussions would follow if they continued supporting the self-help effort. Even in the face of these threats, the cooperative members planted 570 acres of cucumbers, 500 acres of okra, and 1,000 acres of early and late peas, a total of 1 million pounds of produce. "We had a fine early cucumber and okra market," Fink reported. "Prices to producers were good."[75]

On July 5, Shriver notified Lurleen Wallace that he had overridden her veto of the SWAFCA grant, just the third time the OEO director had taken that action. Bertrand Harding, Shriver's deputy, told Wallace that the antipoverty agency could not accept her rejection. Shriver provided Senator Hill with a more detailed explanation for overriding the veto: Investigators had found no links between SWAFCA and SNCC or "any anti-American groups," and giving in to threats by local officials would only encourage future rejections of OEO programs. The antipoverty agency was concerned primarily with "the urgent need for assistance which exists in the community."[76]

After receiving word that the long-awaited OEO grant would be forthcoming, the co-op began to hire consultants, technicians, field specialists for each county, and other support staff. Advertisements stated that "preference for non-technical jobs will be given to members of low-income farm families, then to other rural people." Cooperative leaders advertised for one horticulturist, ten agricultural field specialists, one assistant co-op manager (trainee), two administrative assistants (trainees), one comptroller, secretaries, clerk-typists (trainees), truck drivers, loaders, and graders, receiving six hundred applications for the positions. Johnson contacted churches across the Black Belt, asking for prayers of thanksgiving for SWAFCA's good fortune. "We want to SHARE OUR JOY WITH THE ENTIRE COMMUNITY," the board chairman wrote, "and GIVE THANKS TO GOD and to all those who took up the support of SWAFCA, as well as to the many . . . farmers who worked so hard to bring it into reality." Sounding more like a traditional Bible-Belt Alabamian rather than a Black Power revolutionary, Johnson wanted ministers to ask God to give the co-op's leaders "continued courage and determination" to make the venture a "complete success." He hoped that SWAFCA would "serve ALL in these ten counties— Black and White—Farmer and Non-Farmer—Rich and Poor" and wanted pastors to ask God to "let THIS Co-op be a light of new hope unto the poor and downtrodden everywhere, that they might rise among themselves and be able to come into a new and better life. Doing God's work!"[77]

The cooperative carried on with the work it had begun earlier in the summer. SWAFCA newsletters asked for more cucumbers and announced that the co-op would buy okra, peas, snap beans, crooked-necked squash, and butter beans. As Freeman had promised, Carl Deitemeyer of the USDA's Farmers Cooperative Service came to Selma to help "iron out the kinks that any new cooperative runs into." "This is the most challenging assignment I have ever had in my life," he

Rebirth of the Alabama Blackbelt

Figure 20. The Southwest Alabama Farmers Cooperative Association produced a brochure, *The SWAFCA Story.* In addition to claiming that the venture would bring about the "Rebirth of the Alabama Black Belt," the pamphlet included an address by Joe Johnson, chairman of the co-op's board, and an explanation of its purpose. Although this brochure exuded a positive message—African Americans organizing to create opportunities for themselves and their communities—that in itself threatened the status quo. Anti-Poverty Program Evaluation, Box 5, Community Services Administration Papers (formerly Office of Economic Opportunity), Southeast Regional Office, Record Group 381, National Archives and Records Administration, Southeast Region, Morrow, Ga.

told a reporter. "I am gratified at the leadership the people show." Deitemeyer helped SWAFCA obtain the permits needed to operate a vegetable-marketing business and assisted Orsborn in screening applications submitted by technical experts. By the end of August, a more complete staff had come on board. Deitemeyer also tried to get local USDA program offices involved in educating co-op members. He asked the FHA to begin a "crash program" to answer farmers' questions, and he encouraged county extension agents to set up field demonstrations to teach farmers the details about growing vegetables. By the middle of July, extension agents had already offered assistance in Hale County, where they showed co-op members how to identify vegetables ready for market. After Deitemeyer attended a SWAFCA board meeting, Lewis Black commented, "With this type of help, we can see a new hope for SWAFCA."[78]

The Federation of Southern Cooperatives also contributed to SWAFCA's development in the summer of 1967. Formed as an umbrella group for poor people's cooperatives across the South, the federation received a Ford Foundation

grant to train people in cooperative techniques through the Southern Cooperative Development Project. The federation hired Thelma Craig, Mildred Black
(Lewis's wife), a man named Monroe, Ezra Cunningham, and Albert Turner (on
a part-time basis) as field secretaries to work in Alabama. After spending three
weeks in intensive training and leadership development, these men and women
provided technical support to fledgling poor-people's organizations. The federation assigned Cunningham to work with the SWAFCA board of directors.
He led workshops and leadership training sessions for the co-op's board. To
promote better business practices, new standards for board membership were
established. Any director who missed three consecutive meetings without a
written excuse would be removed. The members of the field staff also showed
the board how to subdue internal disunity, increase member loyalty, and recruit
new members.[79]

After four months of work, the Black Belt cooperative assessed its operations. It had marketed more than a million pounds of produce, receiving higher
prices for cucumbers and peas than members had previously received—six
cents per pound compared to three to four cents per pound. Prior to the formation of the cooperative, farmers could sell okra only on the fresh market,
which would often become overwhelmed. SWAFCA found new markets for
okra, enabling farmers to get a better return on their crops. Cooperative members made two to three times as much per acre in vegetables as they did growing cotton. Fink said that "the very existence of SWAFCA had forced the local
markets and processors to raise their prices because of the competition." During its first three months of operation, SWAFCA received more than fifty-two
thousand dollars from commercial markets for its members' crops. Orsborn
reported that several white farmers joined the co-op after learning that it could
bring in better prices for produce. The OEO grant also enabled the cooperative
to offer its members economic opportunity loans, providing financial support
to farmers who did not have enough land or capital to receive FHA loans. Many
SWAFCA members were in their fifties and sixties and had worked on plantations for thirty or forty years. "All of the production that they made, everything
they did for 30 or 40 years," Orsborn explained, "the credit did not go to [them],
the credit went to the plantation, which means when this fellow is put off of
this place or when he decides to move, he has no history. He can show no basic
method of repaying this loan and he has no security nine times out of ten." The
FHA allowed the co-op to act as a collecting agency, requiring borrowers to
pay 50 percent of their note from daily produce sales, not the standard practice
for FHA loans. Farmers thus could pay expenses incurred in getting crops to
market. Finally, SWAFCA representatives offered members assistance in com-
pleting FHA loan applications. "SWAFCA personnel in each county filled out

the loan applications, and presented them to FHA," Orsborn clarified, "and in nine cases out of ten, I think the loans were approved." Despite these successes, the co-op operated at a loss of $926.69, and the average gross sales per member totaled only $134. By the fall, SWAFCA leaders began to anticipate the 1968 crop, search for the markets for the produce, and identify the changes necessary to make the co-op more profitable.[80]

In addition to agricultural benefits, the cooperative offered intangibles to its members. The board alternated its meeting sites among the co-op's ten counties, and each county organized a chapter that met regularly. Field specialists helped run weekly meetings in each county, presenting films, discussing problems, and conducting other extension activities. These meetings provided members with a chance to learn business skills as well as to practice using democratic principles. The board of directors made all decisions through consensus. One official compared the board of directors "with the perfect democracies of ancient Greek city-states, or with the Swiss cantons in their original form, having an all-powerful legislature consisting of the citizenry as a whole, and weak executive." SWAFCA gave its members a public space in which to gather and discuss issues. By late September, Perry County had a grading station; when the building was not in use for grading, local people used it as a social hall. The cooperative also offered members the chance to work collectively to change long-standing southern agricultural practices. Success in the face of the pressure mounted by local, state, and federal officials gave members confidence and proved that local black people could persevere in spite of these difficulties.[81]

The members of SWAFCA's board of directors and their OEO advisers realized that the cooperative required more money to increase its business operations. To operate profitably, the co-op had to enlarge its sales per member, which meant that the volume of produce had to multiply. SWAFCA needed to invest in capital improvements. Grading and receiving sheds had to be built in each county to avoid crop loss. Transportation problems had to be alleviated by purchasing trucks. Other equipment had to be bought—tractors, lime spreaders, and portable irrigation systems—to assist members in their truck farming endeavors. The co-op had to have more technical assistance to develop better loading patterns, appropriate storage and transit temperatures, and secure ways to get produce to market. The co-op had spent only $178,000 of its OEO grant, but the remaining $222,167 would not cover all the co-op's future needs. The co-op board consequently applied to the FHA for an $850,000 cooperative loan.[82]

In November, SWAFCA celebrated its first anniversary with a Thanksgiving open house. Supporters from the civil rights movement and the agriculture community came from across the country, including administrators from the

Farmers Cooperative Service, USDA Rural Services Division, and the Department of Labor. The National Sharecroppers Fund, the National Council of Churches, the Cooperative League of the United States of America, the ACHR, and Tuskegee Institute also sent representatives. Theodore Berry attended the celebration as the guest of honor. Joe Johnson read telegrams of congratulations sent from Vice President Hubert Humphrey, Secretary of Agriculture Freeman, Secretary of Labor W. Willard Wirtz, Sargent Shriver, and thirteen members of Congress. "The road ahead isn't going to be easy and it is important that you take advantage of every idea," Berry told the crowd. "It fell to my honor to fix my signature to the $400,000 grant to launch the ship of SWAFCA and I am happy to be here to see my faith justified."[83]

In December, SWAFCA received further support from OEO by way of Congress. After debating amendments to the Economic Opportunity Act, federal lawmakers agreed to fund the War on Poverty for two years, a change from its previous annual appropriations. Congress also rejected a proposal that would have given local officials or community action boards veto power over demonstration programs such as SWAFCA's rural readjustment effort. The House and Senate also removed the provision requiring local communities to provide 10 percent of the antipoverty budget in cash. Representative Edith Green (D-OR) attached an amendment that required CAP boards to consist of one-third local elected officials, one-third local civic leaders, and one-third representatives of the poor. Although the Green amendment would rein in some CAPs that had functioned without the support of local officials, this ruling did not apply to demonstration projects. As co-op officials looked ahead, the prospects for 1968 looked good. Lewis Black reported that SWAFCA had secured markets, production surveys had been conducted, and soil tests were under way. The coming year would also see political growth for many Black Belt residents. SWAFCA members would learn some hard lessons in this process, but the co-op would eventually provide a solid base for a third political party.[84]

The following year would be crucial for the co-op. Opposition forces continued to try to thwart its work at every turn, redoubling their efforts in an election year. When co-op leaders negotiated an $852,000 FHA loan, the new monies fostered many elected officials' insecurities.

Déjà Vu All Over Again: 1968, a Year of Challenge

The debate that started in the 1966 statewide elections between the freedom party activists in Dallas, Greene, and Lowndes Counties and the Democratic Party loyalists of the ADC continued in anticipation of the 1968 vote. Some Alabamians felt that the best option was staying committed to the state's Democratic

Party, trying to change it from within. Others thought that working outside of the Alabama Democratic Party offered the only way to alter the state's politics, especially in light of its continued devotion to George Wallace. As it became clear that the former governor would make a run for the presidency, Alabama Democrats faithful to the national party began to work to make sure that the party's national candidate could appear on the state's ballot in the fall. They did not want Wallace to block the national Democratic candidate from the state's presidential ballot.

Two loyalist groups formed, one offering presidential electors for the national convention only and one as a third political party. Birmingham attorney and racial moderate David J. Vann created the Alabama Independent Democratic Party (AIDP) in mid-December 1967 with the blessing of the Alabama Democratic Party and the Democratic National Committee. Vann wanted to provide a mechanism that would enable the national party to prevail at the 1968 Democratic National Convention against those Alabama electors who pledged support to Wallace. Vann's new party would seek only candidates for presidential electors in an effort to obtain convention delegates committed to the national party. Vann thought that forming a full-fledged political party would further weaken Democrats already under siege from Alabama's resurgent Republican Party.[85]

John Cashin, a Huntsville dentist and former board member of the ADC, also wanted to make sure that the state Democrats could participate in the national presidential election. Since 1965, he had wanted to form a statewide third party along the lines of the Mississippi Freedom Democratic Party. The time seemed right for launching such an effort, especially after Joe Reed defeated Cashin in the campaign to become the ADC's chair. Cashin and Alvis Howard Jr., a white insurance executive, formed a biracial party to run candidates for office from the local to the national levels. Both Huntsville men did not trust Vann's efforts, suspecting that he had made an "undercover" arrangement with the state's Democratic Party and had no intention of upsetting the status quo.[86]

On December 15, 1967, Howard, Cashin, and Charles Morgan Jr. filed papers for a state charter to create the National Democratic Party of Alabama (NDPA). Many of the new party's African American members had become disillusioned with the ADC's strategies. The new party's white supporters had been disappointed with the regular Alabama Democratic Party's lack of institutional reforms. For this group, a third party that remained committed to the national organization but put forth progressive measures at home seemed to be the answer. The NDPA offered this new hybrid option. In the Black Belt, the NDPA was different from the 1966 freedom organizations because it held allegiance to the national party. However, the NDPA resembled the earlier groups because it also sought to change Alabama's political culture. Sociologist Hardy Frye has explained that "Cashin hoped to establish himself as the black political leader in Alabama, and the NDPA as the only political choice for black and progressive white Alabamians."[87]

As new political parties developed outside of the Black Belt, SWAFCA's good fortunes began to falter. On March 17, the co-op received word that its FHA loan would come from OEO funds budgeted for the USDA to manage. The cooperative had planned to spend $540,000 on buildings, equipment, and supplies and to use the remainder of the money to establish a revolving fund for the purchase of members' vegetables. Bamberg, however, placed harsh restrictions on the loan before agreeing to release the funds. He wanted SWAFCA to provide him copies of its contracts with vegetable buyers, information about how it would pay for specific crops, a complete list of cooperative members and the acreage each planned to farm, and an explanation of what the co-op would pay its members. In addition to these invasive demands, he wanted to place a lien on all property and equipment purchased by SWAFCA for the duration of the thirty-year loan, and he stipulated that the co-op could not finance any of its members for a period any longer than thirty days. He included in the loan terms a requirement that the cooperative give advance notice of any meeting (including board of directors meetings) to the FHA so that Bamberg's officials might attend. The state FHA also wanted to restrict the co-op from meeting with any other agency to discuss business. If the co-op held such a meeting, FHA administrators had to be invited. Bamberg had a long history of not backing black farmers, and he had not been supportive of the co-op since its inception. He used his powerful position to slow SWAFCA's progress. His actions led many in the cooperative to question the motivations behind these regulations. On April 30, Bamberg testified before the U.S. Commission on Civil Rights in Montgomery, where he revealed his private racial philosophy in social Darwinian language. According to Bamberg, "the laws of the animal kingdom apply," a philosophy that meant that it did no good to help the weak because the strong will take from them, a phenomenon he witnessed every day as he administered the Alabama FHA office. Cooperative leaders tried to renegotiate the supervision of the loan to avoid falling under Bamberg's obstructionist thumb, seeking assistance directly from Washington instead of from the FHA office, but until they could do so, the federal funds would not be forthcoming. The same day that the cooperative received word of its FHA loan, three Alabama Democratic congressmen—George Andrews, Bill Nichols, and Armistead Selden—requested that the Government Accounting Office include SWAFCA in its investigation of OEO's various programs.[88]

As the 1968 primaries approached, many Black Belt residents considered their party options. Although some African American candidates agreed with the concepts of the NDPA, the party was not organized enough for many people to trust its viability. As a result, many black candidates continued to seek office under the state's Democratic Party. RAP director Lewis Black and Marvin Wall of the Southern Regional Council's Voter Education Project conducted a workshop on voter registration and political education in anticipation of the statewide vote. Black helped instruct participants on how to prepare communities for the election by organizing on the precinct and ward levels. He had a vested interest in seeing that more black voters learned how the political structure of an area operated: Mildred Black was running for Place 2 on the Hale County Board of Education. The 1968 primary results resembled those from 1966. Some African American candidates reached runoffs, but most lost. One reporter explained that many black people still had not registered to vote or were too frightened to cast ballots. Some might have stayed home because white Democrats continued to malign the civil rights movement. In his campaign for the U.S. Senate, Armistead Selden of Greensboro spoke out against SWAFCA and OEO. He claimed that issuing grants to the cooperative appeared to be "illegal" because of the involvement of "militant civil rights activists" in its ranks. With such stump speeches, some African Americans in the Black Belt not surprisingly continued to distrust the Democratic Party. Nevertheless, one county witnessed an important victory. Mayor R. Leigh Peagues of Marion, a strong opponent of the War on Poverty and SWAFCA, lost in the primary to C. B. Lockhart. Albert Turner claimed that the black vote had helped Lockhart prevail.[89]

Others in the region received good news from OEO when it funded a second demonstration project, this time in the eastern half of the state. The Southeast Alabama Self-Help Association (SEASHA) formed to serve two thousand members in Barbour, Bullock, Coosa, Crenshaw, Elmore, Lee, Lowndes, Macon, Montgomery, Pike, Russell, and Tallapoosa Counties. One aspect of the cooperative focused on raising feeder pigs. SEASHA also had a federal credit union, a community development and assistance branch, and a program of nonfarm business and industrial development. SEASHA grew out of Tuskegee Institute's earlier involvement in the War on Poverty. Lewis Black offered his technical assistance through the Rural Advancement Project to help the SEASHA board members learn how to operate the cooperative's business meetings. OEO's Greene noted the importance of the two Black Belt cooperatives: "With the funding of SEASHA CAP will have two demonstration projects operating in Alabama and covering a total of twenty-two counties," he told Berry. "Both SWAFCA and SEASHA are concentrating on economic development,"

Greene proudly reported, "in order to give the poor of those counties the option of remaining productively in rural areas." SEASHA did not face the same fierce opposition as SWAFCA, probably because it offered a variety of services and had connections to Tuskegee Institute. Although the cooperative harbored the same potential for grassroots organizing, SEASHA appeared to be less threatening, at least on the surface. It was larger than SWAFCA, but the feeder-pig operation assisted only forty-seven families, and it received advice from the Auburn University Extension Service.[90]

Throughout the summer, SWAFCA faced a troubled future. The FHA loan, which it desperately needed, remained stalled in Washington as the terms were renegotiated. In July, OEO issued a second grant to the co-op, which Albert Brewer, who had assumed the governorship when Lurleen Wallace died of cancer, vetoed at the end of August. As a result, the co-op's financial fate looked bleak. Orsborn made matters worse with a basic managerial philosophy described by one OEO consultant as "compulsive procrastination." He did not order seed and fertilizer on time. When the seeds arrived, they were the wrong variety. Orsborn neglected to rent refrigerated space to store the co-op's produce, and he did not get grading sheds built and equipment bought when needed. The board grew impatient with his management mistakes but feared that releasing him would harm the co-op's chances of getting the FHA loan. Finally, the board asked Orsborn to resign on June 30. In mid-August, however, the SWAFCA board members learned that Orsborn had done even more damage than they had thought. The City Bank of Selma mistakenly sent SWAFCA a Farmers Insurance Fund bank statement that showed that Orsborn had set up a second account in December 1967 for his own personal use. The statement revealed that after he was asked to resign, he transferred seventy-five thousand dollars of SWAFCA's money into his account. The board immediately reported the fraud to OEO and worked quickly to recover the money. Although between Orsborn and SWAFCA's bond insurance coverage, the co-op recouped all of the funds, his illegal activity gave co-op opponents further evidence that the enterprise did not operate as a legitimate business worthy of taxpayer support.[91]

As SWAFCA stood on shaky ground, the NDPA's future also seemed unstable. The Democratic National Convention became the first real battleground where the NDPA could test its strength against the moderate forces of the ADC and the AIDP. This contest demonstrated the great difficulty the NDPA would encounter in unseating the traditional black leaders who had been trying to hold onto their coveted positions as power brokers since the passage of the Voting Rights Act. Vann and Cashin's third-party plans shook up the Alabama Democratic Party. In February, it allowed two black delegates and five African American alternates to run unopposed to serve as convention representatives in the May primary. Joe L. Reed and Alvin Holmes of the ADC and Arthur Shores of Birmingham served as three of the African American electors. State party leaders remained loyal to George Wallace but reasoned that the Democratic National Committee would accept the delegation if it was integrated. State representative Alvin Holmes, a deputy vice chairman of the ADC, later recalled that the battle for delegate seats at the 1968 convention "set the course of the Alabama Democratic Party."[92]

The NDPA conducted its first convention to choose presidential electors and candidates for office on July 20. A group of 126 people, half of them black and half white, gathered in Birmingham. The party chose as its themes racial equality, justice for the poor, an end to the Vietnam War, and freedom from domination by political bosses. Civil rights veterans including Virginia Durr from Montgomery and Ed King of the Mississippi Freedom Democratic Party addressed the crowd. The group accepted an entire slate of congressional candidates, all but one of whom were black. It nominated a white attorney, Robert Schwenn, for U.S. Senate and J. H. Davis for the state's Public Service Commission. Davis, an African American, would challenge Birmingham's Eugene "Bull" Connor on November 5. The party's ten presidential electors came from all over the state and represented both races. The party nominated a total of 130 candidates for local, state, and national office.[93]

The Democratic National Convention took place in Chicago at the end of August. Remembered today for Mayor Richard Daley's violent response to the antiwar protesters camped in Grant Park, the convention stood out for other reasons to the members of the NDPA delegation. The fight over delegate representation took precedence over the pending statewide election. The party sought legitimacy, and recognition from the national party would be one way to get it. "Political change for the state of Alabama—that's what it's all about," explained Jack Zylman, the NDPA's executive secretary. "We're challenging the whole Democratic Party of Alabama—the same party which has been perpetuating racist politics here . . . and which has been helping to oppress the poor black and white people of Alabama for so long." As predicted, both the NDPA and the AIDP protested the seating of the delegates from the Alabama Democratic Party. Cashin's party complained that the electors for the Alabama regulars had already pledged their votes to Wallace. When the convention credentials committee agreed to ask the regulars to sign an oath of loyalty to the national party, a walkout of the ten delegation members who supported Wallace ensued.[94]

The NDPA had the support of northern states, while the AIDP regulars had the backing of southern states. The road to recognition would not be smooth for the NDPA, even though its members were more representative of loyal Democrats. First, the NDPA platform plank opposing the Vietnam War pushed the

White House and Democratic National Committee into the AIDP camp. Second, Senator John Sparkman addressed the credentials committee with a speech reassuring those present that Alabama's party was in transition and embracing necessary racial changes, using the presence of black delegates to prove his point. Finally, the black delegates of the regular party served as mediators for the credentials committee. Since they did not support the NDPA's threat to their position of power, they took a stance against seating either an all-black or an all-white delegation (even though both the regulars and the NDPA electors had biracial delegations). Alvin Holmes, an ADC member and black delegate from the Alabama Democratic Party, lobbied the New York delegation on behalf of the AIDP. "I showed them the scars on my body, on my forehead. Then I asked this man—I asked John Cashin—to name one Civil Rights demonstration that he had participated in his whole life. He stood in silence." This show-and-tell lesson seemed to have the desired results. The credentials committee called an executive session, inviting representatives from the regulars and the AIDP but not the NDPA. The New York delegation voted unanimously to seat the AIDP along with those Alabama regulars who agreed to sign loyalty oaths to the national party. Other delegations followed the Empire State's lead, preventing the NDPA from participating in the convention. Like OEO's initial support of integrated CAPs in places such as Selma, members of the credentials committee looked at an Alabama Democratic Party that had elected black delegates and saw what seemed to be a step in the right direction. Nevertheless, according to one scholar, what had actually taken place was "a manipulation of political resources by Alabama's moderate political leaders to retain state ties to the national party."[95]

The exclusion of the NDPA by Holmes and the other ADC members who served as regular delegates reflected a dynamic that had been building within the Alabama black community since the passage of federal civil rights laws. Members of Cashin's delegation had also taken part in various civil rights demonstrations going back to the 1950s. Pointing out that the NDPA chair lacked scars to prove his authenticity in the civil rights struggle made an emotional appeal that Cashin did not refute well. Historical sociologist Charles Payne has explained that what appeared to be selling out in 1968 "would have been called progress had it happened in 1963." Black Mississippi civil rights veteran Lawrence Guyot had no qualms about working within the Democratic Party to effect change. "The fight wasn't about being politically pure," Payne said, "it was a fight to get in and take over." Alabama politics harbored the same harsh realities. As in Mississippi, "what had been a politics of community," Payne concluded, "became increasingly just politics." The rivalry between the ADC and the NDPA would not end in Chicago but indicated what was at stake and how difficult the fight would be.[96]

To another battle-scarred veteran of southern politics, the 1968 convention did not look so bleak. Virginia Durr wrote to her old friends Clark and Mairi Foreman in late September to explain why she remained hopeful even though the NDPA had not been seated as the official convention delegation. To Durr, what mattered was the fact that new relationships had been forged: "In spite of the violence and shenanigans . . . for the first time for so long there was the beginnings of a new coalition, much broader, deeper and more permanent I believe than ever before since the New Deal, the [Eugene] McCarthy people were great I thought . . . and the young people and the SOUTH." She used a wider lens to make her judgments about the significance of the events in Chicago. "It was so exciting to see the Solid South begin to break up, and Julian Bond emerged as the real leader of the challenge forces in the South. . . . [T]he South is really rising and Black and White were together and got along fine at least in our delegation and I think in most of the Southern delegations." Durr had a strong sense of what the future held. "We know Alabama will go for Wallace in a big way and I think he will get a huge vote," she predicted, "and he and the Republican Party will merge eventually, he is certainly destroying the two party system as he said he would."[97]

Durr chided southern historian C. Vann Woodward for failing to attend the convention. "You really missed it," she wrote; "it was simply wonderful . . . a real watershed, at least for the South. For the first time, the people who voted for years AGAINST THE DEMOCRATIC PARTY got at least some of their comeuppance. Just think of Eastland and Stennis losing the backing of the national Democratic Party and Julian Bond getting even half of [Georgia Governor Lester] Maddox's party, it was really thrilling." She even found the experience of witnessing Sparkman explaining to the credentials committee that Alabama was in transition worth the trip to Chicago. "To hear all of those SOBs who for years have been berating the Democratic Party and . . . the Negro . . . brag about how many black people (they even said "Black" which is now the fashionable word) they had on THEIR DELEGATIONS and how they loved the Democratic party and how they loved the colored people and how there was nothing they wanted as much as to get them active in the Democratic Party, it was really a marvelous joy, and to hear the ones from Alabama cussin' out George Wallace . . . and bragging on how many Negroes they had on their side, the whole thing was worth a lifetime of work and worry." She could be hopeful about the future because "the Southern deceivers (along with the master deceiver, Humphrey) were unmasked." She pinned her hopes on the Democratic Party coming to terms with its past accommodations with southern racism: "I have always thought that if the South could be brought to reckoning that the Democratic Party might be saved."[98]

In early September, the NDPA learned that Alabama's secretary of state, Mabel Amos, disputed the party's qualifications to present candidates for the November election in twenty-four counties. She believed that the NDPA had not strictly followed state law in forming a third party. Voting specialist Martha Witt Smith tried to provide evidence to disqualify the NDPA from the election. Smith wanted to subpoena the lists of voters who cast ballots in the counties under review to prove that some NDPA supporters had voted in the Democratic primary. If this approach did not pass muster with the federal district court, she thought doing nothing might be beneficial in the end because it would split the vote for Humphrey. A threat to white supremacy lurked in this approach, however. She warned Hugh Maddox, the governor's legal adviser, "there is the danger of what could happen if [the NDPA] field[s] local candidates in some of these counties." Later in September, the secretary of state disqualified some of the candidates for county office. Two rejected office seekers had not filed letters of intent, and six sought seats that were not up for election. These mistakes highlighted the new third party's poor organization. Not to be outflanked by hostile state officials, the NDPA asked a federal court to place the party's major candidates on the ballot. Until a full hearing could be held on the matter, the court ordered the state to put the NDPA candidates back on the ballot. Regardless of this decision, Rev. William Branch of Greene County maintained a secure position in his bid on the NDPA ticket for the Fifth Congressional District seat. He had followed the letter of the law, holding a mass meeting in his district on May 7 to qualify as a third-party candidate.[99]

At the full hearing before the district court in mid-October, the NDPA lost its argument by a two-to-one vote. The federal court refused to compel state officials to put more than one hundred NDPA candidates on the ballot. The state argued that its Corrupt Practices Act would be violated if the NDPA succeeded, since the third party had not filed the necessary paperwork. Judge Frank Johnson dissented, stating that the state had invoked this argument "strictly as an afterthought." The U.S. Supreme Court did not have time to hear the case on appeal before the election, so it ruled that Alabama had to put the third-party candidates on the ballot. Although the NDPA won in court, its office seekers had little time to campaign.[100]

The impending elections also influenced SWAFCA's receipt of its second OEO grant. On October 16, Shriver overrode Governor Brewer's veto and issued a $595,751 grant to complete the antipoverty agency's four-year commitment to the demonstration project. Three days later, Dallas County law enforcement officials entered the meeting room at Selma University where SWAFCA was hosting a southeast cooperative workshop and issued injunctions against the board of directors for the co-op. Dallas County circuit court judge James Hare had handed down the injunctions at the request of Mayor Smitherman. Hare's orders against the SWAFCA board of directors, the co-op manager, and the City National Bank of Selma kept the cooperative from accessing any of the money it had received from the federal government. "I feel that it is my obligation to protect the total community in asking that legal action be taken to prevent the further spending of public monies," Smitherman argued, "until it is determined if sound management practices are being used." SWAFCA sued Brewer, Hare, and Smitherman in federal court, though the Justice Department stepped in to try to lift the injunctions. As a result of this action, the cooperative could not pay salaries, buy supplies, or function in any normal business activities. The co-op remained unable to use any of its funds until the Justice Department prevailed in federal court on November 13, eight days after the election.[101]

The November 5 election results brought a feeling of déjà vu to many Black Belt residents. The NDPA was not the only third party seeking office in the region. In Lowndes County, five people ran on the Black Panther ticket. Two men, Jessie Favor and Rev. T. M. Gilchrist, faced no opponents for positions as justices of the peace. John E. Hinson vied for Place 2 on the school board. R. L. Strickland, head of the Lowndes County Title III poverty program, and Charles Smith, a SWAFCA board member, campaigned for seats on the board of revenue. Smith used the co-op as part of his message to voters. "Our county was one of the counties that went to Washington" in support of the cooperative, he said. "They did everything they could to stop a little dab of money from comin' in to help poor folks. That should not be." Smith also wanted to bring better county services to Lowndes's black communities. Despite his message, Smith did not win his bid for office; Strickland and Hinson also lost. The unopposed candidates running under the Black Panther emblem won their seats, as did other African American office seekers running unopposed in Macon and Pike Counties.[102]

The NDPA candidates did not fare as well. Despite the backing of the SCLC and of SNCC's Julian Bond, all the third-party congressional nominees lost by large margins. Seventeen of the ninety-one candidates for other offices won— mostly board of education, constable, justice of the peace, and county board of supervisors. The NDPA showed its strength in two Black Belt counties, Sumter, where eight people won races, and Marengo, where five were victorious. The ADC campaigned openly against the NDPA. Joan Cashin remembered that ADC members told voters, "Don't even think about voting for NDPA; you'll throw away your vote; they are not a legal party." In the second district, Rufus

Lewis of the Montgomery chapter of the ADC came out in support of the white candidate Robert F. Whaley, provoking an increase in black voter turnout that benefited NDPA candidate Rev. Richard Boone. Boone lost to Whaley but earned more votes in Montgomery County, a small moral victory for the NDPA. In Greene County, all the NDPA nominees were left off of the ballot. Probate judge Dennis Herndon claimed that the Supreme Court had never officially notified him of its decision.[103]

Many voters in the region took notice of the NDPA's challenge to the status quo. The seventeen NDPA officeholders put Alabama ahead of all other Deep South states in number of elected black officials. The new third party seemed to offer a greater opportunity than the ADC, which chose to stay in the state's Democratic Party. After two statewide elections had ended in defeat, Lewis Black concluded that he needed to support the NDPA. "The lesson was learned that we ain't going to be able to get out of the primary with the white folks' party," he explained, because "we have no control over the Rooster Party." Black grew tired of the ADC's approach to state politics; he wanted to be involved in a political party that respected the aspirations of African Americans. "ADC is still a backdoor organization. It's not a party. It's just a political organization that's beating on a door that has a dead end." He wanted the ability, offered by the NDPA, to "come together and sit down and choose our own candidates that we were going to put on the whole slate." Clarence Williams, chairman of the DCIFVO, agreed with Black's conclusions, stating, "I feel NDPA is necessary, No. 1 as a challenge to the existing party." Williams realized the necessity of organizing around African American voters. "If we're gonna elect black politicians, we're gonna elect them with the black vote. You can't depend on white voters. This is where it's at, so you have to have the machinery to do that." These expressions of Black Power made sense in counties with large black majorities.[104]

After the 1968 election, Cashin held a state meeting and invited interested organizations. The Hale County Progressive Association sent a delegation. The group elected Elijah Knox as temporary chairman for the county. At a regular Monday night mass meeting of the Progressive Association, the group decided to support the NDPA's efforts. In Dallas County, Joe Johnson, the first chairman of the SWAFCA board, joined Williams in supporting the NDPA. Throughout the Black Belt, the new party continued to tap into existing third-party movements, voter organizations, and civil rights groups. In many cases, people who disagreed with the ADC's tactics sympathized with the NDPA. In other areas, people were spurred to support a third party by the continued defiance of Democratic leaders such as Smitherman and other local elected officials who opposed SWAFCA's OEO grant and FHA loan. As a result, although the NDPA functioned as a biracial party, its goals resonated and it formed its base in the

Black Belt. Durr thought that the third party served an important purpose in the state's political landscape. She hoped that Wallace would leave the Democratic Party and that he and his followers eventually would become Republicans, leaving the NDPA as the true Democrats of Alabama. "There really never has been a two-party system in this country," she explained to some friends. "Wallace is only expressing what has always been, and I think it would be much healthier and happier if he could be forced to join his own party and his followers could be forced OUT OF THE DEMOCRATIC PARTY." She realized, however, that such an accomplishment would take more money and more organizing.[105]

The troubles faced by SWAFCA and the NDPA led many participants to look forward to the end of 1968. With the new year, both organizations received a real boost from the federal government. Six months after the co-op renegotiated the FHA loan with Washington administrators, the co-op and the USDA finally closed the deal. On January 16, 1969, SWAFCA received its first installment of $270,000, which co-op officials used to buy supplies and equipment. Additional loan payments came on March 15, June 15, and July 1. The Black Belt cooperative now had the financial security to operate productively. William Harrison, who had replaced Johnson as board chairman, agreed to serve as the co-op manager, which also put SWAFCA on surer ground after Orsborn's financial mismanagement had been resolved.[106]

On March 25, 1969, the NDPA won a critical argument before the U.S. Supreme Court. The justices ordered that new elections had to be held in Greene County after Herndon's failure to place the NDPA candidates on the November ballot. The county would have four months to prepare for the special election. In anticipation of this vote, the State Sovereignty Commission began to look for ways to remove Alabama from the provisions of the Voting Rights Act of 1965. The executive secretary of the commission worried about the "illiterate Negro voters" whose numbers increased "at an alarming rate." He warned the governor's legal adviser that African Americans "will control the elections in 12 counties by 1970." Martha Witt Smith reasoned that African American voters could not "out-vote whites in any county with the possible exception of Macon, if the literacy test is put back into effect." The Sovereignty Commission failed to remove the state from this federal legislation, and the Greene County election confirmed whites' fears regarding the future.[107]

On July 29, Greene County held a special election for seats on the county commission and the school board. Running on the NDPA ticket, all six black candidates won their elections, including farmers Frenchie Burton, Vassie Knott, Harry C. Means, and Levi Morrow Sr., who joined the county commission and gave blacks a majority on the body. Robert Hines and J. A. Posey Sr. became members of the board of education. Circuit Judge Emmett Hildreth swore in the six officials on August 11. With the assistance of three technical advisers—Orzell Billingsley, Edwin Marger, and Walter Turner—the new commissioners reached out to their constituents, exploring ways to create a county housing authority, build a technical trade school, and enlarge the welfare building where the county distributed food stamps. This election propelled the NDPA into the forefront of Black Belt politics.[108]

In January 1970, the NDPA's executive committee decided to emphasize electing black people to county-level offices as its next step in gaining political legitimacy, something third parties had been attempting since 1966. Throughout the next year, the Black Belt cooperatives supported by OEO provided political organizers with easy access to the grass roots of the rural black community, aiding in the NDPA's consolidation effort. Cunningham remembered that after a SEASHA board meeting had been adjourned, someone asked to discuss county politics. The official minutes of the meeting did not reflect these discussions because the gathering had been adjourned.[109]

SWAFCA leaders assisted in creating and leading rural chapters of the NDPA throughout the Black Belt. Lewis Black joined the Hale County chapter and served on the NDPA's state executive committee. Cunningham became chair of the Monroe County NDPA. Johnson served as the treasurer of the Dallas County chapter. In 1969, the Lowndes County Freedom Party merged with the NDPA and dropped the Black Panther logo. This move made sense because the NDPA shared the political philosophy of electing black people to county offices but lacked the baggage added by the logo, which had been adopted by others facing different circumstances outside of the Deep South. The following year, the DCIFVO joined the NDPA and accepted the party logo—a flying eagle—as its own. Cunningham valued SWAFCA for the network it created. He spoke out in favor of the NDPA to the Panola Land Buyers Cooperative and to members of SWAFCA in Choctaw County. When "you put your hands on people in all ten counties," he explained, "then you can't deal hardly with one problem, you have to touch all of them" through the political process. Cunningham also thought that the NDPA had more relevance for rural Black Belt residents than did the ADC, which received support from better-educated middle- and upper-middle-class black people from across the state.[110]

In his study of the NDPA, sociologist Hardy T. Frye has found that the rural chapters functioned as community-motivating units. Rural black people used the political meetings as social gatherings. Party members arrived early to see friends from the opposite side of the county. Meetings usually opened and closed with brief religious services. Local announcements were made before the political discussion began. "Even school events are something announced, as well as other issues such as the need to join and cooperate with the local farm co-op being established in an adjoining county." The boundaries between social entertainment, economic growth, and political participation blurred during these gatherings, which followed the familiar ways of the grassroots civil rights movement. The Black Belt cooperatives influenced NDPA's success, as its newsletter attested: "The co-op movement in Alabama has to be seen as the principal economic arm of the struggle for freedom just as NDPA is the political arm of the movement." Williams thought that the NDPA was the only Dallas County organization that continued to encourage people to participate in elections: "We try to get some registration done and get some political education and encourage people to participate." An unmistakable connection existed between SWAFCA and other OEO-supported programs in the Black Belt and the NDPA's growth in the Black Belt.[111]

The 1970 elections finally brought to fruition the seeds planted five years earlier. The NDPA ran a full slate of candidates in twenty-five counties and produced winners in several Black Belt areas. Lewis Black remembered that 450 people attended the Hale County Progressive Association meeting for the 1970 NDPA campaign. The party backed 169 candidates, 10 of them white, on the November 3 ballot. Many of these office seekers had ties to the War on Poverty programs. Jessie Brooks, who had been a SWAFCA board member, ran for tax collector in Wilcox County. Robert Scott of Perry County, who had tried to start a CAP program with Turner in 1965, ran for a House seat, as did Johnson of Dallas County's SHAPE and SWAFCA. Robert Strickland of Lowndes, who led his county's Title III adult-education program, and Rev. F. N. Nixon of the Sumter County Movement for Human Rights sought election to the Alabama House. A. D. Bush, a 1968 SWAFCA board member, ran for Dallas County commissioner, and SWAFCA member N. F. Payne sought the Dallas coroner's office. Thomas Gilmore, the SCLC's project director for Greene County, tried again to become sheriff, and Rev. William Branch, the local NAACP leader, ran for Greene County probate judge. Turner campaigned for Perry County probate judge, and Rev. Thomas L. Threadgill, who had been involved with the SCLC's Wilcox County Title III adult-education program, sought to become justice of the peace there. Two opponents of SWAFCA and the independent third-party movement joined the NDPA bandwagon for the 1970 election: Amelia Boynton ran on the NDPA ticket for probate judge, while Orzell Billingsley sought the office of attorney general. His switch to the third party may have indicated his disaffection with the ADC or his chameleon-like political nature, which enabled him to place his loyalties wherever he thought he had the best chance to succeed.[112]

Although only twelve NDPA candidates won in 1970, the November election results revealed a shift in the balance of power in the Black Belt. The color barrier had been broken in the Alabama House of Representatives with the election of two Macon County residents, Democrat Fred Gray and the NDPA's Thomas Reed. John Hulett, former chairman of the Black Panther Party, became the Lowndes County sheriff, and NDPA candidates for circuit clerk and coroner also won in Lowndes. The NDPA captured all the county governmental slots in Greene County, making it the country's only county with an all-black government. Branch became the probate judge, the first African American to hold this position in Alabama since Reconstruction. Gilmore finally won as sheriff in Greene County. Other NDPA Black Belt winners served on boards of education and on boards of revenue and as county clerks.[113]

By 1972, however, the third party had lost some of its steam. At its convention, held at the Research and Training Center of the Federation of Southern Cooperatives in Epes, Alabama, Durr sought to get the party to cooperate with the regular Democrats, telling the delegates, "We've got to decide if you want to be a Black Belt party or a statewide party." She wanted the party to focus on issues that transcended race, gender, and age. Durr's warnings had some merit. Even in the Black Belt, the party began to lose ground. That year, no NDPA candidates won in Hale, Macon, or Sumter. In Wilcox County, four white Democrats narrowly defeated African American NDPA candidates, and in Lowndes County, William Cosby lost his bid for county commission, falling to a Democrat by seventy votes. The one victory went to Charles Smith, a SWAFCA board member and longtime associate of the LCCMHR. Enough time had passed for many black voters to return to the Democratic fold, which offered more patronage through the national and state parties than the NDPA could offer. The year 1972 represented the beginning of the end for the NDPA, which remained active in state politics for another four years but never again repeated the victories of 1970.[114]

SWAFCA continued marketing the vegetables its members grew but never became the economic engine for the region that its members and OEO had hoped. Co-op opponents damaged the organization at crucial junctures in its history, contributing to its inability to become a commercial success. The cooperative also faced difficulties because of its isolation from local USDA officials, who could have offered needed technical assistance. The charged atmosphere of the Black Belt kept the co-op from receiving support that would have been available under more favorable circumstances. SWAFCA also did not curb its high operating costs and did not improve its accounting and business standards. The 1969 Government Accounting Office study of the co-op found that $23,500 could not be accounted for because of these substandard business practices. In

1970, SWAFCA spent $473,000 on overhead expenses and sold $302,000 worth of produce. Such results led some observers to call the project a failure. While in a purely business sense, SWAFCA did not succeed, many farmers across the country operated their farms under similar financial burdens. Beyond the bottom line, it must be acknowledged that other aspects of the co-op's organization helped to change the cultural and political landscape of the Alabama Black Belt.[115]

Both Turner and Cunningham lauded the cooperative for providing local people with the means to stay in the region and avoid being completely uprooted by the agricultural reformation that worked its way through the Black Belt. The co-op's leaders also provided tangible evidence that the racial discrimination practiced by local and county USDA officials could be confronted and changed. Turner helped twelve families, three of them Minter's former tenants, buy land in Dallas County through the Southern Consumers Cooperative, the American Friends Service Committee, and the FHA. SWAFCA's presence in the area led to the FHA softening up in Alabama. Most of these people had their first opportunity to live in their own home, farm their own land, and receive assistance from a USDA farm program. The co-op's continued efforts to make officials in Washington more aware of the problems small farmers faced in rural Alabama led to important hearings like the one held in Montgomery by the U.S. Commission on Civil Rights in 1968. Over seven days, witnesses revealed the injustices present in many federal programs as they operated in Alabama. The blatantly racist statements made by Bamberg, the director of the Alabama FHA, at these hearings led to changes on the state level. The USDA announced his retirement in 1969. With its grading sheds located in ten counties and a two-hundred-thousand-dollar facility off of Highway 80 just outside of Selma, SWAFCA also maintained a physical presence in the Black Belt that reminded everyone in the region of its members' tenacity and their determination to participate as equal members in the community.[116]

SWAFCA also provided its members with an opportunity to participate in a democratically run organization. Joining a cooperative and voting in its business operations showed many members the importance of utilizing their voices in their own affairs. Many of the co-op's board members and officers, never considered leaders prior to SWAFCA's formation, represented the membership quite effectively in negotiations with federal politicians, OEO administrators, and USDA bureaucrats. This type of activity spilled over into the political arena in the various third-party movements across the region. When it became clear that SWAFCA would not produce a Black Power takeover, opposition died down. Mayor Smitherman, however, never changed his mind about the co-op's early mission: "I don't back off from any of what I said," he told a reporter in

1976. "I said it was run by civil righters and used federal grants to perpetuate an activist type organization." However, he conceded, "I believe now they are trying to the best of their ability to work with the small farmer." Of all the federal antipoverty programs in Alabama, SWAFCA played the most significant role in breaking down white political control in the Black Belt.[117]

CHAPTER SEVEN

Old Patterns and New Designs

Evaluating the Community Action Program in the Alabama Black Belt

The war on poverty will be judged, ultimately, more upon its success in mobilizing the poor as an effective force than upon the number of dollars it has placed in their pockets. Political action is an inevitable consequence of anti-poverty programs, for any effort to better the condition of the poor raises fundamental issues of citizenship and political influence. . . . In short, how much political revolution can a publicly funded program afford to sponsor? Localized control of programs—to the extent that this has been possible in the anti-poverty programs—only exacerbates this political dimension. No giver of money can long remain neutral: it must decide how much to give, and to whom, and for what purposes.

    Roger H. Davidson, "The War on Poverty," 1969

By January 1, 1969, antipoverty programs sponsored by the Office of Economic Opportunity (OEO) were operating in all of Alabama's sixty-seven counties. OEO reported that the federal government had invested $96,498,570 over the course of four years to fight poverty in the nation's fourth-poorest state. Yet more than 857,000 Alabamians, or 25 percent of the state's total population and 47 percent of the residents of ten Black Belt counties, continued to live below the federal poverty line. So why did the War on Poverty not accomplish more in Alabama?[1]

The state used the bulk of these funds, $62 million, on twenty-four community action programs (CAPs)—five in the urban centers of Birmingham, Mobile, Montgomery, Huntsville, and Selma and nineteen in the rural parts of the state—and fourteen single-purpose Head Start programs. If the community action program was supposed to be the heart and soul of the antipoverty fight, an examination of what happened in this Deep South state is essential. In many ways, the battle waged in Alabama mirrored the larger war on poverty fought across the country. Some of the worst examples of community action could be found in the state's Black Belt operating alongside some of the most innovative programs that emanated directly from Washington through the Migrant Worker Division and the Demonstration Division of OEO's Community Action Program. Analyzing variations in responses in one state illustrates why the War on Poverty never really had a chance to put down strong roots and flourish. In Alabama, the political culture of state and local politics influenced the way the federal antipoverty effort could be fought. As a result, OEO's diverse programs rarely worked in concert with one another. Programs sponsored by local governments operated in isolation or in competition with programs funded directly by Washington. Federal officials, regional bureaucrats, state employees loyal to the Wallace way of governing, and local people organized at the grass roots all did their part to utilize the federal program to fit their vision of Alabama's future.

Those who remained active in the black freedom movement clearly made significant contributions to their Black Belt communities, but the quality of change would not be what many had anticipated as a consequence of the systemic nature of white supremacy and political corruption that defined Alabama. Under the right circumstances—grassroots activism, an engaged federal bureaucracy, and removal of state interference—the War on Poverty addressed the needs of Alabama's poor, as the Southwest Alabama Farmers Cooperative Association (SWAFCA) proved. The vegetable-producers' cooperative put people to work for themselves and their communities and influenced the direction of local politics in significant ways.

Without these conditions, in a state such as Alabama, the antipoverty effort had no chance, not because a culture of poverty kept poor people dependent on the federal government but because a culture of racism, greed, and cynicism propped up state and local politicians who used federal largesse for their own gain. OEO formed part of the problem because it had to spread its programs quickly across the country to gain congressional authorization for more funding. The agency's southeast regional office did not provide effective oversight or enough technical assistance, enabling Alabama officials to utilize antipoverty funds to maintain destructive traditions that perpetuated poverty. This history helps provide an understanding of the continuing obstacles faced by those in the civil rights movement after 1964. The way public policy is implemented matters as much as the policy itself. Grassroots activism in Alabama proved what could be done to change the direction of the Black Belt, but who held positions of power within the bureaucracy—whether on the federal, state, or local level—and who had economic control in the local community explains why the struggle carries on.

Old Patterns: Community Action in the Alabama Black Belt

In the spring of 1968, the U.S. Commission on Civil Rights held hearings in Montgomery, Alabama, setting in motion a series of events that led to an evaluation of the community action program in that state. Over the course of five days, the commissioners heard ninety-five witnesses describe the slow pace at which federal civil rights laws had been implemented in sixteen counties in the state's Black Belt. Robert W. Saunders, the civil rights coordinator for OEO's southeast regional office, sat through the hearings and concluded that the "white power structure . . . still maintains what amounts to complete control of every facet of public and private life, thereby maintaining a maximum of racial segregation." According to Saunders, "The testimony given by witnesses to the Commission . . . gives substance to the many complaints from black people that progress (for Negroes) is being blocked." He warned OEO's civil rights director in Washington, D.C., that the agency must close the credibility gap between those in need of assistance and the agency.[2]

The testimony of two white people, Augusta Wilkinson, the director of the Dallas County Department of Pensions and Security, and Robert C. "Red" Bamberg, state director of the Farmers Home Administration (FHA), made strong impressions on Saunders. Wilkinson had served in her position since 1944, and her responses revealed an acute case of Jim Crow paternalism. In several instances she referred to "our colored people," and she spoke of how "we have tried through generations to be of help to them." When commissioner Glickstein asked Wilkinson why fewer people received food stamps than had participated in the surplus commodity food program, her answer revealed as much about her racial views as about federal food assistance: "I think that the transportation problem is very acute in our county. As you well know, the Negroes who live out in the county, they are charged $5 to come in to get the food stamps; and also, our older people who are not as interested in the new ways of life as some of the rest of us are, they don't like to come to town, they would rather buy the food from the grocers that they have bought it from for years and years, and they don't have to eat as much, as you well know." Moreover, Dallas County housed its Pensions and Securities Office in an antebellum building that Wilkinson described as "beautifully arranged and beautiful as far as tradition is concerned." Saunders found that "tradition" in her persona, which he described as "a characterization of and a throw-back to the antebellum days of the Old South."[3]

Not surprisingly, given his history of opposing OEO self-help programs such as SWAFCA, Bamberg's answers showed a persistent disregard for civil rights mandates issued from Washington. He had spent his entire adult life working within the agrigovernment world of the U.S. Department of Agriculture (USDA). Bamberg had had a long career in agriculture, beginning in the 1930s and 1940s, when he worked with the Alabama Extension Service. He was then appointed to the USDA's Commodity Credit Advisory Board and the Alabama State Agriculture Stabilization and Conservation Service Commission before being elected as the Alabama commissioner of agriculture, a position he held from 1959 until 1962. In 1964, he became the state's FHA director. When asked how the FHA made its decisions about loaning money to farmers, he explained that his agency's criterion was the ability to repay a loan. "If a man is smaller . . . you can't make him as large a loan as if he was larger." This approach did not coincide with the FHA's mandate to serve as the lending agency of last resort, and it often perpetuated the trap of debt peonage traditionally associated with tenant farming. In 1968, the Alabama FHA office gave 154 white farmers loans averaging $4,200, while 623 black farmers received operating loans averaging $1,300. According to the U.S. Commission on Civil Rights, this median amount offered to black farmers equaled "the value of goods advanced by furnishing merchants every planting season." The FHA in Alabama basically replaced a traditionally bad system with another equally unfair system. A similar pattern emerged in other FHA loan categories. Black farmers lucky enough to secure financing usually received far less than their white neighbors. In Marengo County, seven white farmers received farm ownership loans averaging $24,500, while only one black farmer received an $11,500 farm ownership loan. "Well, it goes back to this," Bamberg testified; "in many cases our nigger population has small acreage. You heard a discussion here today, I believe 167 or 170 acres was the largest land owner that we had. We had one here said he had twelve acres, one said he has two. Well, there is a tremendous difference what we would loan to a man who has a 170 acres, and one who had two or twelve."[4]

Writing to OEO in Washington, Saunders reminded his boss of the obvious fact that "Federal Government agencies are required to deal directly with Civil Rights problems and to apply sanctions where there are extreme cases of failure to comply. There has been an apparent failure to do so." Saunders's outrage makes one wonder what had he been doing for the past four years? As the civil rights coordinator for OEO's southeast region, was this the first time he had heard of Augusta Wilkinson and R. C. "Red" Bamberg? The oversight system maintained by OEO's Atlanta regional office was clearly inadequate. The testimony of C. H. Erskine Smith, the Birmingham attorney who had tried to bring community action to his city in 1964, should have also set off alarm bells for Saunders. "With the exception of Head Start," Smith stated, "a review of the programs of rural CAPs will reveal little that offers promise of fulfilling the objectives of the Economic Opportunity Act of 1964." "In fact," he emphasized, "the only anti-poverty programs which offer a real promise are those which are funded directly from Washington and have by-passed the local CAP and the local power structures." He wanted to make sure the hearings produced results. "We suggest that the Commission compare the programs funded directly from Washington with those that must go through local CAPs and the local power structure. We think that such a comparison might prove significant and revealing." Attempting to do his part, Saunders could only recommend that antipoverty officials do more "to enforce requirements for adequate and representative poor on its programs. There should be more guidance given to Community Action Agencies so that more projects can be implemented to meet the immediate needs of the people."[5]

OEO's southeast regional office had already received a mandate to evaluate the community action agencies (CAAs) within its jurisdiction in late 1967, when Congress amended the Economic Opportunity Act. Saunders's recommendations were timely, but they highlight how little he understood about the way CAP operated in Alabama. Placing more low-income people on CAA boards was only one of the many pressing problems that needed to be addressed. The community action program had also floundered because the Alabama Economic Opportunity Office gained control of this part of the War on Poverty in the state. The agency's director, Matt Colley, cared more about funneling federal money into the hands of people who would impede the progress of the antipoverty law than offering much-needed technical assistance and training to implement the concept of community action across the state. In Alabama, grant proposals that survived the threat of gubernatorial veto and the scrutiny of regional OEO officials were dominated by the governor's office.

Beginning in the spring of 1968, CAAs across Alabama began to receive letters from Atlanta establishing the review procedure. An evaluation team consisting of a field representative from the regional office, a monitoring specialist, a representative from the Alabama technical assistance office, and outside consultants planned to assess how well each CAA mobilized and coordinated local resources and implemented community organization. A review of the on-site evaluations of community action in the Black Belt reveals that the creative effort to fight the War on Poverty was not working because the civil rights laws did little to alter Alabama's political culture. Here was a case of "strategic accommodation" similar to what historian Joseph Crespino has found in Mississippi. By appearing to comply with federal laws and avoiding drawing attention to themselves, white leaders monopolized local poverty programs that rewarded them economically and politically. Corruption and resistance to the community action concept characterized these programs. Instead of maximum feasible participation of the poor in developing new ideas for ending poverty, these

CAAs offered service-oriented welfare that often benefited CAA board members instead of the targeted low-income community. Three CAAs in particular stand out as examples of these twin ills: Tri-County Area 22 Inc., the Eleventh Area of Alabama Opportunity Action Committee, and the City of Selma–Dallas County Economic Opportunity Board.[6]

The manner in which Tri-County Area 22 formed reveals the effort Alabama OEO officials exerted in keeping white racial dominance in their CAP plans. The area originally included four counties—Bullock, Coffee, Pike, and Geneva—in Area 22. After Bullock and Coffee applied separately for CAP funds, the area's boundaries were redrawn to include Butler, Crenshaw, Covington, and Lowndes. When Lowndes pulled out after the LCCMHR sought funds, the three remaining counties formed Tri-County Area 22. Most people in these counties lived in rural areas, and ten thousand families survived on less than three thousand dollars a year. An OEO evaluator visited a family of fifteen in Crenshaw County that lived in a three-room dwelling with only one habitable room. Some of the children should have attended school but "have never been because the bus does not come near the house," the evaluator reported. "Their drinking water comes from a muddy branch some yards down the hill behind the house. The floor of the kitchen is not adequate to support the weight of a stove, consequently the stove is in the back yard where the cooking is done." An OEO consultant found that "there was little industry in the area" and that "many farmers found it more profitable to put acreage in the soil bank, thus increasing the supply of temporary, unskilled, cheap labor." The need clearly was great.[7]

The evaluation of this CAA uncovered a corrupt, ineffective, unimaginative program that was not viable enough to warrant continued OEO support. "While the agency has provided a limited amount of assistance in terms of employment, referrals, and medical aid," the report stated, "there is no evidence that it has made any lasting impact on the causes of poverty in that area, or will do so in the foreseeable future." Some of the more severe problems with this program highlight Alabama's political culture.[8]

This CAA decided to alleviate poverty through home health care that was supposed to include assistance, counseling, and referrals for the rural poor, a family planning component, and an emergency medical program—traditional service-oriented welfare programs that did nothing to address the root causes of poverty. But what looked on paper like a welfare delivery service was in reality the blatant use of federal money for the benefit of those who ran the program. The situation shocked many of the members of the evaluation team. Edward Vaughn found the home health aide program to be a glorified maid service of "predominantly black home health aides giving services to white families." One female Covington County aide asked to serve a paralyzed African American but was told that the person lived too far away. Instead, the aide was assigned to work in the home of a middle-class white woman who lived farther away than the paralyzed person, waxing and polishing the floors and furniture. Investigator Maggie Moody interviewed an elderly black man who lived alone and had been sick. One of his relatives asked the CAA to provide him with assistance at home and help with his medicine. "A male aide was sent out," Moody reported, "and the only thing that he did was carry the report in to the center. He had not gotten any orders to serve this person so the person had not received any assistance." Elenora Hines found that a male aide in Greenville went on a weekly basis to bathe and shave the sheriff's father, and Maggie Moody discovered that the mother of a neighborhood center coordinator in Crenshaw County received a lot of service from aides. Another aide worked two to three hours a week training a goat to pull a cart carrying a polio-afflicted white man. This man's family, "according to rural standards, is modestly well off," Vaughn noted in a confidential memo. "I do not believe that this service is justified when there are so many other problems that need to be attended to throughout the county," he lamented. "This is just further evidence that the administration of this agency has no idea of the concept or the philosophy of community action."[9]

Beyond the problems with the home health care program were the issues surrounding the board of directors and the administration of the CAA. "Board members have been elected by manipulations that could scarcely be called elections," Vaughn wrote. The poor did not comprise one-third of the board members, as required by the Green Amendment. The chairman removed the local representative from the ministerial association from the board without cause. And the Butler County NAACP had been ignored, with Tri-County Area 22 staff denying that a chapter even existed. Vaughn, however, found the chapter president and other board members in just two days. "From our observations," Vaughn stated, "we could find little, if any, meaningful involvement of the poor in the program in policy decision making areas."[10]

The board's authority rested in the hands of its chairman, a man named Scott, who presided over a giveaway program rather than facilitating the maximum feasible participation of the poor. All board members received a $5 fee for attending meetings, but such payments were supposed to go only to board and advisory members from target areas. Mayor Ned Moore owned a local pharmacy and received $7,355 in November 1969 for services rendered to the antipoverty agency. Moore had appointed the drugstore's coowner, Henry Foster, to the CAA board. An employee of the store, Irene Butler, also worked for the CAA and was a friend of Matt Colley, the head of the Alabama Economic Opportunity Office. Even after leaving the CAA, Butler continued to sign vouchers redeemable at the drugstore. A Butler County doctor received

$3,042 for medical services provided to the agency as well as $100 a month rent for Area 22's central offices. Only sixteen women received family planning services from the CAA, so this money essentially duplicated medical services already provided by the county health department. The family planning program employed the doctor's daughter and daughter-in-law as social workers. One social worker explained that family planning was "the main way to keep people off the [Aid to Dependent Children] rolls." Hines noted that "any thought of using this component as anything other than a birth control clinic is alien to its administrators." Another board member, DeLacy Baily, received various payments from the agency for his printing services.[11]

CAA employees admitted to Hines that the program "was not benefitting the poor, and had never done so, and had no intention of ever doing so." Of the rampant conflicts of interest, William Roth wrote, "Most people consider [the CAA] a potential source of income and have spent most of their energies either trying to get a job with it, to insure their job, or to find other ways to milk it financially. Quite a bit of milking, some legal and some not, has already been done." He deduced that this graft was motivated by the fact that it was a federally funded program: local leaders believed that they should "take the program for as much financially as you can. It's a federal government program, and therefore fair game." Roth found the corruption "staggering." He admitted that programs at times had to bend to find acceptance in a community, but from his perspective, "this one has bent too much." Particularly galling was the fact that the CAA had been "turned around to serve the desires of those who are against what it stands for."[12]

For the fiscal year that ended on May 31, 1970, Tri-County Area 22 received $537,363 to operate this failing excuse for community action. This figure nearly equaled the $595,751 that OEO had issued to SWAFCA in 1968—and that program covered ten counties. The differences between the two programs could not have been more stark. One member of the evaluation team wondered why OEO had not responded more quickly to confront the many problems associated with this CAA. Many in the black community told Vaughn that they did not understand how this agency had been "allowed to operate as long as it has with questionable financial activities, an utter disregard for civil rights compliance, nepotism and areas of alleged conflict of interest." The final report laid the blame on the state economic opportunity office and the southeast regional office. "The fault may lie with the satisfactory reports submitted by the previous Field Representative," who worked out of OEO's Atlanta office. The former board chair had reportedly given copies of evidence of the malfeasance to Matt Colley, but his close relationship to Irene Butler meant that no changes would result. The CAA was such a failure that Glenn Humes even suggested that "a simple division of the total funds amongst the 500 poorest families (about $1,000 each) would have a much more positive impact." In the end, he recommended closing the agency because continued funding "would only serve to further tarnish the image of OEO and disillusion its most fervent supporters."[13]

While the Eleventh Area of Alabama Opportunity Action Committee lacked the administrative corruption of Tri-County Area 22, these programs did not honor the intent of community action by ignoring the crucial idea of the maximum feasible participation of the poor. Area 11 originally included Bibb, Chilton, Hale, Perry, and Shelby Counties. After Lewis Black and Albert Turner sought separate antipoverty funds for Hale and Perry Counties, the CAA organized without them. Rural communities dominated these three counties, and census figures classified almost 50 percent of the combined population as poor. African Americans made up only 20 percent of the population served by the CAA, and members of the NAACP chapter in Bibb County told one evaluator that they feared economic reprisals if they pushed for membership on the agency's board. Burton Mullins had served as Area 11's executive director since its inception in early 1966; he was also the director of the Chilton County Soil and Water Conservation District. Given his ties to the USDA, his decision to run the antipoverty program from the top down was not unexpected.[14]

The agency served constituents in three counties through a home health management program for the elderly that employed thirty people—ten from each county—to clean, cook, and provide transportation. These aides also delivered surplus commodities and used clothing to their clients. The assistant director, Belcher Hobson, thought that "this program has done more to aid the poverty-stricken than any other that we have." The CAA also had a production and marketing component that worked with small farmers in the area. A local pickle company contributed seeds to the group at cost so that fifty families could grow cucumbers to sell back to the pickle manufacturer. In 1968 the families involved sold 190,539 pounds of cucumbers. This CAP, therefore, worked to subvert the goals of another Black Belt antipoverty program: the Area 11 CAA provided services and resources to a company that had boycotted SWAFCA growers since the co-op formed in 1967.[15]

After the 1969 evaluation, OEO put the CAA on a four-month probation, giving it time to comply with the rules of community action. "The director is actually running the entire agency," Edwin Marger reported, "with the active support of its chairman and the rubber stamp of the majority of the Board." Marger continued emphatically, "This is absolute POLITICAL PATRONAGE. . . . THERE IS NO COMMUNITY ACTION. . . . There has been practically no changeover in this agency. It is an institution, not an instrument of change." Many workers interviewed admitted that racial segregation continued within the agency. Black home health aides helped black people, and white home health aides helped white people. One African American aide said that he had received no training and had never gotten a raise and that no one had explained civil rights requirements to him. The agency maintained segregated restrooms, and the evaluation found that "Negro staff do not feel they can expect promotions to higher supervisory positions." Ronald E. Allen Sr. reported that both Mullins and Hobson "have strong racial bias": "neither have any conception of the aims of OEO and community action, and both fear the involvement of the poor, particularly the black poor," which they thought would just "stir up trouble." Staff members told Phyllis Maass that they avoided confronting Mullins "since everyone feels he is responsible for the program having been funded at all."[16]

After the initial evaluation, the CAA came to a standstill. Its board, administrators, and staff did not know what to do if the agency had to stop offering welfare-type services to low-income area residents. When the home health management program was shut down, CAA members struggled to create new programs for the community. One consultant suggested that the agency find people who could provide technical assistance and funds, similar to the approach used by the Freedom Quilting Bee handicraft cooperative based in Wilcox County. Allen reported that they "appear completely unable to understand the difference between doing things *for* the poor and helping them to be self-sufficient." Many involved with Area 11 were stunned by the evaluation because OEO had previously allowed the program to operate without "significant criticism or demand for change." Because the results were so shocking, program administrators felt that they had "been singled out for destruction by OEO when they were doing so much good for poor people in general and old people in particular." Mullins and Hobson thought the review and subsequent probation were the result of "unwarranted persecution and personal vindictiveness from OEO employees who conducted the pre-review." According to Maass, "Everyone is wandering aimlessly along in united fashion, with no concept of what community action may be all about, and feeling themselves victims of federal, bureaucratic mistreatment by OEO." Such feelings no doubt were reinforced by earlier accusations emanating from the governor's mansion and from officials within the Alabama Economic Opportunity Office who failed to provide any technical assistance or training that could have brought the CAA more in line with the concept of community action.[17]

Similar problems associated with uninspired, service-oriented welfare delivery appeared in the City of Selma–Dallas County CAA with added difficulties caused by a mayor who had close ties to the Wallace administration and by Selma's traditional black leaders, who were threatened by the changes SWAFCA brought to Alabama's Black Belt. On August 14, 1968, William Holland spent an afternoon in Selma, meeting with Joseph Knight, the director of the city's

CAA, to get a sense of how the program operated. As the supervisor of the Alabama and South Carolina district of OEO's southeast office, Holland probably also wanted to check on the area in the wake of the revelations of mismanagement by SWAFCA's business manager, Calvin Orsborn. OEO's Atlanta regional office had not been actively involved in the creation, support, or oversight of SWAFCA, since funding came directly from Washington through the CAP's Demonstration Division. After the co-op demonstration project was well under way, OEO in Washington asked the southeast regional office to sign off on the program. Holland's office was essentially left out of the loop and consequently supported Selma's CAA in a way that bolstered Mayor Joe Smitherman's opposition to changes wrought by the civil rights movement. So, like the Area 11 CAA, which sponsored programs that competed against the vegetable producers' co-op, Selma's antipoverty agency resisted any effort to work in harmony with SWAFCA. After touring several neighborhood service centers and discussing the possibility of moving into the development of cooperatives and small businesses, Holland recommended that the southeast regional OEO office organize a team of people to provide the CAA with training and technical assistance after its evaluation. He also noted, "This CAA needs careful treatment, since the politics are very difficult." In the end, Holland's office was not up to the task.[18]

The evaluation of Selma's CAP got under way on November 19, 1968, and an OEO official from the Midwest regional office based in Kansas City ran the investigation with the support of personnel from the Alabama and southeast regional OEO offices. In his report, Dwain Alexander noted the community's structural problems that contributed to the impoverishment of so many people in the county: racial discrimination, educational deficiencies, unemployment and underemployment, lack of industrial growth, declining agricultural prosperity, and lack of health facilities. He found that none of these issues had "been addressed by the CAA, and the evaluation indicated that external influences upon the CAA have caused it in many instances to support the causes of poverty." Since the agency's inception, it had lacked credibility in the rural parts of the county. OEO initially rejected the grassroots work of members of Self-Help against Poverty for Everyone (SHAPE) in favor of Smitherman's plan, which meant that the CAA lost the creative energy that SHAPE members had initially offered the program. Instead, authority and control of the antipoverty agency rested in the hands of Smitherman through CAA director Joseph Knight. Because Alexander's evaluation criticized both the Alabama Office of Economic Opportunity and the southeast regional OEO office, his recommendations were not fully embraced.[19]

The Selma CAA developed two programs for the targeted population of Dallas County: Operation Mainstream and Neighborhood Service Centers. Operation Mainstream differed little from the earlier program called Operation

Draino. The new plan sought to train unskilled people for jobs that would benefit both them and the county. Low-income residents would be hired to repair streets, pick up garbage, and maintain city property. In reality, Alexander found that target area employees were actually restoring "the curbing in front of homes in the middle class and well to do white neighborhoods" while being supervised by prison guards, a violation of the Economic Opportunity Act. Prior to Operation Mainstream, convicts had performed this work, which meant that the CAA broke an important maintenance-of-effort clause contained in all OEO contracts. CAA work crews also planted and cared for shrubs, bought from Smitherman's nursery, at a private park and pool. The CAA's purchase of these plants had not followed an established bidding process, a blatant conflict of interest that personally benefited the mayor. Finally, Operation Mainstream workers used lime to sanitize outside toilets throughout the city. A Selma housing ordinance prohibited the renting of houses without indoor plumbing: the CAA work program thus facilitated the violation of local laws and supported the persistence of substandard housing.[20]

The lack of vision was also apparent in the way the CAA utilized its Neighborhood Service Centers. The agency built eight centers to serve as resources for job placement and counseling, community organization, rural recreation, and health education. Training courses were planned for domestic work and gardening, and each center would then be utilized as an employment agency for maids, yard workers, babysitters, and day laborers. As Thaddeus Olive's investigation learned, "This would provide not only job opportunities for the unemployed but also provide a valuable service to the community." But instead of an employment agency, many neighborhood residents wanted a year-round Head Start program. Since the city refused to comply with civil rights laws as required by the early childhood development program, Head Start was out of the question. To get around that mandate, the CAA planned to run kindergartens in the centers, but in practice they became day care programs. The Neighborhood Service Centers failed to accomplish any of the original goals. Staff members did not do community outreach because they were busy monitoring the care of young children. Area residents had not been involved in choosing the locations for the centers, none of the centers were well marked, many served as recreation centers for young people, and there was little evidence of programming for adults. Not surprisingly, Olive found that many poor people living near the eight community centers thought that the "Selma–Dallas County Economic Opportunity Board is carrying out the wishes of the 'establishment' in maintaining the *status quo*." It was clear that none of the Neighborhood Service Center programs had the chance to transform the lives of Dallas County's impoverished. The use of federal funds to train people to continue working in subservient jobs also explains why many in Selma's establishment resented SWAFCA. The co-op fostered economic independence and a productive future, quite a contrast to what the Neighborhood Service Centers and Operation Mainstream offered.[21]

There were also problems with the operation of the CAA's board. The chairman, Dr. J. H. Williams, had joined the board at the recommendation of his pastor, P. H. Lewis of Brown's Chapel African Methodist Episcopal, who had supported the mayor's plan instead of SHAPE's in 1965. Williams was a member of the Chesterfield Club, a civic organization for Selma's black businessmen. He represented the city's traditional black leadership. Williams's blindness to the current circumstances was clear when he told Alexander that he thought the board was "doing a good job prior to the evaluation." The board included representatives of the target areas, but the composite evaluation found that "the process by which they were selected was perfunctory and was implemented to legitimatize the agency." Board member Clarence Williams, a local labor leader and member of SHAPE, explained that the body was hostile to SWAFCA, SHAPE, and the Dallas County Progressive Movement for Human Rights, "the only active organizations that are functioning at this time in Dallas County representing the poor and the target area groups." No one had sought to include poor whites in the program. The board met on a regular basis, but it did not make important operational decisions for the CAA. Alexander stated that on the rare occasion when residents from the target areas confronted the board and the CAA's director, agency leaders felt "free to proceed on their own predetermined course, and, to borrow a quote, they feel 'That it is a little bit of democracy and they like it that way.'" Evidence of the board's complicity could be seen in its choice of legal counsel. In addition to working for the antipoverty agency, McLean Pitts served as the city attorney for Selma, defended Alabama's prosegregation school position in court, and represented plantation owner J. A. Minter in a lawsuit brought by his tenants who sued to get their allotment funds directly from the Agriculture Stabilization and Conservation Service. Olive found that the board had "no priorities, long or short range, for the Selma–Dallas County Economic Opportunity Board." Most board members did not know their duties and responsibilities to the organization. Olive could not find a single board member who could name the locations of the county's Neighborhood Service Centers.[22]

The board did not fulfill its essential purpose of serving as an advocate for the poor through program planning, development, and oversight. This left Knight, Smitherman's handpicked choice as CAA director, to make these decisions. Without the board's direction and supervision, the CAA's business practices did not meet accepted legal standards. The check-signing policy was confusing because each program authorized a different person's signature. Funds for each program were placed in a different bank, purchase orders were not being used, and there was a no-bid policy for large purchases. There were no effective property records, separate personnel folders, job descriptions, or time and attendance records. As a result, money flowed through the CAA without any accountability to OEO.[23]

Alexander submitted his report to the southeast regional office in March 1969, pulling no punches and methodically laying out recommendations to improve Selma's CAP. He called for training for board members so that they could learn how to organize the community around creative ways to fight poverty. Alexander wanted the board to reevaluate all staff members' ability to plan programs with the involvement of the target community. He also urged the OEO regional office to provide better oversight to make sure that its directives were followed and that a true election of representatives of the poor took place. "There appears to be a communication and commitment gap" between OEO and the CAA, he wrote. "It appears that OEO has not fully indicated its position on several matters of policy through the field representatives, its monitoring process, field visits, and correspondence." Finally, he called for the replacement of the field representative from the Atlanta office who had failed to hold the CAA accountable for its actions. He did not hide his frustration with what had been allowed to take place in Selma. "The removal of the CAA Director and the influence of the Mayor will greatly affect the speed with which the CAA can move in a new direction. The assignment of a field representative who is not from the area, and who does not share the same antiquated social beliefs which are currently a predominant part of the problem of poverty in the area, will greatly enhance the opportunities for the CAA's growth."[24]

OEO's Atlanta office responded quickly and defensively. The head of the grants-monitoring section edited Alexander's report, removing language he found to be too hard-hitting. Members of the evaluation team claimed that Alexander had conducted an "investigation" instead of an evaluation and that he "pre-determined [that the] agency should be suspended or closed." They described him as "bruising in interviewing" and contended that he "imposed Kansas City procedures on [the] Selma evaluation." These administrators concluded that Alexander's "approach to evaluation is destructive to [the] CAA" and decided not to send the report to Selma until October 1969, further delaying any accountability. By then, the board members who had ties to SHAPE had persuaded the board to conduct new elections to provide true representation for the poor, but that was not enough to turn the agency around. In November, three field representatives from OEO's southeast regional office visited the CAA and found more corrupt business practices. Four people had been hired for positions that were not in the budget, straining the funds for Neighborhood Service Center programs. CAA officials had failed to complete essential oversight forms. The executive board agreed to hire a woman to work in Wilcox County, knowing that this action violated OEO policy because the county was not part of the area covered by the CAP grant. And a surveyor of housing for the city of Selma was being paid using Neighborhood Service Center funds without the knowledge or approval of the board or staff: only Knight knew about this illegal activity.[25]

OEO's patience with Knight had finally run out. The CAA executive director resigned, and Ed Johnson, an African American, became the acting director of the City of Selma–Dallas County Economic Opportunity Board. Smitherman retaliated for the loss of his puppet in the antipoverty agency by claiming that Johnson was not qualified for the job. In late 1970 the mayor attacked the CAA for discriminating against poor white people because the majority of top jobs in the program were held by African Americans. Using his familiar political theatrics, he locked the doors to the CAA office and posted police guards, saying, "I haven't stopped the program—which is a federal program. I just closed the building—which is a city building." He wanted command of the agency and masked his true motivations to get it back. "We're not being racist," he told newspaper reporters. "We had a white director who went to another job and he ought to be replaced by a white director." At the end of 1970, the problems of the CAA had still not been fixed. Dr. Williams continued to chair the CAA board, and its funds were overdrawn by sixty-two thousand dollars at two Selma banks.[26]

Part of the Problem, Not Part of the Solution

Some common threads help to explain why these Black Belt CAAs functioned for so long without adhering to the spirit or the mandates of the Economic Opportunity Act. First, personnel at OEO's headquarters were divided regarding how CAP should be disseminated across the country. Fred O'R. Hayes, who had questioned community action's ability to work without conflict, pushed for quick funding and for leaving the details of implementing "maximum feasible participation of the poor" for another day. In Alabama, with a powerful governor, loyal state and local bureaucrats, and compliant OEO regional field representatives, that day never came. This hurried approach was reinforced in early 1966 as criticism of antipoverty programs mounted across the nation, with problems associated with the Head Start program operated by the Child Development Group of Mississippi and CAAs in Chicago, Syracuse, and San Francisco that gave strong support to the voices of the poor.[27]

To diffuse local conflict, OEO informed its regional offices that they should allow city or county elected officials to veto all or any portion of a CAA proposal. The directive made clear OEO's compromised approach: "Our policy is to accept a veto where this will produce community action. This policy does not mean that we must accept a veto where the effect will be to prevent community action." What mattered was to get CAAs functioning without too much friction. In the Alabama Black Belt, where city and county officials dominated community action, regional-level bureaucrats took this directive as permission to look the other way when elected officials controlled CAA boards and supported programs that maintained the status quo. As long as the appearance of community action could be documented, programs received funding. After 1966, the regional offices took on more significance, which meant that the Washington OEO stepped back. As a result, even though Sargent Shriver had the power to override a governor's veto, if the governor did not make a fuss, the Washington office did not become involved.[28]

In analyzing events in Alabama, this process can be confusing because Governors George and Lurleen Wallace, along with California Governor Ronald Reagan, vetoed more CAPs than other governors. In fact, George Wallace's actions toward the Birmingham CAA led Congress to amend the Economic Opportunity Act in 1965 to allow OEO's director to override a governor's veto after a thirty-day waiting period. This change seemingly would have led Washington to scrutinize every Alabama grant with an especially critical eye. However, bad publicity hurt OEO's ability to do its job across the country. Thus, as long as national OEO officials remained unaware of blatant racial discrimination and as long as the Alabama governor did not draw further attention to a CAA, funding was assured. The Wallaces used this strategy to their political benefit, reaping much credibility at home for trying to block funding for what they labeled "Black Panther" programs in Lowndes and Wilcox Counties and for SWAFCA and at the same time bringing more than $62 million into the state through CAAs controlled by local politicians. Such was not the case in every southern state. When the mayor of New Orleans wanted to use antipoverty programs to modernize his city and give it a chance to compete with other Sun Belt cities, he chose to work with African Americans to meet that goal. The governor of Louisiana did not stand in his way. The Wallaces chose a more destructive path.[29]

The national organization of the OEO bureaucracy was a second thread that helped to strangle community action in Alabama. OEO's regional offices were not up and running right after the passage of the Economic Opportunity Act. After the southeast office opened, its staff members were responsible for eight states—Alabama, Florida, Georgia, Kentucky, Mississippi, North Carolina, South Carolina, and Tennessee. The Atlanta office divided the region into two-state districts, initially pairing Alabama and South Carolina. Sometime after 1970, a reorganization occurred, and Alabama and Mississippi became a district. The available evidence indicates that the southeast regional office did not have enough staff to watch over a region with the historic legacy of Jim Crow segregation and with an enormous number of people living below the poverty line. As late as 1974, Bob Saunders complained that he lacked the staff to carry out the civil rights mission mandated by the law. For example, in early 1971, only seventeen people worked in the Alabama-Mississippi district, the fewest in any of the southeast region's districts. Saunders also noted that the southeast regional office handled more discrimination complaints than any other OEO region.[30]

The operational duties for each district within an OEO region specifically included supporting the Community Action Program. District staff were supposed to be CAA grantees' primary source of planning and programming guidance. The districts were required to coordinate all phases of the grant application process and to communicate and interpret OEO policies and regulations for grantees. This work included reviewing and evaluating reports from CAAs, conducting periodic on-site visits, participating in grantee evaluation programs, and identifying training and technical assistance needs. The Alabama Black Belt was the poorest part of the state and thus required the most assistance and oversight to enable the community action program to meet its lofty goals of transforming conditions by enabling the poor to be activists for their own benefit. If the Area 22, Area 11, and Selma–Dallas County CAAs are representative, the district staff responsible for Alabama did not do their job, perhaps because of the actions of the field representatives who reported back to the Atlanta regional office.[31]

In 1965, the Atlanta office's Mary Grice worked with Matt Colley, the deputy director of the Alabama Office of Economic Opportunity, to divide Alabama into the areas that paired Black Belt counties with nearby counties that had larger white populations. Grice's understanding of the concept of community action became more clear when she left the Atlanta office to become the director of Alabama's Little River CAP, which operated in Baldwin, Escambia, and Monroe Counties. Evaluation reports noted that she ran the organization with a top-down management style that did not implement the maximum feasible participation of the poor in a meaningful way. The board suffered from conflicts of interest as well. For example, the chairman was also the sheriff of Baldwin County, and he hired CAA staff members as a form of political payoff. When SWAFCA applied for its initial grant in 1967, Grice wrote a letter opposing the co-op, in which Monroe County farmers participated, revealing her fear of self-help programs in the Black Belt: "If these funding of single purpose organizations such as SWAFCA and SEASHA continue, there will be no Community Action left in Alabama and riots and civil disorders will take place in

Alabama." She recommended that each member of the board write a similar letter to CAP director Theodore Berry "as every one of us in the CAP in Alabama are fighting for our lives."[32]

The field representative who worked on Alexander's team evaluating the Selma CAA, Lawrence Duncan Sturm, had a history of discriminatory behavior. While working on the evaluation of the Huntsville CAA, he had made derogatory comments about African Americans to Janet Nussmann, a CAP official from Washington, D.C. She reported that he "lamented the paperwork involved in being a Field Representative, but was quick to add that he would never object to processing Head Start applications because nothing pleased him more than to see those 'cute little brown-eyed niggers learning to brush their teeth.'" He also told Nussmann that he resented "people who feel they have to come down from the North to meddle in the South's affairs." He said, "The Northern cities are the ones that burn; have you ever heard of riots in the South? The South knows how to handle its problems." Sturm even commented that Viola Liuzzo, a Detroit woman who had been murdered while driving marchers home after the 1965 Selma to Montgomery march, had been killed because she "lay down with the colored boys." Nussmann told her bosses that "his attitude alone (especially since it was expressed so freely) is inappropriate and unsuitable for a Federal employee, and particularly a representative of OEO." With officials such as Sturm and Grice responsible for oversight in Alabama, CAAs in the Black Belt could continue to operate in violation of OEO mandates. Not only were there not enough boots on the ground, but the wrong people were wearing those boots.[33]

The final thread contributing to community action's demise in the Black Belt involved the Alabama Economic Opportunity Office. OEO envisioned the director of state offices functioning "as the Governor's principal representative in the State's dealing with OEO, and . . . on all matters related to anti-poverty efforts both within and outside the state." The Office of Economic Opportunity expected these state offices to provide technical assistance to local CAAs, sponsor and operate OEO-funded programs, and help governors coordinate state programs for eliminating poverty. Governor Lurleen Wallace promoted Colley to director of the Alabama Economic Opportunity Office after he had served as deputy director during her husband's administration. While he clearly represented the wishes of Governors George and Lurleen Wallace and later Albert Brewer, these wishes meant that he did not provide technical assistance to or coordinate state programs to eliminate poverty. Instead, he attempted to distribute federal money throughout Alabama without honoring the full intentions of the antipoverty law. On January 15, 1969, Colley wrote to Roy Jones, the Alabama district supervisor in OEO's Atlanta office, "just a line to let you know how much I appreciate your cooperation with this office, and, also, to extend to you congratulations for the fine job you are doing. I am sure that I speak on behalf of the CAP Directors in Alabama. I am also grateful for the close working relationship that we have with your office, and I feel now that we are on our way to really getting the job done within the State of Alabama."[34]

As late as 1970, the southeast regional office had allowed Alabama to maintain a segregated state economic opportunity office. Hayes had permitted this arrangement in an effort to facilitate the creation of state OEO bureaucracies. Six years after the Civil Rights Act passed, OEO officials in Atlanta finally insisted that Alabama integrate the office by incorporating all the technical assistance personnel, who were black and consequently worked in a separate office building, into one office. The governor refused, with his legal adviser claiming that the change would violate the provisions of the state merit system. As a result, Alabama lost federal funding for a state OEO office. Governor Brewer then merged the Alabama Office of Economic Opportunity into the Alabama Development Office, created a year earlier to coordinate regional planning and industrial development across the state.[35]

As early as 1965, civil rights activists in the Black Belt knew that OEO's southeast regional office would not be an ally. Vernon Jordan, a consultant in the Atlanta office, also accepted this fact, and he showed people such as Rev. Francis X. Walter how to bypass the regional office and seek assistance directly from Washington. Without an organized voice from the grass roots and with acquiescent OEO regional officials and an obstructionist state economic opportunity office, the community action program in the Alabama Black Belt reinforced the old patterns of the Jim Crow era.[36]

New Designs: Trying to Construct a Different Alabama Black Belt

Knowing how the local authorities controlled CAP in the Alabama Black Belt makes the results of the antipoverty programs supported directly from Washington through the Migrant Workers Division and the Demonstration Division even more extraordinary. When Washington directly backed programs in the Black Belt, change became possible. The hard-line stance taken by Governors George and Lurleen Wallace eventually enabled the funding of antipoverty programs in the region that had a level of independence from the state and local governments that did not exist anywhere else in the area. Against all odds and many obstacles, local people made something out of the War on Poverty for themselves and confirmed that if most OEO guidelines were followed and local obstructions were minimized, the programs could work. Because these programs proved what could be done, they remained politically vulnerable. "It is hard to see how programs for and by the impoverished could be otherwise," political scientist Roger Davidson has found. This was the case in the Alabama Black Belt because by their very existence, these programs engaged in forms of pressure and antagonism because they reached hundreds of people and offered real opportunities. In Alabama those accustomed to holding the reins of power disliked and resented a federal program that enabled black people to have so much independence.[37]

In 1967, three months after OEO released the funds for the Lowndes County Christian Movement for Human Rights (LCCMHR) Farm Workers Adult Education Program, an arsonist burned down its headquarters, completely destroying the building, equipment, and materials. This attempt to stop the federal antipoverty effort did not succeed: the program operated out of a trailer until a new building could be constructed, and in 1968 OEO in Washington renewed funding for the program with a $225,514 Title III (b) grant that assisted 515 people, including 30 who received on-the-job training for jobs in the building, plumbing, and upholstering trades; 75 who registered for basic education and training; 15 who received instruction for secretarial positions; and 25 who signed up for a nurse's aide training course to work in the new Lowndes County health facility. The remaining participants received basic instruction that would enable them to qualify for future occupational training. By January 1, 1969, the LCCMHR had received grants totaling $466,934 for adult education and pre–vocational training programs.[38]

OEO also supported two other projects in Lowndes County. In the spring of 1968, the Lowndes County Board of Education received $263,401 to operate a full-year Head Start program for 150 children. At that same time, the antipoverty agency extended a planning grant to the Lowndes County Board of Health to develop a comprehensive health care plan to serve the county's poor population. A local general practitioner, Dr. H. H. Meadows, directed the program, and members of the LCCMHR served on its board. The Lowndes County Board of Revenue feared that Washington would fund the health services program without local backing, as it had done with the adult education program. As a result, white officials agreed to accept the project, seeking to maintain some direct connection to it. Six months later, the county received a $1,105,305 Title II grant to establish a neighborhood health center in Hayneville and four health stations throughout the county. During the first year of operation, 6,645 county residents had access to free medical care from the clinic. Patients received dental care, pharmaceutical services, and hospital care, and two full-time physicians provided general medical treatment at the facility. In 1972, the health services program accepted its fifth grant in excess of $1 million. After operating for ten years, the clinic's director reported important results: In 1968, infant mortality in Lowndes County had stood at 54.4 per thousand; in 1979, this figure had dropped to 18 per thousand.[39]

OEO also increased its support of antipoverty programs in Wilcox County. Beyond the first Title III (b) grant, made in November 1966 for adult basic education, the agency issued to the Wilcox County chapter of the Southern Christian Leadership Conference (SCLC) $38,640 for the Southwest Alabama Self-Help Housing Project. Twenty families received assistance in building their own homes in the Alberta and Lower Peachtree areas of the county through the support of a combined FHA/OEO program. State Senator Roland Cooper continued his opposition to the SCLC antipoverty programs, this time claiming that the housing effort would amount to the creation of "a Colored city." Bamberg also tried to stop the program by using the Wilcox County FHA supervisor as a gatekeeper for the housing effort. "This is to inform you we would be in a position to participate with a group of applicants in a self-help housing project," he wrote to Rev. Daniel Harrell, the SCLC field secretary who led the antipoverty program, "if the applicants were considered eligible by our local County Committee and it was determined that the applicants had the ability and time to construct their dwellings." He also informed Harrell that the Title III (b) program would have to have "the legal, financial, and actual capacity and resources to provide the construction supervision of all the work to be done under the direction of our County Supervisor." Finally, setting the bar out of reach, Bamberg told Harrell that "all construction done on self-help housing must meet FHA standards and all loan funds [must] be supervised by the County Supervisor." This was the same county supervisor who had refused or delayed FHA loans to people who had participated in civil rights activities in 1965.[40]

Wilcox County's black residents ignored this resistance and sought help directly from Washington to obtain FHA financing for materials to build their homes. The director of the FHA's Rural Housing Division took an interest in the Wilcox County program, which probably explains why the loans were issued. The FHA approved Daniel Harrell Jr. as a qualified inspector to supervise the overall building project, thus circumventing the problematic Alabama FHA officials. A construction supervisor and two construction assistants worked under Harrell's direction. Project participants had to either work as a farmer or have some form of employment to qualify for the FHA loans. Most of the home builders worked in the pulpwood industry, and when they were not cutting trees, they worked together to build their own homes. Each FHA loan paid for one lot, a water system, and the materials for a house. By 1968, OEO increased its support to the housing program by issuing $72,022 to assist fifty more low-income families acquire decent housing. At the end of the year, OEO reported that Southwest Alabama Self-Help Housing had received $110,134 in grants and had served 420 people.[41]

The antipoverty agency maintained its sponsorship of the basic education project operating in Wilcox County, issuing $244,201 to the Title III (b) program in early 1968. The SCLC's county chairman, Thomas Threadgill, directed the project, which provided farm workers pre–vocational training in auto mechanics, carpentry, electrical work, and sawmill operation so they could enter the paper mill industry or other Manpower Development Training Programs in the area. OEO officials praised this effort for bringing in people from across the county. One antipoverty inspector reported that "the program is the most talked about thing among poor people in the county. Drop in at any country store and the poor Negroes standing out front can tell you about the antipoverty program." Two white men in the area also endorsed the program, which seemed to give it legitimacy from OEO's perspective. Yet their participation had been gained only by special arrangements to maintain the appearance of segregation, which indicated apprehension that these steps toward equality were not universally approved. Camden mayor Reginald Albritton and hardware store owner Sam Aiken served on the SCLC's antipoverty board of directors but for political reasons did not attend board meetings. In 1969, two more grants totaling $546,239 enabled the continuation of the adult education program and a youth services program serving thirty-seven hundred people.[42]

Through his work as director of the Selma Inter-Religious Project (SIP), Rev. Walter provided assistance to the Wilcox County SCLC antipoverty programs. He conducted surveys throughout the county, locating people who had been evicted from their homes because they had participated in civil rights activities. Walter did extensive research in cooperatives as a form of self-help, and he sought advice from people involved in federal programs run by agencies such as OEO and the USDA. He worked to get SWAFCA organized and funded. He attended meetings at places such as Minter's plantation to listen to the struggles of tenant farmers; he drove from the Black Belt to Washington, D.C., to lobby for support in Congress and OEO; and he campaigned to have his important contacts across the country write to urge OEO to endorse the cooperative. He also served on the CAA boards in both Lowndes and Wilcox Counties. Getting to know local people across the Black Belt and making important connections between them and supporters outside the region became a crucial part of his role as SIP director, sustaining the momentum of the civil rights movement.[43]

In 1966 Walter organized the Freedom Quilting Bee handicraft cooperative, which could be viewed as a derivative of the War on Poverty in Wilcox County. His earlier work provided important connections and ideas that helped create the cooperative, even though it was not part of a federal antipoverty program. More than one hundred women from across Wilcox County and parts of Dallas County joined the Freedom Quilting Bee to market their original patchwork quilts. The co-op made significant strides toward improving the lives of its members. Nancy Callahan has reported that after its first nine months of operation "the co-op provided $5,500 in profits to its members, amassed mostly from the sale of $20 and $25 quilts. . . . In fact, the co-op raised family income for some by as much as 25 percent." By April 1967, the cooperative had grossed just over $10,000. With the money earned from her contribution to the co-op, one woman and her husband insulated their new home; others added indoor plumbing to their houses and built on additional rooms. As the cooperative expanded, it received financial support from the Southern Regional Council and the New York Foundation, which enabled the hiring of a business manager to assist with contracts and outside marketing. By 1970, the women received between $45 and $175 for each quilt, depending on the size and pattern. Before the co-op formed, a handmade quilt brought $5. The SIP created a brochure to market the quilts beyond Alabama.[44]

Through contacts initiated by Rev. Walter, the Bee signed various lucrative agreements for work to be completed by the cooperative members. Initially seen in New York City through an auction, the quilts caught the eye of well-known decorators, sparking a renewed nationwide interest in patchwork quilts. Photo spreads of the Alabama quilters' work appeared in national magazines such as *Life, House and Garden,* and *Vogue.* Bloomingdale's commissioned the co-op members to make quilts to the department store's specifications, Sears and Roebuck placed an order for corduroy pillow shams, and both Bonwit Teller and Saks Fifth Avenue ordered baby quilts in the "coat of many colors" design. By early 1969, the handicraft co-op had built a sewing center near the home of Estelle Witherspoon, a leader in the organization, on Route 1 in Alberta. Lee Rose, a white farmer who had long known Witherspoon and her husband, Eugene, sold an acre of land to the Bee. The co-op named its new building the Martin Luther King Jr. Memorial Sewing Center in honor of the slain civil rights leader. By the end of the next year, the cooperative owned twenty-three acres of land; members decided to sell eight lots to black families who needed a place to live. The Bee also created a day care center for children whose mothers sewed with the cooperative. The women supplemented the handicraft operation with a feeder pig program and cattle business. Mennonites assisted the co-op from 1970 until 1981 and often helped with this aspect of the venture. "The cattle have been somewhat of a banking account because whenever they need some cash or extra money," Mennonite Ralph Reinford explained, "they usually sell off a cow or two." The Mennonites did not make decisions for the cooperative; instead,

The Freedom Quilting Bee

Figure 21. In March 1966, Rev. Francis X. Walter helped form the Freedom Quilting Bee handicraft cooperative. More than one hundred women from Wilcox and Dallas Counties joined together to market original patchwork quilts, sunbonnets, pot holders, and other handwork items. Francis X. Walter Personal Papers, Sewanee, Tenn.

Figure 22. The Freedom Quilting Bee's success enabled its members to improve their living standards. For years, Eugene and Estelle Witherspoon and their family used this outhouse, but her work as the co-op manager enabled the Witherspoons to build a house with modern conveniences. Francis X. Walter Personal Papers, Sewanee, Tenn.

members voted on issues including selling livestock and planting crops. The Bee served an important function, becoming the county's largest industry and only job-creating possibility. In 1982 its gross sales totaled $200,000. Working for the co-op enabled many women to become eligible for Social Security benefits. And some of the quilts gained national acclaim beginning in 2002 as part of the Gee's Bend quilt exhibit, which traveled to art museums across the country, including the Museum of Fine Arts in Houston, the Whitney Museum of American Art in New York City, and the High Museum of Art in Atlanta.[45]

In addition to making handicrafts and raising livestock and crops, the Freedom Quilting Bee continued to provide members with leadership training and job experience that benefited the black community beyond the doors of the sewing center. As Witherspoon's assistant, Minnie McMillian Williams acquired skills that she utilized in organizing a student/parent strike against the Wilcox County school system in the fall of 1971 to push for integration. The strike included marches in downtown Camden to protest the slow progress of school desegregation, leading to the arrests of 429 people, including Witherspoon, the manager of the Freedom Quilting Bee.[46]

OEO completed its financing of SWAFCA in October 1968 by sending the cooperative a $595,751 demonstration grant. One year later, the co-op also received an $852,000 FHA loan. As a result of the cooperative's presence, a Dallas County FHA office was set up in January 1968: farmers with smaller acreage finally had access to loans. The FHA supervisor told an OEO investigator that the number of FHA loans increased from 82 in 1967 to 215 in 1968. He thought this increase resulted from "the local office being opened, the action of SWAFCA, and better communication with the rural area." As was the case with Rev. Harrell in Wilcox County, SWAFCA officials were approved to oversee these loans. In this small way, an OEO-supported program began to chip away at Alabama's obdurate USDA institutions. Beyond the producers' cooperative, SWAFCA's original grant application included a community development component. Its organizers wanted to offer self-help housing, education, a cooperative day care, counseling, recreation, economic development through credit unions, insurance programs, farm equipment sales, and business investment. This part of the rebirth of the Black Belt never became reality, a casualty of too little money and too little staff. The FHA stopped financially supporting SWAFCA in 1973, by which time the Nixon administration had made its decisions about the war on poverty. The staff dwindled to five people, and the cooperative had to rely on the Auburn Extension Service for technical support. The co-op maintained its membership base at about two thousand people, and it reduced the production costs of farming for its members by 20 to 30 percent. In 1975, SWAFCA sold $425,000 worth of truck crops, giving almost 80 percent of that money back to its members. In the late 1970s, co-op leader Albert Turner decided to involve the members in raising corn for the production of ethanol, pulling them away from growing cucumbers and other truck crops. This shift into new business eventually led to the cooperative's demise. It closed up its grading sheds and ceased doing business in January 1981.[47]

The antipoverty programs funded directly from Washington through the CAP's Migrant Labor and Demonstration Divisions provided evidence that the War on Poverty could address the needs of the poor in Alabama's Black Belt. These programs represented the positive side of the CAP funding argument. Richard Boone headed the Demonstration Division, and unlike Hayes, Boone wanted maximum feasible participation of the poor to be front-loaded into CAP grants. Absent such participation, federal money would not be released. The local people in the Alabama Black Belt who had ties to the earlier civil rights struggles in the 1960s found important allies within OEO headquarters through Boone's office. When George and later Lurleen Wallace blocked these programs, OEO's Washington bureaucrats eventually found ways to circumvent the intransigence. These CAP administrators also confronted USDA officials and tried to make that federal agency more responsive to the needs of poor farmers. After Black Belt elites blocked the participation of African Americans in the early years of the War on Poverty, Theodore Berry, Bertrand Harding, and Sargent Shriver did not shy away from supporting programs in the region that were operated by civil rights activists or members of third-party political movements. Through this support, these antipoverty programs gave people new options to better their lives and their communities. After these programs received funding and became firmly established, they operated with minimal interference from local authorities and provided an important base for the political empowerment of local black activists. These programs became the catalytic agents Boone had always intended community action to be. But this process did not occur by accident. The committed participation of civil rights activists was essential to the success of the antipoverty programs, as the failures of Black Belt CAAs dominated by the local power structure attest.[48]

When President Richard Nixon entered office in 1969, federal endorsement of OEO programs changed. In contrast to LBJ's expansive rhetoric, the new president stressed how little experts knew about ending poverty. "Precedents are weak and knowledge is uncertain," Nixon said. "How vast is the range of what we do not yet know and how fragile are projections based on social understanding." Instead of carrying on and building from the initial years of fighting poverty, he moved quickly to restructure the antipoverty agency more to his liking. Nixon appointed thirty-six-year-old Congressman Donald Rumsfeld (R-IL) to direct the agency. He quickly spun off programs to other parts of the federal bureaucracy, transferring the Job Corps to the Department of Labor and sending Head Start, Foster Grandparents, and Comprehensive Health Centers to the Department of Health, Education, and Welfare. After the 1972 elections, Nixon decided to dismantle the antipoverty agency altogether. In a March 1, 1973, budget address to Congress, he announced, "Further spending on behalf of [community action] no longer seems necessary or desirable." In late April 1973, OEO's regional offices closed, and by June 30 the federal agency disbanded completely.[49]

Carry It On, Carry It On

The politics in this country is controlled by bigwigs, and these are the people who call the shots. . . . Fortunately, I feel black people are going to make [some] significant strides in politics in this country and in Alabama. . . . This is where it's really at to get down to the nitty-gritty. . . . Some bread-and-butter politics has to be played in this game. Of course black politics has to be played also. . . . This is the only way you're going to defeat the professional politicians.

    Clarence Williams, Dallas County Chairman, National Democratic Party
    of Alabama, 1972

When Congress passed the Economic Opportunity Act on that hot August day in 1964, Lyndon Baines Johnson probably had no idea what his War on Poverty would really accomplish. As many of Dixie's members of Congress had foreseen, in the South the antipoverty fight converged with the civil rights movement to offer economic and political outlets for African Americans. In the face of intimidation and pressure, those who were organized found ways around the intransigence of their state and local lawmakers to try to remake their region.

Beginning in 1965, the continued chicanery of bureaucrats in the Alabama Office of Economic Opportunity, officials with the U.S. Department of Agriculture (USDA), and county and state election authorities signaled that power sharing would not be an option for Black Belt African Americans. Accepting this reality led many of those African Americans to place their hopes in new institutions, where they could utilize their newfound freedom. Alabama-style Black Power emerged organically, like trumpet vines growing in the Black Belt soil, as economics and politics intertwined to proclaim that the region must accept change despite white resistance. "They ain't gonna let us have no power no how," Stokely Carmichael told fellow Student Nonviolent Coordinating Committee (SNCC) activists James Forman and George Green. "It was natural that you would have a Freedom Organization, man. The black man's party. You have no alternative." "We figured we'd be at this two thousand years," Shirley Mesher remembered. "You couldn't go through them, you'd have to go around them, and that's when we started to do our own thing." Black Power was necessary to counter the force of white power.[1]

By 1967, as the attention of the Southern Christian Leadership Conference (SCLC) and SNCC was drawn elsewhere, the remaining Black Belt activists drew on the methods and experience gained from earlier struggles. In some cases, they ran for and won election to office; in other instances, they continued working with civil rights groups based in Alabama. Since 1964, voting and gaining access to political power had been the main goals of direct-action campaigns and community organizing efforts in the area. Throughout the Black Belt, cooperatives taught many people the importance of participating in democratic institutions. "In a cooperative, you have only one vote per member, irregardless to how many shares that member might hold," Lewis Black explained to the U.S. Commission on Civil Rights. He believed that this arrangement was important because some co-op members had never had the opportunity to participate in any community endeavor, "so this gives them the right to feel a part of sharing in the governing of their community in a small way." Because southern black people had for so long been denied the vote, historian Steven Lawson has explained, they "were unwilling to give up on the ballot's potential, especially when they had not yet had a real opportunity to explore its possibilities."[2]

Over time, these efforts translated into new political realities. By the mid-1970s, African Americans held the majority on the Greene and Lowndes County Commissions. Elsewhere in the region, black people were elected sheriff, tax collector, justice of the peace, coroner, and school board member. Political access was supposed to lead to more than black people sitting in official positions. Many hoped that the new political power would translate into better social and economic opportunities for African Americans.

In the years after 1964, black people in the poorest parts of Alabama defined their freedom through their actions both big and small. They expressed their Alabama style of Black Power by using public space to proclaim that times had begun to change. Nine men who spent their adult lives working on J. A. Minter's plantation in Tyler, in Dallas County, sued their landlord in an effort to change USDA policies in the Agriculture Stabilization and Conservation Service (ASCS). They utilized their freedom to access the federal courts in an effort to change an unfair system even though they could sign the court documents only using an X. The nation's highest court finally had to step in to get these men their trial, which meant that Minter had to hire a lawyer and defend his position because of the actions of his former tenants. The members of the Freedom Quilting Bee bought land, sold property to enable others in their community to live decently, protested the slow pace of school integration, and built a permanent structure for their sewing cooperative, naming it after Martin Luther King Jr. Members of the Southwest Alabama Farmers Cooperative Association (SWAFCA) drove to Washington, D.C., to lobby members of Congress. For many of the participants in the effort, this trip constituted their first venture beyond the state line. Co-op members erected vegetable grading sheds that could be seen throughout ten counties in the Black Belt. Members who owned cars or trucks placed bright orange stickers on their bumpers that read: "SWAFCA WHO?? Small Farms Producing Cooperatively in the Alabama Black Belt," "SWAFCA WHAT?? Ask Your Grocer!" and "SWAFCA WHERE?? Across the Black Belt, Headquarters Selma, Alabama." New houses built by local people and funded directly by the Farmers Home Administration (FHA) in Washington could be seen in Alberta and Lower Peachtree in Wilcox County. These houses had indoor plumbing, glass windows, concrete foundations, and insulated walls. The health clinic in Hayneville employed women who had learned secretarial skills through the adult-education program sponsored by the Lowndes County Christian Movement for Human Rights. Many Black Belt residents read a weekly paper, the *Southern Courier,* that reported on a variety of local news neglected by the region's conservative small-town papers. Subscribing to the *Courier* enabled people to learn about third-party politics, school desegregation, antipoverty programs, and social events. This weekly sustained the civil rights movement well after national organizations had turned their attention elsewhere. Reporters kept people in touch with events in otherwise isolated communities across the Black Belt.[3]

By 1968, the Selma Inter-Religious Project (SIP) had grown beyond the work of Rev. Francis X. Walter. New staff joined the project and offered important support to people in the region. An SIP brochure described the organization as "trying not to be a static institution but an Alabama institution, awake to the needs of the progressive people and victimized people in our state. Here the two are the same people. There are not too many like that in Alabama. It's easy to know one another." Young attorneys provided legal services for people in rural areas. Rev. James Corder worked as a community organizer and legal paraprofessional for the SIP in addition to serving as the president of the Pickens County chapter of the National Association for the Advancement of Colored People (NAACP). SIP's lawyers defended people who had been arrested and charged with committing crimes and offered help to people who needed assistance in their business activities. When African Americans were elected to the Greene County Commission after the 1968 election, SIP attorney Jack Drake helped them replace the school superintendent and drafted a desegregation plan accepted by the black community. Drake served as an internal adviser to the Board of County Commissioners and supervised the creation of the Greene County Housing Authority. Finally, in the early 1970s, the SIP hired Marie Daniels and Steve Martin as labor organizers to enroll independent woodcutters in the Gulfcoast Pulpwood Association. Before the labor union was formed, these woodcutters had to sell their timber to a dealer, who then sold the wood to paper companies. These dealers often treated the woodcutters like tenant farmers, keeping them in continuous debt. The new union sought to end this practice. It had black and white members and an integrated board of officers.[4]

Many of these new institutions had ties to antipoverty programs sponsored directly by Washington's Office of Economic Opportunity (OEO). After President Richard M. Nixon closed OEO, an important leverage for community reform disappeared. To debate whether the War on Poverty was won or lost is not useful in evaluating its impact. Antipoverty programs in the Alabama Black Belt could not tackle all the structural problems associated with poverty by 1973. The agricultural revolution that worked its way through the region could not be stopped, and more would have to be done to revive the local economy than SWAFCA or the education and housing programs in Lowndes and Wilcox Counties could address. If the evaluation of the War on Poverty looks only at the individual success of each community program, important overall consequences will be missed as a final conclusion is drawn.

In places such as the Alabama Black Belt, the federal struggle against poverty undermined many aspects of the old order, a fact that should be a part of any assessment of the overall impact of the War on Poverty. In tandem with the civil rights movement, antipoverty programs gave recognition and legitimacy to many people not traditionally seen as capable of influencing change. The poverty programs enabled many African Americans to confront local elites both black and white. The political struggle between black people and white officials in many Black Belt counties nurtured a third-party movement that pushed the Alabama Democratic Party to integrate its ranks. Although most of the third-party incarnations (the Lowndes County Freedom Party, the Dallas County Independent Free Voters Organization, and the National Democratic Party of Alabama) did not reach all of their stated goals, their presence enabled many black people to gain political office in the Black Belt, an accomplishment that should not be minimized. In 1973, *Newsweek* magazine reported on the effect of the Greene County Commission elections: "The black ascendancy was an outright political miracle. Even now both blacks and whites seem too stunned from the historic event to quite know what to do with it." One of the tragedies of the American political system is that those groups that create the opportunity for change quite often do not reap the benefits of their efforts. In

Alabama, the resurgent Alabama Democratic Conference (ADC) became the power broker for the state's black vote, to the detriment of those who were not part of its political machine. Nevertheless, there is value in understanding how the ADC attained its position and what created the context for its ascendancy.[5]

The hope for the rebirth of the Black Belt foundered on the response of whites to the assertiveness and activism of their African American neighbors. In his study of the white southern reaction to civil rights, historian Jason Sokol said that "white southerners played decisive roles in determining the depths, and limits, of change. Better understanding of their actions and beliefs can more fully explain why the civil rights movement failed, or triumphed, where it did." Through this dynamic, white elites contributed to the creation of a collective memory—like the one revealed at the High Museum's Gee's Bend Quilt exhibit—that remained silent on issues of political power, economic dominance, and the politics of distribution. After the passage of the Civil Rights Act, southern local officials and national politicians such as Howard Smith of Virginia, Richard Russell of Georgia, and Strom Thurmond of South Carolina claimed that the federal legislation ended the need for a continued civil rights movement. Others picked up on this new strategy. Like the negative of a Gee's Bend quilt, Alabama's white leaders stitched novel designs using remnants of Jim Crow in their effort to maintain control and power in spite of the new federal civil rights laws. In 1970 George Wallace announced, "Segregation is dead. It's outlawed, and it won't be again." This statement acknowledged that in the era after the implementation of the Voting Rights Act, the consummate politician had to stitch a different design to win reelection as governor. Nevertheless, practical segregation remained, making a society committed to social justice elusive. Just because one of the nation's champions of racial division had pronounced the demise of segregation did not mean that all the remnants of Jim Crow had disappeared. Many people within the state's power structure carried on by using old patterns of racial dominance in fresh designs to preserve their positions in society.[6]

Selma mayor Joe Smitherman stayed in office for thirty-five years by using his contacts with the city's traditional black leaders to his advantage. He often bragged about his ability to get the African American vote, and he even turned former sites of racial conflict into tourist attractions. In his obituary, the *New York Times* reported that at the end of his life, he had his own form of Jim Crow amnesia. "I fought change and all the while I was for it," he told a Selma newspaper reporter. "A political stance is often different from your personal beliefs," he claimed. This statement would surprise those who worked for Self-Help against Poverty for Everyone and SWAFCA and lived through his "political stance." He even participated in the commemorations of Bloody Sunday that became known as the Bridge Crossing Jubilee. In 2007 Julian Bond, a SNCC activist and later national chairman of the NAACP, pointed out that Smitherman's presence at these events demonstrated that voting rights had become politically safe: "If he could come, anybody could come."[7]

Beyond the infamous mayor of Selma, white businessmen also carried on by holding onto the economic purse strings in many Black Belt towns. By owning and managing the region's financial institutions and major businesses, white people maintained authority over land distribution and policies regarding business loans and financing.

The lawsuit involving the Minter tenants provides a case in point. Even when the Supreme Court ruled in favor of the Dallas County plaintiffs in the case, *Clemon Barlow et al. v. B. L. Collins, Executive Director, Alabama Agricultural Stabilization and Conservation Service et al.,* on March 3, 1970, justice was not guaranteed. Time was not on their side. Walter Blocton and Will Williams, two of the nine plaintiffs, had spent their entire lives on Minter's plantation. They and the others who brought suit sought redress for their landlord's use of their ASCS cotton allotment checks so that they could "make a crop." In 1966 the secretary of agriculture, Orville Freeman, changed the definition of what "making a crop" financing would entail, which altered the Food and Agriculture Act of 1965 to permit allotment checks to be used to secure "the payment of cash rent for land used." Under this new regulation, instead of signing over their allotment checks to Minter in exchange for the use of his land, the plaintiffs wanted to use the money to form a cooperative to buy fertilizer, groceries, and other supplies at wholesale rates, bypassing Minter's commissary. When the Supreme Court overruled the district and appellate courts to say these plaintiffs had standing to maintain this lawsuit, the original case moved forward.[8]

According to the plaintiffs, in December 1966, when Minter learned of the lawsuit that would become known as *Clemon Barlow et al. v. J. A. Minter, et al.,* he refused to renew their leases for the next year. Even though the nine tenants had legal representation provided by the Lawyers Constitutional Defense Committee, when they refused to sign their allotment checks over to Minter, they could not stay on the land they had been leasing while they waited for the trial to go forward. If Minter could evict them from the leased farms, they would no longer have a reason to sue for the cotton allotment checks because they were ineligible to participate in that program. The tenants had little ability to seek redress against what appeared to be retaliatory tactics. They had to find places to live and ways to earn a living. In late January 1967, Sinnie Blocton and Walter Blocton asked to be removed from the case. By July 1970, Clemon Barlow had moved to Chicago, and Willie Gilcrest, Otis Hale, Will Moorer, and Will Williams could not be found. Only Arthur Brown and Elijah Green remained as plaintiffs. Because the two men no longer rented land from Minter, their lawyers sought damages for the way he had mistreated them.[9]

The issue to be decided in this case focused on whether assignment of cotton allotment checks could be made to secure an obligation to payment. Minter claimed that he had the right as a citizen "to select who he will finance, how he will finance them and his requirements if he is going to finance them as long as he does not violate any of their civil rights." His attorney, McLean Pitts, also Selma's city attorney, argued that his client's constitutional right as the owner of property trumped the plaintiffs' rights as tenants. "The Defendant Minter has an absolute constitutional right to use and control his private property in any way he sees fit," Pitts asserted, "even in a discriminatory manner, absent some definite legal compulsion to the contrary, which is non-existent in this case." Minter explained that was not retaliating; rather, he made his decisions based on the fact that he would have to change "his whole method of operations for the year 1966" to farm his lands profitably. He wanted to go on a year-by-year basis in anticipation of altering the way he worked his land. Minter planned to begin mechanized farming techniques "that required complete rearrangement of the lands, the doing away with certain houses for the purpose of establishing rows of sufficient distance and allowing sufficient room for large farm machinery equipment to operate." His diversified operation included 475 acres in cotton, 300 acres in soybeans, 100 acres in grain sorghum, 300 acres in uech clover, 35 acres of wheat, 15 acres of oats, 15 acres of sericea, and 1,500 acres in a cattle and hay operation. While this case highlights the agricultural revolution that rolled through the Alabama Black Belt, it also reveals the role played by the civil rights movement in this transformation. Those tenants who sought access to ASCS financing were the ones removed from this new system of farming. "What do a man think he deserves if he works all the time," Will Williams asked in 1966. "Don't he deserve something? I think he do. Yeah, that's what he's workin for . . . to have something, to take care of his family, children, and everything." He explained his exhaustion with the old tenant system he tried to change by joining the lawsuit against his landlord. "Yeah, you don't work for the way it looks like—it's working like a mule: work him, feed him as long as he's workin, when he done gather the crop turn the old mule a loose through the winter to die poor or do any way he wants . . . and they take it all, while you got to do without until the first of March and then start advancing again. Yeah, if you workin, you wouldn't want to be working if you didn't get nothin out of your work. . . . Well, that's the way it is with the colored folk." Under his new arrangement, Minter kept six black tenants and three white tenants, none of whom had sought to change USDA practices.[10]

Minter's economic power enabled him to string this case out for many years after his tenants filed their initial lawsuit. He hired a well-connected attorney to effectively represent his interests. The tenants, while quite courageous in their willingness to confront their landlord and his Old South management traditions, simply could not compete. Brown and Green lost their case on March 29, 1972. Their activism and desire to reverse some of the powerful ways elites distributed property and held onto economic advantages in their community could not contend against someone like J. A. Minter Jr.[11]

Many years would pass before Alabama's state and local officials gave up their allegiance to Jim Crow. Blatant examples of racial discrimination receded, only to be replaced by more clandestine attempts to keep black Alabamians out of the mainstream. As a result, the Black Belt remained a place of racial disharmony that discouraged economic development. This continued division contributed to the persistent impoverishment of the Black Belt, which the War on Poverty could not conquer before President Nixon dismantled OEO.

These patterns of discrimination and misappropriation of assistance continued throughout the 1970s and into the 1980s. The U.S. Commission on Civil Rights monitored the USDA programs in 1971, 1973, and 1975 and found that the USDA did not effectively implement recommendations to remedy these problems. The commission concluded that the "FHA has become increasingly a lender for farmers with large assets, who rely heavily on debt financing to expand their agricultural operations, while taking advantage of inflation, technology, and tax benefits." In 1981, black farmers received only 2.5 percent of the total amount loaned through the FHA. That same year, only seventeen black Alabama farmers received farm ownership loans, a drop from thirty-seven in 1980. The average black farm family received $10,769, while the average white farm family got $64,664. Fourteen years after Robert C. "Red" Bamberg testified in Montgomery, state FHA director Dale Richey did not sound much different. "Sooner or later it becomes a business decision," he explained, ignoring the social function his office was supposed to endorse. "And loans to farmers with little land to operate on are sometime[s] hard to repay. . . . The money is taxpayers' money and has to be repaid." These findings reinforce historian Gilbert Fite's conclusions: "Officials of the USDA and associated agencies . . . never even fired their guns in the war on poverty." Many white officials' fears regarding SWAFCA had been dealt with by the early 1970s. Through the organized attack on the co-op, these local Black Belt elites maintained control of the lucrative USDA programs, resulting in SWAFCA's isolation as it operated without valuable technical assistance that other white farmers routinely received.[12]

Although George Wallace continued to accept federal funds to fight poverty during his second term, other aspects of his administration contributed to the lack of economic growth in the Black Belt. In 1972, poverty programs operating across Alabama received $15,694,372 from OEO, and the governor approved programs regardless of the racial diversity of the sponsoring organizations. The Black Belt received 24.3 percent of the federal antipoverty funds distributed within the state. Nevertheless, without the cooperation of other aspects of the state administration, federal and local activities to fight poverty could not build an economic engine with much horsepower.[13]

So even though black people began to hold elected offices across the region, the new political power did not translate into better economic and social opportunities for their constituents. Such was the case partly because of other aspects of the state bureaucracy and partly because of the continued animosity between the races. When Wallace became governor for the second time in 1970, he appointed Bamberg director of the Alabama Development Office. True to form, in his new position Bamberg did not assign African Americans to the regional industrial development commissions, which worked with local governments to prepare demographic information on counties and to assist cities and counties in acquiring funds for industrial development. In addition, each county had an economic and industrial board that made decisions regarding development; in the Black Belt, only Macon County, home of Tuskegee Institute, had African American representation on these important boards. On the rare occasions when industries located in the region, they usually did not benefit the rural unemployed. One newspaper reported that instead of increasing jobs by bringing in industry, Wallace created jobs only in state and local government, which expanded by 50 percent. These positions usually fell under the state merit system, which could exclude African Americans under the subterfuge that they did not pass the necessary examinations. Unlike new industry, governmental jobs did not contribute to further job creation.[14]

The State Sovereignty Commission was another part of the Alabama bureaucracy that continued to fight against civil rights during the 1970s. Martha Witt Smith persevered in her work as the governor's voting specialist under the State Sovereignty Commission. In 1972, when the state legislature considered the amendment to the U.S. Constitution that would have allowed eighteen-year-olds to vote, she claimed that the change would enable more black people than white people to vote and therefore that Alabama should not support the amendment. The *Alabama Journal* questioned Smith's statistics, since the U.S. Census had discontinued listing age groups by race. After eighteen-year-olds received the vote, Smith tried to hinder their ability to register, telling state registrars that to qualify to vote, students living in college towns had to prove that they planned to remain in these cities after graduation and had to own fixed property in the county where they sought to register.[15]

Smith also continued to utilize her office to obstruct the election of African Americans in the Black Belt. For the 1972 statewide election, she traveled to Lowndes County to instruct the registrars about how to circumvent Alabama attorney general William Baxley's ruling that the same person could help an unlimited number of voters who requested assistance in the voting booth. In a report she titled "Watchers Win It for Whites," Smith claimed that her work enabled all the white candidates to win in their races against the black office seekers from the National Democratic Party of Alabama. The white candidates "could not have won" in Lowndes County "without their good group of poll watchers," she reported. "Neither could they have won if those poll watchers had not known what they could do within the law."[16]

In spite of these state obstructions, black people continued to run for political office and sometimes won. Most African Americans gained seats on the county level, but economic power in the Black Belt resided in the hands of businesspeople and elected officials in the cities and towns. The U.S. Commission on Civil Rights found that industries chose to locate in the towns where white people maintained civic power. For example, in Hayneville, Fort Deposit, Eutaw, and Selma, white officials continued to dominate the most powerful political offices. Some important changes came about on the county level but usually arose through the financial support of the federal government.[17]

Greene County's black county commissioners distributed federal funds for the benefit of their rural constituents in the form of standard housing for displaced tenant farmers, a health clinic, and countywide transportation and sewage systems. Federal funds also sustained the gains made by African American county commissioners in Lowndes County. Across the region, public schools finally stopped segregating students in the mid-1970s. In the aftermath of desegregation enforcement, white people created private academies that catered exclusively to their children. The new dual education system made it difficult to raise local taxes to support public schools because white families did not want to expend any more money on educational systems in which their children did not participate. Many districts consequently came to rely heavily on state and federal assistance. Nevertheless, African American school board members used federal funds to support programs for impoverished students such as free school lunches, Chapter 1 (a program that offers federal funds based on the number of impoverished students living in a school district), and Head Start. Even though public schools became virtually resegregated, this time as all-black institutions, the facilities were better than those available to black students prior to desegregation. The low-income citizens of Dallas, Greene, Lowndes, and Sumter Counties also had improved public health facilities, resources that did not even exist before the 1970s. In some cases, better schools and health clinics translated into improved graduation rates for African Americans and lower infant mortality rates. Yet the reliance on federal assistance could not transform the region.[18]

In the Alabama Black Belt, gaining political office turned out to be an inadequate means for improving the local economy. Many people involved in the civil rights movement and the War on Poverty in the region had pinned their future hopes on political access and civic power. That was the basic message of Stokely Carmichael's initial call for Black Power. Historian Adam Fairclough has analyzed this hope: "In the North, blacks had already discovered that the vote did not eliminate poverty and discrimination. Blacks in the South had still to learn that lesson."[19]

Having been denied admission to so many parts of the power structure, African Americans had reason to believe that holding political office would bring them the keys to the locked doors. Yet after some black people won elected positions, the remaining social problems and the persistent legacy of white supremacy impeded economic progress. When new industries came into the Black Belt, the rural poor lacked the skills necessary to acquire the jobs or the transportation to reach them. In other cases, local banks required higher credit standards from black people seeking loans, preventing some African Americans from starting their own businesses. One black man in Lowndes County received financial backing from a church in Philadelphia, Pennsylvania, after the local bank refused his loan application. This outside help enabled him to operate the Lowndes Wood Products Company, the county's only substantial black-owned business. Alabama's tax structure also did not help in matters of economic development. State lawmakers lured industry with low corporate taxes, which contributed to the state's stingy educational and social welfare systems. All of these factors plus the lack of industry helped to keep the Black Belt impoverished. The unemployment rate for African Americans in the region was typically two to three times that of white people. Consequently, the typical white family earned more than double the amount earned by the typical black family.[20]

As the problems associated with poverty persisted in the Alabama Black Belt, those who had worked in the civil rights movement and participated in War on Poverty programs continued to try to change the region. The unwillingness of Lowndes County banks to offer credit to black customers led the Lowndes County Commission to form a credit union in hopes of creating competition. In 1971, the Emergency Land Fund formed to help African Americans hold onto their land by providing legal assistance, loans, and educational programs. By 1977, Selma attorney Henry Sanders had overseen two hundred cases covering twenty-five thousand acres of land for the fund. He and others tried to remedy problems associated with partition sales, lack of wills, and tax sales that took land away from many black property owners. "Just because some things are legally correct," Sanders explained, "doesn't mean they're morally right. We've found that to be the case in many of these land disputes." In his work with the Emergency Land Fund, Sanders took up the struggle to get the FHA to lend money on a more equitable basis.[21]

The Federation of Southern Cooperatives maintained a presence in the Black Belt at its Rural Training and Research Center based in Epes, in Sumter County. This 1,325-acre facility offered technical assistance to rural people who had formed cooperatives and credit unions. In 1973, more than a hundred co-ops and credit unions from fourteen southern states joined the organization, and more than one thousand members attended training sessions and seminars at the Epes center. Many of the cooperatives that formed the federation began as OEO demonstration projects or CAP programs. The federation had a staff of seventy-five, and fifty co-op managers and bookkeepers received subsidized support from the organization. The demonstration farm had three hundred head of beef cattle, a one-hundred-sow feeder pig project, a goat herd, three experimental greenhouses, and an irrigation system. In 1982, the U.S. Commission on Civil Rights reported that the payroll of the Federation of Southern Cooperatives fluctuated between $200,000 and $1,000,000 annually. The training center also had a dormitory, cafeteria, and classroom so that other groups could use its facilities for conferences. The National Democratic Party of Alabama, the Gulf Coast Pulpwood Association, and the Alabama Coordinating Committee for Minority Economic Development held meetings there. The federation, however, did not reside in harmony with some of its neighbors. Federation officials alleged that the Sumter County commissioners denied the group county services and that a federal grand jury investigation of the organization stemmed from the animosity of local elected officials. The Department of Justice conducted an investigation of the Federation of Southern Cooperatives from December 1979 until May 1981. Although no one received an indictment, the federation spent $1,000,000 defending itself. The inquiry drained the organization's resources and jeopardized its future.[22]

The National Democratic Party of Alabama (NDPA) continued its effort to represent progressive black and white Alabamians. Many people who had been involved in the War on Poverty programs affiliated with this political party to challenge the more accommodationist ADC, but by 1978 the NDPA was no longer active. Those people who had won office under the third-party banner found it difficult to receive state funds outside of the Alabama Democratic Party. When the NDPA disbanded, many rejoined the state's regular Democrats. By 1980, Joe Reed's leadership of the ADC created a formidable force in Alabama's political circles. He created a patronage system mirroring that run by Alabama's white politicians, such as George Wallace. The *Montgomery Advertiser* reported, "The conference's patronage system, which secured blacks positions on government boards and in government jobs, has kept black voters loyal and made the conference strong." In 1985, President Ronald Reagan's Justice Department began to investigate and bring charges of voter fraud against many of the Black Belt African American leaders who were not part of the ADC machine and who had been active in antipoverty programs and third-party movements during the 1960s. Targets of these investigations included John Hulett in Lowndes County, Rev. Thomas Threadgill in Wilcox County, and Albert Turner in Perry County.[23]

Nine black people, including four elected officials, from Greene, Lowndes, Perry, Sumter, and Wilcox Counties responded to these investigations by filing a class-action lawsuit challenging the legitimacy of these federal actions. The Southern Poverty Law Center and the southeastern office of the American Civil Liberties Union represented the plaintiffs, who charged the Reagan officials with being "engaged in a concerted effort to unlawfully interfere with black citizens' associational and political activities" in the Black Belt, contending that the investigations sought to discourage people from voting. The suit also accused federal and local officials of ignoring citizen complaints with regard to election fraud and intimidation committed by political opponents of both races. Federal Bureau of Investigation agents questioned more than a thousand black absentee voters from the Black Belt about the way they had cast their ballots in the 1984 elections, causing the region's residents to wonder where these agents had been during the many decades when whites were threatening and intimidating blacks. Many African Americans in the area viewed the U.S. attorneys' actions as part of the Reagan administration's national effort to reverse twenty years of civil rights gains. According to the Southern Regional Council, the Reagan administration focused on the Alabama Black Belt because "at stake are scores of local elective offices, administrative control of revenues, resources and policies, sufficient clout to secure black participation in government public works contracts and programs, several seats in the Alabama legislature, influence upon the outcome of a US Congressional candidacy, and the margin of difference in a close Senate race." In the wake of this intimidation, people who had been active in antipoverty programs and third-party politics in the Black Belt appeared on the 1986 membership lists of the Alabama New South Coalition, the next incarnation willing to take on the power of the ADC.[24]

Events in the Alabama Black Belt between 1964 and 1972 confirm that the civil rights movement carried on the struggle for racial and economic equality. Charles Payne has concluded that one of the fundamental questions raised by the concept of Black Power was whether American institutions could work for the benefit of black people. The War on Poverty was one of the first federally sponsored programs that intentionally tried to incorporate African Americans into the country's mainstream. In Alabama, the antipoverty effort addressed issues of equality, power, and the politics of distribution. By the mid-1970s, black people had clearly gained admission into one of the nation's most basic institutions, the political party. The tragedy is that the rebirth of the Black Belt that many had envisioned did not come because elected office was just not enough to conquer the issues of economic inequality and political corruption that continued to plague the region. More energy and resources would be required to permit African Americans access to the many institutions that continued to exclude them.[25]

Understanding how the South changed after 1965 requires acknowledging the complexity of the civil rights movement and its larger goals. The movement was a dynamic struggle among those in power, those who traditionally brokered that power, and those who fought to include representatives of people from the grass roots in the power structure. After 1965, the movement carried on, but not necessarily through national heroes and national organizations; instead, the movement shifted to the local level, where people worked it out the hard way. During this period, we can see what people with a lot of courage and few economic resources were able to accomplish to make something meaningful for themselves and their communities. On March 3, 2007, the 2008 presidential campaign came to the Alabama Black Belt. Amid the hoopla of dueling speeches—Senator Hillary Clinton at Selma's First Baptist Church and Senator Barack Obama at Brown's Chapel African Methodist Episcopal—former SCLC activist Rev. Richard Boone offered some advice to the candidates: "They've got to come out and meet the people. And this is where the people are. And the people need help. The more things change, the more they stay the same. We've still got a long way to go."[26]

Notes

Abbreviations

ABP   Albert Boutwell Papers, Birmingham Public Library, Archives and Manuscripts Division, Birmingham, Ala.

ACAI   Alabama Commission of Agriculture and Industries, Administrative Files, 1964–69, Alabama Department of Archives and History, Montgomery

AGAdmAF   Alabama Governor—Administrative Assistants' Files, Alabama Department of Archives and History, Montgomery

AGF   Alabama Governor (1963–79: Wallace, Wallace, Brewer, Wallace) Administrative Files, Alabama Department of Archives and History, Montgomery

AGLAF   Alabama Governor: Legal Advisers' Files, Alabama Department of Archives and History, Montgomery

ASACUSCCR Selma   Open Meeting of the Alabama State Advisory Committee to the U.S. Commission on Civil Rights, Selma, Ala., May 26, 1967, U.S. Commission on Civil Rights Library, Washington, D.C.

HHrgHR10440   U.S. Congress, House of Representatives, Committee on Education and Labor, *Hearings on HR 10440*, 88th Cong., 2nd sess., March 17–20, April 7–10, 13–14, 1964, Part I. Washington, D.C.: U.S. Government Printing Office, 1964.

HTFOHC   Hardy T. Frye Oral History Collection, Ralph Brown Draughon Library, Special Collections and Archives Department, Auburn University, Auburn, Ala.

LBJ Library   Lyndon B. Johnson Library, Austin, Tex.

LBJOHC   Lyndon B. Johnson Library Oral History Collection, Lyndon B. Johnson Library, Austin, Tex.

LH   Lister Hill Papers, W. S. Hoole Special Collections Library, University of Alabama, Tuscaloosa

NAACP Papers   National Association for the Advancement of Colored People Papers, Group III, Library of Congress Manuscript Division, Washington, D.C.

PISF   Public Information Subject Files—General Files, Alabama Department of Archives and History, Montgomery

RBOHC	Ralph Bunche Oral History Collection, Moorland-Spingarn Research Center, Manuscript Division, Howard University, Washington, D.C.
RG 381	Office of Economic Opportunity Papers, Record Group 381, National Archives and Records Administration II, College Park, Md.
RG 381SE	Community Services Administration Papers (formerly Office of Economic Opportunity), Southeast Regional Office, Record Group 381, National Archives and Records Administration, Southeast Region, Morrow, Ga.
SCLC Papers	Southern Christian Leadership Conference Papers, Martin Luther King Jr. Center for Nonviolent Social Change Archives, Atlanta, Ga.
SIP Papers	Selma Inter-Religious Project Papers, Birmingham Public Library, Archives and Manuscripts Division, Birmingham, Ala.
SNCC Papers	Student Nonviolent Coordinating Committee Papers, Microfilm, Auburn Avenue Research Library on African American Culture and History, Atlanta-Fulton Public Library System, Atlanta, Ga.
SRC	Southern Regional Council Papers, Birmingham Public Library, Archives and Manuscripts Division, Birmingham, Ala.
SWAFCA Binder	SWAFCA Binder, Society of Saint Edmund Mission Archives, Selma, Ala.
TSHC	Tutwiler Southern History Collection, Clippings Files, Birmingham Public Library, Birmingham, Ala.
USCCR Mont	Hearing before the U.S. Commission on Civil Rights, Montgomery, Ala., April 27–May 2, 1968, U.S. Commission on Civil Rights Library, Washington, D.C.

Prologue

1. Author's notes, Gee's Bend Quilt Exhibit, High Museum of Art, Atlanta, May 2006.

2. Ibid.; Katz, *Undeserving Poor,* 7.

3. Author's notes.

4. Ibid.

5. Ibid.; Beardsley et al., *Gee's Bend,* 398–99 (Williams's quilt appears on p. 399).

6. Author's notes, Gee's Bend Quilt Exhibit; Callahan, *Freedom Quilting Bee,* 3, 11, 13–18; John Beardsley, "River Island," in Beardsley et al., *Gee's Bend,* 33–34; Jane Livingston, "Reflections on the Art," in Beardsley et al., *Gee's Bend,* 55–57. Walter's work may not have had a place at the High's exhibit because Livingston focused on origins of the women's creativity and practice of their craft. As she wrote, "The Freedom Quilting Bee, established in part because of the already existing presence of a rich quiltmaking culture in Wilcox County, is definitely not what these books and exhibi-

tion are about. In fact, the truly distinctive styles (or substyles) developed by these
women so far predate the quilting bee that there can be literally no argument made
for its influence on the origins of this phenomenon. It is perhaps more significant
that the pressure brought to bear by the quilting bee had as *little* effect as it did on the
best quilts that continued to be made during the late 1960s and afterward." I nevertheless believe that the presence of the Freedom Quilting Bee, while not an influence on the way handmade quilts continued to be stitched by women in the county,
provided an inspiration for self-determination. Livingston seems unsympathetic to
the fact that the bee provided jobs for women who otherwise would have had very
limited economic opportunities. While cooperative members may have changed their
quilt-making techniques to fit a standardized form for a wider market, that did not
mean that when they sewed for themselves away from the bee, they did not retain
their own styles.

7. Blight, *Race and Reunion;* Fahs and Waugh, *Memory of the Civil War.* Blight's
groundbreaking book and Fahs and Waugh's collection of essays have influenced my
ideas on the significance of museums and collective memory.

8. Callahan, *Freedom Quilting Bee,* 42; Ulrich, *Good Wives.* Ulrich's work with material culture as a way to understand the lives of Puritan women has influenced my view
of how these quilts may also express Black Power.

Introduction. How Will Freedom Come?

1. Gay Talese, "Where's the Spirit of Selma Now?" *New York Times Magazine,* May
30, 1965, 9, 41, 44, Box SG13843, Alabama State Sovereignty Commission Papers, Alabama Department of Archives and History, Montgomery.

2. Ibid., 44–45.

3. Matusow, *Unraveling of America;* Walter, Interview, 13–14, RBOHC.

4. Walter, Interview by Author, 1–10, 26–27; Eagles, *Outside Agitator,* 174–75; Walter,
Interview, 43–47, RBOHC.

5. Walter Diary, 7, 64–65, Francis X. Walter Personal Papers, Sewanee, Tenn.

6. Woodward, "What Happened to the Civil Rights Movement?" 29–34; Sullivan,
Freedom Writer, 374–75. Durr is using the term *Pole Cat* to refer to conservative, white,
southern Democrats.

7. Sullivan, *Freedom Writer,* 374–75.

8. Ibid., 374–76.

9. Turner, Interview by Author, 4–6, 12; Black, Interview 6–8, RBOHC.

10. Mesher, Interview, 1–4, 8, 10–11, 16, 18, RBOHC.

11. Kate Harris, "OEO Fight Taken to Capital against Grant to 'Black Power' Group,"
Birmingham News, April 4, 1967, SWAFCA Binder; Louis B. Whitfield to Lister Hill,
June 2, 1967, Box 379, LH; Mesher, Interview, 79–80, RBOHC.

12. Hall, "Long Civil Rights Movement," 1258; Matusow, *Unraveling of America,* 120,
126, 246, 251, 254; Lemann, *Promised Land,* 192, 344; Ronald Eller, War on Poverty
Seminar, April 7, 2005, Center for Appalachian Studies and the Center for Kentucky

History and Politics, Eastern Kentucky University, Richmond; Nicholas D. Kristof, "The Larger Shame," *New York Times,* September 6, 2005.

One. Southern Accents

1. Lyndon Baines Johnson, "Annual Message to the Congress of the State of the Union," January 8, 1964, in *Public Papers of the Presidents . . . Lyndon B. Johnson,* 112–14.

2. Crespino, *In Search of Another Country,* 82; Novak, *Agony of the G.O.P. 1964,* 176–79; Phillips, *Emerging Republican Majority,* 32–33. Phillips corroborates Novak's summation.

3. Whalen and Whalen, *Longest Debate,* 40, 212–13, 215; Dallek, *Flawed Giant,* 120; Crespino, *In Search of Another Country,* 8–9.

4. *Congressional Record,* vol. 110, pt. 14, August 5, 1964, pp. 18634, 19023; Johnson, *Vantage Point,* 81; *Atlanta Constitution,* August 8, 1964.

5. Richard N. Goodwin, *Remembering America,* 258, 260–70; Chafe, *Unfinished Journey,* 237; Unger, *Best of Intentions,* 76; Patterson, *Grand Expectations,* 531, 535; Conkin, *Big Daddy,* 192–93; Moynihan, *Maximum Feasible Misunderstanding,* 29; Heath, *Decade of Disillusionment,* 170–71; Johnson, *Vantage Point,* 72.

6. Dallek, *Lone Star Rising,* 8, 169, 379–81, 518–27; Dallek, *Flawed Giant,* 120.

7. Brauer, "Kennedy, Johnson, and the War on Poverty," 104, 118–19.

8. Fairclough, *To Redeem the Soul of America,* 134–35, 150–53.

9. John F. Kennedy, "Special Message to the Congress on Civil Rights and Job Opportunities," June 19, 1963, in *Public Papers of the Presidents . . . John F. Kennedy,* 483–85, 488; Heath, *Decade of Disillusionment,* 113–14; Miroff, *Pragmatic Illusions,* 225; Matusow, *Unraveling of America,* 120–21; Lampman, Interview, 7–9, LBJOHC; Patterson, *America's Struggle,* 134–35.

10. OEO, Administrative History, vol. 2, Documentary Supplement, *Economic Report of the President,* January 1964, 203–4, RG 381; HHrgHR10440, pt. 1, p. 247; Patricia Sullivan, *Days of Hope,* 64–65; Rogers et al., *Alabama,* 524, 530; Levitan, *Great Society's Poor Law,* 12; Boulard, "Review," 416.

11. McPherson, *Political Education,* 135; Bernstein, *Promises Kept,* 236; Frederickson, *Dixiecrat Revolt,* 215.

12. Conkin, *Big Daddy,* 135; Miroff, *Pragmatic Illusions,* 231; Moynihan, *Maximum Feasible Misunderstanding,* 6; Matusow, *Unraveling of America,* 217; Bernstein, *Guns or Butter,* 106.

13. Kermit Gordon, "Figures for OEO Spending," January 22, 1964, Economic Opportunity Act, Legislative Background, Box 2, LBJ Library; Sundquist, *On Fighting Poverty,* 22–23; Poverty and Urban Policy: Conference Transcript of 1973 Group Discussion of the Kennedy Administration Urban Poverty Programs and Policies, 149, 287, 301–2, John F. Kennedy Library, Boston; Patterson, *America's Struggle,* 141; Bernstein, *Promises Kept,* 27–28, 32; Unger, *Best of Intentions,* 74–75; Califano, *Triumph and Tragedy,* 75; Heath, *Decade of Disillusionment,* 169; Gordon, Interview, Tape 3, pp. 1–4, LBJOHC; Cannon, Interview, 57–58, LBJOHC; Shriver, Interview I, 18–19,

38–39, LBJOHC; Sundquist, Interview, 22–24, LBJOHC. William Capron felt that the $1 billion figure to fight poverty indicated how off the CEA had been in understanding where Johnson wanted to go with this program.

14. Johnson, *Vantage Point,* 76; Califano, *Triumph and Tragedy,* 76; Bernstein, *Promises Kept,* 268; Levitan, *Great Society's Poor Law,* 74; Shriver, Interview I, 34–35, Interview II, 52–53, LBJOHC; Gordon, Interview, Tape 4, p. 9, LBJOHC.

15. O'Reilly, *Nixon's Piano,* 193–95; Sargent Shriver, Speech, National Conference on Religion and Race, Chicago, January 15, 1963, White House Aides Files—Moyers, Box 77, LBJ Library; Bernstein, *Promises Kept,* 270–71.

16. OEO, Administrative History, vol. 1, pt. 1, Narrative History, p. 26, LBJ Library; Johnson, *Vantage Point,* 76; Beschloss, *Taking Charge,* 211.

17. Yarmolinsky, Interview II, 18, Interview III, 5–6, 8, LBJOHC; Shriver, Interview I, 71, LBJOHC; Lampman, Interview, 27–28, 43–44, LBJOHC; John A. Baker, Interview III, 3–4, LBJOHC; Kelly, Interview I, 6, LBJOHC; Levitan, *Great Society's Poor Law,* 29–30; Poverty and Urban Policy: Conference Transcript, 183–84; Moynihan, *Maximum Feasible Misunderstanding,* 98; *Congressional Record,* Extension of Remarks, June 12, 1968, p. E5347; Yarmolinsky, Interview I, 2, LBJOHC; OEO, Administrative History, vol. 1, pt. 1, Narrative History, pp. 49–50; Patricia Sullivan, *Days of Hope,* 1–2, 125; John A. Baker, Interview I, 1, Interview II, 1, 21–22, 24–25, Interview III, 4, LBJOHC; Conway, Interview, 3, 6, LBJOHC; Kelly, Interview II, 11, LBJOHC; Bernstein, *Promises Kept,* 108, 178; Shriver, Interview II, 9–10, LBJOHC; HHrgHR10440, pt. 3, 1509.

18. Patterson, *America's Struggle,* 136; OEO, Administrative History, vol. 1, pt. 1, Narrative History, pp. 37–38; O'Connor, *Poverty Knowledge,* 164; Parker, *John Kenneth Galbraith,* 281–82.

19. "Section by Section Analysis of the Economic Opportunity Act of 1964," n.d., Economic Opportunity Act, Legislative Background, Box 2, LBJ Library; OEO, Administrative History, vol. 1, pt. 1, Narrative History, p. 35; Charles L. Schultze, "Outline of the Poverty Bill and Issues Raised Therein," March 2, 1964, Economic Opportunity Act, Legislative Background, Box 1, LBJ Library; Sundquist, *On Fighting Poverty,* 63.

20. Poverty and Urban Policy: Conference, 231–32, 247–49, 254, 258; Cannon, Interview, 24–25, LBJOHC; Schulman, *Lyndon B. Johnson,* 183.

21. Knapp and Polk, *Scouting the War on Poverty,* 138; Moynihan, *Maximum Feasible Misunderstanding,* 86–87; Shriver, Interview I, 101, LBJOHC; John A. Baker, Interview III, 11, LBJOHC.

22. F. O'R. Hayes, Discussion Draft of "The Role of Indigenous Organizations in Community Action Programs," May 4, 1964, White House Aides Files—Bohen, Box 2, LBJ Library.

23. Ibid.

24. Cannon, Interview, 54–55, LBJOHC; Sundquist, *On Fighting Poverty,* 48–50; Hayes, Discussion Draft of "The Role of Indigenous Organizations in Community Action Programs"; Yarmolinsky, Interview III, 17, LBJOHC; Sundquist, Interview, 57, LBJOHC.

25. Hayes, Discussion Draft of "The Role of Indigenous Organizations in Community Action Programs."

26. "The War on Poverty: A Congressional Presentation," March 17, 1964, 4–5, General Counsel Records Regarding the President's Task Force in the War Against Poverty, Box 7, RG 381.

27. Mary Drake, "Summary," ca. 1969, Anti-Poverty Program Evaluation, Community Action/Anti-Poverty, Box 10, RG 381SE; Rebecca Ward and Pattie Mae Haynes, Testimony, USCCR Mont, 285, 288.

28. "The War on Poverty: A Congressional Presentation," 405; Schultze, "Outline of the Poverty Bill."

29. Sundquist, Interview, 7–8, LBJOHC; John A. Baker, Interview II, 30–31, LBJOHC; Dan T. Carter, *Politics of Rage,* 154; Schultze, "Outline of the Poverty Bill." Baker got the idea for the family farm corporation from the 1937 Bankhead-Jones Farm Tenant Act.

30. "The War on Poverty: A Congressional Presentation," 4–5, 40–41; John A. Baker, Interview II, 26, LBJOHC.

31. Dallek, *Flawed Giant,* 142; Johnson, *Vantage Point,* 74–75.

32. Yarmolinsky, Interview III, 11, Interview II, 9, LBJOHC; Poverty and Urban Policy: Conference Transcript, 249–50; Goldschmidt, Interview, 3–4, LBJOHC; Shriver, Interview I, 76, LBJOHC.

33. Doris Kearns Goodwin, *Lyndon Johnson,* 227; Johnson, *Vantage Point,* 77.

34. *Washington Post,* March 17, 1964, 1964 Scrapbook, 88th Cong., 2nd sess., Phil Landrum Papers, Offices of Susan Landrum and Phil Landrum Jr., Jasper, Ga.; Johnson, *Vantage Point,* 77–78; Califano, *Triumph and Tragedy,* 76; Shriver, Interview II, 45–46, LBJOHC; Pollak, Interview, 14, LBJOHC; Unger, *Best of Intentions,* 91; *Gainesville (Ga.) Daily Times,* March 17, 1964, Poverty Clippings File, Landrum Papers; Tindall with Shi, *America,* 1321.

35. Shriver, Interview II, 46–47, LBJOHC; Donald M. Baker, Interview, Tape 1, p. 1, LBJOHC; Virginia Van der Veer Hamilton, *Lister Hill,* 267; Boulard, "Review," 416; *Congressional Quarterly Almanac,* 88th Cong., 2nd sess., 1964, 20:27.

36. Virginia Van der Veer Hamilton, *Lister Hill,* 236, 249, 253, 255, 266, 291. See also Frederickson, *Dixiecrat Revolt;* Badger, "Southerners Who Refused," 518; Boulard, "Review," 416, 419.

37. HHrgHR10440, pt. 1, p. 433; Bernstein, *Guns or Butter,* 56; OEO, Administrative History, vol. 1, pt. 1, Narrative History, pp. 42–43; Yarmolinsky, Interview III, 33, LBJOHC; Levitan, *Great Society's Poor Law,* 41; Donald M. Baker, Interview, Tape 1, p. 203, LBJOHC; Pollak, Interview, 17, LBJOHC; *Congressional Record,* Extension of Remarks, June 12, 1968, p. E5347. My use of the word *chairman* throughout the book is in the context of the mid-1960s and reflects the dominance of men in public life at the time.

38. HHrgHR10440, pt. 1, p. 19, pt. 3, p. 1521; OEO, Administrative History, vol. 1, pt. 1, Narrative History, pp. 42–44; Drew Pearson Editorial, May 21, 1964, Poverty Clippings File, Landrum Papers.

39. HHrgHR10440, pt. 1, pp. 321–23, 465.

40. Statement, April 8, 1964, Poverty Clippings File, Landrum Papers; HHrgHR10440, pt. 1, p. 379; Marjorie Hunter, "Landrum Defies G.O.P. on Poverty," *New York Times,* April 10, 1964.

41. HHrgHR10440, pt. 3, pp. 1509–10, 1546; Burton A. Weisbrod, "Late Notes on the Poverty Bill," May 20, 1964, Milton Turen, "Legislative Developments on the OEO Legislation," May 6, 1964, Economic Opportunity Act, Legislative Background, Box 1, LBJ Library; Moynihan, *Maximum Feasible Misunderstanding,* 93; MF, "Congressman Carl Albert's Information on the Economic Opportunity Act of 1964," Economic Opportunity Act, Legislative Background, Box 2, LBJ Library; Unger, *Best of Intentions,* 93; OEO, Administrative History, vol. 1, pt. 1, Narrative History, p. 47.

42. U.S. Congress, Senate, Committee on Labor and Public Welfare, *Hearings on S2642,* 54.

43. Ibid., 177, 181, 183–84, 186.

44. Major Amendments to H.R. 11377 [fka H.R. 10440] Made by the Senate Labor and Public Welfare Committee, Anti-Poverty Legislation File, Landrum Papers; Select Subcommittee on Labor and Public Welfare, Executive Meeting Minutes, June 30, 1964, Labor and Public Welfare Committee, Box 444, LH.

45. Shriver, Interview II, 80–81, LBJOHC; Joseph W. Sullivan, "Revolt in Congress: Southerners Become Wary of Supporting Johnson's Program," *Wall Street Journal,* July 29, 1964; Johnson, *Vantage Point,* 80.

46. Sargent Shriver, Memorandum for the President, White House Aides Files—Moyers, Box 39, LBJ Library.

47. *Congressional Record,* vol. 110, pt. 13, July 22, 1964, p. 16659, July 23, 1964, pp. 16722–23, 16727; Gillette, *Launching the War on Poverty,* 130.

48. *Congressional Record,* vol. 110, pt. 13, July 23, 1964, p. 16705; Crespino, *In Search of Another Country,* 104.

49. *Congressional Record,* vol. 110, pt. 13, July 23, 1964, pp. 16726, 16786–787.

50. Ibid., pp. 16727, 16741, 16768, 16790; Gillette, *Launching the War on Poverty,* 129. Gore explained why he voted against the governors' veto: "In programs in which the contractual relationship is between the Federal Government and the municipality or a county or regional organization, I see no justification for interposing the power of the Governor to veto. This is not wise. This is not the practice that has been followed. I see no necessity for starting it now."

51. Yarmolinsky, Interview III, 11–12, LBJOHC; Shriver, Interview II, 76–77, LBJOHC; Cannon, Interview, 55–56, LBJOHC.

52. *Congressional Record,* vol. 110, pt. 13, July 23, 1964, pp. 16706, 16757, 16764; John A. Baker, Interview II, 33, LBJOHC; Patricia Sullivan, *Days of Hope,* 124–29.

53. Joseph W. Sullivan, "Revolt in Congress"; *Congressional Record,* vol. 110, pt. 13, July 23, 1964, pp. 16726, 16786–87. In addition to Gore and Yarborough, the southerners who voted for the bill included Samuel Ervin (D-NC), J. William Fulbright (D-AR), Olin Johnston (D-SC), B. Everett Jordan (D-NC), Russell B. Long (D-LA), Smathers, Herman Talmadge (D-GA), and Herbert S. Walters (D-TN). Those voting against the bill included Harry F. Byrd (D-VA), James O. Eastland (D-MS), Allen J. Ellender (D-LA), Hill, Spessard Holland (D-FL), John L. McClellan (D-AR), Absalom Robertson (D-VA), Richard Russell (D-GA), John Sparkman (D-AL), John Stennis (D-MS), Strom Thurmond (D-SC), and John Tower (R-TX).

54. Johnson, *Vantage Point,* 80; Unger, *Best of Intentions,* 97; Bernstein, *Guns or*

Butter, 109. On July 28, the House Rules Committee voted out the bill. Eight committee members voted yes (all Democrats), and seven opposed (five Republicans and two southern Democrats, Howard Smith [D-VA] and William Colmer [D-MS]).

55. *Congressional Record,* vol. 110, pt. 14, August 5, 1964, p. 18198.

56. Ibid., p. 18208; Unger, *Best of Intentions,* 98.

57. *Congressional Record,* vol. 110, pt. 14, August 5, 6, 7, 1964, pp. 18221, 18263, 18575.

58. Ibid., August 6, 1964, p. 18264; "House Vote on Poverty Bill Planned Today," *Elberton (Ga.) Star,* August 7, 1964, Poverty Clippings File, Landrum Papers.

59. *Congressional Record,* vol. 110, pt. 14, August 6, 1964, p. 18325; *Congressional Quarterly Almanac,* 89th Cong. 1st sess., 1965, 21:406.

60. *Congressional Record,* vol. 110, pt. 14, August 7, 1964, p. 18582.

61. Shriver, Interview II, 85–91, LBJOHC. For other versions of Yarmolinsky's removal, see John A. Baker, Interview III, 15, LBJOHC; Yarmolinsky, Interview II, 38, Interview I, 17–18, LBJOHC; Cannon, Interview, 58–59, LBJOHC; Pollak, Interview, 17–21, LBJOHC; Donald M. Baker, Interview, Tape 1, pp. 7–10, LBJOHC. Most of these accounts give more or less the same details except Donald Baker, who remembered that Shriver had agreed to not recommend Yarmolinsky to the president as OEO's deputy director. See *Birmingham News,* August 14, 17, 21, 1964. Biographical information from L. Mendel Rivers, College of Charleston, www.cofc.edu/~speccoll/lmr.html. In 1952, Rivers supported Eisenhower's bid for president. In 1956 he was the only South Carolina congressman to declare himself a member of the White Citizens' Council.

62. Yarmolinsky, Interview I, 6, 17–18, LBJOHC; Cannon, Interview, 58–59, LBJOHC; Donald M. Baker, Interview, Tape 1, pp. 7–10, LBJOHC; OEO, Administrative History, vol. 1, pt. 1, Narrative History, pp. 49–50; Bernstein, *Guns or Butter,* 109–10; Unger, *Best of Intentions,* 99; Pollak, Interview, 17, LBJOHC.

63. Califano, *Triumph and Tragedy,* 77; Dallek, *Lone Star Rising,* 9; Schlei, Interview, 38, LBJOHC; Patterson, *Grand Expectations,* 589.

64. *Congressional Record,* vol. 110, pt. 14, August 5, 1964, pp. 18634, 19023; Biographical Directory of the U.S. Congress, http://bioguide.congress.gov/scripts/biodisplay; Crespino, *In Search of Another Country,* 104–5. As Governor George Wallace maintained his hold on politics in Alabama, the Democratic Party continued its dominance on the state and local levels.

65. Johnson, *Vantage Point,* 81; Donald M. Baker, Interview, Tape 1, p. 14, LBJOHC; Schlei, Interview, 36, 44, LBJOHC; Sundquist, *On Fighting Poverty,* 4.

66. David C. Carter, "Two Nations." Carter explores the variety of ways President Johnson responded to civil rights issues in the period after the Voting Rights Act passed.

67. Beschloss, *Taking Charge,* 511; Dittmer, *Local People,* 285–86, 290.

68. Beschloss, *Taking Charge,* 511, 534; Dittmer, *Local People,* 296–98, 302. The Mississippi regulars rejected the compromise, as did the Freedom Democrats.

69. Beschloss, *Taking Charge,* 534–35; www.phrases.org.uk/meanings. What the president meant by "dog in a manger" is that the Mississippi delegation was being

spiteful and mean spirited. Its origin comes from a dog that slept in a manger not because it wanted to eat the hay there but to keep other animals from doing so.

70. Beschloss, *Taking Charge,* 467, 510.

71. Session led by Bob Moses, National Endowment for the Humanities, Summer Teaching Institute, "Teaching the African American Freedom Struggle," July 31, 2003, W. E. B. Du Bois Institute, Harvard University, Cambridge, Mass.

72. Crespino, *In Search of Another Country,* 104.

73. Levitan, *Great Society's Poor Law,* 45–46; Kelly, Interview I, 12–14, LBJOHC; Shriver, Interview I, 41, LBJOHC.

Two. At the Crossroads

1. U.S. Commission on Civil Rights, "Civil Rights under Federal Programs: The Civil Rights Act of 1964: An Analysis of Title VI," January 1965, Box SG22384, AGF; OEO, Administrative History, vol. 1, 57, LBJ Library; OEO, Administrative History, vol. 2, Documentary Supplement, 34, 141, Records of the Office of Planning, Research, and Evaluation, Box 106B, RG 381; Kermit Gordon to President, CAP Office of the Director, Subject Files, 1967–70, Box 1, RG 381; Sargent Shriver to Roy Wilkins, March 30, 1965, Box A147, NAACP Papers. The Title VI regulations called for federal departments to develop affirmative measures, file compliance reports, conduct periodic field reviews, accept complaints, conduct investigations and make adjustments, and where necessary terminate funds.

2. OEO Reference Guide, ca. late 1966 for FY 1967, General Counsel Records Regarding the President's Task Force in the War Against Poverty, Box 6, RG 381; Levine, Interview, 22, LBJOHC.

3. Roy Wilkins, "Action Memo: NAACP in the War on Poverty," October 13, 1964, and attachment, "Suggested Implementation of the Anti-Poverty Law by NAACP Units," October 13, 1964, Box A331, NAACP Papers.

4. R[uby] Hurley, "Monthly Report," April 22, 1965, Ruby Hurley, "Report for September from the Southeast Region," September 17, 1965, Box C175, NAACP Papers.

5. Berry, Interview, 9–10, LBJOHC; Jack Gonzales, "State-by-State Southern Rundown," March 9, 1965, CAP Office Records of the Director, State Files 1965–68, Box 1, RG 381; Harold J. Weshow to Sargent Shriver, March 12, 1965, Records of the Office of the Director, Records Relating to the Administration of the Civil Rights Program in the Regions 1965–66, Box 24, RG 381. At this meeting, Shriver first met Theodore Berry, who later became the director of the CAP. Clarence Coleman of the Atlanta Urban League reported to OEO that the Birmingham workshop was well attended by "Negroes and whites from all over the state."

6. Brochure on SCLC's SCOPE Project, n.d., Box SG19970, AGAdmAF; Martin Luther King Jr. to OEO, November 24, 1965, Records of the Office of the Director, Records Relating to the Administration of the Civil Rights Program in the Regions 1965–66, Box 24, RG 381.

7. Frank Prial, "Alabama Area 8, Etowah County," October 20, 1965, Inspection Reports Evaluating Community Action Programs, Box 1, RG 381; "Report to the Board of Directors of the Southern Christian Leadership Conference," April 12–13, 1966, Correspondence 1964–66, Series II, Box 144, SCLC Papers.

8. John Lewis, James Forman, Cleveland Sellers, and Stokely Carmichael to OEO, ca. 1966, Box SG19970, AGAdmAF; Anthony Partridge, "Proposed Grant in Lowndes County," June 3, 1966, Robert W. Saunders to Samuel F. Yette, July 18, 1966, Records of the Office of the Director, Records Relating to the Administration of the Civil Rights Program in the Regions 1965–66, Box 24, RG 381.

9. Kelly, Interview II, 38–39, LBJOHC; Harding, Interview, 15–16, LBJOHC; "OEO, Atlanta, General Observations Made by Regional Staff Officials," May 29, 1967, Bertrand Harding Personal Papers, Box 44, LBJ Library. Jess Merrell, deputy regional director, reported that although the southeast region had no Job Corps facilities, young people from the area were recruited and placed in Job Corps programs elsewhere in the country.

10. Gillette, *Launching the War on Poverty,* 249–51; VISTA Press Conference, Sargent Shriver's Remarks, September 27, 1965, Program Records of the Assistant Director for Civil Rights, Box 1, RG 381; Unger, *Best of Intentions,* 184.

11. "The Quiet Revolution: Second Annual Report Office of Economic Opportunity," 1966, 124–25, White House Aides Files—Gaither, Box 210, LBJ Library; "The Tide of Progress: Third Annual Report of the Office of Economic Opportunity," FY 1967 (June 1966–May 1967), 113, White House Aides Files—Gaither, Box 239, LBJ Library. However, VISTA volunteers working in conjunction with other OEO-sponsored programs made an impact in some southern towns. See Greene, *Praying for Sheetrock;* OEO, Administrative History, vol. 2, Documentary Supplement, 40, Records of the Office of Planning, Research, and Evaluation, Box 106B, RG 381; Unger, *Best of Intentions,* 184; Theodore Berry, "Restrictions on Political Activities—Effect of New Legislation," December 1, 1966, Series XV, CR Box 109, Richard B. Russell Senatorial Papers, Richard B. Russell Library for Political Research and Studies, University of Georgia, Athens; Public Law 90-222, 714; May, Interview, October 6, 1981, 24–25, LBJOHC; Moynihan, *Maximum Feasible Misunderstanding,* 155. OEO originally planned for four thousand volunteers. By the end of the first year, VISTA had placed about eleven hundred.

12. May, Interview, 23–24, 27, LBJOHC; Gillette, *Launching the War on Poverty,* 189; "Poverty Bill Seeks to Coordinate Varied Programs," Congressional Quarterly Fact Sheet on the Anti-Poverty Program, week ending August 7, 1964, Box A331, NAACP Papers; Pollak, Interview, 12–13, LBJOHC; Haddad, "Mr. Shriver," 49; "Ladders of Opportunity," Congressional Presentation on OEO, June 5, 1967, White House Aides Files—Gaither, Box 210, LBJ Library.

13. OEO Reference Guide; OEO, Administrative History, vol. 2, Documentary Supplement, 297–98; Haddad, "Mr. Shriver," 44.

14. Richard W. Boone, "What Is Meaningful Participation?" *Community Development* (National Association for Community Development newsletter), n.d., Harding Papers, Box 59; Paul E. Peterson and J. David Greenstone, "Racial Change and Citizen

Participation: The Mobilization of Low-Income Communities through Community Action," in *Decade of Federal Antipoverty Programs,* ed. Haveman, 258; OEO, Administrative History, vol. 1, pt. 1, Narrative History, 186–87, LBJ Library.

15. Berry, Interview, 34, LBJOHC; "Ladders of Opportunity"; "Poverty: The War within the War," *Time,* May 13, 1966, John Macy Office Files, Box 537, LBJ Library; May, Interview, 21–22, LBJOHC; John G. Wofford, "The Politics of Local Responsibility: Administration of the Community Action Program—1964–1966," in *On Fighting Poverty,* ed. Sundquist, 82–83. May viewed CAAs as a force that would affect rather than bypass the local government structure.

16. Notes for Joint Management Survey 1966, n.d., White House Aides Files—Bohen, Box 2, LBJ Library.

17. Shriver, Interview IV, 37–38, LBJOHC; Gillette, *Launching the War on Poverty,* 204; May, Interview, 18, LBJOHC; Kelly, Interview I, 29–30, LBJOHC.

18. Gillette, *Launching the War on Poverty,* 76, 83–84, 86, 190. Norbert Schlei thought that Conway and his staff "went clear over the edge" in their interpretation of putting the target population in charge. Hal Horowitz believed that CAP personnel "really tried to do what the legislation said, and that came as a surprise to a lot of people." Shriver, Interview II, 9–10, LBJOHC; Conway, Interview, 8–10, 19–20, 24–25, LBJOHC.

19. Biographical information on Richard W. Boone, Office Files of John Macy, Box 51, LBJ Library; Knapp and Polk, *Scouting the War on Poverty,* 23.

20. Staff Information Memorandum 2, ca. 1964, General Counsel Records Regarding the President's Task Force in the War Against Poverty, Box 2, RG 381; Brendan [Sexton] to Ted [Berry], n.d., CAP Office Records of the Director, State Files 1965–68, Box 1, RG 381; Conway, Interview, 25–26, LBJOHC; Gillette, *Launching the War on Poverty,* 84–85, 205–6; Berry, Interview, 25, LBJOHC; "Quiet Revolution," 75.

21. Staff Information Memorandum 2, ca. 1964; Gillette, *Launching the War on Poverty,* 66, 67, 71, 84–85; Yette, Interview by Author, 18; Frederick O'R. Hayes, "Alabama," March 20, 1965, CAP Office Records of the Director, State Files 1965–68, Box 1, RG 381.

22. Donald M. Baker, Interview, Tape 1, 15, LBJOHC; Staff Information Memorandum 2, ca. 1964; Gillette, *Launching the War on Poverty,* 66, 84–85; Cahn and Cahn, Interview, 16, LBJOHC; Hayes, "Alabama"; W. Edward Harris to R. Sargent Shriver, March 13, 1965, Records Relating to the Administration of the Civil Rights Program in the Regions 1965–66, Box 24, RG 381; Open Meeting of Alabama State Advisory Committee to the U.S. Commission on Civil Rights, Alabama Power Company, Demopolis, Ala., July 10, 1965, 263–64, U.S. Commission on Civil Rights Library, Washington, D.C.

23. Staff Information Memorandum 2, ca. 1964; Gillette, *Launching the War on Poverty,* 66, 84–85; Cahn and Cahn, Interview, 16, LBJOHC.

24. OEO, Administrative History, vol. 2, Documentary Supplement, 8, 15; Shriver, Interview IV, 7–8, LBJOHC; Cahn and Cahn, Interview, 43–44, LBJOHC; Levitan, *Great Society's Poor Law,* 71–72; Haddad, "Mr. Shriver," 45.

25. OEO, Administrative History, vol. 1, pt. 1, Narrative History, 203–4; Jonathan Spivak, "Spotlight on Shriver," *Wall Street Journal,* June 4, 1965; Jack Gonzales, "South— Round II," March 4, 1965, CAP Office Records of the Director, State Files 1965–68,

Box 1, RG 381; Haddad, "Mr. Shriver," 45, 50; Shriver, Interview IV, 6–7, LBJOHC; OEO, Administrative History, vol. 2, Documentary Supplement, 15–16; Bill Haddad to John A. Morsell, March 19, 1965, Box A147, NAACP Papers.

26. Gonzales, "State-by-State Southern Rundown"; Shriver, Interview IV, 6, LBJOHC.

27. Shriver, Interview I, 98–99, LBJOHC; Yette, Interview by Author, 8–9, 15; Donald M. Baker, Interview, Tape 1, 16–17, Tape 2, 18, Tape 3, 28–29, 29–30, LBJOHC; OEO, Administrative History, vol. 2, Documentary Supplement, 17–18, 36; Levitan, Great Society's Poor Law, 72; Wofford, "Politics of Local Responsibility," 92. These meetings sometimes digressed into personal attacks on participants. Until OEO regionalized, the General Counsel's Office reviewed every grant with the exception of a few Head Start applications. Baker remembered that the Inspection Division and Civil Rights Division, especially under Haddad and Yette, always wanted at least one more black person to be put on CAA boards. The Inspection Division made sure that CAA bylaws required that meetings be held at times and places convenient to the poor, that there be a 50 percent quorum, that adequate notice of meetings be provided, that the full board of directors have authority to review decisions of the CAA committees, and that committees of the board be as broadly representative as the board itself. Levitan described the process of an inspection examination. Someone from the Inspection Division first would try to verify the validity of the complaint. If the accusation turned out to be justified, a field study would be initiated through a staff investigator.

28. OEO, Administrative History, vol. 1, pt. 1, Narrative History, 203–4; Gonzales, "State-by-State Southern Rundown"; David Swit, "General Civil Rights Policy," June 14, 1965, Inspection Reports 1964–67, Georgia Compilation, Box 21, RG 381; Sugarman, Interview, 8–9, LBJOHC. Gonzales found trouble in each southern state. Governor Wallace threatened to take over the poverty programs in Alabama. Georgia lacked black representation on its CAAs. Mississippi's governor distrusted independent groups creating CAAs, leading OEO to seek to use programs not subject to the governor's veto, such as Title III (b) programs for seasonal and migrant workers or programs sponsored by universities. OEO had high hopes for North Carolina: "This should be the state where the first significant minority representation in OEO programs takes place." South Carolina had a very weak state OEO director. Like North Carolina, however, Tennessee seemed to be a bright spot for OEO in the South; only one county needed watching. Virginia's governor had not even applied for state OEO funds to establish a state technical assistance agency, "the only Southern state to fail to do so."

29. Wofford, "Politics of Local Responsibility," 93; May, Interview, 42–44, LBJOHC; Sugarman, Interview, 7–9, LBJOHC; OEO, Administrative History, vol. 2, Documentary Supplement, 17–18.

30. Yette, Interview by Author, 16, 18.

31. Donald M. Baker, Interview, Tape 1, 17–19, LBJOHC; Kelly, Interview I, 2, 31, LBJOHC; Richard W. Boone to Lyndon Johnson, White House Central Files—Name File, Boone, R., Box 354, LBJ Library; Haddad, "Mr. Shriver," 44; Levitan, Great Society's Poor Law, 72. Haddad resigned in the fall of 1965, Levitan reported, as a "result

of opposition both outside and inside OEO." Boone left OEO by the summer of 1966 to head up the Citizens' Crusade against Poverty, a private-sector organization that worked to create support for the War on Poverty and to keep OEO focused on its commitment to empowering the poor. Yette left in 1967, in part as a result of the fallout from the Child Development Group of Mississippi Head Start Program. Hayes served as the CAP's deputy director under Berry until late 1966, when he became the budget director for New York City. Kelly worked as the assistant director for management, became the acting head of CAP, and then led the Job Corps.

32. Staff Information Memorandum 2, ca. 1964; Gillette, *Launching the War on Poverty,* 84–85; Brendan [Sexton] to Ted [Berry], CAP Office Records of the Director, State Files 1965–68, Box 1, RG 381; Moynihan, *Maximum Feasible Misunderstanding,* 97; Conway, Interview, 16, LBJOHC.

33. Gillette, *Launching the War on Poverty,* 84, 195; Kelly, Interview II, 3–4, LBJOHC; Donald M. Baker, Interview, Tape 1, 8–9, LBJOHC; Berry, Interview, 1, 3, 11, 23, 30–31, 36, LBJOHC; OEO, Administrative History, vol. 2, Documentary Supplement, 459. Conway served as OEO's deputy director until October 1965. He and Shriver worked well together, but not as well as Shriver and Yarmolinsky. OEO had no deputy director from October 1964 through February 1965.

34. Berry, Interview, 20–21, LBJOHC; Donald M. Baker, Interview, Tape 2, 27, LBJOHC. After 1967, Congress gave OEO a two-year authorization.

35. OEO, Administrative History, vol. 2, Documentary Supplement, 36; Donald M. Baker, Interview, Tape 3, 1, LBJOHC; Gillette, *Launching the War on Poverty,* 76, 87; Donald M. Baker, Interview, Tape 1, 13, 19–20, LBJOHC; Wofford, "Politics of Local Responsibility," 78; Gonzales, "State-by-State Southern Rundown." The Inspection Division tried to devise ways to fund programs around the local government. Division representatives asked the General Counsel's Office to see whether Title III (b) programs and direct grants to universities could be used in Mississippi instead of CAP grants, which were subject to the governor's veto.

36. Dittmer, *Local People,* 376; Robert L. Martin, "Dallas County–City of Selma Economic Opportunity Board," June 20, 1966, Inspection Reports Evaluating Community Action Programs, Box 1, RG 381; Robert L. Martin to Edgar May and Robert G. Emond, April 17, 1967, CAP Office Records of the Director, Subject Files 1965–69, Box 70, RG 381.

37. B. B. Mayberry to Sargent Shriver, February 18, 1966, Box SG22403, AGF.

38. Sargent Shriver to All OEO Staff, June 11, 1965, Program Records of the Assistant Director for Civil Rights, Box 7, RG 381; "Fact Sheet on Non-Presidential Appointive Policy and Supporting Positions," "Security Investigation Data for Nonsensitive Position for Edgar May," October 28, 1964, Office Files of John Macy, Box 370, LBJ Library; May, Interview, 1–2, LBJOHC; OEO, Administrative History, vol. 2, Documentary Supplement, 517.

39. OEO, Administrative History, vol. 2, Documentary Supplement, 19–20, 21–22; Sugarman, Interview, 17–18, LBJOHC; Levitan, *Great Society's Poor Law,* 72; May, Interview, 13–14, 45–46, LBJOHC; Shriver, Interview IV, 5, LBJOHC.

40. Samuel Yette, "Need for Involvement of the Office of Inspection in Pre-Grant Review," December 14, 1966, Routing Slip from Sargent Shriver to Edgar May, Samuel Yette, and Frank Sloan, December 18, 1966, Harding Papers, Box 60; May, Interview, 1, LBJOHC.

41. Sargent Shriver, "Policy Statement on OEO 'Newspapers,'" May 11, 1967, Harding Papers, Box 59; Levitan, *Great Society's Poor Law,* 86; May, Interview, 55–56, LBJOHC. May described some of the difficulties of working in CAP: "Community Action at most times at OEO was a place you wanted to go into wearing a helmet all the time, keeping hunched down. You didn't want to get hit by a stray shot. A lot of bickering, but maybe that occurs in every endeavor."

42. Sargent Shriver to George Wallace, November 10, 1964, Box SG22390, AGF; Gonzales, "South—Round II"; Gonzales, "State-by-State Southern Rundown"; Haddad, "Mr. Shriver," 48; "A Nation Aroused: First Annual Report of the Office of Economic Opportunity," 1965, 17, White House Aides Files—McPherson, Box 14, LBJ Library; OEO, Administrative History, vol. 1, pt. 1, Narrative History, 172–73.

43. Gillette, *Launching the War on Poverty,* 190–91; "Nation Aroused," 16; OEO Reference Guide; "How Do You Start the Anti-Poverty Battle at Home?" Government Document GSA DC 65-7709, General Counsel Records Regarding the President's Task Force in the War Against Poverty, Box 2, RG 381; Bill Haddad to Ted Berry, March 30, 1965, CAP Office Records of the Director, State Files 1965–68, Box 1, RG 381.

44. Shriver, Interview IV, 27–28, LBJOHC; Berry, Interview, 24, LBJOHC; Sugarman, Interview, 24, LBJOHC; Cahn and Cahn, Interview, 25, LBJOHC; Notes for Joint Management Survey 1966; Peter Eisinger, "Discussions," in *Decade of Federal Antipoverty Programs,* ed. Haveman, 280.

45. Sugarman, Interview, 23, LBJOHC; Gillette, *Launching the War on Poverty,* 18. A supporter of national-emphasis programs, Sugarman acknowledged one pitfall to using this approach to community action: "The tragedy of it of course, was by the time [communities] were ready to build, there wasn't any money. So many of them never went beyond that Head Start stage." Sugarman served as a deputy associate director of CAP, and he was instrumental in the creation of Head Start. In 1965 he became the associate director of Head Start.

46. Gillette, *Launching the War on Poverty,* 230; Shriver, Interview IV, 37–38, LBJOHC; Berry, Interview, 24, LBJOHC; [Sargent Shriver], "Involvement of the Poor in All OEO Programs," September 9, 1966, White House Aides Files—McPherson, Box 14, LBJ Library. Shriver emphasized the necessity of including the poor "in all our activities, including 'national emphasis programs' like Head Start, Upward Bound, Legal Services, Health Centers, Foster Grandparents, etc. . . . As these national emphasis programs grow in size and diversity, they must not lose their inherent purposes as *Community Action* programs."

47. "Nation Aroused," 31–32; "Project Head Start Fact Sheet," March 1968, Program Records of the Assistant Director for Civil Rights, Box 4, RG 381; Sugarman, Interview, 21, LBJOHC; OEO, Administrative History, vol. 1, pt. 1, Narrative History, 232, 236; Samuel F. Yette to Roy Wilkins, May 10, 1965, William Haddad to Roy Wilkins,

April 14, 1965, Mildred Bond to William Haddad, April 28, 1965, Box A147, NAACP Papers.

48. Patterson, *Grand Expectations,* 570; Bartley, *New South,* 369–70; Grady Poulard, "Current Head Start Picture," May 13, 1967, Program Records of the Assistant Director for Civil Rights, Box 7, RG 381; Shriver, Interview IV, 50–51, LBJOHC. By 1967, most of the 180 summer Head Start applications came from CAAs rather than local school boards. "Local school officials have not all been anxious to promote integration," Poulard reported to Washington.

49. Gillette, *Launching the War on Poverty,* 279; Sugarman, Interview, 26–39, LBJOHC; Dittmer, *Local People,* 370, see also chapter 16; Greenberg, *And the Devil Wore Slippery Shoes;* Payne, *I've Got the Light of Freedom;* Crespino, *In Search of Another Country;* David C. Carter, "Two Nations," chapter 2.

50. "Project Head Start Supplemental Nondiscrimination Conditions," Series VII, Box A370, Herman Talmadge Senatorial Papers, Richard B. Russell Library for Political Research and Studies, University of Georgia, Athens; Gillette, *Launching the War on Poverty,* 290; Open Meeting of Alabama State Advisory Committee to the U.S. Commission on Civil Rights, Alabama Power Company, Demopolis, Ala., July 10, 1965, 253–54.

51. OEO, Administrative History, vol. 2, Documentary Supplement, 16, 23; Don Petit to Bill Haddad, June 15, 1965, White House Aides Files—Moyers, Box 52, LBJ Library.

52. Donald M. Baker, Interview, Tape 2, 12–13, LBJOHC; OEO, Administrative History, vol. 2, Documentary Supplement, 33, 38–39; Pollak, Interview, 27, LBJOHC; Steven Lowenstein, "Employment Discrimination in OEO Funded Programs," June 20, 1966, Records Relating to the Administration of the Civil Rights Program in the Regions 1965–66, Box 34B, RG 381.

53. Donald M. Baker, Interview, Tape 1, 15–16, LBJOHC; Ashmore, "More than a Head Start."

54. Benjamin Hopkins and Willie Hopkins, "Thomas County [Ga.] Head Start," July 6, 1965, Records Relating to the Administration of the Civil Rights Program in the Regions 1965–66, Box 26, RG 381; Open Meeting of Alabama State Advisory Committee to the U.S. Commission on Civil Rights, Alabama Power Company, Demopolis, Ala., July 10, 1965, 253–54; Don[ald] Baker, "Letter to Head Start Grantees," June 17, 1965, Donald M. Baker, "Proposed Letter to All Head Start Grantees," n.d., White House Aides Files—Moyers, Box 56, LBJ Library; Sargent Shriver to Americus City Schools, November 24, 1966, Series VII, Box A370, Talmadge Senatorial Papers; Donald M. Baker, Interview, Tape 1, 27–28, LBJOHC; Theodore Berry to "Dear Head Start Grantee," August 23, 1965, Series XV, Box CR229, Russell Senatorial Papers.

55. Douglas Brown to Sargent Shriver, December 18, 1965, Box 378, LH.

56. Poulard, "Current Head Start Picture"; Al Krumlauf and Ted Jones, "Director's Trip to Atlanta," March 4, 1967, Inspection Reports 1964–67, Box 20, RG 381; Jay B. Boykin to Frank Sloan, June 14, 1967, Box 379, LH; Frank Prial, "Alabama Area 10, Talladega, Clay, and Randolph Counties," October 19, 1965, Inspection Reports Evaluating Community Action Programs, Box 1, RG 381; Herman Talmadge to Sargent Shriver,

January 11, 1966, Series VII, Box A370, Talmadge Senatorial Papers; Margaret Shannon, "Racial Duress Studied by U.S.; Sumter and Americus Accused of Violence to Keep School Bar," *Atlanta Journal*, February 16, 1966. In this case, investigators found that the black people who participated on the CAA executive board were all schoolteachers who were "not about to rock the boat." OEO officials also concluded that this CAA board was quite political: "Jay B. Boykin, the coordinator-elect, is a defeated candidate for probate judge; Robert Keeler, his first assistant[,] is the son of the probate judge. . . . [T]he big board is loaded with local political types." The inspector recommended that OEO push this CAA in the direction of community development "right quick." Shannon uncovered how freedom-of-choice plans really worked: "One Negro father reported being told by his employer-landlord that he would lose his job and home if his child went to the white school," she reported. For a personal history of freedom-of-choice integration, see Curry, *Silver Rights*.

57. Herman Talmadge to Sargent Shriver, January 11, 1966, William G. Phillips to Herman E. Talmadge, March 26, 1966, Series VII, Box A370, Talmadge Senatorial Papers; Sargent Shriver to E. Jean Wise, January 25, 1966, Records Relating to the Administration of the Civil Rights Program in the Regions 1965–66, Box 25, RG 381.

58. HHrgHR10440, pt. 1, p. 11; "Nation Aroused," 47; "Tide of Progress," 81–83. A 1966 amendment to the Economic Opportunity Act raised the maximum outstanding balance for individual loans to thirty-five hundred dollars.

59. U.S. Commission on Civil Rights, *Equal Opportunity in Farm Programs*, 9–10, 15–16; Elizabeth Hutton, Helen Randale, and Pattie Mae Haynes, Testimony, USCCR Mont, 290, 295–98, 300.

60. "Nation Aroused," 47; "Quiet Revolution," 59, 113; "Tide of Progress," 15.

61. May, Interview, 28, LBJOHC; Donald M. Baker, Interview, Tape 1, 13, LBJ Library; Bernstein, *Promises Kept*, 57; J. Francis Pohlhaus to Roy Wilkins, August 25, 1964, Group III, Box A144, NAACP Papers; Sundquist, Interview, 58–60, LBJOHC. Baker anticipated trouble whenever OEO confronted institutional change: "It was going to cause a great deal of difficulty trying to get institutions to change their way of doing business, and I knew that any agency that tried to do it was going to get into trouble." Pohlhaus told Wilkins that "of all government agencies, the Department of Agriculture probably has the most Southern-oriented bureaucracy. In addition it finances grant programs, such as land grant college and farm extension, which are operated completely by the states under a 'separate but unequal' administration."

62. U.S. Commission on Civil Rights, *Equal Opportunity in Farm Programs*, 7–8, 21, 24, 57, 102. The Extension Service received funds from the federal government based on a formula determined by a state's percentage of the national rural and farm population. The Extension Service let county officials determine the location of its office space, which led to separate and unequal county offices for white and black staff. The FHA operated through county committees appointed by the federal government. The Soil Conservation Service held elections to create its board of supervisors, and the ASCS held elections to operate its committees. For more examples of USDA discrimination, see Daniel, "African American Farmers and Civil Rights."

63. U.S. Commission on Civil Rights, *Equal Opportunity in Farm Programs,* 7, 58, 60–61, 79.

64. Ibid., 60–61, 72–73, 100.

65. J. Francis Pohlhaus to Roy Wilkins, August 25, 1964, National Sharecroppers Fund, "Statement on Discriminatory Practices Affecting Programs of the United States Department of Agriculture," August 29, 1963, Box A144, NAACP Papers.

66. U.S. Commission on Civil Rights, *Equal Opportunity in Farm Programs,* 28; John A. Baker, Interview III, 51–52, LBJOHC; Daniel, "African American Farmers and Civil Rights," 8.

67. Orville L. Freeman to Roy Wilkins, July 24, 1964, Agriculture Secretary's Memorandum 1560, "Implementation of Civil Rights Act of 1964," July 10, 1964, J. Francis Pohlhaus, "Meeting with Secretary of Agriculture," August 10, 1964, Box A144, NAACP Papers; U.S. Commission on Civil Rights, *Equal Opportunity in Farm Programs,* 28; Daniel, "African American Farmers and Civil Rights," 6–8.

68. ASACUSSCR; Joseph C. Doherty, "Greene County," March 17, 1965, Howard Bertsch to Lisle Carter, June 1, 1965, Records Relating to the Administration of the Civil Rights Program in the Regions 1965–66, Box 24, RG 381; John A. Baker, Interview III, 51–52, LBJOHC; May, Interview, 13, LBJOHC.

69. Council of Economic Advisers, Administrative History, vol. 1, pp. V-10, V-43, LBJ Library; John A. Baker, Interview III, 49–50, LBJOHC; Public Law 90-222, 691; OEO, Administrative History, vol. 2, Documentary Supplement, 61–62. The Council of Economic Advisers discussed the issue of rural-urban migration throughout 1966 and 1967 and concluded that migration was not really the issue and that moving to the city probably reduced the poverty of rural people. From 1967 to 1968, the council focused on general agricultural policies that contributed to rural poverty. The president did not accept the advice of his economists and went forward with plans to slow rural-urban migration.

70. OEO Reference Guide; "Tide of Progress," 51–52; Sundquist, Interview, 2, 57–58, LBJOHC; Biographical Information on Sundquist, John Macy, "Replacement for Arnold Jones on the TVA Board of Directors," April 4, 1966, Office Files of John Macy, Box 580, LBJ Library; Bernstein, *Promises Kept,* 26–27, 182; John A. Baker, Interview III, 56, LBJOHC.

Three. Wallace's Infrastructure

1. "War on Poverty, in Second Year, Is Slow but Effective in Alabama," *Southern Courier,* October 16–17, 1965; "Editorial Opinion: Funny Thing," *Southern Courier,* May 28, 1966; "What Is the Black Belt?" *Montgomery Advertiser,* October 9, 1938, Box SG6944, PISF; Fite, *Cotton Fields No More,* 183–85. Fite describes the changes in southern agriculture after the 1940s as a revolution that occurred in less than a single generation. He explains that "when technology and science teamed up with better informed farmers, the old agriculture which had resisted change for three-quarters of a century was doomed to oblivion." See also Aiken, *Cotton Plantation South;* Fay Bennett, "The

Condition of Farm Workers and Small Farmers in 1965," Report to the Board of Directors of the National Sharecroppers Fund, Doc. 1382, C-III-60, Reel 59, SNCC Papers; Richard Beard to David J. Lau, September 20, 1968, Box SG8847, ACAI. Bennett found that between 1939 and 1964, 2.4 million farmers disappeared, 95 percent of them small operators with less than twenty-five hundred dollars in annual gross sales, and about one-fourth of those farms were worked by sharecroppers. "Only about 1.5 million small farms are left now," Bennett reported. During the same period, the number of large farmers with gross sales of ten thousand dollars or more rose 2.5 times.

2. Rogers et al., *Alabama*, 522; "Special Report," n.d., Doc. 0273, A-VII-3, Reel 14, SNCC Papers; "Lowndes County, Alabama," September 5, 1965, SNCC Research, Doc. 0688, A-VIII-50, Reel 18, SNCC Papers; "Dallas County Statistics from U.S. Census Figures," n.d., Records Relating to the Civil Rights Program in the Regions 1965–66, Box 24, RG 381; Grafton and Permaloff, *Big Mules and Branchheads*, 47–49; "Political Handbook for Alabama," n.d., Doc. 0913, A-VIII-62, Reel 18, SNCC Papers; "Median Family Income and Median School Years Completed from 1960 Census in Various Black Belt Alabama Counties," Doc. 0394, A-VIII-39, Reel 18, SNCC Papers; Eagles, *Outside Agitator,* 99. The median family incomes for African Americans in these counties were Dallas, $1,393; Greene, $971; Hale, $1,203; Lowndes, $935; Sumter, $1,087; Wilcox, $1,081. The median school years completed for African Americans were Dallas, 5.8; Greene, 5.0; Hale, 5.3; Lowndes, 5.1; Sumter, 5.0; Wilcox, 5.5. In 1946, Alabama passed the Boswell Amendment, which changed the requirements for voter registration so that only those persons who could "understand and explain" any article of the U.S. Constitution could be registered. The amendment gave the local board of registrars the power to determine who could understand and explain.

3. For information on the culture of white supremacy and African Americans' response to it, see Hale, *Making Whiteness;* Litwack, *Trouble in Mind.*

4. Fairclough, *Race and Democracy,* 386, 393; Payne, *I've Got the Light of Freedom,* 361; Dittmer, *Local People,* 363; Cobb, *Most Southern Place on Earth,* 253–76; Germany, *New Orleans after the Promises.*

5. Stephen Pollak to Sargent Shriver, February 22, 1965, Inspection Reports Evaluating Community Action Programs, Box 1, RG 381. Dave Marlin was the Department of Justice official who sent Pollak this information. He explained why his comments were so foreboding: "Pardon the sermon—I've been bouncing around rural Negro homes for a week again and it gets you."

6. Gillette, *Launching the War on Poverty,* 190–91.

7. Rogers et al., *Alabama*, 568, 577; Grafton and Permaloff, *Big Mules and Branchheads,* 45–46, 52; Permaloff and Grafton, "Chop-Up Bill"; Richard Beard, Speech, August 15, 1968, Box SG8856, ACAI. When Governor "Big" Jim Folsom sought tax reform during the 1950s, one of his allies from North Alabama told the legislature that fairer taxes would result in better schools for blacks and thus reduce pressure for integration. According to Flynt, one legislator muffled his microphone and grumbled, "We don't want the black bastards to learn to read and write." Grafton and Permaloff explain that the Black Belt–Big Mule coalition began after the Populist Revolt of the 1890s.

"Black Belt leaders realized that the manipulation of black votes in their counties had to cease. . . . They concluded that the answer was to limit voting rights to those who possessed 'virtue and intelligence.'" Industrialists also hoped to curtail the strength of the growing numbers of industrial workers in the Birmingham region.

8. J. Webb Cocke to A. W. Todd, June 26, 1962, B. V. Hain to A. W. Todd, October 4, 1963, A. W. Todd to James G. Clark Jr., October 3, 1963, A. C. Allen to A. W. Todd, April 13, August 14, 1965, Box SG8845, ACAI; Ruth Hicks to A. W. Todd, December 31, 1962, Box SG8841, ACAI. Allen served on the Dallas County voter registrars board during the tumultuous Selma voting rights campaign. He resigned in April 1965 for health reasons.

9. "Detailed Report—Martha Witt Smith," Pat Houtz, "Controversial Voting Consultant Says Election Laws Are Praised," *Birmingham News,* July 16, 1972, Martha Witt Smith, Report to the Members of the State Sovereignty Commission, December 11, 1972, Martha Witt Smith, "Constitutional Provision on Voter Registration," in Monthly Activity Reports—Martha Witt Smith, 1970–72, Box SG13843, Alabama State Sovereignty Commission Papers, Alabama Department of Archives and History, Montgomery; Cecil J. Jackson Jr. to Albert J. Lingo, July 13, 1964, Box SG22481, AGF; Martha Witt Smith to Montgomery County Board of Registrars, June 30, 1964, Box SG8844, ACAI. Smith requested a permit to carry a gun to protect herself throughout her travels across the state. Jackson explained, "This lady is traveling for us in every county in the State of Alabama and on several occasions has been followed by persons unknown."

10. "History of Voter Registration: Background on Need for Purging Lists," July 24, 1964, 9–10, Box SG8844, ACAI; Testimony on SB 1564 before the Senate Judiciary Committee, Hon. Frank Mizell, Witness, April 2, 1965, Box SG22398, AGF.

11. Gail Falk, "New Federal Examiners Register Negro Voters in Hale, Dallas, Marengo, Lowndes Counties," *Southern Courier,* August 13, 1965; Eagles, *Outside Agitator,* 197; "New Law Spurs Negro Vote Rolls: Registration Advances 16 Per Cent in Six Southern States," *New York Times,* August 5, 1966, Doc. 1122, A-VIII-283, Reel 22, SNCC Papers; Robert E. Smith, "Negro Candidates Plan Races in Many Counties," *Southern Courier,* February 19–20, 1966.

12. SNCC Press Release, September 11, 1965, Doc. 0451, A-VII-3, Reel 14, SNCC Papers.

13. Martha Witt Smith, "Report to the Members of the State Sovereignty Commission"; Alabama State Sovereignty Commission, *Watcher's Handbook,* March 1968, Box SG13843, Alabama State Sovereignty Commission Papers; Eli H. Howell to Judges of Probate, January 21, 1966, Box SG22435, AGF; MacDonald Gallion to Martha Witt Smith, March 7, 1968, Box SG19974, AGAdmAF. A second special session of the Alabama Legislature passed Act 105 on September 30, 1965. It authorized "county governing bodies to require certain identification procedures for all persons who vote in any election held in the county." Alabama legislators were worried that newly registered black voters could use the certificates issued by federal examiners to vote in more than one precinct.

14. George C. Wallace to John Frier, August 17, 1965, George C. Wallace to Mrs. Elmo G. Holloman, October 19, 1965, Box SG22398, AGF.

15. George C. Wallace to Eli Howell, December 29, 1965, Box SG22416, AGF; Nicholas Katzenbach to Alabama Boards of Registrars, January 8, 1966, George C. Wallace to Earl C. Jackson, January 21, 1966, Eli Howell to Cecil Jackson, January 24, 1966, F. D. Reese to Eli Howell, January 25, 1966, Box 22435, AGF.

16. Terry Cowles, "How Judges Reached Decision on Poll Tax," *Southern Courier,* March 12–13, 1966; Annual Report to the Board of Directors of the Southern Christian Leadership Conference, April 12–13, 1966, Box 144, Series II, SCLC Papers; Rogers et al., *Alabama,* 565.

17. Annual Report to the Board of Directors; "Wilcox: 83% Illiterate: Portrait of County with Problems," *Southern Courier,* April 2–3, 1966; I. C. Kuykendall to Hugh Maddox, October 26, 1966, Hulda Coleman to Hugh Maddox, October 28, 1966, School Files D–W (Counties) 1963–67, Box SG20061, AGLAF. Both Kuykendall and Coleman sent Maddox figures on school enrollment that reveal the unequal school systems.

18. "The Civil Rights Act of 1964: Civil Rights under Federal Programs: An Analysis of Title VI," U.S. Commission on Civil Rights Special Publication 1, January 1965, Box SG22384, AGF; Francis Keppell to I. C. Kuykendall, September 20, 1965, School Files D–W (Counties) 1963–67, Box SG20061, AGLAF; "Alabama Council on Human Relations: Alabama Schools Avoid Integration," *Southern Courier,* October 9–10, 1965; ACHR, "A Special Report: The First Year of Desegregation under Title VI in Alabama," September 1965, Box SG21072, Alabama Legislative Commission to Preserve the Peace Papers, Alabama Department of Archives and History, Montgomery. The Muscle Shoals area, which had a large federal presence through the Tennessee Valley Authority, was the state's most progressive area in terms of school integration.

19. ACHR, "Special Report." The $185 represented the amount the state spent per year on each child in the public schools.

20. Edward M. Rudd, "Negro, White Lowndes Parents Wonder about School Integration," *Southern Courier,* August 13, 1965; "Alabama Integrates Its Schools, Switch Peaceful in Most Schools; Trouble in Greene County, Marion," *Southern Courier,* September 4–5, 1965; Mary Wissler, "Judge Finds New Guidelines for Greene School Desegregation," *Southern Courier,* September 24–25, 1966; Monroe County Board of Education School Desegregation Plan, June 15, 1965, Minutes of Hale County Board of Education, August 6, 1965, School Files D–W (Counties) 1963–67, Box SG20061, AGLAF.

21. Statement by Willie Joe White, White Hall, Alabama, July 1965, Doc. 0696, A-VIII-51, Reel 21, SNCC Papers; Statement by Gully Jordan, July 18, 1965, Doc. 0697, A-VIII-51, Reel 21, SNCC Papers; Terry Cowles, "No Proof Negroes Evicted for Registering," *Southern Courier,* June 18–19, 1966; Statement of Robert Harris, July 1965, A-VIII-51, Reel 21, SNCC Papers.

22. Complaint in Civil Action CA 65-580 in the U.S. District Court for the Northern District of Alabama, Western Division, September 8, 1965, Box SG19967, AGAdmAF.

The plaintiffs were represented by Oscar W. Adams Jr., Peter A. Hall, Demetrius C. Newton of Birmingham for Mattye Lee Hutton; Orzell Billingsley Jr. of Birmingham for Richard Lee Richardson, Edward Richardson, Helen Richardson, Phillip Anthony, and Laura D. Chambers; and Jack Greenberg, James M. Natrit III, and Charles Stephen Ralston of New York City for all plaintiffs.

23. Minutes of Hale County Board of Education, January 11, 1966, School Files D–W (Counties) 1963–67, Box SG20061, AGLAF; Michael S. Lottman, "School Reports Knock Alabama," *Southern Courier,* November 6–7, 1965; Department of Health, Education, and Welfare, "Guidelines for School Desegregation: A Summary Explanation of the Revised Statement of Policies for School Desegregation Plans under Title VI of the Civil Rights Act of 1964," March 1, 1966, Reel 24, Series VI, Folder 3, Nonpartisan Voters League Papers, microfilm, University of South Alabama Library, Mobile; Harold Howe II, "An Address on the 1966 Desegregation Guidelines," April 16, 1966, School Files O–T 1964–70, Box SG20058, AGLAF.

24. Minutes of Hale County Board of Education, January 11, 1966; Hulda Coleman to Hugh Maddox, October 28, 1966, Harold Howe II to Fred D. Ramsey, June 3, 1966, L. G. Walker, Note on Perry County Board of Education, September 1, 1966, Harold Howe II to R. H. Vickery, October 13, 1966, School Files D–W (Counties) 1963–67, Box SG20061, AGLAF; Guy S. Kelly to George Wallace, March 9, 1966, School Files A–C 1964–72, Box SG20051, AGLAF; "Everybody Wants to Talk about School Guidelines," *Southern Courier,* May 28–29, 1966; George Wallace to Eli Howell, July 6, 1966, Box SG22416, AGF; Jim Martin to George Wallace, May 31, 1966, Robert E. Jones to George Wallace, June 2, 1966, School Files O–T (Counties) 1964–70, Box SG20058, AGLAF; Carol S. Lottman, "Legislature Convenes; Wallace Goes on TV," *Southern Courier,* July 30–31, 1966; Michael S. Lottman, "Schools under Fire: Wallace Bill to Aid State's Non-Complying Boards," *Southern Courier,* August 20–21, 1966.

25. "A Political Snipe Hunt," *Birmingham News,* August 19, 1966, William O. Bryant, "Passage Expected for Defiance Bill," *Montgomery Advertiser,* August 28, 1966, Tom Mackin, "Wallace Signs Anti-Guidelines Bill as Special Session Comes to End: Legislators Are Selected as Commission Members," *Montgomery Advertiser,* September 3, 1966, "As Night Follows Day," *Montgomery Advertiser,* September 10, 1966, HEW 1964–67, Box SG20053, AGLAF.

26. Michael S. Lottman, "Everybody's Talking about Schools: 'Willing to Go Down Swinging,'" *Southern Courier,* September 3–4, 1966; Bryant, "Passage Expected for Defiance Bill"; Act No. 252, H.446, September 2, 1966, *Alabama Laws,* 373–77; Mackin, "Wallace Signs Anti-Guidelines Bill"; Mary Ellen Gale, "Four Judges Hear Big School Case," *Southern Courier,* December 3–4, 1966. "Alabama Tops in Segregation," *Southern Courier,* December 24–25, 1966. The bill passed by a vote of seventy to sixteen in the House. Supporters came from all regions of the state.

27. Rogers et al., *Alabama,* 454–55; U.S. Commission on Civil Rights, *Equal Opportunity in Farm Programs,* 21, 24; Lowndes County Rural Areas Development Committee, "Overall Economic Development Program: Lowndes County," March 1965, Doc. 0652, A-VIII-50, Reel 18, SNCC Papers.

28. Richard Beard, Speech to FHA Employees, June 13, [1967], Box SG8856, ACAI; A. W. Todd to Julian Brown, August 19, 1964, Box SG8838, ACAI; Daniel, "African American Farmers and Civil Rights," 11–12.

29. U.S. Commission on Civil Rights, *Equal Opportunity in Farm Programs*, 58, 60–61, 72–73, 79, 100; Gail Falk, "'What County Are You from Sir?': Farm Folks Full of Questions," *Southern Courier*, January 29–30, 1966; Daniel, "African American Farmers and Civil Rights," 11–12; Open Meeting of Alabama State Advisory Committee to the U.S. Commission on Civil Rights, Alabama Power Company, Demopolis, Ala., July 10, 1965, 140, 144, 147, 149–50, 124–25, 127–28, U.S. Commission on Civil Rights Library, Washington, D.C.

30. Alabama ASCS Annual Report, 1967, 1, 13, 20, 23–24, 27–28, 38–40, Box SG8857, ACAI; U.S. Commission on Civil Rights, *Equal Opportunity in Farm Programs*, 89; ASACUSCCR Selma, B2, C6–C8.

31. Alabama ASCS Annual Report, 1967, 1; ASCS Background Information Bl. 6, "Farmer Committee Administration of Agriculture Programs," March 1965, Box SG8857, ACAI; U.S. Commission on Civil Rights, *Equal Opportunity in Farm Programs*, 90.

32. U.S. Commission on Civil Rights, *Equal Opportunity in Farm Programs*, 92; Fred M. Acuff to J. L. Lawson, June 18, 1969, Box SG8846, ACAI; Alabama ASCS Annual Report, 1969, Box 8862, ACAI; ASACUSCCR Selma, A7–A8, C11–C12, E1–E6, C12–C13.

33. Richard Beard, Speech at State Conference of ASCS County Committeemen and Office Managers, October 7–9, 1969, Richard Beard, Speech to Members of the Senior Class in Agricultural Business and Economics, Auburn University, March 5, 1969, Box SG8838, ACAI.

34. Alabama Department of Agriculture and Industries, Annual Report, October 1, 1966 through September 30, 1967, Alabama Department of Agriculture and Industries, Biennial Report, October 1, 1963–September 30, 1965, Annual Reports 1946–67, Box 29052, Alabama Department of Archives and History, Montgomery; Richard Beard to Phillip Alampi, December 1, 1967, Box SG8847, ACAI; Richard Beard, "Meeting, Technical Panel, December 11, 1969," December 18, 1969, Box 8860, ACAI; Ira L. Myers, "Meeting August 28, 1969, Tuscaloosa," August 1, 1969, Box 8858, ACAI; James L. Lawson to Members of State Rural Areas Development Committee and Technical Panel, April 16, 1965, October 22, 1964, Richard Beard to R. P. Swofford, August 2, 1968, James L. Lawson to Joe Traylor, September 23, 1964, James L. Lawson to Baker Atterbury, October 2, September 25, 1964, Box SG8847, ACAI; "State Team Looks into Anti-Poverty," *Birmingham News*, October 1, 1964, TSHC.

35. James L. Lawson to John Sparkman, August 17, 1967, James L. Lawson to Lister Hill, May 8, 1967, Box SG8847, ACAI.

36. James L. Lawson to John Sparkman, June 10, 1966, ACAI; James L. Lawson, "Orville Freeman Statement on Hunger and Malnutrition and the USDA's food programs," ca. May 1968, Box 8857, ACAI.

37. James L. Lawson to Richard Daley, September 9, 1968, ACAI; James L. Lawson to Wendell S. Kennedy, December 3, 1968, Box 8846, ACAI.

38. Sargent Shriver to George Wallace, November 10, 1964, Box SG22390, AGF.

39. Memorandum from Claude R. Kirk, n.d., Claude R. Kirk Résumé, n.d., Box SG22390, AGF; Frederick O'R. Hayes, "Alabama," March 20, 1965, CAP Office Records of the Director, State Files 1965–68, Box 1, RG 381; "War on Poverty Drawing Fire: Four Probes On," *Washington Evening Star,* March 31, 1965, Box 378, LH; Ted Bryant, "U.S. Funds on Poverty Withheld from State?" *Birmingham News,* March 22, 1965, TSHC; James Free, "Anti-Poverty Money for State Held Up," *Birmingham News,* March 13, 1965, TSHC; "Editorial: Our Own 'Poverty Program,'" *Birmingham News,* November 30, 1964, Box 37.57, ABP.

40. George C. Wallace to Jack T. Conway, November 4, 1964, Box SG22390, AGF; James Bennett, "Wallace to Discuss Anti-Poverty Program," *Birmingham Post Herald,* September 30, 1964, Box 37.56, ABP; "State Team Looks into Anti-Poverty"; Jim Solomon, Memorandum to Poverty Bill File, October 1, 1964, Box SG22379, AGF; C. Herbert Oliver to George C. Wallace, December 12, 1964, Box SG22390, AGF; Cecil C. Jackson Jr., "Economic Opportunity Act Office," November 20, 1964, Box SG22403, AGF. The governor's advisory committee for economic opportunity consisted of Leonard Beard, director of the Planning and Industrial Development Board; Dr. Ira L. Myers, state health officer; Harold I. Gooch, Bureau of Apprenticeship and Training Division; Ed E. Paid, executive director of the Alabama League of Municipalities; J. F. Ingram, director of vocational education; Rex Roach, director of the Department of Industrial Relations; Ruben K. King, commissioner of pensions and security; Dr. Fred Robertson, director of extension services; James L. Lawson, secretary of the State Rural Area Development Committee; Joe Traylor, executive secretary of the Soil Conservation Committee; and Earl G. Morgan, executive secretary of the governor's office. The Inter-Citizens Committee of Birmingham urged Wallace to appoint a black person to his antipoverty advisory committee.

41. Hayes, "Alabama," March 20, 1965; Claude R. Kirk, memorandum, n.d., Claude R. Kirk, "Progress Report," February 26, 1965, Box SG22390, AGF.

42. Claude Kirk to George Wallace, December 21, 1964, George Wallace to Rex Roach, December 22, 1964, Claude Kirk, "Selton Boyd," February 17, 1965, Bill Jones, "Leroy Porter," February 25, 1965, George Wallace to Claude Kirk, February 18, 1965, Jesse M. Hamil and James E. Hamil to George Wallace, February 28, 1965, George Wallace, "J. O. Barclay of Scottsboro," February 25, 1965, George Wallace, "R. E. Abbes, Jr., Geraldine, Alabama," February 26, 1965, George Wallace, "Charles Rice, Graves Musgrove, Art Haynes," March 1, 1965, George Wallace, "Russell Arnold," March 8, 1965, George Wallace, "Frank Carpenter, New Hope, Alabama," March 15, 1965, Hugh Maddox to Cecil C. Jackson, March 18, 1965, George Wallace, "Betty S. Bryan, Cullman County," April 2, 1965, George Wallace to Charles Weston, April 10, 1965, Box SG22390, AGF; Cecil C. Jackson to Hugh Maddox, October 28, 1965, Box 22403, AGF; George C. Wallace to Cecil Jackson, February 3, 1965, George C. Wallace to Al Lingo, March 12, June 4, 1965, Box SG22304, AGF.

43. Claude R. Kirk, "Economic Opportunity Grants," n.d., Cecil C. Jackson Jr. to Hugh Maddox, October 28, 1965, Hugh Maddox to Jack Hayes, November 2, 1965, Box SG22403, AGF; Frederick O'R. Hayes, "Alabama," March 31, 1965, "Assessment of the

Anti-Poverty Situation in Alabama," April 6, 1965, CAP Office Records of the Director, State Files 1965–68, Box 1, RG 381; Marvin Watson, "Memo from Buford Ellington Poverty Program in Alabama," June 7, 1965, White House Aides Files—Moyers, Box 56, LBJ Library.

44. John F. Collins to Mayors and Managers, March 16, 1964, Joseph N. Langan to John Sparkman, August 21, 1964, Joseph N. Langan to Robert F. Adams Sr., August 20, 1964, Joseph N. Langan, Form Letter, August 29, 1964, Joseph N. Langan to Sargent Shriver, September 4, 1964, Box RG7, S.3, B.10, Joseph Langan Papers, Mobile Municipal Archives, Mobile, Ala.; Jack Conway to "Dear Sir," August 21, 1964, Box RG7, S.3, B.13, Langan Papers; Langan, Interview by Author.

45. David R. Underhill, "Joseph Langan Says and Does Whatever He Believes Is Right," *Southern Courier,* October 3–4, 1965; Dow, "Joseph N. Langan," 4, 10, 13–15, 19–26, 29–32.

46. Mary Grice to Fred Hayes, March 17, 1965, Inspection Reports Evaluating Community Action Programs, Box 1, RG 381.

47. Dow, "Joseph N. Langan," 19, 37–38; Alsobrook, "Alabama's Port City"; Martha McKay, Memorandum, April 15, 1965, Martha McKay, "Preliminary Report on Mobile, Alabama," ca. April 1965, CAP Office Records of the Director, State Files 1965–68, Box 1, RG 381.

48. Resolution 03-018, January 12, 1965, Resolution 03-058, January 26, 1965, RG 7, S.3, B.10, Langan Papers; Bill Haddad to Ted Berry, March 30, 1965, Martha McKay, "Members of Mayor Trimmier's Committee—Mobile, Al.," April 19, 1965, CAP Office Records of the Director, State Files 1965–68, Box 1, RG 381; Charles S. Trimmier, "Review of the Mobile Area Economic Opportunity Commission and Committee," ca. July 1965, Reel 15, Series IV, Folder 177A, Nonpartisan Voters League Papers.

49. Claude Kirk to George Wallace, December 21, 1964, George Wallace to Rex Roach, December 22, 1964, Claude Kirk, "Selton Boyd," February 17, 1965, Box SG22390, AGF; Hayes, "Alabama," March 31, 1965; George Wallace to Sargent Shriver, April 9, 1965, Box SG22390, AGF.

50. Thomas M. Nunan to Susie West, November 24, 1964, "Archbishop Hosts Poverty Meeting," October 22, 1964, Box SG22390, AGF; Nunan, Interview by Author.

51. Thomas M. Nunan to Susie West, November 24, 1964, Box SG22390, AGF; "Archbishop Hosts Poverty Meeting"; Flannery, *Basic Sixteen Documents,* 70, 184, 191–92, 194, 211, 236, 244–45. The Second Vatican Council addressed issues of racial discrimination and economic deprivation. See especially Pope Paul VI, "Pastoral Constitution on the Church in the Modern World," December 7, 1965, http://www.christusrex.org/www1/CDHN/v4.html. See also Southern, *John LaFarge;* "Editorial: Civil Rights Legislation," *Catholic Week,* April 3, 1964; "Editorial: A Noble War," *Catholic Week,* April 10, 1964; "Catholic Agencies Support 'All-Out' War on Poverty," *Catholic Week,* April 24, 1964; "Discrimination and Christian Conscience," November 14, 1958, in *Pastoral Letters,* ed. Nolan, 2:201–6; "Statement on National Race Crisis," April 25, 1968, in *Pastoral Letters,* ed. Nolan, 3:156–60.

52. Thomas J. Toolen to Joseph Langan, October 27, 1964, David Sullivan to Joseph Langan, November 7, 1964, RG7, S.3, B.10, Langan Papers; Nunan, Interview by

Author. Toolen's reticence may have had its roots in the environment he found when he arrived in Alabama as bishop. In 1921, a Catholic priest had been shot on the porch of his rectory in Birmingham by a man who supported the Ku Klux Klan and the True Americans. The murderer was not convicted. Thereafter, Toolen learned to function within the state's segregated culture. As archbishop, he oversaw the construction of many facilities for African Americans that otherwise would not have been erected. Nevertheless, he did not support equality between the races and did not change his position as the civil rights movement roared through Alabama in the 1960s. See Pruitt, "Killing of Father Coyle," 24–25; Feldman, *Politics, Society, and the Klan.* Feldman provides a thorough discussion of anti-Catholic violence in 1920s Alabama.

53. David L. Lollis to William C. Hamilton, July 15, 1964, Box 37.56, ABP; C. H. Erskine Smith Obituary, *Birmingham Post Herald,* July 28, 1973, TSHC; Albert Boutwell, Speech, December 22, 1964, Erskine Smith to Claude Kirk, December 22, 1964, Box 37.57, ABP; "C. H. E. Smith, Civil Rights Advisory Chairman, Dies," July 26, 1973, Unidentified Newspaper Clipping, TSHC; Erskine Smith to Albert Boutwell, March 9, 1965, Box 8.12, ABP. Smith also paid for the filing fees to incorporate BACDEO.

54. Smith, Interview by Author, 1–4, 13–14.

55. Ibid., 3–4, 10; Erskine Smith to John Sparkman, November 2, 1964, Box 15.21, ABP; Eskew, *But for Birmingham,* 166, 182, 256, 277.

56. "Statement of Erskine Smith," January 5, 1965, Box 38.14, ABP; Gillis Morgan, "City's Anti-Poverty Action Could Reach into 42 Areas," *Birmingham News,* Ted Bryant, "Mayor Appoints New Development Group Head War on Poverty Here," *Birmingham Post Herald,* TSHC; Daniel S. Oliver to Bill Hamilton, January 6, 1965, Albert Boutwell to J. Paul Keefe, January 6, 1965, Erskine Smith to Milton Cummings, February 2, 1965, Box 38.14, ABP; Minutes of BACDEO Meeting, January 15, 29, February 12, 1965, Box 38.10, ABP; Erskine Smith to Robert Moore, January 29, 1965, Erskine Smith to Claude Kirk, February 3, 1965, Box 38.14, ABP.

57. Minutes of BACDEO Meeting, February 12, 1965; Erskine Smith to Robert Moore, January 29, 1965, Erskine Smith to Claude Kirk, February 3, 1965, Box 38.14, ABP; Erskine Smith to Jesse Lanier, February 16, 1965, Box 38.15, ABP; "Antipoverty Aid Says Wallace Sought Ouster: Head of Birmingham Program to Resign Today—Tells of Threat to Veto Projects," *New York Times,* March 12, 1965; Jesse Lanier to Erskine Smith, February 17, 1965, Box 8.12, ABP; Jesse Lanier to Bill Jones, February 19, 1965, Box SG22390, AGF.

58. Minutes of BACDEO Meeting, January 22, 1965; Erskine Smith to W. C. Hamilton, February 9, 1965, Box 38.13, ABP; Erskine Smith and Frieda Coggin to George Wallace, February 16, 1965, Claude Kirk to Sargent Shriver, Frieda Coggin, WBRC-TV, WAPI-TV, and Erskine Smith, Box SG22390, AGF.

59. Claude Kirk to Sargent Shriver, Frieda Coggin, WBRC-TV, WAPI-TV, and Erskine Smith, February 25, 1965, Box SG22390, AGF; Claude Kirk to Jack Conway, February 25, 1965, Jack Gonzales, "South—State Control of Community Projects," ca. March 1965, Jack Gonzales, "State-by-State Southern Rundown," March 9, 1965, "Calhoun County, Alabama, County Seat: Anniston," ca. 1965, CAP Office Records of the

Director, State Files 1965–68, Box 1, RG 381; Ted Bryant, "Smith Key to Poverty Funds," *Birmingham News,* ca. March 1965, TSHC.

60. Gillis Morgan, "Poverty Experts Explain Program to 400 Alabamians," *Birmingham News,* February 28, 1965, TSHC; "Agenda: Alabama State Economic Opportunity Conference," February 26–27, 1965, Box 38.15, ABP.

61. Harold J. Wershow to Sargent Shriver, March 12, 1965, Records Relating to the Administration of the Civil Rights Program in the Regions 1965–66, Box 24, RG 381.

62. Charles N. Whitten to George Wallace, February 26, 1965, Box SG22390, AGF; Jesse Lanier to Albert Boutwell, March 1, 1965, "Anti-Poverty Meeting Set by County: Establishment of Committee to be Discussed," *Birmingham Post Herald,* March 2, 1965, "Minutes of the Meeting of the Jefferson County Association of Municipal Mayors," March 3, 1965, Box 38.15, ABP; "Wendell Named Successor: Smith to Resign as Chief of Anti-Poverty Group," *Birmingham News,* March 10, 1965, TSHC; Economic Opportunity, "Progress Report as of March 12, 1965," March 12, 1965, Box SG22390, AGF. Kirk clearly did not understand the various OEO programs. He explained that CAP administrators needed to be "familiar with the various assistance acts passed by the Congress and how to relate such acts to the needs of the community." He said that there were "approximately 115 such acts which included 600 to 700 titles providing for the distribution of approximately $33 billion."

63. Lou Isaacson, "War behind Poverty War: Mayor Asks Smith to Quit," *Birmingham News,* March 7, 1965, TSHC; Erskine Smith to Albert Boutwell, March 9, 1965, Erskine Smith to Members of the BACDEO, March 9, 1965, Box 8.12, ABP; "Smith to Resign as Poverty Chief," *Birmingham Post Herald,* March 10, 1965, TSHC; Albert Boutwell and M. E. Wiggins to Erskine Smith, March 10, 1965, Box 8.12, ABP.

64. Smith, Interview by Author, 10; "Background on Albert Boutwell," Finding Aid, ABP; "Editorial: Erskine Smith 'Case,'" *Birmingham News,* March 9, 1965, TSHC; "Antipoverty Aide Says Wallace Sought Ouster: Head of Birmingham Program to Resign Today—Tells of Threat to Veto Projects," *New York Times,* March 12, 1965.

65. "Antipoverty Aide Says Wallace Sought Ouster."

66. James Prewitt to Albert Boutwell, March 8, 1965, Robert H. Aland to Albert Boutwell, March 18, 1965, Virginia Sparks Volker to Albert Boutwell, March 16, 1965, Box 38.6, ABP; Orzell Billingsley to Albert Boutwell, March 6, 1965, Box 8.12, ABP; Randolph C. Sailor to Sargent Shriver, March 8, 1965, Winthrop R. Wright to Sargent Shriver, March 13, 1965, W. Edward Harris to Sargent Shriver, Marcia Herman-Giddens to W. S. [*sic*] Shriver, Records Relating to the Administration of the Civil Rights Program in the Regions 1965–66, Box 24, RG 381.

67. "Assessment of the Anti-Poverty Situation in Alabama"; Ted Bryant, "Smith Key to Poverty Funds"; Hayes, "Alabama," March 20, 1965; Theodore M. Berry, "Alabama," March 24, 1965, CAP Office Records of the Director, State Files 1965–68, Box 1, RG 381; Resolution of the BACDEO, March 12, 1965, Box 38.6, ABP; Theodore M. Berry, "Birmingham Veto," n.d., CAP Office Records of the Director, State Files 1965–68, Box 1, RG 381.

68. Marjorie Hunter, "Wallace Defied on Poverty Funds: Federal Grants Are Made to Alabama Biracial Groups," *New York Times,* April 14, 1965; Roy Reed, "Wallace Vetoes

a Poverty Grant: Action on Birmingham Aid Is Attributed to Politics," *New York Times,* May 13, 1965; Minutes of BACDEO Meeting, April 23, 1965.

69. Bill Haddad, "Alabama Funding," March 14, 1965, CAP Office Records of the Director, State Files 1965–68, Box 1, RG 381; Hayes, "Alabama," March 20, 1965; Berry, "Alabama"; Marjorie Hunter, "Poverty Teams to Tour Country: 12 Congressmen Will Study Effect of Federal Programs," *New York Times,* March 13, 1965; Free, "Anti-Poverty Money for State Held Up"; Ted Bryant, "U.S. Funds on Poverty Withheld from State?"

70. Kate Harris, "Office Set Up to Help Poverty Applicants," *Birmingham News,* May 30, 1965, TSHC; Hayes, "Alabama," March 20, 1965; Economic Opportunity, "Summary of Counties in the State in Regard to Forming CAP under the Economic Opportunity Act," ca. March 1965, Box SG22390, AGF; Alex S. Pow to Brendon Sexton, May 24, 1965, [Earl] Redwine, "Alabama Technical Assistance Corporation," April 27, 1965, Brendon Sexton, "Alabama Technical Assistance Corporation," June 9, 1965, CAP Office Records of the Director, State Files 1965–68, Box 1, RG 381; Ev[erett] Crawford, "Technical Assistance in Alabama," June 23, 1966, Frank K. Sloan, "State T/A Refunding for Alabama," February 10, 1967, CAP Office Records of the Director, State Files 1965–68, Box 14, RG 381.

71. George Wallace to Sargent Shriver, December 30, 1966, Box SG22403, AGF; "General Swofford Named State OEO Director," *Birmingham News,* December 31, 1965, TSHC; Crawford, "Technical Assistance in Alabama"; Ralph P. Swofford Jr. to Frank Sloan, April 21, 1966, Box SG22403, AGF; Everett Crawford, "Alabama STA Funds," July 14, 1966, Everett Crawford, "Alabama Technical Assistance," February 21, 1967, CAP Office Records of the Director, State Files 1965–68, Box 14, RG 381, Theodore M. Berry, "Alabama TA," February 27, 1967; Sloan, "State T/A Refunding for Alabama"; Albert P. Brewer to Roy E. Batchelor, June 23, 1970, Box SG21318, AGF. OEO officials worried about what to do with the Alabama State Technical Assistance Office. Crawford reasoned that if OEO canceled the program, there was no college or university in the state that "could mount the TA effort which is not under some degree of State control." Issuing the program to a private contractor was subject to the governor's veto. Crawford recommended not refunding and providing the technical assistance through OEO in Washington.

72. "Assessment of the Anti-Poverty Situation in Alabama"; Jack C. Gallalee to Lister Hill, October 4, 1965, Box 378, LH; "Archbishop's Letter on Integration of Schools," *Catholic Week,* April 24, 1964; Albert S. Foley, "Some Historical Aspects of the Ministry of Service in the Black Community of Mobile," ca. 1971, Folder Mobile Black Ministry, Albert S. Foley, S.J., Papers, Spring Hill College Library and Archives, Mobile, Ala.; Thomas D. Weise to "Dear Friends," November 19, 1964, Meeting of Archbishop Toolen's Anti-Poverty Committee, July 25, 1967, Box RG7, S.3, B.10, Langan Papers; "Mobile Area Community Action Committee, Inc.—Planning Committee," n.d., Reel 13, Series IV, Folder 40, Nonpartisan Voters League Papers; Markham Ball, "Problems in Insuring Equal Opportunity in EOA Programs in Alabama," July 12, 1965, Records Relating to the Administration of the Civil Rights Program in the Regions 1965–66, Box 24, RG 381; Jack Gonzales, "South Round II," March 4, 1965, CAP Office Records of the Director, State Files 1965–68, Box 1, RG 381. The public schools in Mobile also

received a Head Start grant, but OEO delayed its funding because the school district refused to integrate its facilities.

73. "Assessment of the Anti-Poverty Situation in Alabama."

74. Jack Gonzales, "Requested Report on Huntsville, Alabama—HS 0155," August 13, 1965, Inspection Reports 1964–67, Head Start, Box 88, RG 381.

75. Bill Haddad to Sargent Shriver, August 17, 1965, Inspection Reports 1964–67, Head Start, Box 88, RG 381; Jack Gonzales, "CAP 3076 Application (Troy, Al) CAP [Area 23]," October 20, 1965, Frank Prial, "Area 11, Alabama—Shelby, Bibb, Chilton, Perry, and Hale Counties," October 11, 1965, Inspection Reports Evaluating CAP, Box 1, RG 381; Francis X. Walter Diary, October 4, 1965, 6–9, Francis X. Walter Personal Papers, Sewanee, Tenn.

76. "Editorial: Mayor Lanier, Anti-Poverty," *Birmingham News,* May 3, 1965, TSHC; George Wallace to Sargent Shriver, May 7, 1965, Box 22390, AGF.

77. Governor's Office Press Release, ca. May 1965, Box SG22390, AGF; Bob Martin, "Huntsville, Alabama (Preliminary Report)," April 5, 1965, Frank Prial, "Huntsville, Madison County, Alabama," November 1, 1965, Bill Seward and Al From, "Huntsville, Alabama, CAP," July 20, 1966, A. Frank Grimsley Jr., "Calhoun County–Anniston, Alabama Program," April 2, 1965, Inspection Reports Evaluating CAP, Box 1, RG 381; "Calhoun County, Alabama, County Seat."

78. Kaffer, Interview by Author; Weise, Interview by Author; Langan, Interview by Author; Nunan, Interview by Author.

79. George M. Cox, "Thousands of Area Catholics in Tribute to Christ the King," *Mobile Register,* October 31, 1966.

80. Reed, "Wallace Vetoes a Poverty Grant"; "After Wallace Vetoes U.S. Allocation to City, Poverty Group to Try Again for Funds," *Birmingham Post Herald,* May 13, 1965, "Conversation between [W. C.] Hamilton and Lee Lendt, CAP Operations," CAP Office Records of the Director, State Files 1965–68, Box 1, RG 381; Ted Bryant, "Drennen Blasts Action—Poverty Fund Veto by Wallace Attacked," *Birmingham Post Herald,* May 14, 1965, TSHC; Minutes of BACDEO Meeting, May 18, 1965; Minutes of Meeting of the Jefferson County Committee for Economic Opportunity, June 18, 1965, Box 38.21, ABP.

81. "Conversation between Erskine Smith and Lee Lendt, CAP Operations," May 13, 1965, CAP Office Records of the Director, State Files 1965–68, Box 1, RG 381; Erskine Smith to Albert Boutwell, May 28, 1965, Alan T. Drennen Jr., "Erskine Smith's Letter of May 28, 1965," June 1, 1965, Box 38.16, ABP; Minutes of Meeting of the Jefferson County Committee for Economic Opportunity, June 11, October 29, 1965, Box 38.22, ABP; "Poverty Plan Is Approved," *Birmingham Post Herald,* October 21, 1965, TSHC; Minutes of Meeting of the Jefferson County Committee for Economic Opportunity, October 26, 1965, Box 38.29, ABP; Sheldon Schaffer to George Wallace, November 2, 1965, Hugh Maddox, "Letter from Earl Morgan with Reference to Erskine Smith Appointment," November 17, 1965, Box 22403, AGF.

82. "Administrative Confidential re: Governor's Veto," ca. May 14, 1965, CAP Office Records of the Director, State Files 1965–68, Box 1, RG 381; "State Poverty Veto Periled: Amendment Takes Aim at Governors," *Birmingham Post Herald,* May 14, 1965, TSHC;

Marjorie Hunter, "House Group Votes Poverty-Veto Curb," *New York Times,* May 14, 1965; Marjorie Hunter, "Governors to Get Antipoverty Veto: House Panel Limits Power as It Votes to Pass Bill," *New York Times,* May 21, 1965; "Editorial: The Anti-Poverty Veto," *Birmingham News,* May 21, 1965, TSHC.

83. B. B. Mayberry to Sargent Shriver, February 18, 1966, Box SG22403, AGF.

84. John Robert Lewis, "Some Comments on the Civil Rights Movement," *New York Herald Tribune,* May 23, 1965, Doc. 0327, A-VII-3, Reel 14, SNCC Papers; Martin Luther King Jr. to "Dear Friend," March 1964, Box A212, NAACP Papers.

Four. In Selma's Wake

1. Bruce Gordon, "Field Report from Selma, Alabama," November 9, 1963, Doc. 0368, A-VIII-39, Reel 18, SNCC Papers; Walter Stafford, "SNCC Selma Workshop Report," December 13–16, 1963, Doc. 0382, A-IV-331, Reel 9, SNCC Papers; "Special Report," n.d., Doc. 0273, A-VII-3, Reel 14, SNCC Papers; Silas Norman and John Love, "Selma, Alabama," March 1965, Doc. 1093, A-VIII-70, Reel 18, SNCC Papers; "The Selma Story as of January 28, 1965 3:30 p.m. EST," Box 148, Series II, SCLC Papers; SNCC Press Release, March 7, 1965, Doc. 0282, A-VII-3, Reel 14, SNCC Papers. The Selma Campaign and subsequent march to Montgomery are covered in Carson, *In Struggle;* Garrow, *Protest at Selma* (figures of march participants and King's quotations from 115–17); Fairclough, *To Redeem the Soul of America;* Gaillard, *Cradle of Freedom.*

2. Norman and Love, "Selma, Alabama"; John Robert Lewis and Silas Norman Jr. to Martin Luther King Jr., March 7, 1965, A-I-31, Reel 1, SNCC Papers; Chafe, *Unfinished Journey,* 316–17; Paul Good, "Voting Rights Drive Endangered by Conflicting Negro Leadership," *Washington Post,* March 12, 1965, Box A212, NAACP Papers. Lewis and Norman explained to King that SNCC had agreed with SCLC to organizational autonomy while both groups worked in the Selma area. The two organizations would cooperate, however, in strategy discussions, decision making, legal affairs, and press relations. The SNCC leaders blamed key SCLC staff for the breakdown of this cooperative relationship.

3. "Alabama Staff Workshop," April 21–23, 1965, Doc. 1213, A-X-10, Reel 36, SNCC Papers. Bevel attended this workshop and explained that the Selma project "took a lot of energy out of SCLC staff" and that "King wanted a rest" (Garrow, *Protest at Selma,* 118–20).

4. "Random Notes taken at June 5th SCOPE County Leaders' Conference, Atlanta," June 8, 1965, A-XVII-156, Reel 44, SNCC Papers; "Alabama Staff Workshop"; Agenda Orientation Session, SCLC, Summer Community Organization Political Education, June 14–19, 1965, Doc. 0455, A-XVII-156, Reel 44, SNCC Papers; "Major State Civil Rights Projects Seek Voter Registration, Education," *Southern Courier,* July 16, 1965; SCOPE Brochure, Folder 129, Series IV, Reel 15, Nonpartisan Voters League Papers, microfilm, University of South Alabama Library, Mobile; "The Summer Community Organization and Political Education Project of the SCLC," *Southern Student*

Organizing Committee Newsletter, May 1965, Box SG19972, AGAdmAF; Mesher, Interview, 316, RBOHC.

5. "Random Notes"; Henry Clay Moorer, "Community Reports: Registration in Greenville, Eufaula," *Southern Courier,* August 20, 1965; Don Mose, "SCOPE Returns," *Southern Courier,* November 20–21, 1965; SCLC Executive Staff Meeting, August 26–28, 1965, A-I-31, Reel 1, SNCC Papers; Ed Strickland to Mrs. E. L. Wallace, June 23, 1965, Box SG21074, Alabama Legislative Commission to Preserve the Peace Papers, Alabama Department of Archives and History, Montgomery. The Alabama Legislative Commission to Preserve the Peace kept a watchful eye on SCOPE's activities. Ed Strickland, the commission's staff director, thought SCOPE was composed of a "number of individuals who have cooperated openly with Communist fronts."

6. Frank Prial, "Area 11, Alabama—Shelby, Bibb, Chilton, Perry, and Hale Counties," October 11, 1965, Inspection Reports Evaluating Community Action Programs, Box 1, RG 381; Roy Reed, "Alabama Negroes Jab at Status Quo: Press Angry White Minority for a Cut of the Power Pie," *New York Times,* August 2, 1965, A-VIII-43, Reel 18, SNCC Papers.

7. Clarence Shelton, "Community Reports: Greensboro," *Southern Courier,* July 16, 1965; "Alabama Staff Workshop"; SNCC Report from Hale County, July 16, 1965, Doc. 0038, A-VIII-28, Reel 18, SNCC Papers; Edward M. Rudd, "Gas Scatters Demonstrators in Greensboro," *Southern Courier,* July 30, 1965; SNCC Press Release, "Two Churches Fire-Bombed," July 21, 1965, Doc. 0420, A-VII-3, Reel 14, SNCC Papers; Hale County Report, July 23, 1965, Doc. 0039, A-VIII-28, Reel 18, SNCC Papers; State of Alabama Department of Public Safety Investigative and Identification Division, "Individuals Active in Civil Disturbances," vol. 3, ca. 1965, Box SG22414, AGF.

8. Rudd, "Gas Scatters Demonstrators in Greensboro"; Hale County Report, July 26, 1965, Doc. 0043, A-VIII-28, Reel 18, SNCC Papers; Reed, "Alabama Negroes Jab at Status Quo"; Motion for Preliminary Injunction in Civil Action 3807-65 in the U.S. District Court for the Southern District of Alabama, Northern Division, July 29, 1965, Box SG19967, AGAdmAF.

9. Reed, "Alabama Negroes Jab at Status Quo"; Motion for Preliminary Injunction; Order, Judgment, Decree in Civil Action 3807-65, August 13, 1965, Box SG19967, AGAdmAF; Gail Falk, "New Federal Examiners Register Negro Voters in Hale, Dallas, Marengo, Lowndes Counties," *Southern Courier,* August 13, 1965; O. B. Green, "Community Reports: Greensboro," *Southern Courier,* August 20, 1965; Fairclough, *To Redeem the Soul of America,* 264, 268.

10. SCLC Executive Staff Meeting, August 26–28, 1965; Turner, Interview by Author, 6–7; Fairclough, *To Redeem the Soul of America,* 232, 256; "Proposal for Alabama Staff Submitted by Rev. Harold A. Middlebrook," September 1965, Records of the Voter Education Project, 1964–66, Series II, Box 146, SCLC Papers; "Alabama Staff," September 24, 1965, Records of Direct Action Alabama 1965, Series II, Box 147, SCLC Papers.

11. "Annual Report to the Board of Directors of the SCLC," April 12–13, 1966, Correspondence 1964–66, Series II, Box 144, SCLC Papers; Bernard S. Lee, "Montgomery Report," November 8, 1965, Office Files, Series II, Box 165, SCLC Papers; Rogers

et al., *Alabama,* 565. Turner reported that "Negro registration in Alabama has nearly tripled from 85,000 at the beginning of the 1965 drive to approximately 250,000 today." Turner's report may have been slightly overstated. Flynt's research indicates that fewer than 250,000 were registered by 1966: "Alabama's black registration between 1960 and 1965 increased from 66,000 to 113,000; by 1969 it had more than doubled to 295,000. In 1965, 23.5 percent of Alabama's eligible blacks were registered; by 1970 the figure was 65.4 percent."

12. Lawrence C. Johnson, James Carter Lenys, and Albert Turner to Sargent Shriver, August 4, 1965, Records Relating to the Administration of the Civil Rights Program in the Regions 1965–66, Box 24, RG 381. Major W. R. Jones, "State of Alabama Department of Public Safety Investigative and Identification Division Report on February 18, 1965, Marion, Alabama," February 25, 1965, Box SG22394, AGF; Prial, "Area 11"; Garrow, *Protest at Selma,* 61, 65–66.

13. Lewis Black, "Alabama Report—Rural Advancement Project," ca. late 1966, Box 41.2.7.3.22, SRC; "Two Young Men with Big Plans: Greensboro," *Southern Courier,* February 19–20, 1966; Daphna Simpson, "In Greensboro Only $42.50 Started Their Credit Union," *Southern Courier,* May 7–8, 1966; Prial, "Area 11."

14. Lewis Black, Lawrence Johnson, Albert Turner, James Carter, Joe Hamilton, and A. T. Days to Earl Redwine, August 23, 1965, Frank Prial, Memorandum, October 7, 1965, Burton Mullins to John Sparkman, September 25, 1965, Inspection Reports Evaluating CAP, Box 1, RG 381; Prial, "Area 11"; Economic Opportunity, "Progress Report as of March 12, 1965," March 12, 1965, Economic Opportunity, "Summary of Counties in the State in Regard to Forming CAP . . . ," n.d., Box SG22390, AGF. Mullins complained to Sparkman that Matt Colley and Mary Grice called the meeting of the five counties so they would form Area 11. Before this May meeting, Shelby, Bibb, and Chilton had planned to submit a plan for these three counties alone. "We people in the five Counties certainly did not create Area 11," Mullins explained.

15. Prial, "Area 11." Mayor Peagues listed the leaders of the "militant Negroes" as Turner, Liona Langford, James Carter, Lucy Foster, and Rev. R. W. Johnson. Prial felt that the mayor was "unswerving in his determination not to deal with any of the militant Negroes."

16. Prial, "Area 11"; Edward M. Rudd, "Race Complicates Black Belt Anti-Poverty Plans," *Southern Courier,* October 16–17, 1965. Poole thought that the White Citizens' Council served as a force of moderation in Hale County. "If it hadn't been for the Council," he said, "there would have been a lot of killing around here." He believed that the councils "channel into rallies and meetings red-neck energies that might be expended on night-riding."

17. Lewis Black, Lawrence Johnson, Albert Turner, James Carter, Joe Hamilton, and A. T. Days to Earl Redwine, August 23, 1965, Frank Prial, Memorandum, October 7, 1965, Inspection Reports Evaluating CAP, Box 1, RG 381.

18. Harvey Burg to SNCC, February 11, 1965, Doc. 0001, A-VIII-26, Reel 18, SNCC Papers; Steven Antler to "Gentlemen," n.d., Doc. 0479, A-IV-213, Reel 7, SNCC Papers; Frye, *Black Parties and Political Power,* 23, 24, 27, 29, 32; Tersh Boasberg, "Alabama,"

August 19, 1965, Records Relating to the Administration of the Civil Rights Program in the Regions 1965–66, Box 24, RG 381; Mrs. G. H. Billingsley to Randolph T. Blackwell, October 20, 1965, Series II, Box 144, SCLC Papers; Program, Statewide Meeting of the ADCI, Mobile, Alabama, April 11–12, 1965, 1102.1.2. "A," *Birmingham World* Files, Emory O. Jackson Collection, Birmingham Civil Rights Institute, Birmingham, Ala.; Executive Committee of the Alabama Democratic Conference, Statement Regarding the Antipoverty Program in Alabama, August 29, 1965, Box Correspondence—Democratic Party Organization, Jackson Collection. Burg worked with Billingsley when the ADC challenged the seating of the Alabama delegation at the 1964 Democratic National Convention. He worked through the Law Students Civil Rights Research Council, which formed out of a group of law students who had participated in Freedom Summer in Mississippi. It had chapters at Columbia, Georgetown, Harvard, Yale, New York University, Howard, George Washington University, the University of Pennsylvania, Cornell, Rutgers, and Boston College.

19. Harvey Burg to Randolph T. Blackwell, August 30, 1965, Series II, Box 144, SCLC Papers; Frank Prial, Memorandum, October 7, 1965, Inspection Reports Evaluating Community Action Programs, Box 1, RG 381; "Sumpter [*sic*] Co.," ca. 1966, Doc. 1167, A-VII-72, Reel 18, SNCC Papers. Prial said that Burg "knows more about Negroes in Hale and Perry County than any white man I met in Alabama."

20. Prial, Memorandum, October 7, 1965, Inspection Reports Evaluating Community Action Programs, Box 1, RG 381.

21. "Voters Hard to Reach in County Like Perry," *Southern Courier,* April 30–May 1, 1966; Bob Valder to J. Edwin Stanfield, February 14, 1966, Box 41.1.1.1.30, SRC.

22. "SNCC Programs for 1965," February 23, 1965, Doc. 0403, A-II-4, Reel 3, SNCC Papers; Executive Committee Meeting in Holly Springs, Mississippi, April 12–14, 1965, A-II-4, Reel 3, SNCC Papers; Carson, *In Struggle,* 162.

23. SNCC Press Release, "SNCC Workers Move to 'Bama Counties," n.d., Doc. 0110, A-XV-15, Reel 37, SNCC Papers; "SNCC Presently Known to Project Director in Alabama, Including Assignments Given Last Saturday and Sunday," March 15, 1965, A-IV-351, Reel 9, SNCC Papers; SNCC Press Release, "SNCC Expands Alabama Vote Drive," March 5, 1965, Doc. 0283, A-VII-3, Reel 14, SNCC Papers; Norman and Love, "Selma, Alabama"; Executive Committee Meeting in Holly Springs, Mississippi, April 12–14, 1965; "Alabama Staff Workshop."

24. Stokely Carmichael, Speech to the Southern Student Organizing Committee Conference, Gammon, ca. 1965, A-I-70, Reel 3, SNCC Papers.

25. Garrow, *Protest at Selma,* 117; "Viola Liuzzo: Wife of Teamster Business Agent Murdered in Civil Rights Struggle," *International Teamster Magazine,* April 1965, Box SG19968, AGAdmAF; Lowndes County Rural Areas Development Committee, "Overall Economic Development Program: Lowndes Co.," March 1965, Doc. 0652, A-VIII-50, Reel 18, SNCC Papers.

26. "Alabama Staff Workshop"; Eagles, *Outside Agitator,* 127; "Lowndes Marks a Year Full of Historic Change," *Southern Courier,* April 2–3, 1966; Carson, *In Struggle,* 165–66.

27. "Alabama Staff Workshop"; "Lowndes Marks a Year"; Carson, *In Struggle,* 165–66; Transcript of Conversation between Stokely Carmichael, James Forman, and George Greene, "Riding in the Car from Atlanta to Tuskegee," February 19, 1966, Doc. 1168, A-XV-9, Reel 36, SNCC Papers.

28. Eagles, *Outside Agitator,* 122–23, 126–27; Robert L. Martin, "Lowndes County Christian Movement for Human Rights Lowndes County, Alabama—Migrant Grant," July 23, 1966, Inspection Reports Evaluating Community Action Programs, Box 2, RG 381. Complete coverage of the civil rights movement in Birmingham appears in Eskew, *But for Birmingham.*

29. Martin, "Lowndes County Christian Movement"; Eagles, *Outside Agitator,* 120, 124; Jack Nelson, "'Convicted Criminal' Just a Scared Youth," *Washington Post,* July 28, 1966, CAP Office Records of the Director, State Files 1965–68, Box 9, RG 381.

30. Eagles, *Outside Agitator,* 123–24; Martin, "Lowndes County Christian Movement."

31. Eagles, *Outside Agitator,* 125–26.

32. Ibid., 126; Martin, "Lowndes County Christian Movement." Cosby was born in Lowndes County, served in the military, and worked as a part-time tenant farmer. His wife owned a grocery business. Jackson was a Lowndes-born farmer who served as chairman of the county co-op and had an income of less than two thousand dollars a year.

33. John Hulett, Frank Miles Jr., and Lillian S. McGill to R. Sargent Shriver, August 8, 1965, Records Relating to the Administration of the Civil Rights Program in the Regions 1965–66, Box 24, RG 381; Chair, LCCMHR, "Poverty Program Report," ca. July 1966, Doc. 1182, A-XV-9, Reel 36, SNCC Papers.

34. "Explanation of Initial Efforts of Forming Poverty Program in Lowndes County," ca. August 1965, Doc. 0827, A-VIII-55, Reel 18, SNCC Papers; Chair, LCCMHR, "Poverty Program Report"; M. E. Marlette to John Sparkman, July 18, 1966, Box SG19970, AGAdmAF.

35. LCCMHR to Theodore Berry and Sargent Shriver, August 22, 1965, CAP Office Records of the Director, State Files 1965–68, Box 1, RG 381; Eagles, *Outside Agitator,* 179.

36. Orzell Billingsley Jr. to Earl Redwine, August 24, 1965, John Hulett to CAP, OEO, August 22, 1965, CAP Office Records of the Director, State Files 1965–68, Box 1, RG 381; Chair, LCCMHR, "Poverty Program Report."

37. Edward M. Rudd, "Negro Farmers Must Use the Vote Well to Win in This Fall's ASCS Elections," *Southern Courier,* September 25–26, 1965; National Sharecroppers Fund, *The South's Revolution: Challenge to the Nation,* ca. 1962, Doc. 1395, C-III-60, Reel 59, SNCC Papers; Fay Bennett, "The Condition of Farm Workers in 1962," Doc. 0346, A-IV-270, Reel 8, SNCC Papers; SNCC Press Release, "Baldwin and Rustin to Address SNCC Conference," November 22, 1963, Doc. 0055, A-VII-3, Reel 14, SNCC Papers; Dittmer, *Local People,* 333–35; SNCC, "Some Thoughts on the ASCS Elections COFO Worker after 1964 Elections," Doc. 0449, A-VIII-145, Reel 20, SNCC Papers; "ASCS Meeting Held in Mobile," *Southern Courier,* August 20, 1965.

38. Eagles, *Outside Agitator,* 135–37; Fay Bennett to "Friend," August 15, 1963, Doc. 0329, A-IV-270, Reel 8, SNCC Papers; Fay Bennett to James Foreman, October 7, 1963, Doc. 0334, A-IV-270, Reel 8, SNCC Papers; Brochure from SNCC's Fourth Annual Conference on Food and Jobs, November 29–December 1, 1963, Doc. 0049, A-VII-3, Reel 14, SNCC Papers.

39. Elmo Holder to B. L. Collins, July 18, 1965, Bruce Rogow to Ray Fitzgerald, July 19, 1965, A-VIII-143, Reel 20, SNCC Papers.

40. Janet [Jemott] to Muriel, ca. August 1965, Doc. 0181, A-XV-19, Reel 37, SNCC Papers; Cleophus Hobbs, Hale County Report, August 4, 1965, Doc. 0046, A-VIII-28, Reel 18, SNCC Papers; Cleophus Hobbs and Terry Shaw, Hale County Report, August 26, 1965, Doc. 0051, Lowndes County Weekly Report, August 5, 1965, A-VIII-28, Reel 18, SNCC Papers; Eddie C. Smith Affidavit, August 23, 1965, Doc. 0114, A-VIII-29, Reel 18, SNCC Papers.

41. B. L. Collins to Elmo Holder, August 10, 1965, B. L. Collins, "SNCC Questions on Committee Elections," August 24, 1965, Doc. 0384, A-VIII-143, Reel 20, SNCC Papers; SNCC Press Release, "Illegalities Charged in Alabama ASCS Elections," November 5, 1965, Doc. 0460, A-VII-3, Reel 14, SNCC Papers.

42. Staff Newsletter, August 1, 1964, Doc. 0023, A-VII-6, Reel 15, SNCC Papers; "Farmer Committees," n.d., Doc. 1399, C-III-60, Reel 59, SNCC Papers; "Hale County Daily Report—First ASCS meeting," July 14, 1965, A-VIII-28, Reel 18, SNCC Papers; Janet [Jemott] and Tina [Harris] to Muriel and Cleve [Sellers], September 11, 1965, Doc. 1226, A-XV-10, Reel 36, SNCC Papers; Janet [Jemott] and Tina [Harris] to Silas [Norman], Muriel, staff, ca. September 1965, Doc. 0182, A-XV-19, Reel 37, SNCC Papers; Daniel, "African American Farmers and Civil Rights," 18. The flyer said, "JOIN your county agriculture committee. VOTE to help determine marketing uses and acreage allotments. ELECT committee men who will work for the good of the committee. You farmers, are directly affected by federal programs and can have your say about how these programs are run locally. Ideas and policies and programming must come from the grassroots. If you wish representatives of the Student Nonviolent Coordinating Committee will gladly go with you to the meetings of your county agriculture committee."

43. "A Paper for the People," *Southern Courier,* July 16, 1965; Rolinson, *Grassroots Garveyism,* 81; Rudd, "Negro Farmers"; Edward M. Rudd, "Farmers Plan ASCS Races," *Southern Courier,* October 30–31, 1965; Memorandum to Friends of SNCC, "ASCS Elections," November 5, 1965, Doc. 0659, C-IV-1, Reel 60, SNCC Papers. The *Southern Courier* played an important role in sustaining the civil rights movement in Alabama. Not only did it let people know what was happening across the state, but it also served as a source of pride that bolstered people's courage and commitment to change.

44. "SNCC Program: ASCS Elections, 1965," November 5, 1965, Doc. 0660, C-IV-1, Reel 60, SNCC Papers; Rudd, "Farmers Plan ASCS Races."

45. Memorandum to Friends of SNCC, "ASCS Elections"; SNCC Press Release, "Illegalities Charged"; SNCC Press Release, "Alabama ASCS Elections Held Today,"

November 15, 1965, Doc. 0465, A-VII-3, Reel 14, SNCC Papers; "SNCC Program: ASCS Elections, 1965." Barbour County did not file a complete report.

46. Memorandum to Friends of SNCC, "ASCS Elections"; SNCC Press Release, "Illegalities Charged"; SNCC Press Release, "Alabama ASCS Elections Held Today"; "SNCC Program: ASCS Elections, 1965"; ASCS Affidavits from Lowndes County, Alabama for ASCS Elections, ca. fall 1965, Doc. 0069, A-XVII-6, Reel 42, SNCC Papers; Edward M. Rudd, "Moves Hurt Negroes in ASCS Campaign," *Southern Courier,* November 13–14, 1965.

47. "SNCC Program: ASCS Elections 1965"; J. Edwin Stanfield to Orville Freeman, September 27, 1965, Robert S. Valder to H. D. Godfrey, September 28, 1965, Box 41.1.1.1.29, SRC. The ACHR also tried to get the USDA to pay close attention to the upcoming ASCS elections. J. Edwin Stanfield, executive director, warned secretary of agriculture Orville Freeman "that unless the USDA takes strong, immediate, positive steps, another Department of Agriculture program will serve to continue the oppression of and discrimination against Negro farmers, tenants, and sharecroppers." Stanfield gave Freeman specific examples of what was needed for a fair ASCS election to take place in Alabama and noted that white leaders "will use *every* method at their disposal to deprive the Negro farmer, tenant and sharecropper of their rightful participation in the ASCS election process." Finally, Robert Valder, the ACHR's associate director, wrote to the ASCS administrator in Washington to warn that personal commitment by rural leaders to be fair would not be enough to guarantee compliance with the ASCS regulations. He suggested "the personal presence of officials of the Federal government with the will to use maximum enforcement" as essential to attain "full and free participation by all people in all USDA programs."

48. SNCC Press Release, "Fraud Charged in Alabama ASCS Elections," November 19, 1965, Doc. 0466, A-VII-3, Reel 14, SNCC Papers; Edward M. Rudd, "Local ASCS Committees Integrated in 3 Counties," *Southern Courier,* November 20–21, 1965.

49. Stokely Carmichael, Affidavit re: ASCS Elections in Lowndes County during 1965 Voting, March 11, 1966, Doc. 0460, A-VIII-145, Reel 20, SNCC Papers; Eagles, *Outside Agitator,* 254; SNCC Press Release, "Fraud Charged"; John Lewis to Orville Freeman, November 30, 1965, Doc. 0926, A-I-31, Reel 1, SNCC Papers.

50. William N. Seabron, "Complaint of Discrimination in the Alabama ASCS Community Elections in Greene, Hale, Lowndes, and Wilcox Counties," November 22, 1965, Doc. 0068, A-XVII-6, Reel 42, SNCC Papers; Eagles, *Outside Agitator,* 135–37; Doug and Tina Harris to Kenneth K. Marshall, December 2, 1965, Doc. 0115, C-I-1, Reel 53, SNCC Papers.

51. Edward M. Rudd, "Freedom City, Alabama: Lowndes Families Start Tent Village," *Southern Courier,* January 8–9, 1966; SNCC Press Release, December 28, 1965, Doc. 0241, A-VII-3, Reel 14, SNCC Papers; "News of the Field No. 1," March 29, 1966, Doc. 0025, A-VII-16, Reel 17, SNCC Papers; Doug and Tina Harris to Kenneth K. Marshall, December 2, 1965, Doc. 0115, C-I-1, Reel 53, SNCC Papers; Elmo Holder, "People Help Themselves thru COOPS," n.d., Doc. 0419, A-VIII-144, Reel 20, SNCC Papers.

52. "Wilcox Plans Big Housing Project," *Southern Courier,* August 28–29, 1965; Leonard R. Mitchell to Randolph T. Blackwell, December 3, 1965, Series II, Box 146, SCLC Papers; Edward M. Rudd, "After Registering to Vote Wilcox Farmers Find Freedom Comes Fast," *Southern Courier,* January 22–23, 1966.

53. Fairclough, *To Redeem the Soul of America,* 147–48, 233; Robert L. Martin, "Wilcox County, Alabama—Expansion of Preliminary Report," July 26, 1966, John Cook to "Dear Friend," September 29, 1965, Inspection Reports Evaluating Community Action Programs, Box 1, RG 381; "Annual Report," April 12–13, 1966; Rudd, "Race Complicates Black Belt Anti-Poverty Plans"; John Cook, Thomas L. Threadgill, Carl Jones, Daniel Harrell, and Albert Gordon to Samuel Yette, October 12, 1965, Records Relating to the Administration of the Civil Rights Program in the Regions 1965–66, Box 24, RG 381; John Cook, Albert Gordon, Daniel Harrell Jr., Thomas Threadgill, and Carl D. Jones to Bob Martin, October 29, 1965, Inspection Reports Evaluating Community Action Programs, Box 1, RG 381; Roland Cooper to Sargent Shriver, October 12, 1965, Samuel F. Yette to John Cook, December 1, 1965, Records Relating to the Administration of the Civil Rights Program in the Regions 1965–66, Box 24, RG 381; Kate Harris, "Surprise Appointments—More Irregularities Popping Up in Wilcox County OEO Grant," *Birmingham News,* July 24, 1966, TSHC.

54. Walter, Interview by Author, 1–12, 26–27; Eagles, *Outside Agitator,* 174–75; Walter, Interview, 10–11, 43–47, RBOHC; SIP, "Help for Decent Housing in Black Belt Alabama," ca. 1966, Box 41.2.16.3.40, SRC. Walter's mother had a great influence on his racial awareness. He also heard Dr. Martin Luther King Jr. speak in Mobile prior to the Montgomery Bus Boycott, read Gunnar Myrdal's *American Dilemma,* and studied Gandhi's philosophy. Walter did not want to run from Alabama. "I've always been an inward grappler," he explained. "I have what I call the reverse Groucho Marx syndrome. Marx said he would not belong to a club that would elect him as a member. I will never leave an organization that wants to get rid of me. Yeah, I have a lot of hostility, an anger, it's just free floating. And this civil rights, not civil rights but the issue of racism in the church or distinction of persons would be the more theological term, which is totally foreign to the understanding of the body of Christ, just afforded me moral and legitimizing ways to use my anger." The SIP formally organized in October 1965 to nurture the relationship between religious institutions and the civil rights movement in Selma and the Black Belt. Four religious groups sponsored the project—the National Catholic Conference for Inter-Racial Justice, the National Council of Churches of Christ Committee on Religion and Race, the Synagogue Council of America, and the Unitarian-Universalist Association.

55. Francis X. Walter Diary, 7, 61, Francis X. Walter Personal Papers, Sewanee, Tenn.; Walter, Interview, 38–39, RBOHC; Southeastern Regional OEO, Chart of the Office Structure, 38.30, ABP; Mew-soong Li to Orzell Billingsley, February 15, 1966, Box "Correspondence," Jackson Collection; Rogers et al., *Alabama,* 487. The farming cooperative idea had deep roots in Wilcox County. As part of the New Deal, a cooperative was organized in Gee's Bend under the Farm Security Administration.

56. Walter Diary, 73–75; Mew-soong Li to Orzell Billingsley, February 15, 1966, Box "Correspondence," Jackson Collection.

57. Walter Diary, 64–65, 68–70, 73–75, 81–82. On January 2, Walter served as the "official greeter" for Attorney General Nicholas Katzenbach when he visited Brookley Air Force Base in Mobile. Walter sat with Katzenbach on the platform for his speech at the Mobile Municipal Auditorium. The Episcopal priest took this opportunity to have an impromptu meeting with Katzenbach along with Leroy Randolph of Wilcox County. "I told him of the 25 depositions from harassed tenants sent by us to Washington, asked him to start proceedings such as those in West Feliciana Parish. . . . I added that we were telling people to stay on the land until thrown off. He said 'Good—that's a help.' . . . I think he also said at the time that it was helpful for eviction preceding to come from the land first in other words people shouldn't move just at the demand of their landlords."

58. Daniel Harrell, "Special Report, Wilcox County," in "Annual Report," April 12–13, 1966.

59. Rudd, "Freedom City, Alabama"; "The Housing Committee of LCCMHR Will Be Elected by the Participants in the Housing Program," November 22, 1965, Doc. 1109, A-VIII-22, Reel 17, SNCC Papers; "The Alabama Program of Poverty," ca. 1966, Doc. 1140, A-VIII-22, Reel 17, SNCC Papers; HHrgHR10440, pt. 1, p. 11; "A Nation Aroused: First Annual Report of the Office of Economic Opportunity," 1965, 47, White House Aides Files—McPherson, Box 14, LBJ Library; "The Tide of Progress: Third Annual Report of the Office of Economic Opportunity," FY 1967 (June 1966–May 1967), 81–83, White House Aides Files—Gaither, Box 239, LBJ Library; Jack Gonzales, "South—Round II," March 4, 1965, CAP Office Records of the Director, State Files 1965–68, Box 1, RG 381; Anthony Partridge, "Proposed Grant in Lowndes County," June 3, 1966, Records Relating to the Administration of the Civil Rights Program in the Regions 1965–66, Box 24, RG 381; Levine, *Poor Ye Need Not Have*, 51–52.

60. Partridge, "Proposed Grant in Lowndes County"; Handwritten Note regarding Wilcox County, Alabama, February 28, [1966], Records of the Office of the Director, Records Relating to the Administration of the Civil Rights Program in the Regions 1965–66, Box 24, RG 318; Harrell, "Special Report"; SIP, "Help for Decent Housing"; Press Release, ca. June 28, 1966, "Wilcox County, Alabama (Seasonal Farm Workers) Grant Announcement," OEO Press Release, "Lowndes and Wilcox Cos., Alabama, Receive First Title III-B Grants for Seasonal Farm Workers," ca. June 1966, Box 378, LH. Partridge warned Shriver about this interpretation of Title III (b). "The use of section 311 to serve non-migrant seasonal workers reflects a fairly broad interpretation of that section," he explained. Yet he thought that Congressman Harlan Hagen of California, who had written the language for this section of the act, wanted programs to be included for "those families in which the head of household migrated while the rest of the family stayed home." He also argued that using the broad definition fit in with the agency's budget submission for Title III. Finally, he reasoned that migrant and nonmigrant seasonal farm workers constituted "a homogeneous class" that OEO

should address as one population. "They are tied to the same economy, characterized by both the seasonal nature of the work and the declining need for labor, and they not uncommonly work in the fields side by side."

61. Harrell, "Special Report"; SIP, "Help for Decent Housing"; Press Release, "Wilcox County, Alabama (Seasonal Farm Workers) Grant Announcement"; OEO Press Release, "Lowndes and Wilcox Cos., Alabama."

62. Greene County Community Fund, ca. 1965, Doc. 0489, SNCC Greene County Newsletter, n.d., Doc. 0495, A-VIII-40, Reel 18, SNCC Papers; Daphna Simpson, "Greene County Negroes Bypass FHA Troubles," *Southern Courier,* June 11–12, 1966.

63. Gail Falk, "'What County Are You from Sir?': Farm Folks Full of Questions," *Southern Courier,* January 29–30, 1966; ACHR, Quarterly Report, October–December 1965, Box 41.1.2.1.36, SRC; Bob Valder to J. Edwin Stanfield, January 19, 1966, Ed Stanfield, "Alabama Council, Annual Meeting, February 4–5, 1966," February 7, 1966, Ed Stanfield to Robert Valder, February 7, 1966, Box 41.1.1.1.30, SRC; ACHR, Quarterly Report, January–March 1966, Box 41.1.2.1.36, SRC; "Two Young Men with Big Plans."

Five. In the Rurals

1. "News of the Field No. 1," March 29, 1966, Doc. 0025, A-VII-16, Reel 17, SNCC Papers; Bill Mahoney, "'SNICK' in Alabama," ca. 1966, Doc. 0970, A-VIII-66, Reel 18, SNCC Papers; Robert E. Smith, "Visiting Federal Official Hears Complaints about Voting Law," *Southern Courier,* October 9–10, 1965; Martin Luther King Jr., "SCLC Voter Registration," February 1966, Series IV, Reel 15, Nonpartisan Voters League Papers, microfilm, University of South Alabama Library, Mobile; John Lewis, Statement on 1966, December 30, 1965, A-I-37, Reel 1, SNCC Papers; Transcript of Conversation between Stokely Carmichael, James Forman, and George Greene, "Riding in the Car from Atlanta to Tuskegee," February 19, 1966, Doc. 1168, A-XV-9, Reel 36, SNCC Papers. "In general," the report explained, "SNCC is urging people to run as representatives of Freedom parties, while the SCLC (Martin Luther King)—is backing those who are running in the Democratic primaries with support of the Alabama Democratic Conference." Alabama SNCC staff charged the ADC with being disinterested in the plight of their "brothers who live in rural and city slums."

2. John Klein, "Civil Rights Leaders Disagree on Using Votes in Black Belt," *Southern Courier,* January 22–23, 1966; Michael S. Lottman, "Gov. Wallace Seeks Four More Years," *Southern Courier,* October 9–10, 1965; Gail Falk, "Wallace Stumps . . . and SCLC Plans," *Southern Courier,* October 23–24, 1965; Mary Ellen Gale, "Succession Bill Loses, 18 to 14," *Southern Courier,* October 30–31, 1965; "The Race for Governor Is On," *Southern Courier,* March 5–6, 1966.

3. Certificate of Incorporation of the LCCMHR, November 22, 1965, Box SG22401, AGF; Edward M. Rudd, "New Political Group in Lowndes to Name Own Negro Candidates," *Southern Courier,* January 1–2, 1966; Bill Mahoney, "Fact Sheet—Lowndes County, Alabama Tent City," February 5, 1966, Doc. 0671, A-VIII-50, Reel 18, SNCC Papers; Transcript of Conversation between Stokely Carmichael, James Forman, and

George Greene; SNCC Press Release, December 28, 1965, Doc. 0241, SNCC Press Release, December 29, 1965, Doc. 0242, A-VII-3, Reel 14, SNCC Papers; "News of the Field No. 1," February 23, 1966, Doc. 0001, A-VII-15, Reel 17, SNCC Papers. The board of directors included John Hulett, William J. Cosby, Lillian S. McGill, Josephine Wagner, Jesse W. Favor, and Elvie McGill. Some of their stated objectives included "to promote and strive for the improvement and betterment of all public facilities and services within the community" and "to cooperate with county, town, and other officials, and with other civic and public organizations for the general welfare of the entire community."

4. Edward M. Rudd, "Freedom City, Alabama: Lowndes Families Start Tent Village," *Southern Courier,* January 8–9, 1966; "The Housing Committee of LCCMHR Will Be Elected by the Participants in the Housing Program," November 22, 1965, Doc. 1109, A-VIII-22, Reel 17, SNCC Papers; "The Alabama Program of Poverty," ca. 1966, Doc. 1140, A-VIII-22, Reel 17, SNCC Papers; Jack Gonzales, "South—Round II," March 4, 1965, CAP Office Records of the Director, State Files 1965–68, Box 1, RG 381; Anthony Partridge, "Proposed Grant in Lowndes County," June 3, 1966, Records Relating to the Administration of the Civil Rights Program in the Regions 1965–66, Box 24, RG 381.

5. "Alabama Program of Poverty"; R. L. Strickland to Sargent Shriver, March 22, 1966, Doc. 0779, A-VIII-54, Reel 18, SNCC Papers; Partridge, "Proposed Grant in Lowndes County"; Transcript of Conversation between Stokely Carmichael, James Forman, and George Greene.

6. Courtland Cox, draft of article that later became SNCC brochure, *What Would It Profit a Man? A Report on Alabama,* ca. 1966, Doc. 1174, A-XV-9, Reel 36, SNCC Papers; "Background on the Development of Political Strategy and Political Education in Lowndes County, Alabama," July 1966, Doc. 0672, A-VIII-50, Reel 18, SNCC Papers; Rudd, "New Political Group"; "Notes on Lowndes County Freedom Organization," n.d., Doc. 1155, A-VIII-71, SNCC Papers; VanDeburg, *New Day in Babylon,* 124.

7. Stokely Carmichael, "What We Want," *New York Review of Books,* 1966, later printed by SNCC as *Power and Racism,* A-I-49, Reel 2, SNCC Papers; Eagles, *Outside Agitator,* 255–56.

8. Stokely Carmichael, "Who Is Qualified?" *New Republic,* January 8, 1966, A-I-49, SNCC Papers; Carmichael, "What We Want"; Mahoney, "'SNICK' in Alabama."

9. Complaint in Civil Action 2322-N, U.S. District Court for the Middle District of Alabama, January 3, 1966, Motion to Dismiss in Civil Action 2322-N, U.S. District Court for the Middle District of Alabama, March 31, 1966, Box SG19969, AGAdmAF; Terry Cowles, "No Proof Lowndes Negroes Evicted for Registering," *Southern Courier,* June 18–19, 1966. The plaintiffs in the county official lawsuits were Lillian S. McGill, Jessie Mae McGill, Sarah B. Logan, John Hulett, Mattie Moorer, William Cosby, Clara Maull, Frank Miles Jr., Sidney Logan Jr., Charles Smith, Napoleon Nelson, Jesse W. Favor, Hattie Lee, and Clara McNeans. Judges Rives, Grooms, and Johnson dismissed the motion on March 31, 1966, claiming that "the community has a substantial interest in stable elections and the prompt determination of their validity." The judges thought that making all the elections invalid would be too disruptive to the orderly transition

of government. Finally, they thought that the plaintiffs could find relief in a fairly short amount of time—two and a half years—for most of their grievances to be taken care of through the 1966 and 1968 elections. Speaking for the court, Johnson said that there was "absolutely no evidence" that the white landowners evicted their tenants because they had registered to vote. The civil rights lawyers were ordered to pay all the court costs connected with the case.

10. Opinion in Civil Action No. 2288-N, U.S. District Court for the Middle District of Alabama Northern Division, *John Hulett v. Honorable J. B. Julian Justice of the Peace,* Lowndes County, February 5, 1966, Decree in Civil Action No. 2263-N, U.S. District Court for the Middle District of Alabama, Northern Division, *Gardenia White et al. v. Bruce Crook et al.,* February 7, 1966, Box SG19969, AGAdmAF.

11. "Editorial: One Good Reason," *Southern Courier,* February 12–13, 1966; "Stu House Reports from Selma, Alabama," February 13, 1966, Doc. 1049, A-VIII-70, Reel 18, SNCC Papers; "News of the Field No. 1," February 23, 1966. Lee's home burned.

12. "County Reports," ca. March 1966, Doc. 0023, A-VIII-27, Reel 18, SNCC Papers; Rudd, "New Political Group"; Larry Freudiger, "Lowndes Party Elects Officers," *Southern Courier,* April 9–10, 1966; "Is This the Party You Want? White Supremacy for the Right Democratic Party of Alabama," ca. 1966, Doc. 0759, A-VIII-53, Reel 18, SNCC Papers; Background Information on Freedom Elections Alabama, May 3, 1966, Doc. 0346, A-VIII-37, Reel 18, SNCC Papers; Transcript of Conversation between Stokely Carmichael, James Forman, and George Greene.

13. Frye, *Black Parties and Political Power,* 32; Jack Nelson, "Negro Split Endangers Vote Success in South: Militant 'Black Panther' Movement Seen Helping Known Segregationists on Ballot," *Los Angeles Times,* April 24, 1966, Doc. 1110, A-VIII-71, Reel 18, SNCC Papers.

14. Frye, *Black Parties and Political Power,* 24; Orzell Billingsley, Remarks at the Semiannual Meeting of the ADC, November 6, 1965, Box 144, Series II, SCLC Papers; Robert E. Smith and Stephen E. Cotton, "Negro Leaders Reveal How They Worked Strategy with Democrats," *Southern Courier,* January 29–30, 1966; Stephen E. Cotton, "Party 'Loyalists' Erase White Supremacy Tag," *Southern Courier,* January 29–30, 1966.

15. "Flowers Gets Support of Both Negro Groups," *Southern Courier,* April 23–24, 1966; Thornton, *Dividing Lines,* 30, 56, 63, 100–101, 139, 388, 390, 409, 511, 515. Rufus Lewis worked in the Montgomery Improvement Association during the Montgomery Bus Boycott. He nominated Martin Luther King Jr., his pastor at Dexter Avenue Baptist, to lead the association, served as the director of the car pool organized to provide transportation for those staying off the buses, and worked on voter registration as a part of the campaign to end segregation on the city's buses. Thornton reports that "Lewis's control of the Alabama Democratic Conference and his consequent command of party patronage gradually delivered ascendancy to him" in the struggle with E. D. Nixon, Lewis's longtime rival. Joe L. Reed was Lewis's protégé; he subsequently became the chair of Alabama State University's board of trustees. Lewis eventually won a seat in the Alabama legislature. Peter Hall worked with Billingsley on important cases focus-

ing on the discrimination of Alabama jury pools that did not allow African Americans to serve. They represented William Earl Fikes in a 1953 trial in Dallas County. Thornton explains that "Hall and Billingsley's NAACP sponsorship, their aggressive conduct toward white authority, and their attacks on the patterns of white supremacy had caused white Selma to close ranks." Hall and Billingsley also represented Rev. Louis L. Anderson in a 1959 trial that took place in Selma. Hall was appointed Birmingham's first black municipal judge in the 1970s.

16. John Klein, "SCLC Proposes Political Group," *Southern Courier,* March 5–6, 1966; Albert Turner, "State Field Secretary Report for Alabama for 1965–1966," April 12–13, 1966, Series II, Box 144, SCLC Papers; Francis X. Walter Diary, October 29, 1965, 38–40, Francis X. Walter Personal Papers, Sewanee, Tenn. Turner reported that the new coalition offered "a new unity . . . among Negroes in Alabama." Walter also noted Williams's difficult personality. "I don't blame anyone for resisting Hosea's dogmatic egomania," he noted.

17. Klein, "SCLC Proposes Political Group"; John Klein, "Leaders in 15 Counties Meet to Plan Bloc Vote: Mobile, Montgomery Absent," *Southern Courier,* March 12–13, 1966; David R. Underhill, "Political Confederation Lays Plans to Decide Who Gets Negro Vote," *Southern Courier,* April 2–3, 1966; "Editorial: Have a Seat, Hosea," *Southern Courier,* April 16–17, 1966; Stephen E. Cotton, "Politicians, Leaders Fight over 'the Negro Vote,'" *Southern Courier,* April 9–10, 1966.

18. Underhill, "Political Confederation Lays Plans"; "Annual Report to the Board of Directors of the SCLC," April 12–13, 1966, Series II, Box 144, SCLC Papers.

19. Gay Talese, "Where's The Spirit of Selma Now?" *New York Times Magazine,* May 1965, Box SG13843, Alabama State Sovereignty Commission Papers, Alabama Department of Archives and History, Montgomery.

20. Claude Kirk, "Progress Report," February 26, 1965, Economic Opportunity, "Progress Report as of March 12, 1965," March 12, 1965, Box SG22390, AGF; Frederick O'R. Hayes, "Alabama," March 31, 1965, CAP Office Records of the Director, State Files, 1965–68, Box 1, RG 381; Fairclough, *To Redeem the Soul,* 261; "Selma Wonders after Reese Arrest," *Southern Courier,* July 16, 1965; David M. Gordon, "Selma: Quiet after the Battle," *Southern Courier,* July 23, 1965. On January 11, 1965, the Selma City Council and the county revenue board approved a resolution to seek OEO funds. The director of OEO's Atlanta regional office reported that the Selma antipoverty committee was disappointed when it learned that OEO would not fund its program unless the board itself was biracial. The board had discarded its initial plans for a biracial board because its members feared that Governor Wallace would veto the project.

21. Fairclough, *To Redeem the Soul,* 261; "Annual Report," April 12–13, 1966; "Alabama Staff Workshop," April 21–23, 1965, Doc. 1213, A-X-10, Reel 36, SNCC Papers; Dallas County Independent Free Voters League Flyer, Doc. 0226, A-VIII-32, Reel 18, SNCC Papers; "Special Report No. 4: Selma and Dallas County, Alabama: A Statistical Roundup," March 1965, Doc. 0061, C-I-1, Reel 53, SNCC Papers; "Method for Selecting Board of Directors—Adopted at SHAPE General Meeting," December 8, 1965, Inspection Reports Evaluating CAP, Box 1, RG 381.

22. Doug Harris, Tina Harris, and Janet Jermott, "Over 200 at East Selma People's Convention," July 23, 1965, Doc. 1062, A-VIII-70, Reel 18, SNCC Papers; "East Selma Newsletter, What Rights Do We Have as Citizens?" August 9, 1965, Doc. 0181, A-XV-19, Reel 37, SNCC Papers.

23. Mesher, Interview by Author, 10–12.

24. Robert L. Martin, "Dallas County–City of Selma Economic Opportunity Board," June 20, 1966, Inspection Reports Evaluating CAP, Box 1, RG 381; "Selma Program Offers Free Food to Needy," *Southern Courier*, October 16–17, 1965; Shirley Mesher to Colonel Decker, October 27, 1965, Docs. 0208 and 0209, A-VIII-31, Reel 18, SNCC Papers.

25. John Klein, "Dan River Mills Charged with Job Discrimination," *Southern Courier*, February 12–13, 1966; "Annual Report," April 12–13, 1966; Thornton, *Dividing Lines*, 493–97. At least twenty black people had completed a training course for spinners and weavers sponsored by Dan River Mills and operated through the Manpower Development Training Act of 1962. A Dan River employee told a reporter, "They're actually hiring people out there who have never seen those machines before, and they don't hire the colored folks that have been trained." Thornton reports, "Primarily as a result of these two acquisitions, between 1963 and 1967, Dallas County's annual industrial payroll more than doubled, from $7.2 million to $14.6 million."

26. Mesher, Interview by Author, 14, 16–17; "Annual Report," April 12–13; Robert E. Smith, "Rights Lawyers Open Selma Office," *Southern Courier*, June 18–19, 1966; *Clemon Barlow et al. v. J. A. Minter Jr. et al.*, Civil Action No. 4482-67, U.S. District Court for the Southern District of Alabama, Northern Division, Answers to Interrogatories, July 21, 1970, *Clemon Barlow v. J. A. Minter Jr.*, U.S. District Court, Mobile, Ala., Civil Case Files ACC 021-73A2029, Case 4482-67, National Archives and Records Administration, Southeast Region, Morrow, Ga.; Walter, Interview, 39–41, RBOHC.

27. "Annual Report," April 12–13, 1966; Mesher, Interview by Author, 17–18.

28. John A. Baker to Harold A. Middlebrook, July 18, 1965, Chuck Fager to Randolph Blackwell, July 31, 1965, Records of the Voter Education Project 1964–66, Series II, Box 146, SCLC Papers; Doug Harris, Tina Harris, Janet Jermott, and Jim to Silas Norman, August 3, 1965, Doc. 1061, A-VIII-70, Reel 18, SNCC Papers; Edward M. Rudd, "Race Complicates Black Belt Anti-Poverty Plans," *Southern Courier*, October 16–17, 1965; Frank Prial, "Alabama Contact," November 7, 1965, Inspection Reports Evaluating CAP, Box 1, RG 381.

29. Edward M. Rudd and Mary Ellen Gale, "Two Fronts in the War on Poverty: 1. A Successful Meeting in Selma 2. Disputes Block Macon Program," *Southern Courier*, October 23–24, 1965; Martin, "Dallas County–City of Selma Economic Opportunity Board"; Frank Prial, "Alabama Contact," November 7, 1965, Inspection Reports Evaluating CAP, Box 1, RG 381. OEO's initial support of the SCLC group caused its leaders to think that it had quasi-official status, even though it had yet to file an application with the antipoverty agency. OEO later reported that the agency's technical assistance also "put pressure on Mayor Smitherman, who proved much less inflexible than had originally been thought."

30. Martin, "Dallas County–City of Selma Economic Opportunity Board";
Edward M. Rudd, "Poverty Dispute in Selma," *Southern Courier,* November 13–14, 1965;
David R. Underhill, "Governor Wallace Comes Out Fighting, Hits Attacks on Local
Government," *Southern Courier,* August 28–29, 1965.

31. Edward M. Rudd, "Mayor: I'll See Selma Negroes of 'Good Faith,'" *Southern Courier,* December 18–19, 1965; Walter Diary, November 9, 1965, 47, November 16, 1965, 53.

32. Martin, "Dallas County–City of Selma Economic Opportunity Board"; "Method
for Selecting Board of Directors," December 8, 1965. Martin's memo includes a list of
SHAPE board members.

33. Rudd, "Mayor: I'll See Selma Negroes"; Ernest M. Bradford to Joe T. Smitherman,
December 15, 1965, Inspection Reports Evaluating CAP, Box 1, RG 381; Joe T. Smitherman to Ernest Bradford, December 21, 1965, Records Relating to the Administration of
the Civil Rights Program in the Regions 1965–66, Box 24, RG 381.

34. Rudd, "Poverty Dispute in Selma"; Martin, "Dallas County–City of Selma Economic Opportunity Board"; N. A., "Selma, Alabama," January 15, 1966, Inspection
Reports Evaluating CAP, Box 1, RG 381.

35. Mahoney, "'SNICK' in Alabama"; John Klein, "Selma Negroes Wonder, What
Did Mayor Mean?" *Southern Courier,* February 5–6, 1966; "Stu House Reports." Klein
reported that Mesher thought that OEO would grant funds to an independent organization such as SHAPE if it truly represented the whole community. Klein said that
"there seemed to be a vague fear among the poorer Negro members of SHAPE that
dealing with whites appointed by the mayor meant poor Negroes would have a small
part in the planning and operation of the program."

36. Mahoney, "'SNICK' in Alabama"; Klein, "Selma Negroes Wonder"; "Stu House
Reports."

37. Walter, Interview, 24–25, RBOHC.

38. Ibid., 26–28.

39. "Editorial: Antipoverty Probe?" *Selma Times Journal,* March 10, 1966, Box A147,
NAACP Papers; Martin, "Dallas County–City of Selma Economic Opportunity Board";
Walter, Interview, 32–33, RBOHC.

40. Joseph S. Knight Résumé, March 25, 1966, Inspection Reports Evaluating CAP,
Box 1, RG 381; Martin, "Dallas County–City of Selma Economic Opportunity Board."

41. Ernest M. Bradford, "Protest from the People of Dallas County Regarding the
Community Action Program by Dallas County SHAPE," March 29, 1966, Ernest M.
Bradford to Samuel Yette, March 31, 1966, Records Relating to the Administration of
the Civil Rights Program in the Regions 1965–66, Box 24, RG 381; "Selma's Poor Object
to Poverty Set-Up," *Southern Courier,* April 9–10, 1966; Martin, "Dallas County–City
of Selma Economic Opportunity Board"; Thornton, *Dividing Lines,* 482, 491. Bradford
was very upset that SHAPE members had been chosen to serve on the CAA and not
directly elected. He asked that an investigation be carried out "by high-level officials
from Washington, D.C. and that it be done in public." Bradford even sent a protest
letter to President Johnson. OEO reported that local people believed that Mesher was
the real power behind SHAPE.

42. Anonymous to Bill [and] Gwen, March 16, 1966, Anonymous to Bill, March 17, 1966, Doc. 0066, A-VIII-28, Reel 18, SNCC Papers; Larry Freudiger, "A Rally in Selma," *Southern Courier,* April 16–17, 1966; SNCC News Release, "Dallas County Independent Voters League," March 17, 1966, A-VIII-71, Reel 18, SNCC Papers; John Klein, "Dallas County Voters Start Third Party," *Southern Courier,* March 19–20, 1966; Walter, Interview, 32–35, RBOHC. Walter explained that when "SHAPE workers as a committee of DCVL really got out there in the bushes and worked and found all these rural people and got them to create something—I think they used political precincts and got these people to elect their delegates to the CAP board from their precinct. And they got all these people who had never gotten involved in a Negro organization before. . . . At this point SHAPE was deep into politics as I saw, it happened to give birth to a political arm, a natural thing."

43. "Rev. Reese Cleared of Charges in Selma," *Southern Courier,* April 9–10, 1966; "Selma Wonders after Reese Arrest"; Klein, "Dallas County Voters."

44. Tina Harris, "Freedom Organizations in Alabama," April 21, 1966, Doc. 0543, A-VII-3, Reel 14, SNCC Papers; Larry Freudiger, "Dick Gregory: Selma," *Southern Courier,* April 16–17, 1966; "First They Listened, Then They Danced," *Southern Courier,* April 16–17, 1966.

45. Freudiger, "Rally in Selma"; Terry Cowles, "Tenants Say Planter Won't Share Payments in U.S. Cotton Plan," *Southern Courier,* April 2–3, 1966; Willis, *Lay My Burden Down.* Moorer's group evolved out of the evictions from the Minter Plantation.

46. Tina Harris, "Freedom Organizations in Alabama"; "Dallas County Independent Free Voters Organization Information," n.d., Doc. 1136, A-VIII-22, Reel 17, SNCC Papers; Clarence Williams Jr. to Cleveland Sellers, n.d., Doc. 1249, A-XV-10, Reel 36, SNCC Papers; Transcript of Conversation between Stokely Carmichael, James Foreman, and George Greene.

47. Note Regarding Richmond Flowers, n.d., A-VIII-52, Reel 18, SNCC Papers; Eagles, *Outside Agitator,* 196, 200, 204–5, 225. Flowers sent mixed messages with regard to his racial moderation. He spoke out in favor of prosecuting Coleman for Daniels's murder but he also testified before the U.S. Supreme Court against the constitutionality of the Voting Rights Act.

48. Tina Harris, "Freedom Organization in Alabama"; Selma Office, "Daily Reports," ca. 1966, Doc. 0423, A-VIII-39, Reel 18, SNCC Papers; Hugh Merrill, "King Criticizes Panthers," *Birmingham News,* April 27, 1966, Box SG6944, PISF; Selma Office, "Request from Bob Mants as to Who Is Doing What in Alabama," ca. 1966, Doc. 0427, A-VIII-39, Reel 18, SNCC Papers; Notes on DCIFVO, ca. spring 1966, A-VIII-71, Reel 18, SNCC Papers; Dallas County Report, n.d., Doc. 0073, A-VIII-28, Reel 18, SNCC Papers; Tom Lankford, "'Black Power' Lowndes Heard First Cry," *Birmingham News,* July 20, 1966, Box SG6944, PISF.

49. Michael S. Lottman, "How Did Your County Vote?" *Southern Courier,* May 7–8, 1966; Michael S. Lottman, "Slim Chance for Negroes to Win Legislative Races," *Southern Courier,* May 7–8, 1966; Robert E. Smith, "Negro Candidates Plan Races in Many Counties: Four Start Try for Legislature," *Southern Courier,* February 19–20, 1966;

"Alabama Candidates Running for Public Office in the May Primaries," May 1966, Box 165, Series IV, SCLC Papers; "Voters Hard to Reach in County Like Perry," *Southern Courier,* April 30–May 1, 1966; Bob Valder to J. Edwin Stanfield, February 14, 1966, Bob Valder to Lewis Black, February 23, 1966, Box 41.1.1.1.30, SRC; Willis, *Lay My Burden Down.* Lewis Black had planned to run for a seat in the Alabama House of Representatives but changed his mind when he realized the campaign would conflict with his new position as the director of the Rural Advancement Project. The quotation from LeRoy Randolph appears in Willis's film. Although Randolph is not named, Francis Walter identified him as we watched the documentary together.

50. Daphna Simpson, "Gilmore vs. Sheriff Lee in Greene County Election," *Southern Courier,* March 26–27, 1966; "Alabama Candidates Running for Public Office"; Robin Reisig, "More to Come in Greene," *Southern Courier,* November 12–13, 1966; "Alabama Freedom Candidates," May 3, 1966, A-VIII-70, Reel 18, SNCC Papers; Greene County Report, May 2, 1966, Doc. 0067, A-VIII-28, Reel 18, SNCC Papers. Sheriff Lee did not wear a uniform and did not carry a gun. Someone from his family had been sheriff for forty-five consecutive years. In mid-March he had appointed a black cattle farmer as a deputy. He admitted, "The federal government has forced me to be moderate."

51. "Big Political Day in Dallas County," *Southern Courier,* April 30–May 1, 1966; "Alabama Candidates Running for Public Office"; SNCC Press Release, May 4, 1966, Doc. 0552, A-VII-3, Reel 14, SNCC Papers; "News of the Field No. 3 from the New York Office of SNCC," May 6, 1966, Doc. 0030, A-VII-16, Reel 17, SNCC Papers; Dallas County Report, ca. 1966, Doc. 0065, A-VIII-28, Reel 18, SNCC Papers; Dallas County Report, May 2, 1966, Doc. 0067, A-VIII-28, Reel 18, SNCC Papers; Lottman, "Slim Chance." The DCVL backed Lawrence Williams for tax collector, Robert E. H. J. Perry and Rev. J. D. Hunter for court of county revenues, and Rev. S. J. Brown for coroner. The DCIFVO candidates included Addie Lind for tax assessor, Horace Griffin for tax collector, Agatha Harville for Selma District, Roosevelt McElroy for West Dallas District, Wilmer Walker for Southside District, A. D. Bush for Fort District, George Sallie and Norma E. Day for county school board, and Nathan Payne for coroner. Mesher wrote to the postal department to notify Crum's bosses that he intended to seek political office. The letter did not make it to Washington before the May 3 primary, which made it difficult for him to run for office and keep his job. On May 3, Crum had not decided what he would do.

52. Willis, *Lay My Burden Down.*

53. SNCC Press Release, May 4, 1966, Doc. 0552, A-VII-3, Reel 14, SNCC Papers; "Panther Party Meeting Today at Hayneville," *Alabama Journal,* May 3, 1966, Box SG6944, PISF; "And Now It's the Voters' Turn: Mass Meeting Day Tuesday for Lowndes County Party," *Southern Courier,* April 30–May 1, 1966; Larry Freudiger, "Lowndes Third Party Attracts 900, Nominates Logan to Face Sheriff," *Southern Courier,* May 7–8, 1966, Box SG21071, Alabama Legislative Commission to Preserve the Peace Papers, Alabama Department of Archives and History, Montgomery.

54. SNCC Press Release, "Report on Alabama Elections," May 6, 1966, Doc. 0553, A-VII-3, Reel 14, SNCC Papers; SNCC Press Release, n.d., A-VIII-71, Reel 18, SNCC

Papers; Daphna Simpson, "Losing Negroes Protest Greene County Election," *Southern Courier,* May 14–15, 1966; NAACP Legal Defense and Educational Fund, "LDF Challenges Irregularities in Alabama Primary Elections: Asks Court to Void Greene County Contest," May 27, 1966, Doc. 1116, A-VIII-71, Reel 18, SNCC Papers; Stephen E. Cotton, "Negro Voters All over State Say, 'I Waited,' but No Negro Candidates Able to Say, 'I Won': Several to Face Run-Off Races," *Southern Courier,* May 7–8, 1966; Robert L. Martin, "Supplemental Report on Wilcox County, Alabama," August 4, 1966, Inspection Reports Evaluating CAP, Box 1, RG 381. SNCC reported that 235,348 black Alabamians had registered to vote before the primary. But 100,000 additional white people had registered since the passage of the Voting Rights Act, for a total of 1,175,122. The NAACP filed suit on behalf of Gilmore, McShan, Branch, and Kirksey, alleging that there were fewer than 1,500 qualified voters living in Greene County but that at least 1,789 ballots had been cast. White illiterates were allowed to use sample ballots, but black voters were not.

55. Willis, *Lay My Burden Down;* Lottman, "How Did Your County Vote?"; Lottman, "Slim Chance"; SNCC Press Release, "Report on Alabama Elections"; Daphna Simpson, "Gilmore Waits for the Election Results: 'Baby, We've Got to Make It,'" *Southern Courier,* May 7–8, 1966; Mary Ellen Gale, "Macon Sheriff Nominee Takes Victory in Stride," *Southern Courier,* June 4–5, 1966; Norrell, *Reaping the Whirlwind,* 188–201; Michael S. Lottman, "Kirksey Is Only Negro to Win Outside Macon," *Southern Courier,* June 4–5, 1966; "Baker Named Winner, but Clark Can Fight," *Southern Courier,* May 28–29, 1966; Mary Wissler, "How Big Is a Mass Meeting? Gilmore and McShan Off Ballot in Greene County," *Southern Courier,* October 22–23, 1966; Reisig, "More to Come in Greene"; Photo Caption, *Southern Courier,* June 25–26, 1966; SNCC Press Release, "Report on Alabama Elections." "By George—No Run-Off," *Southern Courier,* May 7–8, 1966. In Dallas County, all black candidates in the Democratic primary were defeated. Henry McCaskill reached the runoff for Hale County sheriff but lost in the May 31 election. Perry County's Patt J. Davis, Rev. Obie Scott Jr., Willie Lester Martin, Ison Atkins, and Albert Turner reached runoffs but lost on May 31. Lonnie Brown faced State Senator Roland Cooper in the runoff for the Nineteenth District seat but lost. Macon County faced issues similar to those in Dallas County, with the city of Tuskegee having a more middle-class-oriented political organization and the county not sharing those values. Norrell explains that Amerson's election resulted from the rural black community's support. The sheriff was the most important county official for rural people. Charles Gomillion, leader of the Tuskegee Civil Association, thought that the last office to be occupied by a black person should be the sheriff. The other five Choctaw County winners were Nellie M. Steele, William Harrison, Lucille Hayden, Marshall Ruffin, and Christine Hopkins.

56. "Rights Staff Studies Vote 'by the Sea,'" *Southern Courier,* May 14–15, 1966; Terry Cowles, "SCLC Moves Out of Alabama," *Southern Courier,* June 4–5, 1966; Mesher, "Annual Report," April 12–13, 1966; Smith, "Rights Lawyers Open Selma Office."

57. Carson, *In Struggle,* 200–203; "Black Panther Party to Import Observers," *Alabama Journal,* May 24, 1966, Box SG6944, PISF; Dittmer, *Local People,* 392; Listing of SNCC Staff and Assignments, May 1966, Doc. 1064, A-III-1, Reel 3, SNCC Papers;

Minutes of the Central Committee Meeting, October 22–23, 1966, Doc. 0604, A-II-11, Reel 3, SNCC Papers.

58. Dittmer, *Local People,* 389, 392; Carson, *In Struggle,* 209–10; Stokely Carmichael on *Face the Nation,* June 19, 1966, A-I-63, Reel 2, SNCC Papers.

59. Carmichael on *Face the Nation.*

60. Ibid.; Lerone Bennett Jr., "Stokely Carmichael, Architect of Black Power," *Ebony,* July 1966, A-I-48, Reel 2, SNCC Papers; Carmichael, "What We Want." Carmichael's arguments about Black Power in these articles resembled what he said on *Face the Nation.*

61. Alice L. Moore to Stokely Carmichael, August 10, 1966, Stokely Carmichael to Alice L. Moore, August 22, 1966, A-I-52, Reel 2, SNCC Papers.

62. George C. Wallace to Sargent Shriver, July 18, 1966, Box SG19970, AGAdmAF; Nelson Lichtenstein and Robert E. Smith, "$500,000 to Civil Rights Groups," *Southern Courier,* July 16–17, 1966, Box SG21071, Alabama Legislative Commission to Preserve the Peace Papers; OEO Press Release, "Wilcox County, Alabama (Seasonal Farm Workers)," ca. June 28, 1966, OEO Press Release, "Lowndes County, Alabama LCCMHR Grant," ca. June 28, 1966, Box 378, LH; Frank K. Sloan, "Lowndes and Wilcox Counties, Alabama," August 5, 1966, Inspection Reports Evaluating CAP, Box 2, RG 381; "SCLC Aide Gets Alabama Poverty Post," *Birmingham News,* July 14, 1966, TSHC; Fairclough, *To Redeem the Soul,* 257, 316–17, 335; Chairman to Members of the LCCMHR, n.d., Doc. 1182, A-XV-9, Reel 36, SNCC Papers. Green joined the SCLC staff in 1965 as director of the Citizenship Education Program.

63. Samuel Yette to Sargent Shriver, June 15, 1966, Records Relating to the Administration of the Civil Rights Program in the Regions 1965–66, Box 24, RG 381; Partridge, "Proposed Grant in Lowndes County"; OEO Press Release, "Lowndes and Wilcox Counties, Alabama, Receive First Title III-B Grants for Seasonal Farm Workers," ca. July 1966, Box 378, LH; "OEO Gives Aid for Training Programs," *Birmingham News,* July 14, 1966, TSHC; Note to File on Ken Valis, July 1966, Inspection Reports Evaluating CAP, Box 2, RG 381.

64. George C. Wallace to Sargent Shriver, July 18, 1966 (2), Box SG19970, AGAdmAF; Dan T. Carter, *Politics of Rage,* 232; Edwin Strickland, "Report of the Alabama Legislative Commission to Preserve the Peace Requested by Governor George C. Wallace," July 14, 1966, Box SG21074, Alabama Legislative Commission to Preserve the Peace Papers. The Alabama Legislative Commission to Preserve the Peace was a legislative creature formed by the governor in 1963 with the purpose of exposing the "entire scope of the subversive apparatus" that threatened the state of Alabama. Its legislative leader, Representative John Hawkins, thought the civil rights movement was "the vanguard of the revolutionary thrust of international Communism."

65. George C. Wallace, Statement, July 19, 1966, Box SG22401, AGF.

66. Ibid.; "Poverty Off in Washington Grant ¼ Million, Governor Not Informed," n.d., Box 19970, AGAdmAF.

67. Marty to Cecil [Jackson] and Hugh [Maddox], n.d., Box SG19966, AGAdmAF; Samuel Eichold to George C. Wallace, July 21, 1966, Mr. and Mrs. Stanton Hawkins to

George C. Wallace, July 23, 1966, Box SG22401, AGF; Nettie P. Hightower to George C. Wallace, July 20, 1966, Box SG22403, AGF.

68. "Editorial: Black Panthers in the Trough," *Alabama Journal,* July 21, 1966, Box SG6944, PISF; "Editorial: End These Two Projects," *Birmingham Post-Herald,* July 21, 1966, Box 373, LH; "Editorial: Black Power," WSFA-TV Channel 12 Montgomery, July 19, 1966, "Editorial: Black Power and the War on Poverty," WSFA-TV Channel 12 Montgomery, July 21, 1966, "Editorial: Black Progress," WSFA-TV Channel 12 Montgomery, July 22, 1966, "Editorial: No Aid for the Mob," *Dallas Morning News,* July 22, 1966, "Negro Killer in OEO Job," *Muncie (Ind.) Star,* July 20, 1966, Box 22401, AGF.

69. Mrs. Gilchrist Shirley to Lister Hill, July 18, 1966, Records Relating to the Administration of the Civil Rights Program in the Regions 1965–66, Box 24, RG 381; Hugh Merrill, "Strickland Interview Recalled New Poverty-Panther Links," *Birmingham News,* July 31, 1966, Box SG6944, PISF. Merrill reported that the Federal Alcohol and Tobacco Tax unit in Birmingham searched Strickland's home in March and found no automatic rifle, or any illegal firearms.

70. Lister Hill to Sargent Shriver, July 18, 1966, Lister Hill to Crowell A. Pate Jr., July 25, 1966, Box 378, LH; Glenn Andrews to Sargent Shriver, July 21, 1966, Sargent Shriver to Glenn Andrews, August 23, 1966, Records Relating to the Administration of the Civil Rights Program in the Regions 1965–66, Box 24, RG 381; Kate Harris, "Surprise Appointments—More Irregularities Popping Up in Wilcox County Grant," *Birmingham News,* July 24, 1966, Al Fox, "Blames Democrats—Martin Says Lowndes Case 'Typical Abuse,'" *Birmingham News,* July 22, 1966, TSHC.

71. Robert W. Saunders, "Lowndes and Wilcox Counties, Alabama," July 18, 1966, John Dean, "Lowndes and Wilcox Counties, Alabama," July 29, 1966, Theodore M. Berry, "Contacts Made with Dr. M. L. King's Office," July 21, 1966, Records Relating to the Administration of the Civil Rights Program in the Regions 1965–66, Box 24, RG 381; Hugh Merrill, "War inside the Poverty War: Tried to Tell Superiors Alabama OEO Director Admits Charges True," *Birmingham News,* July 22, 1966, "Editorial: Questions Needing Answers," *Birmingham News,* July 24, 1966, TSHC; Sloan, "Lowndes and Wilcox Counties, Alabama."

72. "Statement by Sargent Shriver in Reply to Communications from Governor George C. Wallace of Alabama, Concerning Anti-Poverty Grants to Lowndes and Wilcox Counties, Alabama," July 20, 1966, Box 378, LH; Inspection Reports Evaluating CAP, Box 2, RG 381; Edwin Graves, "OEO Chief Rejects 'Black Power' Tie-In," *Birmingham News,* July 20, 1966, Edwin Graves, "On Lowndes Grant: OEO Chief Denies Wallace's Charges," *Birmingham News,* July 21, 1966, TSHC. Shriver made it clear to Wallace that Carmichael had never "expressed an opinion to OEO publicly or privately on this grant" and that the SNCC activist was not "associated in any official capacity with the LCCMHR Inc." Shriver told Wallace that his charges against Strickland were serious but that "an official pardon from the Governor of Alabama exonerating an individual of such a crime . . . would also be important evidence."

73. Chairman to Members of the LCCMHR, n.d., Doc. 1182, A-XV-9, Reel 36, SNCC Papers; Martin Luther King Jr. to Sargent Shriver, July 27, 1966, Inspection Reports

Evaluating CAP, Box 2, RG 381; "King Urges Shriver to Release OEO Funds," *Birmingham News,* July 29, 1966, TSHC; Robert S. Valder to Sargent Shriver, July 27, 1966, Lewis Black to Sargent Shriver, July 29, 1966, Francis X. Walter and Mel Dubin to Sargent Shriver, July 21, 1966, Records Relating to the Administration of the Civil Rights Program in the Regions 1965–66, Box 24, RG 381.

74. Theodore Berry, "CAP Position on Grant to Lowndes County," July 27, 1966, Robert L. Martin, "Lowndes County and Wilcox County—Migrant Program," July 29, 1966, Edgar May, "Lowndes County," August 2, 1966, Inspection Reports Evaluating CAP, Box 2, RG 381.

75. Robert L. Martin, "Wilcox County, Alabama—Preliminary Report," July 25, 1966, Bob Martin to Noel Klores, August 22, 1966, Edgar May, "Wilcox County, Alabama," July 27, 1966, Inspection Reports Evaluating CAP, Box 1, RG 381; Martin, "Supplemental Report"; "Progress Secret: OEO Still Probing Lowndes Fund Case," *Birmingham News,* July 31, 1966, TSHC.

76. Alice Moore to Stokely Carmichael, August 29, 1966, A-I-52, Reel 2, SNCC Papers; Viola Bradford, "Freedom Candidates Campaign in Lowndes," *Southern Courier,* October 22–23, 1966; Michael S. Lottman, "Tuesday—Day of Decisions: High Hopes in Lowndes," *Southern Courier,* November 5–6, 1966.

77. Viola Bradford, "Samson Crum Withdraws from Dallas Sheriff Race," *Southern Courier,* October 8–9, 1966; Dallas County Independent Free Voters Organization Flyer, ca. 1966, Doc. 0119, A-VIII-29, Reel 18, SNCC Papers; Dallas County Independent Free Voters Organization Advertisement, *Southern Courier,* November 5–6, 1966; "November 8 Nears—Political Plots Thicken," *Southern Courier,* October 22–23, 1966; James Chisum, "Negro Voter May Cast Deciding Ballot Tuesday," *Birmingham News,* November 6, 1966, Box SG6975, PISF. DCIFVO candidates included Addie Lily for tax assessor; Horace D. Griffin Sr. for tax collector; N. F. Payne for coroner; A. D. Bush for member, court of county revenues, Fork District; Agatha Harville for member, court of county revenues, City of Selma District; Roosevelt McElroy for member, court of county revenues, West Dallas District; Wilmer Walker for member, court of county revenues, Southside District; and George Sallie for member, board of education, Dallas County, Place 3. The DCVL was not the only black organization to support Wallace. The Jefferson County Progressive Democratic Conference also endorsed her, reportedly as a means of aiding the national Democratic Party.

78. "Carmichael to Go before Judge Today," *Birmingham News,* November 18, 1966, "Three 'Black Power' Advocates Go on Trial in Selma Today," *Alabama Journal,* November 22, 1966, Box SG6944, PISF; Viola Bradford, "Lowndes: A Good Day to Go Voting, but Black Panther Candidates Lose," *Southern Courier,* November 12–13, 1966; SNCC Press Release, "Election Reports (Ga, Al, Miss)," November 10, 1966, Doc. 0584, A-VII-3, Reel 14, SNCC Papers.

79. Viola Bradford, "Lowndes"; SNCC Press Release, "Election Reports (Ga, Al, Miss)"; "Dallas: DCIFVO Head Not Discouraged," *Southern Courier,* November 12–13, 1966; Viola Bradford, "Election Aftermath in Lowndes: 'Sold His People for a Coke,'" *Southern Courier,* November 19–20, 1966.

80. Mary Ellen Gale, "Amerson Elected Macon Sheriff Despite Sadler Write-In Effort," "Helps to Be a Lady and a Democrat," *Southern Courier,* November 12–13, 1966; Reisig, "More to Come in Greene."

81. "Revised Draft of Mr. Shriver's Statement on Wilcox and Lowndes," ca. November 1966, Records Relating to the Administration of the Civil Rights Program in the Regions 1965–66, Box 24, RG 381; OEO Press Release, "Lowndes County, Alabama Receives Title III-B Grant for Seasonal Farm Workers," November 17, 1966, Inspection Reports Evaluating CAP, Box 2, RG 381; James Free, "Shriver Releases Protested Grants," *Birmingham News,* November 18, 1966, TSHC.

82. OEO Press Release, "The OEO Today Announced a Federal Anti-Poverty Grant to Dallas County in Alabama," ca. August 1966, Box 378, LH; Robert L. Martin to Edgar May and Robert G. Emond, April 17, 1967, CAP Office Records of the Director, Subject Files 1965–69, Box 70, RG 381; Daphna Simpson, "Greene County Negroes Bypass FHA Troubles," *Southern Courier,* June 11–12, 1966.

Six. Agriculture Is More Than Farming

1. Robin Reisig, "Farmers Lose Land in Greene County," *Southern Courier,* January 14–15, 1967; Aiken, *Cotton Plantation South,* 225–26.

2. Aiken, *Cotton Plantation South,* 100–102, 110, 119–20, 130–31; Fite, *Cotton Fields No More,* 166, 183–85, 194; ASACUSSCCR Selma, O2–O3, N13–N14. Aiken sets the two phases of agriculture mechanization as 1935–42 and 1963–74. The Alamo Land Company, a soybean agribusiness, offered to buy land in Greene County at double the going rental rate.

3. Robin Reisig, "Block Factory in Greene County Plans to Build $3,500 Houses," *Southern Courier,* February 11–12, 1967; Reisig, "Farmers Lose Land"; VanDeburg, *New Day in Babylon,* 124.

4. Dittmer, *Local People,* 365. People involved in the civil rights movement had promoted the idea of forming cooperatives in Mississippi. A group of farmers formed an okra co-op in Panola County, and Jesse Morris of SNCC created the Poor People's Corporation "to assist low-income groups to initiate and sustain self-help projects of a cooperative nature."

5. USCCR Mont, 180; Turner, Interview by Author, 12; Cunningham, Interview by author, 16–17; Frye, *Black Parties and Political Power,* 62–63; ASACUSCCR Selma, N9–N10.

6. ACHR, "Rural Advancement Project Director," n.d., Box 41.1.1.1.32, SRC. The Southern Regional Council provided Black with research and publication facilities, and the National Sharecroppers Fund offered him training, technical advice and assistance, and programming aid.

7. Terry Cowles, "Farm Talk: New Rules Tell Farmer, Share Cotton Payments," *Southern Courier,* March 26–27, 1966; ASACUSCCR Selma, F11–F12, P26, L27–L28, X7–X8. Alabama state ASCS officials explained that any tenant who assigned his diversion payment to his landlord could "go to the office and find out exactly how much was

taken out of his payment, and what difference" remained. But many tenants did not know that this information was kept on file, and many tenants were intimidated by the idea of checking up on their landlords' transactions through an agency of the federal government.

8. ASACUSCCR Selma, A1–A7, R12–R14. Williams's house did not have running water; it was probably more like a sharecropper's dwelling.

9. Ibid., R18–R22.

10. Ibid.; "Advisory Committee," *Southern Courier,* April 2–3, 1966; NAACP Press Release, "Destitute Alabama Families Receive NAACP Assistance," February 5, 1967, Box 45, CAP Office Records of the Director, Subject Files 1965–69, RG 381; Robin Reisig, "Sumter Farmers Lose Their Homes 'Don't Know Where We're Going,'" *Southern Courier,* May 20–21, 1967; Zippert, Interview by Author, 32–33; Lewis Black, Quarterly Report, April–June 1968, January–February 1968, Box 41.1.2.1.37, SRC. Black worked with the Southern Development Cooperative to raise money for the Panola farmers. The American Friends Service Committee gave them fifteen thousand dollars, which the cooperative used to purchase land that had been foreclosed. The courts took three years to approve the sale. The farmers ended up with 1,164 acres and gave a parcel to the Federation of Southern Cooperatives for its training center.

11. Terry Cowles, "Tenants Say Planter Won't Share Payments in U.S. Cotton Plan," *Southern Courier,* April 2–3, 1966; ASACUSCCR Selma, I6–I7, I9, I11–I13; J. A. Minter and Sons Gin Company Records, Ralph Brown Draughon Library, Special Collections and Archives Department, Auburn University, Auburn, Ala.; Willis, *Lay My Burden Down.* Evidence indicates that Barlow ginned with Minter in 1945. Others who became involved in a lawsuit against Minter that arose from these ASCS changes are also found in these gin records dating back to 1945, including Otis Hale, Will Moorer, Elijah Green, Arthur Brown, Wil Gilcrest, Sinnie Blocton, Walter Blocton, and Will Williams.

12. ASACUSCCR Selma, I14–I18; Cowles, "Tenants Say Planter Won't Share Payments."

13. "News of the Field No. 8," April 13, 1966, Doc. 0540, A-VII-3, Reel 14, SNCC Papers; Rodney Karr, "Mrs. Moorer Goes to Washington: 'Like I Told the Vice-President,'" *Southern Courier,* April 23–24, 1966; Cowles, "Tenants Say Planter Won't Share."

14. Cowles, "Tenants Say Planter Won't Share."

15. ASACUSCCR Selma, I5, I16–I17; Robert E. Smith, "Rights Lawyers Open Selma Office," *Southern Courier,* June 18–19, 1966; Estelle Fine, "Appeals Judge Agrees with Dallas Farmers," *Southern Courier,* June 8–9, 1968; U.S. Commission on Civil Rights, "Staff Report: Voting and Political Participation by Blacks in the Sixteen Alabama Hearing Counties," Hearings Transcript, Montgomery, Alabama, April 27–May 2, 1968, 936–37. In June 1967, Federal District Judge Frank M. Johnson Jr. ruled that the Minter tenants could not sue the federal government but could seek judgment against Minter. In June 1968, U.S. Fifth Circuit Court of Appeals Judge Elbert P. Tuttle indicated his sympathies for the tenants' arguments. "I would think the government would be here to confess error," he told Norman Knopf, attorney for the federal government.

16. Bob Valder to Stokely Carmichael, June 6, 1966, Doc. 0457, A-I-52, Reel 2, SNCC; ASACUSCCR Selma, B19–B20, F4, F10–F11, N7, O2–O3; Lewis Black and Bob Valder, "Summary Report on an Evaluation of the Voter Education Project's Citizenship Education Grant to the ACHR for the 1966 ASCS Elections in Alabama," Box 41.2.7.3.22, SRC.

17. Stokely Carmichael to William M. Seabron, July 25, 1966, A-I-52, Reel 2, SNCC Papers; Nelson Lichtenstein, "ASCS: 'A Gut Issue,'" *Southern Courier,* July 30–31, 1966; "Bar to Farm Vote in Alabama Asked: Negro Group's Suit Seeks U.S. Court Injunction," *New York Times,* August 10, 1966, Doc. 0462, A-VIII-145, Reel 20, SNCC Papers; Nelson Lichtenstein, "Court Extends ASCS Elections; Ballots Not Due until September 15," *Southern Courier,* August 13–14, 1966. Carmichael wanted the USDA to oversee the election in Lowndes County: "We do not intend to have you tell us next year that the election is invalid," he told the official.

18. "Threatened after Testifying: ASCS Witness Flees State," *Southern Courier,* August 20–21, 1966; ASACUSCCR Selma, C18–C19. Agee moved to Memphis to live with relatives to avoid being killed.

19. ACHR, "A Partial Quarterly Report, July–September 1966," Box 41.1.2.1.36, SRC; Black and Valder, "Summary Report." Black spent more money in the counties with higher percentages of African American voters, which seemed to offer the best chance of electing black farmers to office. Those counties were Greene, Lowndes, Macon, Sumter, and Wilcox. The RAP project also assisted Choctaw, Clarke, Dallas, Hale, Marengo, Monroe, and Perry Counties.

20. Black and Valder, "Summary Report"; Mary Ellen Gale, "Negroes Lose ASCS in Bullock; Election to Be Re-Run in Macon," *Southern Courier,* September 24–25, 1966.

21. ACHR, Quarterly Report, October–December 1966, Box 41.1.2.1.36, SRC; Black and Valder, "Summary Report"; "No Negroes Elected to New ASCS County Committees," *Southern Courier,* October 8–9, 1966. The Macon ASCS elections were redone in October.

22. ACHR, Quarterly Report, October–December 1966; Black and Valder, "Summary Report"; "No Negroes Elected"; ASACUSCCR Selma, B7–B8, H22–H25, R4–R5, V1–V8, X17.

23. "No Negroes Elected"; Black and Valder, "Summary Report." Despite the failure to elect any African Americans to the county committee, Black and Valder found some good that came out of their effort. They thought that more people had become aware of the importance of the ASCS program; the county coordinators received important training in conducting a countywide election effort; and some gains occurred in most of the Black Belt counties.

24. ASACUSCCR Selma, L20, P41, S7–S9, X14; Alabama ASCS Annual Report 1967, 3–4, Box SG8857, ACAI.

25. "No Negroes Elected"; Black and Valder, "Summary Report."

26. ASACUSCCR Selma, H4–H8, H35–H36; Wayne Hurder, "Negro Farmers Bury Their Cotton Crops," *Southern Courier,* September 30, 1966.

27. ASACUSCCR Selma, H8–H9, H13–H14, H17–H18, H21, H32–H35, T4–T5.

28. ACHR, Quarterly Report, April–June 1966; Lewis Black, Alabama Report, ca. late 1966, Box 41.2.7.3.22, SRC; Cunningham, Interview by Author, 1–3; Reisig, "Sumter Farmers Lose Their Homes"; Turner, Interview by Author, 1, 3; Payne, *I've Got the Light of Freedom,* 330. The civil rights activists who formed the CDGM also viewed the project as a way to provide work for people who had lost their jobs because of their activism.

29. SWAFCA to Sargent Shriver, July 28, 1966, "The Southwest Alabama Farmers Cooperative (SWAFCA)," July 28, 1966, Inspection Reports Evaluating CAP, Box 1, RG 381.

30. State Work Plan and Fund Request to USDA from Alabama Department of Agriculture and Industries, Project No. ALA-A-7, ca. 1966, James L. Lawson to [M. R.] Glasscock, January 14, 1965, Box SG8847, ACAI; M. R. Glasscock to County Extension Chairs in Mobile, Wilcox, Limestone, Chilton, Colbert, and Lauderdale Counties, November 17, 1965, Richard Beard to Walter Sinsel, July 12, 1967, Box SG8846, ACAI; Auburn University Extension Service, "Fruits and Vegetables for Processing in Alabama," n.d., "How Assembly Markets Can Be Used More Effectively to Meet the Requirements of Large Buyers and to Improve Producers' Returns," October 20, 1967, Box SG8856, ACAI; "State Farm Cooperatives Do Record $9 Million Business," *Birmingham News,* August 13, 1965, TSHC; Fite, *Cotton Fields No More,* 13; Aiken, *Cotton Plantation South,* 54–55, 74; "Southwest Alabama Farmers Cooperative Association (SWAFCA)"; Turner, Interview by Author, 11–12. Turner remembered that Mesher first contacted OEO and that she was involved in writing the grant proposal.

31. John A. Baker, Interview III, 49–50, LBJOHC; Aiken, *Cotton Plantation South,* 246; Theodore M. Berry to Sargent Shriver, April 14, 1967, CAP Office Records of the Director, Subject Files 1965–69, Box 45, RG 381.

32. Theodore M. Berry to Sargent Shriver, April 14, 1967, CAP Office Records of the Director, Subject Files 1965–69, Box 45, RG 381; Lewis Black, ACHR RAP Report for January–March 1967, Box 41.2.7.3.22, SRC; ACHR Quarterly Report, October–December 1966; Plan for Agricultural Readjustment Program, ca. December 1966, Inspection Reports Evaluating CAP, Box 1, RG 381; Minutes of Southwest Alabama Cooperative Association Meeting, January 5, 1967, Box 41.2.7.3.22, SRC; Mesher, Interview by Author, 12. Joe R. Johnson had been active in the Dallas County grassroots group, SHAPE, and when Dallas County residents tried to obtain a CAP grant. He had close ties to Mesher.

33. Plan for Agricultural Readjustment Program; B. L. Collins to Joe Johnson, January 13, 1967, CAP Office Records of the Director, Subject Files 1965–69, Box 45, RG 381; Minutes of Southwest Alabama Cooperative Association Meeting, Dallas County, January 14, 1967, Box 41.2.7.3.22, SRC. B. L. Collins, state executive director of the ASCS program, declined the invitation to come to the meeting, explaining, "We do not feel the matters you plan to discuss come within the scope of our Agency's responsibilities."

34. Minutes of Southwest Alabama Cooperative Association Meeting, Dallas County, January 14, 1967. Many state- and national-level USDA officials had been named as codefendants in *Barlow v. Minter.* Merkeson may have offered assistance to the co-op as a way to counter the agriculture secretary's status as a defendant in the case.

35. Black, ACHR RAP Report, January–March 1967; Turner, Interview by Author, 12; Joseph Bradford, "Contacts in Alabama, January 13–14, 1967," Box 378, LH; Bertrand Harding to Joseph S. Knight, May 9, 1967, Program Records of the Assistant Director for Civil Rights, Box 1, RG 381. After SWAFCA received an OEO grant, Harding explained why the agency had ignored Bradford's warnings: "Since that time the proposal has undergone many changes. As currently written, the project gives every indication of being economically feasible." He clarified that OEO did not require unanimity in its project appraisals, especially when demonstration projects were under review. "Of the six field representatives that OEO sent to Alabama to examine the project, Dr. Bradford was alone in questioning the proposal's economic feasibility."

36. Black, ACHR RAP Report, January–March 1967; Theodore M. Berry to Sargent Shriver, April 14, 1967, SWAFCA Multi-County Board Members, CAP Office Records of the Director, Subject Files 1965–67, Box 45, RG 381; Reisig, "Sumter Farmers Lose Their Homes"; Robin Reisig, "'Fighting to Stay on the Land' Farmers Joining New Cooperative," *Southern Courier,* February 18–19, 1967. The other nine board members were Anthony Butler from Choctaw County, Searcy Hill from Hale County, Earnest Essex and Horace Jones from Marengo County, Prince Black and Fred Mims from Monroe County, William Palmer from Sumter County, and Eddie Witherspoon and Will Burrell from Wilcox County.

37. "SWAFCA Land and Crop Information," March 17, 1967, Rural Services Division of CAP, "Rural Opportunities: Cooperatives: How Farmer Cooperative Service Can Help," October 1967, CAP Office Records of the Director, Subject Files 1965–69, Box 45, RG 381; "Black Belt Tempest: Politics and Poverty: In the Beginning, a Girl's Curiosity about Soil Testing—Then Tempest," *Birmingham News,* June 12, 1967, Box 379, LH; Black, ACHR RAP Report, January–March 1967; Mesher, Interview by Author, 11, 22, 43; Clara Walker, Testimony, USCCR Mont, 174–75. Louise and Freeman Berry participated in the same way as the Walkers—she ran the farm while he worked somewhere else.

38. Black, ACHR RAP Report, January–March 1967; SWAFCA Meeting with State FHA, February 16, 1967, Box 41.2.7.3.22, SRC.

39. Fite, *Cotton Fields No More,* 86, 160, 177; John A. Baker, Interview III, 49–50, 53–55, LBJOHC; Daniel, "African American Farmers and Civil Rights," 4–5; Robert C. Bamberg to Richard Beard, February 1, 1967, Box SG8851, ACAI; "Robert Chalmers Bamberg, Jr.," Alabama Academy of Honor, http://www.archives.state.al.us/famous/academy/r_bamber.html. Fite offers two reasons why the FHA denied credit to SWAFCA members. First, since the 1920s, a stereotype of black farmers prevailed in the South that held that they were "unable to implement improved practices . . . because of their ignorance and need for close supervision." Some white officials even thought that black people could grow only "a few staple crops." Second, the initial rationale behind the USDA farm support programs had been to support the family farm. As the programs became more developed, however, they primarily assisted commercial farmers.

40. Theodore M. Berry to Sargent Shriver, April 14, 1967, CAP Office Records of the Director, Subject Files 1965–69, Box 45, RG 381; Turner, Interview by Author, 1; Richard Beard to Joe Johnson, March 31, 1967, Box SG8852, ACAI; Highlight Memorandum for SWAFCA Initial Grant Application, March 14, 1967, CAP Office Records of the Director, Subject Files 1965–69, Box 45, RG 381; Lewis Black, Report on the RAP, ca. 1967, Box 41.2.7.3.23, SRC; Black, ACHR RAP Report, January–March 1967; David R. Underhill, "John Hulett Tells New York People about Lowndes Freedom Party," *Southern Courier,* March 11–12, 1967; Kate Harris, "OEO Fight Taken to Capital against Grant to 'Black Power' Group," *Birmingham News,* April 4, 1967, SWAFCA Binder.

41. John V. Wilson, "From Black Belt—Poverty Plan Foes Gather in Capital," *Birmingham Post Herald,* April 5, 1967, SWAFCA Binder. The *Post Herald* reported that SWAFCA was the first program of its type in the nation.

42. Biographical Directory of the U.S. Congress, http://bioguide.congress.gov/scripts/biodisplay; "Resistance to Collective Is Being Organized Here," *Selma Times Journal,* March 31, 1967, "Resolution Opposes Grant—Eight Counties Share Protest," *Selma Times Journal,* April 3, 1967, SWAFCA Binder; Joe T. Smitherman and B. A. Reynolds to Lister Hill, ca. March 1967, Box 378, LH; Don F. Wasson, "Proposed Co-op Creates Furor: Civil Rights Coverup, Claim Local Officials," *Montgomery Advertiser,* SWAFCA Binder; Kate Harris, "OEO Fight Taken to Capital"; Payne, *I've Got the Light of Freedom,* 343; Howard A. Glickstein, Statement, USCCR Mont, 184. The CDGM faced similar opposition from Mississippi elected officials when it applied for a Head Start grant, but unlike the CDGM, the ten-county SWAFCA region utilized approximately $16 million in ASCS funding alone. Smitherman had reason to be concerned.

43. Roy Reed, "Leaders of Negro Farm Co-op in Alabama Go to Washington to Seek Funds," *New York Times,* April 12, 1967, CAP Office Records of the Director, Subject Files 1965–69, Box 45, RG 381; "Resolution Opposes Grant"; "Overview of April 5, 1967, Meeting of Alabama Delegation to Oppose SWAFCA Grant," Box 378, LH; John V. Wilson, "By OEO Official—Probe of Co-Op Project Promised," *Birmingham Post Herald,* April 6, 1967, SWAFCA Binder; Wasson, "Proposed Co-op Creates Furor"; Kate Harris, "OEO Fight Taken to Capital"; Wilson, "From Black Belt"; Alabama Legislative Commission to Preserve the Peace, "Southwest Alabama Farmers Cooperative Association," ca. April 1967, Box 378, LH; "White Officials Attack SWAFCA, but Co-op Leaders Confident," *Southern Courier,* April 8–9, 1967, SWAFCA Binder. Those who attended the Washington meeting included R. C. Hadly, King-Pharr Canning Company; L. B. Whitfield III, W & W Pickle Company; W. H. Knight, probate judge of Hale County; Crowell Pate Jr., mayor of Lowndesboro; Bill Dannelly, probate judge of Wilcox County; Frank Thomas, Marengo County commissioner; B. A. Reynolds, probate judge of Dallas County; Joe T. Smitherman, mayor of Selma; Leigh Pegues, mayor of Marion; Joe Knight, director, Dallas County–City of Selma CAA; and R. P. Swofford, state OEO office. Other members of Congress who attended included U.S. Senator John Sparkman of Alabama and U.S. Representatives Armistead Selden, William Nichols, Tom Bevill, and Jack Edwards, also from Alabama.

44. Rogers et al., *Alabama*, 568, 577; Grafton and Permaloff, *Big Mules and Branch-heads*, 52; Permaloff and Grafton, "Chop-Up Bill"; Lister Hill to R. C. Handley, April 5, 1967; Louis B. Whitfield Jr. to Lister Hill, ca. April 3, April 13, 1967, Box 379, LH; Turner, Interview by Author, 1–2; Richard Beard, Speech to Farm Equipment Dealers Annual Meeting, November 30, 1967, Richard Beard, Speech to FHA Employees, Box SG8856, ACAI; Lurleen B. Wallace, "Speech before the Legislature of Alabama in Joint Session Assembled, First Special Session," March 30, 1967, Box SG22453, AGF.

45. SAI Report from the Alabama Legislative Commission to Preserve the Peace, "Organizations Operating in the Southeastern U.S. Whose Purposes or Programs Might Cause Breach of the Peace or Pose Problems for Law Enforcement," January 15, 1967, Edwin Strickland, "Confidential Report to Governor George C. Wallace," September 13, 1966, Edwin Strickland to Lurleen B. Wallace, March 21, 1967, Box SG21074, Alabama Legislative Commission to Preserve the Peace Papers, Alabama Department of Archives and History, Montgomery; James Free, "OEO Urged Not to OK Grant for Farmers Co-Op," *Birmingham News,* April 5, 1967; Dan T. Carter, *Politics of Rage,* 232–33. One of the issues that the opposition brought up at the OEO meeting was SWAFCA's request for two-way radios for five trucks. Opponents feared that the radios would be used for "civil rights and political activities." Most SWAFCA members lacked telephones, and the cooperative needed to communicate with its officials in each of the ten counties. Carter has found that the Peace Commission was not known for its accuracy in its investigations: "Incompetence, indeed, sheer stupidity, characterized the day-to-day operations of the Peace Commission." Although its reports were often egregiously inaccurate, the Peace Commission continued to do damage when reporters circulated its findings in newspaper articles that legitimized its claims.

46. Rogers et al., *Alabama,* 573; Dan T. Carter, *Politics of Rage,* 232; John H. Hawkins Jr., report, April 4, 1967, Box SG21074, Alabama Legislative Commission to Preserve the Peace Papers; Fairclough, *Race and Democracy,* 301; Chris Waddle, "Woman behind SWAFCA Is Illusive," *Birmingham Post Herald,* June 19, 1968, SWAFCA Binder; "Overview of April 5, 1967, Meeting."

47. Robert Walters, "OEO Faces Controversy over Alabama Co-Op," *Washington Star,* April 12, 1967, SWAFCA Binder; Aiken, *Cotton Plantation South,* 251; "Overview of April 5, 1967, Meeting"; Louis B. Whitfield to Lister Hill, June 2, 1967, Box 379, LH.

48. Highlight Memorandum for SWAFCA Initial Grant Application; Turner, Interview by Author, 2–3; Fairclough, *Race and Democracy,* 385; Robin Reisig, "'To Hell with Laws of U.S.,'" *Southern Courier,* April 1–2, 1967.

49. Donald K. Hess to Theodore M. Berry, May 25, 1967, CAP Office Records of the Director, Subject Files 1965–69, Box 45, RG 381; Rogers et al., *Alabama,* 562; "White Officials Attack SWAFCA"; Frye, *Black Parties and Political Power,* 103; Payne, *I've Got the Light of Freedom,* 340–41, 358, 361; Dittmer, *Local People,* 378, 381; Kate Harris, "Minister Tells OEO Personnel in Co-op Protested by Negro," *Birmingham News,* May 14, 1967, SWAFCA Binder; "OEO Wigglers," *Selma Times Journal,* May 30, 1967, SSE. Payne and Dittmer document similar splits in Mississippi black politics after 1965 when the CDGM and the Mississippi Action for Progress vied to serve as the "new

face of the freedom movement" in the state. According to Payne, a loss of moral clarity affected the entire movement. Goals seemed to shift without being clearly articulated; "it had become more difficult to say what the movement was trying to do. . . . [S]ome of what was called selling out in 1968 would have been called progress had it happened in 1963." The rift that occurred between the DCVL and SWAFCA's supporters fits this example. After OEO announced that SWAFCA would receive the grant, Reese traveled to Washington to protest, primarily because of Mesher's involvement with the project.

50. "White Officials Attack SWAFCA"; Orzell Billingsley Jr. to Ira Kaye, April 3, 1967, CAP Office Records of the Director, State Files 1965–68, Box 14, RG 381; Maurice A. Dawkins, "Inspection Requirements," April 11, 1967, Program Records of the Assistant Director for Civil Rights, Box 8, RG 381; Theodore M. Berry, "Orzell Billingsley," October 3, 1967, CAP Office Records of the Director, State Files 1965–68, Box 14, RG 381; Michael S. Lottman, "Lewis, Mrs. Johnson Hit Co-op, but Gomillion Indicates Approval," *Southern Courier,* April 15–16, 1967; C. W. to Don, "SWAFCA," May 5, 1967, Box 379, LH; Frye, *Black Parties and Political Power,* 42–43, 160–61. Not every member of the "traditional Negro leadership class" spoke out against SWAFCA. Longtime activist C. G. Gomillion of Tuskegee said he was inclined to be in favor of SWAFCA. "Any folk in any county who can establish and operate a cooperative ought to have the opportunity to do it," he said. "If local people are interested enough to try to establish one, they should receive all the help they can get."

51. Frye, *Black Parties and Political Power,* 42–43; Berry, "Orzell Billingsley." By the fall of 1967, OEO reported that Billingsley "has generally not been a supporter of OEO programs and policies. . . . Mr. Billingsley supported the Wallaces in the last election and considers most of the Negroes now working in OEO programs to be irresponsible and radical."

52. "How Will OEO Funds Be Spent? By Whom?" *Selma Times Journal,* April 9, 1967, "That Co-op," *Birmingham Post Herald,* April 6, 1967, SWAFCA Binder; "SWAFCA Deserves a Try," *Southern Courier,* April 15–16, 1967.

53. "OEO Cooperation on Protest Is Pleasing," *Selma Times Journal,* April 6, 1967, SWAFCA Binder; Wilson, "From Black Belt."

54. Bertrand M. Harding to Joseph S. Knight, May 9, 1967, L. Sylvester Odum to Theodore M. Berry and Maurice Dawkins, April 7, 1967, Theodore M. Berry to Sargent Shriver, April 14, 1967, CAP Office Records of the Director, Subject Files 1965–69, Box 45, RG 381; William Selover, "Negro Cooperative Triggers Test," *Christian Science Monitor,* May 17, 1967, Box 379, LH.

55. "Priests Approve of Co-op Plans," *Selma Times Journal,* April 6, 1967, SWAFCA Binder; "White Officials Attack SWAFCA"; John Crowley to Sargent Shriver, April 3, 1967, CAP Office Records of the Director, Subject Files 1965–69, Box 45, RG 381.

56. Black, ACHR RAP Report, January–March 1967; Robert Swann to Peter Michelson, March 27, 1967, CAP Office Records of the Director, Subject Files 1965–69, Box 45, RG 381; Black, Report on the RAP; Beth Wilcox, "SWAFCA Leaders Answer White Officials' Charges," *Southern Courier,* May 20–21, 1967, SWAFCA Binder. Al Ulmer

of the Southern Regional Council helped SWAFCA secure these loans. Twenty-five people from Atlanta cosigned the loan for one thousand dollars each.

57. Reed, "Leaders of Negro Farm Co-op"; Joe Johnson and Calvin Orsborn to Sargent Shriver, ca. April 1967, Isabel Schmitz-Dumont and Joan Mulder to Sargent Shriver, April 10, 1967, SIP Newsletter, April 12, 1967, CAP Office Records of the Director, Box 45, RG 381; Beth Wilcox, "Co-op Members Wait for Decision on Grant," *Southern Courier,* May 6–7, 1967; Selover, "Negro Cooperative Triggers Test."

58. OEO Press Release, "Farm Cooperative Grant to Ten Alabama Counties," May 11, 1967, Program Records of the Assistant Director for Civil Rights, Speeches, Box 1, RG 381; Bertrand M. Harding to Joseph S. Knight, May 9, 1967, L. Sylvester Odum to Theodore M. Berry and Maurice Dawkins, April 7, 1967, Theodore M. Berry to Sargent Shriver, April 14, 1967, John Dean to Ira Kaye, March 28, 1967, SWAFCA Statement of CAP Grant, Section 207 Demonstration, ca. May 1967, "Response to Research Program Planning and Evaluation's Objections," n.d., CAP Office Records of the Director, Subject Files 1965–69, Box 45, RG 381; Selover, "Negro Cooperative Triggers Test." SWAFCA originally wanted five hundred thousand dollars for a two-phase project, with the first phase the producing and marketing cooperative and the second phase a rural development project for health care, vegetable processing, credit unions, and other similar programs. OEO officials decided to concentrate only on the first phase of the grant application.

59. Theodore M. Berry, "Proposed Grant to SWAFCA," April 14, 1967, CAP Office Records of the Director, Subject Files 1965–69, Box 45, RG 381. Berry was ready to fund SWAFCA by April 14. "This has been a complex and difficult project to develop," he told Shriver, "but it holds great promise for OEO."

60. Donald K. Hess, "SWAFCA," April 11, 1967, John A. Baker, "SWAFCA Project," April 13, 1967, CAP Office Records of the Director, Subject Files 1965–69, Box 45, RG 381.

61. John A. Baker, Interview III, 22–28, LBJOHC; Edward A. Tenenbaum to Gerson M. Greene, April 11, 1967, Genie Gans to Gerson Greene, "'Outside' Review of SWAFCA Proposal," April 12, 1967, CAP Office Records of the Director, Subject Files 1965–69, Box 45, RG 381. Tenenbaum liked the fact that SWAFCA was a self-help initiative. "Much can be done *with* the people of underdeveloped areas, but very little of lasting benefit can be done *for* them," he told Greene. Edward Hollander of Robert R. Nathan Associates told OEO that SWAFCA was the kind of program OEO should be doing. Both men advised OEO that technical service would be the key to SWAFCA's success.

62. Robert L. Martin, "SWAFCA," April 17, 1967, CAP Office Records of the Director, Subject Files 1965–69, Box 70, RG 381; Frank K. Sloan to Bertrand M. Harding, April 28, 1967, Bertrand Harding to Sargent Shriver, May 3, 1967, Louis Lloyd Anderson to Sargent Shriver, April 9, 1967, CAP Office Records of the Director, Subject Files 1965–69, Box 45, RG 381. Harding used Smitherman's actions to respond to a request from Reynolds and Nichols, who presented Harding with a new proposal under which the Selma CAP would operate some of SWAFCA's functions. Harding responded that

the "Mayor's actions did little to increase our faith in the viability and independence of the CAA." He told Shriver, "I think we've got a good whip here."

63. Donald M. Baker, Interview, Tape 4, 8–9, LBJOHC; Lister Hill, Press Release, May 26, 1967, Box 379, LH; Wilcox, "Co-op Members Wait"; Dittmer, *Local People*, 379; Crespino, *In Search of Another Country*, 19; Califano, *Triumph and Tragedy*, 56. Hill refused to send an aide to investigate the co-op because that would be "meddling" in local politics. LBJ also disliked Wallace, which may have freed OEO from worrying about confronting his wife.

64. Schulman, *Lyndon B. Johnson and American Liberalism*, 113; HHrgHR10440, pt. 1, 259; Theodore M. Berry to Sargent Shriver, April 14, 1967, CAP Office Records of the Director, Subject Files 1965–69, Box 45, RG 381; OEO Press Release, May 11, 1967, Maurice A. Dawkins to Sargent Shriver, May 11, 1967, Maurice A. Dawkins to Floyd McKissick, May 15, 1967, Program Records of the Assistant Director for Civil Rights, Box 1, RG 381. OEO compiled statistics on rural migration for 1960–64: "Within the ten county area that would be affected by this proposed project members of SWAFCA have already identified 300 families that have lost, or will shortly lose, their farms. The proposed project attempts to demonstrate a method for arresting this unfortunate trend." One item on the agenda for a June 1 meeting with civil rights leaders was whether SWAFCA could be duplicated in Georgia and Mississippi. Dawkins also told McKissick that SWAFCA "has many civil rights implications and as a demonstration project, might have very significant impact on the future of the rural South."

65. Walt Robbins to Maurice Dawkins, April 15, 1967, Office of Civil Rights Correspondence with Regional Civil Rights Leaders, Box 7, RG 381; Dittmer, *Local People*, 381.

66. "'Black Panther' OEO Grant Provokes Anger in Selma," *Birmingham News*, May 11, 1967, TSHC; "Noon Bulletin," *Selma Times Journal*, May 11, 1967, "State Officials to Join Protest against OEO," *Selma Times Journal*, May 12, 1967, Jim McGregor, "Governor Promises Veto of Grant to Farm Co-op," *Montgomery Advertiser*, May 12, 1967, Frank Brock and Mac Porterfield, "Poverty Fund Veto Vowed," *Birmingham Post Herald*, May 12, 1967, SWAFCA Binder; Selover, "Negro Cooperative Triggers Test."

67. "Selma Mayor Probes Action Possibility," *Montgomery Advertiser*, May 12, 1967, Kate Harris, "Mayor Asks FBI Probe Anti-Poverty Officials," *Birmingham News*, May 17, 1967, Box 379, LH; "State Officials to Join Protest"; "State Alleges Link of SNCC, Grant," *Birmingham News*, May 15, 1967, TSHC; Mac Porterfield, "SNCC Plot Charge Made," *Birmingham Post Herald*, May 15, 1967, TSHC; Wilcox, "SWAFCA Leaders Answer"; "Hysteria over SWAFCA," *Southern Courier*, May 20–21, 1967; Donald J. Cronin to James L. Lawson, May 25, 1967, Box SG8847, ACAI; ASACUSCCR Selma, H26–H27, N13; "OEO Slates Another Probe," *Birmingham News*, June 7, 1967, TSHC. Editors encouraged defenders of SWAFCA to write to Shriver expressing support for the cooperative. They thought one of the strongest features of the grant was the fact that local officials were not involved with SWAFCA. Lawson suggested that Hill issue a statement against the cooperative after Smitherman's press conference. Donald Baker told Senator Hill that the material Smitherman found in the briefcase dealt with another proposed Alabama co-op rather than SWAFCA.

68. "State Officials to Join Protest"; Brock and Porterfield, "Poverty Fund Veto Vowed"; "Selma Mayor Probes Action Possibility." The Wilcox County SCLC had campaigned against Cooper in the 1966 elections; Hawkins sponsored the Legislative Commission to Preserve the Peace.

69. "Black Belt Tempest: Politics and Poverty: Is New Group of Poor Farmers or Boondoggle and Spawner of Strife?" *Birmingham News,* June 11, 1967, SWAFCA Binder; "Black Belt Tempest: Politics and Poverty: In the Beginning, a Girl's Curiosity about Soil Testing"; "Black Belt Tempest: Politics and Poverty," *Birmingham News,* June 13, 1967, Box 379, LH; "Black Belt Tempest: Politics and Poverty," *Birmingham News,* June 14, 1967, Box SG6944, PISF; "Black Belt Tempest: Politics and Poverty: Co-op Head Depicts Area's Dire Need," *Birmingham News,* June 15, 1967, Box 379, LH; Turner, Interview by Author, 11; R. C. Bamberg, Testimony, USCCR Mont, 238. In the June 11 article, the *News* described Mesher as "a plump, busy, aggressive young woman." It further maligned her when it said, "Mesher, by choice and even profession, is a civil rights worker; a welfare sympathist; an activist; confidant and advisor to the Negro, and a girl who, of recent date, has learned how to make soil test[s]." Turner thought the press focused harshly on SWAFCA: "They never let up on SWAFCA, they fought it from day one. . . . They fought anything they thought was progressive." In 1968 the Alabama Farm Home Administration employed 203 people, of whom 5 were black. USDA state programs could not really claim to be fully integrated.

70. "OEO Grant Is Vetoed by Lurleen," *Birmingham Post Herald,* June 9, 1967, TSHC; Robert E. Baker, "OEO Grant to Co-op in Alabama Stirs Clash," *Washington Post,* May 11, 1967, CAP Office Records of the Director, Subject Files 1965–69, Box 45, RG 381; "Lurleen Warns Shriver She'll Take OEO Probe to Congress," *Birmingham News,* June 17, 1967, TSHC; Lurleen Wallace to Sargent Shriver, June 16, 1967, CAP Office Records of the Director, Subject Files 1965–69, Box 45, RG 381; "ASCS Program Will Be Held Here Two Days," *Selma Times Journal,* May 24, 1967, SWAFCA Binder; Beth Wilcox, "At Selma Hearings: Farmers Hit ASCS," *Southern Courier,* June 3–4, 1967; Robin Reisig, "Something's Wrong with Greene Juries—Jelinek," *Southern Courier,* June 10–11, 1967. Wallace's claim that a Black Power group wanted to assassinate her referred to a comment by Carmichael, who was no longer the chairman of SNCC. He told black people in Birmingham that if they were given guns to go to Vietnam, they should use them instead on "Lurleen, George, and Little Junior." The Alabama Advisory Committee to the U.S. Commission on Civil Rights held open meetings regarding the ASCS program in Alabama while Wallace decided on the SWAFCA grant. Some of the recommendations and testimony heard at these hearings could have also contributed to her veto of the cooperative's proposal. At the same time, Jelinek brought a suit against the Greene County jury system, thereby threatening to pull down another plank in the white supremacy barricade in the Black Belt. Jelinek openly supported SWAFCA.

71. Turner, Interview by Author, 10–13; Cunningham, Interview by Author, 3–6, 8; Williams, Interview, HTFOHC; Johnson, Interview, HTFOHC; SIP Newsletter, April 12, 1967, CAP Office Records of the Director, Subject Files 1965–69, Box 45, RG 381.

72. Lewis Black, Quarterly Report, April–June 1967, Box 41.2.1.37, SRC; Black, ACHR RAP Report, January–March 1967; Black, Report on the RAP, ca. 1967; Beth Wilcox, "Farm Head Tours South; What's a Negro Cucumber?" *Southern Courier,* July 1–2, 1967; Cunningham, Interview by Author, 11. Cunningham remembered that Detroit's Vlasic Pickle Company accepted SWAFCA's cucumbers. He too blamed Alabama officials for cutting off the co-op's markets. Specifically, Cunningham thought that Governor Wallace told buyers to stay away from SWAFCA because it had stolen the cucumber market from Whitfield.

73. Black, Report on the RAP, ca. 1967; "Black Belt Tempest: Politics and Poverty: In the Beginning, a Girl's Curiosity about Soil Testing."

74. "Secretary's Trip Smells of Politics Says Mayor: 'He'd Be Welcome Here,'" *Selma Times Journal,* June 25, 1967, James Free, "About 'Gestures'—Freeman Tour Causes Buzzing," *Birmingham News,* July 2, 1967, "Freeman Bullets through Selma on Extended Tour," Unidentified Newspaper Clipping, June 29, 1967, Mac Porterfield, "Freeman Takes Hard Look at State Poor," *Birmingham Post Herald,* June 29, 1967, SWAFCA Binder; Black, Report on the RAP, ca. 1967; Beth Wilcox, "SWAFCA Gains from Secretary Freeman's Visit," *Southern Courier,* July 29–30, 1967; Tom Cosgrove, "SWAFCA," June 27, 1967, CAP Office Records of the Director, Subject Files 1965–69, Box 45, RG 381. Freeman had asked OEO to wait until he returned from the Black Belt before announcing SWAFCA's receipt of the grant.

75. Sargent Shriver to Joe T. Smitherman, June 30, 1967, Box 379, LH; Wilcox, "Farm Head Tours South"; Continental-Allied Company, Monthly Evaluation Report on SWAFCA, No. 1, October 18, 1967, CAP Office Records of the Director, Subject Files 1965–69, Box 45, RG 381; Cunningham, Interview by Author, 11; Turner, Interview by Author, 9; Dan T. Carter, *Politics of Rage,* 234; Thomas F. Hill, "In 10 County Area Farm Expert Helps Set up Farm Co-op," *Birmingham News,* July 23, 1967, SWAFCA Binder; Calvin Orsborn, Testimony, USCCR Mont, 175. Carter has explained that the real muscle behind the Peace Commission was the antisubversive unit of the state Department of Public Safety. It is not known if the troopers who stopped the SWAFCA trucks were part of this unit, but it would not be surprising if state officials supported this harassment.

76. "Veto Overruled on SWAFCA," *Birmingham News,* July 6, 1967, "OEO Overrides Veto on Farmers' Co-op," *Birmingham Post Herald,* July 7, 1967, TSHC; Selover, "Negro Cooperative Triggers Test"; Lister Hill to Joe T. Smitherman, July 5, 1967, Box 379, LH; Jim McGregor, "OEO Overrides Veto of Antipoverty Aid," *Montgomery Advertiser,* July 6, 1967, "Co-op Gets the Money," *Birmingham Post Herald,* July 7, 1967, SWAFCA Binder. A total of seventeen programs had been vetoed by governors to date. Shriver had previously overridden one veto by the governor of Mississippi and one by George Wallace. The editors of the *Post Herald* wondered how the cooperative could use the four hundred thousand dollars since planting season had almost passed. This again provides evidence that the newspaper did not investigate before making statements about SWAFCA. It was clear that farming had been under way since May.

77. "SWAFCA Jobs," *Southern Courier,* June 10–11, 1967; Robin Reisig, "Cabinet Member Meets Farmers: 'We Have to Stick Together,'" *Southern Courier,* July 15–16,

1967, "Farmers Finally Get OK," *Southern Courier*, July 7–8, 1967, Joe R. Johnson to "Dear Pastor," July 1967, SWAFCA Newsletter, July 9, 1967, SWAFCA Binder.

78. SWAFCA Newsletter, July 9, 1967, SWAFCA Binder; Wilcox, "SWAFCA Gains"; Hill, "In 10 County Area"; Rural Services Division of CAP, "Rural Opportunities"; Polly G. Lester and A. V. Smith to Richard Beard, September 21, 1967, Box SG8849, ACAI; Lewis Black, Report, July 15–22, 1967, Box 41.2.7.3.23, SRC; Black, Report on the RAP, ca. 1967; Sargent Shriver to Orville Freeman, September 6, 1967, CAP Office Records of the Director, Subject Files, 1965–69, Box 45, RG 381.

79. Lewis Black, Report, July 24–29, 1967, August 1967, Box 41.2.7.3.23, SRC; Lewis Black, Annual Report 1967, Box 41.2.7.3.24, SRC; Cunningham, Interview by Author, 6–9; Marshall and Godwin, *Cooperatives and Rural Poverty*, 49–50.

80. Continental-Allied Company, Monthly Evaluation Report on SWAFCA, No. 1; James Free, "In South Alabama: OEO-Supported Farm Co-op Spends over $2 to Make $1," *Birmingham News*, October 13, 1967, TSHC; Stephen Darst, "SWAFCA Means Prosperity for 'Black Belt' Farmers," *Oklahoma Courier*, January 1, 1968, SWAFCA Binder; Calvin Orsborn, Testimony, USCCR Mont, 178–79, 185. Through September 4, 1967, SWAFCA handled 593,082 pounds of pickling cucumbers, 52,703 pounds of fresh market cucumbers, 438,029 pounds of okra, 142,941 pounds of southern peas, 409 pounds of butter beans, and 2,200 pounds of sweet potatoes.

81. Continental-Allied Company, Monthly Evaluation Report on SWAFCA, No. 1; Continental-Allied Company, Monthly Evaluation Report on SWAFCA, No. 2, January 8, 1968, CAP Office Records of the Director, Subject Files 1965–69, Box 45, RG 381; Polly G. Lester and A. V. Smith, "SWAFCA," December 4, 1967, Box SG8849, ACAI; "Okra for SWAFCA," *Southern Courier*, September 30–October 1, 1967.

82. Continental-Allied Company, Monthly Evaluation Report on SWAFCA, No. 1; Gerson M. Greene, "SWAFCA 'Open House,'" CAP Office Records of the Director, Subject Files 1965–69, Box 45, RG 381. Ed Tenenbaum of Continental-Allied thought SWAFCA really needed $1.7 million to meet its future needs, while OEO's Gerson M. Greene estimated that SWAFCA required $1.2 million. USDA staff working in Selma thought $400,000 would be enough.

83. Joe Johnson to Sargent Shriver, October 31, 1967, Theodore M. Berry to Joe R. Johnson, November 17, 1967, Gerson M. Greene to Theodore M. Berry, November 17, 1967, Rural Services Division of OEO, "Rural Opportunities—SWAFCA Celebrates First Year," January 1968, CAP Office Records of the Director, Subject Files 1965–69, Box 45, RG 381.

84. James Free, "After Original $400,000 Spent, SWAFCA's Federal Funds to End," *Birmingham News*, November 5, 1967, SWAFCA Binder; James Free, "Antipoverty Program Takes a Cut, about $5.5 Million in Alabama," *Birmingham News*, November 19, 1967, TSHC; "Projects in South Survive," *Southern Courier*, December 9–10, 1967; Black, Annual Report 1967.

85. Frye, *Black Parties and Political Power*, 73–74; Bob Labaree, "To Oppose Wallace: New Party Is Formed," *Southern Courier*, December 16–17, 1967; "Alabama Democrats: Loyalists Still Swapping Jabs," *Birmingham News*, March 24, 1968, TSHC; Peggy Roberson, "On July 20: National Democrat Group to Name Slate Here," *Birmingham News*,

July 12, 1968, TSHC. The AIDP's incorporation papers stated that the "party shall have no members. Persons supporting the political efforts of the corporation shall retain their membership in previously established political parties and shall be free to support the candidates of other political parties for public office."

86. Frye, *Black Parties and Political Power,* 24; Cynthia Smith, "ADC Gains Reputation as Political Power," *Alabama Journal and Advertiser,* February 3, 1985, Box SG6938, PISF; Bob Labaree, "Alabama Gets 2nd 'Loyal' Party," *Southern Courier,* January 20–21, 1968.

87. Frye, *Black Parties and Political Power,* 34, 36, 120; VanDeburg, *New Day in Babylon,* 127–28.

88. Kate Harris, "Co-op to Be Required to Show Soundness," *Birmingham News,* March 17, 1968, SWAFCA Binder; James Free, "SWAFCA Probe Promised," *Birmingham News,* March 17, 1968, SWAFCA Binder; Olga Boikess and William Kopit, "Proposed Terms of SWAFCA Loan," April 3, 1968, CAP Office Records of the Director, Subject Files 1965–69, Box 70, RG 381; "Black Belt Negroes in Servitude, Is Charge," *Birmingham Post Herald,* June 15, 1968, SWAFCA Binder; "Will Administer Directly: U.S. Bypasses State in Loan to SWAFCA," *Birmingham News,* June 16, 1968, TSHC; Michael S. Lottman, "On Central Alabama Discrimination: Commission Asks Action," *Southern Courier,* June 22–23, 1968; Orsborn, Testimony, USCCR Mont, 183. Although FHA administrators thought these regulations seemed normal, SWAFCA and OEO officials disagreed. Because Bamberg had worked closely with King Pharr and Whitfield vegetable processors, SWAFCA's leaders were wary of his intentions. Bamberg did not help his case when he appeared before the U.S. Commission on Civil Rights Hearings in Montgomery on April 30, 1968, where, according to the head of the commission, he "made abundantly clear . . . his low opinion of the abilities of Negro farmers." Staff director William Taylor described the FHA official's "private philosophy." When the FHA administrators in Washington finally agreed to oversee the SWAFCA loan from USDA headquarters, Bamberg's testimony was cited as one reason for agreeing to SWAFCA's request.

89. Frye, *Black Parties and Political Power,* 93; Jerry Roden, "Report of the Workshop on Voter Registration and Education: Resource Persons, Lewis Black, Director of RAP, and Marvin Wall, Director of Research Voter Education Project," Box 41.2.1.3.15, SRC; Election Flyer for Mildred Black, Board of Education Place No. 2, Box 41.2.7.3.24, SRC; James Bennett, "Selden Lashes OEO for Grant to Co-op," *Birmingham Post Herald,* March 7, 1968, SWAFCA Binder; Estelle Fine, "Where Did Votes Go?" *Southern Courier,* August 24–25, 1968.

90. Gerson M. Greene to Theodore M. Berry, "Need for Research on Impact of Alabama Development Programs on Rural-Urban Migration," CAP Office Records of the Director, Subject Files 1965–69, Box 69, RG 381; James L. Lawson, "Meeting, TICEP and SEASHA, June 13, 1968," June 14, 1968, Box SG8847, ACAI; Mary Ellen Gale, "'When You Try to Help the Poor, You Need to Know All You Can,'" *Southern Courier,* December 9–10, 1967; Zippert, Interview by Author, 5; Lewis Black, Report, October 1967, Box 41.1.2.7.3.23, SRC; William L. Hamilton, *Study of Rural Cooperatives,* 27–28.

91. Albert Brewer to Theodore M. Berry, August 23, 1968, Box SG21317, Alabama Governor—Administrative Files of Alabama Development Office, Alabama

Department of Archives and History, Montgomery; Theodore M. Berry, "SWAFCA Report," May 20, 1968, Gerson M. Greene, "SWAFCA Report," June 3, 1968, Theodore M. Berry, "SWAFCA," June 12, 1968, Job K. Savage, "SWAFCA's Latest Marketing Problem," July 3, 1968, Theodore M. Berry, "Mismanagement of SWAFCA Federal Funds," August 16, 1968, Gerson M. Greene, "Mismanagement of SWAFCA Funds," August 15, 1968, Terry J. Tondro to Fred M. Vinson Jr., August 20, 1968, CAP Office Records of the Director, Subject Files 1965–69, Box 70, RG 381; Rogers et al., *Alabama,* 576; Continental-Allied Company, Monthly Evaluation Report on SWAFCA, No. 6, June 6, 1968, CAP Office Records of the Director, Subject Files 1965–69, Box 45, RG 381. SWAFCA was not held responsible for Orsborn's theft of federal funds. The bank allowed his transactions without the proper resolutions and permitted him to make withdrawals from the SWAFCA account when he no longer had the authority to sign the co-op's checks.

92. "And the Beat Goes On: 3 Delegations Trying to Represent Alabama," *Southern Courier,* August 24–25, 1968; John C. Diamante, "At Democratic Convention: Wins and Losses," *Southern Courier,* August 31–September 1, 1968; Cynthia Smith, "ADC Gains Reputation." The Alabama Democratic Party had not had an integrated convention delegation since Reconstruction.

93. Roberson, "On July 20"; Bob Labaree, "National Democratic Party Plans Challenge to Wallace," *Southern Courier,* July 27–28, 1968; "NDPA Files List of 130 Candidates," Unidentified Newspaper Clipping, September 6, 1968, TSHC. The presidential electors were E. D. Bouler, Rev. William Branch, Virginia Durr, R. E. Cordray, J. H. Davis, George Deboer, Jack Drake, Billy Joe Robinson, Robert Schwenn, and James Williams.

94. "And the Beat Goes On"; Diamante, "At Democratic Convention"; Al Fox, "Demo Delegation: NDPA to Challenge Whoever Wins Control," *Birmingham News,* April 23, 1972, TSHC; Frye, *Black Parties and Political Power,* 86.

95. Frye, *Black Parties and Political Power,* 85; Diamante, "At Democratic Convention"; Cynthia Smith, "ADC Gains Reputation"; Fox, "Demo Delegation"; Frye, *Black Parties and Political Power,* 79.

96. Payne, *I've Got the Light of Freedom,* 358–59, 362; Frye, *Black Parties and Political Power,* 160–61.

97. Patricia Sullivan, *Freedom Writer,* 406–7.

98. Ibid., 403–5. In a letter to Jessica Mitford, Durr explained the source of her hope for the future of southern politics after attending the convention in Chicago. "After living so long in Alabama under Wallace and his kind, I suppose I am rather used to a police state and think things are actually getting better, or at least there is more opposition."

99. "NDPA Files List of 130 Candidates"; Martha Witt Smith to Hugh Maddox, September 18, 1968, Box SG22451, AGF; Michael S. Lottman, "NDPA Candidates Off Ballot—Or Are They?" *Southern Courier,* September 21–22, 1968.

100. Michael S. Lottman, "NDPA Still Kept Off Ballot; Johnson, Wallace May Help," *Southern Courier,* October 19–20, 1968; Michael S. Lottman, "'Need a Black Person

to Represent Blacks,'" *Southern Courier,* October 26–27, 1968; Frye, *Black Parties and Political Power,* 86.

101. OEO Press Release, "OEO Continues Support of SWAFCA-Al Co-op," July 17, 1968, Box 379, LH; "Selma Mayor May Seek Injunction: SWAFCA Given $595,751," *Birmingham Post Herald,* October 16, 1968, Writ of Injunction and Bill of Complaint, *Joe T. Smitherman v. SWAFCA et al.,* Circuit Court of Dallas County, Alabama, October 18, 1968, "SWAFCA Enjoined from Expending Further Funds," *Selma Times Journal,* October 20, 1968, Box SG20058, AGLAF; "Legal Action Eyed to Stall SWAFCA," *Birmingham News,* October 17, 1968, TSHC; "Stop Spending, Court Tells Coop," *Birmingham News,* October 24, 1968, TSHC; SWAFCA Press Release, "SWAFCA Takes Court Action against Injunction," October 30, 1968, Olga Boikess to Carl Eardley, November 4, 1968, CAP Office Records of the Director, Subject Files 1965–69, Box 81, RG 381; "U.S. Court Delays SWAFCA Hearing," Unidentified Newspaper Clipping, November 13, 1968, Box 11, Alumni and Development Office Records, RG 385, Ralph Brown Draughon Library, Special Collections and Archives Department, Auburn University, Auburn, Ala.

102. Michael S. Lottman, "Still Faces Problems: Freedom Party Tries for Lowndes Offices," *Southern Courier,* October 26–27, 1968; Michael S. Lottman, "Boone's Strong Showing Whips Whaley in County," *Southern Courier,* November 9–10, 1968.

103. Frye, *Black Parties and Political Power,* 87; Lottman, "Boone's Strong Showing"; Patricia Sullivan, *Freedom Writer,* 410.

104. Frye, *Black Parties and Political Power,* 94; Black, Interview, 4–8, 13–14, HTFOHC; Williams, Interview, HTFOHC.

105. Frye, *Black Parties and Political Power,* 8–10, 56; Williams, Interview, HTFOHC; Johnson, Interview, HTFOHC; Black, Interview, 1–2, HTFOHC; Payne, *I've Got the Light of Freedom,* 359, 362; Patricia Sullivan, *Freedom Writer,* 411. Payne found similar dynamics within the black community in Mississippi. Older leaders such as Charles Evers and Aaron Henry worked with the Democratic Party, whereas younger activists felt betrayed by the national party.

106. "SWAFCA, FHA in Accord," *Selma Times Journal,* June 18, 1968, SWAFCA Binder; Herbert L. Tyson, "FHA Loan to SWAFCA," January 17, 1969, CAP Office Records of the Director, Subject Files 1965–69, Box 81, RG 381; Nick Horrock, "By Rep. Nichols: SWAFCA Loan Blasted," *Birmingham Post Herald,* January 16, 1969, SWAFCA Binder. Assistant secretary of agriculture John Baker had been influential in helping SWAFCA renegotiate the terms of the FHA loan. SWAFCA received $310,000 on March 15, $242,000 on June 15, and $30,000 on July 1.

107. Frye, *Black Parties and Political Power,* 94–95; "An Example for Greene: Macon Bi-Racial Government Working," *Birmingham News,* August 5, 1969, Box 6.5, Birmingham Police Surveillance Files, Birmingham Public Library, Archives and Manuscripts Division, Birmingham, Ala.; Albert J. Winfield to Hugh Maddox, April 24, 1969, Box SG22652, AGF.

108. "Example for Greene"; Frank Sikora, "6 Win in Official Canvass: Negro Winners in Greene Will Be Sworn in August 11," *Birmingham News,* August 2, 1969, "Crowd Sees

Greene 'Historic Occasion,'" *Birmingham News,* August 11, 1969, Frank Sikora, "Advisers, Judge Help New Greene Officials," *Birmingham News,* August 14, 1969, Box 6.5, Birmingham Police Surveillance Files; Frye, *Black Parties and Political Power,* 157.

109. Frye, *Black Parties and Political Power,* 97; Cunningham, Interview by Author, 17–18, 30.

110. Frye, *Black Parties and Political Power,* 51, 61–64, 104; Williams, Interview, HTFOHC; Johnson, Interview, HTFOHC; Eagles, *Outside Agitator,* 256; Cleaver and Katsiaficas, *Liberation, Imagination, and the Black Panther Party,* introduction; Judson L. Jeffries, "An Unexamined Chapter of Black Panther History," in *Black Power,* ed. Jeffries, 185–223. The Black Panther Party in Oakland, California, took another approach to militancy based on an urban context of hypermasculine armed resistance. Its members called for revolutionary change in America because they saw the entire system as corrupt and in need of restructuring.

111. Frye, *Black Parties and Political Power,* 66–67; Williams, Interview, HTFOHC; Johnson, Interview, HTFOHC; Cunningham, Interview by Author, 29–30.

112. Clint Claybrook, "Strategy of First Full Slate by NDPA Seems to Be Avoiding Ticket Splitting," *Birmingham News,* August 3, 1970, TSHC; Black, Interview, 1–2, 4–10, HTFOHC; Frank Bruer, "NDPA Certifies Candidates for 169 November Races," *Birmingham Post Herald,* September 2, 1970, TSHC; Al Fox, "From Governor to JP: NDPA Fields 174 Candidates for General Election Ballot," *Birmingham News,* September 2, 1970, TSHC; "'Team Effort,' Says Dr. Cashin of Race," *Birmingham Post Herald,* August 3, 1970, TSHC; Bob Hawkins, "Party Tags Take on Significance in Dallas Vote," *Selma Times Journal,* November 4, 1970.

113. James Bennett, "Two Negroes Elected: Legislature to Be Integrated 1st Time since Reconstruction," *Birmingham Post Herald,* November 5, 1970, TSHC; "NDPA Candidates Likely Lowndes Sheriff Winner," *Selma Times Journal,* November 4, 1970; Hawkins, "Party Tags Take on Significance"; "NDPA Challengers," *Birmingham News,* November 4, 1970; Clint Claybrook, "NDPA Takes Greene County, All Black Candidates Elected," *Birmingham News,* November 4, 1970; Frye, *Black Parties and Political Power,* 122. Bush and Payne lost, as did Nixon. Albert Turner lost his race for Perry County probate judge.

114. Jonathan Steele, "The Black Sheriff of Mean County, Alabama," *Guardian,* May 1, 1977, TSHC; Waylon Smithey, "Names Miami Delegates: NDPA Convention Picks Candidate List," *Birmingham News,* May 28, 1972, TSHC; Al Fox, "NDPA Slipping? Vote Indicates It," *Birmingham News,* November 9, 1972, TSHC; "NDPA Drive to Win Major County Office Sidetracked," *Birmingham Post Herald,* November 9, 1972, TSHC.

115. Mike Harris, "Coop Struggling to Aid Farmers as 'Black Power' Fears Fizzle," *Birmingham Post Herald,* January 28, 1976; Aiken, *Cotton Plantation South,* 349. Aiken declared SWAFCA a failure in his survey of the region.

116. Turner, Interview by Author, 10; Cunningham, Interview by Author, 16–17; Beth Wilcox, "In Dallas County: Farmers Get Loans to Buy Land," *Southern Courier,* March 23–24, 1968; "Charles Griffin and Family: A Story of Land," *Southern Courier,* April 27–28, 1968; Chris Waddle, "SWAFCA Helps 12 Operate 300-Acre Farm," *Birming-*

ham Post Herald, June 20, 1968, SWAFCA Binder; Fite, *Cotton Fields No More,* 224–25; Richard Beard and M. D. Gilmer to John A. Garrett, April 25, 1969, Box SG8860, ACAI.

117. Mike Harris, "Coop Struggling to Aid Farmers"; Frank Sikora, "Justice Probe: Black Coops Asked to Produce Records," *Birmingham News,* February 5, 1980, TSHC; Cunningham, Interview by Author, 1, 13–14; Turner, Interview by Author, 12.

Seven. Old Patterns and New Designs

1. OEO, "Alabama Summary," January 1, 1969, Records of the Field Office, CAP, Ala. and S.C. District Offices, Box 6, RG 381SE; Census of 1969 Incomes, All Residential Locations, Choctaw, Dallas, Greene, Hale, Lowndes, Marengo, Monroe, Perry, Sumter, Wilcox Counties, Alabama, 1960 Poverty Statistics, Box 1, RG 381SE; U.S. Bureau of the Census, *Tables—Persons by Poverty Status in 1969, 1979, 1989 by State.* Beyond community action, the state used $504,186 on VISTA workers, $847,054 on adult basic education, $4,057,290 on rural loans, and $28,821,096 on bureau of work programs. The percentage of people living in poverty in the ten Black Belt counties ranged from Greene County with 65 percent to Dallas County with 40 percent.

2. USCCR Mont, 1–3; Robert W. Saunders, "Report of U.S. Civil Rights Commission's Hearings in Montgomery, Ala.," May, 6, 1968, Office of Civil Rights Program Records of the Assistant Director for Civil Rights, Box 9, RG381. The sixteen counties studied included Autauga, Barbour, Bullock, Butler, Choctaw, Clarke, Dallas, Greene, Hale, Lowndes, Macon, Marengo, Monroe, Perry, Sumter, and Wilcox.

3. USCCR Mont, 304–5, 308, 311; Robert W. Saunders to Maurice A. Dawkins, May 6, 1968, Program Records of the Assistant Director for Civil Rights, Box 9, RG 381.

4. USCCR Mont, 225–27, 230–31; "Brown Promoted by FHA; Bamberg Succeeds Him," *Montgomery Advertiser,* August 8, 1964, TSHC.

5. Robert W. Saunders to Maurice A. Dawkins, May 6, 1968, Program Records of the Assistant Director for Civil Rights, Box 9, RG 381; Erskine Smith, Testimony, USCCR Mont, 19.

6. William W. Suttle to Norman H. Davis, April 24, 1968, Anti-Poverty Program Evaluation, Community Action/Anti-Poverty, Box 2, RG 381SE; William Suttle to Ralph P. Swofford, August 5, 1968, Anti-Poverty Program Evaluation, Community Action/Anti-Poverty, Box 9, RG 381SE; Crespino, *In Search of Another Country,* 11–12.

7. Glenn K. Humes, "Composite Evaluation Report on Tri-County Area 22, Inc., Greenville, Al.," March 3–6, 1970, Elenora Hines, "Evaluation Report, Tri-County Area 22, Inc.," Anti-Poverty Program Evaluation, Community Action/Anti-Poverty, Box 14, RG 381SE.

8. Humes, "Composite Evaluation Report."

9. Ibid.; Edward Vaughn, "Evaluation Report, Tri-County Area 22, Inc.," March 1970, Maggie Moody, "Evaluation Report on the Tri-County Area 22, Inc.," March 3–6, 1970; Edward Vaughn, "Goat Training," March 17, 1970, Anti-Poverty Program Evaluation, Community Action/Anti-Poverty, Box 14, RG 381SE; Hines, "Evaluation Report."

10. Vaughn, "Evaluation Report."

11. Humes, "Composite Evaluation Report"; Vaughn, "Evaluation Report"; Glenn K. Humes to District Supervisor, Alabama OEO/SE Regional Office, March 10, 1970, William F. Roth Jr., "Evaluation Report for Tri-County Area 22 Agency," Anti-Poverty Program Evaluation, Community Action/Anti-Poverty, Box 14, RG 381SE; Hines, "Evaluation Report."

12. Hines, "Evaluation Report"; Roth, "Evaluation Report."

13. Glenn K. Humes to District Supervisor, Alabama OEO/SE Regional Office, March 10, 1970, Anti-Poverty Program Evaluation, Community Action/Anti-Poverty, Box 14, RG 381SE; Humes, "Composite Evaluation Report"; Vaughn, "Evaluation Report."

14. Ronald E. Allen Sr., "A Composite Report," Eleventh Area of Alabama Opportunity Action Committee, June 24–26, 1970, Anti-Poverty Program Evaluation, Community Action/Anti-Poverty, Box 19, RG 381SE; Jean H. Crooks, Memorandum for Record, August 13, 1969, handwritten notes about Eleventh Area CAP Form 75, revised September 23, 1969, Records of the Field Office, CAP, Ala. and S.C. District Offices, Box 2, RG 381SE.

15. OEO, "Alabama Summary"; Neighborhood Referral Service Monthly Report, Eleventh Area of Alabama, October 21, 1968, Records of the Field Office, CAP, Ala. and S.C. District Offices, Box 2, RG 381SE.

16. Edwin Marger, "Compliance Reviews for Monitoring and Evaluation Teams," May 12–13, 1969, Individual Report of Interview for Employee Grantee or Other Component as Part Of Compliance Review, ca. 1969, Records of the Field Office, CAP, Ala. and S.C. District Offices, Box 2, RG 381SE; Eleventh Area of Alabama Opportunity Action Committee, "Composition Evaluation Report," January 6–9, 1970, Ronald E. Allen Sr., "Evaluation Report, Eleventh Area," January 1969, Phyllis A. Maass, "Evaluation—11th Area of Alabama," Antipoverty Program Evaluation, Community Action/Anti-Poverty, Box 7, RG 381SE.

17. Eleventh Area of Alabama Opportunity Action Committee, "Composition Evaluation Report"; Allen, "Evaluation Report, Eleventh Area"; Maass, "Evaluation"; Handwritten Notes about Area 11, June 16, 1969, Records of the Field Office, CAP, Ala. and S.C. District Offices, Box 2, RG 381SE.

18. William Holland, Handwritten Field Trip Report, August 14, 1968, Records of the Field Office, CAP, Ala. and S.C. District Offices, Box 2, RG 381SE.

19. Dwain Alexander, "Official Report of On-Site Findings," Dallas County–Selma Economic Opportunity Board, November 19–22, 1968, Anti-Poverty Program Evaluation, Community Action/Anti-Poverty, Box 5, RG 381SE.

20. Ibid.; "Comments by Dwain Alexander," November 25, 1968, Anti-Poverty Program Evaluation, Community Action/Anti-Poverty, Box 5, RG 381SE.

21. "Comments by Dwain Alexander"; Thaddeus Olive Jr., "Assignment Report," November 19, 1968, Selma–Dallas County Economic Opportunity Board, Andre W. Moore, "Assignment Report," Selma–Dallas County Economic Opportunity Board, November 19, 1968, Donald Thielke to Dwain Alexander, December 5, 1968, Anti-Poverty Program Evaluation, Community Action/Anti-Poverty, Box 5, RG 381SE. The

eight centers were located in Selmont, Carver, Bogu Chitti, Hobbs, Basco, East Selma, E. M. Brown, and Old Town.

22. Alexander, "Official Report of On-Site Findings"; Olive, "Assignment Report"; Dwain Alexander, handwritten notes from investigation for Selma–Dallas County evaluation, November 21, 1968, Anti-Poverty Program Evaluation, Community Action/ Anti-Poverty, Box 5, RG 381SE.

23. Alexander, "Official Report of On-Site Findings."

24. Ibid.

25. "Official Report of On-Site Findings," Selma–Dallas County Economic Board, Handwritten Phone Message from Andre Moore and Thad Olive, November 25, 1968; Tom Duncan to Members of the Selma Evaluation Team, March 20, 1969, Anti-Poverty Program Evaluation, Community Action/Anti-Poverty, Box 5, RG 381SE; Joseph White to J. M. Williams, December 3, 1969, Records of the Field Office, CAP, Ala. and S.C. District Offices, Box 2, RG 381SE.

26. "To Discuss Bias Charge: Smitherman Meeting with OEO Board," *Birmingham News,* October 30, 1970, TSHC; "Atlanta Officials' Order; Selma OEO Office Given 45 Days for Hiring More Whites," October 31, 1970, Unidentified Newspaper Clipping, TSHC.

27. Davidson, "War on Poverty," 5.

28. Ibid.

29. Ibid., 3, 8–9; Germany, *New Orleans after the Promises.* Davidson reports that "altogether, thirty vetoes were invoked in ten states during OEO's first three years, or one for every 550 grants made. Governors Wallace of Alabama . . . and Ronald Reagan of California were the champion vetoers, accounting for three of every five vetoes."

30. Louise Bradley to John A. Dyer, January 14, 1971, Regional Offices, Organizations Planning Files, Box 5, RG 381SE; Bob Saunders to William Walker, March 19, 1974, Regional Offices, Organizations Planning Files, Box 3, RG 381SE.

31. "Functional Statements, Region IV, Atlanta Office of Economic Opportunity," October 1971, Regional Offices, Organizational Planning Files, Box 4, RG 381SE.

32. Volt Technical Corporation, Report on Assignment No. 3-GA-016-MO-120 (Little River Community Action Agency), August 29, 1968, Anti-Poverty Program Evaluations, Community Action/Anti-Poverty, Box 9, RG 381SE; Mary Y. Grice to All Board Members, August 21, 1967, 1044.2.2, SIP Papers.

33. Janet Nussmann, "Alleged Racist Attitudes of a Member of the CAP Staff," February 3, 1969, Regional Offices, Organizations Planning Files, Box 3, RG 381SE; Evaluation Team of City of Selma–Dallas County Economic Opportunity Board, Anti-Poverty Program Evaluation, Community Action/Anti-Poverty, Box 5, RG 381SE. Nussmann noted to her boss that "someone from Region VI"—probably Alexander— "was on the Selma Evaluation and is preparing a similar report against Sturm. Hugh knows this; at first I didn't take these remarks serious. . . . After a couple of days I began to take him serious. I'll stand behind what I'll say."

34. Davidson, "War on Poverty," 4–5; Matthew C. Colley to Roy Jones, January 15, 1969, Records of the Field Office, CAP, Ala. and S.C. District Offices, Box 6, RG 381SE.

35. Hugh Maddox to Alabama Program Development Committee, July 29, 1969, Box SG8858, ACAI; Kate Harris, "8 Planning Districts Set Up by State," *Birmingham News,* August 4, 1970, Box SG6938, PISF; J. E. Mitchell Jr. to Matthew Colley, June 30, 1970, J. E. Mitchell Jr. to Richard Holmes, July 1, 1970, J. E. Mitchell Jr. to Roy E. Batchelor, July 17, 1970, Box SG19970, AGAdmAF.

36. Francis X. Walter Diary, October 4, 1965, 6–9, Francis X. Walter Personal Papers, Sewanee, Tenn.; Southeastern Regional Office of Economic Opportunity, Chart of the Office Structure, 38.30, ABP. Jordan worked as a consultant in the Community Action Division under the regional manager, John Dean.

37. Davidson, "War on Poverty," 11–13.

38. Mac Porterfield, "FBI Agents Probing in Hayneville: Ex-Church Used by Controversial Poverty Groups," *Birmingham Post Herald,* March 13, 1967, TSHC; Stokely Carmichael, "Church Bombings: The American Way of Racism," A-I-70, Reel 3, SNCC Papers; OEO Press Release, "Lowndes County, Alabama Migrants and Seasonal Farm Workers," ca. early 1968, Box 379, LH.

39. OEO Press Release, "Head Start Grant to Lowndes County Board of Education," ca. spring 1968, Box 379, LH; Lurleen Wallace to Frank K. Sloan, August 10, 1967, Lurleen Wallace to Theodore M. Berry, August 19, 1967, Box SG22422, AGF; *Congressional Record,* April 1, 1968, p. E2476, Box 537, Office Files of John Macy, LBJ Library; OEO Contract, Grant, and Loan Announcement, May 8, 1968, OEO Press Release, "Lowndes County, Alabama to Get Comprehensive Health Care Program," ca. spring 1968, Box 379, LH; "Medical Care Begins for Lowndes People," *Southern Courier,* November 9–10, 1968; Ed Strickland to Lurleen Wallace, March 21, 1967, Box SG21074, Alabama Legislative Commission to Preserve the Peace Papers, Alabama Department of Archives and History, Montgomery; James M. Fallows, "Lowndes Health Officials Deny It: Something Wrong in Project?" *Southern Courier,* August 17–18, 1968; Phyllis Wesley, "Tour Visits Poor, Hungry in 4 Counties: The Passing Throng," *Montgomery Advertiser,* May 31, 1979, Box SG6979, PISF. The Lowndes County Board of Education had been operating a summer Head Start program in 1967. The Peace Commission spoke out against the early plans for the health care facility because it thought one of OEO's support personnel had been an organizer for the National Farm Workers Association in California.

40. Kate Harris, "With Anti-Poverty Money, U.S. Financing All-Negro City in Wilcox," *Birmingham News,* May 28, 1967, "Wilcox OEO Mishandled, Is Charge," *Birmingham Post Herald,* May 29, 1967, Kate Harris, "Under Antipoverty Program: FHA OKs 11 Pleas for Homes," *Birmingham News,* July 6, 1967, TSHC; Robert C. Bamberg to Daniel Harrell, September 23, 1966, 1044.2.3, SIP Papers; Everett P. Wenrick, "Findings and Recommendations Based on a Study of Economic Intimidation and Discrimination in Wilcox County, Alabama," December 12, 1965, 1044.2.15, SIP Papers.

41. Kate Harris, "Under Antipoverty Program"; USCCR Mont, 124–29, 131; OEO Press Release, "Southwest Alabama Self-Help Housing, Inc., Camden, Alabama (Migrants)," June 1, 1968, Box 379, LH; OEO, "Alabama Summary."

42. OEO Press Release, "Wilcox County, Alabama (Migrant and Seasonal Farm Workers)," ca. early 1968, Box 379, LH; Al From to Edgar May, "Wilcox County Veto,"

September 6, 1967, CAP Records of the Director, State Files 1965–89, Box 14, RG 381; OEO, "Alabama Summary."

43. Trinity Parish Newsletter, January–February 1973, 1044.1.39, SIP Papers; "Community Action Program Application for Southwest Alabama Self-Help Housing Inc.," 1044.2.3, SIP Papers; Wenrick, "Findings and Recommendations"; Francis X. Walter, "SIP Contacted for SWAFCA," 1044.2.2, SIP Papers; John D. Price to Lyndon Johnson, April 8, 1967, 1044.2.2, SIP Papers; Walter Diary.

44. Callahan, *Freedom Quilting Bee*, 31, 46, 63, 67; Trinity Parish Newsletter, January–February 1973, 1044.1.39, SIP Papers.

45. Callahan, *Freedom Quilting Bee*, 65, 66, 71, 92, 95, 105, 107, 110, 113, 135, 136, 244; Beardsley et al., *Gee's Bend*, 34, 178; SIPBrochure, ca. early 1970s, 1044.1.39, SIP Papers.

46. Callahan, *Freedom Quilting Bee*, 136; Beardsley et al., *Gee's Bend*, 34–35.

47. OEO Press Release, "OEO Continues Support of SWAFCA—Al Co-op," July 17, 1968, Box 379, LH; Herbert L. Tyson, "FHA Loan to SWAFCA," January 17, 1969, CAP Office Records of the Director, Subject Files 1965–69, Box 81, RG 381; Donald Thielke to Dwain Alexander, December 5, 1968, Anti-Poverty Evaluation, Community Action/Anti-Poverty, Box 5, RG 381SE; Fay Bennett, Memorandum on Meeting with OEO Officials re: SWAFCA, April 11, 1967, 1044.2.2, SIP Papers; Frank Sikora, "Justice Probe: Black Coops Asked to Produce Records," *Birmingham News*, February 5, 1980, TSHC; Cunningham, Interview by Author, 1, 13–14; Turner, Interview by Author, 12.

48. Davidson, "War on Poverty," 12–13. The idea of a catalytic agent comes from Davidson, who appraises community action: "Finally, it is next to impossible to assess the relation of the war on poverty to the social movements of the 1960s—including the rise and demise of the civil rights movement, the advent of Black Power, and the ghetto riots. OEO officials . . . are circumspect in evaluating the impact of antipoverty programs on institutional change." An internal OEO memorandum described the findings of an evaluation of CAP: "Based on assessments of observers in a sample of 47 locales, the study found favorable developments in almost all cities; in almost ⅔rds of the cases, CAA's played some role in the changes. If valid, the findings hardly constitute grounds for crediting OEO with eliminating poverty, but, given the limitations of publicly funded efforts, they are grounds for the modest conclusion that OEO has been a useful catalytic agent."

49. Kenneth W. Munden, "The Office of Economic Opportunity in the Nixon Administration," 1973, 18–20, 24, 369–70, 374–76, Records of the Office of Planning, Research, and Evaluation, Box 107, RG 381; White House Press Release, April 21, 1969, Bertrand Harding to All Employees, April 21, 1969, CAP Office Records of the Director, Subject Files, 1964–70, Box 2, RG 381.

Conclusion. Carry It On, Carry It On

1. Stokely Carmichael, James Forman, and George Green, Transcript of Conversation, "Riding in the Car from Atlanta to Tuskegee," February 19, 1966, Doc. 1168, A-XV-9, Reel 36, SNCC Papers; Mesher, Interview by Author, 25–26.

2. USCCR Mont, 592–93; Lawson, *In Pursuit of Power,* 90. Black saw a strong connection between what people learned in cooperatives and in politics. "Anything that you have is political, whether or not people want to admit it, but the mere idea of them voting one vote per person to vote for a candidate in his particular cooperative has some politics within it."

3. SWAFCA bumper stickers, CAP Office Records of the Director, Subject Files 1965–69, Box 70, RG 381. The *Southern Courier* is available on microfilm at the Ralph Brown Draughon Library, Special Collections and Archives Department, Auburn University, Auburn, Ala.

4. Trinity Parish Newsletter, January–February 1973, 1044.1.39, SIP Papers; SIP Brochure, 1044.1.39, SIP Papers.

5. Sokol, *There Goes My Everything,* 266.

6. Lawson, *In Pursuit of Power,* 270–71; Davis, Interview, October 28, 1980, 9, Ralph Brown Draughon Library, Special Collections and Archives Department, Auburn University, Auburn, Ala.; Sokol, *There Goes My Everything,* 9; Katz, *Undeserving Poor,* 7.

7. Douglas Martin, "Joseph Smitherman, Mayor in Selma Strife, Dies at 75," *New York Times,* September 13, 2005; Scott Shepard, "Clintons, Obama Join Selma Jubilee," *Atlanta Journal-Constitution,* March 4, 2007; U.S. Commission on Civil Rights, "Fifteen Years Ago," 83.

8. *Barlow v. Collins,* 397 U.S. 159 (1970), http://www.justia.us/us/397/159/case.html; *Clemon Barlow v. J. A. Minter Jr.,* U.S. District Court, Mobile, Ala., Civil Case Files ACC 021-73A2029, Case 4482-67, National Archives and Records Administration, Southeast Region, Morrow, Ga. In addition to Walter Blocton and Will Williams, the other seven plaintiffs were Clemon Barlow, Sinnie Blocton, Arthur Brown, Willie Gilcrest, Elijah Green, Otis Hale, and Will Moorer.

9. *Barlow v. Minter:* Memorandum in Support of Plaintiffs' Motion for a Preliminary Injunction, December 30, 1966, Answer of Defendant, J. A. Minter Jr., March 2, 1967, Motion for Continuance of Pretrial and of Case, June 13, 1970.

10. *Barlow v. Minter:* Plaintiffs' Memorandum in Opposition to Motion to Dismiss of Defendants Freeman, Godfrey, and Collins, February 20, 1967, Memorandum in Support of Motion to Dismiss the Complaint as to Defendant Minter, ca. February 1967, Joint Pretrial Document, September 2, 1970; Willis, *Lay My Burden Down.*

11. *Barlow v. Minter:* Order, March 29, 1972.

12. U.S. Commission on Civil Rights, "The Decline of Black Farming in America," 9, 133–34, 179–80; Frank Sikora, "Help Urged for Black Farmers," *Birmingham News,* June 6, 1982, TSHC; Fite, *Cotton Fields No More,* 224–25.

13. "OEO Grants Accepted by the State of Alabama for 1972," Box SG21328, Alabama Governor—Administrative Files of Alabama Development Office, Alabama Department of Archives and History, Montgomery; USCCR Mont, 19.

14. R. C. Bamberg, "Economic Opportunity Grants," February 1, 1971, Box SG21317, Alabama Governor—Administrative Files of Alabama Development Office; U.S. Commission on Civil Rights, "Fifteen Years Ago," 83; Ray Jenkins, "Editorial: Development

Office Padded Figures on Industrial Growth, Columnist Says," *Montgomery Advertiser,* January 6, 1974, Box SG6938, PISF.

15. "The Statistical Panjandrum," *Alabama Journal,* February 22, 1972, Box SG13843, Alabama State Sovereignty Commission Papers, Alabama Department of Archives and History, Montgomery.

16. Martha Witt Smith, "Lowndes County Election (Watchers Win It for Whites)," December 11, 1972, Box SG13843, Alabama State Sovereignty Commission Papers.

17. U.S. Commission on Civil Rights, "Fifteen Years Ago," 82–84.

18. Ibid, 3–10, 14–17, 43, 45, 53–55, 62, 76–77, 80. As late as 1982, no black people had been elected to the county commissions of Sumter, Dallas, Marengo, Monroe, and Wilcox.

19. Mesher, Interview by Author, 25; Fairclough, *Race and Democracy,* 428.

20. U.S. Commission on Civil Rights, "Fifteen Years Ago," 5–10, 58–60, 78–79; Rogers et al., *Alabama,* 591, 597.

21. U.S. Commission on Civil Rights, "Fifteen Years Ago," 59–60; Frank Sikora, "Southern Blacks: Fighting to Keep Their Land," *Birmingham News,* December 16, 1977, TSHC; Sikora, "Help Urged for Black Farmers."

22. U.S. Commission on Civil Rights, "Fifteen Years Ago," 79–80; Federation of Southern Cooperatives, "Statement to the National Advisory Committee on Economic Opportunity," February 7, 1973, Reel 27, Box 10, Folder 8, Nonpartisan Voters League Papers, microfilm, University of South Alabama Library, Mobile.

23. James Free, "Busy Rebuilding: National Democrats Handle Problems with Realism," *Birmingham News,* March 25, 1973, TSHC; Lou Elliott, "ADC Gives Alabama Blacks Influence in Politics through State Organization," *Montgomery Advertiser,* March 2, 1980, Peggy Roberson, "ADC Called Hub of Black Influence in Alabama," *Montgomery Advertiser,* Box SG6938, PISF; Rogers et al., *Alabama,* 591; Tullos, "Crackdown in the Black Belt," 1–2.

24. Tullos, "Crackdown in the Black Belt," 3; Frye, *Black Parties and Political Power,* 169–70.

25. Payne, *I've Got the Light of Freedom,* 436.

26. Shepard, "Clintons, Obama Join Selma Jubilee."

Bibliography

MANUSCRIPTS

Athens, Georgia
Richard B. Russell Library for Political Research and Studies, University of Georgia
    Richard B. Russell Senatorial Papers
    Herman Talmadge Senatorial Papers

Atlanta, Georgia
Auburn Avenue Research Library on African American Culture and History, Atlanta-
    Fulton Public Library System
    Papers of the Student Nonviolent Coordinating Committee, Microfilm
Martin Luther King Jr. Center for Nonviolent Social Change Archives
    Southern Christian Leadership Conference Papers

Auburn, Alabama
Ralph Brown Draughon Library, Special Collections and Archives Department,
    Auburn University
    Alumni and Development Office Records
    J. A. Minter and Sons Gin Company Records, 1948–82

Austin, Texas
Lyndon B. Johnson Library
    Council of Economic Advisers, Administrative History, vol. 1
    Economic Opportunity Act, Legislative Background
    Bertrand Harding Personal Papers
    John Macy Office Files
    Office of Economic Opportunity, Administrative History
    White House Aides Files—Bohen
    White House Aides Files—Gaither
    White House Aides Files—McPherson
    White House Aides Files—Moyers

Birmingham, Alabama
Birmingham Public Library, Archives and Manuscripts Division
    Birmingham Police Surveillance Files

Albert Boutwell Papers
Selma Inter-Religious Project Papers
Southern Regional Council Papers
Birmingham Public Library
Tutwiler Southern History Collection, Clippings Files
Birmingham Civil Rights Institute, Archives Division
Emory O. Jackson Collection

Boston, Massachusetts
John F. Kennedy Library
Poverty and Urban Policy: Conference Transcript of 1973 Group Discussion of the
Kennedy Administration Urban Policy Programs and Policies

College Park, Maryland
National Archives and Records Administration II
Office of Economic Opportunity Papers, Record Group 381

Jasper, Georgia
Offices of Susan Landrum and Phil Landrum Jr.
Phil Landrum Papers

Mobile, Alabama
Mobile Municipal Archives
Joseph Langan Papers
Spring Hill College Library and Archives
Albert S. Foley, S.J., Papers
University of South Alabama Library
Papers of the Nonpartisan Voters League, microfilm

Montgomery, Alabama
Alabama Department of Archives and History
Alabama Commission of Agriculture and Industries, Administrative Files 1964–69
Alabama Governor—Administrative Assistants' Files
Alabama Governor—Administrative Files of Alabama Development Office
Alabama Governor (1963–79: Wallace, Wallace, Brewer, Wallace), Administrative
Files
Alabama Governor—Legal Adviser's Files
Alabama Legislative Commission to Preserve the Peace Papers
Alabama State Sovereignty Commission Papers
Department of Agriculture and Industries, Annual Reports, 1946–67
Public Information Subject Files—General Files

Morrow, Georgia
National Archives and Records Administration, Southeast Region
  Community Services Administration Papers (formerly Office of Economic
    Opportunity), Southeast Regional Office, Record Group 381
  U.S. District Court, Mobile, Alabama, Civil Case Files ACC 021-73A2029, Case
    4482-62, *Barlow v. Minter*

Selma, Alabama
Society of Saint Edmund Mission Archives
  SWAFCA Binder

Sewanee, Tennessee
Francis X. Walter Personal Papers
  Francis X. Walter Diary, October 1, 1965–June 27, 1969

Tuscaloosa, Alabama
W. S. Hoole Special Collections Library, University of Alabama
  Lister Hill Papers

Washington, D.C.
Library of Congress Manuscript Division
  National Association for the Advancement of Colored People Papers
U.S. Commission on Civil Rights Library
  "The Decline of Black Farming in America," February 1982
  "Fifteen Years Ago . . . Rural Alabama Revisited," December 1983
  Hearings in Montgomery, Alabama, April 27–May 2, 1968
  Meeting of the Alabama State Advisory Committee to the U.S. Commission on Civil
    Rights, Alabama Power Company, Demopolis, Alabama, July 10, 1965
  Open Meeting of the Alabama State Advisory Committee, U.S. Commission on Civil
    Rights, Selma, Alabama, May 26, 1967

INTERVIEWS AND ORAL HISTORIES

Interviews by Author
Ezra Cunningham, May 7, 1992, Beatrice, Alabama
Sara Kaffer, May 20, 1998, Mobile, Alabama
Joseph Langan, July 28, 1998, Mobile, Alabama
Shirley Mesher, July 21, 2005, Seattle, Washington
Tom Nunan, September 24, 1998, Alexandria, Virginia
Paul G. Smith, May 9, 1998, Birmingham, Alabama
Albert Turner, April 30, 1992, Marion, Alabama
Francis X. Walter, October 22, December 16, 1999, Birmingham, Alabama
Thomas Weise, July 3, 1998, Phenix City, Alabama

Samuel F. Yette, December 12, 1996, Silver Spring, Maryland
John Zippert, February 23, 1992, Eutaw, Alabama

Ralph Brown Draughon Library, Special Collections and Archives Department, Auburn University, Auburn, Alabama
Neil O. Davis, October 28, 1980

Hardy T. Frye Oral History Collection, Ralph Brown Draughon Library, Special Collections and Archives Department, Auburn University, Auburn, Alabama
Lewis Black
Joe R. Johnson
Clarence Williams

Moorland-Spingarn Research Center, Manuscript Division, Howard University, Washington, D.C., Ralph Bunche Oral History Collection
Lewis Black, October 1967, Hale County, Alabama
Agatha Harville, August 16, 1969, Selma, Alabama
Shirley Mesher, 1968, Selma, Alabama
Stanley Smith, April 25, 1967, Tuskegee, Alabama
Francis X. Walter, August 1969, Selma, Alabama

Lyndon B. Johnson Library, Austin, Texas, Lyndon B. Johnson Oral History Collection
Donald M. Baker, February 24, 1969, Interview Tape 1; March 5, 1969, Interview Tape 2, Tape 3, Tape 4
John A. Baker, April 21, 1981, Interview I, II, III
Theodore M. Berry, February 15, 1969, Interview I
Edgar S. Cahn and Jean Camper Cahn, December 10, 1980, Interview I
William B. Cannon, May 21, 1982
Jack T. Conway, August 13, 1980, Interview I
Elizabeth Wickendon Goldschmidt, November 6, 1974, Interview II
Kermit Gordon, January–April 1969, Interview Tape 1, 2, 3, 4
Bertrand Harding, November 20, 1968, Interview Tape 1
Lyndon Baines Johnson, February 1, 1973, "The Last Interview" CBS Television
William P. Kelly, April 4, 1969, Interview I; April 11, 1969, Interview II
Robert Lampman, May 24, 1983
Robert A. Levine, February 26, 1969, Interview Tape 1
Edgar May, October 6, 1981
Stephen J. Pollak, January 29, 1969, Interview II
Norbert A. Schlei, May 15, 1980
R. Sargent Shriver, August 20, 1980, Interview I; October 23, 1980, Interview II; February 7, 1986, Interview IV

Jule M. Sugarman, March 14, 1969
James L. Sundquist, April 7, 1969, Interview I
Adam Yarmolinsky, July 13, 1970, Interview I; October 21, 1980, Interview II, III

U.S. GOVERNMENT DOCUMENTS

Congressional Record: Proceedings and Debates of the 88th Congress, Second Session. Vol. 110, pts. 13–14. Washington, D.C.: U.S. Government Printing Office, 1964.
Public Law 90-222, Economic Opportunity Amendments of 1967, December 23, 1967.
Public Papers of the Presidents of the United States, Lyndon B. Johnson Containing the Public Messages, Speeches, and Statements of the President 1963–1964. Book 1, November 22, 1963 to June 30, 1964. Washington, D.C.: U.S. Government Printing Office, 1965.
Public Papers of the Presidents of the United States, John F. Kennedy, Containing the Public Messages, Speeches, and Statements of the President, January 20 to December 31, 1961. Washington, D.C.: U.S. Government Printing Office, 1962.
U.S. Bureau of the Census. *Current Population Reports.* Series P-60, no. 68, *Poverty in the United States: 1959 to 1968.* Washington, D.C.: U.S. Government Printing Office, 1969.
U.S. Bureau of the Census. *Tables—Persons by Poverty Status in 1969, 1979, 1989 by State.* http://www.census.gov/hhes/www/poverty/census/cphl162.html.
U.S. Commission on Civil Rights. *Equal Opportunity in Farm Programs: An Appraisal of Services Rendered by Agencies of the United States Department of Agriculture.* Washington, D.C.: U.S. Government Printing Office, 1965.
U.S. Congress. House of Representatives. Committee on Education and Labor. *Hearings on H.R. 10440.* 88th Cong., 2nd sess., March 17–20, April 7–10, 13–14, 1964. Washington, D.C.: U.S. Government Printing Office, 1964.
U.S. Congress. Senate. Committee on Labor and Public Welfare. *Hearings on S. 2642.* 88th Cong., 2nd sess., June 17, 18, 23, 25, 1964. Washington, D.C.: U.S. Government Printing Office, 1964.

STATE OF ALABAMA GOVERNMENT DOCUMENT

Alabama Laws (and Joint Resolutions) of the Legislature of Alabama at the Special Session of 1966. Montgomery: State of Alabama, 1966.

NEWSPAPERS AND PERIODICALS

Alabama Journal
Atlanta Constitution
Atlanta Journal
Birmingham News

Birmingham Post Herald
Catholic Week of Alabama
Christian Science Monitor
Clarkesville (Georgia) Tri County Advertiser
Dallas Morning News
Elberton (Georgia) Star
Gainesville (Georgia) Daily Times
Los Angeles Times
Montgomery Advertiser
New York Herald Tribune
New York Times
Selma Times Journal
Southern Courier
Wall Street Journal
Washington Evening Star
Washington Post

DOCUMENTARY

Willis, Jack, producer. *Lay My Burden Down: A Look at the Life of the Southern Rural Negro.* NET Journal, National Education Television, 1966.

BOOKS AND ARTICLES

Aaron, Henry J. *Politics and the Professors: The Great Society in Perspective.* Washington, D.C.: Brookings Institution, 1978.

Aiken, Charles S. *The Cotton Plantation South since the Civil War.* Baltimore: Johns Hopkins University Press, 1998.

Ashmore, Susan Youngblood. "More Than a Head Start: The War on Poverty, Civil Rights, and Catholic Charities in Mobile, Alabama, 1964–1970." In *The New Deal and Beyond: Social Welfare in the South since 1930,* edited by Elna C. Green. Athens: University of Georgia Press, 2003.

Badger, Tony. "Southerners Who Refused to Sign the Southern Manifesto." *Historical Journal* 42, no. 2 (June 1999): 517–34.

Bartley, Numan V. *The New South, 1945–1980: The Story of the South's Modernization.* Baton Rouge: Louisiana State University Press, 1995.

Beardsley, John, William Arnett, Paul Arnett, and Jane Livingston. *Gee's Bend: The Women and Their Quilts.* Atlanta: Tinwood, 2002.

Bernstein, Irving. *Guns or Butter: The Presidency of Lyndon Johnson.* New York: Oxford University Press, 1996.

———. *Promises Kept: John F. Kennedy's New Frontier.* New York: Oxford University Press, 1991.

Beschloss, Michael R., ed. *Taking Charge: The Johnson White House Tapes, 1963–1964.* New York: Simon and Schuster, 1997.

Blight, David W. *Race and Reunion: The Civil War in American Memory.* Cambridge: Belknap Press of Harvard University Press, 2001.

Boulard, Garry. "Review: The Failure of the Southern Moderates." *American Quarterly* 40, no. 3 (September 1988): 415–21.

Brauer, Carl. "Kennedy, Johnson, and the War on Poverty." *Journal of American History* 69, no. 1 (June 1982): 98–119.

Burgess, Ernest W., and Donald J. Bogue. *Contributions to Urban Sociology.* Chicago: University of Chicago Press, 1964.

Califano, Joseph A., Jr. *The Triumph and Tragedy of Lyndon Johnson: The White House Years.* New York: Simon and Schuster, 1991.

Callahan, Nancy. *The Freedom Quilting Bee.* Tuscaloosa: University of Alabama Press, 1987.

Carson, Clayborne. *In Struggle: SNCC and the Black Awakening of the 1960s.* Cambridge: Harvard University Press, 1981.

Carter, Dan T. *The Politics of Rage: George Wallace, the Origins of the New Conservatism, and the Transformation of American Politics.* New York: Simon and Schuster, 1995.

Chafe, William H. *The Unfinished Journey: America since World War II.* 2nd ed. New York: Oxford University Press, 1991.

Cleaver, Kathleen, and George Katsiaficas, eds. *Liberation, Imagination, and the Black Panther Party: A New Look at the Panthers and Their Legacy.* New York: Routledge, 2001.

Cobb, James C. *The Most Southern Place on Earth: The Mississippi Delta and the Roots of Regional Identity.* New York: Oxford University Press, 1992.

Conkin, Paul K. *Big Daddy from the Pedernales: Lyndon Baines Johnson.* Boston: Twayne, 1986.

Crespino, Joseph H. *In Search of Another Country: Mississippi and the Conservative Counterrevolution.* Princeton: Princeton University Press, 2007.

Curry, Constance. *Silver Rights.* New York: Harcourt Brace, 1995.

Dallek, Robert. *Flawed Giant: Lyndon Johnson and His Times, 1961–1973.* New York: Oxford University Press, 1998.

———. *Lone Star Rising: Lyndon Johnson and His Times, 1908–1960.* New York: Oxford University Press, 1991.

Daniel, Pete. "African American Farmers and Civil Rights." *Journal of Southern History* 73, no. 1 (February 2007): 3–38.

Davidson, Roger H. "The War on Poverty: Experiment in Federalism." *Annals of the American Academy of Political and Social Science* 385 (September 1969): 1–13.

Dittmer, John. *Local People: The Struggle for Civil Rights in Mississippi.* Urbana: University of Illinois Press, 1994.

Eagles, Charles W. *The Civil Rights Movement in America.* Jackson: University Press of Mississippi, 1986.

———. *Outside Agitator: Jon Daniels and the Civil Rights Movement in Alabama.* Chapel Hill: University of North Carolina Press, 1993.

Eskew, Glenn T. *But for Birmingham: The Local and National Movements in the Civil Rights Struggle.* Chapel Hill: University of North Carolina Press, 1997.

Evans, Rowland, and Robert Novak. *Lyndon B. Johnson: The Exercise of Power.* New York: New American Library, 1968.

Fahs, Alice, and Joan Waugh, eds. *The Memory of the Civil War in American Culture.* Chapel Hill: University of North Carolina Press, 2004.

Fairclough, Adam. *Race and Democracy: The Civil Rights Struggle in Louisiana, 1915–1972.* Athens: University of Georgia Press, 1995.

———. *To Redeem the Soul of America: The Southern Christian Leadership Conference and Martin Luther King, Jr.* Athens: University of Georgia Press, 1987.

Feldman, Glenn. *Politics, Society, and the Klan in Alabama, 1915–1949.* Tuscaloosa: University of Alabama Press, 1999.

Fite, Gilbert C. *Cotton Fields No More: Southern Agriculture, 1865–1980.* Lexington: University Press of Kentucky, 1984.

———. *Richard B. Russell, Jr., Senator from Georgia.* Chapel Hill: University of North Carolina Press, 1991.

Fitzgerald, Sally, ed. *The Habit of Being: The Letters of Flannery O'Connor.* New York: Farrar, Straus, Giroux, 1979.

Flannery, Austin, ed. *The Basic Sixteen Documents: Vatican Council II Constitutions, Decrees, Declarations.* Northport, N.Y.: Costello, 1996.

Frederickson, Kari. *The Dixiecrat Revolt and the End of the Solid South, 1932–1968.* Chapel Hill: University of North Carolina Press, 2001.

Frye, Hardy T. *Black Parties and Political Power: A Case Study.* Boston: Hall, 1980.

Gaillard, Frye. *Cradle of Freedom: Alabama and the Movement That Changed America.* Tuscaloosa: University of Alabama Press, 2004.

Galbraith, John Kenneth. *The Affluent Society.* Boston: Houghton Mifflin, 1958.

Garrow, David J. *Protest at Selma: Martin Luther King, Jr., and the Voting Rights Act of 1965.* New Haven: Yale University Press, 1978.

Germany, Kent. *New Orleans after the Promises: Poverty, Citizenship, and the Search for the Great Society.* Athens: University of Georgia Press, 2007.

Gillette, Michael L. *Launching the War on Poverty: An Oral History.* New York: Twayne, 1996.

Goodwin, Doris Kearns. *Lyndon Johnson and the American Dream.* New York: St. Martin's, 1976, 1991.

Goodwin, Richard N. *Remembering America: A Voice from the Sixties.* Boston: Little, Brown, 1988.

Grafton, Carl, and Anne Permaloff. *Big Mules and Branchheads: James E. Folsom and Political Power in Alabama.* Athens: University of Georgia Press, 1985.

Greenberg, Polly. *And the Devil Wore Slippery Shoes: A Biased Biography of the Child Development Group of Mississippi.* London: Macmillan, 1969.

Greene, Melissa Fay. *Praying for Sheetrock.* New York: Fawcett Columbine, 1991.

Haddad, William F. "Mr. Shriver and the Savage Politics of Poverty." *Harper's Magazine,* December 1965, 43–50.

Hale, Grace Elizabeth. *Making Whiteness: The Culture of Segregation in the South, 1890–1940.* New York: Pantheon, 1998.

Hall, Jacquelyn Dowd. "The Long Civil Rights Movement and the Political Uses of the Past." *Journal of American History* 91, no. 4 (March 2005): 1233–63.

Hamilton, Virginia Van der Veer. *Lister Hill: Statesman from the South.* Chapel Hill: University of North Carolina Press, 1987.

Hamilton, William L. *A Study in Rural Cooperatives: Final Report: Analysis.* Cambridge, Mass.: Abt, 1973.

Harrington, Michael. *The Other America: Poverty in the United States.* New York: Macmillan, 1962.

Haveman, Robert H., ed. *A Decade of Federal Antipoverty Programs: Achievements, Failures, and Lessons.* New York: Academic, 1977.

Heath, Jim F. *Decade of Disillusionment: The Kennedy-Johnson Years.* Bloomington: Indiana University Press, 1975.

Horwitt, Sanford D. *Let Them Call Me a Rebel: Saul Alinsky—His Life and Legacy.* New York: Knopf, 1989.

Jacoway, Elizabeth, Dan T. Carter, Lester C. Lamon, and Robert C. McMath, eds. *The Adaptable South: Essays in Honor of George Brown Tindall.* Baton Rouge: Louisiana State University Press, 1991.

Jeffries, Judson L., ed. *Black Power: In the Belly of the Beast.* Urbana: University of Illinois Press, 2006.

Johnson, Lyndon Baines. *The Vantage Point: Perspectives of the Presidency, 1963–1969.* New York: Holt, Rinehart, and Winston, 1971.

Joseph, Peniel E. *Waiting 'Til the Midnight Hour: A Narrative History of Black Power in America.* New York: Holt, 2006.

Katz, Michael B. *The Undeserving Poor: From the War on Poverty to the War on Welfare.* New York: Pantheon, 1989.

King, Martin Luther, Jr. *Where Do We Go from Here: Community or Chaos?* New York: Harper Collins, 1967.

Knapp, Daniel, and Kenneth Polk. *Scouting the War on Poverty: Social Reform Politics in the Kennedy Administration.* Lexington, Mass.: Heath, 1971.

Kobrin, Solomon. "The Chicago Area Project: A Twenty-five-Year Assessment." *Annals of the American Academy of Political and Social Sciences* 322 (March 1959): 22.

Kotlowski, Dean J. *Nixon's Civil Rights: Politics, Principle, and Policy.* Cambridge: Harvard University Press, 2001.

Lawson, Steven F. *In Pursuit of Power: Southern Blacks and Electoral Politics, 1965–1972.* New York: Columbia University Press, 1985.

Lawson, Steven F., and Charles Payne. *Debating the Civil Rights Movement, 1945–1968.* Lanham, Md.: Rowman and Littlefield, 1998.

Lemann, Nicholas. *The Promised Land: The Great Black Migration and How It Changed America.* New York: Knopf, 1991.

Levine, Robert A. *The Poor Ye Need Not Have with You: Lessons from the War on Poverty.* Cambridge: MIT Press, 1970.

Levitan, Sar A. *Federal Aid to Depressed Areas: An Evaluation of the Area Redevelopment Administration.* Baltimore: Johns Hopkins University Press, 1964.

————. *The Great Society's Poor Law: A New Approach to Poverty.* Baltimore: Johns Hopkins University Press, 1969.

Litwack, Leon F. *Trouble in Mind: Black Southerners in the Age of Jim Crow.* New York: Knopf, 1998.

Marris, Peter, and Martin Rein. *Dilemmas of Social Reform: Poverty and Community Action in the United States.* 2nd ed. Chicago: Aldine, 1973.

Marshall, Ray, and Lamond Godwin. *Cooperatives and Rural Poverty in the South.* Baltimore: Johns Hopkins University Press, 1971.

Matusow, Allen J. *The Unraveling of America: A History of Liberalism in the 1960s.* New York: Harper and Row, 1984.

MacDonald, Dwight. "Our Invisible Poor." *New Yorker,* January 19, 1963, 82–96.

McPherson, Harry. *A Political Education: A Washington Memoir.* Austin: University of Texas Press, 1972, 1988, 1995.

Miroff, Bruce. *Pragmatic Illusions: The Presidential Politics of John F. Kennedy.* New York: McKay, 1976.

Morris, Willie. *New York Days.* New York: Back Bay, 1993.

Moynihan, Daniel Patrick. *Maximum Feasible Misunderstanding: Community Action in the War on Poverty.* New York: Free Press, 1969.

Nolan, Hugh J., ed. *Pastoral Letters of the United States Catholic Bishops.* Vol. 2, 1941–61. Washington, D.C.: National Conference of Catholic Bishops, U.S. Catholic Conference, 1983.

————. *Pastoral Letters of the United States Catholic Bishops.* Vol. 3, 1962–74. Washington, D.C.: National Conference of Catholic Bishops, U.S. Catholic Conference, 1983.

Norrell, Robert J. *Reaping the Whirlwind: The Civil Rights Movement in Tuskegee.* New York: Vintage, 1985.

Novak, Robert D. *The Agony of the G.O.P. 1964.* New York: Macmillan, 1965.

O'Connor, Alice. *Poverty Knowledge: Social Science, Social Policy, and the Poor in Twentieth-Century United States History.* Princeton: Princeton University Press, 2001.

O'Reilly, Kenneth. *Nixon's Piano: Presidents and Racial Politics from Washington to Clinton.* New York: Free Press, 1995.

Parker, Richard. *John Kenneth Galbraith: His Life, His Politics, His Economics.* New York: Farrar Straus Giroux, 2005.

Patterson, James T. *America's Struggle against Poverty, 1900–1985.* Cambridge: Harvard University Press, 1981, 1986.

————. *Grand Expectations: The United States, 1945–1974.* New York: Oxford University Press, 1996.

Payne, Charles M. *I've Got the Light of Freedom: The Organizing Tradition and the Mississippi Freedom Struggle.* Berkeley: University of California Press, 1995.

————. "'The Whole United States Is Southern!': *Brown v. Board* and the Mystification of Race." *Journal of American History* 91, no. 1 (June 2004): 83–91.

Permaloff, Anne, and Carl Grafton. "The Chop-Up Bill and the Big Mule Alliance." *Alabama Review* 43, no. 4 (October 1990): 243–69.

Phillips, Kevin P. *The Emerging Republican Majority*. New York: Anchor, 1969.

Quadagno, Jill. *The Color of Welfare: How Racism Undermined the War on Poverty*. New York: Oxford University Press, 1994.

Pruitt, Paul M., Jr. "The Killing of Father Coyle: Private Tragedy, Public Shame." *Alabama Heritage*, no. 30 (Fall 1993): 24–37.

Rogers, William Warren, Robert David Ward, Leah Rawls Atkins, and Wayne Flynt. *Alabama: The History of a Deep South State*. Tuscaloosa: University of Alabama Press, 1994.

Rolinson, Mary G. *Grassroots Garveyism: The Universal Negro Improvement Association in the Rural South, 1920–1927*. Chapel Hill: University of North Carolina Press, 2007.

Roper, John Herbert, ed. *C. Vann Woodward: A Southern Historian and His Critics*. Athens: University of Georgia Press, 1997.

Schlesinger, Arthur M., Jr. *A Thousand Days: John F. Kennedy in the White House*. Boston: Houghton Mifflin, 1965.

Schrecker, Ellen. *Many Are the Crimes: McCarthyism in America*. Boston: Little, Brown, 1998.

Schulman, Bruce J. *Lyndon B. Johnson and American Liberalism: A Brief Biography with Documents*. Boston: Bedford Books of St. Martin's, 1995.

Seeger, Pete, and Bob Reiser. *Everybody Says Freedom*. New York: Norton, 1989.

Sokol, Jason. *There Goes My Everything: White Southerners in the Age of Civil Rights, 1945–1975*. New York: Knopf, 2006.

Sorensen, Theodore. *"Let the Word Go Forth": The Speeches, Statements, and Writings of John F. Kennedy*. New York: Delacorte, 1988.

Southern, David W. *John LaFarge and the Limits of Catholic Interracialism, 1911–1963*. Baton Rouge: Louisiana State University Press, 1996.

Sullivan, Patricia. *Days of Hope: Race and Democracy in the New Deal Era*. Chapel Hill: University of North Carolina Press, 1996.

———, ed. *Freedom Writer: Virginia Foster Durr, Letters from the Civil Rights Years*. New York: Routledge, 2003.

Sundquist, James L., ed. *On Fighting Poverty: Perspectives from Experience*. New York: Basic Books, 1969.

———. *Politics and Policy: The Eisenhower, Kennedy, and Johnson Years*. Washington, D.C.: Brookings Institution, 1968.

Thornton, J. Mills, III. *Dividing Lines: Municipal Politics and the Struggle for Civil Rights in Montgomery, Birmingham, and Selma*. Tuscaloosa: University of Alabama Press, 2002.

Tindall, George B. *The Emergence of the New South, 1913–1945*. Baton Rouge: Louisiana State University Press, 1967.

Tindall, George B., with David Shi. *America: A Narrative History*. 3rd ed. Vol. 2. New York: Norton, 1991.

Tullos, Allen. "Crackdown in the Black Belt: Not-So-Simple Justice." *Southern Changes: The Journal of the Southern Regional Council* 7, no. 2 (1985): 1–5.

Ture, Kwame, and Charles V. Hamilton. *Black Power: The Politics of Liberation*. New York: Vintage, 1967, 1992.

Ulrich, Laurel Thatcher. *Good Wives: Image and Reality in the Lives of Women in Northern New England, 1650–1750.* New York: Vintage, 1991.

Unger, Irwin. *The Best of Intentions: The Triumph and Failure of the Great Society under Kennedy, Johnson, and Nixon.* New York: Doubleday, 1996.

VanDeberg, William L. *New Day in Babylon: The Black Power Movement and American Culture, 1965–1975.* Chicago: University of Chicago Press, 1992.

Whalen, Charles, and Barbara Whalen. *The Longest Debate: A Legislative History of the 1964 Civil Rights Act.* Cabin John, Md.: Seven Locks, 1985.

Wicker, Tom. "George Wallace: A Gross and Simple Heart." *Harper's Magazine,* April 1967, 41–49.

Woodward, C. Vann. *Thinking Back: The Perils of Writing History.* Baton Rouge: Louisiana State University Press, 1986.

———. "What Happened to the Civil Rights Movement?" *Harper's Magazine,* January 1967, 29–37.

THESES AND DISSERTATIONS

Alsobrook, David E. "Alabama's Port City: Mobile during the Progressive Era, 1896–1917." Ph.D. diss., Auburn University, 1983.

Carter, David. "Two Nations: Social Insurgency and National Civil Rights Policy-Making in the Johnson Administration, 1965–1968." Ph.D. diss., Duke University, 2001.

Dow, Patsy Busby. "Joseph N. Langan: Mobile's Racial Diplomat." Master's thesis, University of South Alabama, 1993.

Index

222, 355n76; on Wallace's smear campaign, 189

Bizzell, Jack, 198

Black, Lewis: activism of, 127, 134, 201–8, 246, 248; experience of, 129–30, 151; as RAP director, 201, 239; SWAFCA organizer, 12, 216

Black, Mildred, 234, 239

Black, Prince, 230

Black Belt: all-white ASCS committees in, 207, 346n23; and Area 22 Committee for OEO grants, 139–40, 258; and Big Mule coalition, 89, 312n7; CAA demonstration programs in, 63; civil rights movement in, 87–88, 290–91; COAPO representatives in, 163; evaluation of antipoverty programs in, 254–78 passim; geographic area of, *xv,* 12; historical reassessment of, 14–16; industrialization in, 165–66, 274–77; motivated by civil rights movement, 124–26; OEO programs in, 57, 122; racial disharmony in, 288–89; reconstruction efforts in, 271–79; and resistance to antipoverty programs, 86–89; SEASHA program in, 239–40; after Selma to Montgomery march, 151–52; and statewide elections, 153–54; successes and failures in, 196–97, 281–94; SWAFCA in, 199–200, 209–16; tenant farmer evictions in, 10, 146–50, 158, 166, 176, 198–201, 333–34n9; Voting Rights Act in, 91–92, 124–26, 177–97; working outside the system in, 134–40; working within the system in, 126–34. *See also* racial discrimination/segregation

Black Belt elites, opposed to SWAFCA, 217–18, 349n43

black citizens. *See* African Americans

Black Panther Party: logo of, 157; Lowndes County candidates of, 245; political campaign tactics of, 180–81; as radical, 217–18. *See also* freedom parties; Lowndes County Freedom Party

Black Power: Alabama-style, 154–60, 232, 246, 281–83; misunderstandings of, 186; and 1968 election, 246; in political cartoon, *191;* in Selma, 163–77

Blackwell, Randolph, 164

Block, Robert W., 112

Blocton, Sinnie, 286, 366n8

Blocton, Walter, 286

Bloody Sunday, on Edmund Pettus Bridge, 114, 124–25, 285

Bloomingdale's, sells Freedom Quilting Bee quilts, 275

Bokulich, Paul, 199, 211

Bond, Julian, 175, 243, 285–86

Bonwit Teller, sells Freedom Quilting Bee quilts, 275

Boone, Richard: as CAP official, 62–63, 278; and Citizens Crusade against Poverty, 199, 204; on maximum feasible participation, 60; on national-emphasis programs, 73; resignation of, 307n31

Boone, Rev. Richard: as NDPA candidate, 246; as SCOPE worker, 126

Boston Globe, 185

Boulard, Gerry, 35

Boutwell, Albert, 109–10, 113–14, 120

Boynton, Amelia, 132, 220, 249

Boynton, Bruce, 220

Brademas, John, 122

Bradford, Ernest, 168–70, 173–74, 176

Bradford, Joseph, 21, 211, 349n35

Bradley, Sam, 139

Branch, Alberta, 179

Branch, William, 151, 197, 249–50

Brassfield, Clinton, 131

Brauer, Carl, 22

Brewer, Albert, 196, 240, 244

Bridge Crossing Jubilee, 285

Bridges, Jack, 207

Bronstein, Alvin J., 203–4

Brooks, Jessie, 249

Brown, Arthur, 166, 205, 286, 366n8

Brown, Douglas, 78

Brown, Holmes, 115

Brown, Ken, 155

Brown, Lonnie, 178

Brown's Chapel AME Church, 171, 174

Bullock County, 118, 178, 258

Burg, Harvey, 132–34, 139, 326nn18–19

Burns, Haydon, 45

Burton, Frenchie, 247

Bush, A. D., 165, 174, 249

Butler, Irene, 259–60